Business and Society

Stakeholders, Ethics, Public Policy

Business and Society

Stakeholders, Ethics, Public Policy

Thirteenth Edition

Anne T. Lawrence
San José State University

James Weber
Duquesne University

Boston   Burr Ridge, IL   Dubuque, IA   Madison, WI   New York   San Francisco   St. Louis
Bangkok   Bogotá   Caracas   Kuala Lumpur   Lisbon   London   Madrid   Mexico City
Milan   Montreal   New Delhi   Santiago   Seoul   Singapore   Sydney   Taipei   Toronto

The McGraw·Hill Companies

BUSINESS & SOCIETY: STAKEHOLDERS, ETHICS, PUBLIC POLICY
International Edition 2011

Exclusive rights by McGraw-Hill Education (Asia), for manufacture and export. This book cannot be re-exported from the country to which it is sold by McGraw-Hill. This International Edition is not to be sold or purchased in North America and contains content that is different from its North American version.

10 09 08 07 06 05 04 03
20 15 14 13 12 11
CTP BJE

When ordering this title, use ISBN 978-007-128936-8 or MHID 007-128936-4

Printed in Singapore

www.mhhe.com

About the Authors

Anne T. Lawrence   *San José State University*

Anne T. Lawrence is a professor of organization and management at San José State University. She holds a Ph.D. from the University of California–Berkeley and completed two years of postdoctoral study at Stanford University. Her articles, cases, and reviews have appeared in many journals, including the *Academy of Management Review, Administrative Science Quarterly, Journal of Management Education, Case Research Journal, Business and Society Review, Research in Corporate Social Performance and Policy,* and *Journal of Corporate Citizenship.* Her cases in business and society have been reprinted in many textbooks and anthologies. She has served as guest editor of the *Case Research Journal* and as president of both the North American Case Research Association (NACRA) and the Western Casewriters Association. She received the Emerson Center Award for Outstanding Case in Business Ethics (2004) and the Curtis E. Tate Award for Outstanding Case of the Year (1998 and 2009). At San José State University, she was named Outstanding Professor of the Year in 2005.

James Weber   *Duquesne University*

James Weber is a professor of management and business ethics and chair of the management department at Duquesne University. He also serves as senior fellow and founding director of the Beard Center for Leadership in Ethics and coordinates the Masters of Science in Leadership and Business Ethics program at Duquesne. He holds a Ph.D. from the University of Pittsburgh and has taught at the University of San Francisco, University of Pittsburgh, and Marquette University. His areas of interest and research include managerial and organizational values, cognitive moral reasoning, business ethics, ethics training and education, eastern religions' ethics, and corporate social audit and performance. He was recognized by the Social Issues in Management division of the Academy of Management with the Best Paper Award in 1989 and 1994. He has served as division and program chair of the Social Issues in Management division of the Academy of Management. He has also served as president and program chair of the International Association of Business and Society (IABS) and is a member of the Society for Business Ethics. He is on the editorial board of *Business Ethics Quarterly* and is the Senior Associate Editor of the *Journal of Organizational Moral Psychology.*

Preface

In a world economy that is becoming increasingly integrated and interdependent, the relationship between business and society is becoming ever more complex. The globalization of business, the emergence of civil society organizations in many nations, and new government regulations and international agreements have significantly altered the job of managers and the nature of strategic decision making within the firm.

At no time has business faced greater public scrutiny or more urgent demands to act in an ethical and socially responsible manner than at the present. Consider the following:

- The global financial crisis of 2008–2009—highlighted by the failure of major business firms, unprecedented intervention in the economy by many governments, and the fall from grace of numerous prominent executives—focused a fresh spotlight on issues of corporate responsibility and ethics. Around the world, people and governments are demanding that executives do a better job of serving shareholders and the public. Once again, policymakers are actively debating the proper scope of government oversight in such wide-ranging arenas as health care, financial services, and manufacturing. Management educators are placing renewed emphasis on issues of business leadership and accountability.

- A host of new technologies have become part of the everyday lives of billions of the world's people. Advances in the basic sciences are stimulating extraordinary changes in agriculture, telecommunications, and pharmaceuticals. Businesses can now grow medicine in plants, embed nanochips in tennis rackets, and communicate with customers overseas over the Internet and wireless networks. Technology has changed how we interact with others, bringing people closer together through social networking, instant messaging, and photo and video sharing. These innovations hold great promise. But they also raise serious ethical issues, such as those associated with genetically modified foods, stem cell research, or use of the Internet to exploit or defraud others or to censor free expression. Businesses must learn to harness new technologies, while avoiding public controversy and remaining sensitive to the concerns of their many stakeholders.

- Businesses in the United States and other nations are transforming the employment relationship, abandoning practices that once provided job security and guaranteed pensions in favor of highly flexible but less secure forms of employment. The Great Recession caused job losses across broad sectors of the economy in the United States and many other nations. Many jobs, including those in the service sector, are being outsourced to the emerging economies of China, India, and other nations. As jobs shift abroad, transnational corporations are challenged to address their obligations to workers in far-flung locations with very different cultures and to respond to initiatives, like the United Nations' Global Compact, that call for voluntary commitment to enlightened labor standards and human rights.

- Ecological and environmental problems have forced businesses and governments to take action. An emerging consensus about the risks of global warming, for example, is leading many companies to adopt new practices, and once again the nations of the world have taken up the challenge of negotiating an international treaty to limit the emissions of greenhouse gases. Many businesses have cut air pollution, curbed solid waste, and designed products to be more energy-efficient. A better understanding of how human activities affect natural resources is producing a growing understanding that economic growth must be achieved with environmental protection if development is to be sustainable.

- Many regions of the world are developing at an extraordinary rate. Yet the prosperity that accompanies economic growth is not shared equally. Personal income, health care, and educational opportunity are unevenly distributed among and within the world's nations. The tragic pandemic of AIDS in sub-Saharan Africa and the threat of a swine or avian flu epidemic have compelled drug makers to rethink their pricing policies and raised troubling questions about the commitment of world trade organizations to patent protection. Many businesses must consider the delicate balance between their intellectual property rights and the urgent demands of public health, particularly in the developing world.

- In many nations, legislators have questioned business's influence on politics. Business has a legitimate role to play in the public policy process, but it has on occasion shaded over into undue influence and even corruption. In the United States, reforms of campaign finance and lobbying laws have changed the rules of the game governing how corporations and individuals can contribute to and influence political parties and public officials. Technology offers candidates and political parties new ways to reach out and inform potential voters. Businesses the world over are challenged to determine their legitimate scope of influence and how to voice their interests most effectively in the public policy process.

The new thirteenth edition of *Business and Society* addresses this complex agenda of issues and their impact on business and its stakeholders. It is designed to be the required textbook in an undergraduate or graduate course in Business and Society; Business, Government, and Society; Social Issues in Management; or the Environment of Business. It may also be used, in whole or in part, in courses in Business Ethics and Public Affairs Management. This new edition of the text is also appropriate for an undergraduate sociology course that focuses on the role of business in society or on contemporary issues in business.

The core argument of *Business and Society* is that corporations serve a broad public purpose: to create value for society. All companies must make a profit for their owners. Indeed, if they did not, they would not long survive. However, corporations create many other kinds of value as well. They are responsible for professional development for their employees, innovative new products for their customers, and generosity to their communities. They must partner with a wide range of individuals and groups in society to advance collaborative goals. In our view, corporations have multiple obligations, and all stakeholders' interests must be taken into account.

A Tradition of Excellence

Since the 1960s, when Professors Keith Davis and Robert Blomstrom wrote the first edition of this book, *Business and Society* has maintained a position of leadership by discussing central issues of corporate social performance in a form that students and faculty have found engaging and stimulating. The leadership of the two founding authors, and later of Professor William C. Frederick and James E. Post, helped *Business and Society* to achieve a consistently high standard of quality and market acceptance. Thanks to these authors' remarkable eye for the emerging issues that shape the organizational, social, and public policy environments in which students will soon live and work, the book has added value to the business education of many thousands of students.

Business and Society has continued through several successive author teams to be the market leader in its field. The current authors bring a broad background of business and society research, teaching, consulting, and case development to the ongoing evolution of the text. The new thirteenth edition of *Business and Society* builds on its legacy of market leadership by reexamining such central issues as the role of business in society, the nature of corporate responsibility and global citizenship, business ethics practices, and the complex roles of government and business in a global community.

For Instructors

For instructors, this textbook offers a complete set of supplements. An extensive instructor's resource manual—fully revised for this edition—includes lecture outlines, discussion case questions and answers, tips from experienced instructors, and extensive case teaching notes. A computerized test bank and PowerPoint slides for every chapter are also provided to adopters. A video supplement, compiled especially for the thirteenth edition, features recent segments from the *NewsHour with Jim Lehrer,* produced by the Public Broadcasting Service. These videos may be used to supplement class lectures and discussions.

Business and Society is designed to be easily modularized. An instructor who wishes to focus on a particular portion of the material may select individual chapters or cases to be packaged in a Primis custom product. Sections of this book can also be packaged with other materials from the extensive Primis database, including articles and cases from the Harvard Business School, to provide exactly the course pack the instructor needs.

For instructors who teach over the Internet and for those who prefer an electronic format, this text may be delivered online, using McGraw-Hill's eBook technology. eBooks can also be customized with the addition of any of the materials in Primis's extensive collection.

For Students

Business and Society has long been popular with students because of its lively writing, up-to-date examples, and clear explanations of theory. This textbook has benefited greatly from feedback over the years from thousands of students who have used the material in the authors' own classrooms. Its strengths are in many ways a testimony to the students who have used earlier generations of *Business and Society.*

The new thirteenth edition of the text is designed to be as student-friendly as always. Each chapter opens with a list of key learning objectives to help focus student reading and study. Numerous figures, exhibits, and real-world business examples (set as blocks of colored type) illustrate and elaborate the main points. A glossary at the end of the book provides definitions for bold-faced and other important terms. Internet references, greatly expanded for this edition, and a full section-by-section bibliography guide students who wish to do further research on topics of their choice, and subject and name indexes help students locate items in the book.

Additional student resources are also available via the book's Online Learning Center at www.mhhe.com/lawrence13e, including self-grading quizzes and chapter review material.

New For The Thirteenth Edition

Over the years, the issues addressed by *Business and Society* have changed as the environment of business itself has been transformed. This thirteenth edition is no exception, as readers will discover. Some issues have become less compelling and others have taken their place on the business agenda, while others endure through the years.

The thirteenth edition has been thoroughly revised and updated to reflect the latest theoretical work in the field and the latest statistical data, as well as recent events. Among the new additions are

- New discussion of theoretical advances in stakeholder theory, corporate citizenship, public affairs management, corporate governance, social performance auditing, social investing, reputation management, business partnerships, and corporate philanthropy.
- Treatment of practical issues, such as social networking, digital medical records, bottom of the pyramid, social entrepreneurship, advocacy and issue advertising, as well as the latest developments in the regulatory environment in which businesses operate.
- New discussion cases and full-length cases on such timely topics as the subprime mortgage meltdown, toy safety, Internet censorship in China, plant-based medicines, corporate board scandals, activist investing, sweatshop labor, corporate ethics programs, YouTube content, and tobacco regulation.

Finally, this is a book with a vision. It is not simply a compendium of information and ideas. The new edition of *Business and Society* articulates the view that in a global community, where traditional buffers no longer protect business from external change, managers can create strategies that integrate stakeholder interests, respect personal values, support community development, and are implemented fairly. Most important, businesses can achieve these goals while also being economically successful. Indeed, this may be the *only* way to achieve economic success over the long term.

Anne T. Lawrence

James Weber

Acknowledgments

We are grateful for the assistance of many colleagues at universities in the United States and abroad who over the years have helped shape this book with their excellent suggestions and ideas. We also note the feedback from students in our classes and at other colleges and universities that has helped make this book as user-friendly as possible.

We especially wish to acknowledge the assistance of several esteemed colleagues who provided detailed reviews for this edition. These reviewers are Kathleen Rehbein of Marquette University, Joseph Petrick of Wright State University, Harry Van Buren of the University of New Mexico–Albuquerque, Bruce Paton of San Francisco State University, Heather Elms of American University, Jacob Park of Green Mountain College, Tara Ceranic of the University of San Diego, Warren Wee of Hawaii Pacific University–Honolulu, Gwendolyn Alexis of Monmouth University, Norma Johansen of Scottsdale Community College, Nicholas Miceli of Concord University, Timothy Durfield of Citrus College, Wendy Eager of Eastern Washington University, Diane Swanson of Kansas State University, and Paul Drass of Marshall University.

In addition, we are grateful to the many colleagues who over the years have generously shared with us their insights into the theory and pedagogy of business and society. In particular, we thank Sandra Waddock of Boston College, Joerg Andriof of Warwick University, Craig Fleisher of the University of New Brunswick–St. John, Margaret J. Naumes of the University of New Hampshire, Michael Johnson-Cramer and Jamie Hendry of Bucknell University, John Mahon and Stephanie Welcomer of the University of Maine, Ann Svendsen of Simon Fraser University, Robert Boutilier of Robert Boutilier & Associates, Kathryn S. Rogers of Pitzer College, Anne Forrestal of the University of Oregon, Kelly Strong of Iowa State University, Daniel Gilbert of Gettysburg College, Gina Vega of Merrimack College, Craig Dunn and Brian Burton of Western Washington University, Lori V. Ryan of San Diego State University, Bryan W. Husted of York University, Sharon Livesey of Fordham University, Barry Mitnick of the University of Pittsburgh, Virginia Gerde and David Wasieleski of Duquesne University, Robbin Derry of the University of Lethbridge, Linda Ginzel of the University of Chicago, Jerry Calton of the University of Hawaii–Hilo, H. Richard Eisenbeis of the University of Southern Colorado (retired), Anthony J. Daboub of the University of Texas at Brownsville, Asbjorn Osland of San José State University, Linda Klebe Trevino of Pennsylvania State University, Mary Meisenhelter of York College of Pennsylvania, Steven Payne of Georgia College and State University, Amy Hillman and Gerald Keim of Arizona State University, Jeanne Logsdon and Shawn Berman of the University of New Mexico, Barbara Altman of the University of North Texas, Karen Moustafa of Indiana University–Purdue University Fort Wayne, Deborah Vidaver-Cohen of Florida International University, Lynda Brown of the University of Montana, Kirk O. Hanson of Santa Clara University, Kathleen A. Getz of American University, Martin Calkins of the University of Massachusetts–Boston, Jennifer J. Griffin and Mark Starik of The George Washington University, Frank Julian of Murray State University, Gordon Rands of Western Illinois University, and Diana Sharpe of Monmouth University.

These scholars' dedication to the creative teaching of business and society has been a continuing inspiration to us.

Thanks are also due to Murray Silverman and Tom E. Thomas of San Francisco State University, Pierre Batellier and Emmanuel Raufflet of HEC Montreal, and Jeanne McNett of Assumption College, who contributed cases to this edition. Bill Sodeman of Hawaii Pacific University provided invaluable assistance by sharing his expertise in drafting the two technology chapters in this edition. Bill enlightened us on many recent technological developments, including emerging trends in social networking.

A number of research assistants and former students have made contributions throughout this project for which we are appreciative. Among the special contributors to this project were Patricia Morrison of Grossmont College and Okan Sakar and Jacob Fait of Duquesne University, who provided research assistance, and Stephanie Glyptis and David Wasieleski of Duquesne University, who assisted in preparing the instructor's resource manual and ancillary materials.

We wish to express our continuing appreciation to William C. Frederick, who invited us into this project many years ago and who has continued to provide warm support and sage advice as the book has evolved through numerous editions. James E. Post, a former author of this book, has also continued to offer valuable intellectual guidance to this project.

We continue to be grateful to the excellent editorial and production team at McGraw-Hill. We offer special thanks to Dana Woo and Laura Hurst Spell, our sponsoring editors, for their skillful leadership of this project. Jaime Halteman headed the excellent marketing team. We also wish to recognize the able assistance of Jonathan Thornton, editorial coordinator, and Harvey Yep, project manager, whose ability to keep us on track and on time has been critical. Paul Ducham, publisher; Brent Gordon, editor-in-chief; Cathy Tepper, media project manager; Debra Sylvester, production supervisor; Peter de Lissovoy, copy editor; and JoAnne Schopler, who designed the book cover, also played key roles. Each of these people has provided professional contributions that we deeply value and appreciate.

Anne T. Lawrence

James Weber

Brief Contents

Contents

Business
in Society

CHAPTER ONE

The Corporation and Its Stakeholders

Business corporations have complex relationships with many individuals and organizations in society. The term *stakeholder* refers to all those that affect, or are affected by, the actions of the firm. An important part of management's role is to identify a firm's relevant stakeholders and understand the nature of their interests, power, and alliances with one another. Building positive and mutually beneficial relationships across organizational boundaries can help enhance a company's reputation and address critical social and ethical challenges. In a world of fast-paced globalization, shifting public expectations and government policies, growing ecological concerns, and new technologies, managers face the difficult challenge of achieving economic results while simultaneously creating value for all of their diverse stakeholders.

This Chapter Focuses on These Key Learning Objectives:

- Understanding the relationship between business and society and the ways in which business and society are part of an interactive system.
- Considering the purpose of the modern corporation.
- Knowing what a stakeholder is and who a corporation's market and nonmarket stakeholders are.
- Conducting a stakeholder analysis and understanding the basis of stakeholder interests and power.
- Recognizing the diverse ways in which modern corporations organize internally to interact with various stakeholders.
- Analyzing the forces of change that continually reshape the business and society relationship.

Walmart has been called "a template for 21st century capitalism." In each period of history, because of its size and potential impact on many groups in society, a single company often seems to best exemplify the management systems, technology, and social relationships of its era. In 1990, this company was U.S. Steel. In 1950, it was General Motors. Now, in the 2010s, it is Walmart.[1]

In 2009, Walmart was the largest private employer in the world, with 2.1 million employees worldwide. The company operated 7,390 facilities in 14 countries and had annual sales of $404 billion. The retailer was enormously popular with customers, drawing them in with its great variety of products under one roof and "save money, live better" slogan; 176 million customers worldwide shopped there every week. Economists estimated that Walmart had directly through its own actions and indirectly through its impact on its supply chain saved American shoppers $287 billion annually, about $957 for every person in the United States.[2] Shareholders who invested early were richly rewarded; the share price rose from 5 cents (split adjusted) when the company went public in 1970 to a high of $63 in 2008. (Walmart's stock, like that of many other companies, fell during the financial crisis of 2008–2009.) Walmart was a major customer for 61,000 suppliers worldwide, ranging from huge multinationals to tiny one-person operations.

Yet, Walmart had become a lightning rod for criticism from many quarters, charged with hurting local communities, discriminating against women, and driving down wages and working conditions. Consider the following:

- In 2004, the City Council in Inglewood, California, a predominantly African-American and Hispanic suburb of Los Angeles, voted down a proposed Walmart mega-store on a 60-acre parcel near the Hollywood racetrack. The city expressed concern that the development would adversely impact small businesses, traffic, public safety, and wages. This was only one of many communities that mobilized to block Walmart's entry in the 2000s.
- The same year, a federal judge ruled that a lawsuit charging Walmart stores with discrimination against women could go forward as a class action. The case charged that women at Walmart were paid less than men in comparable positions, received fewer promotions into management, and waited longer to move up than men did. (This case is further discussed in Chapter 17.) If the decision ultimately went against Walmart, the cost to the company could be in the hundreds of millions of dollars.
- In 2008, a critical documentary called *Walmart Nation* was released, featuring a former Miss America speaking out against the treatment of women by Walmart. This followed an earlier film, called *Walmart: The High Cost of Low Prices*. Among its embarrassing allegations was that many Walmart workers had to apply for public assistance because their wages, which averaged less than $10 an hour, were so low.

Lee Scott, the company's CEO, commented in an interview with *BusinessWeek*, "We always believed that if we sat here in Bentonville [the company's headquarters] and took care of our customers and took care of associates that the world itself would leave us alone." That, he acknowledged, was no longer the case. "We have to continue to evolve

---

[1] Nelson Lichtenstein, "Wal-Mart : A Template for Twenty-First Century Capitalism," in *Wal-Mart: The Face of Twenty-First Century Capitalism*, ed. Nelson Lichtenstein (New York: The New Press, 2006), pp. 3–30.

[2] Global Insight, "The Price Impact of Wal-mart: An Update through 2006," September 4, 2007.

in how we operate and how we interface with society," he said.[3] In an effort to shore up its reputation, the company increased its health insurance for workers, offered grants to small businesses, and donated to wildlife habitat restoration. It also adopted ambitious environmental goals to reduce waste, use more renewable energy, and sell more sustainable products, and began reporting to the public on its progress.[4]

Walmart's experience illustrates, on a particularly large scale, the challenges of managing successfully in a complex global network of stakeholders. The company's actions affected not only itself, but also many other people, groups, and organizations in society. Customers, suppliers, employees, stockholders, creditors, business partners, and local communities all had a stake in Walmart's decisions. Walmart had to learn just how difficult it could be to simultaneously satisfy multiple stakeholders with diverse and, in some respects, contradictory interests.

Every modern company, whether small or large, is part of a vast global business system. Whether a firm has 50 employees or 50,000—or, like Walmart, more than 2 million—its links to customers, suppliers, employees, and communities are certain to be numerous, diverse, and vital to its success. This is why the relationship between business and society is important to understand for both citizens and managers.

Business and Society

Business today is arguably the most dominant institution in the world. The term *business* refers here to any organization that is engaged in making a product or providing a service for a profit. Consider that in the United States today there are over 5 million businesses, based on the number that file tax returns with the government, and in the world as a whole, there are uncounted millions more. Of course, these businesses vary greatly in size and impact. They range from a woman who helps support her family by selling handmade tortillas by the side of the road in Mexico City for a few pesos, to ExxonMobil, a huge corporation that employs 81,000 workers and earns annual revenues approaching $400 billion in 200 nations worldwide.

Society, in its broadest sense, refers to human beings and to the social structures they collectively create. In a more specific sense, the term is used to refer to segments of humankind, such as members of a particular community, nation, or interest group. As a set of organizations created by humans, business is clearly a part of society. At the same time, it is also a distinct entity, separated from the rest of society by clear boundaries. Business is engaged in ongoing exchanges with its external environment across these dividing lines. For example, businesses recruit workers, buy supplies, and borrow money; they also sell products, donate time, and pay taxes. This book is broadly concerned with the relationship between business and society. A simple diagram of the relationship between the two appears in Figure 1.1.

As the Walmart example that opened this chapter illustrates, business and society are highly interdependent. Business activities impact other activities in society, and actions by various social actors and governments continuously affect business. To manage these interdependencies, managers need an understanding of their company's key relationships and how the social and economic system of which they are a part affects, and is affected by, their decisions.

---

[3] "Can Walmart Fit into a White Hat?" *BusinessWeek*, October 3, 2005; and extended interview with Lee Scott available online at *www.businessweek.com*.

[4] "2009 Global Sustainability Report," *www.walmartstores.com/sustainability*.

FIGURE 1.1
Business and Society: An Interactive System

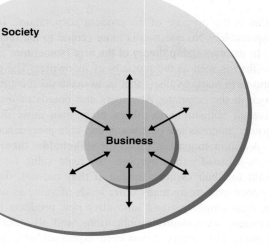

A Systems Perspective

General systems theory, first introduced in the 1940s, argues that all organisms are open to, and interact with, their external environments. Although most organisms have clear boundaries, they cannot be understood in isolation, but only in relationship to their surroundings. This simple but powerful idea can be applied to many disciplines. For example, in botany, the growth of a plant cannot be explained without reference to soil, light, oxygen, moisture, and other characteristics of its environment. As applied to management theory, the systems concept implies that business firms (social organisms) are embedded in a broader social structure (external environment) with which they constantly interact. Corporations have ongoing boundary exchanges with customers, governments, competitors, the media, communities, and many other individuals and groups. Just as good soil, water, and light help a plant grow, positive interactions with society benefit a business firm.

Like biological organisms, moreover, businesses must adapt to changes in the environment. Plants growing in low-moisture environments must develop survival strategies, like the cactus that evolves to store water in its leaves. Similarly, a long-distance telephone company in a newly deregulated market must learn to compete by changing the products and services it offers. The key to business survival is often this ability to adapt effectively to changing conditions. In business, systems theory provides a powerful tool to help managers conceptualize the relationship between their companies and their external environments.

Systems theory helps us understand how business and society, taken together, form an **interactive social system**. Each needs the other, and each influences the other. They are entwined so completely that any action taken by one will surely affect the other. They are both separate and connected. Business is part of society, and society penetrates far and often into business decisions. In a world where global communication is rapidly expanding, the connections are closer than ever before. Throughout this book we discuss examples of organizations and people that are grappling with the challenges of, and helping to shape, business–society relationships.

The Stakeholder Theory of the Firm

What is the purpose of the modern corporation? To whom, or what, should the firm be responsible?[5] No question is more central to the relationship between business and society.

In the **ownership theory of the firm** (sometimes also called property or finance theory), the firm is seen as the property of its owners. The purpose of the firm is to maximize its long-term market value—that is, to make the most money it can for shareholders who own stock in the company. Managers and boards of directors are agents of shareholders and have no obligations to others, other than those directly specified by law. In this view, owners' interests are paramount and take precedence over the interests of others.

A contrasting view, called the **stakeholder theory of the firm**, argues that corporations serve a broad public purpose: to create value for society. All companies must make a profit for their owners; indeed, if they did not, they would not long survive. However, corporations create many other kinds of value as well, such as professional development for their employees and innovative new products for their customers. In this view, corporations have multiple obligations, and all stakeholders' interests must be taken into account. This approach has been expressed well by the pharmaceutical company Novartis, which states in its code of conduct that it "places a premium on dealing fairly with employees, commercial partners, government authorities, and the public. Success in its business ventures depends upon maintaining the trust of these essential stakeholders."[6]

Supporters of the stakeholder theory of the firm make three core arguments for their position: *descriptive, instrumental,* and *normative.*[7]

The *descriptive argument* says that the stakeholder view is simply a more realistic description of how companies really work. Managers have to pay keen attention, of course, to their quarterly and annual financial performance. Keeping Wall Street satisfied by managing for growth—thereby attracting more investors and increasing the stock price—is a core part of any top manager's job. But the job of management is much more complex than this. In order to produce consistent results, managers have to be concerned with producing high-quality and innovative products and services for their customers, attracting and retaining talented employees, and complying with a plethora of complex government regulations. As a practical matter, managers direct their energies toward all stakeholders, not just owners.

The *instrumental argument* says that stakeholder management is more effective as a corporate strategy. A wide range of studies have shown that companies that behave responsibly toward multiple stakeholder groups perform better financially, over the long run, than those that do not. (This empirical evidence is further explored in Chapters 3 and 4.) These findings make sense, because good relationships with stakeholders are themselves a source of value for the firm. Attention to stakeholders' rights and concerns can help produce motivated employees, satisfied customers, and supportive communities, all good for the company's bottom line.

The *normative argument* says that stakeholder management is simply the right thing to do. Corporations have great power and control vast resources; these privileges carry with them a duty toward all those affected by a corporation's actions. Moreover, all stakeholders,

---

[5] One summary of contrasting theories of the purpose of the firm appears in Margaret M. Blair, "Whose Interests Should Corporations Serve," in Margaret M. Blair and Bruce K. MacLaury, *Ownership and Control: Rethinking Corporate Governance for the Twenty-First Century* (Washington, DC: Brookings Institution, 1995), ch. 6, pp. 202–34. More recently, these questions have been taken up in James E. Post, Lee E. Preston, and Sybille Sachs, *Redefining the Corporation: Stakeholder Management and Organizational Wealth* (Palo Alto, CA: Stanford University Press, 2002).

[6] Novartis Corporation Code of Conduct, online at *www.novartis.com.*

[7] The descriptive, instrumental, and normative arguments are summarized in Thomas Donaldson and Lee E. Preston, "The Stakeholder Theory of the Corporation: Concepts, Evidence and Implications," *Academy of Management Review* 20, no. 1 (1995), pp. 65–71. See also Post, Preston, and Sachs, *Redefining the Corporation,* ch. 1.

not just owners, contribute something of value to the corporation. A skilled engineer at Microsoft who applies his or her creativity to solving a difficult programming problem has made a kind of investment in the company, even if it is not a monetary investment. Any individual or group who makes a contribution, or takes a risk, has a moral right to some claim on the corporation's rewards.[8]

A basis for both the ownership and stakeholder theories of the firm exists in law. The legal term *fiduciary* means a person who exercises power on behalf of another—that is, who acts as the other's agent. In U.S. law, managers are considered fiduciaries of the owners of the firm (its stockholders) and have an obligation to run the business in their interest. These legal concepts are clearly consistent with the ownership theory of the firm. However, other laws and court cases have given managers broad latitude in the exercise of their fiduciary duties. In the United States (where corporations are chartered not by the federal government but by the states), most states have passed laws that permit managers to take into consideration a wide range of other stakeholders' interests, including those of employees, customers, creditors, suppliers, and communities. In addition, many federal laws extend specific protections to various groups of stakeholders, such as those that prohibit discrimination against employees or grant consumers the right to sue if harmed by a product.

In other nations, the legal rights of nonowner stakeholders are often more fully developed than in the United States. For example, a number of European countries—including Germany, Norway, Austria, Denmark, Finland, and Sweden—require public companies to include employee members on their boards of directors, so that their interests will be explicitly represented. Under the European Union's so-called harmonization statutes, managers are specifically permitted to take into account the interests of customers, employees, creditors, and others.

In short, while the law requires managers to act on behalf of stockholders, it also gives them wide discretion—and in some instances requires them—to manage on behalf of the full range of stakeholder groups. The next section provides a more formal definition and an expanded discussion of the stakeholder concept.

The Stakeholder Concept

The term **stakeholder** refers to persons and groups that affect, or are affected by, an organization's decisions, policies, and operations.[9] The word *stake*, in this context, means an interest in—or claim on—a business enterprise. Those with a stake in the firm's actions include such diverse groups as customers, employees, stockholders, the media, governments, professional and trade associations, social and environmental activists, and nongovernmental organizations. The term *stakeholder* is not the same as *stockholder*, although the words sound similar. Stockholders—individuals or organizations that own shares of a company's stock—are one of several kinds of stakeholders.

Business organizations are embedded in networks involving many participants. Each of these participants has a relationship with the firm, based on ongoing interactions. Each

---

[8] Another formulation of this point has been offered by Robert Phillips, who argues for a principle of stakeholder fairness. This states that "when people are engaged in a cooperative effort and the benefits of this cooperative effort are accepted, obligations are created on the part of the group accepting the benefit" [i.e., the business firm]. Robert Phillips, *Stakeholder Theory and Organizational Ethics* (San Francisco: Berrett-Koehler, 2003), p. 9 and ch. 5.

[9] The term *stakeholder* was first introduced in 1963 but was not widely used in the management literature until the publication of R. Edward Freeman's *Strategic Management: A Stakeholder Approach* (Marshfield, MA: Pitman, 1984). For more recent summaries of the stakeholder theory literature, see Thomas Donaldson and Lee E. Preston, "The Stakeholder Theory of the Corporation: Concepts, Evidence, Implications," *Academy of Management Review*, January 1995, pp. 71–83; Max B. E. Clarkson, ed., *The Corporation and Its Stakeholders: Classic and Contemporary Readings* (Toronto: University of Toronto Press, 1998); and Abe J. Zakhem, Daniel E. Palmer, and Mary Lyn Stoll, *Stakeholder Theory: Essential Readings in Ethical Leadership and Management* (Amherst, NY: Prometheus Books, 2008).

of them shares, to some degree, in both the risks and rewards of the firm's activities. And each has some kind of claim on the firm's resources and attention, based on law, moral right, or both. The number of these stakeholders and the variety of their interests can be large, making a company's decisions very complex, as the Walmart example illustrates.

Managers make good decisions when they pay attention to the effects of their decisions on stakeholders, as well as stakeholders' effects on the company. On the positive side, strong relationships between a corporation and its stakeholders are an asset that adds value. On the negative side, some companies disregard stakeholders' interests, either out of the belief that the stakeholder is wrong or out of the misguided notion that an unhappy customer, employee, or regulator does not matter. Such attitudes often prove costly to the company involved. Today, for example, companies know that they cannot locate a factory or store in a community that strongly objects. They also know that making a product that is perceived as unsafe invites lawsuits and jeopardizes market share.

Market and Nonmarket Stakeholders

Business interacts with society in many diverse ways, and a company's relationships with various stakeholders differ. **Market stakeholders** are those that engage in economic transactions with the company as it carries out its primary purpose of providing society with goods and services. (For this reason, market stakeholders are also sometimes called *primary* stakeholders.)

Figure 1.2 shows the market stakeholders of business. Each relationship is based on a unique transaction, or two-way exchange. Stockholders invest in the firm and in return receive the potential for dividends and capital gains. Creditors lend money and collect

FIGURE 1.2
Market Stakeholders of Business

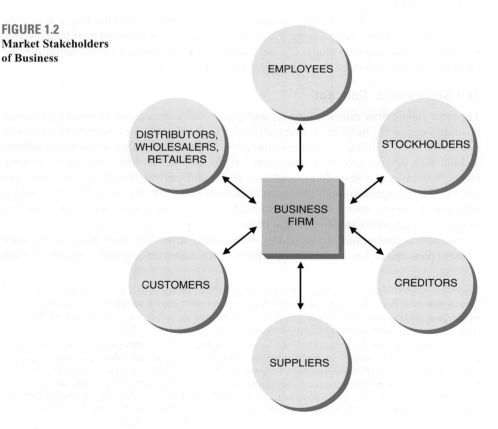

Exhibit 1.A

Are Managers Stakeholders?

Are managers, especially top executives, stakeholders? This has been a contentious issue in stakeholder theory.

On one hand, the answer clearly is "yes." Like other stakeholders, managers are impacted by the firm's decisions. As employees of the firm, managers receive compensation—often very generous compensation, as shown in Chapter 14. Their managerial roles confer opportunities for professional advancement, social status, and power over others. Managers benefit from the company's success and are hurt by its failure. For these reasons, they might properly be classified as employees on the perimeter of the stakeholder wheel, as shown in Figure 1.2.

One the other hand, top executives are agents of the firm and are responsible for acting on its behalf. In the stakeholder theory of the firm, their role is to integrate stakeholder interests, rather than to promote their own more narrow, selfish goals. For these reasons, they might properly be classified in the center of the stakeholder wheel, as representatives of the firm.

Management theory has long recognized that these two roles of managers potentially conflict. The main job of executives is to act for the company, but all too often they act primarily for themselves. Consider, for example, the many top executives of Merrrill Lynch, Enron, and WorldCom who enriched themselves personally at the expense of shareholders, employees, customers, and other stakeholders. The challenge of persuading top managers to act in the firm's best interest is further discussed in Chapter 14.

payments of interest and principal. Employees contribute their skills and knowledge in exchange for wages, benefits, and the opportunity for personal satisfaction and professional development. In return for payment, suppliers provide raw materials, energy, services, and other inputs; and wholesalers, distributors, and retailers engage in market transactions with the firm as they help move the product from plant to sales outlets to customers. All businesses need customers who are willing to buy their products or services. These are the fundamental market interactions every business has with society.

The puzzling question of whether or not managers should be classified as stakeholders along with other employees is discussed in Exhibit 1.A.

Nonmarket stakeholders, by contrast, are people and groups who—although they do not engage in direct economic exchange with the firm—are nonetheless affected by or can affect its actions. Figure 1.3 shows the nonmarket stakeholders of business (also called *secondary* stakeholders by some theorists). Nonmarket stakeholders include the community, various levels of government, nongovernmental organizations, the media, business support groups, and the general public. The natural environment is generally not considered a stakeholder, because it is not a social group, but is represented in Figure 1.3 by nongovernmental organizations, including those dedicated to environmnental issues.

The classification of government as a nonmarket, or secondary, stakeholder has been controversial in stakeholder theory. Most theorists say that government is a nonmarket stakeholder (as does this book) because it does not normally conduct any direct market exchanges (buying and selling) with business. However, money often flows from business to government in the form of taxes and fees, and sometimes from government to business in the form of subsidies or incentives. Moreover, some businesses—defense contractors for example—*do* sell directly to the government and receive payment for goods and services rendered. For this reason, a few theorists have called government a market stakeholder of business. And, in a few cases, the government may take a direct ownership stake in a company—as the U.S. government did recently when it invested in several banks and auto companies, becoming a shareholder of these firms. The unique relationship between government and business is discussed throughout this book.

FIGURE 1.3
Nonmarket Stakeholders of Business

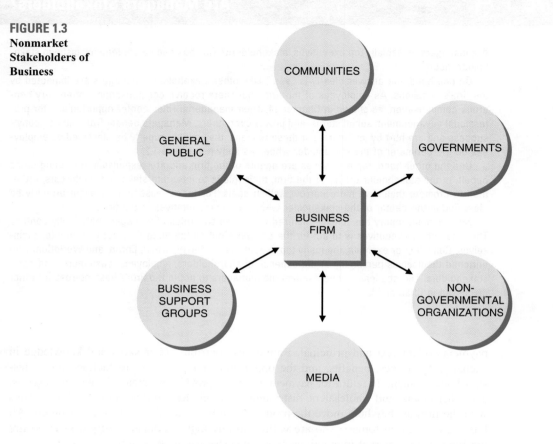

Both Figures 1.2 and 1.3 should be understood as very simplified ways of understanding the real world. These diagrams show the business firm as, in effect, the center of a system, like the sun with its planets in the solar system. They also illustrate the firm's relationship to each stakeholder, but not stakeholders' relationships with each other. Many now believe that a more accurate way to visualize the relationship is to show the business firm embedded in a complex network of stakeholders, many of which have independent relationships with each other.[10] This alternative image of the business firm and its stakeholders—as a network with many nodes—is shown in Figure 1.4.

Nonmarket stakeholders are not necessarily less important than others, simply because they do not engage in direct economic exchange with a business. On the contrary, interactions with such groups can be critical to a firm's success or failure, as shown in the following example:

In 2001, a company called Energy Management Inc. (EMI) announced a plan to build a wind farm about six miles off the shore of Cape Cod, Massachusetts, to supply clean, renewable power to New England customers. The project, called Cape Wind, immediately generated intense opposition from socially prominent residents of Cape Cod and nearby islands, who were concerned that its 130 wind turbines would spoil the view and get in the way of boats. Opponents of the

---

[10] Timothy J. Rowley, "Moving beyond Dyadic Ties: A Network Theory of Stakeholder Influence," *Academy of Management Review* 22, no. 4 (October 1997).

FIGURE 1.4
**A Stakeholder
Network**

Source: Adapted from Ann C.
Svendsen and Myriam Laberge,
"Convening Stakeholder
Networks: A New Way of
Thinking, Being, and
Engaging," *Journal of
Corporate Citizenship* 19
(Autumn 2005). Used by
permission.

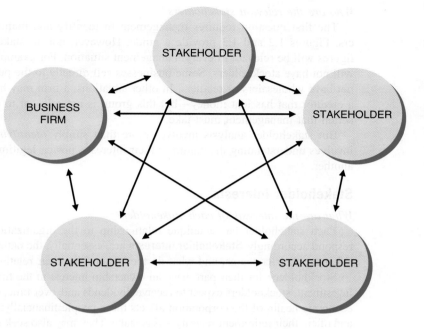

project were able to block its progress for almost a decade. In 2009, although
Cape Wind had cleared some legal hurdles and obtained preliminary permits, the
wind farm had still not been built.[11]

In this instance, the community was able to block the company's plans, even though
it did not have a market relationship with it. Moreover, market and nonmarket areas of
involvement are not always sharply distinguished; often, one shades into the other. For
example, the environmental effect of an automobile may be of concern both to a customer (a market stakeholder) and to the entire community (a nonmarket stakeholder),
which experiences cumulative air pollution emitted from cars.

Of further note, some individuals or groups may play multiple stakeholder roles. Some
theorists use the term *role sets* to refer to this phenomenon. For example, one person
may work at a company, but also live in the surrounding community, own shares of company stock in his or her 401(k) retirement account, and even purchase the company's
products from time to time. This person has several stakes in a company's actions.

Later sections of this book (especially Chapters 14 through 19) will discuss in more
detail the relationship between business and its various stakeholders.

Stakeholder Analysis

An important part of the modern manager's job is to identify relevant stakeholders and
to understand both their interests and the power they may have to assert these interests.
This process is called **stakeholder analysis**. It asks four key questions, as follows.

---

[11] The Web site of the project is at *www.capewind.org*. The story of the opposition to Cape Wind is told in Robert
Whitcomb and Wendy Williams, *Cape Wind: Money, Celebrity, Energy, Class, Politics, and the Battle for Our Energy
Future* (New York: PublicAffairs, 2008).

Who are the relevant stakeholders?

The first question requires management to identify and map the relevant stakeholders. Figures 1.2 and 1.3 provide a guide. However, not all stakeholders listed in these figures will be relevant in every management situation. For example, a privately held firm will not have stockholders. Some businesses sell directly to the public, and therefore will not have wholesalers or retailers. In other situations, a firm may have a stakeholder—say, a creditor that has lent money—but this group is not relevant to a particular decision or action that management must take.

But stakeholder analysis involves more than simply *identifying* stakeholders; it also involves understanding the nature of their interests, power, legitimacy, and links with one another.

Stakeholder Interests

What are the interests of each stakeholder?

Each stakeholder has a unique relationship to the organization, and managers must respond accordingly. **Stakeholder interests** are, essentially, the nature of each group's stake. What are their concerns, and what do they want from their relationship with the firm?[12]

Stockholders, for their part, have an ownership interest in the firm. In exchange for their investment, stockholders expect to receive dividends and, over time, capital appreciation. The economic health of the corporation affects these people financially; their personal wealth—and often, their retirement security—is at stake. They may also seek social objectives through their choice of investments. Customers, for their part, are most interested in gaining fair value and quality in exchange for the purchase price of goods and services. Suppliers, likewise, wish to receive fair compensation for products and services they provide. Employees, in exchange for their time and effort, want to receive fair compensation and an opportunity to develop their job skills. Governments, public interest groups, and local communities have another sort of relationship with the company. In general, their stake is broader than the financial stake of owners, customers, and suppliers. They may wish to protect the environment, assure human rights, or advance other broad social interests. Managers need to understand these complex and often intersecting stakeholder interests.

Stakeholder Power

What is the power of each stakeholder?

Stakeholder power means the ability to use resources to make an event happen or to secure a desired outcome. Experts have recognized four types of stakeholder power: *voting power, economic power, political power,* and *legal power.*

Voting power means that the stakeholder has a legitimate right to cast a vote. Stockholders typically have voting power proportionate to the percentage of the company's stock they own. Stockholders typically have an opportunity to vote on such major decisions as mergers and acquisitions, the composition of the board of directors, and other issues that may come before the annual meeting. (Stockholder voting power should be distinguished from the voting power exercised by citizens, which is discussed below.)

In 2008, Carl Icahn, a billionaire financier and investor, sought to exercise his voting power as a shareholder of Yahoo! Icahn, who owned about 5 percent of the company's shares, proposed his own slate of candidates for the board of directors. Icahn wanted control of the board in order to promote his position that

---

[12] A full discussion of the interests of stakeholders may be found in R. Edward Freeman, *Ethical Theory and Business* (Englewood Cliffs, NJ: Prentice Hall, 1994).

Yahoo! should seriously consider selling part of its business to Microsoft—a step that the company's CEO and current board opposed. Icahn reached out to other shareholders, asking for their support for his slate on the grounds that a sale to Microsoft would boost Yahoo!'s stock price. Icahn finally called off his challenge after Yahoo! agreed to add Icahn and two of his associates to the board.[13]

Customers, suppliers, and retailers have *economic power* with the company. Suppliers can withhold supplies or refuse to fill orders if a company fails to meet its contractual responsibilities. Customers may refuse to buy a company's products or services if the company acts improperly. Customers can boycott products if they believe the goods are too expensive, poorly made, or unsafe. Employees, for their part, can refuse to work under certain conditions, a form of economic power known as a strike or slowdown. Economic power often depends on how well organized a stakeholder group is. For example, workers who are organized into unions usually have more economic power than do workers who try to negotiate individually with their employers.

Governments exercise *political power* through legislation, regulations, or lawsuits. While government agencies act directly, other stakeholders use their political power indirectly by urging government to use its powers by passing new laws or enacting regulations. Citizens may also vote for candidates that support their views with respect to government laws and regulations affecting business, a different kind of voting power than the one discussed above. Stakeholders may also exercise political power directly, as when social, environmental, or community activists organize to protest a particular corporate action.

Finally, stakeholders have *legal power* when they bring suit against a company for damages, based on harm caused by the firm—for instance, lawsuits brought by customers for damages caused by defective products, brought by employees for damages caused by workplace injury, or brought by environmentalists for damages caused by pollution or harm to species or habitat. After Enron collapsed, many institutional shareholders, such as state pension funds, joined together to sue to recoup some of their losses.

Activists often try to use all of these kinds of power when they want to change a company's policy. For example, human rights activists wanted to bring pressure on Unocal Corporation to change its practices in Burma, where it had entered into a joint venture with the government to build a gas pipeline. Critics charged that many human rights violations occurred during this project, including forced labor and relocations. In an effort to pressure Unocal to change its behavior, activists organized protests at stockholder meetings (*voting power*), called for boycotts of Unocal products (*economic power*), promoted local ordinances prohibiting cities from buying from Unocal (*political power*), and brought a lawsuit for damages on behalf of Burmese villagers (*legal power*). These activists increased their chances of success by mobilizing many kinds of power. This combination of tactics eventually forced Unocal to pay compensation to people whose rights had been violated and to fund education and health care projects in the pipeline region.[14]

Exhibit 1.B provides a schematic summary of some of the main interests and powers of both market and nonmarket stakeholders.

Stakeholder Coalitions

An understanding of stakeholder interests and power enables managers to answer the final question of stakeholder analysis: *How are coalitions likely to form?*

---

[13] "Yahoo Will Add Icahn to Its Board," *The Wall Street Journal,* July 22, 2008; and "Icahn Finalizes Proposed Slate for Yahoo," *The Wall Street Journal,* July 15, 2008.

[14] Further information about the campaign against Unocal is available at *www.earthrights.org/unocal.*

Exhibit 1.B

Stakeholders: Nature of Interest and Power

Stakeholder	Nature of Interest— Stakeholder Wishes To:	Nature of Power— Stakeholder Influences Company By:
Market Stakeholders		
Employees	■ Maintain stable employment in firm ■ Receive fair pay for work ■ Work in safe, comfortable environment	■ Union bargaining power ■ Work actions or strikes ■ Publicity
Stockholders	■ Receive a satisfactory return on investments (dividends) ■ Realize appreciation in stock value over time	■ Exercising voting rights based on share ownership ■ Exercising rights to inspect company books and records
Customers	■ Receive fair exchange: value and quality for money spent ■ Receive safe, reliable products	■ Purchasing goods from competitors ■ Boycotting companies whose products are unsatisfactory or whose policies are unacceptable
Suppliers	■ Receive regular orders for goods ■ Be paid promptly for supplies delivered	■ Refusing to meet orders if conditions of contract are breached ■ Supplying to competitors
Retailers/ wholesalers	■ Receive quality goods in a timely fashion at reasonable cost ■ Offer reliable products that consumers trust and value	■ Buying from other suppliers if terms of contract are unsatisfactory ■ Boycotting companies whose goods or policies are unsatisfactory
Creditors	■ Receive repayment of loans ■ Collect debts and interest	■ Calling in loans if payments are not made ■ Utilizing legal authorities to repossess or take over property if loan payments are severely delinquent

Not surprisingly, stakeholder interests often coincide. For example, consumers of fresh fruit and farmworkers who harvest that fruit in the field may have a shared interest in reducing the use of pesticides, because of possible adverse health effects from exposure to chemicals. When their interests are similar, stakeholders may form coalitions, temporary alliances to pursue a common interest. **Stakeholder coalitions** are not static. Groups that are highly involved with a company today may be less involved tomorrow. Issues that are controversial at one time may be uncontroversial later; stakeholders that are

Stakeholder	Nature of Interest— Stakeholder Wishes To:	Nature of Power— Stakeholder Influences Company By:
Nonmarket Stakeholders		
Communities	■ Employ local residents in the company ■ Ensure that the local environment is protected ■ Ensure that the local area is developed	■ Refusing to extend additional credit ■ Issuing or restricting operating licenses and permits ■ Lobbying government for regulation of the company's policies or methods of land use and waste disposal
Nongovermental organizations	■ Monitor company actions and policies to ensure that they conform to legal and ethical standards, and that they protect the public's safety	■ Gaining broad public support through publicizing the issue ■ Lobbying government for regulation of the company
Media	■ Keep the public informed on all issues relevant to their health, well-being, and economic status ■ Monitor company actions	■ Publicizing events that affect the public, especially those that have negative effects
Business support groups (e.g., trade associations)	■ Provide research and information that will help the company or industry perform in a changing environment	■ Using staff and resources to assist company in business endeavors and development efforts ■ Providing legal or "group" political support beyond that which an individual company can provide for itself
Governments	■ Promote economic development ■ Encourage social improvements ■ Raise revenues through taxes	■ Adopting regulations and laws ■ Issuing licenses and permits ■ Allowing or disallowing industrial activity
The general public	■ Protect social values ■ Minimize risks ■ Achieve prosperity for society	■ Supporting activists ■ Pressing government to act ■ Condemning or praising individual companies

dependent on an organization at one time may be less so at another. To make matters more complicated, the process of shifting coalitions does not occur uniformly in all parts of a large corporation. Stakeholders involved with one part of a large company often have little or nothing to do with other parts of the organization.

In recent years, coalitions of stakeholders have become increasingly international in scope. Communications technology has enabled like-minded people to come together quickly, even across political boundaries and many miles of separation. Cell phones, blogs, e-mail, faxes, and social networking sites have become powerful tools in the hands of groups that monitor how multinational businesses are operating in different locations around the world.

In 2000, the Mexican government canceled plans for a salt plant in a remote area on the Pacific coast, after groups from around the world rallied to oppose it. The proposed plant was a joint venture of Mitsubishi (a multinational corporation based in Japan) and the Mexican government. Together, they wanted to create jobs, taxes, and revenue by mining naturally occurring salt deposits along the Baja California coast. Environmentalists attacked the venture on the grounds that it would hurt the gray whales that migrated every year to a nearby lagoon to give birth to their young. In the past, such objections would probably have attracted little attention. But critics were able to use the Internet and the media to mobilize over 50 organizations worldwide to threaten a boycott of Mitsubishi. One million people sent protest letters to "save the gray whale." Although Mitsubishi was convinced that the whales would continue to thrive near the salt works, it found its plans blocked at every turn.[15]

This example illustrates how international networks of activists, coupled with the media's interest in such business and society issues, make coalition development and issue activism an increasingly powerful strategic factor for companies. Nongovernmental organizations regularly meet to discuss problems such as global warming, human rights, and environmental issues, just as their business counterparts do. Today, stakeholder coalitions are numerous in every industry and important to every company.

Stakeholder Salience and Mapping

Some scholars have suggested that managers pay the most attention to stakeholders possessing greater **salience**. (Something is *salient* when it stands out from a background, is seen as important, or draws attention.) Stakeholders stand out to managers when they have power, legitimacy, and urgency. The previous section discussed various forms of stakeholder power. *Legitimacy* refers to the extent to which a stakeholder's actions are seen as proper or appropriate by the broader society. *Urgency* refers to the time sensitivity of a stakeholder's claim—that is, the extent to which it demands immediate action. The more of these three attributes a stakeholder possesses, the greater the stakeholder's salience and the more likely that managers will notice and respond.[16]

Managers can use the salience concept to develop a **stakeholder map**, a graphical representation of the relationship of stakeholder salience to a particular issue. Figure 1.5 presents a simple example of a stakeholder map. The figure shows the position of various stakeholders on a hypothetical issue—whether or not a company should shut down an underperforming factory in a community. The horizontal axis represents each stakeholder's position on this issue—from "against" (the company should not shut the plant) to "for" (the company should shut the plant). The vertical axis represents the salience of the stakeholder, an overall measure of that stakeholder's power, legitimacy, and urgency. In this example, the company's creditors (banks) are pressuring the firm to close the plant. They have high salience, because they control the company's credit line and are urgently

---

[15] H. Richard Eisenbeis and Sue Hanks, "When Gray Whales Blush," case presented at the annual meeting of the North American Case Research Association, October 2002.

[16] Ronald K. Mitchell, Bradley R. Agle, and Donna J. Wood, "Toward a Theory of Stakeholder Identification and Salience: Defining the Principle of Who and What Really Counts," *Academy of Management Review* 22, no. 4 (1997), pp. 853–86.

FIGURE 1.5
Stakeholder Map of a Proposed Plant Closure

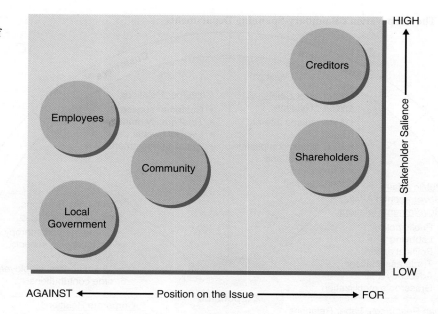

demanding action. Shareholders, who are powerful and legitimate (but not as urgent in their demands), also favor the closure. On the other side, employees urgently oppose shuting the plant, because their jobs are at stake, but they do not have as much power as the creditors and are therefore less salient. Local government officials and local businesses also wish the plant to remain open, but have lower salience than the other stakeholders involved.

A stakeholder map is a useful tool, because it enables managers to see quickly how stakeholders feel about an issue and whether salient stakeholders tend to be in favor or opposed. It also helps managers see how stakeholder coalitions are likely to form, and what outcomes are likely. In this example, company executives might conclude from the stakeholder map that those supporting the closure—creditors and shareholders—have the greatest salience. Although they are less salient, employees, local government officials, and the community all oppose the closure and may try to increase their salience by working together. Managers might conclude that the closure is likely, unless opponents organize an effective coaliton. This example is fairly simple; more complex stakeholder maps can represent network ties among stakeholders, the size of stakeholder groups, and the degree of consensus within stakeholder groups.[17]

The Corporation's Boundary-Spanning Departments

How do corporations organize internally to respond to and interact with stakeholders? **Boundary-spanning departments** are departments, or offices, within an organization that reach across the dividing line that separates the company from groups and people in society.

---

[17] For two different approaches to stakeholder mapping, see David Saiia and Vananh Le, "Mapping Stakeholder Salience," presented at the International Association for Business and Society, June 2009; and Robert Boutilier, *Stakeholder Politics: Social Capital, Sustainable Development, and the Corporation* (Sheffield, UK: Greenleaf Publishing, 2009), chs. 6 and 7.

FIGURE 1.6 The Corporation's Boundary-Spanning Departments

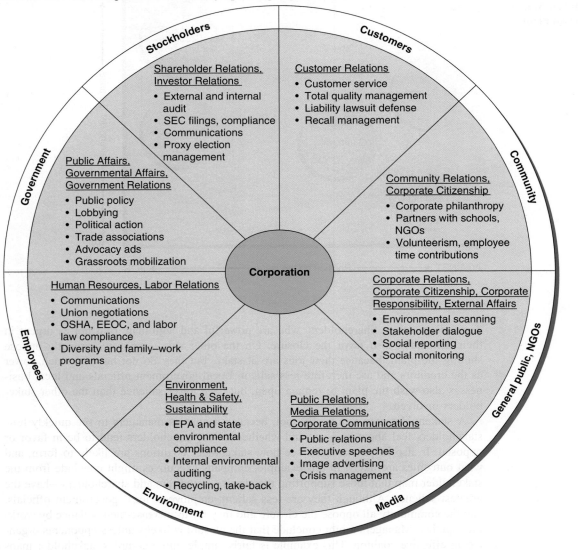

Building positive and mutually beneficial relationships across organizational boundaries is a growing part of management's role.

Figure 1.6 presents a list of the corporation's market and nonmarket stakeholders, alongside the corporate departments that typically have responsibility for engaging with them. As the figure suggests, the organization of the corporation's boundary-spanning functions is complex. For example, in many companies, departments of public affairs or government relations interact with elected officials and regulators. Departments of investor relations interact with shareholders; human resources with employees; customer relations with customers; and community relations with the community. Specialized departments of environment, health, and safety may deal with environmental compliance and worker health and safety, and public relations or corporate communications with the media. Many of these specific departments will be discussed in more detail in later chapters.

The Dynamic Environment of Business

A core argument of this book is that *the external environment of business is dynamic and ever changing*. Businesses and their stakeholders do not interact in a vacuum. On the contrary, most companies operate in a swirl of social, ethical, global, political, ecological, and technological change that produces both opportunities and threats. Figure 1.7 diagrams the six dynamic forces that powerfully shape the business and society relationship. Each of these forces is introduced briefly below and will be discussed in more detail later in this book.

Changing societal expectations. Everywhere around the world, society's expectations of business are changing. People increasingly expect business to be more responsible, believing companies should pay close attention to social issues and act as good citizens in society. New public issues constantly arise that require action. Increasingly, business is faced with the daunting task of balancing its social, legal, and economic obligations, seeking to meet its commitments to multiple stakeholders. These changes in society's expectations of business, and how managers have responded, are described in Chapter 2 and 3.

Growing emphasis on ethical reasoning and actions. The public also expects business to be ethical and wants corporate managers to apply ethical principles or values—in other words, guidelines about what is right and wrong, fair and unfair, and morally correct—when they make business decisions. Fair employment practices, concern for

FIGURE 1.7
Forces That Shape the Business and Society Relationship

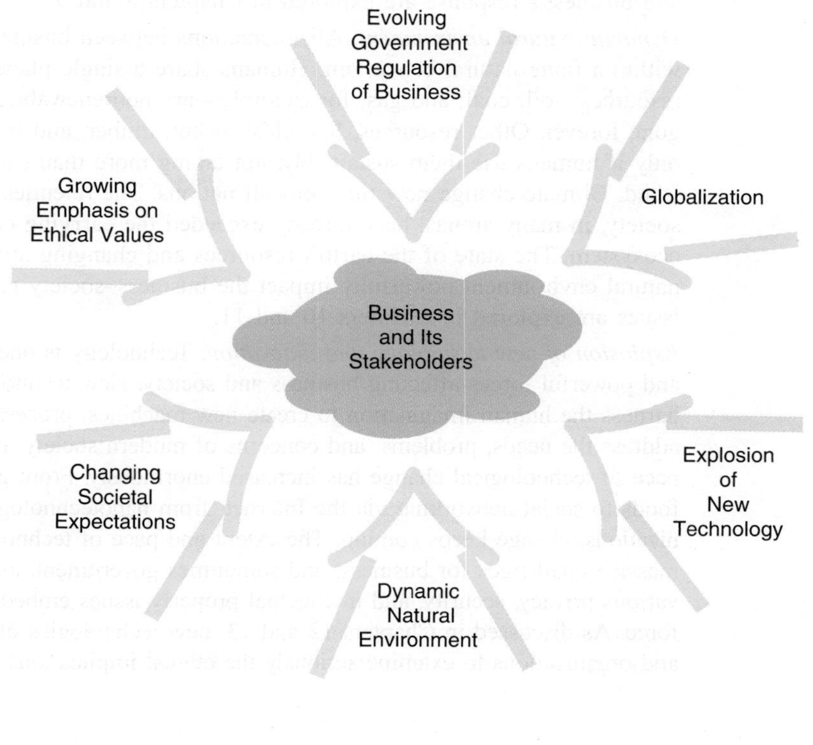

consumer safety, contribution to the welfare of the community, and human rights protection around the world have become more prominent and important. Business has created ethics programs to help ensure that employees are aware of these issues and act in accordance with ethical standards. The ethical challenges faced by business, both domestically and abroad—and business's response—are discussed in Chapters 4 and 5.

Globalization. We live in an increasingly integrated world economy, characterized by the unceasing movement of goods, services, and capital across national borders. Large transnational corporations do business in scores of countries. Products and services people buy every day in the United States or Germany may have come from Indonesia, Haiti, or Mexico. Today, economic forces truly play out on a global stage. A financial crisis on Wall Street can quickly impact economies around the world. Societal issues—such as the race to find a cure for HIV/AIDS, the movement for women's equality, or the demands of citizens everywhere for full access to the Internet—also cut across national boundaries. Environmental issues, such as ozone depletion and species extinction, affect all communities. Globalization challenges business to integrate their financial, social, and environmental performance. Chapters 6 and 7 address globalization and business firms' efforts to become better global citizens.

Evolving government regulations and business response. The role of government has changed dramatically in many nations in recent decades. Governments around the world have enacted a myriad of new policies that have profoundly constrained how business is allowed to operate. Government regulation of business periodically becomes tighter, then looser, much as a pendulum swings back and forth. Because of the dynamic nature of this force, business has developed various strategies to influence elected officials and government regulators at federal, state, and local levels. Business managers understand the opportunities that may arise from active participation in the political process. The changing role of government, its impact, and business's response are explored in Chapters 8 and 9.

Dynamic natural environment. All interactions between business and society occur within a finite natural ecosystem. Humans share a single planet, and many of our resources—oil, coal, and gas, for example—are nonrenewable. Once used, they are gone forever. Other resources, like clean water, timber, and fish, are renewable, but only if humans use them sustainably, not taking more than can be naturally replenished. Climate change now threatens all nations. The relentless demands of human society, in many arenas, have already exceeded the carrying capacity of the earth's ecosystem. The state of the earth's resources and changing attitudes about the natural environment powerfully impact the business–society relationship. These issues are explored in Chapters 10 and 11.

Explosion of new technology and innovation. Technology is one of the most dramatic and powerful forces affecting business and society. New technological innovations harness the human imagination to create new machines, processes, and software that address the needs, problems, and concerns of modern society. In recent years, the pace of technological change has increased enormously. From genetically modified foods to social networking via the Internet, from nanotechnology to wireless communications, change keeps coming. The extent and pace of technological innovation pose massive challenges for business, and sometimes government, as they seek to manage various privacy, security, and intellectual property issues embedded in this dynamic force. As discussed in Chapters 12 and 13, new technologies often force managers and organizations to examine seriously the ethical implications of their use.

Creating Value in a Dynamic Environment

These powerful and dynamic forces—fast-paced changes in societal and ethical expectations, the global economy, government policies, the natural environment, and new technology—establish the context in which businesses interact with their many market and nonmarket stakeholders, as discussed in Chapters 14 to 19. This means that the relationship between business and society is continuously changing in new and often unpredictable ways. Environments, people, and organizations change; inevitably, new issues will arise and challenge managers to develop new solutions. To be effective, corporations must meet the reasonable expectations of stakeholders and society in general. A successful business must meet *all* of its economic, social, and environmental objectives. A core argument of this book is that *the purpose of the firm is not simply to make a profit, but to create value for all its stakeholders.* Ultimately, business success is judged not simply by a company's financial performance but by how well it serves broad social interests.

Summary

- Business firms are organizations that are engaged in making a product or providing a service for a profit. Society, in its broadest sense, refers to human beings and to the social structures they collectively create. Business is part of society and engages in ongoing exchanges with its external environment. Together, business and society form an interactive social system in which the actions of each profoundly influence the other.

- According to the stakeholder theory of the firm, the purpose of the modern corporation is to create value for all of its stakeholders. To survive, all companies must make a profit for their owners. However, they also create many other kinds of value as well for their employees, customers, communities, and others. For both practical and ethical reasons, corporations must take all stakeholders' interests into account.

- Every business firm has economic and social relationships with others in society. Some are intended, some unintended; some are positive, others negative. Stakeholders are all those who affect, or are affected by, the actions of the firm. Some have a market relationship with the company, and others have a nonmarket relationship with it.

- Stakeholders often have multiple interests and can exercise their economic, political, and other powers in ways that benefit or challenge the organization. Stakeholders may also act independently or create coalitions to influence the company. Stakeholder mapping is a technique for graphically representing stakeholders' relationship to an issue facing a firm.

- Modern corporations have developed a range of boundary-crossing departments and offices to manage interactions with market and nonmarket stakeholders. The organization of the corporation's boundary-spanning functions is complex. Most companies have many departments specifically charged with interacting with stakeholders.

- A number of broad forces shape the relationship between business and society. These include changing societal and ethical expectations; redefinition of the role of government; a dynamic global economy; ecological and natural resource concerns; and the transformational role of technology and innovation. To deal effectively with these changes, corporate strategy must address the expectations of all of the company's stakeholders.

Key Terms

boundary-spanning departments, *17*
business, *4*
general systems theory, *5*
interactive social system, *5*
ownership theory of the firm, *6*

society, *4*
stakeholder, *7*
stakeholder analysis, *11*
stakeholder coalitions, *14*
stakeholder interests, *12*
stakeholder (market), *8*

stakeholder (nonmarket), *9*
stakeholder map, *16*
stakeholder power, *12*
stakeholder salience, *16*
stakeholder theory of the firm, *6*

Internet Resources

www.businessweek.com   *BusinessWeek*
www.economist.com   *The Economist*
www.fortune.com   *Fortune*
www.nytimes.com   *The New York Times*
www.wsj.com   *The Wall Street Journal*
www.bloomberg.com   Bloomberg
www.ft.com   *Financial Times (London)*
www.cnnmoney.com   CNN Money

Discussion Case: *A Brawl in Mickey's Backyard*

Outside City Hall in Anaheim, California—home to the theme park Disneyland—dozens of protestors gathered in August 2007 to stage a skit. Wearing costumes to emphasize their point, activists playing "Mickey Mouse" and the "evil queen" ordered a group of "Disney workers" to "get out of town." The amateur actors were there to tell the city council in a dramatic fashion that they supported a developer's plan to build affordable housing near the world-famous theme park—a plan that Disney opposed.

"They want to make money, but they don't care about the employees," said Gabriel de la Cruz, a banquet server at Disneyland. De la Cruz lived in a crowded one-bedroom apartment near the park with his wife and two teenage children. "Rent is too high," he said. "We don't have a choice to go some other place."

The Walt Disney Company was one of the best-known media and entertainment companies in the world. In Anaheim, the company operated the original Disneyland theme park, the newer California Adventure, three hotels, and the Downtown Disney shopping district. The California resort complex attracted 24 million visitors a year. The company as a whole earned more than $35 billion in 2007, about $11 billion of which came from its parks and resorts around the world, including those in California.

Walt Disney, the company's founder, had famously spelled out the resort's vision when he said, "I don't want the public to see the world they live in while they're in Disneyland. I want them to feel they're in another world."

Anaheim, located in Orange County, was a sprawling metropolis of 350,000 that had grown rapidly with its tourism industry. In the early 1990s, the city had designated two square miles adjacent to Disneyland as a special resort district, with all new development restricted to serving tourist needs, and pumped millions of dollars into upgrading the area. In 2007, the resort district—5 percent of Anaheim's area—produced more than half its tax revenue.

Housing in Anaheim was expensive, and many of Disney's 20,000 workers could not afford to live there. The median home price in the community was more than $600,000, and a one-bedroom apartment could cost as much as $1,400 a month. Custodians at the park earned around $23,000 a year, restaurant attendants around $14,000. Only 18 percent of resort employees lived in Anaheim. Many of the rest commuted long distances by car and bus to get to work.

The dispute playing out in front of City Hall had begun in 2005, when a local developer called SunCal had arranged to buy a 26-acre site in the resort district. (The parcel was directly across the street from land Disney considered a possible site for future expansion.) SunCal's plan was to build around 1,500 condominiums, with 15 percent of the units set aside for below-market-rate rental apartments. Because the site was in the resort district, the developer required special permission from the city council to proceed.

Affordable housing advocates quickly backed SunCal's proposal. Some of the unions representing Disney employees also supported the idea, as did other individuals and groups drawn by the prospect of reducing long commutes, a contributor to the region's air pollution. Backers formed the Coalition to Defend and Protect Anaheim, declaring that "these new homes would enable many . . . families to live near their places of work and thereby reduce commuter congestion on our freeways."

Disney, however, strenuously opposed SunCal's plan, arguing that the land should be used only for tourism-related development such as hotels and restaurants. "If one developer is allowed to build residential in the resort area, others will follow," a company spokesperson said. "Anaheim and Orange County have to address the affordable housing issue, but Anaheim also has to protect the resort area. It's not an either/or." In support of Disney's position, the chamber of commerce, various businesses in the resort district, and some local government officials formed Save Our Anaheim Resort District to "protect our Anaheim Resort District from non-tourism projects." The group considered launching an initiative to put the matter before the voters.

The five-person city council was split on the issue. One council member said that if workers could not afford to live in Anaheim, "maybe they can move somewhere else . . . where rents are cheaper." But another disagreed, charging that Disney had shown "complete disregard for the workers who make the resorts so successful."

Sources: "Disneyland Balks at New Neighbors," *USA Today,* April 3, 2007; "Housing Plan Turns Disney Grumpy," *The New York Times,* May 20, 2007; "In Anaheim, the Mouse Finally Roars," *Washington Post,* August 6, 2007; and "Not in Mickey's Backyard," *Portfolio,* December 2007.

Discussion Questions

1. What is the issue in this case?
2. Who are the relevant market and nonmarket stakeholders in this situation?
3. What are the various stakeholders' interests? Please indicate if each stakeholder is in favor of, or opposed to, SunCal's proposed development.
4. What sources of power do the relevant stakeholders have?
5. Based on the information you have, draft a stakeholder map of this case. What conclusions can you draw from the stakeholder map?
6. What possible solutions to this dispute might emerge from dialogue between SunCal and its stakeholders?

Managing Public Issues and Stakeholder Relationships

Businesses today operate in an ever-changing external environment, where effective management requires anticipating emerging public issues and engaging positively with a wide range of stakeholders. Whether the issue is growing concerns about global warming, water scarcity, child labor, animal cruelty, or Internet privacy, managers must respond to the opportunities and risks it presents. To do so effectively often requires building relationships across organizational boundaries, learning from external stakeholders, and altering practices in response. Effective management of public issues and stakeholder relationships builds value for the firm.

This Chapter Focuses on These Key Learning Objectives:

- Evaluating public issues and their significance to the modern corporation.
- Applying available tools or techniques to scan an organization's multiple environments.
- Describing the steps in the issue management process and determining how to make the process most effective.
- Identifying who is responsible for managing public issues and the skills required to do so effectively.
- Understanding how businesses can build collaborative relationships with stakeholders through engagement, dialogue, and network building.
- Identifying the benefits of stakeholder engagement to the business firm.

IKEA is the Swedish home furnishings retailer known for its distinctive yellow and blue big-box stores and stylish, inexpensive, and environmentally sound products. The firm's mission is "to create a better everyday life for the many people." About 15 years ago, the company's managers were startled by a documentary, broadcast on European television, showing young children in South Asia working under deplorable conditions making handwoven rugs. The program named IKEA as one of several rug importers from that region. Shortly afterward, activists held protests outside several IKEA stores, demanding that it halt child labor in its supply chain. As the company's area manager for carpets later commented, "The use of child labor was not a high-profile public issue at the time. . . . We were caught completely unaware."

Rather than ignore the issue, IKEA responded by sending a legal team to Geneva to consult with the International Labor Organization. It promptly adopted a clause in all supply contracts which stated that any supplier employing children under legal working age would be immediately terminated. The company also reached out to UNICEF (the United Nations Children's Fund) and Save the Children (a child advocacy group) for further guidance about what actions to take.

After extensive consultation, IKEA decided to fund a community development project in villages in the carpet-manufacturing region of northern India, which had been depicted in the documentary. Administered by UNICEF, the project provided alternative schooling, community loans, and vaccinations as a way to avoid the economic necessity for children to work. The company also integrated child labor issues into its established supplier auditing programs (set up initially to track environmental compliance) and instituted regular reviews of its rug suppliers. It later created a position of children's ombudsman to handle children's issues at the firm.

In 2009, IKEA made yet another financial contribution to UNICEF for Indian community development, bringing its total giving over more than a decade to $180 million. A representative of UNICEF reflected that "IKEA's investment in children's well-being, despite the downturn in the global economy, sets a high standard for corporate partnership."[1]

IKEA's creative engagement with stakeholders on the issue of child labor went far beyond what was legally required. But it improved the firm's reputation with both customers and suppliers, avoided more serious conflict with activists, and produced positive outcomes that the company might not have been able to achieve on its own. IKEA had recognized an issue, reached out to stakeholders, and made a difference.

Public Issues

A **public issue** is any issue that is of mutual concern to an organization and one or more of its stakeholders. (Public issues are sometimes also called *social issues* or *sociopolitical issues*.) They are typically broad issues, often impacting many companies and groups, and of concern to a significant number of people. Public issues are often contentious—different groups may have different opinions about what should be done about them. They often, but not always, have public policy or legislative implications.

The emergence of a new public issue—such as concerns about child labor, mentioned in the opening example of this chapter—often indicates there is a *gap* between what the firm wants to do or is doing and what stakeholders expect. In the IKEA example, the company was sourcing products from suppliers who used child labor, a practice that offended many of its customers. Scholars have called this the **performance–expectations gap**.

---

[1] "IKEA Gives UNICEF $48 Million to Fight India Child Labor," *Reuters News Service,* February 24, 2009; and Christopher A. Bartlett, Vincent Dessain, and Anders Sjoman, "IKEA's Global Sourcing Challenge: Indian Rugs and Child Labor (A) and (B)," Cases # 9-906-414 and #9-906-415, 2006.

FIGURE 2.1
The Performance–Expectations Gap

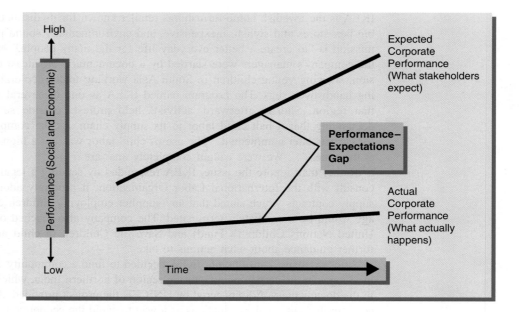

Stakeholder expectations are a mixture of people's opinions, attitudes, and beliefs about what constitutes reasonable business behavior. Managers and organizations have good reason to identify emergent expectations as early as possible. Failure to understand stakeholder concerns and to respond appropriately will permit the performance–expectations gap to grow: the larger the gap, the greater the risk of stakeholder backlash or of missing a major business opportunity. The performance–expectations gap is pictured in Figure 2.1.

Emerging public issues are both a risk and an opportunity. They are a risk because issues that firms do not anticipate and plan for effectively can seriously hurt a company. A classic example of this was Monsanto, which developed seeds for genetically modified corn, soybeans, and other crops in the late 1990s. Although the products were well accepted in the United States, they sparked intense opposition from European consumers, who objected to eating food that had been genetically engineered. Monsanto, which had not anticipated the depth of the opposition it would face, encountered numerous national regulations banning its products from the European marketplace. (This situation is further discussed in Chapter 13.)

On the other hand, correctly anticipating the emergence of an issue can confer a competitive advantage. Toyota was one of the first firms to recognize that growing public concern about the environment and related government regulations would spur demand for fuel-efficient and low-emission vehicles. As a result, the company got an early start on developing gas–electric engines and is today the leading producer of such vehicles. In 2008, Toyota announced that it had sold 1 million Priuses since the hybrid car's introduction, exceeding all expectations.[2]

Understanding and responding to changing societal expectations is a business necessity. As Mark Moody-Stuart, former managing director of Royal Dutch/Shell, put it in an interview, "Communication with society . . . is a commercial matter, because society is your customers. It is not a soft and wooly thing, because society is what we depend on for our living. So we had better be in line with its wishes, its desires, its aspirations, its dreams."[3]

---

[2] "Prius: Over 1 Million Sold," *BusinessWeek* blog, May 15, 2008, at *http://blogs.businessweek.com.*

[3] Interview conducted by Anne T. Lawrence, "Shell Oil in Nigeria," interactive online case published by *www.icase.co.*

Every company faces many public issues. Some emerge over a long period of time; others emerge suddenly. Some are predictable; others are completely unexpected. Some companies respond effectively; others do not. Consider the following recent examples of public issues and companies' responses:

- *Climate change*: Lafarge, a French multinational cement company, wanted to expand its operations in East Africa. But the company recognized that 5 percent of all man-made carbon dioxide emissions, a key contributor to global warming and a growing public concern, came from the cement industry. Lafarge promised to experiment with new production processes to reduce the levels of carbon dioxide emissions by 20 percent per ton, while bringing employment and business opportunities to remote villages in the region.[4]

- *Executive pay*: When AIG, the world leader in insurance and financial services, paid out $165 million in executive bonuses, the public outcry was loud. American taxpayers objected to the company's use of a portion of its $85 billion in government bailout money to enrich its top managers. Congress considered passing a new income tax at a rate of 90 percent on executive bonuses for managers who worked for firms receiving a government bailout. Although the new tax was never imposed, most AIG managers eventually returned their bonuses, succumbing to public pressure and the threat of taxation.[5]

- *Food safety*: Outbreaks of E. coli, salmonella, and other food-borne illnesses were on the rise in the 2000s. One analyst warned, "The food safety process is collapsing [in the United States]." Urgent calls for action by consumer advocates, health care professionals, and political figures led to new and more stringent government standards for the processing and storage of vegetables and other food products. Many growers, food companies, and restaurants scrambled to catch up with the new rules.[6]

- *Privacy*: Privacy advocates in the United Kingdom, where laws were more stringent than in the United States, protested the introduction of Google's Street View, an addition to the search firm's popular mapping service. Street View shows a driver's-eye view of the ground level of streets, buildings, and people. Google collected the images using specially equipped cameras mounted on cars. British law prohibited the photography of people on the street without their explicit permission.[7]

The public issues that garner the most public attention change over time, sometimes emerging with surprising suddenness. For this reason, companies track them closely. (Various methods they use to do so are discussed later in this chapter.) For the past several years, the consulting firm McKinsey has tracked the opinions of top executives around the world on which issues they believe will be most important to the public in the next five years. In the 2008 survey, environmental issues, including climate change, jumped to the top of the list. Fifty-seven percent of executives expected that environmental issues would garner attention in the next five years (up sharply from 31 percent just two years earlier). Other issues cited by a fifth or more of the executives were privacy and data security, demand for safer and more healthful products, health care and other employee benefits, and job losses from offshoring.[8]

---

[4] "Fueling the Debate," *Ethical Performance Best Practice* 12 (2008), pp. 6–7.

[5] "House Approves 90% Tax on Bonuses after Bailouts," *The New York Times*, March 20, 2009, *www.nytimes.com*.

[6] "Dangerous Sealer Stayed on Shelves after Recall," *The New York Times*, October 8, 2007, *www.nytimes.com*.

[7] "Google Faces 'Street View Block,'" *BBC News*, July 4, 2008, *newsvote.bbc.co.uk;* and "Google Pulls Some Street Images," *BBC News*, March 20, 2009, *newsvote.bbc.co.uk.*

[8] "From Risk to Opportunity: How Global Executives View Sociopolitical Issues," *McKinsey Quarterly*, October 2008. Based on a survey of 1,453 CEOs and top-level executives in 78 countries, conducted in September 2008. Multiple responses were possible.

Exhibit 2.A

Leading Emerging Issues as Perceived by Top Executives

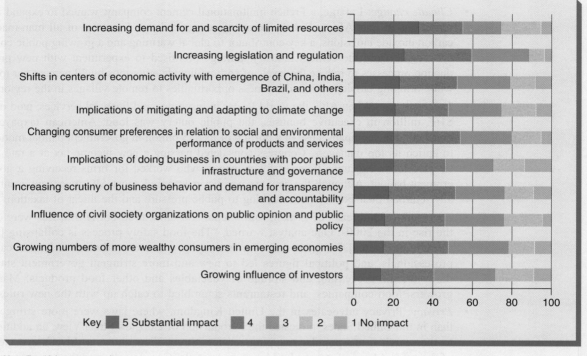

To what extent are the following trends likely to impact your organization over the next three to five years (by presenting either risks or opportunities or both)?

Increasing demand for and scarcity of limited resources

Increasing legislation and regulation

Shifts in centers of economic activity with emergence of China, India, Brazil, and others

Implications of mitigating and adapting to climate change

Changing consumer preferences in relation to social and environmental performance of products and services

Implications of doing business in countries with poor public infrastructure and governance

Increasing scrutiny of business behavior and demand for transparency and accountability

Influence of civil society organizations on public opinion and public policy

Growing numbers of more wealthy consumers in emerging economies

Growing influence of investors

Key ■ 5 Substantial impact   ■ 4   ■ 3   ■ 2   ■ 1 No impact

Note: Top 10 issues presented.

Source: Exhibit 1, "The Business Impact of Trends in the External Environment," p. 13 in European Academy of Business in Society, *Developing the Global Leader of Tomorrow* (United Kingdom: Ashridge, December 2008). Based on a global survey of 194 CEOs and senior executives in September–October 2008. Used by permission.

Another study, conducted in 2008 by the the European Academy of Business in Society (EABIS), also asked top executives which societal trends they anticipated would impact their firms the most over the next three to five years. Their responses showed them to be concerned about a very wide range of issues, from tougher regulations to climate change, shortages of resources, changing demographics, and rising activism by nongovernmental organizations and investors, as shown in Exhibit 2.A.[9]

Environmental Analysis

As new public issues arise, businesses must respond. Organizations need a systematic way of identifying, monitoring, and selecting public issues that warrant organizational action because of the risks or opportunities they present. Organizations rarely have full control of a public issue because of the many factors involved. But it is possible for the organization to create a management system that identifies and monitors issues as they emerge.

To identify those public issues that require attention and action, a firm needs a framework for seeking out and evaluating environmental information. (In this context,

[9] European Academy of Business in Society, *Developing the Global Leader of Tomorrow* (United Kingdom: Ashridge, December 2008). Based on a global suvey of 194 CEOs and senior executives in September–October 2008.

FIGURE 2.2
**Eight Strategic
Radar Screens**

Source: Karl Albrecht,
*Corporate Radar: Tracking
Forces That Are Shaping Your
Business* (New York: American
Management Association,
2000).

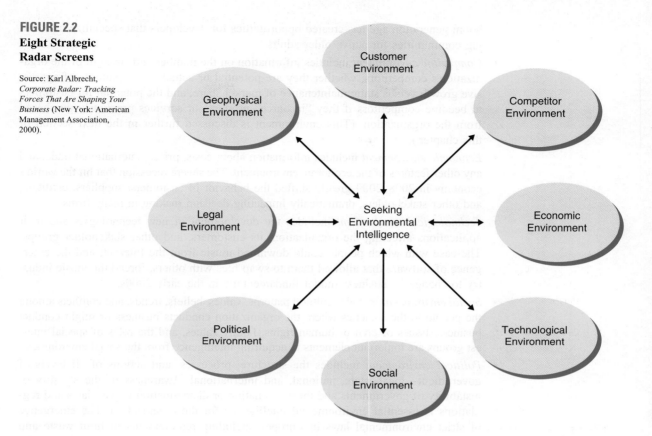

environmental means *outside the organization*; in Chapters 10 and 11, the term refers to the natural environment.) **Environmental analysis** is a method managers use to gather information about external issues and trends, so they can develop an organizational strategy that minimizes threats and takes advantage of new opportunities.

Environmental intelligence is the acquisition of information gained from analyzing the multiple environments affecting organizations. Acquiring this information may be done informally or as a formal management process. If done well, this environmental intelligence can help an organization avoid crises and spot opportunities.

According to management scholar Karl Albrecht, scanning to acquire environmental intelligence should focus on eight *strategic radar screens.*[10] Radar is an instrument that uses microwave radiation to detect and locate distant objects, which are often displayed on a screen; law enforcement authorities use radar, for example, to track the speed of passing cars. Albrecht uses the analogy of radar to suggest that companies must have a way of tracking important developments that are outside of their immediate view. He identifies eight different environments that managers must systematically follow. These are shown in Figure 2.2 and described next:

- *Customer environment* includes the demographic factors, such as gender, age, marital status, and other factors, of the organization's customers as well as their social values or preferences. For example, the "graying" of the population as members of the baby

[10] Adapted from Karl Albrecht, *Corporate Radar: Tracking the Forces That Are Shaping Your Business* (New York: American Management Association, 2000).

boom generation age has created opportunities for developers that specialize in building communities for active older adults.

- *Competitor environment* includes information on the number and strength of the organization's competitors, whether they are potential or actual allies, patterns of aggressive growth versus static maintenance of market share, and the potential for customers to become competitors if they "insource" products or services previously purchased from the organization. (This environment is discussed further in the next section of this chapter.)

- *Economic environment* includes information about costs, prices, international trade, and any other features of the economic environment. The severe recession that hit the world's economy in 2008–2009 greatly shifted the behavior of customers, suppliers, creditors, and other stakeholders, dramatically impacting decision making in many firms.

- *Technological environment* includes the development of new technologies and their applications affecting the organization, its customers, and other stakeholder groups. The ease with which people could download music from the Internet, and the emergence of software that allowed them to swap files with others, forced the music industry to change its business model fundamentally in the early 2000s.

- *Social environment* includes cultural patterns, values, beliefs, trends, and conflicts among the people in the societies where the organization conducts business or might conduct business. Issues of civil or human rights, family values, and the roles of special interest groups are important elements in acquiring intelligence from the social environment.

- *Political environment* includes the structure, processes, and actions of all levels of government—local, state, national, and international. Awareness of the stability or instability of governments and their inclination or disinclination to pass laws and regulations is essential environmental intelligence for the organization. The emergence of strict environmental laws in Europe—including requirements to limit waste and provide for recycling at the end of a product's life—have caused firms all over the world that sell to Europeans to rethink how they design and package their products.

- *Legal environment* includes patents, copyrights, trademarks, and considerations of intellectual property, as well as antitrust considerations and trade protectionism and organizational liability issues. Repeated violations of intellectual property laws landed Russia and China at the top of an international watch list of 12 countries. Countries that remained on the list and did not show significant efforts to comply with the law risked having their trade agreements revoked.

- *Geophysical environment* relates to awareness of the physical surroundings of the organization's facilities and operations, whether it is the organization's headquarters or its field offices and distribution centers, and the organization's dependence and impact on natural resources such as minerals, water, land, or air. Growing concerns about global warming and climate change, for example, have caused many firms to seek to improve their energy efficiency.

The eight strategic radar screens represent a system of interrelated segments, each one connected to and influencing the others.

Companies do not become experts in acquiring environmental intelligence overnight. New attitudes have to be developed, new routines learned, and new policies and action programs designed. Many obstacles must be overcome in developing and implementing the effective scanning of the business environments. Some are structural, such as the reporting relationships between groups of managers; others are cultural, such as changing traditional ways of doing things. In addition, the dynamic nature of the business environments requires organizations to continually evaluate their environmental scanning procedures.

Competitive Intelligence

One of the eight environments discussed by Albrecht is the competitor environment. The term **competitive intelligence** refers to the systematic and continuous process of gathering, analyzing, and managing external information about the organization's competitors that can affect the organization's plans, decisions, and operations. The acquisition of this information benefits an organization by helping it better understand what other companies in its industry are doing. Competitive intelligence enables managers in companies of all sizes to make informed decisions ranging from marketing, research and development, and investing tactics to long-term business strategies. "During difficult times, excellent competitive intelligence can be the differentiating factor in the marketplace," explained Paul Meade, vice president of the research and consulting firm Best Practices. "Companies that can successfully gather and analyze competitive information, then implement strategic decisions based on that analysis, position themselves to be ahead of the pack."[11]

Clearly, numerous ethical issues are raised in the acquisition and use of competitive intelligence. Business managers must be aware of these issues, often clarified in the organization's code of ethics.[12] The importance of ethical considerations when collecting competitive intelligence cannot be understated. One instance where the perceived value of competitive intelligence was so great that an employee conspired to sell information to a competitor was the focus of a sensational trial, as described next:

> Joya Williams, former secretary to Coca-Cola's global brand director, was sentenced to eight years in prison, longer than the federal sentencing guidelines recommended (five years and three months), for attempting to steal trade secrets from her employer. Judge J. Owen Forrester based his decision for a longer sentence on his belief that "this is the kind of offense that cannot be tolerated in our society." Williams was convicted of stealing confidential documents and sample products from Coca-Cola and giving them to two others as part of a conspiracy to sell the items to rival Pepsi. Williams was reportedly in debt, unhappy at her job, and hoping to receive a big payday from the sale. The conspiracy failed when Pepsi turned over to the FBI a letter it received informing them that Coca-Cola's trade secrets were to be sold to the highest bidder.[13]

As the Coca-Cola attempted theft story indicates, the perceived value of trade secrets or other information may be so great that businesses or their employees may be tempted to use unethical or illegal means to obtain such information (or provide it to others). However, competitive intelligence acquired ethically remains one of the most valued assets sought by businesses.

The Issue Management Process

Once a company has identified a public issue and detects a gap between society's expectations and its own practices, what are its next steps? Proactive companies do not wait for something to happen; they actively manage issues as they arise. The process of doing so is called **issue management**. The **issue management process**, illustrated in Figure 2.3,

---

[11] See Best Practices report at *www.benchmarkingreports.com/competitiveintelligence*.

[12] For information about the professional association focusing on competitive intelligence, particularly with attention to ethical considerations, see the Society of Competitive Intelligence Professionals' Web site at *www.scip.org*.

[13] "Ex-Secretary Gets 8-Year Term in Coca-Cola Secrets Case," *The New York Times Online*, May 24, 2007, *www.nytimes.com*; and "Ex-Secretary at Coke Guilty of Trade-Secrets Theft," *The New York Times Online*, February 3, 2007, *www.nytimes.com*.

FIGURE 2.3
The Issue
Management Process

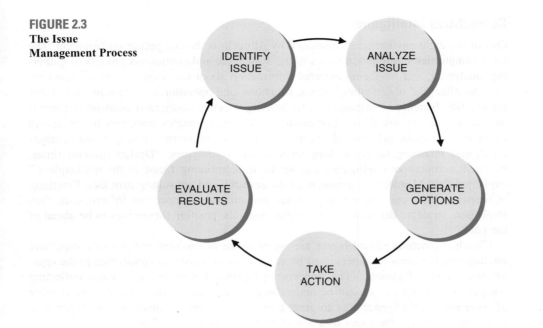

has five steps or stages.[14] Each of these steps is explained below, using the example of McDonald's response to emerging stakeholder concerns about the humane treatment of farm animals raised for food. As the largest buyer of beef and the second largest buyer of chicken in the United States, McDonald's was vulnerable to stakeholder pressure on this issue, but also was well positioned to take action and move ahead of its competitors. But, as this example also illustrates, even a strong corporate response does not completely close an issue, since it may arise again in a new form.

Identify Issue

Issue identification involves anticipating emerging concerns, sometimes called "horizon issues" because they seem to be just coming up over the horizon like the first morning sun. Sometimes managers become aware of issues by carefully tracking the media, experts' views, activist opinion, and legislative developments to identify issues of concern to the public. Normally, this requires attention to all eight of the environments described in Figure 2.2. Organizations often use techniques of data searching, media analysis, and public surveys to track ideas, themes, and issues that may be relevant to their interests all over the world. They also rely on ongoing conversations with key stakeholders. Sometimes, awareness of issues is forced on companies by lawsuits or protests by activists who hold strong views about a particular matter.

In 1997, a judge handed down a decision in a legal dispute between McDonald's and several of the company's critics in the United Kingdom, calling the company "culpabl[y] responsible for cruel practices [toward animals]." People for the Ethical Treatment of Animals (PETA), an animal rights organization based in the United States, immediately followed up with a campaign against McDonald's and

---

[14] Other depictions of the development and management of public issues may be found in Rogene Buchholz, *Public Issues for Management,* 2nd ed. (Englewood Cliffs, NJ: Prentice Hall, 1992); Robert Heath, *Strategic Issues Management* (Thousand Oaks, CA: Sage, 1997); and Eli Sopow, *The Critical Issues Audit* (Leesburg, VA: Issues Action Publications, 1994).

other fast-food companies. The group charged, among other things, that chickens used to produce McNuggets were crammed by the tens of thousands into sheds that stank of ammonia fumes from accumulated waste, suffered broken bones from being bred to be top-heavy, and were slaughtered by having their throats slit while still conscious. PETA wrote the McDonald's CEO and campaigned publicly for its goals, including sponsoring shareholder resolutions, placing provocative ads, and mounting public demonstrations to pressure McDonald's and other fast-food companies to change their practices.

McDonald's had been aware of the animal welfare issue for some time and had held discussions with organizations such as Animal Rights International. But PETA's challenge elevated the urgency to the company of the issue of humane treatment of animals and put it squarely on the agenda of managers.

Analyze Issue

Once an issue has been identified, its implications must be analyzed. Organizations must understand how the issue is likely to evolve, and how it is likely to affect them. For each company, the ramifications of the issue will be different.

How the animal welfare issue affected McDonald's was complex. On one hand, the company was concerned about public perception, and did not want customers to turn away because of concerns about the mistreatment of cows, pigs, and chickens used for food. On the other hand, it was also concerned about maintaining standards for food quality and keeping down costs. An added complexity was that McDonald's did not raise its own animals for slaughter, but relied on a network of suppliers for its meat, including such major firms as Tyson, ConAgra, and National Beef. In order to influence the treatment of animals, it would need to collaborate closely with companies in its supply chain.

A result of the issue analysis process for McDonald's was an understanding that it would need to work with ranchers, poultry farmers, meat processors, and others to address its stakeholders' concerns.

Generate Options

An issue's public profile indicates to managers how significant an issue is for the organization, but it does not tell them what to do. The next step in the issue management process involves generating, evaluating, and selecting among possible options. This requires complex judgments that incorporate ethical considerations, the organization's reputation and good name, and other nonquantifiable factors.

The company began discussions with Temple Grandin, a renowned academic expert, to consider possible options. Grandin had developed a methodology for objectively measuring animal welfare in slaughterhouses and audit protocols based on these measures. McDonald's vice president for corporate responsibility later recalled the "magic moment" in 1997 when Grandin presented her concept of an audit program to company managers. "We saw it as something that had tremendous potential," he commented. The company began experimenting with slaughterhouse audits (inspections) in 1999, to see how the system might work in practice. The company also sought to learn more about animal welfare on the thousands of farms that supplied chickens, cows, and pigs to its meat processing partners. In 2000, McDonald's convened an Animal Welfare Council of experts to continue to advise the company and explore other possible options.

Selecting an appropriate response often involves a creative process of considering various alternatives and rigorously testing them to see how they work in practice.

Take Action

Once an option has been chosen, the organization must design and implement a plan of action.

In 2001, the company issued a set of guiding principles for animal welfare, affirming the company's belief that "animals should be free from abuse and neglect" and that animal welfare is "an integral part of an overall quality assurance program that makes good business sense." The company also formalized its audit program, completing 500 audits worldwide of beef, poultry, and pork processing plants in 2002. In the small number of cases where the results were "not acceptable," the company required the facility to take corrective action. The company also sponsored animal welfare training for its suppliers to bring them on board.

Evaluate Results

Once an organization has implemented the issue management program, it must continue to assess the results and make adjustments if necessary. Many managers see issue management as a continuous process, rather than one that comes to a clear conclusion.

McDonald's continued to talk with animal welfare organizations, examine its own practices, and try new approaches. In 2005, the company launched a study of the feasibility of using a more humane way to slaughter chickens, called controlled-atmosphere killing, or CAK. Standard industry practice had been to hang chickens by their feet on a conveyer line and move them through a vat of water charged with electricity. In CAK, by contrast, oxygen in the air was slowly replaced by an inert gas. PETA responded by withdrawing a shareholder proposal that had criticized McDonald's for using a method that was cruel to animals. "McDonald's agreed to do what we asked it to do, and it agreed to do it sooner than we asked," said a PETA spokesperson.[15]

This example illustrates the complexity of the issue management process. Figure 2.3 is deliberately drawn in the form of a loop. When working well, the issue management process continuously cycles back to the beginning and repeats, pulling in more information, generating more options, and improving programmatic response. Such was the case with the concern over the slaughtering of chickens. McDonald's 2005 report concluded that "current standards for animal welfare are appropriate . . . at this time," and that "the application of CAK in commercial environments is still in the early stages of development." Thus, McDonald's did not change its policy of how chickens were prepared for their use in their restaurants.

In February 2009, nine years after calling a truce with McDonald's, PETA began a new offensive against the fast-food chain and the public issue arose again, calling for renewed attention by McDonald's management.

A PETA spokesperson argued that McDonald's had ignored the technological developments of the past few years and that the CAK process was "by far the most humane way to kill a chicken." The animal rights advocates said that there was no reason to hang a chicken upside down and shock it with electricity when a

---

[15] "McD Seeks a Less Cruel Way to Kill Chickens," *Nation's Restaurant News*, January 24, 2005, pp. 1–2.

Exhibit 2.B

Is Issue Management an Art or a Science?

A recent opinion article by Tony Jacques, issue manager for the Dow Chemical Company in Asia-Pacific and a board member of the Issue Management Council, published in the *Journal of Public Affairs*, offered the provocative thesis that issue management often overemphasizes technique and underemphasizes creative problem solving. Jacques pointed out that many of the techniques used to manage issues were highly systematized, involving computerized data scanning, media analysis, and information storing and sharing. The purpose, he suggested, was to "reduce variation and eliminate defects." This approach, Jacques argued, was wrong-headed. In his view, issue management "by definition deals with problems which are often subjective, highly emotive, prone to political whim, demanding judgment and compromise, and where 'perception is reality' and there is seldom a 'right answer.'" Data analysis can be useful in identifying issues, but not in determining what to do about them. For that, creative problem solving is required. Jacques concluded, "The reality is that issue management is neither all art nor all science. It has elements of both art and science . . . [T]he desired outcome of getting the balance right is not to deliver the perfect process but to deliver genuine bottom line . . . outcomes."

Source: Tony Jacques, "Issue Management: Process versus Progress," *Journal of Public Affairs* 6, no. 1 (February 2006), pp. 69–74.

more humane and effective method was available. PETA believed that McDonald's had the influence to pressure its chicken suppliers to modify their plants to use the gas, or CAK, process.[16]

In the four years since McDonald's had issued its report, the dynamic environment had changed—demonstrating that the management of public issues also is a dynamic process. McDonald's had to revisit the issue, which had changed as technology had evolved, and then analyze the issue and generate a new set of viable options for action.

Contemporary issue management is truly an interactive process, as forward-thinking companies must continually engage in a dialogue with their stakeholders about issues that matter, as McDonald's has learned. The new challenge from PETA jump-started another round of discussions between company representatives and animal rights activists. As a result, all parties have continued to learn from one another.[17] Managers must not only implement programs, but continue to reassess their actions to be consistent with both ethical practices and long-term survival.

Is the issue management process an art or a science? One practitioner's observations are presented in Exhibit 2.B.

Organizing for Effective Issue Management

Who manages public issues? What departments and people are involved? There is no simple answer to this question. Figure 1.6, presented in Chapter 1, showed that the modern corporation has many boundary-spanning departments. Which part of the organization is mobilized to address a particular emerging issue often depends on the nature of

---

[16] "McDonald's Draws PETA Protests over Chicken Processing," *Chicago Tribune*, February 17, 2009, www.chicagotribune.com.

[17] Information on McDonald's responsible purchasing is available online at *http://www.mcdonalds.com/usa/good/products.html*. Information on PETA's campaign against McDonald's is available online at *www.mccruelty.com*. Dr. Temple Grandin's Web site is *www.grandin.com*.

the issue itself. For example, if the issue has implications for public policy or government regulations, the public affairs or government relations department may take a leadership role. (The public affairs department is futher discussed in Chapter 9.) If the issue is an environmental one, the department of sustainability or environment, health, and safety may take on this role. Some companies combine multiple issue management functions in an office of external relations or corporate affairs. The following example illustrates how one company has organized to manage emerging public issues:

> Unilever, a transnational corporation based in the Netherlands and the United Kingdom, makes laundry detergent, shampoo, toothpaste, tea, ice cream, frozen foods, and many other consumer products. The company's chairman and board of directors (called an executive committee in Europe) have overall responsibility for managing external relations at the corporate level. A committee of the board called the External Affairs and Corporate Relations Committee is charged with this specific responsibility. A full-time corporate development director is responsible for working with other managers around the world. For example, in Canada, this role is held by an executive whose title is manager of environmental and corporate affairs. This job is described on the company's Web site as "creating a link between the company and its local communities." Unilever's external relations activities are organized and coordinated at many levels—from the board down to the business unit.[18]

A corporation's issue management activities are usually linked to both the board of directors and to top management levels. One study showed that these executives believed that overall responsibility for managing sociopolitical issues should rest at the top. Fifty-six percent reported that the CEO or chair *did* take the lead in this area, but 74 percent thought the CEO or chair *should* take the lead.[19] Some companies assign responsibility for issue management to members of their boards of directors. Thirty percent of major companies have an external relations committee of the board of directors.[20] About half of all companies have "informal systems" in place for coordinating work on public issues across the organization; 28 percent have "fully integrated management structures," and 16 percent of companies have a "formal system for setting priorities and coordinating activities." Only 7 percent have little or no coordination.[21] These findings reflect the growing importance of public issues and executives' perception of the need to closely engage in issue management with strategic oversight at top levels of the corporation.

What kinds of managers are best able to anticipate and respond effectively to emerging public issues? What skill sets are required? In 2008, the European Academy of Business in Society (EABIS) undertook a major study of leaders in companies participating in the United Nations Global Compact. (This initiative, discussed in more detail in Chapter 7, is a set of basic principles covering labor, human rights, and environmental standards, to which companies can voluntarily commit.) The researchers were interested in the knowledge and skills required of what they called the "global leader of tomorrow."

They found that effective global leadership on these public issues required three basic capabilities, as schematically diagrammed in Exhibit 2.C. The first was an understanding of the changing business *context*—emerging environmental and social trends affecting

---

[18] Information on Unilever's corporate structure is available online at *www.unilever.com/company/corporatestructure*.

[19] "The McKinsey Global Survey of Business Executives: Business and Society," *McKinsey Quarterly,* January 2006, Exhibit 3.

[20] Foundation for Public Affairs, *The State of Corporate Public Affairs* (Washington, DC: FAP, 2005).

[21] Foundation for Public Affairs, *The State of Corporate Public Affairs 2008–2009* (Washington, DC: FAP, 2008).

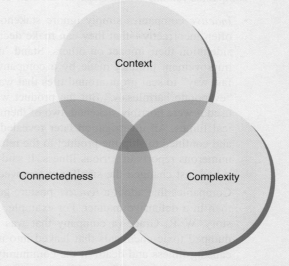

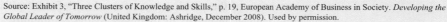

Source: Exhibit 3, "Three Clusters of Knowledge and Skills," p. 19, European Academy of Business in Society. *Developing the Global Leader of Tomorrow* (United Kingdom: Ashridge, December 2008). Used by permission.

the firm. These trends include various changes in the external environment discovered through use of strategic radar screens, discussed earlier in this chapter. The second was an ability to lead in the face of *complexity*. Many emerging issues, the researchers found, were surrounded by ambiguity; to deal with them, leaders needed to be flexible, creative, and willing to learn from their mistakes. The final capability was *connectedness:* the ability to understand actors in the wider political landscape and to engage with external stakeholders in dialogue and partnership.

We turn next to the topic of connectedness—how managers in today's corporations engage with stakeholders in the management of public issues.

Stakeholder Engagement

One of the key themes of this book is that companies that actively engage with stakeholders do a better job of managing a wide range of issues than companies that do not. In the McDonald's example presented earlier in this chapter, one of the reasons that the company was quite successful in its response to the emerging issue of animal welfare was that it consulted widely with stakeholders. (This process is often ongoing, as McDonald's experienced when changing technology required the firm to reestablish critical dialogues with its stakeholders.) This section will further explore the various forms the business–stakeholder relationship takes, when stakeholder engagement is likely to occur, and how managers can engage with stakeholders most effectively.

Stages in the Business–Stakeholder Relationship

Over time, the nature of business's relationship with its stakeholders often evolves through a series of stages. Scholars have characterized these stages as *inactive*, *reactive*, *proactive*, and *interactive*, with each stage representing a deepening of the relationship.

Sometimes, companies progress through this sequence from one stage to the next; other companies remain at one stage or another, or move backward in the sequence.[22]

- *Inactive* companies simply ignore stakeholder concerns. These firms may believe— often incorrectly—that they can make decisions unilaterally, without taking into consideration their impact on others. Stand 'n Seal Grout Sealer, a do-it-yourself home improvement product made by a company called BRTT, promised a "revolutionary fast way" to seal grout around tiles that was safe to use since any excess spray would "evaporate harmlessly." But the product was hardly harmless: dozens of people who used it were horribly sickened, two of them fatally, after breathing in dangerous chemical fumes. An investigation later revealed that BRTT tried to play down the hazard and contined to ship the product to the retailer Home Depot even after it had received numerous reports of serious illness. It said it had reformulated the product—although it had just changed the smell, not removed the hazardous ingredients.[23]

- Companies that adopt a *reactive* posture generally act only when forced to do so, and then in a defensive manner. For example, in the film *A Civil Action*, based on a true story, W. R. Grace (a company that was later bought by Beatrice Foods) allegedly dumped toxic chemicals that leaked into underground wells used for drinking water, causing illness and death in the community of Woburn, Massachusetts. The company paid no attention to the problem until forced to defend itself in a lawsuit brought by a crusading lawyer on behalf of members of the community.

- *Proactive* companies try to anticipate stakeholder concerns. These firms use the environmental scanning practices described earlier in this chapter to identify emerging public issues. They often have specialized departments, such as public affairs, community relations, consumer affairs, and government relations, to manage stakeholder relationships. These firms are much less likely to be blindsided by crises and negative surprises. Stakeholders and their concerns are still, however, considered a problem to be managed, rather than a source of competitive advantage.

- Finally, an *interactive* stance means that companies actively engage with stakeholders in an ongoing relationship of mutual respect, openness, and trust. For example, pharmaceutical giant GlaxoSmithKline announced in 2008 that it would fully disclose the results of clinical trials of drugs it was developing for the market, citing their desire to "cultivate a culture of openness and trust." Firms with this approach recognize that positive stakeholder relationships are a source of value and competitive advantage for the company. They know that these relationships must be nurtured over time. The term **stakeholder engagement** is used to refer to this process of ongoing relationship building between a business and its stakeholders.

Drivers of Stakeholder Engagement

When are companies most likely to engage with stakeholders—that is, to be at the interactive stage? What drives companies further along in this sequence?

Stakeholder engagement is, at its core, a *relationship*. The participation of a business organization and at least one stakeholder organization is necessary, by definition, to constitute engagement. In one scholar's view, engagement is most likely when both the company

[22] This typology was first introduced in Lee Preston and James E. Post, *Private Management and Public Policy* (Englewood Cliffs, NJ: Prentice Hall, 1975). For a more recent discussion, see Sandra Waddock, *Leading Corporate Citizens: Visions, Values, and Value Added*, 2nd ed. (New York: McGraw-Hill, 2006), ch. 1.

[23] "Dangerous Sealer Stayed on Shelves after Recall," *The New York Times*, October 8, 2008.

FIGURE 2.4
Drivers of Stakeholder Engagement

Source: Adapted from Anne T. Lawrence, "The Drivers of Stakeholder Engagement: Reflections on the Case of Royal Dutch/Shell, *Journal of Corporate Citizenship*, Summer 2002, pp. 71–85.

	Company	Stakeholder(s)
Goal	To improve corporate reputation; to earn a license to operate; to win approval of society	To change corporate behavior on an issue of concern
Motivation	Needs stakeholder involvement because of their expertise or control of critical resources	Governmental campaigns, protest perceived as inadequate to change corporate behavior
Organizational capacity	Top leaders committed to engagement; well-funded department of external (stakeholder) affairs	Experienced staff; core group of activists committed to dialogue with business

and its stakeholders have an urgent and important *goal*, the *motivation* to participate, and the *organizational capacity* to engage with one another. These three elements are presented in Figure 2.4.

Goals

For stakeholder engagement to occur, both the business and the stakeholder must have a problem that they want solved. The problem must be both important and urgent. Business is often spurred to act when it recognizes a gap between its actions and public expectations, as discussed earlier. The company may perceive this gap as a reputational crisis or a threat to its license to operate in society. For their part, stakeholders are typically concerned about an issue important to them—whether child labor, animal cruelty, environmental harm, or something else—that they want to see addressed.

Motivation

Both sides must also be motivated to work with one another to solve the problem. For example, the company may realize that the stakeholder group has technical expertise to help it address an issue. Or it needs the stakeholder's approval, because the stakeholder is in a position to influence policymakers, damage a company's reputation, or bring a lawsuit. Stakeholders may realize that the best way actually to bring about change is to help a company alter its behavior. In other words, both sides depend on each other to accomplish their goals; they cannot accomplish their objectives on their own. (Theorists sometimes refer to this as *interdependence*.)

Organizational Capacity

Each side must have the organizational capacity to engage the other in a productive dialogue. For the business, this may include support from top leadership and an adequately funded external affairs or comparable department with a reporting relationship to top executives. It may also include an issue management process that provides an opportunity for leaders to identify and respond quickly to shifts in the external environment. For the stakeholder, this means leadership or a significant faction that supports dialogue and individuals or organizational units with expertise in working with the business community.

In short, engagement is most likely to occur where both companies and stakeholders perceive an important and urgent problem, see each other as essential to a solution, and have the organizational capacity to interact with one another.

Making Engagement Work Effectively

Companies have experimented with various engagement processes. These range from informal to formal, and from one-time-only interactions to fully institutionalized relationships. Engagement may take the form of focus groups, individual or small group interviews, surveys, key-person meetings, or advisory councils. In any event, the firm must invite stakeholders to participate, provide a forum for discussion, and sometimes offer financial or logistical support.

Sun Microsystems is an example of a company that has begun to institutionalize its stakeholder engagement process. The company has formed a Corporate Social Responsibility Stakeholder Committee, composed of representatives of major customers, investors, and environmental and human rights organizations. The company schedules regular telephone consultations, as well as face-to-face meetings, to air issues of common concern. During a discussion of the global nature of the business, one stakeholder team member suggested that the company adopt a human rights policy. After broad consultation, Sun did so—becoming one of just a few firms to have such a policy.

Marcy Scott Lynn, Sun's director of corporate sustainability and responsibility, commented, "Working with external stakeholder groups allows Sun to get direct and meaningful feedback on the social and environmental aspects of our business performance. Admittedly, it isn't always easy to hear what they have to say, nor are we able to commit to all the things they ask of us. But every interaction we have with the stakeholder team so far has led to progress for Sun."[24]

The process of engagement can take many forms, but it often involves dialogue with stakeholders. One management theorist has defined dialogue as "the art of thinking together."[25] In **stakeholder dialogue**, a business and its stakeholders come together for face-to-face conversations about issues of common concern. There, they attempt to describe their core interests and concerns, reach a common definition of the problem, invent innovative solutions for mutual gain, and establish procedures for implementing solutions. To be successful, the process requires that participants express their own views fully, listen carefully and respectfully to others, and open themselves to creative thinking and new ways of looking at and solving a problem. The promise of dialogue is that together, they can draw on the understandings and concerns of all parties to develop solutions that none of them, acting alone, could have envisioned or implemented.[26]

BC Hydro, the third-largest electric utility in Canada, serves residents in British Columbia and sells power to other provinces and states throughout the Pacific Northwest. Over 90 percent of the company's output comes from hydroelectric dams. BC Hydro ran into stiff opposition from locals when it set out to build a new power plant on the Alouette River. Rather than ignore these complaints, the company convened a stakeholder committee, with representation from the local community, First Nations bands (aboriginal peoples), environmentalists, and local regulators. Over many months of dialogue, the committee hammered out a

---

[24] Author interview, July 8, 2009.

[25] William Isaacs, *Dialogue and the Art of Thinking Together* (New York: Doubleday, 1999).

[26] This section draws on the discussion in Anne T. Lawrence and Ann Svendsen, *The Clayoquot Controversy: A Stakeholder Dialogue Simulation* (Vancouver: Centre for Innovation in Management, 2002). The argument for the benefits of stakeholder engagement is fully developed in Ann Svendsen, *The Stakeholder Strategy: Profiting from Collaborative Business Relationships* (San Francisco: Berrett-Koehler, 1998).

plan for the river that permitted more power generation, but also provided for protection of fish and wildlife, recreational use, and flood control. The group also set up an ongoing governance process, so stakeholders could continue to be consulted in future decisions. Today, BC Hydro has stakeholder dialogues in progress in many locations across the province.[27]

Stakeholder Networks

Dialogue between a single firm and its stakeholders is sometimes insufficient to address an issue effectively. Corporations sometimes encounter public issues that they can address effectively only by working collaboratively with other businesses and concerned persons and organizations in **stakeholder networks**. One such issue that confronted Nike, Inc., was a growing demand by environmentally aware consumers for apparel and shoes made from organic cotton.

> Cotton, traditionally cultivated with large quantities of synthetic fertilizers, pesticides, and herbicides, is one of the world's most environmentally destructive crops. In the late 1990s, in response both to consumer pressure and to its own internal commitments, Nike began for the first time to incorporate organic cotton into its sports apparel products. Its intention was to ramp up slowly, achieving 5 percent organic content by 2010. However, the company soon encountered barriers to achieving even these limited objectives. Farmers were reluctant to transition to organic methods without a sure market, processors found it inefficient to shut down production lines to clean them for organic runs, and banks were unwilling to lend money for unproven technologies. The solution, it turned out, involved extensive collaboration with groups throughout the supply chain—farmers, cooperatives, merchants, processors, and financial institutions—as well as other companies that were buyers of cotton, to facilitate the emergence of a global market for organic cotton. The outcome was the formation in 2003 of a new organization called the Organic Exchange, in which Nike has continued to play a leading role.[28]

In this instance, Nike realized that in order to reach its objective, it would be necessary to become involved in building a multi-party, international network of organizations with a shared interest in the issue of organic cotton.

The Benefits of Engagement

Engaging interactively with stakeholders—whether through dialogue, network building, or some other process—carries a number of potential benefits.[29]

Stakeholder organizations bring a number of distinct strengths. They are often aware of shifts in popular sentiment before companies are, and are thus able to alert companies to emerging issues. For example, as described earlier in this chapter, People for the Ethical Treatment of Animals (PETA) brought the issue of animal cruelty to McDonald's

---

[27] We are indebted to Ann Svendsen for this example. More information is available at *www.bchydro.com*.

[28] The Web site for the Organic Exchange is *www.organicexchange.org*. Nike's description of its efforts is available online at *www.nike.com/nikebiz*. This case is discussed in Ann C. Svendsen and Myriam Laberge, "Convening Stakeholder Networks: A New Way of Thinking, Being, and Engaging," *Journal of Corporate Citizenship* 19 (Autumn 2005), pp. 91–104.

[29] The following paragraph is largely based on the discussion in Michael Yaziji and Jonathan Doh, *NGOs and Corporations: Conflict and Collaboration* (Cambridge, UK: Cambridge University Press, 2009), ch. 7, "Corporate–NGO Engagements: From Conflict to Collaboration," pp. 123–45.

attention and encouraged the firm to address it proactively. Stakeholders often operate in networks of organizations very different from the company's; interacting with them gives a firm access to information in these networks. Stakeholders often bring technical or scientific expertise in their area of concern. Finally, when stakeholders agree to work with a company on implementing a mutually agreed-upon solution, they can give the resulting work greater legitimacy in the eyes of the public. For example, when Coca-Cola partnered with the World Wildlife Fund, an environmental group, to address stakeholder concerns about the company's impact on water quality and access—a story told in the discussion case at the end of this chapter—its efforts were more believable to many than if it had undertaken this initiative on its own.

In short, stakeholder engagement can help companies learn about society's expectations, draw on outside expertise, generate creative solutions, and win stakeholder support for implementing them. It can also disarm or neutralize critics and improve a company's reputation for taking constructive action. On the other hand, corporations that do *not* engage effectively with those their actions affect may be hurt. Their reputation may suffer, their sales may drop, and they may be prevented from taking action. The need to respond to stakeholders has only been heightened by the increased globalization of many businesses and by the rise of technologies that facilitate fast communication on a worldwide scale.

Companies are learning that it is important to take a strategic approach to the management of public issues, both domestically and globally. This requires thinking ahead, understanding what is important to stakeholders, scanning the environment, and formulating action plans to anticipate changes in the external environment. Effective issue management requires involvement by both professional staff and leaders at top levels of the organization. It entails communicating across organizational boundaries, engaging with the public, and working creatively with stakeholders to solve complex problems.

Summary

- A public issue is an issue that is of mutual concern to an organization and one or more of the organization's stakeholders. Emerging public issues present a risk, but they also present an opportunity, because companies that correctly anticipate and respond to them can often obtain a competitive advantage.

- The eight strategic radar screens (the customer, competitor, economic, technological, social, political, legal, and geophysical environments) enable public affairs managers to assess and acquire information regarding their business environments. Managers must learn to look outward to understand key developments and anticipate their impact on the business.

- The issue management process includes identification and analysis of issues, the generation of options, action, and evaluation of the results.

- In the modern corporation, the issue management process takes place in many boundary-spanning departments. Some firms have a department of external affairs or corporate relations to coordinate these activities. Top management support is essential for effective issue management.

- Stakeholder engagement involves building relationships between a business firm and its stakeholders around issues of common concern. It may involve dialogue, network building, or partnerships.

- Engaging with stakeholders benefits businesses by bringing in expertise, enhancing legitimacy, and generating creative solutions to common problems.

Key Terms

competitive
intelligence, *31*
environmental analysis, *29*
environmental
intelligence, *29*

issue management, *31*
issue management
process, *31*
performance–expectations
gap, *25*

public issue, *25*
stakeholder dialogue, *40*
stakeholder
engagement, *38*
stakeholder network, *41*

**Internet
Resources**

www.wn.com/publicissues
www.nifi.org
www.un.org/en/globalissues
www.issuemanagement.org
www.scip.org
www.wfs.org
www.globalissues.org
http://dir.yahoo.com/Society_and
_Culture/issues_and_Causes

World News, Public Issues
National Issues Forum
United Nations, Global Issues
Issue Management Council
Society of Competitive Intelligence Professionals
World Future Society
Global Issues
Yahoo's list of issues

Discussion Case: *Coca-Cola's Water Neutrality Initiative*

In the middle to late 2000s, Coca-Cola faced an emerging issue: its corporate impact on water quality, availability, and access around the world.

The Coca-Cola Company (TCCC) was the world's largest beverage company. The company operated in more than 200 countries, providing 1.6 billion servings a day of carbonated beverages, juices and juice drinks, bottled water, and ready-to-drink coffees and teas. The company also partnered with around 300 bottlers, independent companies that manufactured various Coca-Cola products under franchise. More than 70 percent of the company's revenue came from outside the United States.

Water was essential to Coca-Cola's business. The company and its bottlers used around 80 billion gallons of water worldwide every year. Of this, about two-fifths went into finished beverages, and the rest was used in the manufacturing process—for example, to wash bottles, clean equipment, and provide sanitation for employees. Water supplies were also essential to the production of many ingredients in its products, such as sugar, corn, citrus fruit, tea, and coffee. Coca-Cola's chairman and CEO put it bluntly when he commented that unless the communities where the company operated had access to water, "we haven't got a business."

In 2003, Coca-Cola was abruptly reminded of the impact of its water use on local communities. The Center for Science and the Environment, a think tank in India, charged that Coca-Cola products there contained dangerous levels of pesticide residues. Other activists in India charged that the company's bottling plants used too much water, depriving local villagers of supplies for drinking and irrigation. In 2004, local officials shut down a Coca-Cola bottling plant in the state of Kerala, saying it was depleting groundwater, and an Indian court issued an order requiring soft-drink makers to list pesticide residues on their labels. In the United States, the India Resource Center took up the cause, organizing a grassroots campaign to convince schools and colleges to boycott Coca-Cola products.

Water was also emerging as a major concern to the world's leaders. In the early 21st century, more than 1 billion people worldwide lacked access to safe drinking water. Water consumption was doubling every 20 years, an unsustainable rate of growth. By 2025, one-third of the world's population was expected to face acute water shortages. The secretary general of the United Nations highlighted water stress as a major cause of disease, rising food prices, and regional conflicts such as the one in Darfur, Sudan, and called on national governments and corporations to take steps to address the issue.

Coca-Cola fought the challenges to its operations in India, but it also began to take a serious look at the water issue. The company undertook a comprehensive study, surveying its global operations to assess its water management practices and impacts. It also reached out to other stakeholders, including the World Wildlife Fund, the Nature Conservancy, the World Business Council for Sustainable Development, UNESCO, CARE, and various academic experts, to seek their advice. As the leader of TCCC's water stewardship initiative later explained, the company also "sat down with each of our top bottlers, all of our operating groups, and really walked through all aspects of water and really understood where they were coming from and reached consensus though a very deliberate process." Internally, it built a set of Web-based tools to allow its bottlers to benchmark against others and learn from the best practices of their peers.

In 2007, TCCC announced a goal of *water neutrality*, defined as "returning to nature and communities an amount of water equal to what we use in our beverages and their production." This goal would be accomplished in three ways: reduce, recycle, and replenish. The company would reduce its own use of water by running its operations more efficiently. It said it would discharge water used in manufacturing only if it were clean enough to support aquatic life—treating its wastewater itself where local authorities were unable to do so. Finally, the company would replenish the balance of the water it used (for example, as an ingredient in bottled beverages) by participating in various water conservation projects globally. To help it do so, Coca-Cola announced a partnership with the World Wildlife Fund, providing an initial $20 million to the environmental group to support projects such as river conservation, rainwater collection, and efficient irrigation.

"If we do not act responsibly, society will not give us the social license to continue to operate," said Coca-Cola's CEO. "[Water neutrality] is an aspirational goal, but behind it is work that's already taken place. . . . You focus on the areas which are relevant to your business. . . . Water is clearly a relevant area. And that then gets employee engagement and legitimization from the shareholders as well."

Sources: Business for Social Responsibility, "Drinking It In: The Evolution of a Global Water Stewardship Program at The Coca-Cola Company," March 2008; "The Coca-Cola System Announced New Global Targets for Water Conservation and Climate Protection in Partnership with WWF," press release, October 30, 2008; "Ban Warns Business on Looming Water Crisis," *Financial Times (London)*, January 25, 2008; "Coke Aims to Improve Water Recycling; Proposal Marks a Bid to Address Criticism in Developing Nations," *The Wall Street Journal*, June 6, 2007; "World Economy: Running Dry," *The Economist*, August 28, 2008; "Coca-Cola in India," in Michael Yaziji and Jonathan Doh, *NGOs and Corporations* (Cambridge, UK: Cambridge University Press, 2009), pp. 115–19; and *The Coca-Cola Company 2007/2008 Sustainability Review*, at *www.thecoca-colacompany.com/citizenship/pdf/2007-2008_sustainability_review.pdf*.

Discussion Questions

1. What was the public issue facing The Coca-Cola Company in this case? What stakeholders were concerned, and how did their expectations differ from the company's performance?

2. If you applied the strategic radar screens model to this case, which of the eight environments would be most significant, and why?

3. Apply the issue management life cycle process model to this case. Which stages of the process can you identify in this case?

4. How did TCCC use stakeholder engagement and dialogue to improve its response to this issue, and what were the benefits of engagement to the company?

5. In your opinion, did TCCC respond appropriately to this issue? Why or why not?

CHAPTER THREE

Corporate Social Responsibility

Corporate social responsibility is the idea that businesses interact with the organization's stakeholders for social good while they pursue economic goals. Both market and nonmarket stakeholders expect businesses to be socially responsible, and many companies have responded by making social goals a part of their overall business operations. What it means to act in socially responsible ways is not always clear, thus producing controversy about what constitutes such behavior, how extensive it should be, and what it costs to be socially responsible.

This Chapter Focuses on These Key Learning Objectives:

- Understanding the role of big business and its responsible use of corporate power in a democratic society.
- Knowing where and when the idea of social responsibility originated.
- Assessing how business meets its economic and legal obligations while being socially responsible.
- Evaluating the limits of corporate social responsibility while maximizing social benefits.
- Examining the critical arguments for and against corporate social responsibility.
- Recognizing socially responsible best practices.

Do managers have a responsibility to their stockholders? Certainly they do, because the owners of the business have invested their capital in the firm, exhibiting the ownership theory of the firm presented in Chapter 1. Do managers also have a responsibility, a *social* responsibility, to their company's other market and nonmarket stakeholders—the people who live where the firm operates, who purchase the firm's product or service, or who work for the firm? Does the stakeholder theory of the firm, described in detail in Chapter 1, expand a firm's obligations to include multiple stakeholders present in an interactive social system? Generally, yes, but while managers may have a clear responsibility to respond to all stakeholders, just how far should this responsibility go?

> After a massive earthquake shook the Sichuan Province in China, Pfizer joined other multinational corporations by pledging to send up to RMB 10 million (approximately $1.4 million) in medicine and financial assistance to relief organizations operating in the region. "We were devastated to hear about the rising death tolls and escalating number of injuries," said Ahmet Esen, country manager of Pfizer China. "Pfizer will work closely with the Chinese government to provide assistance to victims of the disaster."
>
> One hundred IBM employees set out in teams of eight for Ghana, Turkey, Romania, the Philippines, Tanzania, and Vietnam for a management development exercise organized by the company's citizenship group as part of the Corporate Service Corps program. IBM employees traveling to Ghana helped small businesses make their operations more professional. Another team in Turkey helped entrepreneurs obtain small business loans. The Vietnam-bound team created a training program on information technology to help local businesses there. The company viewed the Corporate Service Corps as a way to learn how well employees worked with strangers, in strange lands, on unfamiliar projects. More than 5,500 IBM employees applied for the 100 positions in the program.
>
> Microsoft demonstrated its commitment to expanding its global reach by offering a stripped-down version of Windows, Office, and other software for $3 to people living in developing countries through its Microsoft Unlimited Potential program. The software in the $3 package would normally retail at around $150. Microsoft chairman Bill Gates said that the company recognized that people in these countries have a growing appetite for technology but have very limited budgets. The program was also offered to low-income communities in developed nations, such as the United States.[1]

Are the efforts described above examples of corporate social responsibility, how businesses merge their social goals with solid economic objectives, or are these inappropriate uses of corporate assets—finances, personnel, and product? If these are examples of good business practice, how far should an organization go to help those in society in need of their support? How much is too much?

This chapter describes the role business plays in society, introduces the notion of corporate social responsibility, and describes how this obligation began. How organizations address and balance their multiple responsibilities—economic, legal, and social—is an ongoing challenge. What are the advantages and drawbacks of being socially responsible? Whether businesses are large or small, make goods or provide services, operate at

---

[1] "Pfizer Extends 10 Million Yuan to Earthquake Victims and Relief Efforts in China," *Medical News Today*, May 13, 2008, *http://www.medicalnewstoday.com/articles/107591.php*; "Volunteering Abroad to Climb at I.B.M.," *The New York Times*, March 26, 2008, *www.nytimes.com*; "The Globe Is IBM's Classroom," *BusinessWeek*, March 23 and 30, 2009, pages 56–57; and "Software by Microsoft Is Nearly Free for the Needy," *The New York Times*, April 19, 2007, *www.nytimes.com*.

The B Lab is a nonprofit organization created to certify and rate "B Corporations" (as in "be" good) through a B Ratings System. The organization developed and promotes a legal framework that institutionalizes stakeholder interests within existing corporate law; recruits and promotes B Corporations; and helps B Corporations access purpose-driven capital markets. So what is a "B Corporation"? To be recognized as a B Corporation, there are three steps:

- Step 1: The organization must complete the B Survey, which measures the organization against a new standard for social and environmental performance. If the organization receives 80 out of 200 points, it can proceed to step 2.
- Step 2: The organization must amend its governing documents to incorporate stakeholder interests. A legal roadmap is provided by B Lab for organizations to follow to ensure that the social and environmental values are "baked into the DNA of the company."
- Step 3: The final step makes the certification of the organization official—it is a B Corporation. The benefits of becoming a B Corporation, as well as the expectations of organizations with this distinction, are described in a simple two-page sheet.

The certified organization is expected to adopt the B Corporation Declaration of Interdependence, which states, "We envision a new sector of the economy which harnesses the power of the private enterprise to create public benefit. . . . [and] We hold these truths to be self-evident: that we must be the change we seek in the world; that all business ought to be conducted as if people and place mattered; that, through their products, practices, and profits, businesses should aspire to do no harm and benefit all; to do so requires that we act with the understanding that we are each dependent upon another and thus responsible for each other and future generations."

Dansko (literally translated as "Danish shoe"), a California apparel footwear and accessories manufacturer, became a Founding B Corporation. The company explains that it sought the certification for the same reason it acquired the LEED Certification on its company's building—to resource and learn from the broad-based, independent, third-party benchmarking standards that these organizations could provide.

Method Products is another Founding B Corporation. This San Francisco–based cleaning products company already runs its business in a values-driven manner, building social and environmental benefit into its products. Being a B Corporation, according to Method's management, allows the company to build that ethos into the legal backbone of the company so that the values will never be compromised.

Sources: B Corporation Web site, *www.bcorporation.net;* "How to B Good," Miller-McCune.com, November–December 2008, pp. 53–59.

home or abroad, willingly try to be socially responsible or fight against it all the way, there is no doubt that the public expects businesses to understand and act on their responsibility to all of their stakeholders in the society in which they operate. One organization, B Lab, attempts to measure and certify social responsibility, or *good corporations*, as shown in Exhibit 3.A.

Corporate Power and Responsibility

Undeniably, businesses, especially large corporations—whether by intention or accident, and whether for good or evil—play a major role in all that occurs in society. The power exerted by the world's largest business organizations is obvious and enormous. This influence, termed **corporate power**, refers to the capability of corporations to influence government, the economy, and society, based on their organizational resources.

FIGURE 3.1
The 10 Largest Global Corporations, 2009

Source: "*Fortune* Global 500," CNN Money.com, *money.cnn.com/magazines/fortune/global500/2009/full_list.*

Rank (by revenue)	Company	Revenues (U.S. $ millions)	Profits (U.S. $ millions)
1	Walmart Stores	$378,799	$12,731
2	ExxonMobil	372,824	40,610
3	Royal Dutch Shell	355,782	31,331
4	BP	291,438	20,845
5	Toyota Motor	230,201	15,042
6	Chevron	210,783	18,688
7	ING Group	201,516	12,649
8	Total	187,280	18,042
9	General Motors	182,347	−38,732
10	ConocoPhillips	178,558	11,891

Power is often a function of size, and by almost any measure used, the world's largest business enterprises are impressively big, as shown in Figure 3.1. As measured by revenue, the "big five" in 2009 were Walmart, ExxonMobil, Royal Dutch Shell, BP, and Toyota Motor. The three most profitable companies in the top 10—during a period of rapidly rising oil prices—were all in the petroleum industry: ExxonMobil, Royal Dutch Shell, and BP.

One way to get a sense of the economic power of the world's largest companies is to compare them with nations. Figure 3.2 shows some leading companies alongside countries whose total gross domestic product is about the same as these companies' revenue. The revenues of automaker Toyota Motor, for example, are about equal to the entire economic output of Venezuela. Walmart's are about the size of the economy of Norway; and BP's are about the size of the economy of Denmark.

The size and global reach of major transnational corporations such as Walmart and the others listed in Figure 3.2 give them tremendous power. Through their ever-present marketing, they influence what people want and how they act around the world. We count on corporations for job creation; much of our community well-being; the standard of living

FIGURE 3.2
Comparison of Annual Sales Revenue and the Gross Domestic Product for Selected Transnational Corporations and Nations, 2007, in $ Billions*

Sources: "*Fortune* Global 500," CNN Money.com, *money.cnn.com/magazines/fortune/global500/2009/full_list*; and World Bank data, *www.worldbank.org.*

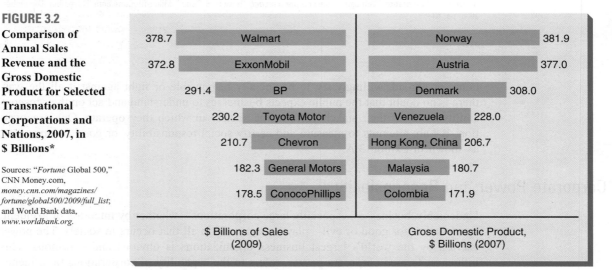

*2009 $ billions of sales compared to 2007 gross domestic product in $ billions.

we enjoy; the tax base for essential municipal, state, and national services; and our needs for banking and financial services, insurance, transportation, communication, utilities, entertainment, and a growing proportion of health care. These corporations have the resources to make substantial contributions to political campaigns, as discussed in Chapter 9, thus influencing the policies of governments. They dominate not only the traditional domains of product manufacture and service delivery, but also increasingly reach into such traditionally public sector activities as education, law enforcement, and the provision of social services.

The following well-known quotation, frequently appearing in journals for business executives, challenges its readers to assume a responsible role for business in society:

> Business has become . . . the most powerful institution on the planet. The dominant institution in any society needs to take responsibility for the whole. . . .
> Every decision that is made, every action that is taken, must be viewed in light of that kind of responsibility.[2]

The tremendous power of the world's leading corporations has both positive and negative effects.[3] A big company may have definite advantages over a small one. It can command more resources, produce at a lower cost, plan further into the future, and weather business fluctuations somewhat better. Globalization of markets can bring new products, technologies, and economic opportunities to developing societies. And yet, the concentration of corporate power can also harm society. Huge businesses can disproportionately influence politics, shape tastes, and dominate public discourse. They can move production from one site to another, weakening unions and communities. These companies can also use their economic influence to collude to fix prices, divide markets, and quash competition in ways that can negatively affect consumer choices, employment opportunities, or the creation of new businesses.

Many people are concerned about the enormous influence of business. In a recent Harris Interactive poll, 85 percent of those surveyed said that big companies have too much power, especially in terms of their influence on our government policymakers in Washington. Since 1994, between 80 and 90 percent of the Americans polled every year or so said that big business had too much power.[4] The focused power found in the modern business corporation means that every action it takes can affect the quality of human life—for individuals, for communities, and for the entire globe. The obligation this gives rise to is often referred to as the *iron law of responsibility*. The **iron law of responsibility** says that in the long run, those who do not use power in ways that society considers responsible will tend to lose it.[5]

---

[2] David C. Korten, "Limits to the Social Responsibility of Business," *The People-Centered Development Forum*, article 19, June 1, 1996.

[3] For two classic analyses of corporate power, see Alfred C. Neal, *Business Power and Public Policy* (New York: Praeger, 1981); and Edwin M. Epstein and Dow Votaw, eds., *Rationality, Legitimacy, Responsibility: Search for New Directions in Business and Society* (Santa Monica, CA: Goodyear, 1978). More recent treatments may be found in David C. Korten, *When Corporations Rule the World* (San Francisco: Berrett-Koehler, 1996); Carl Boggs, *The End of Politics: Corporate Power and the Decline of the Public Sphere* (New York: Guilford Press, 2000); and Alastair McIntosh, *Soil and Soul: People versus Corporate Power* (London: Aurum Press, 2004).

[4] "Very Large Majorities of Americans Believe Big Companies, PACs, Political Lobbyists and the News Media Have Too Much Power and Influence in D.C.," *The Harris Poll*, Harris Interactive, March 12, 2009.

[5] This concept first appeared in Keith Davis and Robert Blomstrom, *Business and Its Environment* (New York: McGraw-Hill, 1966).

Given the virtually immeasurable power in the hands of the leaders of large, global corporations, stakeholders throughout the social system expect business to take great care in wielding its power responsibly for the betterment of society. McKinsey and Company discovered that 95 percent of the CEOs polled in their global study believe that "society has higher expectations for business to take on public responsibilities than it had five years ago." About 60 percent of the CEOs believe that these expectations will increase even more over the next five years.[6] All societies are now affected by corporate operations. As a result, social responsibility has become a worldwide expectation.

The Meaning of Corporate Social Responsibility

Corporate social responsibility (CSR) means that a corporation should act in a way that enhances society and its inhabitants and be held accountable for any of its actions that affect people, their communities, and their environment. This concept is based in the root of the term *responsibility*, meaning "to pledge back," creating a commitment to give back to society and the organization's stakeholders.[7] It implies that harm to people and society should be acknowledged and corrected if at all possible. It may require a company to forgo some profits if its social impacts seriously hurt some of its stakeholders or if its funds can be used to have a positive social impact.

The Many Responsibilities of Business

Being socially responsible does not mean that a company must abandon its other missions. As discussed later in this chapter, a business has many responsibilities: economic, legal, and social. In a worldwide survey of CEOs, 72 percent of executives polled said they sought to embed social and environmental issues into the organization's core strategies and operations.[8] Therefore, the challenge for management is to understand the interrelationships that exist among their responsibilities so that a comprehensive corporate strategy emerges embodying each of the organization's obligations.[9] At times these responsibilities will be in tension; at other times they will blend together to better the firm and actually make it more profitable. Thus, having multiple and sometimes competing responsibilities does not mean that socially responsible firms cannot be as profitable as others that are less responsible; some are and some are not.

Social responsibility requires companies to balance the benefits to be gained against the costs of achieving those benefits. Many people believe that both business and society gain when firms actively strive to be socially responsible. Others are doubtful, saying that taking on social tasks weakens business's competitive strength. The arguments on both sides of this debate are presented later in this chapter.

---

[6] "CEOs on Strategy and Social Issues," *The McKinsey Quarterly*, October 2007, p. 1

[7] For a more complete discussion of the roots of corporate social responsibility and how it is practiced, see Jerry D. Goldstein and Andrew C. Wicks, "Corporate and Stakeholder Responsibility: Making Business Ethics a Two-Way Conversation," *Business Ethics Quarterly* 17 (2007), pp. 375–98. Also see Florian Wettstein, "Beyond Voluntariness, beyond CSR: Making a Case for Human Rights and Justice," *Business and Society Review*, 2009, pp. 125–52.

[8] "CEOs on Strategy and Social Issues," p. 7.

[9] The understanding of the interrelations among business's obligations is discussed in Jared D. Harris and R. Edward Freeman, "The Impossibility of the Separation Thesis," *Business Ethics Quarterly* 18 (2008), pp. 541–48. Michael E. Porter and Mark R. Kramer also discuss the link between competitive advantage and corporate social responsibility in "Strategy and Society," *Harvard Business Review*, December 2006, pp. 78–92.

How Corporate Social Responsibility Began

In the United States, the idea of corporate social responsibility appeared around the start of the 20th century. Corporations at that time came under attack for being too big, too powerful, and guilty of antisocial and anticompetitive practices. Critics tried to curb corporate power through antitrust laws, banking regulations, and consumer protection laws.

Faced with this social protest, a few farsighted business executives advised corporations to use their power and influence voluntarily for broad social purposes rather than for profits alone. Some of the wealthiest business leaders—steelmaker Andrew Carnegie is a good example—became great philanthropists who gave much of their wealth to educational and charitable institutions. Others, like automaker Henry Ford, developed paternalistic programs to support the recreational and health needs of their employees. (A recent example is Warren Buffet, who in 2006 gave the bulk of his $44 billion fortune to the Bill and Melinda Gates Foundation and four other philanthropic organizations.) These business leaders believed that business had a responsibility to society that went beyond or worked along with their efforts to make profits.[10]

As these early ideas about business's expanded role in society gained influence, two broad principles emerged: the *charity principle* and the *stewardship principle*. They are described in the following sections of this chapter. These principles shaped business thinking about social responsibility during the 20th century and are the foundation stones for the modern idea of corporate social responsibility.

The Charity Principle

The **charity principle**, the idea that the wealthiest members of society should be charitable toward those less fortunate, is of course a very ancient notion. When Andrew Carnegie and other wealthy business leaders endowed public libraries, supported settlement houses for the poor, gave money to educational institutions, and contributed funds to many other community organizations, they were continuing this long tradition of being "my brother's keeper."

> Andrew Carnegie and John D. Rockefeller are usually credited with pioneering the path of the great modern philanthropists. For some years, the world's newspapers kept score on their giving. *The London Times* reported that in 1903 Carnegie had given away $21 million, Rockefeller $10 million. In 1913, *The New York Herald* ran a final box score: Carnegie, $332 million; Rockefeller, $175 million. All this was before the income tax and other tax provisions had generated external incentives to giving. The feeling of duty to the public good arose from inner sources.[11]

This kind of private aid to the needy members of society was especially important in the early decades of the last century. At that time, there was no Social Security, Medicare, unemployment pay, or United Way. There were few organizations capable of counseling troubled families, sheltering women and children who were victims of physical abuse, aiding alcoholics, treating the mentally ill or the disabled, or taking care of the destitute. When wealthy industrialists reached out to help others such as these, they were accepting

---

[10] Harold R. Bowen, *Social Responsibility of the Businessman* (New York: Harper, 1953); and Morrell Heald, *The Social Responsibility of Business: Company and Community, 1900–1960* (Cleveland: Case Western Reserve Press, 1970). For a history of how some of these business philanthropists acquired their wealth, see Matthew Josephson, *The Robber Barons: The Great American Capitalists* (New York: Harcourt Brace, 1934).

[11] Michael Novak, *Business as a Calling: Work and the Examined Life* (New York: The Free Press, 1996), p. 197.

some measure of responsibility for improving the conditions of life in their communities. In doing so, their actions helped counteract critics who claimed that business leaders were uncaring and interested only in profits.

Before long, when it was recognized that many community needs outpaced the riches of even the wealthiest persons and families, or beginning in about the 1920s, much of the charitable load was taken on by business firms themselves rather than by the owners alone. Business leaders often gave vigorous support to this form of corporate charity, urging all firms and their employees to unite their efforts to extend aid to the poor and the needy. Businesses built houses, churches, schools, and libraries, provided medical and legal services, and gave to charity.

Today, for some business firms, corporate social responsibility means participating in community affairs by making similar kinds of charitable contributions. The Giving USA Foundation reported that total U.S. charitable contributions were more than $307 billion in 2008.[12] Although many corporations today make generous contributions, as will be further discussed in Chapter 18, most observers nowadays believe that corporate social responsibility encompasses much more than just charity.

The Stewardship Principle

Many of today's corporate executives see themselves as stewards, or trustees, who act in the general public's interest. Although their companies are privately owned and they try to make profits for the stockholders, business leaders who follow the **stewardship principle** believe they have an obligation to see that everyone—particularly those in need or at risk—benefits from their firms' actions. According to this view, corporate managers have been placed in a position of public trust. They control vast resources whose use can affect people in fundamental ways. Because they exercise this kind of crucial influence, they incur a responsibility to use those resources in ways that are good not just for the stockholders alone but for society generally. In this way, they have become stewards, or trustees, for society, as well as for the natural environment. As such, they are expected to act with a special degree of responsibility in making business decisions.[13]

This kind of thinking has eventually produced the modern theory of stakeholder management, which was described in the opening chapter of this book. According to this theory, corporate managers need to interact skillfully with all groups that have a stake in what the corporation does. If they do not do so, their firms will not be fully accepted by the public as legitimate.

> HP Brazil, a subsidiary of Hewlett-Packard, developed the Digital Garage project where the firm collaborated with local Brazilian foundations and youth clubs to provide young Brazilians from less privileged backgrounds the tools to develop self-esteem, creativity, sociability, entrepreneurship, leadership, citizenship, teamwork, and IT skills. HP Brazil management recognized their stewardship responsibility to serve as volunteer mentors and tutors for the local youths and to empower young people with skills to enable them to participate in the growing technological society.[14]

---

[12] Giving USA Foundation (formerly AAFRC), *Giving USA 2009* (Indianapolis, IN: Center on Philanthropy at Indiana University, 2009), p. 1 .

[13] Two early statements of this stewardship-trustee view are Frank W. Abrams, "Management's Responsibilities in a Complex World," *Harvard Business Review*, May 1951; and Richard Eells, *The Meaning of Modern Business* (New York: Columbia University Press, 1960).

[14] "HP Wins International Corporate Conscience Award," HP press release, *www.hp.com/hpinfo*.

FIGURE 3.3
Evolving Phases of Corporate Social Responsibility

	Phases of Corporate Social Responsibility	CSR Drivers	CSR Policy Instruments
CSR₁ 1950s–1960s	**Corporate Social Stewardship** Corporate philanthropy—acts of charity Managers as public Trustee-stewards Balancing social pressures	Executive conscience Company image/reputation	Philanthropic funding Public relations
CSR₂ 1960s–1970s	**Corporate Social Responsiveness** Social impact analysis Strategic priority for social response Organizational redesign and training for responsiveness Stakeholder mapping and implementation	Social unrest/protest Repeated corporate misbehavior Public policy/government regulation Stakeholder pressures Think tank policy papers	Stakeholder strategy Regulatory compliance Social audits Public affairs function Governance reform Political lobbying
CSR₃ 1980s–1990s	**Corporate/Business Ethics** Foster an ethical corporate culture Establish an ethical organizational climate Recognize common ethical principles	Religious/ethnic beliefs Technology-driven value changes Human rights pressures Code of ethics Ethics committee/officer/audits Ethics training Stakeholder negotiations	Mission/vision/values Statements CEO leadership ethics
CSR₄ 1990s–2000s	**Corporate/Global Citizenship** Stakeholder partnerships Integrate financial, social, and environmental performance Identify globalization impacts Sustainability of company and environment	Global economic trade/investment High-tech communication networks Geopolitical shifts/competition Ecological awareness/concern NGO pressures	Intergovernmental compacts Global audit standards NGO dialogue Sustainability audits/reports

Source: Adapted from William C. Frederick, *Corporation, Be Good! The Story of Corporate Social Responsibility* (Indianapolis, IN: Dog Ear Publishing, 2006). Used with permission.

William C. Frederick, a leading scholar and a coauthor of several earlier editions of this book, described in a recent book how business understanding of corporate social responsibility has evolved over the past half century. During each of four historical periods, corporate social responsibility has had a distinct focus, set of drivers, and policy instruments, as shown in Figure 3.3. Frederick explained that the most recent phase of corporate social responsibility is called *corporate citizenship*. (Chapter 7 will explore this concept more fully.)

Balancing Economic, Legal, and Social Responsibilities

Social responsibility is embraced by some organizations and treated at arm's length by others. However, social responsibility is not a business organization's sole responsibility. In addition, as a member of a civil society, organizations have legal obligations, as well as economic responsibilities, to their owners and other stakeholders affected by the financial well-being of the firm. Any organization or manager must seek to juggle these multiple responsibilities—economic, legal, and social. The belief that the business of business is

FIGURE 3.4

Business Executives' View of the Role of Business in Society

Percentage of business executives who believe that business organizations should . . .

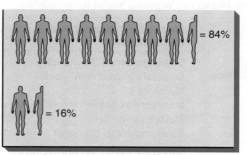

Balance their responsibility to their investors with their responsibilities to other business stakeholders = 84%

Primarily focus on maximizing their investors' returns while staying within the law of society = 16%

Source: For a more detailed discussion of these views, see "The McKinsey Global Survey of Business Executives: Business and Society," *McKinsey Quarterly,* January 2006. Based on a survey of 4,238 executives (more than a quarter of CEOs or other top executives) in 116 countries, conducted in December 2005.

solely to attend to stockholders' return on investment and make a profit is no longer widely held, as Figure 3.4 suggests. Rather, many business executives believe the key challenge facing their organizations today is to meet their multiple economic and social responsibilities simultaneously.

> Never was the balancing of multiple responsibilities more evident than when Jeffrey Immelt, chairman and CEO at General Electric, announced before 200 corporate officers that it would take four things to keep the company on top: execution, growth, great people, and *virtue.* Immelt appointed the company's first vice president for corporate citizenship, Bob Corcoran, to take his message globally to GE's suppliers, customers, and employees. Within a year after Immelt's announcement, GE had performed more than 3,100 labor, health, environmental, and safety audits and opened up discussions with socially responsible investment funds. GE launched a global philanthropic program by providing health care to people in the poorest areas of Ghana.[15]

A business must manage its economic responsibilities to its stockholders, its legal requirements to societal laws and regulations, and its social responsibilities to various stakeholders. Although these obligations may conflict at times, a successful firm is one whose management finds ways to meet each of its critical responsibilities and develops strategies to enable these obligations to reinforce each other.

Economic and Social Responsibilities: Enlightened Self-Interest

Being socially responsible by meeting the public's continually changing expectations requires wise leadership at the top of the corporation. Companies with the ability to recognize profound social changes and anticipate how they will affect operations have proven to be survivors. They get along better with government regulators, are more open to the needs of the company's stakeholders, and often cooperate with legislators as new laws are developed to cope with social problems.

> In 2006, Gap, Inc., joined a number of other companies in launching (Product) Red. Specific products were earmarked, and 50 percent of the profits from these sales were sent to The Global Fund to fight AIDS, tuberculosis, and malaria in Africa. Is this just another act of charity? Not so, says Gap on its Web site: "This isn't charity. It's a new way of doing business."

[15] "Money and Morals at GE," *Fortune,* November 15, 2004, pp. 176–82.

Gap management argues that this is simply good for business. The products themselves are appealing, but Gap customers have told management that they want their dollars to do more, and thus (Product) Red was born. Customers know that their spending also helps others.

Employee morale is also up at Gap, according to Dan Henkle, senior vice president of global responsibility at Gap. "Our employees love the fact that we're doing something like this. Everyone wants to be involved in some way, shape or form."[16] Gap is committed to the program since it integrates its commitment to its shareholders, customers, and employees, as well as its long-standing commitment to helping others in need around the world.

The actions taken by Gap are an example of a business organization's leaders being guided by **enlightened self-interest**. Gap recognizes the long-term rewards to the company from its global involvement through an enhanced reputation, customer loyalty, employee satisfaction, and global community support. According to this view, it is in a company's self-interest in the long term to provide true value to its customers, to help its employees to grow, and to behave responsibly as a global corporate citizen.[17]

Do socially responsible companies sacrifice profits by working conscientiously to promote the social good? Do they make higher profits, better-than-average profits, or lower profits than corporations that ignore the public's desires for a high and responsible standard of social performance?

Scholars have explored this issue for two decades, with mixed results. In 2003, researchers at the University of Iowa conducted a rigorous review of 52 prior studies of the relationship between corporate social responsibility and firm performance. They found that most of the time, more responsible companies also had solid financial results; the statistical association was highly to modestly positive across the range of all prior studies. The authors concluded, "Corporate virtue, in the form of social responsibility and, to a lesser extent, environmental responsibility is likely to pay off."[18] In short, most of the time, social responsibility and financial performance go together, although there may be some conditions under which this is not true.

Any social program—for example, an in-company child care center, a drug education program for employees, or the lending of company executives as advisers to community agencies—will usually impose immediate monetary costs on the participating company. These short-run costs certainly have a potential for reducing the company's profits unless the social activity is designed to make money, which is not usually the purpose of these programs. Therefore, a company may sacrifice short-run profits by undertaking social initiatives, but what is lost in the short run may be gained back over a longer period. For example, if a drug education program prevents or reduces on-the-job drug abuse, then the resulting lower employee turnover, fewer absences from work, healthier workforce, and fewer accidents and injuries may increase the firm's productivity and lower health insurance costs. In that case, the company may actually experience an

---

[16] "Getting Engaged," *The CRO, www.thecro.com*, October 19, 2006.

[17] Jeff Frooman, "Socially Irresponsible and Illegal Behavior and Shareholder Wealth," *Business & Society*, September 1997, pp. 221–49, argues that the negative effects on shareholder wealth when a firm acts irresponsibly support the enlightened self-interest view: act responsibly to promote shareholders' interests.

[18] Mark Orlitzky, Frank Schmidt, and Sara Rynes, "Corporate Social and Financial Performance: A Meta-analysis," *Organization Studies*, 2003, pp. 403–41. Also investigating this issue are Marc Orlitzky and John D. Benjamin, "Corporate Social Performance and Firm Risk: A Meta-analytic Review," *Business & Society*, 2001, pp. 369–96; and for a contrarian view see Idris Mootee, "The Impact of Corporate Social Responsibility—From Creating Customer Goodwill to Influencing Social Standards," Futurelab, *blog.futurelab.net/2008/12*.

increase in its long-run profits, although it had to make an expensive outlay to get the program started.

Legal Requirements versus Corporate Social Responsibility

Accompanying a firm's economic responsibility to its stockholders are its **legal obligations**. As a member of society, a firm must abide by the laws and regulations governing the society. How are a firm's legal obligations related to its social responsibilities? Laws and regulations are enacted to ensure socially responsible conduct by businesses. The standards of behavior expected by society are embodied in that society's laws. Can't businesses voluntarily decide to be socially responsible? Of course, but legal rules set minimum standards for businesses to follow. Some firms go beyond the law; others seek to change the law to require competitors to be more socially responsible.

Laws and regulations help create a level playing field for businesses that compete against one another. By requiring all firms to meet the same social standards—for example, the safe disposal of hazardous wastes—government prevents one firm from gaining a competitive advantage over its rivals by acting irresponsibly. If a company dumped its wastes carelessly, it would risk lawsuits, fines, and possible jail terms for some of its managers and employees and unfavorable publicity for its actions.

Businesses that comply with laws and public policies are meeting a minimum level of social responsibility expected by the public. According to one leading scholar of corporate social performance, even legal compliance is barely enough to satisfy the public:

> The traditional economic and legal criteria are necessary but not sufficient conditions of corporate legitimacy. The corporation that flouts them will not survive; even the mere satisfaction of these criteria does not ensure the corporation's continued existence . . .
>
> Thus, social responsibility implies bringing corporate behavior up to a level where it is in congruence with currently prevailing social norms, values, and performance expectations. . . . [Social responsibility] is simply a step ahead—before the new societal expectations are codified into legal requirements.[19]

Stockholder Interests versus Other Stakeholder Interests

Top-level managers, along with a corporation's board of directors, are generally expected to produce as much value as possible for the company's owners and investors. This can be done by paying high dividends regularly and by running the company in ways that cause the stock's value to rise. Not only are high profits a positive signal to Wall Street investors that the company is being well run—thereby increasing the stock's value—but those profits also make possible the payment of high dividends to stockholders. Low profits have the opposite effect and put great pressure on managers to improve the company's financial performance.

However, stockholders are not the only stakeholder group that management must keep in mind. As reported in a recent survey of CEOs from around the world, the investment community ranked *ninth* among stakeholders who will have significant impact on the company's management of societal expectations. Employees have the greatest influence, according to the CEOs polled, followed by consumers, governments, local communities, government agencies, media, NGOs, and boards of directors.[20]

---

[19] S. Prakash Sethi, "A Conceptual Framework for Environmental Analysis of Social Issues and Evaluation of Business Response Patterns," in S. Prakash Sethi and Cecilia M. Falbe, eds., *Business and Society: Dimensions of Conflict and Cooperation* (Lexington, MA: Lexington Books, 1987), pp. 42–43.

[20] "CEOs on Strategy and Social Issues," p. 2.

Exhibit 3.B

The Limits of Corporate Social Responsibility

"It is easy to understand why big business has embraced corporate social responsibility with such verve. It makes for good press and reassures the public. . . . [B]ut the pressures operating on [corporations] to lure and keep consumers and investors haven't eased one bit. In supercapitalism, they *cannot* be socially responsible, at least not to any significant extent. . . . No company can 'voluntarily' take on an extra cost that its competitors don't also take on—which is why, under supercapitalism, regulations are the only means of getting companies to do things that hurt their bottom lines."—Robert B. Reich, *Supercapitalism: The Transformation of Business, Democracy, and Everyday Life* (New York: Alfred A. Knopf, 2007), pp. 170 and 204.

"CSR . . . is now a big, growing industry, seen as a vital tool in promoting and improving the public image of some of the world's largest corporations. In simple terms, companies make loud, public commitments to principles of ethical behavior and undertake 'good works' in the communities in which they operate. . . . The problem is that companies frequently use such initiatives to defend operations or ways of working which come in for public criticism . . . CSR, in other words, can become merely a branch of PR [public relations]. . . . Christian Aid is saying that CSR is a completely inadequate response to the sometimes devastating impact that multinational companies can have in an ever-more globalized world—and that is actually used to mask that impact."—Christian Aid, "Behind the Mask: The Real Face of Corporate Social Responsibility," *www.christian-aid.org.uk*, January 2004. Used by permission.

"Business leaders today say their companies care about more than profit and loss, that they feel responsible to society as a whole, not just to their shareholders. Corporate social responsibility is their new creed, a self-conscious corrective to earlier greed-inspired visions of the corporation. Despite this shift, the corporation itself has not changed. . . . Corporate social responsibility . . . holds out promises of help, reassures people, and sometimes works. We should not, however, expect very much from it. A corporation can do good only to help itself do well, a profound *limit* on just how much good it can do."—Joel Bakan, *The Corporation: The Pathological Pursuit of Profit and Power* (New York: The Free Press, 2004), pp. 28, 50. Used by permission.

"[P]recisely because CSR is voluntary and market-driven, companies will engage in CSR only to the extent that it makes business sense for them to do so. . . . Unlike government regulation, it cannot force companies to make unprofitable but socially beneficial decisions. In most cases, CSR only makes business sense if the costs of more virtuous behavior remain modest. This imposes important constraints on the resources that companies can spend on CSR, and limits the improvements in corporate social and environmental performance that voluntary regulation can produce."—David J. Vogel, *The Market for Virtue: The Potential and Limits of Corporate Social Responsibility* (Washington, DC: The Brookings Institution, 2005), p. 4. Used by permission.

This broader view that includes multiple stakeholders tends to put more emphasis on the long-run profit picture rather than an exclusive focus on immediate financial returns. When this happens, dividends paid to stockholders may be less than they desire, and the value of their shares may not rise as rapidly as they would like. These are the kinds of risks faced by corporate managers who have a legal responsibility to produce high value for the company's stockholder-owners but who also must try to promote the overall interests of the entire company. Putting all of the emphasis on short-run maximum profits for stockholders can lead to policies that overlook the interests and needs of other stakeholders. Managers may also downgrade social responsibility programs that increase short-run costs, although it is well known that the general public strongly approves of socially responsible companies.

As a response to the conflict between long- and short-term profit making, an enlightened self-interest point of view may be the most useful and practical approach. That means that incurring reasonable short-run costs to undertake socially responsible activities that benefit both the company and the general public in the long run is acceptable.[21] Some critics of corporate social responsibility argue that these efforts are merely superficial or cosmetic, not truly addressing the social problems claimed as targets or being responsive to the real objectives of business. Some of these opinions are presented in Exhibit 3.B.

The Corporate Social Responsibility Debate

As we have seen, there are various views about business's social responsibilities and these views evolve over time. The arguments for and against corporate social responsibility are detailed next and summarized in Figure 3.5. When you have been exposed to arguments on both sides of the debate, you will be in a better position to judge business actions in our social environment and to make more balanced business judgments in your own career.

Arguments for Corporate Social Responsibility

Who favors corporate social responsibility? Many business executives believe it is a good idea. As shown earlier in Figure 3.4, a global survey of business executives conducted in 2005 found that 84 percent agreed that large corporations should generate high returns to investors but balance this with their economic and social responsibilities. Clearly, many social groups that seek to preserve the environment, protect consumers, safeguard the safety and health of employees, prevent job discrimination, and forestall invasions of privacy through the Internet stress the importance of social responsibility by business, but so also do groups that look to business to maintain a strong return on their financial investments. Government officials also support CSR in that they ensure corporate compliance with laws and regulations that protect the general public from abusive business practices. In other words, both businesspeople and citizens, both supporters and critics of business have reasons for wanting businesses to act in socially responsible ways.

Balances Corporate Power with Responsibility

Today's business enterprise possesses much power and influence. Most people believe that responsibility must accompany power, whoever holds it. This obligation, presented

FIGURE 3.5
The Pros and Cons of Corporate Social Responsibility

Arguments for Corporate Social Responsibility	Arguments against Corporate Social Responsibility
Balances corporate power with responsibility.	Lowers economic efficiency and profit.
Discourages government regulation.	Imposes unequal costs among competitors.
Promotes long-term profits for business.	Imposes hidden costs passed on to
Improves business value and reputation.	stakeholders.
Corrects social problems caused by business.	Requires skills business may lack.
	Places responsibility on business rather
	than individuals.

[21] For an interesting discussion of this view see Moses L. Pava, "Why Corporations Should *Not* Abandon Social Responsibility," *Journal of Business Ethics*, 2008, pp. 805–12.

earlier in this chapter, is the *iron law of responsibility*. Businesses committed to social responsibility are aware that if they misuse the power they have, they might lose it. Corporations' reputations and to some extent even their independence have recently taken a hit in the economic downturn as dozens of national governments have rushed in to bolster their countries' economies and failing financial markets (see Chapter 8), an example of how managers' misuse of corporate power and the lack of responsibility as trustees of the public's wealth result in their loss of power.

Discourages Government Regulation

One of the most appealing arguments in favor of CSR for business supporters is that voluntary social acts may head off increased government regulation. Some regulation may reduce freedom for both business and society, and freedom is a desirable public good. In the case of business, regulations tend to add economic costs and restrict flexibility in decision making. From business's point of view, freedom in decision making allows business to maintain initiative in meeting market and social forces.

Two scholars, Bryan Husted and Jose de Jesus Salazar, examined how well firms performed if they voluntarily developed a social responsibility strategy versus being coerced by government or some other external force to act to benefit society. They found that firms enjoyed significant strategic advantages and maximized social benefit to their communities when they voluntarily and freely developed a social strategy rather than acting under coercive pressure.[22]

This view is also consistent with political philosophy that wishes to keep power as decentralized as possible in a democratic society. From this perspective, government is already a massive institution whose centralized power and bureaucracy threaten the balance of power in society. Therefore, if business by its own socially responsible behavior can discourage new government restrictions, it is accomplishing a public good as well as its own private good.

For example, the natural juice producer Odwalla took fast action after a number of people became sick after drinking its juice products, which were contaminated with E. Coli bacteria. To improve the safety of its fresh juice drinks, Odwalla began voluntarily to pasteurize (heat-treat) them. The company hoped that by doing so it would avoid strict and often more costly government regulation of its production processes.

Promotes Long-Term Profits for Business

At times, social initiatives by business produce long-run business profits. In 1951 a New Jersey judge ruled in a precedent-setting case, *Barlow et al. v. A.P. Smith Manufacturing*, that a corporate donation to Princeton University was an *investment* by the firm, and thus an allowable business expense. The rationale was that a corporate gift to a school, though costly in the present, might in time provide a flow of talented graduates to work for the company. The court ruled that top executives must take "a long-range view of the matter" and exercise "enlightened leadership and direction" when it comes to using company funds for socially responsible programs.[23]

---

[22] Bryan W. Husted and Jose de Jesus Salazar, "Taking Friedman Seriously: Maximizing Profits and Social Performance," *Journal of Management Studies* 43 (2006), pp. 75–91.

[23] *Barlow et al. v. A.P. Smith Manufacturing* (1951, New Jersey Supreme Court), discussed in Clarence C. Walton, *Corporate Social Responsibility* (Belmont, CA: Wadsworth, 1967), pp. 48–52.

A classic example of the long-term benefits of social responsibility was the Johnson & Johnson Tylenol incident in the 1980s, when several people died after they ingested Extra-Strength Tylenol capsules laced with the poison cyanide. To ensure the safety of its customers, Johnson & Johnson immediately recalled the product, an action that cost the firm millions of dollars in the short term. The company's production processes were never found defective. Customers rewarded Johnson & Johnson's responsible actions by continuing to buy its products, and in the long run the company once again became profitable.

In one of the opening examples of this chapter, the leadership at Pfizer believed that in the long term, its commitment to helping those in medical need and supporting governments and public health organizations in Asia after the earthquake in China would strengthen the company's financial performance by enhancing its global image and possibly attracting new customers.

Improves Business Value and Reputation

The social reputation of the firm is often viewed as an important element in establishing trust between the firm and its stakeholders. **Reputation** refers to desirable or undesirable qualities associated with an organization or its actors that may influence the organization's relationships with its stakeholders.[24] Rating Research, a British firm, created a "reputation index" to measure a company's social reputation. The index evaluates critical intangible assets that constitute corporate reputation and broadly disseminates these ratings to interested parties.

A firm's reputation is a valuable intangible asset, as it prompts repeat purchases by loyal consumers and helps to attract and retain better employees to spur productivity and enhance profitability. Employees who have the most to offer may be attracted to work for a firm that contributes to the social good of the community, or is more sensitive to the needs and safety of its consumers, or takes better care of its employees. Research has confirmed that a firm's "good deeds" or reputation increases its attractiveness to employees.[25] Thus, a company may benefit from being socially responsible by improving the quality of people it attracts as employees. In this sense, the company's social reputation is one of its intangible assets that add to the organization's wealth.

A concern for company reputation is found at the highest levels of business organizations worldwide. Sixty-five percent of CEOs surveyed in a Korn/Ferry International poll said that it was their personal responsibility to manage their company's reputation. Corporate boards are putting more pressure on CEOs to build corporate reputation. When choosing a successor, the CEOs responding to the survey overwhelmingly agreed (97 percent) that when seeking a new leader of the firm, boards place more weight than ever on a candidate's ability to protect and enhance the company's reputation.[26]

Corrects Social Problems Caused by Business

Many people believe business has a responsibility to compensate society for the harm it has sometimes caused. If consumers are injured due to a product defect, the manufacturer

---

[24] The definition of *reputation* is adapted from John F. Mahon, "Corporate Reputation: A Research Agenda Using Strategy and Stakeholder Literature," *Business & Society* 41, no. 4 (December 2002), pp. 415–45. For the "reputation index," see Charles Fombrun, *Reputation: Realizing Value from the Corporate Image* (Cambridge, MA: Harvard University Press, 1996) and Rating Research LLC, *www.ratingresearch.com.*

[25] Rebecca A. Luce, Alison E. Barber, and Amy J. Hillman, "Good Deeds and Misdeeds: A Mediated Model of the Effect of Corporate Social Performance on Organizational Attractiveness," *Business & Society* 40, no. 4 (2001), pp. 397–415.

[26] "CEOs Taking Greater Responsibility for Corporate Reputations," *Ethics Newsline*, Institute for Global Ethics, October 20, 2003, *www.globalethics.org.*

is responsible. If a business does not voluntarily recognize its responsibility, the courts will often step in to represent society and its interests. When a business pollutes the environment, the cleanup is the responsibility of that firm, as seen in the following example:

> At the insistence of the Environmental Protection Agency and thousands of concerned citizens, General Electric accepted responsibility for dredging New York's Hudson River to rid the waterway of much of the 1.3 million pounds of toxic PCBs that had been dumped there since the 1940s. Since the mid-1970s, PCBs had been linked to premature birth defects and cancer, particularly to those people who consumed contaminated fish. Although the government had stopped General Electric from continuing to dump PCBs into the river since 1975, the company had assumed no responsibility for cleaning up its mess until 2002. Since then the company's proactive environmental response has cost the firm more than $1 billion, as of 2007.[27]

As General Electric learned from its experience in this case, it is often much less expensive to avoid causing problems, such as chemical pollution, than to correct them afterward.

Arguments against Corporate Social Responsibility

Who opposes corporate social responsibility? The economist Milton Friedman famously stated in 1970, "There is only one responsibility of business, namely to use its resources and engage in activities designed to increase its profits."[28] Some people in the business world—such as the 16 percent of CEOs in the survey shown in Figure 3.4 who believe that the appropriate role of business is to provide the highest possible returns to shareholders while obeying all laws and regulations—clearly agree with this view. Some fear that the pursuit of social goals by business will lower firms' economic efficiency, thereby depriving society of important goods and services. Others are skeptical about trusting business with social improvements; they prefer governmental initiatives and programs. According to some of the more radical critics of the private business system, social responsibility is nothing but a clever public relations smokescreen to hide business's true intentions to make as much money as possible. See Figure 3.5 again for some of the arguments against corporate social responsibility, discussed next.

Lowers Economic Efficiency and Profits

According to one argument, any time a business uses some of its resources for social purposes, it risks lowering its efficiency. For example, if a firm decides to keep an unproductive factory open because it wants to avoid the negative social effect that a plant closing would have on the local community and its workers, its overall financial performance may suffer. The firm's costs may be higher than necessary, resulting in lower profits. Stockholders may receive a lower return on their investment, making it more difficult for the firm to acquire additional capital for future growth. In the long run, the firm's efforts to be socially responsible by keeping the factory open may backfire.

---

[27] For a thorough discussion of this issue see "Hudson River PCBs," U.S. Environmental Protection Agency Web site, *www.epa.gov/hudson*; and "Hudson River Cleanup," General Electric's Web site, *www.ge.com/news/our_viewpoints/hudson_river_cleanup.html*.

[28] Milton Friedman, "The Social Responsibility of Business Is to Increase Its Profits," *New York Times Magazine*, September 13, 1970.

Business managers and economists argue that the business of business is business. Businesses are told to concentrate on producing goods and services and selling them at the lowest competitive price. When these economic tasks are done, the most efficient firms survive. Even though corporate social responsibility is well-intended, such social activities lower business's efficiency, thereby depriving society of higher levels of economic production needed to maintain everyone's standard of living.[29]

Imposes Unequal Costs among Competitors

Another argument against social responsibility is that it imposes greater costs on more responsible companies, putting them at a competitive disadvantage. Consider the following scenario:

> A manufacturer operating in multiple countries wishes to be more socially responsible worldwide and decides to protect its employees by installing more safety equipment at its plants than local law requires. Other manufacturers in competition with this company do not take similar steps, choosing to install only as much safety equipment as required by law. As a result their costs are lower, and their profits higher. In this case, the socially responsible firm penalizes itself and even runs the risk of going out of business, especially in a highly competitive market.

This kind of problem becomes acute when viewed from a global perspective, where laws and regulations differ from one country to the next. If one nation requires higher and more costly pollution control standards, or stricter job safety rules, or more stringent premarket testing of prescription drugs than other nations, it imposes higher costs on business. This cost disadvantage means that competition cannot be equal. Foreign competitors who are the least socially responsible will actually be rewarded because they will be able to capture a bigger share of the market.

Imposes Hidden Costs Passed On to Stakeholders

Many social proposals undertaken by business do not pay their own way in an economic sense; therefore, someone must pay for them. Ultimately, society pays all costs. Some people may believe that social benefits are costless, but socially responsible businesses will try to recover all of their costs in some way. For example, if a company chooses to install expensive pollution abatement equipment, the air may be cleaner, but ultimately someone will have to pay. Stockholders may receive lower dividends, employees may be paid less, or consumers may be charged higher prices. If the public knew that it would eventually have to pay these costs, and if it knew how high the true costs were, it might not be so insistent that companies act in socially responsible ways. The same might be true of government regulations intended to produce socially desirable business behavior. By driving up business costs, these regulations often increase prices and lower productivity, in addition to making the nation's tax bill higher.

Requires Skills Business May Lack

Businesspeople are not primarily trained to solve social problems. They may know about production, marketing, accounting, finance, information technology, and personnel work, but what do they know about inner-city issues or world poverty or violence in schools? Putting businesspeople in charge of solving social problems may lead to unnecessarily expensive and poorly conceived approaches. A global survey of senior business executives on social responsibility found that "only 11 percent [of the companies who have developed

---

[29] This argument is most often attributed to Milton Friedman, ibid., pp. 33, 122–26.

a CSR strategy] have made significant progress in implementing the strategy in their organization."[30] Thus one might question the effectiveness and efficiency of businesspeople seeking to address social responsibility problems. Business analysts might be tempted to believe that methods that succeed in normal business operations will also be applicable to complex social issues, even though different approaches may work better in the social arena.

A related idea is that public officials who are duly elected by citizens in a democratic society should address societal issues. Business leaders are not elected by the public and therefore do not have a mandate to solve social problems. In short, businesspeople do not have the expertise or the popular support required to address what are essentially issues of public policy.

Places Responsibility on Business Rather Than Individuals

The entire idea of *corporate* responsibility is misguided, according to some critics. Only *individual persons* can be responsible for their actions. People make decisions; organizations do not. An entire company cannot be held liable for its actions, only those individuals who are involved in promoting or carrying out a policy. Therefore, it is wrong to talk about the social responsibility of *business* when it is the social responsibility of *individual businesspersons* that is involved. If individual business managers want to contribute their own personal money to a social cause, let them do so; but it is wrong for them to contribute their company's funds in the name of corporate social responsibility.[31]

Together, the above arguments claim that the attempt to exercise corporate social responsibility places added burdens on both business and society without producing the intended effect of social improvement or produces it at excessive cost.

Award-Winning Corporate Social Responsibility Practices

Recognition of corporate social responsibility by business has increased dramatically. Since 2000, academic scholars have teamed with KLD Research and Analytics to assess and score businesses' stakeholder relations to create a list of the "100 Best Corporate Citizens." Three companies were recognized in each of the nine years: Intel, Starbucks, and Cisco Systems. In 2009, the highest scores were achieved by Bristol Myers-Squibb, General Mills, IBM, Merck, and Hewlett-Packard. These companies earned the designation of "good corporate citizens" because of their attention to multiple stakeholder relations. The most heavily weighted categories focused on the environment, employees, climate change, human rights, and financial performance.[32]

A study of how Americans ranked companies' reputations, carried out by Harris Interactive, found in 2008 that 71 percent of those polled said that the reputation of corporate America as ethically or socially responsible businesses was "poor." (This study was conducted *before* the financial crisis gained momentum in late 2008.) However, some companies were able to buck the trend and establish themselves in the minds of the American public as having a solid reputation. Google replaced Microsoft at the top of the list of firms with the best reputations, with Microsoft falling from first in 2007 to tenth in 2008. Other firms in the top five for 2008 were Johnson & Johnson (number one from 1997 through

---

[30] "Corporate Social Responsibility: Unlocking the Value," *www.ey.com/Global.*

[31] This argument, like the "lowers economic efficiency and profits" argument, often is attributed to Friedman, "Social Responsibility of Business."

[32] For a complete listing of the 100 Best Corporate Citizens for 2009 and the methodology used for these rankings, see "CRO's 100 Best Corporate Citizens 2009," *The CRO,* January/February 2009, *www.thecro.com.*

2006), Intel, General Mills, and Kraft Foods. Harris Interactive ranked responses to six factors to come up with the reputational index: social responsibility, emotional appeal, financial performance, products and services, vision and leadership, and workplace environment. Google ranked in the top five for all six categories. Ken Powell, CEO of General Mills, said, "In the end, we believe the most important measure is trust. General Mills values its reputation tremendously, and we constantly strive to remain worthy of the trust of our customers, consumers, employees, investors, and community."[33]

The Center for Corporate Citizenship at Boston College invited business organizations to submit their citizenship story in a one- to three-minute video. The FedEx video was announced as the winner of the first Corporate Citizenship Film Festival in 2009. The video demonstrated how the company used its transportation and logistics skills to meet the needs of communities around the world.[34] Business managers also conducted their own assessment of corporate reputation and citizenship performance. *Fortune* magazine's America's Most Admired list annually identifies companies that are admired by their *peers* for their social responsibility. In 2009 Apple topped the *Fortune* rankings for the first time, followed by Berkshire Hathaway, Toyota, Google, and the *Fortune* list's perennial company, Johnson & Johnson, which has been in the top five every year since 1997.[35]

Besides how a firm looks in the eyes of the public, GovernanceMetrics set out in 2002 to assess business organizations' risk after shady accounting practices and lack of corporate governance by senior leadership, as seen at Enron and other notable companies, cost investors billions of dollars. GovernanceMetrics rates nearly 4,000 publicly traded companies globally, grading them on more than 400 variables, from financial statements to training for directors. Less than 1 percent of the companies evaluated earn the top grade of a "10" on a 10-point scale, yet Chevron and Sun Microsystems did achieve this score. GovernanceMetrics says that highly ranked companies outperform others since "Good governance translates into trust, and trust determines what you're willing to pay," explains chief executive Howard Sherman.[36]

These companies exemplify some of the best of corporate social responsibility practices in an era when firms are increasingly being called upon to move beyond rhetoric and put their commitment to social and environmental responsibility into action. They are meeting the public's expectations that the use of corporate power can enhance the well-being of the organization's stakeholders as well as serve the business organization's interests.

Summary

- The world's largest corporations are capable of wielding tremendous influence, at times even more than national governments, due to their economic power. Because of this potential influence, the organizations' stakeholders expect businesses to enhance society when exercising their power.

- The idea of corporate social responsibility in the United States was adopted by business leaders in the early 20th century. The central themes of social responsibility have been charity—which means giving aid to the needy—and stewardship—acting as a public trustee and considering all corporate stakeholders when making business decisions.

[33] "Americans Rank Corporate Reputation and Google Lands on Top," *brand*curve*, June 23, 2008, *www.brandcurve.com*.

[34] "FedEx Takes Off with Top Honors in First Corporate Citizenship Film Festival," *Web Wire*, April 2, 2009, *www.webwire.com*. To view all of the film festival's videos see *www.BCCorporateCitizenship.org/filmfestival*.

[35] For the complete list of the *Fortune* magazine America's Most Admired list see *Fortune's* Web site at *cnnmoney.com*, *money.cnn.com/magazine/fortune/mostadmired/2009/index.html*.

[36] "Finding the Best Measure of 'Corporate Citizenship,'" *The Wall Street Journal*, July 2, 2007, *online.wsj.com*. Also see GovernanceMetrics' Web site at *www.gmiratings.com*.

- Socially responsible businesses should attempt to balance economic, legal, and social obligations. Following an enlightened self-interest approach, a firm may be economically rewarded while society benefits from the firm's actions. Abiding by legal requirements can also guide businesses in serving various groups in society.

- Managers should consider all of the company's stakeholders and their interests, not only their shareholders. Management's central goal is to promote the interests of all stakeholders by pursuing multiple company goals. This broader, more complex task emphasizes the long-run objectives and performance of the firm.

- Corporate social responsibility is a highly debatable notion. Some argue that its benefits include discouraging government regulation, promoting long-term profitability for the firm, and enhancing the company's reputation. Others believe that it lowers efficiency, imposes undue costs, and shifts unnecessary obligations to business.

- Many organizations have developed metrics for assessing and recognizing socially responsible best practices. At the core of many of these measures is trust.

Key Terms

charity principle, *51*
corporate power, *47*
corporate social
responsibility, *50*

enlightened
self-interest, *55*
iron law of
responsibility, *49*

legal obligations, *56*
reputation, *60*
stewardship
principle, *52*

Internet Resources

www.asyousow.org/csr	As You Sow Foundation, Corporate Social Responsibility
www.bsr.org	Business for Social Responsibility
www.businessinsociety.eu	The Business in Society Gateway
www.cbsr.ca	Canadian Business for Social Responsibility
www.csreurope.org	CSR Europe
www.csr-search.net	CSR News
www.csrwire.com	The Newswire of Corporate Social Responsibility
www.instituteforphilanthropy.org.uk	Institute for Philanthropy
www.mallenbaker.net/csr	Corporate Social Responsibility News and Resources

Discussion Case: *Timberland's Model of Corporate Social Responsibility*

Timberland is a manufacturer of rugged outdoor boots, clothing, and accessories. Founded in 1918 in Boston by an immigrant shoemaker named Nathan Swartz, the company has been run for almost a century by three generations of the Swartz family. Today, the company sells its products in department and specialty stores as well as in its own retail outlets in North America, Europe, Asia, South Africa, Latin America, and the Middle East. Although the company was taken public in 1987, the Swartz family and its trusts and charitable foundations continue to hold about 48 percent of Timberland stock. The company's mission embodies a strong social responsibility theme: ". . . to equip people to make a difference in their world. We do this by creating outstanding products and by trying to make a difference in the communities where we live and work."

In 1989, Timberland was approached by City Year, an urban service corps for young people, with a request for a donation of boots. Jeff Swartz, grandson of the founder and CEO, said yes and also agreed to join the corps for half a day of community service. Swartz later described his experience:

> I found myself, not a mile from our headquarters, . . . face to face with a vision [of] America not unlike the one that drew my grandfather to leave Russia in steerage so many years ago. I spent four hours with the corps members from City Year and some young recovering drug addicts in a group home. I painted some walls and felt the world shaking under my feet. In America? At this time of plenty? Children on drugs? Behind my desk again, safe no longer, moved by my own sense of purpose, having served albeit briefly, all that mattered was figuring out how service could become part of daily life at Timberland.

What started with 50 pairs of boots grew to over $10 million in support, allowing City Year to expand to 18 cities across the United States and in South Africa.

Infected with a sense of commitment to helping others, Swartz worked over the next several years with others at Timberland to create a unique program demonstrating social responsibility called Path to Service. Formally launched in 1992, the program provides employees with numerous opportunities for community involvement from engaging youth in art and cultural education in Kliptown, South Africa, to rural medicine outreach in Santiago, Dominican Republic, to creating a 30-mile bike path along the seacoast of New England. As soon as they are hired, employees are granted up to 40 hours of paid time per year to participate in company-sponsored community service activities. Although participation is voluntary, almost 95 percent do so, and most cite the program as one of the most valuable benefits offered by the company. Since the program began, employees have contributed over 500,000 hours of service.

In 2008, the Path to Service program evolved into Timberland's Community Greening program, where GREEN stands for Grassroots, Reduce–reuse–recycle, Engagement, Education, and Neutral (carbon neutral). Timberland plans to build 15 community gardens worldwide and refurbish 80 playgrounds by 2009, utilizing the more than 76,000 employee volunteer service hours.

Timberland also makes cash and in-kind contributions. The company has a goal of contributing over 2 percent of its pretax income annually and makes grants to many nonprofit organizations, including many of those it aids through its service projects. Timberland also routinely donates its shoes and clothing. It is the official outfitter of City Year and sent 25,000 pairs of shoes to Afghanistan so that children returning to school there after the war would have proper footwear.

Recently Timberland focused on sustainability issues. It advocates an ambitious goal of becoming carbon neutral by 2010, meaning that it will eliminate or offset its own carbon footprint by reducing emissions at its facilities. Timberland is aggressively moving toward this goal as seen in its Ontario, California, distribution center where 60 percent of its power is generated through the installation of new solar panels. The solar installation reduces greenhouse gas emissions by an estimated 480,000 pounds annually. The Timberland plant in the Dominican Republic installed a wind turbine and solar heating panels to provide approximately 30,000 kilowatt-hours of clean, renewable energy each year.

Swartz explained the meaning of Timberland's various service and philanthropic initiatives this way:

> At Timberland, doing well and doing good are not separate or separable efforts. Every day, everywhere, we compete in the global economy. At the center of our efforts is the premise of service, service to a truth larger than self, a demand more pressing even than this quarter's earnings. While we are absolutely accountable to our shareholders, we also recognize and accept our responsibility to share our strength—to work, in the context of our for-profit business, for the common good.

Sources: Based on author interviews and information from the company's Web site at *www.timberland.com*. Both quotations are from Jeff Swartz, "Doing Well and Doing Good: The Business Community and National Service," *The Brookings Review* 20, no. 4 (Fall 2002).

Discussion Questions

1. How would you characterize Timberland's exercise of its corporate power in society? Is Timberland engaging multiple stakeholders in its business operations? If so, how?

2. Has Timberland balanced its economic and social responsibilities through its various programs, such the Path to Service program and sustainability goals? Are the company's programs examples of enlightened self-interest?

3. What impact to do think the current economic recession may have on Timberland's social programs?

4. How would you improve Timberland's corporate social responsibility program?

PART TWO

Business and Ethics

CHAPTER FOUR

Ethics and Ethical Reasoning

People who work in business frequently encounter and must deal with on-the-job ethical issues. Being ethical is important to the individual, the organization, and the global marketplace in today's business climate. Managers and employees alike must learn how to recognize ethical dilemmas and know why they occur. In addition, they need to be aware of the role their own ethical character plays in their decision-making process, as well as the influence of the ethical character of others. Finally, managers and employees must be able to analyze the ethical problems they encounter at work to determine an ethical resolution to these dilemmas.

This Chapter Focuses on These Key Learning Objectives:

- Defining ethics and business ethics.
- Evaluating why businesses should be ethical.
- Knowing why ethical problems occur in business.
- Identifying managerial values as influencing ethical decision making.
- Recognizing how people's spirituality influences their ethical behavior.
- Understanding stages of moral reasoning.
- Analyzing ethical problems using generally accepted ethics theories.

Bernard Madoff admitted in open court in March 2009 that he spent half of his business life running a Ponzi scheme, a fraudulent investment operation that pays returns to investors from their own money or money paid by subsequent investors rather than from any actual profit earned. "I knew what I was doing was wrong, indeed criminal," admitted Madoff. "When I began the Ponzi scheme, I believed it would end shortly and I would be able to extricate myself and my clients." Clearly Madoff was unable (or unwilling) to break free from the fraudulent activities that ultimately led to investment losses estimated at $65 billion, the largest in history. Madoff was convicted of 11 counts of fraud, money laundering, perjury, and theft and given the maximum sentence of 150 years in prison, which for the 70-year-old Madoff means life behind bars. The government also required Madoff to forfeit $170 billion in assets, an amount that reflects all the money that Madoff moved through his bank accounts during the decades of his criminal career.

Madoff had apparently assembled an ill-trained and inexperienced clerical staff to run the operations and had directed them to generate false and fraudulent documents. Madoff had ordered his staff to lie to regulators and supplied them with false records. He had also shuffled hundreds of millions of dollars from bank to bank to create the illusion of active trading. Madoff used money gathered from the Ponzi scheme to support his personal stock trading ventures.

While some victims of Madoff's scheme were grateful to see justice done, others believed Madoff should have been more forthcoming in an account of his actions. Alexandra Penny said, "He is gaming the system once again. We know nothing—all he has given up is his disgusting, loathsome self."[1]

With the Madoff debacle as a backdrop, this chapter explores the meaning of ethics, explains why businesses should be ethical, identifies the different types of ethical problems that occur in business, and focuses on an ethical decision-making framework influenced by the core elements of an individual's ethical character. Then in Chapter 5 we will build on this with a discussion of how ethical performance in business can be improved by strengthening the organization's culture and climate and by providing organizational safeguards, such as policies, training, and reporting procedures.

The Meaning of Ethics

Ethics is a conception of right and wrong conduct. It tells us whether our behavior is moral or immoral and deals with fundamental human relationships—how we think and behave toward others and how we want them to think and behave toward us. **Ethical principles** are guides to moral behavior. For example, in most societies lying, stealing, deceiving, and harming others are considered to be unethical and immoral. Honesty, keeping promises, helping others, and respecting the rights of others are considered to be ethically and morally desirable behavior. Such basic rules of behavior are essential for the preservation and continuation of organized life everywhere.

These notions of right and wrong come from many sources. Religious beliefs are a major source of ethical guidance for many. The family institution—whether two parents, a single parent, or a large family with brothers and sisters, grandparents, aunts, cousins, and other kin—imparts a sense of right and wrong to children as they grow up. Schools and schoolteachers, neighbors and neighborhoods, friends, admired role models, ethnic groups, and the ever-present electronic media and the Internet influence what we believe to be

---

[1] Information and quotations are from "Madoff Will Plead Guilty; Faces Life for Swindle," *The New York Times*, March 11, 2009, *www.nytimes.com;* "Madoff Goes to Jail after Guilty Pleas," *The New York Times*, March 13, 2009, *www.nytimes.com;* and "Madoff Is Sentenced to 150 Years for Ponzi Scheme," *The New York Times*, June 30, 2009, *www.nytimes.com.*

right and wrong in life. The totality of these learning experiences creates in each person a concept of ethics, morality, and socially acceptable behavior. This core of ethical beliefs then acts as a moral compass that helps guide a person when ethical puzzles arise.

Ethical ideas are present in all societies, organizations, and individual persons, although they may vary greatly from one to another. Your ethics may not be the same as your neighbor's; one particular religion's notion of morality may not be identical to another's; or what is considered ethical in one society may be forbidden in another society. These differences raise the important and controversial issue of **ethical relativism**, which holds that ethical principles should be defined by various periods of time in history, a society's traditions, the special circumstances of the moment, or personal opinion. In this view, the meaning given to ethics would be relative to time, place, circumstance, and the person involved. In that case, the logical conclusion would be that there would be no universal ethical standards on which people around the globe could agree. However, for companies conducting business in several societies at one time, whether or not ethics is relevant can be vitally important; we discuss these issues in more detail in Chapter 5.

For the moment, however, we can say that despite the diverse systems of ethics that exist within our own society and throughout the world, all people everywhere do depend on ethical systems to tell them whether their actions are right or wrong, moral or immoral, approved or disapproved. Ethics, in this basic sense, is a universal human trait, found everywhere.

What Is Business Ethics?

Business ethics is the application of general ethical ideas to business behavior. Business ethics is not a special set of ethical ideas different from ethics in general and applicable only to business. If dishonesty is considered to be unethical and immoral, then anyone in business who is dishonest with stakeholders—employees, customers, stockholders, or competitors—is acting unethically and immorally. If protecting others from harm is considered to be ethical, then a company that recalls a dangerously defective product is acting in an ethical way. To be considered ethical, business must draw its ideas about what is proper behavior from the same sources as everyone else in society. Business should not try to make up its own definitions of what is right and wrong. Employees and managers may believe at times that they are permitted or even encouraged to apply special or weaker ethical rules to business situations, but society does not condone or permit such an exception. In a recent study conducted by the Ethics Resource Center, researchers found that observations of unethical conduct in the workplace were on the rise, as shown in Figure 4.1.

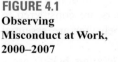

FIGURE 4.1
Observing Misconduct at Work, 2000–2007

Source: *National Business Ethics Survey,* Ethics Resource Center, Washington, DC, 2007.

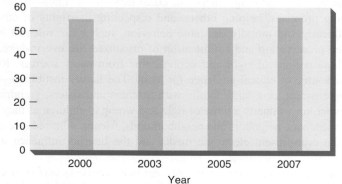

 Percentage of employees reporting misconduct at work

FIGURE 4.2
Why Should Business Be Ethical?

To meet demands of business stakeholders.
To enhance business performance.
To comply with legal requirements.
To prevent or minimize harm.
To promote personal morality.

The Ethics Resource Center report concluded that the combination of high rates of misconduct with low management awareness and few ethics and compliance programs led to a "treacherous ethics landscape." The top three types of observed misconduct were conflicts of interest, abusive or intimidating behavior, and lying to employees. The report also said that employees increasingly distrusted top managers and the information they provided. This hostile work environment had contributed to an increase in observations of unethical behavior at work, beyond the average of 56 percent of employees observing unethical behavior at work to more than 90 percent of employees observing misconduct.[2]

Why Should Business Be Ethical?

Why should business be ethical? What prevents a business firm from piling up as much profit as it can, in any way it can, regardless of ethical considerations? Figure 4.2 lists the major reasons why business firms should promote a high level of ethical behavior.

Meet Demands of Business Stakeholders

In Chapter 3, we mentioned one reason businesses should be ethical when discussing social responsibility. Organizational stakeholders demand that businesses exhibit high levels of ethical performance and social responsibility. On a positive note, many employees believe that their firms are addressing these stakeholder demands. About three-fourths of employees surveyed in 2007 believed their firms were considering the environment, employee well-being, and the interests of society and the community.[3]

Some businesses know that meeting stakeholders' expectations is good business. When a company upholds ethical standards, consumers may conduct more business with the firm and the stockholders may benefit as well, as illustrated by the Co-operative Bank, a retail bank based in Manchester, United Kingdom, whose slogan is "Customer led, ethically guided."

> The Co-operative Bank revealed that it had turned away $12 million in business annually from firms whose policies violated the bank's ethical standards, saying the loss was more than made up by income from consumers who supported the bank's strong ethical stand. The bank's policies precluded it from lending funds to firms that were involved in animal testing, nuclear power, unfair labor practices, or weapons production. Nonetheless, Co-operative Bank has experienced strong growth in profitability, increased customer deposits, and other positive financial measures for years while maintaining this tough ethical stance.[4]

---

[2] *National Business Ethics Survey*, Ethics Resource Center, Washington, DC, 2007, pp. 1–2.

[3] Ibid., p. 19.

[4] "U.K. Bank Forgoes Business—But Not Profits—Due to Ethical Stance," *Ethics Newsline*, Institute for Global Ethics, May 10, 2004, *www.globalethics.org/newsline;* and financial reports available at the company's Web site, *www.co-operativebank.co.uk.*

Enhance Business Performance

Some people argue that another reason for businesses to be ethical is that it enhances the firm's performance, or simply: *ethics pays.*

Empirical studies have supported the economic benefits of being perceived as an ethical company. In a New Zealand–based report analyzing the results of 52 previous studies, researchers found a significant relationship between corporate financial performance and ethical performance. "Businesses that are ethical leaders attract and retain the best employees, increase sales and customer loyalty, strengthen relationships with suppliers, enhance corporate citizenship and goodwill throughout the community and perform better financially for shareholders," the researcher concluded.[5]

Companies that recognize the value of ethical behavior by their employees reward their behavior in a variety of ways.

At Walmart, they created the "Award for Ethical Courage" program. Begun in 2006, employees of the company annually nominate others who have demonstrated "extraordinary courage by doing the right thing when faced with a difficult ethical dilemma." These nominees are evaluated by the Company's Global Ethics Office staff, and a number of employees are singled out for recognition at the annual company awards ceremony. Among those honored in 2006 were Leslie Durairaja, ethical standards operations managers for the Middle East, Africa, and the European region, who led an investigation of potential ethical violations in factories in Jordan; Dee Dee Hernandez, who alerted the company to mismanagement of funds at the Walmart Foundation, despite the fact that the individual guilty of the wrongdoing was Hernandez's close friend; and Kathy Stowe, who went to the manager in charge to report her concerns over questionable spending practices observed in a specific department.[6]

Whether at the organizational or individual level, businesses increasingly are recognizing that ethics pays and are encouraging ethical behavior through rewards programs and other incentives or commendations. Business executives recognize that ethical actions can directly affect their organization's bottom line, and have chosen to reward these actions accordingly.

It is also clear that "the lack of ethics costs." Researchers have identified that costs to the company go far beyond the government's fines. In a study conducted by the University of Washington's business school, researchers found that "companies that have cooked their books [misstated accounting information] lose 41 percent of their market value after news spreads about their misdeeds." Although penalties assigned to the firms for unethical action are relatively small, averaging $23.5 million per firm, the reputational damage to the company is calculated to be 7.5 times the amount of the penalties imposed by government.[7]

[5] Rodger Spiller, "Ethics Pays—But Can It Be Taught?" *New Zealand Management,* 2007, p. 10. For an Italian-based study investigating the relationship between consumer behavior and ethics see Sandro Castaldo, Francesco Perrini, Nicola Misani, and Antonio Tencati, "The Missing Link between Corporate Social Responsibility and Consumer Trust: The Case of Fair Trade Products," *Journal of Business Ethics* 84 (2009), pp. 1–15.

[6] "Walmart Honors Ethical Courage by Associates," *Newsletter,* Ethics and Compliance Officers Association, November 29, 2006, *www.theecoa.org.*

[7] "Cooked Books, Fried Reputation: Study," *Ethics Newsline,* Institute for Global Ethics, November 20, 2006, *www.globalethics.org.* Also see Jonathan M. Karpoff, D. Scott Lee, and Gerald S. Martin, "The Cost to Firms of Cooking the Books," *Journal of Financial and Quantitative Analysis,* 2008, pp. 581–611.

Comply with Legal Requirements

Doing business ethically is also often a legal requirement. Two legal requirements, in particular, provide direction for companies interested in being more ethical in their business operations. Although they apply only to U.S.-based firms, these legal requirements also provide a model for firms that operate outside the United States.

The first is the **U.S. Corporate Sentencing Guidelines**, which provide a strong incentive for businesses to promote ethics at work.[8] The sentencing guidelines come into play when an employee of a firm has been found guilty of criminal wrongdoing and the firm is facing sentencing for the criminal act, since the firm is responsible for actions taken by its employees. To determine the sentencing, the judge computes a culpability (degree of blame) score using the guidelines, based on whether or not the company has

1. Established standards and procedures to reduce criminal conduct.
2. Assigned high-level officer(s) responsibility for compliance.
3. Not assigned discretionary authority to "risky" individuals.
4. Effectively communicated standards and procedures through training.
5. Taken reasonable steps to ensure compliance—monitor and audit systems, maintain and publicize reporting system.
6. Enforced standards and procedures through disciplinary mechanisms.
7. Following detection of offense, responded appropriately and prevented reoccurrence.

Companies that have taken these steps, or most of them, receive lesser sentences, such as lower fines.

> The impact of the sentencing guidelines was felt by Hoffman-LaRoche. The multinational pharmaceutical company pleaded guilty to a price-fixing conspiracy in the vitamins market that spanned nine years and was fined $500 million. Although this was a significant financial blow to the firm, the government noted that the sentencing guidelines permitted a fine as high as $1.3 billion against Hoffman-LaRoche. The sentence was reduced because Hoffman-LaRoche had met many of the sentencing guidelines directives.

In 2005 the U.S. Supreme Court weakened this legal requirement when the court ruled that federal judges were not required to follow the federal sentencing guidelines but could rely upon them in an advisory role.[9] However, many firms have developed and maintain ethics and compliance programs based on the Sentencing Commission's "seven steps" (see above).

Another legal requirement imposed upon U.S. businesses is the **Sarbanes-Oxley Act** of 2002.[10] Born from the ethics scandals at Enron, WorldCom, Tyco, and others, this law seeks to ensure that firms maintain high ethical standards in how they conduct and monitor business operations. For example, the Sarbanes-Oxley Act requires executives to

---

[8] For a thorough discussion of the U.S. Corporate Sentencing Guidelines, see Dan R. Dalton, Michael B. Metzger, and John W. Hill, "The 'New' U.S. Sentencing Commission Guidelines: A Wake-Up Call for Corporate America," *Academy of Management Executive*, 1994, pp. 7–13; and Dove Izraeli and Mark S. Schwartz, "What Can We Learn from the U.S. Federal Sentencing Guidelines for Organizational Ethics?" *Journal of Business Ethics*, 1998, pp. 1045–55.

[9] "High Court Ruling Casts Doubt on Federal Sentencing Guidelines," *The Wall Street Journal*, January 12, 2005, online.wsj.com.

[10] See Howard Rockness and Joanne Rockness, "Legislated Ethics: From Enron to Sarbanes-Oxley, the Impact on Corporate America," *Journal of Business Ethics*, 2005, pp. 31–54; and Alix Valenti, "The Sarbanes-Oxley Act of 2002: Has It Brought About Changes in the Boards of Large U.S. Corporations?" *Journal of Business Ethics*, 2008, pp. 401–12.

In September 2007, 69 accounting firms and their partners were charged with violating provisions of the Sarbanes-Oxley Act by not registering with the Public Company Accounting Oversight Board (PCAOB). According to Linda Chatman Thomsen of the PCAOB, "The actions we take today protect investors and will deter future violations of Sarbanes-Oxley's registration provision." Some the violators settled with the SEC, while others were censured or paid fines.

Yet, despite the SEC and PCAOB's aggressive compliance efforts, a number of provisions within the Sarbanes-Oxley Act have loosened recently. In 2006, the SEC developed new and more lenient guidelines on how Section 404 is implemented. Many corporate leaders complained that Section 404, requiring companies to review their own systems for ensuring financial reports and then have them verified by outside auditors, was cumbersome and expensive. Some auditors were interpreting this provision so literally that they were asking management to account for such things as who has access to an office key. Critics of the Sarbanes-Oxley Act responded that the loosening of the rules may encourage more companies to go public in the United States or foreign companies to list their stock on American exchanges.

In 2007, another round of regulation loosening occurred when the SEC provided a more relaxed set of guidelines applied to small businesses and their compliance with the Sarbanes-Oxley Act. The new rules allow for more internal initiatives, rather than external auditing examinations, in discovering where financial controls are working or not and where areas of fraud or other financial violations are more likely to occur. Previously, under the SEC rules, small businesses relied on auditors hired by the firms to verify if they were Sarbanes-Oxley compliant.

Sources: "SEC Charges Accountants and Firms with Sarbanes-Oxley Violations," *The New York Times*, September 14, 2007, *www.nytimes.com;* "Business Wins Its Battle to Ease a Costly Sarbanes-Oxley Rule," *The Wall Street Journal*, November 10, 2006, *online.wsj.com;* and "SEC Revises Its Standards for Corporate Audits," *The New York Times*, May 24, 2007, *www.nytimes.com.*

vouch for the accuracy of a firm's financial reports and requires them to pay back bonuses based on earnings that are later proved fraudulent. The act also established strict rules for auditing firms. Recent changes in regulatory interpretation of the Sarbanes-Oxley Act are shown in Exhibit 4.A.

After the passage of the Sarbanes-Oxley Act, experts estimated that compliance costs were likely to total $7 billion annually for firms governed by the legislation. In fact, Sarbanes-Oxley compliance costs have been declining, partly due to the changes in the SEC rules described in Exhibit 4.A, and partly due to the need for fewer employee hours needed to process compliance activities. In the first year of compliance, costs averaged $4.51 million per firm, according to a survey by the Financial Executives International. By 2006, the third year companies had to follow the Sarbanes-Oxley rules, costs fell 23 percent, to an average of $2.92 million per company.[11]

Although costs are declining, most CEOs believe that the Sarbanes-Oxley Act was "an overreaction to the ethical failures of a handful of executives" and was unhealthy for the business environment. In a study of American CEOs in 2008, 74 percent of the executives said that the act had done nothing to improve ethical standards at their businesses. Sixty-eight percent agreed that the act was burdensome and unnecessary.[12]

European financial officers also were critical of the Sarbanes-Oxley Act. Nearly 90 percent of the 236 European CFOs questioned believed that these regulations offered no

[11] "Costs to Comply with Sarbanes Decline Again," *The Wall Street Journal*, May 16, 2007, *online.wsj.com.*

[12] *The National Survey of CEOs on Business Ethics,* Georgia State University's Center for Ethics and Corporate Responsibility and Clemson University's Robert J. Rutland Institute for Ethics, 2008, available online at *robinson.gsu.edu/files/ethics/2008CEO_Survey.pdf.*

benefits. Forty percent believed them to be an outright hindrance, increasing time and cost commitments for no positive results. However, a columnist for the *Financial Times*, Morgen Witzel, argued that "there are many benefits to be gained from a positive approach to regulation." He mentioned better investor and customer relations, enhanced internal processes, greater efficiencies, and the opportunity for proactive organizations to shape the regulatory agenda. [13] One example of possible benefits arising from compliance to the Sarbanes-Oxley Act provisions is shown in the following example:

> University of Pittsburgh Medical Center (UPMC) voluntarily accepted this regulatory standard established by Sarbanes-Oxley, despite the fact that, as a private firm, it was not governed by the act. In a reported push to improve its corporate governance and the transparency of its operations to the public, UPMC's Chairman G. Nicholas Beckwith III said the organization was "on schedule to become one of the first academic medical centers in the country to comply with the most rigorous provisions of Sarbanes-Oxley." UPMC recognized that voluntary compliance might yield unexpected benefits through improved efficiency and set a standard for transparency for nonprofit organizations.
>
> The public trust appeared to be key for Beckwith and his management of UPMC. "Who owns us? The entire Western Pennsylvania region owns us. That's the people we are accountable to," explained Robert Cindrich, Chief Legal Officer, who chaired the UPMC audit committee. "Nick [Beckwith] really defined us as an asset belonging to the region."
>
> Compliance with the Sarbanes-Oxley Act benefited UPMC in several ways. For example, billing shops at three different health care facilities were standardized and consolidated in one place. Forecasting and accounting information was available faster, and supply chain management improved. Best of all for UPMC, the cost of compliance was much less than anticipated. UPMC budgeted $6 million for Sarbanes-Oxley compliance efforts, but CFO Rob DeMichiei stated that out-of-pocket expenses would likely be less than $1 million. The anticipated savings easily exceeded the cost of compliance, and the endeavor brought peace of mind to the organization's leaders. "I can't tell you how much better we feel about our internal controls," said DeMichiei.[14]

Prevent or Minimize Harm

Another reason businesses and their employees should act ethically is to prevent harm to the general public and the corporation's many stakeholders. One of the strongest ethical principles is stated very simply: *Do no harm.* A company that is careless in disposing of toxic chemical wastes that cause disease and death is breaking this ethical injunction. Many ethical rules operate to protect society against various types of harm, and businesses are expected to observe these commonsensical ethical principles.

The recent notorious examples of outright greed and other unethical behavior by managers in the financial community contributed in part to the current economic recession in the United States and around the world. These managers' unethical actions were responsible for significant harm to many stakeholders in society. Investors' portfolios lost considerable value, retirees saw their nest eggs dwindle, hundreds of thousands of

[13] "The Virtues of Compliance over Complaint," *Financial Times*, January 15, 2006, *www.ft.com*.

[14] Material and quotations for this example were provided by Kris B. Mamula, "UPMC Seeks Nonprofit First: Experts Hail Sarbanes-Oxley Compliance Effort," *Pittsburgh Business Times*, October 28, 2005, *www.bizjournals.com/pittsburgh;* and Christopher Snowbeck, "UPMC Draws Line at Children's in New Effort at Corporate Compliance," *Pittsburgh Post-Gazette*, January 14, 2006, p. A9.

employees lost their jobs, and many small business owners were unable to stay in business. The costs resulting from these unethical behaviors devastated many in our society, and it will require years of effort and hard work to rebuild from this damage.

A 2008 report by the Association of Certified Fraud Examiners (ACFE) indicates how serious the costs of unethical action can be:

> The ACFE report uncovered 959 cases of occupational fraud with a median loss of $175,000 per case, and more than one-quarter of the frauds involved losses of at least $1 million. Participants in the survey estimated that U.S. organizations lose 7 percent of their annual revenues to fraud, or approximately $994 billion each year. Small businesses are especially vulnerable, suffering the largest median losses for all organizations in the ACFE study.[15]

Promote Personal Morality

A final reason for promoting ethics in business is a personal one. Most people want to act in ways that are consistent with their own sense of right and wrong. Being pressured to contradict their personal values creates emotional stress. Knowing that one works in a supportive ethical climate contributes to one's sense of psychological security.

> More than one in three American employees reportedly have left their jobs because they disagreed with a company's business ethics, a survey conducted by the LRN Corporation found. According to the study, "A majority of workers—94 percent—say it is 'critical' or 'important' that the company they work for is ethical." Eighty-two percent said they would prefer to be paid less but work for a company with ethical business practices than receive higher pay at a company with questionable ethics. "Our findings confirm that companies with a commitment to ethical conduct enjoy distinct advantages in the marketplace, including attracting and retaining talent," said LRN's CEO Dov Seidman.[16]

Why Ethical Problems Occur in Business

If businesses have so many reasons to be ethical, why do ethical problems occur? Although not necessarily common or universal, ethical problems occur frequently in business. Finding out what causes them is one step toward minimizing their impact on business operations and on the people affected. Some of the main reasons are summarized in Figure 4.3 and are discussed next.

Personal Gain and Selfish Interest

Desire for personal gain, or even greed, causes some ethics problems. Businesses sometimes employ people whose personal values are less than desirable, who will put their own welfare ahead of all others, regardless of the harm done to other employees, the company, or society.

A manager or employee who puts his or her own self-interest above all other considerations is called an **ethical egoist**.[17] Self-promotion, a focus on self-interest to the point

---

[15] *2008 Report to the Nation on Occupational Fraud and Abuse,* Association of Certified Fraud Examiners, *www.acfe.com.*

[16] "Study: Workers Will Quit over Ethics," LRN Corporation, August 3, 2006, *www.centralvalleybusinesstimes.com.*

[17] For a compact discussion of ethical egoism, see Tom L. Beauchamp and Norman E. Bowie, *Ethical Theory and Business,* 7th ed. (Upper Saddle River, NJ: Prentice Hall, 2004), pp. 12–16; and Laura P. Hartman and Joe DesJardins, *Business Ethics: Decision-Making for Personal Integrity and Social Responsibility* (New York: McGraw-Hill, 2008), p. 83.

FIGURE 4.3
Why Ethical
Problems Occur in
Business

Reason	Nature of Ethical Problem	Typical Approach	Attitude
Personal gain and selfish interest	Selfish interest versus others' interests	Egotistical mentality	"I want it!"
Competitive pressures on profits	Firm's interest versus others' interests	Bottom-line mentality	"We have to beat the others at all costs!"
Conflicts of interest	Multiple obligations or loyalties	Favoritism mentality	"Help yourself and those closest to you!"
Cross-cultural contradictions	Company's interests versus diverse cultural traditions and values	Ethnocentric mentality	"Foreigners have a funny notion of what's right and wrong."

of selfishness, and greed are traits commonly observed in an ethical egoist. The ethical egoist tends to ignore ethical principles accepted by others, believing that ethical rules are made for others. Altruism—acting for the benefit of others when self-interest is sacrificed—is seen to be sentimental or even irrational. "Looking out for number one" is the ethical egoist's motto, as the Madoff example with which we began this chapter and the following stories show:

> Consider the actions of Dennis Kozlowski, former CEO of Tyco. New York prosecutors charged Kozlowski with stealing more than $170 million from the company. Kozlowski was also accused of borrowing $270 million from a company loan program intended to help him pay taxes, but he improperly used 90 percent of this money for personal expenses, such as yachts, jewelry, fine art, and real estate. Kozlowski was sentenced to up to 25 years in a New York state prison in 2005.

> In another case of personal greed taking precedence over the integrity of company property, Thomas Coughlin, former vice chairman of Walmart, pleaded guilty to five counts of wire fraud and one count of filing a false tax return and was sentenced to 27 months of home detention, five years probation, 1,500 hours of community service, and a $50,000 fine and $400,000 restitution. (Coughlin could have been sentenced to 28 years in prison and fined $1.35 million, but the judge cited Coughlin's lack of a criminal record and poor health for a lighter sentence.) Coughlin was a protégé of Walmart founder Sam Walton and earned more than $1 million in base salary and more than $3 million in bonuses in his final year as the company's vice chairman of the board of directors. He admitted that he had embezzled $500,000 from the company to purchase snakeskin boots, hunting trips, care for his hunting dogs, upgrades for his pickup truck, and liquor.[18]

---

[18] "Kozlowski, Swartz Sentenced to Up to 25 Years in Prison," *The Wall Street Journal,* September 19, 2005, *online.wsj.com;* "Ex-Walmart Vice Chairman Pleads Guilty in Fraud Case," *The Wall Street Journal,* January 31, 2006, *online.wsj.com;* and "Ex-Vice Chairman of Walmart Stores Avoids Prison Term," *The Wall Street Journal,* February 4, 2008, *online.wsj.com.*

Competitive Pressures on Profits

When companies are squeezed by tough competition, they sometimes engage in unethical activities to protect their profits. This may be especially true in companies whose financial performance is already substandard. Research has shown that managers of poor financial performers and companies with financial uncertainty are more prone to commit illegal acts. In addition, intense competitive pressure in the global marketplace has resulted in unethical activity, such as the practice of price fixing.

> Three of the world's largest manufacturers of computer and video screens, Sharp, LG, and Chunghwa, pleaded guilty to criminal price-fixing charges and paid fines totaling $585 million. The industry leaders were concerned that the prices for these electronic devices were dropping too quickly and could cause serious financial setbacks for the companies. The Justice Department, when imposing the substantial fine, said that the price fixing had artificially created higher prices for televisions, cellphones, and other electronic products using liquid crystal displays, which were ultimately paid by millions of American consumers. The manufacturers' products were used in Apple iPods, Motorola Razr cellphones, and Dell laptops and computer monitors.[19]

Conflicts of Interest

Ethical challenges in business often arise in the form of conflicts of interest. A **conflict of interest** occurs when an individual's self-interest conflicts with acting in the best interest of another, when the individual has an obligation to do so.[20] For example, if a purchasing agent directed her company's orders to a firm from which she had received a valuable gift, even if this firm did not offer the best quality or value, she would be accused of unethical behavior because of a conflict of interest. In this situation, she would have acted to benefit herself, rather than in the best interests of her employer. A failure to disclose a conflict of interest represents deception in and of itself and may hurt the person or organization on whose behalf judgment has been exercised. Many ethicists believe that even the *appearance* of a conflict of interest should be avoided, because it undermines trust.

Both individuals and organizations can be in a conflict of interest. In recent years, much attention has been focused on organizational conflicts of interest in the accounting profession. When an accounting firm audits the books of a public company, it has an obligation to shareholders to provide an honest account of the company's financial health. Sometimes, though, accounting firms may be tempted to overlook irregularities to increase their chances of attracting lucrative consulting work from the same company. This conflict is now significantly curtailed by provisions in the Sarbanes-Oxley Act, which restricts accounting firms from providing both audit and consulting services to the same client.

Many cases of financial fraud illustrate conflicts of interest, in which opportunities for self-enrichment by senior managers conflict with the long-term viability of the firm and the best interests of employees, customers, suppliers, and stockholders. The case

---

[19] "3 Flat-Screen Makers Plead Guilty to Trying to Keep Prices High," *The New York Times,* November 12, 2008, *www.nytimes.com;* and "Makers of LCD Screens Plead Guilty to Price Fixing," *The Wall Street Journal,* November 13, 2008, *online.wsj.com.*

[20] Based on John R. Boatright, *Ethics and the Conduct of Business,* 6th ed. (Upper Saddle River, NJ: Prentice Hall, 2009), pp. 123–24.

"Moody's Credit Ratings and the Subprime Mortgage Meltdown," which appears at the end of this book, describes an organizational conflict of interest in which a company was paid by the firms whose bonds it rated, rather than by the buyers of these bonds. Many firms seek to guard against the dangers inherent in conflicts of interest by including prohibitions of any such practices in their codes of ethics, as discussed in Chapter 5.

Cross-Cultural Contradictions

Some of the knottiest ethical problems occur as corporations do business in other societies where ethical standards differ from those at home. Today, the policymakers and strategic planners in all multinational corporations, regardless of the nation where they are headquartered, face this kind of ethical dilemma. Consider the following situation:

> The pesticide methyl parathion is officially banned or restricted in many countries including the United States, China, Malaysia, Indonesia, and Cambodia. The World Health Organization has classified methyl parathion as "extremely hazardous." The chemical can be fatal for humans if swallowed, inhaled, or absorbed through the skin. Yet, methyl parathion and nearly 50 other dangerous pesticides are being sold in Thailand and Vietnam and, from there, being illegally exported to Cambodia. Cambodian farmers argue that they need the pesticides to increase agricultural production, despite the lack of protective safety equipment or procedures for properly disposing of used containers. Multinational companies that manufacture the chemicals say that they are not responsible because they do not directly market to Cambodia.[21]

This episode raises the issue of *ethical relativism,* which was defined earlier in this chapter. Although the foreign sales of methyl parathion to Thailand and Vietnam were *legal,* were they *ethical?* Is dumping unsafe products by any measure *ethical* if it is not forbidden by the receiving nation, especially if the companies know that the products are exported to another country where farmers there mishandle the products and use them without safety precautions? *Are multinational companies ethically responsible for what happens to their products, even though they are being sold legally? Which standards or whose ethical standards should be the guide?*

As business becomes increasingly global, with more and more corporations penetrating overseas markets where cultures and ethical traditions vary, these cross-cultural questions will occur more frequently.

The Core Elements of Ethical Character

The ethical analysis and resolution of ethical dilemmas in the workplace significantly depend on the ethical character and moral development of managers and other employees. Good ethical practices not only are possible, but also become normal with the right combination of these components.

Managers' Values

Managers are key to whether a company and its employees will act ethically or unethically. As major decision makers, they have more opportunities than others to create an ethical tone for their company. The values held by managers, especially the top-level managers, will serve as models for others who work at the company.

[21] "Bayer Pesticides Cause Poisoning in Cambodia," CBGnetwork, September 25, 2001, *www.pmac.net/bayer_cambodia.html.*

Unfortunately, according to a 2009 opinion poll, Americans hold a dim view of business executives' and managers' values. A majority—60 percent—of the 2,000 American adults polled gave Wall Street executives poor grades when it came to honesty and ethics. Other executives did not fare much better, with 49 percent receiving poor grades. Of the 110 executives included in the poll, only 19 percent gave themselves poor grades for leadership, with 53 percent rating themselves as fair and 27 percent as good.

In an annual Gallup poll that rated 21 occupations for honesty and ethics, nurses—for the seventh straight year—came out on top. Notably, the only significant change for any occupation in 2008 from the 2007 results was for bankers, whose ratings of "high" or "very high" honesty and ethics dropped from 35 to 23 percent.[22]

Differences in ethical values were found among European employees. Researchers discovered that workers in the United Kingdom are among the most honest in Europe, avoiding ethical breaches more commonly detected in France, Germany, and Spain. Only 14 percent of U.K. workers approve of taking office supplies home for personal use—the lowest of workers from all 12 countries surveyed—and 21 percent approve of using office software at home—second lowest in the survey.[23]

However, across the Atlantic, studies generally show that most U.S. managers focus on themselves and are primarily concerned about being competent. They place importance on values such as having a comfortable and exciting life and being capable, intellectual, and responsible. Researchers also found that new CEOs tend to be more self-interested and short-term focused, possibly in an effort to immediately drive up company profits, rather than valuing long-term investments in research and development or capital expenditures. However, some managers show a strong concern for values that include others, living in a world at peace, or seeking equality among people. One out of four managers emphasize this other set of values: moral values. These managers place greater importance on the value of forgiving others, being helpful, and acting honestly.[24]

But what about future managers? A survey of 759 graduating MBA students from 11 top business schools in the United States reported that "a company's CSR performance is a major factor when selecting a new employer." These MBA students said they were willing to sacrifice a portion of their salary to work for a firm that shares their outlook. These results mirror another study, undertaken by Net Impact, an international group of MBA and graduate students who believe corporations should work for social good. Of the more than 2,000 MBA students surveyed, nearly 80 percent said they wanted to find socially responsible employment in their careers and 59 percent said they would seek out such a job immediately after graduation. Seventy-eight percent believed that classes in ethics and social responsibility should be a part of their business school training.[25]

Spirituality in the Workplace

A person's **spirituality**—that is, a personal belief in a supreme being, religious organization, or the power of nature or some other external, life-guiding force—has always been a part of the human makeup. In 1953 *Fortune* published an article titled "Businessmen

[22] "Wall Street Rates Poorly for Ethics, Honesty," *Reuters,* February 27, 2009, *uk.reuters.com;* and "Nurses Shine, Bankers Slump in Ethics Ratings," *Ethics Newsline,* Institute for Global Ethics, November 24, 2008, *www.globalethics.org.*

[23] "U.K. Workers Give High Marks for Employees' Ethics: Survey," *Ethics Newsline,* Institute for Global Ethics, September 12, 2005, *www.globalethics.org.*

[24] See James Weber, "Managerial Value Orientations: A Typology and Assessment," *International Journal of Value-Based Management,* 1990, pp. 37–54; and Jeffrey S. Harrison and James O. Fiet, "New CEOs Pursue Their Own Self-Interests by Sacrificing Stakeholder Value," *Journal of Business Ethics,* 1999, pp. 301–8.

[25] "CEOs of Tomorrow Demand Green and Ethical Employers," *BusinessGreen,* July 21, 2008, *www.businessgreen.com;* and "Business Students Portrayed as Ethically Minded in Study," *Financial Times,* October 25, 2006, *www.ft.com.*

on Their Knees" and claimed that American businessmen (women generally were excluded from the executive suite in those days) were taking more notice of God. More recently cover stories in *Fortune, BusinessWeek,* and other business publications have documented a resurgence of spirituality or religion at work. Academic journals also have recognized spirituality in the workplace with special issues featuring this topic in the *Journal of Organizational Change Management* and *Leadership Quarterly.* Scholars have created the Faith at Work Scale to combine and simplify the more than 150 measures of individual religiosity and spirituality, with a particular focus on how these values influence workplace behavior.[26]

As far back as 1976, scholars have found a positive relationship between an organization's economic performance and attention to spiritual values. Scholars found that spirituality positively affects employee and organizational performance by enhancing intuitive abilities and individual capacity for innovation, as well as increasing personal growth, employee commitment, and responsibility. Best-selling books have touted the importance of being sensitive to employees' values and spirituality as a success path. Ethical leadership and ethical cultures in organizations based on a strong sense of spirituality are seen as necessary and productive. As Jack Hawley explains, "All leadership is spiritual because the leader seeks to liberate the best in people and the best is always linked to one's higher self."[27]

Organizations have responded to the increased attention to spirituality and religion at work by attempting to accommodate their employees.

The chief diversity officer at PricewaterhouseCoopers found office space in their Asia-Pacific region facility to provide a prayer room for their Muslim employees. In the United States, employers are required by law to make substantial accommodations for their employees' religious practices, as long as it does not create major hardships for the organization. Ford's Interfaith Network, a group of employees focusing on religious issues, successfully lobbied the company to install sinks designed for the religious washings that Muslim employees perform.

British Airways' policy that employees must wear any jewelry under their uniform came under challenge when an employee began to wear a cross on a chain over her uniform. Initially the airline banned this action, but after an appeal by the employee that prompted substantial negative publicity in the London newspapers and from the Anglican Church, the company changed its policy to allow symbols of faith to be worn as lapel pins or on chains around an employee's neck.[28]

Most companies use chaplains on an outsourced basis from secular employee assistance programs or from chaplaincy providers such as Marketplace Ministries, a nonprofit concern that provides about 1,000 Protestant chaplains to more than 240 companies nationwide. Other firms, such as Tyson Foods, found it worthwhile to have a chaplain on staff full-time. When a Tyson employee told his boss that he had a drug problem, the

[26] See Monty L. Lynn, Michael J. Naughton, and Steve VanderVeen, "Faith at Work Scale (FWS): Justification, Development, and Validation of a Measure of Judeo-Christian Religion in the Workplace," *Journal of Business Ethics* (2009), 85 pp. 227–43.

[27] The quotation from Hawley is from Jack Hawley, *Reawakening the Spirit at Work: The Power of Dharmic Management* (San Francisco: Berrett-Koehler, 1993), p. 5. Studies establishing a link between spirituality and spiritual values and economic performance include J. Richard Hackman and Greg Oldham, "Motivation through the Design of Work: A Test of a Theory," *Organizational Behavior and Human Performance* 16 (1976), pp. 250–79; Melvin W. Reder, "Chicago Economics: Permanence and Change," *Journal of Economic Literature,* 1982, pp. 1–38; and Christopher P. Neck and John F. Milliman, "Thought Self-Leadership: Finding Spiritual Fulfillment in Organizational Life," *Journal of Managerial Psychology,* 1994, pp. 9–16.

[28] "When Religious Needs Test Company Policy," *The New York Times,* February 25, 2007, www.nytimes.com.

supervisor sent the employee to the chaplain. The employee thought, "What could he do? Offer me a prayer?" The chaplain met with the employee and over the next few months helped the employee enroll in a drug rehabilitation program, find a drug counselor, and attend Narcotics Anonymous meetings. The spread of the practice of including chaplains within the organization demonstrates the understanding that firms need to embrace their employees' religious or spiritual characteristics as part of who they are as employees, not something relegated to places of worship alone.

However, others disagree with the trend toward a stronger presence of religion in the workplace. They hold the traditional belief that business is a secular—that is, nonspiritual—institution. They believe that business is business, and spirituality is best left to churches, synagogues, mosques, and meditation rooms, not corporate boardrooms or shop floors. This, of course, reflects the separation of church and state in the United States and many other countries.

Others note that ethical misconduct or greed is often cloaked in the robes of religion. Scandals involving religious leaders, such as sexual abuse by Catholic priests or fraud committed by self-interested television evangelists, have caused many people to be wary of religion whether at work or elsewhere.

Beyond the philosophical opposition to bringing spirituality into the business environment, procedural or practical challenges arise. Whose spirituality should be promoted? The CEO's? *With greater workplace diversity comes greater spiritual diversity, so which organized religion's prayers should be cited or ceremonies enacted? How should businesses handle employees who are agnostics or atheists (who do not follow any religion)?*

Opponents of spirituality at work point to the myriad of implementation issues as grounds for keeping spirituality out of the workplace. Nonetheless, many believe that religion is making inroads into the workplace. Employees are becoming more accustomed to seeing a Bible on a work desk or hearing someone at work respond to a casual "How's it going?" with an earnest "I'm blessed."

Just as personal values and character strongly influence employee decision making and behavior in the workplace, so does personal spirituality, from all points on the religious spectrum, impact how businesses operate.

Managers' Moral Development

People's values and spirituality exert a powerful influence on the way ethical work issues are treated. Since people have different personal histories and have developed their values and spirituality in different ways, they are going to think differently about ethical problems. This is as true of corporate managers as it is of other people. In other words, the managers in a company are likely to be at various **stages of moral development**. Some will reason at a high level, others at a lower level.

A summary of the way people grow and develop morally is diagrammed in Figure 4.4. From childhood to mature adulthood, most people move steadily upward in their moral reasoning capabilities from stage 1. Over time, they become more developed and are capable of more advanced moral reasoning, although some people never use the most advanced stages of reasoning in their decision processes.

At first, individuals are limited to an ego-centered focus (stage 1), fixed on avoiding punishment and obediently following the directions of those in authority. (The word *ego* means "self.") Slowly and sometimes painfully, the child learns that what is considered to be right and wrong is pretty much a matter of reciprocity: "I'll let you play with my toy, if I can play with yours" (stage 2). At both stages 1 and 2, however, the individual is mainly concerned with his or her own pleasure. The self-dealings of Bernard Madoff, Dennis Kozlowski, and Thomas Coughlin, described earlier in this chapter, exemplify

FIGURE 4.4
Stages of Moral Development and Ethical Reasoning

Source: Adapted from Lawrence Kohlberg, *The Philosophy of Moral Development* (New York: Harper & Row, 1981).

Age Group	Development Stage and Major Ethics Referent	Basis of Ethics Reasoning
Mature adulthood	**Stage 6** Universal principles: justice, fairness, universal human rights	Principle-centered reasoning
Mature adulthood	**Stage 5** Moral beliefs above and beyond specific social custom: human rights, social contract, broad constitutional principles	Principle-centered reasoning
Adulthood	**Stage 4** Society at large: customs, traditions, laws	Society- and law-centered reasoning
Early adulthood, adolescence	**Stage 3** Social groups: friends, school, coworkers, family	Group-centered reasoning
Adolescence, youth	**Stage 2** Reward seeking: self-interest, own needs, reciprocity	Ego-centered reasoning
Childhood	**Stage 1** Punishment avoidance: punishment avoidance, obedience to power	Ego-centered reasoning

ego-centered reasoning. By taking money from their companies for personal use, they benefited themselves and their immediate families, without apparent concern for others.

In adolescence the individual enters a wider world, learning the give-and-take of group life among small circles of friends, schoolmates, and similar close-knit groups (stage 3). Studies have reported that interaction within groups can provide an environment that improves the level of moral reasoning. This process continues into early adulthood. At this point, pleasing others and being admired by them are important cues to proper behavior. Most people are now capable of focusing on other-directed rather than self-directed perspectives. When a manager "goes along" with what others are doing or what the boss expects, this would represent stage 3 behavior. On reaching full adulthood—the late teens to early 20s in most modern, industrialized nations—most people are able to focus their reasoning according to society's customs, traditions, and laws as the proper way to define what is right and wrong (stage 4). At this stage, a manager would seek to follow the law; for example, he or she might choose to curtail a chemical pollutant because of government regulations mandating this.

Stages 5 and 6 lead to a special kind of moral reasoning. At these highest stages, people move above and beyond the specific rules, customs, and laws of their own societies. They are capable of basing their ethical reasoning on broad principles and relationships, such as human rights and constitutional guarantees of human dignity, equal treatment, and freedom of expression. In the highest stage of moral development, the meaning of right and wrong is defined by universal principles of justice, fairness, and the common rights of all humanity. For example, at this stage, an executive might decide to pay wages above the minimum required by law, because this is the morally just thing to do.[29]

[29] For details and research findings, see Lawrence Kohlberg, *The Philosophy of Moral Development* (San Francisco: Harper & Row, 1981); and Anne Colby and Lawrence Kohlberg, *The Measurement of Moral Judgment, Volume I: Theoretical Foundations and Research Validations* (Cambridge: Cambridge University Press, 1987).

Researchers have consistently found that most managers typically rely on criteria associated with reasoning at stages 3 and 4, although some scholars argue that these results may be slightly inflated.[30] Although they may be capable of more advanced moral reasoning that adheres to or goes beyond society's customs or law, managers' ethical horizons most often are influenced by their immediate work group, family relationships, or compliance with the law. The development of a manager's moral character can be crucial to a company. Some ethics issues require managers to move beyond selfish interest (stages 1 and 2), beyond company interest (stage 3 reasoning), and even beyond sole reliance on society's customs and laws (stage 4 reasoning). Needed is a manager whose personal character is built on a caring attitude toward all affected, recognizing others' rights and their essential humanity (a combination of stage 5 and 6 reasoning). The moral reasoning of upper-level managers, whose decisions affect companywide policies, can have a powerful and far-reaching impact both inside and outside the company.

Analyzing Ethical Problems in Business

Underlying an ethical decision framework is a set of universal ethical values or principles, notions that most people anywhere in the world would hold as important. While a list of ethical principles may be exhaustive, these five values seem to be generally accepted and are present in most ethical dilemmas: do no harm, be fair and just, be honest, respect others' rights, and do your duty/act responsibly. Business managers and employees need a set of decision guidelines that will shape their thinking when on-the-job ethics issues occur. The guidelines should help them (1) identify and analyze the nature of an ethical problem and (2) decide which course of action is likely to produce an ethical result. The following four methods of ethical reasoning can be used for these analytical purposes, as summarized in Figure 4.5.

FIGURE 4.5
Four Methods of Ethical Reasoning

Method	Critical Determining Factor	An Action Is Ethical When . . .	Limitations
Virtues	Values and character	It aligns with good character	Subjective or incomplete set of good virtues
Utilitarian	Comparing benefits and costs	Net benefits exceed net costs	Difficult to measure some human and social costs; majority may disregard rights of the minority
Rights	Respecting entitlements	Basic human rights are respected	Difficult to balance conflicting rights
Justice	Distributing fair shares	Benefits and costs are fairly distributed	Difficult to measure benefits and costs; lack of agreement on fair shares

[30] James Weber and Janet Gillespie, "Differences in Ethical Beliefs, Intentions, and Behaviors," *Business & Society,* 1998, pp. 447–67; and James Weber and David Wasieleski, "Investigating Influences on Managers' Moral Reasoning," *Business & Society,* 2001, pp. 79–111.

FIGURE 4.6
Lists of Moral Values across Time

Plato and Aristotle, 4th century B.C.	St. Thomas Aquinas, 1225–1274	Benjamin Franklin, 1706–1790	Robert Solomon, 1942–2007
• Courage • Self-control • Generosity • Magnificence • High-mindedness • Gentleness • Friendliness • Truthfulness • Wittiness • Modesty	• Faith • Hope • Charity • Prudence • Justice • Temperance • Fortitude • Humility	• Cleanliness • Silence • Industry • Punctuality • Frugality	• Honesty • Trust • Toughness

Sources: Plato and Aristotle's values are from Steven Mintz, "Aristotelian Virtue and Business Ethics Education," *Journal of Business Ethics,* 1996, pp. 827–38; St. Thomas Aquinas's values are from Manuel G. Velasquez, *Business Ethics: Concepts and Cases,* 6th ed. (Upper Saddle River, NJ: Prentice Hall, 2006), pp. 110–11; Benjamin Franklin's values, from the American Industrial Revolution era, are from Peter McMylor, *Alisdair MacIntyre: Critic of Modernity* (London: Routledge, 1994); and Robert Solomon's moral values can be found in Robert C. Solomon, *Ethics and Excellence: Cooperation and Integrity in Business* (New York: Oxford University Press, 1992), pp. 207–16.

Virtue Ethics: Pursuing a "Good" Life

Some philosophers believe that the ancient Greeks, specifically Plato and Aristotle, developed the first ethical theory, which was based on values and personal character. Commonly referred to as **virtue ethics**, it focuses on character traits that a good person should possess, theorizing that moral values will direct the person toward good behavior. Virtue ethics is based on a way of being and on valuable characteristics rather than on rules for correct behavior. Moral virtues are habits that enable a person to live according to reason, and this reason helps the person avoid extremes. Aristotle argued, "Moral virtue is a mean between two vices, one of excess and the other of deficiency, and it aims at hitting the mean in feelings, desires, and action."[31] A variety of people have suggested lists of moral values over the years as shown in Figure 4.6.

As indicated in Figure 4.6, Plato, Aristotle, Aquinas, Franklin, and Solomon have slightly different views of what guides a moral or virtuous person. This suggests that to some extent what counts as a moral virtue depends on one's personal beliefs. However, most scholars believe that there is a great deal of agreement on the question of who is acting as the virtuous person, as summed up by business ethicist Manuel Velasquez: "An action is morally right if in carrying out the action the agent exercises, exhibits, or develops a morally virtuous character, [as opposed to] develops a morally vicious character."[32]

> When placing virtue ethics in a business context, ethicist Robert Solomon explains, "The bottom line of the Aristotelian approach to business ethics is that we have to get away from 'bottom line' thinking and conceive of business as an essential part of the good life, living well, getting along with others, having a sense of self-respect, and being a part of something one can be proud of."[33]

[31] For discussions of virtue ethics see Richard DeGeorge, *Business Ethics,* 6th ed. (Upper Saddle River, NJ: Prentice Hall, 2008), pp. 106–11; and Laura P. Hartman and Joe DesJardins, *Business Ethics: Decision-Making for Personal Integrity and Social Responsibility* (New York: McGraw-Hill, 2008), pp. 83–87.

[32] Manuel G. Velasquez, *Business Ethics: Concepts and Cases,* 6th ed. (Upper Saddle River, NJ: Prentice Hall, 2006), p. 113.

[33] Robert C. Solomon, *Ethics and Excellence: Cooperation and Integrity in Business* (New York: Oxford University Press, 1992), p. 104.

However, others argue that virtue ethics is not really an ethics at all, not a thoroughly developed ethical system of rules and guidelines, but rather a system of values that form good character. Virtue ethics also suffers from this challenge: whose values? As noted in Figure 4.6, different people offer different sets of values to define virtue ethics. What if these values conflict or the list is incomplete? Does a set of values provide a sufficient framework to resolve the most complex ethical dilemmas found in global business? Does a manager sometimes have to be or seem to be "the bad person" or do or seem to do "a bad thing" for the sake of some ultimate ethical good? Would this be virtuous or vicious?[34]

That is, could a moral person decide to close a plant? Would the decision maker, using values espoused by Aristotle or Franklin or Solomon, shut down a plant and lay off workers? Would virtue ethics help a manager close a plant in a way that is virtuous and supportive of the workers about to be laid off?

Utility: Comparing Benefits and Costs

Another approach to ethics emphasizes *utility*, or the overall amount of good that can be produced by an action or a decision. This ethical approach is called **utilitarian reasoning**. It is often referred to as cost–benefit analysis because it compares the costs and benefits of a decision, a policy, or an action. These costs and benefits can be economic (expressed in dollar amounts), social (the effect on society at large), or human (usually a psychological or emotional impact). After business managers add up all the costs and benefits and compare them with one another, the net cost or the net benefit should be apparent. If the benefits outweigh the costs, then the action is ethical because it produces the greatest good for the greatest number of people in society. If the net costs are larger than the net benefits, then it is probably unethical because more harm than good is produced. If there is more than one option where the benefits outweigh the costs, and thus multiple ethical options for the utilitarian reasoner, then the decision maker would select the alternative where the greatest benefit would be achieved.

The main drawback to utilitarian reasoning is the difficulty of accurately measuring both costs and benefits. Some things can be measured in monetary terms—goods produced, sales, payrolls, and profits—but others more intangible are trickier, such as employee morale, psychological satisfaction, or the worth of a human life. Human and social costs are particularly difficult to measure with precision. But unless they can be measured, the cost–benefit calculations will be incomplete, and it will be difficult to know whether the overall result is good or bad, ethical or unethical. Another limitation of utilitarian reasoning is that the majority may override the rights of those in the minority. Since utilitarian reasoning is primarily concerned with the end results of an action, managers using this reasoning process often fail to consider the means taken to reach the end.

Despite these drawbacks, cost–benefit analysis is widely used in business. Because this method works well when used to measure economic and financial outcomes, business managers sometimes are tempted to rely on it to decide important ethical questions without being fully aware of its limitations or the availability of still other methods that may improve the ethical quality of their decisions.

How would a utilitarian decision maker decide to close a plant? Using utilitarian reasoning, the decision maker must consider all the benefits (improving the company bottom line, higher return on investment to the investors, etc.) versus the costs (employee layoffs, reduced economic activity to the local community, etc.).

[34] For a critique of virtue ethics see Boatright, *Ethics and the Conduct of Business,* pp. 80–81.

Rights: Determining and Protecting Entitlements

Human rights are another basis for making ethical judgments. A right means that a person or group is entitled to something or is entitled to be treated in a certain way. The most basic human rights are the rights to life, safety, free speech, freedom, being informed, due process, and property, among others. Denying those rights or failing to protect them for other persons and groups is normally considered to be unethical. Respecting others, even those with whom we disagree or dislike, is the essence of human rights, provided that others do the same for us. This approach to ethical reasoning holds that individuals are to be treated as valuable ends in themselves just because they are human beings. Using others for your own purposes is unethical if, at the same time, you deny them their goals and purposes.

The main limitation of using rights as a basis of ethical reasoning is the difficulty of balancing conflicting rights. For example, an employee's right to privacy may be at odds with an employer's right to protect the firm's assets by testing the employee's honesty. Rights also clash when U.S. multinational corporations move production to a foreign nation, causing job losses at home but creating new jobs abroad. In such cases, whose job rights should be respected?[35]

Despite this kind of problem, the protection and promotion of human rights is an important ethical benchmark for judging the behavior of individuals and organizations. Surely most people would agree that it is unethical to deny a person's fundamental right to life, freedom, privacy, growth, and human dignity. By defining the human condition and pointing the way to a realization of human potentialities, such rights become a kind of common denominator of ethical reasoning, setting forth the essential conditions for ethical actions and decisions.

Would someone using human rights reasoning decide to close a plant? When using human rights reasoning, the decision maker must consider the rights of all affected (the right to a livelihood for the displaced workers or business owners in the local community versus the right of the employees to be informed of the layoffs and plant closing versus the right of the managers to the freedom to make decisions they believe are within their duty to the company, etc.).

Justice: Is It Fair?

A fourth method of ethical reasoning concerns **justice**. A common question in human affairs is, Is it fair or just? Employees want to know if pay scales are fair. Consumers are interested in fair prices when they shop. When new tax laws are proposed, there is much debate about their fairness—where will the burden fall, and who will escape paying their fair share?[36] After the U.S. government bailed out several big banks and insurance companies in 2008–2009, many people wondered if it was fair that some of their top executives continued to receive big bonuses while their employees, shareholders, and bondholders suffered—and taxpayers absorbed the cost.

Justice, or fairness, exists when benefits and burdens are distributed equitably and according to some accepted rule. For society as a whole, social justice means that a

---

[35] For a discussion of ethical rights, see ibid., pp. 36–39; and Velasquez, *Business Ethics: Concepts and Cases*, pp. 71–84.

[36] For an interesting discussion of "what is fair?" see Patrick Primeaux and Frank P. LeVeness, "What is Fair: Three Perspectives," *Journal of Business Ethics* 84 (2009), pp. 89–102.

society's income and wealth are distributed among the people in fair proportions. A fair distribution does not necessarily mean an equal distribution. Most societies try to consider people's needs, abilities, efforts, and the contributions they make to society's welfare. Since these factors are seldom equal, fair shares will vary from person to person and group to group. Justice reasoning is not the same as utilitarian reasoning. A person using utilitarian reasoning adds up costs and benefits to see if one is greater than the other; if benefits exceed costs, then the action would probably be considered ethical. A person using justice reasoning considers who pays the costs and who gets the benefits; if the shares seem fair (according to society's rules), then the action is probably just.

Is it just to close a plant? Using justice reasoning, a decision maker must consider the distribution of the benefits (to the firm, its investors, etc.) versus the costs (to the displaced employees, local community, etc.). To be just, the firm closing the plant might decide to accept additional costs for job retraining and outplacement services for the benefit of the displaced workers. The firm might also decide to make contributions to the local community over some period of time to benefit the local economy, in effect to balance the scales of justice in this situation.

Applying Ethical Reasoning to Business Activities

Anyone in the business world can use these four methods of ethical reasoning to gain a better understanding of ethical issues that arise at work. Usually, all four can be applied at the same time. Using only one of the four methods is risky and may lead to an incomplete understanding of all the ethical complexities that may be present. It also may produce a lopsided ethical result that will be unacceptable to others.

Once the ethical analysis is complete, the decision maker should ask this question: Do all of the ethics approaches lead to the same decision? If so, then the decision or policy or activity is probably ethical. If the application of all ethics theories result in a "no, this is not ethical," then you probably are looking at an unethical decision, policy, or activity. The reason you cannot be *absolutely* certain is that different people and groups (1) may honestly and genuinely use different sources of information, (2) may rely on different values or definitions of what is a virtuous character, (3) may measure costs and benefits differently, (4) may not share the same meaning of justice, or (5) may rank various rights in different ways. Nevertheless, any time an analyst obtains a consistent result when using all of the approaches, it indicates that a strong case can be made for either an ethical or an unethical conclusion.

What happens when the application of the four ethical approaches does not lead to the same conclusion? A corporate manager or employee then has to assign priorities to each method of ethical reasoning. What is most important to the manager, to the employee, or to the organization—virtue, utility, rights, or justice? What ranking should they be given? A judgment must be made, and priorities must be determined. These judgments and priorities will be strongly influenced by a company's culture and ethical climate. Some will be sensitive to people's needs and rights; others will put themselves or their company ahead of all other considerations.

The importance of being attentive to ethical issues at work and the ability to reason to an ethical resolution of these knotty dilemmas have always been important but today are essential given the increasing ethical scrutiny of business and the grave consequences for unethical behavior in the workplace. Employees do not work in a vacuum. The organization where they work and the culture that exists within any organization exert significant influence on the individual as an ethical decision maker. Businesses are making significant efforts to improve the ethical work climates in their organizations and are providing safeguards to encourage ethical behavior by their employees, as the next chapter discusses.

Summary

- Ethics is a conception of right and wrong behavior, defining for us when our actions are moral and when they are immoral. Business ethics is the application of general ethical ideas to business behavior.

- Ethical business behavior is demanded by business stakeholders, enhances business performance, complies with legal requirements, prevents or minimizes harm, and promotes personal morality.

- Ethics problems occur in business for many reasons, including the selfishness of a few, competitive pressures on profits, the clash of personal values and business goals, and cross-cultural contradictions in global business operations.

- Managers' on-the-job values tend to be company-oriented, assigning high priority to company goals. Managers often value being competent and place importance on having a comfortable or exciting life, among other values.

- Individual spirituality can greatly influence how a manager understands ethical challenges; increasingly it is recognized that organizations must acknowledge employees' spirituality in the workplace.

- Individuals reason at various stages of moral development, with most managers focusing on personal rewards, recognition from others, or compliance with company rules as guides for their reasoning.

- People in business can analyze ethics dilemmas by using four major types of ethical reasoning: virtue ethics, utilitarian reasoning, rights reasoning, and justice reasoning.

Key Terms

Internet Resources

Discussion Case: *The Warhead Cable Test Dilemma*[37]

It was Monday morning at Bryson Corporation's cable division assembly plant. Stanton Wong, the quality supervisor, had been worrying all weekend about a directive he had received from his boss before leaving work on Friday. Harry Jackson, the plant manager and a vice president of operations, had told Stanton unambiguously to disregard defects in a batch of laminated cable they had produced for a major customer, a military contractor. Now, Stanton was wondering what if anything he should say or do.

Bryson Corporation was a large conglomerate headed by an aggressive CEO who had established a track record of buying and turning around low-performing manufacturing firms. Harry Jackson had been sent to the cable plant shortly after it had been acquired, and he was making headway rescuing what had been a marginal operation. The word in the plant was that corporate was pleased with his progress.

Harry ran the plant like a dictator, with nearly absolute control, and made sure everyone inside and outside the organization knew it. Harry would intimidate his direct reports, yelling at and insulting them at the least provocation. He harassed many of the young women in the office and was having an affair with one of the sales account managers.

Stanton's two-year anniversary on the job had just passed. He was happy with his progress. He felt respected by the factory workers, by management colleagues, and often even by Harry. His pay was good enough that he and his wife had felt confident to buy a house and start a family. He wanted to keep his reputation as a loyal employee. He had decided early on that he was not about to challenge Harry. At least, that was Stanton's approach until the warhead cable issue came along.

The warhead cable was part of a fuse system used in missiles. In the production process, a round cable was formed into a flat, ribbon-like shape by feeding it through a lamination machine and applying specific heat, speed, and pressure. The flattened cable was then cut into specific lengths and shapes and shipped to the customer, a defense contractor.

As part of his quality control duties, Stanton used a standard procedure called an elevated heat seal test to ensure the integrity of the product. The cable was bent at a 90-degree angle and placed in an oven at 105 degrees C for seven hours. If the seal did not delaminate (pop open at the corners), then the product passed the test. This procedure was usually performed on cable from early runs while the lamination machine operator was still producing a batch. That way, if there was a problem, it could be spotted early and corrected.

When a batch of cable was ready for shipment, Stanton was responsible for preparing a detailed report of all test results. The customer's source inspector, Jane Conway, then came to the plant and performed additional sample testing there. On inspection days, Jane tended to arrive around 9:00 a.m. and spend the morning reviewing Stanton's test data. Typically, she would pull samples from each lot and inspect them. She rarely conducted her own elevated heat seal test, however, relying instead on Bryson's test data. Stanton and Jane often had lunch together at a nearby restaurant and then finished up the paperwork in the afternoon.

The prior week, during a very busy time, a large order for the warhead cable came in with a short turnaround period. Stanton tested a sample taken from an early lot and had good results. But his testing on Friday revealed problems. Of 10 samples, two failed.

[37] By Jeanne McNett, Assumption College. The event described in this case is real, but the names of the individuals and the company have been disguised. An earlier version of this case was presented at the 2005 annual meeting of the North American Case Research Association. Used by permission. © 2006 Jeanne McNett and the North American Case Research Association.

That afternoon, Stanton went to Harry's office with the failed samples to show him the delamination. Before Stanton could say a word, Harry called in the production manager and cursed him out. He then turned to Stanton and said, "Let's wait and see if the source inspector catches this problem." Stanton reminded him that typically the source inspector didn't perform this particular test. Harry responded, "Well, most of the samples passed." Stanton replied, "Yes, but some failed. That shows inconsistency in the lot. The protocol requires that a test failure be reported for such results."

Harry had already made up his mind. "Don't tell me what I can and cannot do! The decision is mine to make, and what I have decided is that we will see if the source inspector finds the failure!"

All weekend, Stanton worried about Harry's directive. Bryson cables were used to manufacture fuses in missiles. Stanton thought about several people he knew from high school, who were now on active duty in a war zone overseas. He thought about possible harm to innocent civilians or even to U.S. service members if a missile misfired. He wondered if anyone in the parent corporation could help, but did not know anyone there to call.

Discussion Questions

1. Why should the Bryson Corporation act ethically in this situation? What are the potentially negative repercussions of acting unethically?

2. What stage of moral development do you think Stanton Wong is at? What about Harry Jackson? Why do you think so?

3. What do you think Stanton should do now, and why? Use each of the methods of ethical reasoning presented in the chapter to consider what action is ethical.

4. What steps could the company take to prevent a situation like this from occurring in the future?

CHAPTER FIVE

Organizational Ethics and the Law

Faced with increasing pressure to create an ethical and law-abiding environment at work, businesses can take tangible steps to improve their ethical performance. The organization's culture and ethical work climate play a central role in promoting ethics at work. Ethical situations arise in all areas and functions of business, and often professional associations seek to guide managers in addressing these challenges. Corporations can also implement ethical safeguards such as ethics policies, ethics and compliance officers, internal reporting mechanisms, and employee ethics training. In addition to developing a comprehensive ethics program, corporations must of course follow the laws of the nation. This can become a complex challenge when facing different customs and regulations around the world. Although ethics and the law are not exactly the same, both are important emphases for businesses, especially when operating in the global marketplace.

This Chapter Focuses on These Key Learning Objectives:

- Classifying an organization's culture and ethical climate.
- Recognizing ethics challenges across the multiple functions of business.
- Creating effective ethics policies, ethics training programs, ethics reporting mechanisms, and similar safeguards.
- Assessing the strengths and weaknesses of a comprehensive ethics program.
- Understanding how to conduct business ethically in the global marketplace.
- Identifying the differences between ethics and the law.

B. Ramalinga Raju, founder and chairman of Satyam Computer Services, one of India's largest information services outsourcing companies with a third of the *Fortune* 500 as its clients, admitted to making up more than 10,000 employees' names to siphon money from the company and to using his elderly mother's name to buy land with the cash. In total, Raju said he stole about $1 billion in cash through his imaginary employees. "Employees are just code numbers in our system," explained a Satyam Computer Services manager who was given immunity to assist the government in its investigation. "You can create any amount of them. All you need to do is make sure the income tax is properly deducted."

The Satyam fraud, called "India's Enron" by some, prompted the World Bank to blacklist Satyam from future business with the bank for its alleged unethical practices. India's Prime Minister, Manmohan Singh, called the Satyam events "a blot on our corporate image . . . indicating how fraud and malfeasance in one company can inflict suffering on many and can also tarnish India's image more broadly." Months after the scandal surfaced, the new Satyam board auctioned off 51 percent of the company as it pledged to start fresh and emerge from this ethical embarrassment.[1]

In the United States, India, Europe, and around the world, dozens and dozens of other companies have been charged with accounting fraud, mishandling investors' funds, market improprieties, and many other illegal activities. *Why are business executives, managers, and employees repeatedly being caught conducting illegal and unethical activities? What could Satyam Computer Services have done to minimize or prevent the fraud perpetrated by its founder and chairman? Could the company have set in place systems or programs to monitor workplace activities to detect illegal or unethical behavior?*

Corporate Ethical Climates

Personal values and moral character play key roles in improving a company's ethical performance, as discussed in Chapter 4. However, they do not stand alone, because personal values and character can be affected by a company's culture and ethical climate.

The terms *culture* and *climate* are often used interchangeably and, in fact, are highly interrelated. **Corporate culture** is a blend of ideas, customs, traditional practices, company values, and shared meanings that help define normal behavior for everyone who works in a company. Culture is "the way we do things around here." Two experts testify to its overwhelming influence:

> Every business—in fact every organization—has a culture . . . [and it] has a powerful influence throughout an organization; it affects practically everything—from who gets promoted and what decisions are made, to how employees dress and what sports they play. . . . When [new employees] choose a company, they often choose a way of life. The culture shapes their responses in a strong, but subtle way.[2]

In most companies, a moral atmosphere can be detected. People can feel which way the ethical winds are blowing. They pick up subtle hints and clues that tell them what behavior is approved and what is forbidden. The unspoken understanding among employees of

---

[1] Quotations and information for this example are from "Satyam Chief Is Accused of Falsifying Size of Work Force, Then Stealing Payroll," *The New York Times*, January 23, 2009, www.nytimes.com; and "Indian Executive Is Said to Have Siphoned Cash," *The New York Times*, January 18, 2009, www.nytimes.com.

[2] Terrence E. Deal and Allan A. Kennedy, *Corporate Cultures: The Rites and Rituals of Corporate Life* (Reading, MA: Addison-Wesley, 1982), pp. 4, 16.

FIGURE 5.1   **The Components of Ethical Climates**

Ethical Criteria	Focus of Individual Person	Organization	Society
Egoism (self-centered approach)	Self-interest	Company interest	Economic efficiency
Benevolence (concern-for-others approach)	Friendship	Team interest	Social responsibility
Principle (integrity approach)	Personal morality	Company rules and procedures	Laws and professional codes

Source: Adapted from Bart Victor and John B. Cullen, "The Organizational Bases of Ethical Work Climates," *Administrative Science Quarterly* 33 (1988), p. 104.

what is and is not acceptable behavior is called an **ethical climate**. It is the part of corporate culture that sets the ethical tone in a company. One way to view ethical climates is diagrammed in Figure 5.1. Three distinct ethical criteria are *egoism* (self-centeredness), *benevolence* (concern for others), and *principle* (respect for one's own integrity, for group norms, and for society's laws) and parallel the levels of moral development developed by Lawrence Kohlberg and discussed in Chapter 4. These ethical criteria can be used to describe how individuals, a company, or society at large approach various moral dilemmas.

For example, if a manager approaches ethics issues with benevolence in mind, he or she would emphasize friendly relations with an employee, stress the importance of team play and cooperation for the company's benefit, and recommend socially responsible courses of action. However, a manager using egoism would be more likely to think first of promoting the company's profit and striving for efficient operations at all costs, as illustrated by the following example:

> By 2006, a culture of protecting the firm at all costs was firmly embedded at Siemens AG, a German engineering firm. From 2002 to 2006, the company paid about $40 to $50 million in bribes *annually*. According to a senior Siemens accountant and target of the bribery prosecution, the payments were "to maintain the competitiveness of Siemens overseas. . . . It was about keeping the business unit alive and not jeopardizing thousands of jobs overnight." Siemens reportedly paid the following bribes: $5 million to win a mobile phone contract in Bangladesh, $12.7 million in Nigeria for government telecommunication contracts, at least $40 million in Argentina to win a $1 billion contract to product national identity cards, $20 million to build power plants in Israel, $16 million for urban rail lines in Venezuela, $14 million for medical equipment contracts in China, and nearly $2 million to Saddam Hussein and other leaders in Iraq. "Bribery was Siemens's business model. Siemens had institutionalized corruption," said a German criminal investigator working on the case. In the aftermath of the bribery prosecution, Siemens's new chief executive officer, Peter Loscher, pledged "to recover the firm's ethical culture. Performance with ethics—this is not a contradiction, it is a must."[3]

Researchers have found that multiple ethical climates, or subclimates, may exist within one organization. For example, one company might include managers who often interact with the public and government regulators, using a principle-based approach,

[3] "At Siemens, Bribery Was Just a Line Item," *The New York Times*, December 21, 2008, *www.nytimes.com;* and "New Siemens Chief Says Firm Will Recover Its 'Ethical Culture,'" *Ethics Newsline*, Institute for Global Ethics, July 9, 2007, *www.globalethics.org.*

compared to another group of managers, whose work is geared toward routine process tasks and whose focus is mainly egotistic—higher personal pay or company profits.[4]

Corporate ethical climates can also signal to employees that ethical transgressions are acceptable. By signaling what is considered to be right and wrong, corporate cultures and ethical climates can pressure people to channel their actions in certain directions desired by the company. This kind of pressure can work both for and against good ethical practices.

Business Ethics across Organizational Functions

Not all ethics issues in business are the same. Because business operations are highly specialized, ethics issues can appear in any of the major functional areas of a business firm. Accounting, finance, marketing, information technology, and other areas of business all have their own particular brands of ethical dilemmas. In many cases, professional associations in these functional areas have attempted to define a common set of ethical standards, as discussed next.

Accounting Ethics

The accounting function is a critically important component of every business firm. By law, the financial records of publicly held companies are required to be audited by a certified professional accounting firm. Company managers, external investors, government regulators, tax collectors, and labor unions rely on such public audits to make key decisions. Honesty, integrity, and accuracy are absolute requirements of the accounting function. Thus, the scandals that rocked the accounting industry and led to the demise of Arthur Andersen hit the integrity of this professional group hard.

Accountants often are faced with conflicts of interest, introduced in Chapter 4, where loyalty or obligation to the company (the client) may be divided or in conflict with self-interest (of the accounting firm) and the interests of others (shareholders and the public). For example, while conducting an audit of a company, should the auditor look for opportunities to recommend to the client consulting services that the auditor's firm can provide? Sometimes, accounting firms may be tempted to soften their audit of a company's financial statements if the accounting firm wants to attract the company's nonaudit business. For this reason, the Sarbanes-Oxley Act severely limits the offering of nonaudit consulting services by the auditing firm.

> The issue of conflicts of interest was at the core of the decision made by management at PricewaterhouseCoopers (PWC), one of the largest accounting firms in the United States and Canada, to withdraw as the auditor for the Royal Bank of Canada. PWC leadership cited a concern over a possible conflict of interest since it was worried that it might have violated auditor independence rules when it performed nonaudit work for a subsidiary of the Royal Bank, even though the work accounted for less than $150,000 in services. Peter Currie, CFO for PWC, said that the firm made a "bad judgment" when it assured Royal Bank executives that its independent audit status would not be jeopardized by its consulting work for the Royal Bank subsidiary.[5]

---

[4] James Weber, "Influences upon Organizational Ethical Subclimates: A Multi-departmental Analysis of a Single Firm," *Organization Science* 6 (1995), pp. 509–23.

[5] "PricewaterhouseCoopers Withdraws from Audit Role, Citing Conflict of Interest," *Ethics Newsline*, Institute for Global Ethics, September 29, 2003, *www.globalethics.org*.

Other ethical issues appear in the accounting industry, with accounting fraud being one of the most visible and involving the largest amount of money. While many examples of accounting fraud have appeared in the United States during the past few years, lapses in accounting ethics can be found elsewhere.

Kanebo Limited, a Japanese household goods company, reported that it had inflated its profits by $1.37 billion over four years. These errors were found during an internal investigation that uncovered a lengthy period of bogus bookkeeping, sparking an investigation by the Tokyo Stock Exchange. Kanebo's accounting fraud was the largest in Japan involving a nonfinancial firm.[6]

Government regulators, particularly in Europe, responded strongly to the U.S. accounting scandals of the recent past by tightening their grip over auditors in their countries. The European Union created the International Accounting Standards (IAS). These standards are seen as essential by the European regulators for the integration of European Union capital markets and for the global convergence of accounting standards. But, more recently, a call for more broadly accepted international accounting standards was announced. Many proponents of the International Financial Reporting Standards (IFRS), including the Obama administration, believe these standards should replace the current Generally Accepted Accounting Principles (GAAP) that govern U.S. accounting practices. At a time when corporate financial mismanagement has shaken the American public's and Wall Street financial analysts' confidence in the American business system, the questions of company oversight, accountability, and transparency are at the forefront and give support for a new international accounting system. Others argue that the rush to adopt international accounting standards by the United States would hurt the standing of the United States in the world's capital markets by undermining the U.S. regulatory system and negatively impact securities issuers.[7]

Even before the IFRS proposal was made and the debate over its merits arose, professional accounting organizations, such as the American Institute of Certified Public Accountants and the Financial Accounting Standards Board, developed generally accepted accounting principles whose purpose is to establish uniform standards for reporting accounting and auditing data. In 1993, the American Institute for Certified Public Accountants (AICPA) dramatically changed its professional code by requiring CPAs to act as whistle-blowers when detecting "materially misstated" financial statements or face losing their license to practice accounting. In 2003, on the heels of the Sarbanes-Oxley Act, the AICPA sought input from its members as it revised its Rule 101—Independence guideline.

Examples of this profession's efforts toward promoting ethics are shown in Exhibit 5.A. Spurred by the increasing threat of liability suits filed against accounting firms and the desire to reaffirm professional integrity, these standards go far toward ensuring a high level of honest and ethical accounting behavior.[8]

---

[6] "Japanese Firm Admits $1.37 Billion Accounting Fraud," *Ethics Newsline*, Institute for Global Ethics, April 18, 2005, *www.globalethics.org.*

[7] See the *International Accounting Standards*, The European Commission, *europa.eu.int*; and for a discussion of the proposed International Financial Reporting Standards see "The Rush to International Accounting," *The New York Times* blog, September 11, 2008, *norris.blogs.nytimes.com*, and "Ready for Global Financial Standards?" *Pittsburgh Post-Gazette*, March 22, 2009, *www.post-gazette.com.*

[8] For several excellent examples of ethical dilemmas in accounting, see Leonard J. Brooks and Paul Dunn, *Business & Professional Ethics for Directors, Executives and Accountants*, 5th ed. (Mason, OH: South-Western Cengage Learning, 2010); and Ronald Duska and Brenda Duska, *Accounting Ethics* (Malden, MA: Blackwell, 2003).

Financial Ethics

Within companies, the finance department and its officers are typically responsible for managing the firm's assets and for raising capital—for example, by issuing stocks and bonds. Financial institutions, such as commercial banks, securities firms, and so forth, assist in raising capital and managing assets for both individuals and institutions. Whether working directly for a business or in a firm that provides financial services, finance professionals face a particular set of ethical issues.

Financial ethics have been the focus of particular attention recently in the wake of the bank failures of 2008, which many believed to be a major cause of the severe recession that began that year. Violations of ethical conduct involving the backdating of stock options were uncovered or under investigation at 115 different firms, resulting in prison terms and fines:

Nancy Heinen, former Apple general counsel, admitted to concealing improper backdating of stock options for various senior managers, including the chief executive Steven Jobs. Heinen agreed to pay $2.2 million to settle the federal charges. Former executive Carole Argo of SafeNet, maker of computer network security products, was fined $1 million and sentenced to six months in prison for securities fraud for backdating millions of dollars' worth of employee stock options grants. Gregory Reyes, former chief executive at Brocade Communication Systems, was sentenced to 21 months in prison and fined $15 million for backdating stock option awards for Brocade employees.

Dozens of other cases were pending trial or being settled out of court. Analysts estimate that the backdating scandal could be one of the largest in the history of financial fraud. (See Exhibit 14.A on stock options trading.)[9]

Other ethical lapses in the financial community were highly visible in 2008 when the corruption and graft led to the financial decline in the United States and around the world:

- The magnitude of client fraud, as described in the opening example of Chapter 4, involving Bernard Madoff and his Ponzi scheme.
- The manipulation of the firm's accounting system by Satyam's founder Raju to create thousands of fictitious employees for his personal extravagant lifestyle, described in this chapter's opening example.
- The insider trading ring of a former Morgan Stanley compliance officer, senior UBS research executive, three employees from Bear Stearns, and a Bank of America employee that led to millions of dollars in illegal profits for those involved.
- The infamous illegal and irresponsible trading conducted at Societe Generale by rogue trader Jerome Kerviel that resulted in more than $8 billion in losses for the firm.[10]

These and other lapses in ethical conduct are evident despite efforts by the finance professions to foster an ethical environment. As shown in Exhibit 5.A, the highly regarded Chartered Financial Analyst Institute, which oversees financial executives performing many different types of jobs in the financial discipline, emphasizes self-regulation as the

[9] "Former Apple Executive Settles Backdating Suit," *The New York Times*, August 15, 2008, *www.nytimes.com;* "Backdating Case Brings a Prison Term," *The New York Times*, January 29, 2008, *www.nytimes.com;* and "Reyes Gets 21 Months in Prison In Stock-Option Backdating Case," *The Wall Street Journal*, January 16, 2008, *online.wsj.com.* For a comprehensive summary of the backdating investigations see "Options Scorecard," *The Wall Street Journal*, October 16, 2006, *online.wsj.com.*

[10] "13 Accused of Trading as Insiders," *The New York Times*, March 2, 2007, *www.nytimes.com;* and "Societe Generale Seeks to Raise $8 Billion," *The New York Times*, February 12, 2008, *www.nytimes.com.*

Exhibit 5.A

Professional Codes of Conduct in Accounting and Finance

AMERICAN INSTITUTE OF CERTIFIED PUBLIC ACCOUNTANTS (AICPA)

Code of Professional Conduct

These Principles of the Code of Professional Conduct of the American Institute of Certified Public Accountants express the profession's recognition of its responsibilities to the public, to clients, and to colleagues. They guide members in the performance of their professional responsibilities and express the basic tenets of ethical and professional conduct. The Principles call for an unswerving commitment to honorable behavior, even at the sacrifice of personal advantage.

- Responsibilities—In carrying out their responsibilities as professionals, members should exercise sensitive professional and moral judgments in all their activities. . . .
- The Public Interest—Members should accept the obligation to act in a way that will serve the public interest, honor the public interest, and demonstrate commitment to professionalism. . . .
- Integrity—To maintain and broaden public confidence, members should perform all professional responsibilities with the highest sense of integrity. . . .
- Objectivity and Independence—A member should maintain objectivity and be free of conflicts of interest in discharging professional responsibilities. A member in public practice should be independent in fact and appearance when providing auditing and other attestation services. . . .
- Due Care—A member should observe the profession's technical and ethical standards, strive continually to improve competence and the quality of services, and discharge professional responsibility to the best of the member's ability. . . .
- Scope and Nature of Services—A member in public practice should observe the Principles of the Code of Professional Conduct in determining the scope and nature of services to be provided.*

CHARTERED FINANCIAL ANALYST (CFA)®

Summary from CFA Institute Code of Ethics and Standards of Professional Conduct

Members of CFA Institute (including Chartered Financial Analyst® (CFA®) charterholders) and candidates for the CFA designation ("Members and Candidates") must:

- Act with integrity, competence, diligence, respect, and in an ethical manner with the public, clients, prospective clients, employers, employees, colleagues in the investment profession, and other participants in the global capital markets.
- Place the interests of clients, the interests of their employer, and the integrity of the investment profession above their own personal interests.

best path for ethical compliance. In 2006, the National Association of Securities Dealers and the New York Stock Exchange asked Wall Street finance companies to self-regulate what constitutes excessive client entertainment. After a number of regulatory investigations, the general belief among regulators was that the industry was best equipped to determine what was excessive when it came to gifts offered to clients. There are, however, skeptics who do not believe the industry can self-regulate when it comes to monitoring gifts, entertainment, and other incentive perks.[11] Clearly in 2009 the preference for self-regulation gave way to government-mandated compliance with regulatory standards, as discussed in detail in Chapters 8 and 14.

---

[11] "Party Tab: Wall Street to Set Limits on Gifts," *The Wall Street Journal*, January 24, 2006, *online.wsj.com*. For several good examples of other financial ethics issues, see Larry Alan Bear and Rita Maldonado-Bear, *Free Markets, Finance, Ethics, and Law* (Englewood Cliffs, NJ: Prentice Hall, 1994); and John R. Boatright, ed., *Ethics in Finance* (Malden, MA: Blackwell, 1999).

- Use reasonable care and exercise independent professional judgment when conducting investment analysis, making investment recommendations, taking investment actions, and engaging in other professional activities.
- Practice and encourage others to practice in a professional and ethical manner that will reflect credit on themselves and the profession.
- Promote the integrity of, and uphold the rules governing, global capital markets.
- Maintain and improve their professional competence and strive to maintain and improve the competence of other investment professionals.

The Standards of Professional Conduct include:

- Professionalism, which discusses knowledge of the law, independence and objectivity, misrepresentation, and misconduct.
- Integrity of capital markets, which discusses material nonpublic information and market manipulation.
- Duties to clients, which discusses loyalty, prudence and care, fair dealing, suitability, performance presentation, and preservation of confidentiality.
- Duties to employers, which discusses loyalty, additional compensation arrangements, and responsibilities of supervisors.
- Investment analysis, recommendations, and action, which discusses diligence and reasonable basis, communication with clients and prospective clients, and record retention.
- Conflicts of interest, which discusses disclosure of conflicts, priority of transactions, and referral fees.
- Responsibilities as a CFA Institute member or CFA candidate, which discusses conduct as members and candidates in the CFA program and reference to CFA Institute, the CFA designation, and the CFA program.[†]

* Reprinted with permission from the AICPA Code of Professional Conduct, copyright © 2008 by the American Institute of Certified Public Accountants, Inc. For a full text of the professional code for American Certified Public Accountants, see *www.aicpa.org*.

† Copyright 2005, CFA Institute. Reproduced with permission from CFA Institute. All Rights Reserved. For full text see *www.cfapubs.org/doi/pdf/10.2469/ccb.v2005.n8.4568*.

Marketing Ethics

Marketing refers to advertising, distributing, and selling products or services. Within firms, the marketing department is the functional area that typically interacts most directly with customers. Outside the firm, advertising agencies and other firms provide marketing services to businesses. The complex set of activities involved in marketing generates its own distinctive ethical issues.

One issue in marketing ethics is the honesty and fairness in advertising. Nestlé, the Swiss-based multinational food company, tried to capitalize on consumers' interest in supporting small businesses and farmers in developing countries by promoting their Partner's Blend brand coffee as a "fair trade" product. Some thought Nestlé's efforts were misleading. Mike Brady, a consumer activist at Baby Milk Action, commented,

"The dishonesty of Nestlé's approach is all too familiar. Nestlé's advertisement and Web site for its Fairtrade product implies it will have a significant impact on farmers in El Salvador and that the company's activities in the coffee industry are ethical. The truth is only about 200 farmers in El Salvador supply coffee for Partners' Blend and over 3 million farmers globally who are dependent on Nestlé remain outside the Fairtrade system." Brady continued, "Nestlé is . . . partly responsible for forcing down prices to suppliers, driving many into poverty, while its own profits have soared. Recently, I interviewed a researcher from Colombia who told me 150,000 coffee farming families have lost their livelihoods due to Nestlé's policies."[12]

In addition to the general ethical questions that surround the marketing or advertising of products to consumers, consumer health and safety are another key ethics issue in marketing.

Nokia, the world's largest cellphone maker, warned its customers in 2007 that 46 million of its handsets contained batteries made in China that could overheat and even be dislodged during recharging. Short circuits generated by defective batteries had occurred only 100 times and none resulted in serious injury or property damage, yet Nokia offered to replace the batteries at no cost to its customers.

Apple thought it was offering a good deal to potential customers by reducing the cost of the new iPhone by $200, just two months after it initially went on sale but did not sell at the levels anticipated. Customers who purchased the iPhone when it first came out at the higher price were angry. In response, Apple sought to satisfy its customers by announcing it would give a $100 credit for Apple Stores to anyone who purchased an iPhone at the original $599 price.[13]

As shown in these examples, many businesses are quick to correct ethical problems as they emerge. Chapter 15 discusses several other issues in marketing ethics, including deceptive advertising, firm liability for consumer injury, and a firm's responsibility for the unethical use of products by buyers.

To improve the ethics of the marketing profession, the American Marketing Association (AMA) has adopted a code of ethics for its members, as shown in Exhibit 5.B. The AMA code advocates professional conduct guided by ethics, adherence to applicable laws, and honesty and fairness in all marketing activities. The code also recognizes the ethical responsibility of marketing professionals to the consuming public and specifically opposes such unethical practices as misleading product information, false and misleading advertising claims, high-pressure sales tactics, bribery and kickbacks, and unfair and predatory pricing. These code provisions have the potential for helping marketing professionals translate general ethical principles into specific working rules.[14]

Information Technology Ethics

One of the most complex and fast-changing areas of business ethics is in the field of information technology. Ethical challenges in this field involve invasions of privacy; the collection and storage of, and access to, personal and business information, especially

---

[12] The Brady quote and Nestlé's response can be found at "Nestlé's Reported to UK Advertising Standards Authority over Dishonest Fairtrade Product Advertisement," *Organic Consumers Association,* December 7, 2005, *www.organicconsumers.org.*

[13] "46 Million Nokia Cell Batteries Defective," *The New York Times,* August 14, 2007, *www.nytimes.org;* and "Apple Offers $100 Store Credit; Jobs Apologies to iPhone Users," *The Wall Street Journal,* September 6, 2007, *online.wsj.com.*

[14] The AMA Code for Market Researchers and a discussion of numerous marketing ethics issues can be found in Patrick E. Murphy and Gene R. Laczniak, *Ethical Marketing: Cases and Readings* (Upper Saddle River, NJ: Prentice Hall, 2006); and D. Kirk Davidson, *The Moral Dimension of Marketing: Essays on Business Ethics* (Mason, OH: Thomson, 2002).

AMERICAN MARKETING ASSOCIATION (AMA)

Code of Ethics

Members of the American Marketing Association (AMA) are committed to ethical professional conduct. They have joined together in subscribing to this Code of Ethics embracing the following topics:

- Responsibilities . . . —Marketers must accept responsibility for the consequences of their activities and make every effort to ensure that their decisions, recommendations, and actions function to identify, serve, and satisfy all relevant publics: customers, organizations, and society.

- Honesty and Fairness—Marketers shall uphold and advance the integrity, honor, and dignity of the marketing profession.

- Rights and Duties of Parties . . . —Participants in the marketing exchange process should be able to expect that (1) products and services offered are safe and fit for their intended uses; (2) communications about offered products and services are not deceptive; (3) all parties intend to discharge their obligations, financial and otherwise, in good faith; and (4) appropriate internal methods exist for equitable adjustment and/or redress of grievances concerning purchases.

- Organizational Relationships—Marketers should be aware of how their behavior may influence or impact the behavior of others in organizational relationships. They should not demand, encourage, or apply coercion to obtain unethical behavior in their relationships with others.

Any AMA members found to be in violation of any provision of this Code of Ethics may have his or her Association membership suspended or revoked.*

ASSOCIATION FOR COMPUTING MACHINERY (ACM)

Code of Ethics and Professional Conduct

Preamble. Commitment to ethical professional conduct is expected of every member (voting members, associate members, and student members) of the Association for Computing Machinery (ACM).

This code, consisting of 24 imperatives formulated as statements of personal responsibility, identifies the elements of such a commitment. It contains many, but not all, issues professionals are likely to face. . . . The code and its supplemental guidelines are intended to serve as a basis for ethical decision making in the conduct of professional work. Secondarily, they may serve as a basis for judging the merit of a formal complaint pertaining to violation of professional ethical standards.

The general imperatives for ACM members include contribute to society and human well-being, avoid harm to others, be honest and trustworthy, be fair and take action not to discriminate, honor property rights including copyrights and patents, give proper credit for intellectual property, respect the privacy of others, and honor confidentiality.

Adherence of professionals to a code of ethics is largely a voluntary matter. However, if a member does not follow this code by engaging in gross misconduct, membership in ACM may be terminated.[†]

* Adapted with permission from the American Marketing Association's Code of Ethics, published by the American Marketing Association. For a full text of the professional marketing code, see www.ama.org.

[†] Copyright © 1997, Association for Computing Machinery, Inc. A full text of the ACM code of ethics can be found at www.acm.org/constitution/code.

through e-commerce transactions; confidentiality of electronic mail communication; copyright protection regarding software, music, and intellectual property; and numerous others. New advances in technology foster new ethical challenges.

Jason Smathers, an engineer at America Online (AOL), was arrested and charged with stealing 92 million e-mail addresses of AOL customers and selling them to spammers that were marketing penis enlargement pills and online gambling sites. Sean Dunaway, accused of brokering the e-mail lists, was also arrested. Under the U.S. "CAN-SPAM Law," enacted in 2004, Smathers and Dunaway each faced a maximum sentence of five years in prison and a fine of $250,000 or twice the gross gain from their activities.

Ethical breaches challenging IT professionals are expanding to include the global community. In one incident, a vast electronic spying operation infiltrated computers around the world and stole documents from hundreds of government and private corporate offices, including files from the computer belonging to the Dalai Lama, the religious leader of Buddhism. Investigators believed that although the spy ring had operated for less than two years, at least 1,295 computers in 103 countries were infiltrated. The operating system, called GhostNet, focused mostly on governments of South Asian and Southeast Asian countries.[15]

As discussed in later chapters of this book, the explosion of information technology has raised serious questions of trust between individuals and businesses. In response to calls by businesspeople and academics for an increase in ethical responsibility in the information technology field, professional organizations have developed or revised professional codes of ethics, as shown in Exhibit 5.B.[16]

Other Functional Areas

Production and operations functions, which may seem remote from ethics considerations, have also been at the center of some ethics storms. Flawed manufacturing designs or the lack of upkeep and inspection of transportation equipment, for example, were at the core of major ethical breaches and caused serious harm to the public. Worker safety is another critical ethical issue in the production and operations functions of businesses.

After a series of mine disasters killed 16 miners in one month, the governor of West Virginia ordered a "time-out" and suspended production in all 544 mines in the state, the nation's second leading coal-producing state. Those concerned with the miners' safety pointed to the lack of safety precautions, education, and equipment that may have contributed to many of these accidents and the resulting fatalities. The governor ordered extensive safety inspections of the operations of the mines, and more than 6,000 miners were provided with updated safety training.[17]

Ethics issues also arise in purchasing and supply management departments. Similar to the other professional associations, whose codes of ethical conduct are presented in Exhibits 5.A and 5.B, the Institute for Supply Management (ISM) revised its professional code of ethics in 2005. Its code advocates "loyalty to your organization, justice to those with whom you deal, and faith in your profession." The professional code denotes 12 principles and standards "to encourage adherence to an uncompromising level of integrity."[18]

---

[15] "AOL Worker Is Accused of Selling 93 Million E-Mail Names," *The New York Times,* June 24, 2004, *www.nytimes.com;* and "Vast Spy System Loots Computers in 103 Countries," *The New York Times,* March 29, 2009, *www.nytimes.com.*

[16] For further discussion of ethics in information technology see Sara Baase, *A Gift of Fire: Social, Legal and Ethical Issues for Computing and the Internet,* 3rd ed. (Upper Saddle River, NJ: Prentice Hall, 2008); and Richard Spinello, *Cyber Ethics: Morality and Law in Cyberspace,* 3rd ed. (Sudbury, MA: Jones and Bartlett, 2006).

[17] "West Virginia Mines Take Safety Timeout," CNN.com, February 2, 2006, *www.cnn.com.*

[18] All quotations are from the Institute for Supply Management's Principles and Standards of Ethical Supply Management Conduct, available to members of the association at *www.ism.ws.*

Efforts by professional associations to guide their members toward effective resolution of ethical challenges make one point crystal clear: All areas of business, all people in business, and all levels of authority in business encounter ethics dilemmas from time to time. Ethics issues are a common thread running through the business world. Specific steps that businesses can take to make ethics work are discussed next.

Making Ethics Work in Corporations

Any business firm that wishes to do so can improve the quality of its ethical performance. Doing so requires a company to build ethical safeguards into its everyday routines. This is sometimes called *institutionalizing ethics*. How frequently organizations adopt these safeguards is shown in Figure 5.2.

Building Ethical Safeguards into the Company

Managers and employees need guidance on how to handle day-to-day ethical situations; their own personal ethical compass may be working well, but they need to receive directional signals from the company. Several organizational steps can be taken to provide this kind of ethical awareness and direction.

Lynn Sharp Paine, a Harvard Business School professor, has described two distinct approaches to ethics programs: a compliance-based approach and an integrity-based approach. A compliance-based program seeks to avoid legal sanctions. This approach emphasizes the threat of detection and punishment in order to channel employee behavior in a lawful direction. Paine also described an integrity-based approach to ethics programs. Integrity-based ethics programs combine a concern for the law with an emphasis on employee responsibility for ethical conduct. Employees are told to act with integrity and conduct their business dealings in an environment of honesty and fairness. From these values a company will nurture and maintain business relationships and will be profitable.[19]

Researchers found that both approaches lessened unethical conduct, although in somewhat different ways. Compliance-based ethics programs increased employees' willingness

FIGURE 5.2
Organizations' Ethics Safeguards at Work*

Ethics Safeguard	Southwest Pennsylvania Organizations (1996)	Ethics Resource Center (2005)	Greater Omaha Alliance for Business Ethics (2008)
Promoted ethics at work	71%		
Developed code of ethics	57	86%	62%
Created ethics office/advice	17	65	
Established ethics hotline	9	73	45
Offered ethics training	20	69	30
Conducted audit/evaluation	11	67	

* The Southwestern Pennsylvania Organizations survey looked at organizations in that region of all sizes (30 percent of the sampled organizations had fewer than 50 employees, and 22 percent had more than 1,000 employees) and at multiple industry groups (health care, finance, manufacturing, etc.). The Ethics Resource Center contacted employees working for companies of all sizes (48 percent from large firms and 69 percent from for-profit organizations). The Greater Omaha survey investigated practices of businesses in the region with a wide range of sizes (58 percent had fewer than 50 employees and 10 percent had more than 1,000 employees).

Sources: Beard Center for Leadership in Ethics, *Ethics Initiatives in Southwestern Pennsylvania: A Benchmarking Report* (Pittsburgh: Duquesne University, 1999); Ethics Resource Center, *National Business Ethics Survey: How Employees View Ethics in Their Organizations* (Washington, DC: Ethics Resource Center, 2005); and Greater Omaha Alliance for Business Ethics, *2008 Organizational Ethics Survey* (Omaha: Creighton University, 2008).

[19] Lynn Sharp Paine, "Managing for Organizational Integrity," *Harvard Business Review,* March–April 1994, pp. 106–17.

to seek ethical advice and sharpened their awareness of ethical issues at work. Integrity-based programs, for their part, also increased employees' sense of integrity, commitment to the organization, willingness to deliver bad news to supervisors, and their perception that better decisions were made.[20]

Former SEC Chairman Christopher Cox, in response to the severe recession that began in 2008, said, "Compliance programs have made huge strides in recent years in becoming more formalized and more robust. . . . Now more than ever, companies need to take a long-term view on compliance and realize that their fiduciary responsibility requires constant commitment to investors. That means sustaining their support for compliance during this market turmoil, and beyond it as well."[21]

Top Management Commitment and Involvement

Research has consistently shown that the "tone at the top"—the example set by top executives—is critical to fostering ethical behavior. When senior-level managers and directors signal employees, through their own behavior, that they believe ethics should receive high priority in all business decisions, they have taken a giant step toward improving ethical performance throughout the company.

> The Ethics Resource Center reported in 2007 that an organization's culture is shaped by ethical leadership, supervisor reinforcement, peer commitment to ethics, and embedded ethical values. It also found that only about half of the firms surveyed had an ethical or ethical-leaning culture. In fact, despite serious efforts by top management toward enhancing the workplace culture in the post-Enron era, by 2007 the number of companies with unethical or unethical-leaning cultures was about the same as during the pre-Enron era. The Center concluded that "the lack of commitment to strong [ethical] cultures coupled with the increased tendency toward weak [unethical] cultures has likely led to the rise in observed misconduct and deep resistance by employees to report [misconduct]."

A survey conducted by The Conference Board found that board of directors' involvement in ethics and compliance programs jumped from 21 percent in 1987 to 96 percent in 2005.[22] One reason for this increased involvement may be due to a program launched in 2004, as described next.

> The Business Roundtable, an association of chief executive officers, created an Institute for Corporate Ethics to develop and conduct training programs for CEOs, boards of directors, and senior managers. "This Institute is a bold investment that will bring together the best educators in the field of ethics, active business leaders, and business school students to forge a new and lasting link between ethical behavior and business practices," pledged Business Roundtable Cochairman Franklin Raines, chairman and CEO of Fannie Mae.[23]

[20] Gary R. Weaver and Linda Klebe Trevino, "Compliance and Values Oriented Ethics Programs: Influences on Employees' Attitudes and Behavior," *Business Ethics Quarterly* 9 (1999), pp. 315–35.

[21] Christopher Cox, Address to the 2008 *COOutreach* National Seminar, November 13, 2008, *http://www.sec.gov/news/speech/2008/spch111308cc.htm.*

[22] "More Corporate Boards Involved in Ethics Programs," *Ethics Newsline,* Institute for Global Ethics, October 26, 2006, *www.globalethics.com.*

[23] "Nation's Top CEOs Announce Plans for Center on Corporate Ethics," *Ethics Newsline,* Institute for Global Ethics, January 20, 2004, *www.globalethics.com.*

Drafted by Judge Elbert Gary, the first chairman of United States Steel Corporation, and distributed throughout the company in 1909, The Gary Principles stated the following:

- I believe that when a thing is right, it will ultimately and permanently succeed.
- The highest rewards come from honest and proper practice. Bad results come in the long run from selfish, unfair, and dishonest conduct.
- I believe in competition . . . that the race should be won by the swiftest, and that success should come to him who is most earnest and active and persevering.
- I believe that no industry can permanently succeed that does not treat its employees equitably and humanely.
- I believe thoroughly in publicity. The surest and wisest of all regulation is public opinion.
- If we are to succeed in business, we must do it on principles that are honest, fair, lawful, and just.
- We must put and keep ourselves on a platform so fair, so high, so reasonable, that we will attract the attention and invite and secure the approval of all who know what we are doing.
- We do not advocate combinations or agreements in restraint of trade, nor action of any kind which is opposed to the laws or to the public welfare.
- We must never forget that our rights and interests are and should be subservient to the public welfare, that the rights and interests of the individual must always give way to those of the public.

Reproduced with permission of United States Steel Corporation.

Whether the issue is sexual harassment, honest dealing with suppliers, or the reporting of expenses, the commitments (or lack thereof) by senior management and the employees' immediate supervisor and their involvement in ethics as a daily influence on employee behavior are the most essential safeguards for creating an ethical workplace.

Ethics Policies or Codes

As shown in Figure 5.2, many U.S. businesses have **ethics policies or codes**, especially large firms. An example of one of the first corporate ethics codes is shown in Exhibit 5.C. The purpose of such codes is to provide guidance to managers and employees when they encounter an ethical dilemma. The rationales underlying the ethics policies differ from country to country. In the United States and Latin America, it was found that policies were primarily *instrumental*—that is, they provided rules and procedures for employees to follow in order to adhere to company policies or societal laws. In Japan, most policies were found to be a mixture of *legal compliance* and *statements of the company's values and mission*. The *values and mission* policies also were popular with European and Canadian companies.[24]

Typically, ethics policies cover issues such as developing guidelines for accepting or refusing gifts from suppliers, avoiding conflicts of interest, maintaining the security of proprietary information, and avoiding discriminatory personnel practices. Sometimes groups of organizations band together to draft ethics policies, as U.S. and European defense contractors did in 2006. Spurred by weapons acquisition scandals from 1995 to 2005, businesses involved in defense contract procurement developed voluntary ethical standards that would apply to defense contract work in the United States or Europe. These

---

[24] Ronald C. Berenbeim, *Global Corporate Ethics Practices: A Developing Consensus* (New York: Conference Board, 1999).

standards created uniform anticorruption rules, including requirements for internal monitoring of operations and procurement bidding and guidelines for self-reporting that go beyond international or national laws and regulations.[25]

Researchers have found that a written ethics policy, while an important contributor, is insufficient by itself to bring about ethical conduct. Companies must circulate ethics policies frequently and widely among employees and external stakeholder groups (for example, customers, suppliers, or competitors). The creation of an ethics policy must be followed up with employee training so that the policy's provisions actually influence day-to-day company activities.[26]

Ethics and Compliance Officers

Ethical lapses in large corporations throughout the 1980s prompted many firms to create a new position: the **ethics and compliance officer**. A second surge of attention to ethics and the creation of ethics offices came in response to the 1991 U.S. Corporate Sentencing Guidelines, discussed in Chapter 4. Finally, the recent wave of corporate ethics scandals and the passage of the Sarbanes-Oxley Act have again turned businesses' attention toward entrusting ethical compliance and the development and implementation of ethics programs to an ethics or compliance officer or ombudsperson. From 2000 to 2004, the number of members in the Ethics Officers Association doubled from 632 to more than 1,200 members and remained at that level through 2009. To reflect the growing number of compliance officers heading companies' ethics programs, this association changed its name to the Ethics and Compliance Officers Association.

> According to a survey of its members, ethics and compliance officers have been entrusted with reducing the risks to the company of employee misconduct (79 percent), ensuring commitment to corporate values (75 percent), and establishing a better corporate culture (68 percent). Keith Darcy, executive director of the ECOA, explained, "Organizations are increasingly recognizing the importance of their ethics and compliance office [and offices], not just in a time of crisis, but as an integral part of day-to-day business." A 2006 ECOA study found that ethics officers' salaries increased 12 percent in one year. Top ethics executives are receiving compensation comparable to other executive-level jobs and are receiving significant amounts of long-term incentives, such as stock options.[27]

Ethics Reporting Mechanisms

In some companies, when employees are troubled about some ethical issue but may be reluctant to raise it with their immediate supervisor, they can turn to their company's **ethics reporting mechanisms** and place a call on the company's ethics assist line or helpline (the new preferred term to hotline or crisis line). Ethics reporting systems

[25] "U.S., European Defense Firms Push for Voluntary Ethics Code," *The Wall Street Journal*, July 17, 2006, *online.wsj.com*.

[26] Betsy Stevens, "Communicating Ethical Values: A Study of Employee Perceptions," *Journal of Business Ethics* 20 (1999), pp. 113–20. For examples of codes, see Ivanka Mamic, *Implementing Codes of Conduct* (Sheffield, UK: Greenleaf Publishing, 2004); and Oliver F. Williams, C.S.C., ed., *Global Codes of Conduct: An Idea Whose Time Has Come* (Notre Dame, IN: University of Notre Dame Press, 2000).

[27] "EOA Survey: Companies Seeking to Integrate Ethics through the Whole Organization," *Ethikos*, July–August 2001, pp. 1–3, 16; and "Pay for Top Corporate Ethics Officers Rising Quickly," *Ethics Newsline*, Institute for Global Ethics, October 10, 2006, *www.globalethics.org*. For additional information on ethics and compliance officers, see Joe Murphy, "Defining the Role of Chief Ethics and Compliance Officer: A Step Forward, *Ethikos*, November/December 2007, pp. 1–3; and for a critical view of ethics and compliance officers, see "Are Ethics Officers 'Window Dressing'?" *Ethics Newsline*, Institute for Global Ethics, October 30, 2006, *www.globalethics.org*.

typically have three uses: (1) to provide interpretations of proper ethical behavior involving conflicts of interest and the appropriateness of gift giving, (2) to create an avenue to make known to the proper authorities allegations of unethical conduct, and (3) to give employees and other corporate stakeholders a way to discover general information about a wide range of work-related topics. An ethics reporting mechanism may work with other ethics safeguards, such as at Raytheon where the assist line served as an early warning system for the need to develop a new ethics training program for the firm's supervisors.

This approach is more common, found in more than 83 percent of all organizations with 500 or more employees, according to the National Business Ethics Survey conducted by the Ethics Resource Center. The growth of ethics reporting mechanisms is partly due to Section 301 of the Sarbanes-Oxley Act, which since 2002 has required companies to provide employees with a mechanism to report potentially criminal misconduct to top managers and the board. Companies are learning how to make these mechanisms more effective, as illustrated by the following example:

> Shell Oil Company, based in Houston, Texas, implemented a hotline that was available to employees only from 8 a.m. to 5 p.m., Monday through Fridays. The response was decidedly cool—*a total of only 32 calls in seven years*, while the company employed 30,000 workers. Shell changed the name of the reporting mechanism to a "helpline," and it was staffed by Global Compliance Services on a full-time, seven-day, 24-hour basis. By the next year Shell's helpline was averaging 117 calls annually. Why the increase? "We advertised the helpline," recalled Danna Walton, Shell's senior counsel. The company distributed helpline brochures to employees. Company ethics and compliance officers posted signs around the workplace. The helpline number was printed on every other page of the company's code of conduct. It was promoted on the company's Web site. The company assured employees that allegations would be investigated and acted upon if something was found to be amiss. "You've got to make people understand that you're going to do something about it" when they make a report, said Walton. If not, they will stop using the mechanism.[28]

Ethics officers say more and more employees are willing to use their companies' ethical reporting mechanisms. In 2006, U.S.-based companies reported that 8.3 incidents per 1,000 employees were logged through the organizations' reporting mechanisms, up about 14 percent from 2004. Smaller organizations had fewer calls per employee, possibly indicating that a more informal approach is used there than in larger, multinational organizations. Most employee calls, 65 percent, were serious enough to warrant an investigation and 45 percent resulted in the organization taking corrective action. The ethics and compliance officer never really knows what to expect when monitoring calls to the helpline, as the following example showed:[29]

> "Oh, boy, this is one of those days," thought the ethics officer at a midsized manufacturing firm when she received a call on the ethics helpline that a toilet in the company's administration building was overflowing. She called maintenance and they found that someone had clogged up the toilet drain. When the same call was received a week later, the ethics officer knew she had to investigate. Through interviews with personnel who worked on that floor, she discovered that the supervisor had refused to allow workers to take bathroom breaks when needed, and an employee had boasted that "he was going to get

---

[28] "Developing Effective Helplines: Shell Oil and Lubrizol," *Ethikos*, September–October 2005, pp. 5–7, 17.

[29] *2007 Corporate Governance and Compliance Hotline Benchmarking Report*, Security Executive Council, p. 10.

even with his supervisor and plug up the toilet" to attract attention to unsafe working conditions. The call about the overflowing toilet and subsequent investigation allowed the ethics officer to address the real "ethical issue," counsel the supervisor, and repair the deteriorating working conditions at her company.[30]

Ethics Training Programs

Another step companies can take to build in ethical safeguards is to offer **employee ethics training**. This is generally the most expensive and time-consuming element of an ethics program. Smaller firms often ignore ethics training; studies have shown that only 20 to 40 percent of such businesses offer it to their employees. Larger businesses, by contrast, usually conduct regular ethics training in the areas of antitrust compliance, sexual harassment avoidance, or adherence to the company's code of conduct. Most ethics and compliance training programs focus on making sure employees know what the law requires and the company expects. Few firms, however, systematically measure the effectiveness of this effort. A new approach to employee ethics training is emerging among global firms, as described by the Ethical Corporate Institute research report:

> Online training has emerged as the most widely used form of training over the last 5 to 10 years. Web-based training guarantees that training is uniform and consistent and employee participation is closely monitored. Online training, however, is not a complete solution. In-person is needed and takes many forms: classroom settings, workshops, staff meetings, and leader speeches. Training is shown to be most effective when multiple methods are employed.[31]

Typically, ethics training is offered to managers, rather than the rank and file. Recently, more senior management and the members of the board of directors have become involved in their company's ethics training, to comply with the Sarbanes-Oxley Act of 2002. Management training also can be rather creative, as seen at Waste Management:[32]

> Since 2000, Waste Management, North America's largest provider of comprehensive waste and environmental services, has distributed a weekly, two-page newspaper called *WMMonday* to its 50,000 employees. The weekly newspaper is produced in three languages, English, Spanish, and French Canadian. Waste Management uses the paper as a means to communicate with its employees about core organizational values and to reinforce the importance of ethics, compliance, and consumer and community relations. Topics for articles in *WMMonday* have ranged from whether or not to sell a 1981 baby's car seat at a garage sale (it did not meet current federal safety regulatory requirements) to whether an executive could accept a Stetson cowboy hat as a gift for presenting a speech on ethics. The conversational or "folksy" tone of *WMMonday* communicates to employees that attention to ethics is an everyday issue at Waste Management.[33]

---

[30] Based on an interview with an ethics and compliance officer who requested that her firm and her identity remain anonymous.

[31] See *Best Practices for Designing Effective Ethics Programmes,* Ethical Corporation Institute, March 2009, at *www.ethicalcorpinstitute.com/ectraining.*

[32] Beard Center for Leadership in Ethics, *Ethics Initiatives in Southwestern Pennsylvania: A Benchmarking Report* (Pittsburgh: Duquesne University, 1996); and Ethics Resource Center, *National Business Ethics Survey: How Employees View Ethics in Their Organizations* (Washington, DC, 2005). Also see Jeffrey M. Kaplan and Rebecca Walker, "Thinking about Training," *Ethikos,* March/April 2008, pp. 7–10, 13.

[33] "Waste Management's 'Core Values,'" *Ethikos,* November/December 2007, pp. 7–9.

Ethics Audits

Some firms have attempted to assess the effectiveness of their ethical safeguards by documenting evidence of increased ethical employee behavior. One technique used is an **ethics audit**. In such an audit, the auditor—either a hired outside consultant or an internal employee—is required to note any deviations from the company's ethics standards and bring them to the attention of the audit supervisor. Often the managers of each operating entity are required to file a report with the auditor on the corrective action they have taken to deal with any deviations from the standards that emerged in the prior year's audit. Managers also report on the written procedures they established for informing new employees of the standards and for providing ongoing reviews of the standards with other employees.

Sometimes, ethics audits are provided by other firms that specialize in carrying out this function. Macroinnovation Associates, for example, offers what it calls its Openness Audit™, an independent advisory service aimed at supporting the needs of ethics officers and other executives concerned with corporate accountability, transparency, and governance. According to the company, the audit is a management tool that profiles the policies, programs, and practices behind information and knowledge processing in a firm.

Although United Technologies objected to the term *ethics audit,* the company did embrace the value of assessing the effectiveness of its ethics compliance program. "There is no such thing as an ethics audit," according to United Technologies' vice president of business practices. "What we do are system audits." The system audit at UT examined the controls in place at its business units for preventing compliance and ethics irregularities. These often included a *desk audit* where auditors went into a sales manager's actual office to see if they could find any so-called red flags. The UT auditors also looked into the manager's file cabinets, correspondence, and e-mail.[34]

Comprehensive Ethics Programs

Experts believe that integrating various ethics safeguards into a comprehensive program is critically important. When all six components discussed in this chapter—top management commitment, ethical policies or codes, compliance officers, reporting mechanisms, training programs, and audits—are used together, they reinforce each other and become more effective. In an Ethics Resource Center survey of U.S. employees, only 26 percent reported that their employer had developed a comprehensive, six-element ethics program. The startling discovery, however, was the dramatic impact a comprehensive ethics program, along with a strong ethical culture, had in creating an ethical work environment for employees. People working at a firm with a comprehensive ethics program were more likely to report ethical misconduct in the workplace to the appropriate company authority and to be satisfied with the company's investigation of and response to charges of ethical misconduct. In contrast, firms with only an ethics policy or code were often perceived as less ethically responsible and less able to address ethical misconduct in the workplace than firms without any ethical safeguards.[35] An example of a strong values-based ethics program is described in the discussion case at the end of this chapter.

---

[34] "Audits Reduce Compliance Risk at United Technologies," *Ethikos,* March–April 2001, pp. 12–13.

[35] See Joshua Joseph, *2000 National Business Ethics Survey, Volume I: How Employees Perceive Ethics at Work* (Washington, DC: Ethics Resource Center, 2000).

Corporate Ethics Awards

Firms are honored for their efforts to create an ethical climate and improve ethical performance. In 2002 *Business Ethics* magazine created a new Living Economy Award, based on the work of theorist David Korten, author of *The Post-Corporate World*. In his work, Korten has emphasized the need to build a living economy based on firms that focus on fair profits rather than maximum profits and that are locally based, stakeholder-owned, democratically accountable, life-serving, and operated on a human scale. Among the Living Economy Award winners were

- The White Dog Café, a $5 million café in Philadelphia that paid living wages to all employees, including dishwashers, and purchased humanely raised meat from local family farmers.
- Organic Valley, a $156 million, 633 farmer–owned cooperative located in LaFarge, Wisconsin.
- Chroma Technology Corporation, a global high-technology manufacturer of optic filters, where no employee is paid more than $75,000 or less than $37,500, there are no designated managers, and employees hold seats on the board of directors.
- Weaver Street Cooperative, a North Carolina natural foods cooperative and café, honored for its sustainable products, community focus, and democratic governance.

Ethisphere Magazine recognizes and rewards ethical leadership and business practices worldwide and each spring ranks companies within their industry according to their Ethical Quotient (EQ) score. The EQ score comprises 20 percent corporate citizenship and responsibility performance; 10 percent corporate governance adherence; 15 percent for innovation that contributes to the public's well-being; 5 percent for exemplary leadership to the industry; 15 percent based on executive leadership; 20 percent for the firm's legal, regulatory, and reputation track record; and 15 percent designated to the internal systems and ethics and compliance program developed at the firm. Among the winners selected in 2009 as the world's most ethical companies was Unilever, which attributes the strength of its program to "the fact that employees deep within the organization can look to their immediate supervisors as examples of ethical leadership. It is here that an ethical culture is cultivated and the standards and values of Unilever's Code of Business Principles are given meaning," explained Iskah Singh, Unilever's associate general counsel.[36]

Covalence, a Geneva-based organization, developed an ethical reputation index based on 45 criteria, including labor standards, waste management, product social utility, and human rights policies. In 2009, they announced their ranking of 541 multinational companies and HSBC was ranked number one, followed by Intel, Unilever, Marks & Spencer, Xerox, Alcoa, Rio Tinto, General Electric, Dell Computer, and DuPont.[37]

These and other award-winning firms provide the foundation for a collection of corporate ethics role models. Their commitment to ethical values and efforts to establish effective ethics programs demonstrate that firms can be financially successful and ethically focused.

---

[36] For the complete explanation of *Ethisphere's* Most Ethical Companies rating system see *www.ethicsphere.com.*

[37] Profiles on the Living Economy Award winners are from the 2002 through 2004 issues of *Business Ethics* at *www.thecro.com.* For information on the other ethics ranking systems see *Ethisphere Magazine* at *www.ethicsphere.com;* and Covalence's Web site at *www.covalence.ch.*

Ethics in a Global Economy

Doing business in a global context raises a host of complex ethical challenges. Examples of unethical conduct by business employees are reported from nearly every country. One example of unethical activity is **bribery**, a questionable or unjust payment often to a government official to ensure or facilitate a business transaction. Bribery is found in nearly every sector of the global marketplace.

A Berlin-based watchdog agency, Transparency International, annually publishes a survey that ranks corruption by country according to perceptions of executives and the public. Countries where having to pay a bribe is least likely included Denmark, New Zealand, Sweden, Singapore, Finland, Switzerland, and Iceland. At the other end of the index countries most likely to demand or accept bribes were Somalia, Myanmar, Iraq, Haiti, Afghanistan, Sudan, Guinea, and Chad. The United States ranked 18th on the list of 180 countries, with the United Kingdom 16th, Canada 9th, Germany 14th, Japan tied for 18th, France 23rd, Italy 55th, China 72nd, India 85th, and Russia 147th.[38]

An analysis of Transparency International's Corruption Perceptions Index (CPI) by a business scholar revealed that bribe taking was more likely in countries with low per capita income, low salaries for government officials, and less variation in income distribution. The report also argued that "a legalistic approach, by itself, is unlikely to be effective in curbing bribery," since the culture of the society plays an important role in the occurrence of bribery. What may be effective in combating bribery is an integrative approach of economic advancement policies, social investment in education, and friendly business policies to foster economic growth, in addition to anticorruption laws and punishments to combat bribery while seeking to enhance economic development and gradual cultural adjustments.[39]

What are the costs to business of working in environments where corruption is endemic and bribes are expected? In Russia, one study showed that the amount of bribes paid to government officials was roughly equal to the nation's entire revenues—about $240 billion annually. The high costs of corruption are also evident in countries that typically do not demand bribery to conduct business, such as the United Kingdom. A U.K. survey reported that nearly half of the 350 businesses surveyed said they had lost a deal because a competitor paid someone a bribe. About 1 in 10 firms said that paying a bribe could account for half of the cost of a project. A third of the survey respondents feared that the use of bribery to close deals would probably increase over the next 10 years.[40]

A recent study by the World Bank estimated the cost of corruption to be more than $1 *trillion* worldwide annually. Stemming the tide of corruption, especially throughout Asia, is seen as a necessity for economic development. Daniel Kaufman of the World Bank stated, "Combating graft is essential to long-term economic growth. Nations that have visibly cracked down on corruption, such as Hong Kong and Singapore, have received real economic benefits in return." Kaufman

---

[38] Transparency International Corruption Perceptions Index 2008, *www.transparency.org.*

[39] Rajib Sanyal, "Determinants of Bribery in International Business: The Cultural and Economic Factors," *Journal of Business Ethics 59* (2005), pp. 139–45.

[40] "Corruption Rife in International Business, Says New Survey," *Ethics Newsline,* Institute for Global Business, October 16, 2006, *www.globalbusiness.org.*

further noted abundant evidence of a *development dividend* for countries that fight corruption.[41]

Corruption was so bad in Romania and Bulgaria that the European Union required the governments there to take significant steps to curb corruption and violence or risk losing their provisional seats in the EU. Government officials were ordered to accelerate their anticorruption efforts and streamline the backlog of cases awaiting action in their court systems.

Efforts to Curtail Unethical Practices

Numerous efforts are under way to curb unethical business practices throughout the world. The most common control is through government intervention and regulation. Efforts to address unethical business behavior often begin with national governments, which can enact stiff legislative controls, but recently include efforts by international organizations.

One of the most widespread and potentially powerful efforts to combat bribery was initiated by the Organization for Economic Cooperation and Development (OECD). The OECD treaty called on member countries to take steps to deter, prevent, and combat the bribery of public officials in foreign countries. As of 2009, 38 countries had ratified the treaty, meaning that bribery is a crime in the country and punishable by the courts. After suffering global embarrassment and potential loss of business due to governmental corruption, the Chinese government launched an effort to combat corruption, as shown in Exhibit 5.D.

In past years, various international organizations, such as the International Labour Organization and the United Nations, have attempted to develop an international code of conduct for multinational corporations. These efforts have emphasized the need for companies to adhere to universal ethical guidelines when conducting business throughout the world. These codes are discussed further in Chapter 7.

At the country level, numerous countries are addressing the challenge of combating corruption and bribery. A coalition of groups across Nigeria called for "zero tolerance" toward corruption. The call came from the anticorruption forum organized by the committee for the Defense of Human Rights in 2007 that declared, "Corruption is fundamentally an economic and political question which is continuously fertilized by poverty and can only be effectively addressed by a progressive, legitimate, and people-driven government." The Philippine government, also plagued with corruption scandals, announced that it would no longer tolerate graft and in 2008 began an investigation into allegations of more than $130 million in kickbacks involving a state telecommunications deal with a Chinese firm. The head of the Bangladesh anticorruption commission declared an all-out war against graft in 2007. Hasan Mashhud Crowdhury argued that corruption was a drag on his nation's economic growth and called on Bangladesh citizens to "raise your voice whenever you see any unethical or illegal activities . . . An inactive civil society is enough for destroying the entire society." In Singapore, a country where bribery has been on the decline, the government announced in 2007 that it would raise the salaries of ministerial-level officials on average 60 percent—a total cost of $1.25 million. Singaporean government officials explained that high salaries are necessary to attract talent to these jobs and to ward off threats of corruption.[42]

[41] "Fighting Corruption May Produce 'Development Dividend' for Nations," *Ethics Newsline,* Institute for Global Ethics, December 22, 2008, *www.globalethics.org.*

[42] Quotations from "Corruption and Chaos Top News from Pakistan and Bangladesh," *Ethics Newsline,* Institute for Global Ethics, November 13, 2007, *www.globalethics.org;* and "Corruption Probes Worldwide Focus on Political, Economic Reforms," *Ethics Newsline,* Institute for Global Ethics, May 21, 2007, *www.globalethics.org.*

Exhibit 5.D

Anticorruption Efforts in China

Anticorruption experts and global business executives point out that corruption and bribery are at epidemic proportions in China. In a one-year period, between July 1, 2007, and June 30, 2008, 148 bribery attempts were reported and subsequently investigated by TRACE, a U.S.-based organization dedicated to antibribery compliance. TRACE reported that 85 percent of these instances of attempted bribery were demands requested by individuals affiliated with the Chinese government, including the police and court judges. Of the 117 reports that specified a monetary range for the bribe demand, more than half were for amounts of more than $1,000 and 6 percent of bribes requested more than $500,000. The Carnegie Endowment for Peace concluded that corruption in China imposes crippling costs on the country's economy and threatens to undermine its political stability.

In an effort to control bribery among its administrative officials, in 2007 China created a new National Corruption Prevention Bureau, charged with fighting corruption. China's President Hu Jinto helped launch the anticorruption campaign by saying that his government "would focus on improving ethics education, reforming legal procedures, arresting high-profile offenders, and cracking down on crimes that most affect the public interest." This initiative enabled China to meet commitments to the United Nations Convention Against Corruption—which led some critics to speculate that these efforts were mostly political posturing on the world stage.

But the Chinese government showed its seriousness when it executed Zheng Xiaoyu, the former head of the State Food and Drug Administration. Zheng admitted to accepting $850,000 in bribes to grant approval for hundreds of medicines, although some drugs were proven to be fakes and others did not pass the regulatory standards for safety. Cao Wenzhuang, who was in charge of drug registration approvals at the State Food and Drug Administration in China, was also sentenced to death in 2007 for accepting more than $300,000 in bribes. Cao was given a two-year reprieve to allow him to seek a lighter sentence of life in prison.

Sources: "China May Create a National Anti-Corruption Bureau," *Ethics Newsline,* Institute for Global Ethics, February 20, 2007, *www.globalethics.org;* "China Sentences Official to Death for Corruption," *The New York Times,* July 7, 2007, *ww.nytimes.com;* "China Quick to Execute Drug Official," *The New York Times,* July 11, 2007, *www.nytimes.com;* and "Bribe Demands in China," *Ethisphere,* 2008, *www.ethisphere.com.*

Executives representing U.S.-based companies are prohibited by the **U.S. Foreign Corrupt Practices Act** (FCPA) from paying bribes to foreign government officials, political parties, or political candidates. To achieve this goal, the FCPA requires U.S. companies with foreign operations to adopt accounting practices that ensure full disclosure of the company's transactions. In 2009, Robert Khuzamii, head of the SEC's Division of Enforcement, announced that his "agency will put more attention on the Foreign Corrupt Practices Act" through proactive investigations, working more closely with foreign counterparts, and taking a more global approach to violations of the act.[43]

Yet defense contractors and other U.S.-based businesses do not always comply with the antibribery Foreign Corruption Practices Act, as shown in the following examples:

- York International agreed to pay $10 million to the U.S. government to resolve allegations that its employees paid bribes to the pre-war Iraqi government in exchange for contracts to supply air conditioning devices to government buildings.

- Baker Hughes, a global oil services company, pleaded guilty to bribing Kazakhstan officials to win oil field contracts in 2007. The company paid $44.1 million in penalties and forfeitures, the largest penalty at the time under the Foreign Corrupt Practices Act.

- In 2009, Halliburton and its former KBR subsidiary agreed to pay $579 million in fines to settle criminal and regulatory charges for bribing foreign officials to win

[43] "More Heat Coming," *Foreign Corrupt Practices Act blog,* August 10, 2009, *fcpablog.blogspot.com.*

[handwritten margin note:] According to the text "Business & Society stakeholder, Ethics, Public policy" page 115 that

$6 billion in construction contracts in Nigeria. For more than 10 years, company executives paid $182 million to Nigerian officials to secure contracts for building a liquefied natural gas complex.[44]

Some people question the effectiveness of governmental legislation or corporate policies. Rather than establishing rules, some businesses, including Motorola and Reebok, are trying to educate and motivate their employees worldwide to both respect the customs of other nations and adhere to basic ethical principles of fairness, honesty, and respect for human rights. Shell Oil publishes a report card documenting the number of employees disciplined or fired, as well as contracts voided, because of bribery-related actions.[45] Some who study international business ethics say that such higher standards of ethics already exist. Thomas Donaldson, a leading ethics scholar, has outlined a set of fundamental human rights—including the rights to security, freedom of movement, and subsistence income—that should be respected by all multinational corporations. These standards and other ethical values are at the core of the development of transnational codes of conduct promoted by the United Nations and other international organizations.[46]

Ethics, Law, and Illegal Corporate Behavior

It is important when discussing specific ways to improve business's ethical performance to consider the relationship of laws and ethics. Some people have argued that the best way to assure ethical business conduct is to insist that business firms obey society's laws. However, this approach is not as simple as it seems.

Laws and ethics are not quite the same. Laws are similar to ethics because both define proper and improper behavior. In general, laws are a society's attempt to formalize—that is, to reduce to written rules—the general public's ideas about what constitutes right and wrong conduct in various spheres of life. Ethical concepts—like the people who believe in them—are more complex than written rules of law. Ethics deal with human dilemmas that frequently go beyond the formal language of law and the meanings given to legal rules. Sometimes businesses or industries preempt legislation and voluntarily adopt ethically based practices:

> The Interactive Digital Software Association, which represents video game makers, established a five-category system that was voluntarily adopted by the industry to inform consumers of the intended target audience. The video game industry also agreed to provide content warnings, such as mild profanity, and to use warning symbols.

This example suggests that following laws cannot always define proper action—that is, what is ethical or unethical. Although laws attempt to codify a society's notions of right

---

[44] "York International Fined $10 Million for U.S. Foreign Corrupt Practices Act Violations," *Ethisphere Ethics News and Commentary Blog*, October 4, 2007, ethisphere.com; "Baker Hughes Admits to Oversees Bribery," *The New York Times*, April 27, 2007, www.nytimes.com; and "More Annals of Global Greed Inc.," *The New York Times*, February 15, 2009, www.nytimes.com.

[45] For a description of Motorola's global ethics program, see R. S. Moorthy, Richard T. DeGeorge, Thomas Donaldson, William J. Ellos, Robert C. Solomon, and Robert B. Textor, *Uncompromising Integrity: Motorola's Global Challenge* (Schaumberg, IL: Motorola University Press, 1998); also see Reebok's company policies on human rights at www.reebok.com/about_reebok/human_rights; and Shell Oil's program was featured in "Controlling Corruption," *The CRO*, August 2008, www.thecro.com.

[46] For a complete list of fundamental human rights, see Thomas Donaldson, *The Ethics of International Business* (New York: Oxford University Press, 1989).

and wrong, they are not always able to do so completely. Obeying laws is usually one way of acting ethically, and the public generally expects business to be law-abiding. But at times, the public expects business to recognize that ethical principles are broader than laws. Because of the imperfect match between laws and ethics, business managers who try to improve their company's ethical performance need to do more than comply with laws.

Corporate Lawbreaking and Its Costs

Although estimates vary, lawbreaking in business may cause serious financial losses to the firms, often inflicted by the company's own employees.

> More than half of all U.S. companies were victims of some type of fraudulent activity or crime in 2005 and 2006, suffering an average loss of over $2.8 million, according to the PricewaterhouseCoopers Global Economic Crime Survey. Two law professors estimated that corporate crimes in the form of faulty goods, monopolistic practices, and other law violations annually cost American consumers between $174 billion and $231 billion. Ten percent of the $1 trillion spent on U.S. health care is believed lost due to fraud every year.[47]

White-collar crime, illegal acts committed by employees or business professionals such as fraud, insider trading, embezzlement, or computer crime, accounts for more than 330,000 arrests each year in the United States, despite significant attention to prevent this type of crime. The FBI estimates that white-collar crime costs the United States more than $300 billion annually.[48]

The United States is not the only nation suffering losses from illegal acts. German officials believe that more than 50 billion marks ($29.07 billion) a year is lost from the German economy as a result of inflated accounting, tax evasion, and illegal kickbacks. The PricewaterhouseCoopers global survey on crime reported that total fraud loss incurred by businesses in the United Kingdom doubled to £1.75 million. Businesses in the United Kingdom that experienced fraud were hit on average 15 times in a 24-month period, twice the global average and three times more than the average across Western Europe.[49]

> In response to the economic costs of criminal activity and spurred by the passage of the Sarbanes-Oxley Act, the U.S. Justice Department announced new sentencing guidelines for criminals who harm more than 250 victims, who substantially jeopardize the health of a financial institution or publicly traded company, or who break securities laws while serving as a director or officer of a public firm. "Crimes in the suites will be treated the same [as] or more seriously than crimes in the streets," warned U.S. district judge Ruben Castillo.

The Justice Department changed its policy so that fewer executives convicted of white-collar crimes would serve their time in halfway houses and similar low-security facilities. Rather, these white-collar criminals are now sent to federal penitentiaries. "The prospect of prison, more than any other sanction, is feared by white-collar criminals and has a powerful deterrent effect," said Deputy Attorney General Larry Thompson.[50]

[47] For more information on the costs of corporate crime see the PricewaterhouseCoopers Global Economic Crime Survey at: *wwwpwc.com.*

[48] See the National White Collar Crime Center for additional information at *www.nw3c.org.*

[49] See the PricewaterhouseCoopers Global Economic Crime Survey at *www.pwc.com.*

[50] "U.S. Stiffens Sentences for White-Collar Criminals," *Ethics Newsline,* Institute for Global Ethics, January 13, 2003, *www.globalethics.org/newsline.*

But there is still an unanswered question: "Does crime pay?" Although Bernard Madoff, B. Ramalinga Raju of Satyam Computer Services, Dennis Kozlowski of Tyco, and Bernie Ebbers of WorldCom received stiff penalties for their criminal deeds, consider the fates of these other executives who also committed illegal acts:

- Global Crossing founder Gary Winnick pocketed millions from allegedly fraudulent stock sales and faced no criminal or civil charges at all.
- Investment banker Frank Quattrone had his conviction and 18-month prison sentence overturned on appeal and will keep most of his $200 million made through allegedly questionable initial public offerings.
- Andrew Wiederhorn, CEO of Fog Cutter Capital Group, was sentenced to 18 months in prison after pleading guilty to two felony counts involving a $160 million loan by his company that resulted in its financial collapse. The firm's board of directors voted to keep Wiederhorn on the company's payroll, so while in jail he will receive $2.5 million in compensation.[51]

In a Conference Board–supported survey, 62 percent of the executives responding said that executives who leave their firm because of major violations of ethics and compliance codes "get a financial package and go." So, while the risks are great, some evidence supports the adage "crime does pay," although governmental and business efforts may seek to change this situation in the future.

Yet the more likely lesson to be learned from the outcomes for many of the recent business ethics scandals is that "crime does *not* pay." There are serious consequences for acting unethically and illegally, as the "perp walks" portrayed in the media of business executives going off to jail in handcuffs would indicate. Therefore, businesses have taken significant measures to foster an ethical environment in the workplace and to provide mechanisms to ensure their employees know what is the "right thing to do" and consistently act in an ethical manner.

Summary

- A company's culture and ethical climate tend to shape the attitudes and actions of all who work there, sometimes resulting in high levels of ethical behavior and at other times contributing to less desirable ethical performance.
- Not all ethical issues in business are the same, but ethical challenges occur in all major functional areas of business. Professional associations for each functional area often attempt to provide a standard of conduct to guide practice.
- Companies can improve their ethical performance by creating a values-based ethics program that relies on top management leadership and organizational safeguards, such as ethics policies or codes, ethics and compliance offices and officers, ethics training programs, ethics reporting mechanisms, and ethics audits.
- Companies that have a comprehensive, or multifaceted, ethics program often are better able to promote ethical behavior at work and avoid unethical action by employees.
- Ethical issues, such as bribery, are evident throughout the world, and many international agencies and national governments are actively attempting to minimize such unethical behavior through economic sanctions and international codes.

[51] "White-Collar Crime: Who Does Time?" *BusinessWeek*, February 6, 2006, pp. 60–61; "Windfalls Are Common in Ousters over Alleged Ethics Violations," *The Wall Street Journal*, November 25, 2003, p. B8; and "Convicted CEO Will Get $2.5 Million Salary Plus a Bonus While Serving Prison Time," *SFGate.com*, August 2, 2004, *www.sfgate.com*.

- Although laws and ethics are closely related, they are not the same; ethical principles tend to be broader than legal principles. Illegal behavior by businesses and employees imposes great costs on business generally and the general public.

Key Terms	bribery, *113*	ethics audit, *111*	U.S. Foreign Corrupt
	corporate culture, *95*	ethics policies or	Practices Act, *115*
	employee ethics	codes, *107*	white-collar crime, *117*
	training, *110*	ethics reporting	
	ethical climate, *96*	mechanisms, *108*	
	ethics and compliance	laws, *116*	
	officer, *108*		

Internet Resources	www.TheCRO.com	*The CRO Magazine*
	www.dii.org	Defense Industry Initiative on Business Ethics and Conduct
	www.theecoa.org	Ethics & Compliance Officers Association
	www.ethicaledge.com	Ethics and Policy Integration Centre
	www.ethicscan.on.ca	EthicScan, Toronto-based ethics clearinghouse
	ethisphere.com	Ethisphere Institute
	www.ethics.org/resources	Ethics Resource Center
	www.globalethics.org	Institute for Global Ethics
	www.integrity-interactive.com	Integrity Interactive Company
	www.business-ethics.org	International Business Ethics Institute
	www.corporatecompliance.org	Society of Corporate Compliance and Ethics
	www.tranparency.org	Transparency International

Discussion Case: *Alcoa's Core Values in Practice*

Alcoa began under the name of the Pittsburgh Reduction Company in 1888, changing its name to the Aluminum Company of America (Alcoa) in 1907. The company was originally founded on a $20,000 investment to capitalize on Charles Martin Hall's invention to smelt bauxite ore into the metal known as aluminum. Within a few years, Alcoa had developed into a model of large-scale vertical integration with control over all the inputs to aluminum production.

Since its inception, Alcoa had a very strong values-based culture. Employees learned early in their careers that every decision they made and everything they did must be aligned with the company's values. In 1985, Fred Fetterolf, then president, decided the company needed to document the values that all employees must live by: Integrity; Environment, Health, and Safety; Customer; Accountability; Excellence; People; and Profitability.

In the 1990s Alcoa's CEO, Paul O'Neill, communicated his unswerving belief in the importance of health and safety—one of the company's core values. As is the case with many large organizations, Alcoa had implemented a global ethics and compliance program, and the focus on health and safety was interwoven through the company's program. The Alcoa program included all the basic elements specified in the U.S. Federal

Sentencing Guidelines and Sarbanes-Oxley Act. Alcoa had an ethics and compliance officer who reported to the company's CEO and board of directors, a global code of conduct, continuous ethics and compliance training for all employees, and a global helpline reporting system, to name just a few. Overall, the company emphasized that the program's tools must be understandable by all employees, must support the company's strong value system, and must be continually reinforced by management.

For example, in addition to continuous safety training and education programs, it was the norm at Alcoa to start all business meetings with an identification of exits, the evacuation plans in the event of an emergency, and other safety procedures. Although specific safety procedures differed among Alcoa's various businesses, corporate headquarters required all of its units to meet the same overall goal: zero work-related injuries and illnesses. Some managers felt that this was an unreachable target, saying that "accidents are inevitable." But the company has come close. In 2009, Alcoa's lost workday rate was 0.118. (This number represents the number of injuries and illnesses resulting in one or more days away from work per 100 full-time workers.) In the 12-month period ending April 30, 2009,

- 44.2 percent of Alcoa's 242 locations worldwide had zero recordable injuries.
- 76.0 percent of Alcoa's 242 locations worldwide had zero lost workdays.
- 99.9 percent of Alcoa employees had zero lost workdays.

Alcoa was rapidly closing the gap between its safety record and that of DuPont, which had long been the benchmark for safety among American industrial companies. This achievement was especially significant since Alcoa had completed several substantial acquisitions during this time in many countries whose safety regulations had not yet matured to the level of those in the United States.

O'Neill took this message outside of Alcoa, as well. In meetings with analysts and other outside parties, he always highlighted Alcoa's progress in health and safety. O'Neill explained that Alcoa's emphasis on safety and the reduction of workplace injuries was not based on grandstanding or self-promotion, but rather on a genuine concern for employees.

The emphasis on safety had deep meaning to Alcoa's management team. The company's management firmly believed that no employees should be forced to work in an environment where their safety and the safety of other employees might be jeopardized. Alcoa's management supported the ethical principle that no employees should leave work in a worse condition than when they arrived. Once the change toward safety at work became "the way we do things around here" and was embedded in the Alcoa culture, the process used to achieve this culture could be duplicated throughout Alcoa's value chain. O'Neill's point was simply that the processes used to achieve success in safety were not grand initiatives or episodic programs but rather were the result of persistent attention to changing behaviors and could be duplicated throughout the organization. Alcoa's vision was "Alcoa Aspires to Be the Best Company in the World." Being the best at everything, for O'Neill and Alcoa employees, required continuous improvement as everyone strove toward an ideal goal of perfection.

In 1996, activist shareholders raised allegations at the annual meeting that health and safety conditions at one of Alcoa's Mexican facilities had deteriorated. The Catholic Sister who spoke at the meeting concluded by saying that "the company's behavior in Mexico was inconsistent with its widely publicized values." The company promptly launched an investigation, and O'Neill himself personally visited the plant. Although the company learned that many of the issues raised at the annual meeting were unfounded, it also discovered that a few injury incidents and the subsequent actions taken by local managers were not reported to corporate headquarters, as required by company policy. Meetings held with local government officials over safety incidents at the facility were also not reported, even though the results of these meetings indicated Alcoa was in compliance with all appropriate laws and regulations.

Given these facts, O'Neill concluded that although the business unit management's response to the safety incidents uncovered in the investigation was adequate, there was "a breach of the letter and spirit of our communication practices with respect to major incidents." O'Neill further noted "there was a serious lack of understanding when it came to incident classification, reporting, and recordkeeping of occupational illnesses." The lack of reporting these safety incidents to others in the company was critical to O'Neill, since others in the company were denied the opportunity to learn and possibly prevent similar occurrences at other Alcoa facilities.

O'Neill decided that a change of leadership at the facility was necessary, and he fired the facility's manager. He did so in spite of the manager's stellar record of increased sales and profitability and high marks for quality and customer satisfaction. In an open letter to the entire company, O'Neill concluded by saying, "It is imperative that there be no misperceptions about our values. It is equally imperative that we all learn from this. Full compliance with both the letter—and spirit—of our policies is imperative. Anything less is unacceptable."

Sources: Quotations by Paul O'Neill are from his July 3, 1996, memo to all Alcoa business unit presidents and subsequently distributed to all Alcoa managers. This case was developed with the assistance of long-time Alcoa employee Perry Minnis, formerly the Global Director of Ethics, Compliance, and Advisory Services at Alcoa before his retirement from the company.

Discussion Questions

1. How would you classify Alcoa's ethical work climate? Which ethical criterion, as shown in Figure 5.1, was used by the company: egoism (self-centered), benevolence (concern for others), or principles (integrity approach)? Or, using Professor Paine's two distinct ethics approaches, as discussed in this chapter, was Alcoa's approach more compliance or integrity?

2. What role did top management commitment play in developing the ethical work climate and organizational performance seen at Alcoa? What other ethical safeguards are mentioned in the case to support the company's efforts at developing a strong ethical culture?

3. Was O'Neill justified in terminating the manager for his lack of reporting the workplace accidents, even though no serious harm resulted from the workplace incident?

4. Can Alcoa's "values in practice" be adopted by other organizations as a universal set of ethical standards leading to ethical employee behavior?

PART THREE

Business in a Globalized World

The Challenges of Globalization

The world economy is becoming increasingly integrated, and many businesses have extended their reach beyond national borders. Yet the process of globalization is controversial, and the involvement of corporations in other nations is not always welcome. Doing business in diverse political and economic systems poses difficult challenges. When a transnational corporation buys resources, manufactures products, or sells goods and services in multiple countries, it is inevitably drawn into a web of global social and ethical issues. Understanding what these issues are and how to manage them through collaborative action with governments and civil society organizations is a vital skill for today's managers.

This Chapter Focuses on These Key Learning Objectives:

- Defining globalization and classifying the major ways in which companies enter the global marketplace.
- Recognizing the major drivers of the globalization process and the international financial and trade institutions that have shaped this process in recent decades.
- Analyzing the benefits and costs of the globalization of business.
- Identifying the major types of political and economic systems in which companies operate across the world and the special challenges posed by doing business in diverse settings.
- Assessing how businesses can work collaboratively with governments and the civil sector to address global social issues.

In 2000, a bitter dispute erupted in Bolivia over control of a very basic commodity—water. As part of a program of privatization promoted by the World Bank, the government of Bolivia had auctioned off the water utility of Cochabamba, the nation's third-largest city. The buyer was a consortium controlled by the U.S. construction and engineering firm Bechtel. Under the terms of the deal, Bechtel agreed to improve the badly dilapidated water system. In exchange, the company received exclusive rights to all the water in the city, including the underground aquifer, and was guaranteed a minimum 15 percent annual return on its investment. The company moved in, began the upgrades, and promptly hiked water rates—stunning local households and small businesses who were then expected to pay up to a quarter of their income for basic water service. A broad coalition quickly formed, and people took to the streets by the thousands. The army moved in and declared a state of siege. Faced with a popular insurrection, the Bolivian government informed Bechtel that it had revoked the contract. The company retaliated by filing a complaint with the World Bank, demanding $25 million in compensation. This was an amount that Bolivia, a landlocked nation high in the Andes and the poorest country in South America, could hardly afford. In 2005, Bechtel finally dropped its claim in the face of intense public pressure in Bolivia and around the world.[1]

This extraordinary episode captures much of the turmoil and controversy that surrounds the globalization of business and its far-reaching social impacts. We live in a world that seems increasingly small, more connected, and highly interdependent. It is a world in which transnational companies such as Bechtel often bring precious technical know-how, capital, and managerial experience to poorer nations deeply in need of these resources. Yet corporate involvement abroad often involves challenging social and ethical issues. In this case, Bechtel had to proceed in the context of World Bank mandates over which it had, at best, indirect control. It faced contradictory stakeholder expectations, confusing norms about subsidies for basic services, and a surprise military intervention. Moreover, it failed almost completely to anticipate any of this or to resolve the problem effectively when it arose. How companies can best negotiate the difficult challenges of doing business in a global world is the subject of this chapter.

The Process of Globalization

Globalization refers to the increasing movement of goods, services, and capital across national borders. Globalization is a *process*—that is, an ongoing series of interrelated events. International trade and financial flows integrate the world economy, leading to the spread of technology, culture, and politics. Thomas Friedman, a columnist for *The New York Times* and a well-known commentator, has described globalization as a *system* with its own internal logic:

> Globalization is not simply a trend or a fad but is, rather, an international system. It is the system that has now replaced the old Cold War system, and, like that Cold War system, globalization has its own rules and logic that today directly or indirectly influence the politics, environment, geopolitics, and economics of virtually every country in the world.[2]

Firms can enter and compete in the global marketplace in several ways. Many companies first build a successful business in their home country, and then export their

[1] William Finnegan, "Leasing the Rain," *The New Yorker*, April 8, 2002, pp. 43–53. Updates may be found at the Web site of the Democracy Center, *www.democracyctr.org*.

[2] Thomas L. Friedman, *The Lexus and the Olive Tree* (New York: Anchor Books, 2000), p. ix.

products or services to buyers in other countries. In other words, they develop *global market channels* for their products. Nokia, for example, began in Finland, but now sells its cellular phones and other products all over the world. Other firms begin in their home country, but realize that they can cut costs by locating some or all of their *global operations* in another country. This decision leads to establishing manufacturing plants or service operations abroad. Sometimes, companies own their own factories and offices overseas; sometimes, they subcontract this work to others. For example, in the apparel and shoe industries, companies such as Nike, Gap, and Guess have extensive networks of subcontractors outside the United States who make products of their design. Finally, a third strategy involves purchasing raw materials, components, or other supplies from sellers in other countries. In other words, these companies develop *global supply chains*. Although they do not make entire products overseas, they source supplies that are then assembled in the home country.

These three strategies of globalization can be summarized in three words: *sell, make,* and *buy*. Today, many companies have all three elements of global business—market channels, manufacturing operations, and supply chains.

Major Transnational Corporations

According to United Nations estimates, there are about 79,000 **transnational corporations (TNCs)** operating in the modern global economy (defined by the United Nations as firms that control assets abroad). These corporations, in turn, have 10 times that number of affiliates, meaning suppliers, subcontractors, retailers, and other entities with which they have some business relationship. These affiliates collectively produce 11 percent of global gross domestic product (GDP) and employ 82 million workers.[3] The interconnectedness of the world's businesses is a major reason why the financial crisis that started in 2008 spread so quickly to almost all corners of the globe.

Although many firms conduct business across national boundaries, most global commerce is carried out by a small number of powerful firms. Who are these leading transnational corporations? Figure 6.1 lists the top 10 nonfinancial transnational corporations, ranked in order of the value of the foreign assets they control. Leading the list is General Electric, the American electrical equipment and electronics conglomerate. Rounding out the group are several of the world's leading oil companies, automakers, and telecommunications and retail firms. The world's major financial institutions also extend across the globe; Citigroup, the largest of these (now partially owned by the U.S. government), has 506 foreign affiliates in 75 host counties.

Another important aspect of globalization is the worldwide flow of capital. **Foreign direct investment (FDI)** occurs when a company, individual, or fund invests money in another country—for example, by buying shares of stock in or lending money to a foreign firm. The world economy is increasingly bound together by such cross-border flows of capital. In 2007, FDI reached $1,833 billion, an all-time high, although it dropped about 10 percent in 2008 as the world economy fell into financial crisis. An emerging trend in foreign direct investment is the rise of *sovereign wealth funds*. These are funds operated by governments to invest their foreign currency reserves. They are most commonly operated by nations that export large amounts of oil and manufactured goods; the largest are run by the United Arab Emirates (Abu Dhabi), Kuwait, Norway, China, and Singapore. In recent years, sovereign wealth funds have made significant cross-border investments.

---

[3] United Nations, *World Investment Report 2008: Transnational Corporations and the Infrastructure Challenge* (New York: United Nations, 2008).

FIGURE 6.1

The World's Top 10
Nonfinancial
Transnational
Corporations,
Ranked by Foreign
Assets

Source: United Nations, *World Investment Report 2008*, Annex Table A.I.15, p. 220. All data are for the year 2006.

Corporation	Home Economy	Industry	Foreign Assets (in $ millions)
General Electric	United States	Electrical equipment	$442,278
BP	United Kingdom	Petroleum	170,326
Toyota Motor	Japan	Motor vehicles	164,627
Royal Dutch/Shell	United Kingdom/ Netherlands	Petroleum	161,122
ExxonMobil	United States	Petroleum	154,993
Ford Motor	United States	Motor vehicles	131,062
Vodafone	United Kingdom	Petroleum	126,190
Total	France	Petroleum	120,645
Electricite de France	France	Electricity, gas, and water	111,916
Walmart Stores	United States	Retail	110,199

The Acceleration of Globalization

Global commerce has taken place for hundreds of years, dating back to the exploration and colonization of Africa, Asia, and the Americas by Europeans beginning in the 15th century. But it is during the past 65 years or so, since the end of World War II, that global commerce has truly transformed the world's economy. According to the World Bank, about one-fourth of all goods and services produced worldwide are sold to other nations, rather than domestically; this is almost double the percentage in 1960. In other words, the world's economy is becoming increasingly integrated, as an ever-higher share of output is being exported across national borders.[4] In earlier years, most exports were of goods; an important recent trend is the globalization of services, such as travel, insurance, financial, and information services.

The acceleration of globalization has been driven by several factors:

- *Technological innovation:* Sophisticated software, Internet, fiber optics, wireless, and satellite technologies, among others, have made it easier and faster for companies to communicate with employees, partners, and suppliers all over the globe in real time. In the words of Thomas Friedman, the world has become increasingly "flat," as technology has leveled the playing field and allowed all to participate on an equal footing in global commerce.[5]

- *Transportation systems:* Improvements in transportation—from air freight, to high-speed rail, to new generations of oceangoing vessels—enable the fast and cheap movement of goods and services from one place to another.

- *The rise of major transnational corporations:* Big, well-capitalized firms are better equipped to conduct business across national borders than smaller, local companies.

- *Social and political reforms:* Critical changes, including the rise of dynamic growth economies on the Pacific Rim and the collapse of the former communist states of central and eastern Europe, have opened new regions to world trade.

---

[4] Current data on exports of goods and services as a percentage of gross domestic product are available at *www.devdata.worldbank.org.*

[5] Thomas Friedman, *The World Is Flat: A Brief History of the Twenty-First Century* (New York: Farrar, Straus and Giroux, 2005).

Volkswagen, Renault, Audi, and other European car companies have shifted much of their production across the former Iron Curtain that divided communist and noncommunist Europe, drawn by the availability of cheap skilled labor, from assemblers to engineers. The VW Touareg and Porsche Cayenne are now made in Slovakia, the Renault Logan in Romania, and the Audi TT roadster in Hungary. The Asian companies Toyota, Kia, and Suzuki have followed suit, also building cars in central and eastern Europe. The concentration of auto factories in the region has gone so far that some have begun to call it "Detroit East."[6]

Finally, the process of globalization has also been spurred by the rise of international financial and trade institutions that stabilize currencies and promote free trade. These institutions are discussed in the next section.

International Financial and Trade Institutions

Global commerce is carried out in the context of a set of important **international financial and trade institutions (IFTIs)**. The most important of these are the World Bank, the International Monetary Fund, and the World Trade Organization. By setting the rules by which international commerce is transacted, these institutions increasingly determine who wins and who loses in the global economy.

The **World Bank (WB)** was set up in 1944, near the end of World War II, to provide economic development loans to its member nations. Its main motivation at that time was to help rebuild the war-torn economies of Europe. Today, the World Bank is one of the world's largest sources of economic development assistance; it provided almost $25 billion in loans in 2008 for roads, dams, power plants, and other infrastructure projects, as well as for education, health, and social services. The bank gets its funds from dues paid by its member countries and from money it borrows in the international capital markets. Representation on the bank's governing board is based on economic power; that is, countries have voting power based on the size of their economies. Not surprisingly, the United States and other rich nations dominate the bank.

The World Bank often imposes strict conditions on countries that receive its loans, to make sure the debtor countries can pay back what they owe. These conditions, called *structural adjustment plans,* may include demands that governments cut spending, devalue their currencies, increase exports, liberalize financial markets, reduce wages, and remove agricultural price subsidies. These conditions often lead to hardship, particularly for the poor. Critics charge that developing countries are unfairly burdened by these conditions. They also say that poor countries are often hard pressed to pay back principal and interest on World Bank loans.

The World Bank's sister organization is the **International Monetary Fund (IMF)**. Founded at the same time as the bank (and today residing across the street from it in Washington, DC), the IMF has a somewhat narrower purpose: to make currency exchange easier for member countries so that they can participate in global trade. It does this by lending foreign exchange to member countries. Like the World Bank, the IMF imposes strict conditions on governments that receive its loans. Some observers think that over the years, the IMF has become even harsher than the World Bank in the conditions it imposes.

One country that has been particularly hard hit by IMF conditions is Jamaica, a developing island nation in the Caribbean. In exchange for IMF loans, Jamaica

---

[6] "Slovak Car Industry Set to Boost Output in 2008," *Reuters,* February 26, 2008; and "Detroit East: Eastern Europe Is Becoming the World's New Car Capital," *BusinessWeek,* August 1, 2005.

By the mid-2000s, many developing countries had accumulated huge debts to the World Bank, the IMF, and other lenders. The total amount of money owed was almost $3 trillion.

One of the unintended consequences of past loans was persistent poverty, because a large share of many nations' earnings went to pay off debt rather than to develop the economy or improve the lives of citizens. (Imagine an individual who accumulates a large credit card debt, and then has to use most of his income just to make payments, rather than saving money or buying things he needs now.) One of the troubling aspects about developing nations' debt was that in some cases the original loans never even helped the people of these countries. Some funds were used to buy arms, bolster oppressive regimes, or personally enrich dictators such as Marcos of the Philippines and Suharto of Indonesia.

Some people felt that developing nations ought to pay off their debts, just as individuals have to pay off their credit cards. But others believed that accumulated debt imposed such a huge burden on poor nations that if something was not done they would never be able to develop. Many activists—including the popular rock star Bono—advocated debt forgiveness. In this approach, international financial institutions would permit debtor nations to "declare bankruptcy" and start over. One of the best-known organizations advocating debt relief, Jubilee USA, took its name from a passage in the Old Testament that called for the forgiveness of debt every 50 years, on the occasion of a celebration called a *jubilee* at which the community celebrated its unity.

In 2005, the G-8 (the eight industrialized nations France, Germany, Italy, Japan, the United Kingdom, the United States, Canada, and Russia, as well as the European Union) called for the cancelation of debt owed by heavily indebted poor countries to the World Bank, IMF, and African Development Fund. By 2009, more than $70 billion in debt relief had been extended to 33 heavily indebted countries, and these nations' payments had been cut in half.

However, problems remained. Poor countries still owed billions, and the world financial crisis weakened their ability to pay. So-called *vulture funds* took advantage of this situation by buying up the debt of countries such as Zambia, Nicaragua, and Cameroon for pennies on the dollar and suing them to recover unpaid debts. A World Bank study found $1.8 billion in pending lawsuits against countries where people lived on less than $1 a day. Debt relief campaigners have called for legislation to shut down the vulture funds' activities.

Sources: For more information on recent debt reduction initiatives and on the Jubilee Debt Reduction Campaign, see *www.worldbank.org, www.imf.org,* and *www.jubileeusa.org*. Comprehensive statistics on external debt are available at *www.jedh.org*.

agreed to a number of conditions, including opening up its borders to free trade with other nations. The problem was that Jamaican dairy, poultry, vegetable, and fruit farmers were unable to compete with the United States, whose meat and produce were produced more efficiently by large agribusiness companies. The result was that many Jamaican farms failed, and the country became increasingly reliant on imports to feed its people. Jamaica fell into an increasing spiral of debt, its citizens became poorer, and the country found it increasingly difficult to repay its IMF loans.[7]

Recently, major lending organizations, including the IMF, have begun to extend **debt relief** to some poor nations, a subject that is explored in Exhibit 6.A.

The final member of the triumvirate of IFTIs is the **World Trade Organization (WTO)**. The WTO, founded in 1995 as a successor to the General Agreement on Tariffs and Trade (GATT), is an international body that establishes the ground rules for trade among nations. Most of the world's nations are members of the WTO, which is based in Switzerland. Its major objective is to promote free trade—that is, to eliminate barriers to trade among nations,

---

[7] *Life and Debt,* a film by Stephanie Black. For more information, see *www.lifeanddebt.org.*

Is trade among nations really free when governments aid their own producers? This issue has been at the heart of an ongoing dispute within the World Trade Organization over farm subsidies.

The European Union, the United States, and Japan all provide generous agricultural subsidies. In the mid to late 2000s, for example, the U.S. government paid farmers between $7 billion and $16 billion a year to support production of a range of commodities, including cotton, wheat, rice, and peanuts (the amount varied with the price of commodities each year). The farm lobby strongly backed these subsidies, which it said were necessary to protect the rural way of life. Critics, however, said that subsidies allowed farmers to "dump" their products on world markets at artificially reduced prices, competing unfairly with agricultural products from poor countries that could not afford similar support payments.

In the cotton industry, for example, every acre under cultivation in the United States received an annual government payment of around $230. Elimination of these payments, according to one economic analysis, would raise the world price of cotton by 26 percent. Particularly hurt by U.S. cotton subsidies were poor farmers in west and central Africa, where more than 10 million people depended on this crop for their livelihoods. In a painful irony, the U.S. government provided more dollars to its own cotton farmers than to all of Africa in the form of development aid.

In 2005, ruling on a complaint brought by Brazil with support from several African nations, the WTO declared that the United States and other countries would have to end their cotton subsidies. "These rulings are a triumph for developing countries and a warning bell for rich countries who consistently flout the rules at the WTO and whose unfair systems are creating misery and poverty for millions," said a representative of Oxfam International. The ruling did not put an end to the broader controversy over farm subsidies, however. Disagreements between rich and poor nations over the terms of agriculture trade were a main reason that the Doha round of WTO negotiations collapsed in 2008.

Sources: "The Doha Round . . . and Round . . . and Round," *The Economist,* August 2, 2008; "The Cotton Debate: A Global Industry Argues over Government Subsidies," *The National Peace Corps Association Worldview,* Fall 2005; "Busted: World Trade Watchdog Declares EU and U.S. Farm Subsidies Illegal," Oxfam International, September 9, 2004; "Cultivating Poverty: The Impact of U.S. Cotton Subsidies on Africa," Oxfam International, 2002, available online at *www.oxfam.org;* " "WTO Agreement on Agriculture: A Decade of Dumping," Institute for Agriculture and Trade Policy, 2005, available online at *www.globalpolicy.org.*

such as quotas, duties, and tariffs. Unlike the WB and the IMF, the WTO does not lend money or foreign exchange; it simply sets the rules for international trade. The WTO conducts multi-year negotiations, called *rounds,* on various trade-related topics, rotating its meetings among different cities. The most recent negotiations—called the Doha round, because they were launched in Doha, Quatar—collapsed in 2008, after negotiators were unable to reach agreement on a number of proposals to help the world's poor. An issue of great contention in the Doha round, involving agricultural subsidies, is profiled in Exhibit 6.B.

Under the WTO's most favored nation rule, member countries may not discriminate against foreign products for any reason. All import restrictions are illegal unless proven scientifically—for example, on the basis that a product is unsafe. If countries disagree about the interpretation of this or any other WTO rule, they can bring a complaint before the WTO's Dispute Settlement Body (DSB), a panel of appointed experts, which meets behind closed doors. In 2009, for example, China complained to the DSB that India had tried to ban imports of Chinese toys to protect its own toy industry, a possible violation of WTO rules.[8] Usually, member countries comply voluntarily with the DSB's rulings. If they do not, the DSB can allow the aggrieved nation to take retaliatory measures, such

---

[8] "China Upset about India Toy Ban, Likely to Ask WTO for Settlement," *BBC Monitoring Asia Pacific,* February 4, 2009.

as imposing tariffs.[9] Rulings are binding; the only way a decision can be overruled is if every member country opposes it.

These three international financial and trade institutions are important because no business can operate across national boundaries without complying with the rules set by the WTO, and many businesses in the developing world are dependent on World Bank and IMF loans for their very lifeblood. The policies these institutions adopt, therefore, have much to do with whether globalization is perceived as a positive or negative force, a subject to which we turn next.

The Benefits and Costs of Globalization

Globalization is highly controversial. One need only look at television coverage of angry protests at recent meetings of the World Trade Organization, World Bank, and International Monetary Fund to see that not all people and organizations believe that globalization—at least as currently practiced—is a positive force. Yet, many others feel that globalization holds tremendous potential for pulling nations out of poverty, spreading technological innovation, and allowing people everywhere to enjoy the bounty generated by modern business. Clearly, some benefit from globalization, while others do not. In this section, we present some of the arguments advanced by both sides in the debate over this important issue.

Benefits of Globalization

Proponents of globalization point to its many benefits. One of the most important of these is that globalization tends to increase economic productivity. That means, simply, that more is produced with the same effort.

Why should that be? As the economist David Ricardo first pointed out, productivity rises more quickly when countries produce goods and services for which they have a natural talent. He called this the *theory of comparative advantage*. Suppose, for example, that one country had a climate and terrain ideally suited for raising sheep, giving it an advantage in the production of wool and woolen goods. A second country had a favorable combination of iron, coal, and water power that allowed it to produce high-grade steel. The first country would benefit from trading its woolen goods for the second country's steel, and vice versa; and the world's economy overall would be more productive than if both countries had tried to make everything they needed for themselves. In other words, in the context of free trade, specialization (everyone does what they are best at) makes the world economy as a whole more efficient, so living standards rise.

Many countries today have developed a specialization in one or another skill or industry. India, with its excellent system of technical education, has become a world powerhouse in the production of software engineers. France and Italy, with their strong networks of skilled craftspeople and designers, are acknowledged leaders in the world's high fashion and footwear design industries. The United States, with its concentration of actors, directors, special effects experts, and screenwriters, is the global headquarters for the movie industry.

Comparative advantage can come from a number of possible sources, including natural resources; the skills, education, or experience of a critical mass of people; or an existing production infrastructure.

[9] Bruce Wilson, "Compliance by WTO Members with Adverse WTO Dispute Settlement Rulings: The Record to Date," *Journal of International Economic Law* 10, no. 2 (2007).

Globalization also tends to reduce prices for consumers. If a shopper in the United States goes into Walmart to buy a shirt, he or she is likely to find one at a very reasonable price. Walmart sources its apparel from all over the world, enabling it to push down production costs. Globalization also benefits consumers by giving them access to a wide range of diverse goods and the latest "big thing." Teenagers in Malaysia can enjoy the latest Tom Cruise or Will Smith movie, while American children can play with new Nintendo Wii games from Japan.

For the developing world, globalization also brings benefits. It helps entrepreneurs the world over by giving all countries access to foreign investment funds to support economic development. Globalization also transfers technology. In a competitive world marketplace, the best ideas and newest innovations spread quickly. Multinational corporations train their employees and partners how to make the fastest computer chips, the most productive food crops, and the most efficient lightbulbs. In many nations of the developing world, globalization has meant more manufacturing jobs in export sectors and training for workers eager to enhance their skills.

The futurist Allen Hammond identifies two additional benefits of globalization. First, he says that world trade has the potential of supporting the spread of democracy and freedom:

> The very nature of economic activity in free markets . . . requires broad access
> to information, the spread of competence, and the exercise of individual decision
> making throughout the workforce—conditions that are more compatible with free
> societies and democratic forms of government than with authoritarian regimes.[10]

Second, according to Hammond, global commerce can reduce military conflict by acting as a force that binds disparate peoples together on the common ground of business interaction. "Nations that once competed for territorial dominance," he writes, "will now compete for market share, with money that once supported military forces invested in new ports, telecommunications, and other infrastructure." In this view, global business can become both a stabilizing force and a conduit for Western ideas about democracy and freedom.

Costs of Globalization

If globalization has all these benefits, why are so many individuals and organizations so critical of it? The answer is complex. Just as some gain from globalization, others are hurt by it. From the perspective of its victims, globalization does not look nearly so attractive.

One of the costs of globalization is job insecurity. As businesses move manufacturing across national borders in search of cheaper labor, workers at home are laid off. Jobs in the domestic economy are lost as imports replace homemade goods and services.

> In the American South, tens of thousands of jobs in the textile industry have
> been lost over the past several decades, as jobs have shifted to low labor cost
> areas of the world, leaving whole communities devastated. In 2003, Pillowtex,
> the last remaining major textile company operating in the region, declared bank-
> ruptcy and shut down 16 plants, citing intense foreign competition. Pillowtex
> (formerly Fieldcrest Cannon) had at one time been the world's largest producer
> of household textiles like towels, sheets, and blankets.

---

[10] Allen Hammond, *Which World? Scenarios for the 21st Century* (Washington DC: Island Press, 1998), p. 30.

In the past, mainly manufacturing was affected by the shift of jobs abroad; today, clerical, white-collar, and professional jobs are, too. Many customer service calls originating in the United States are now answered by operators in the Philippines and India. The back office operations of many banks—sorting and recording check transactions, for example—are done in India and China. Aircraft manufacturers are using aeronautical specialists in Russia to design parts for new planes. By one estimate, as many as 3.3 million white-collar jobs will be outsourced from the United States to lower-wage countries by 2015.[11] Even when jobs are not actually relocated, wages may be driven down because companies facing foreign competition try to keep their costs in check. Much of the opposition to globalization in affluent nations comes from people who feel their own jobs, pay, and livelihoods threatened by workers abroad who can do their work more cheaply.

Not only workers in rich countries are affected by globalization. When workers in Indonesia began organizing for higher wages, Nike Corporation moved much of its production to Vietnam and China. Many Indonesian workers lost their jobs. Some call this feature of global capitalism the "race to the bottom."

Another cost of globalization is that environmental and labor standards may be weakened as companies seek manufacturing sites where regulations are most lax. Just as companies may desire locations offering the cheapest labor, they may also search for locations with few environmental protections; weak regulation of occupational health and safety, hours of work, and discrimination; and few rights for unions. For example, the so-called gold coast of southeastern China has become a world manufacturing center for many products, especially electronics. One journalist offered the following description of a young worker there:

> Pan Qing Mei hoists a soldering gun and briskly fastens chips and wires to motherboards streaming past on a conveyor belt. Fumes from the lead solder rise past her face toward a ventilating fan high above the floor of the spotless factory. Pan, a 23-year-old migrant worker, said the fumes made her lightheaded when she first arrived from a distant farm village three years ago. Now she's used to them—just as she's used to the marathon shifts, sometimes 18 hours a day.[12]

Weak health and safety and environmental regulations—and lax enforcement of the laws that do exist—are a major draw for the companies that manufacture in factories in China's industrial zones.

A related concern is that the World Trade Organization's most favored nation rules make it difficult for individual nations to adopt policies promoting environmental or social objectives, if these have the effect of discriminating against products from another country.

One incident that provoked considerable controversy involved protection for endangered sea turtles. In response to concerns voiced by consumers and environmentalists, the United States passed a law that required shrimp trawlers to use nets equipped with special devices that allowed turtles to escape. It also banned the import of wild shrimp from nations that did not require such devices. Shortly thereafter, Thailand, Pakistan, Malaysia, and India brought a complaint before the WTO, saying that the U.S. law violated trade rules by discriminating against their shrimp (which were caught without protection for sea turtles). The WTO ruled against the United States and ordered it to either change its law or pay compensation to the other nations for lost trade.

---

[11] "Is Your Job Next?" *BusinessWeek*, February 3, 2003, pp. 50–60.
[12] "Cheap Products' Human Cost," *San Jose Mercury News*, November 24, 2002.

Critics of globalization say that incidents such as this one show that free trade rules are being used to restrict the right of sovereign nations to make their own laws setting environmental or social standards for imported products.

Another cost of globalization is that it erodes regional and national cultures and undermines cultural, linguistic, and religious diversity. In other words, global commerce makes us all very much the same. Is a world in which everyone is drinking Coke, watching Hollywood movies, listening to an iPod, and wearing Gap jeans a world we want, or not? Some have argued that the deep **anti-Americanism** present in many parts of the world reflects resentment at the penetration of the values of dominant U.S.-based transnational corporations into every corner of the world.

With respect to the point that globalization promotes democracy, critics charge that market capitalism is just as compatible with despotism as it is with freedom. Indeed, transnational corporations are often drawn to nations that are governed by antidemocratic or military regimes, because they are so effective at controlling labor and blocking efforts to protect the environment. For example, Unocal's joint-venture collaboration to build a gas pipeline with the military government of Myanmar (Burma), a notorious abuser of human rights, may have brought significant financial benefits to the petroleum company.

Figure 6.2 summarizes the major points in the discussion about the costs and benefits of globalization.

What is public opinion on these issues? A survey of almost 10,000 people in 18 countries around the world in 2007 found that people in 14 countries thought that the free market economic system was best (people in Turkey, France, Russia, and Chile disagreed). Support for the free enterprise system had fallen somewhat from a survey taken two years earlier, perhaps reflecting growing instability in the world economy. At the same time, solid majorities in most countries also favored strong government regulations to protect the environment and the rights of workers, consumers, and shareholders. Although broad consensus about the free market system remained, most people polled felt it worked best when coupled with strong government oversight.[13]

This discussion raises the very real possibility that globalization may benefit the world economy as a whole, while simultaneously hurting many individuals and localities. An

FIGURE 6.2
Benefits and Costs of Globalization

Benefits of Globalization	Costs of Globalization
Increases economic productivity.	Causes job insecurity.
Reduces prices for consumers.	Weakens environmental and labor standards.
Gives developing countries access to foreign investment funds to support economic development.	Prevents individual nations from adopting policies promoting environmental or social objectives, if these discriminate against products from another country.
Transfers technology.	Erodes regional and national cultures and undermines cultural, linguistic, and religious diversity.
Spreads democracy and freedom, and reduces military conflict.	Is compatible with despotism.

[13] The full survey results are available at *www.worldpublicopinion.org.*

ongoing challenge to business, government, and society is to find ways to extend the benefits of globalization to all, while mitigating its adverse effects.[14]

Doing Business in a Diverse World

Doing business in other nations is much more than a step across a geographical boundary; it is a step into different social, political, cultural, and economic realities. As shown in Chapters 1 and 2, even businesses operating in one community or one nation cannot function successfully without considering a wide variety of stakeholder needs and interests. When companies operate globally, the number of stakeholders to be considered in decision making, and the diversity of their interests, increases dramatically.

Comparative Political and Economic Systems

The many nations of the world differ greatly in their political, social, and economic systems. One important dimension of this diversity is how power is exercised—that is, the degree to which a nation's people may freely exercise their democratic rights. **Democracy** refers broadly to the presence of political freedom. Arthur Lewis, a Nobel laureate in economics, described it this way: "The primary meaning of democracy is that all who are affected by a decision should have the right to participate in making that decision, either directly or through chosen representatives." According to the United Nations, democracy has four defining features:[15]

- Fair elections, in which citizens may freely choose their leaders from among candidates representing more than one political party.
- Independent media, in which journalists and citizens may express their political views without fear of censorship or punishment.
- Separation of powers among the executive, legislative, and judicial branches of government.
- An open society where citizens have the right to form their own independent organizations to pursue social, religious, and cultural goals.

One of the truly remarkable facts about the past century has been the spread of democratic rights for the first time to many nations around the world. Consider, for example, that at the beginning of the 20th century *no* country in the world had universal suffrage (all citizens could vote); today, the majority of countries do. One hundred and forty of the world's nearly 200 countries now hold multiparty elections, the highest number ever. The collapse of communist party rule in the former Soviet Union and its satellites in eastern and central Europe in the early 1990s was followed by the first open elections ever in these countries. These changes have led some observers to call the end of the 20th century the "third wave of democracy."

On the other hand, many countries still lack basic democratic rights. Single-party rule by communist parties remains a reality in China, Vietnam, Cuba, and the People's Democratic Republic of Korea (North Korea). **Military dictatorships**, that is, repressive regimes ruled by dictators who exercise total power through control of the armed forces,

[14] For recent arguments for and against globalization, and on strategies to make the world's governing institutions more effective, see Jagdish Bhagwati, *In Defense of Globalization* (New York: Oxford University Press, 2007); and Joseph E. Stiglitz, *Making Globalization Work* (New York: W.W. Norton, 2007).

[15] United Nations Development Programme, *Human Development Report 2000* (New York: Oxford University Press, 2000), ch. 3, "Inclusive Democracy Secures Rights," pp. 56–71. The quotation from Arthur Lewis appears on p. 56.

are in place in, among others, Myanmar, Sudan, Uzbekistan, and Eritrea.[16] The rights of women to full societal participation—and the rights of all citizens to organize in support of cultural and religious goals—are restricted in a number of Arab states, including Iran, Syria, and Saudi Arabia. According to United Nations estimates, 106 countries still limit important civil and political freedoms.

Even in some countries that are formally democratic, people perceive that they have little influence on policy. A survey of citizens in 65 countries conducted by Gallup International showed that only about a third said their country was "governed by the will of the people," even though most of these countries held open elections.[17]

The degree to which human rights are protected also varies widely across nations. *Human rights*, introduced in Chapter 4, refer broadly to the rights and privileges accorded to all people, simply by virtue of being human—for example, the rights to a decent standard of living, free speech, religious freedom, and due process of law, among others. Fundamental human rights have been codified in a number of international agreements, the most important of which is the Universal Declaration of Human Rights of 1948.[18] The second half of the 20th century was a period of great advances in human rights in many regions, and over half of the world's nations have now ratified *all* of the United Nations' human right covenants. Nonetheless, many human rights problems remain. Consider the following examples:

- Almost 10 million children die each year before their fifth birthday. Most of these deaths are preventable.[19]
- Gross violations of human rights have not been eliminated. *Genocide*, mass murder of innocent civilians, has occurred all too recently in Rwanda, Iraq, Bosnia and Herzegovina, the Congo, and Sudan.
- Close to 1 million people are trafficked into forced labor every year. Eighty percent of these are women and girls, most of whom are forced into prostitution.[20]
- Minority groups and indigenous peoples in many nations still lack basic political and social rights. In Nepal, the life expectancy of "untouchables," the lowest caste, is fully 15 years less than that of Brahmins, the highest caste.

The absence of key human rights in many nations remains a significant issue for companies transacting business there. The challenge facing Google, as it debated whether or not to establish a search service in China—a country with serious human rights concerns, including censorship of the Internet—is presented in a case at the end of this book.

Another dimension of difference among nations today is how economic assets are controlled—that is, the degree of economic freedom. On one end of the continuum are societies in which assets are privately owned and exchanged in a free and open market. Such **free enterprise systems** are based on the principle of voluntary association and exchange. In such a system, people with goods and services to sell take them voluntarily to the marketplace, seeking to exchange them for money or other goods or services. Political and economic freedoms are related: as people gain more control over government decisions

---

[16] For profiles of the dictators of these nations, see David Wallechinsky, "*Parade's* Annual List of the World's 10 Worst Dictators," *Parade,* February 15, 2009.

[17] For the most recent Gallup "Voice of the People" poll data, see *www.voice-of-the-people.net.*

[18] For more information on the Universal Declaration of Human Rights and other United Nations agreements on human rights, see the Web site of the U.N. High Commissioner for Human Rights at *www.unhchr.ch.*

[19] United Nations Children's Fund (UNICEF) data on child mortality are available online at *www.childinfo.org.*

[20] Data are available at *www.humantrafficking.org.*

Exhibit 6.C

China: A Case of Authoritarian Capitalism?

Democracy, a *political* system in which citizens choose their own leaders and may openly express their ideas, and capitalism, an *economic* system in which the means of creating wealth are privately owned and controlled, have historically often developed in tandem. The two are not always coupled, however. During the early years of the 20th century, for example, capitalism coexisted with nondemocratic, fascist governments in Germany, Spain, and Japan. More recently, scholars have coined the term "authoritarian capitalism" to refer to modern states that combine elements of a market economy with political control by nonelected elites. A prime example is China. In its drive for economic development, the Chinese government has granted considerable freedom to private individuals to own property, invest, and innovate. The result has been very rapid growth in much of the country over the past two decades. At the same time, the Chinese communist authorities have vigorously held onto political power and suppressed dissent. In what direction will China and other authoritarian capitalist nations evolve in the future? "Some believe these countries could ultimately become liberal democracies through a combination of internal development, increasing affluence, and outside influence," commented political scientist Azar Gat. "Alternatively, they may have enough weight to create a new nondemocratic but economically advanced Second World."

Sources: Azar Gat, "The Return of the Authoritarian Capitalists," *International Herald Tribune,* June 14, 2007; and "The Return of Authoritarian Great Powers," *Foreign Affairs,* July/August 2007.

they often press for greater economic opportunity; open markets may give people the resources to participate effectively in politics. But this is not always the case. The particular situation of China with respect to political and economic freedom is explored in Exhibit 6.C.

At the other end of the continuum are systems of **central state control**, in which economic power is concentrated in the hands of government officials and political authorities. The central government owns the property that is used to produce goods and services. Private ownership may be forbidden or greatly restricted, and most private markets are illegal. Very few societies today operate on the basis of strict central state control of the economy. More common is a system of mixed free enterprise and central state control in which some industries are state controlled, and others are privately owned. For example, in Nigeria, the oil industry is controlled by a government-owned enterprise that operates in partnership with foreign companies such as Shell and Chevron, but many other industries are privately controlled. In the social democracies of Scandinavia, such as Norway, the government operates some industries but not others. In the United States, the government temporarily took partial ownership in some banks, including Citigroup, as they faltered during the financial crisis.

The Heritage Foundation, a conservative think tank, has scored the nations of the world according to an *index of economic freedom* defined as "the fundamental rights of every human being to control his or her own labor and property." In economically free societies, governments "refrain from coercion or restraint of liberty beyond the extent necessary to protect and maintain liberty itself." Among the freest nations in 2009, by this measure, were Hong Kong, Singapore, and Australia; among the most repressed were Cuba, Zimbabwe, and—the least free in the world—North Korea.[21]

Nations also differ greatly in their overall levels of economic and social development. Ours is a world of great inequalities. To cite just one simple measure, the richest 1 percent

[21] Available at *www.heritage.org.*

of people in the world receive as much income annually as the poorest 57 percent. The lives of a software engineer in Canada, say, and a subsistence farmer in Mali (in central Africa) could not be more different. The engineer would have a life expectancy of 80 years, access to excellent medical care, and a comfortable home in an affluent suburb. His children would likely be healthy, and they could look forward to a college education. The farmer, by contrast, could expect to live only to age 53, probably could not read or write, and would earn an annual income of around $1,000 (U.S.)—in good years when his crops did not fail. He would likely not have access to clean drinking water, and his children would be poorly nourished and unprotected by vaccination against common childhood illnesses. Several of his children would die before reaching adulthood.[22] Even as the world has become freer politically and economically, inequality has grown; the gaps between the richest and poorest nations are rising, as are gaps between the richest and poorest people in many nations.

Meeting the Challenges of Global Diversity

As the preceding discussion suggests, transnational corporations today do business in a world of staggering diversity and complexity. Not surprisingly, the wide range of political, social, and economic environments in which business operates poses complex and challenging questions for managers, such as the following, for example:

- If a company does business in a nation that does not grant women equal rights, such as Saudi Arabia, for example, should that company hire and promote women at work, even if this violates local laws or customs?
- Should a company enter into a business joint venture with a government-owned enterprise if that government has a reputation for violating the human rights of its own citizens? For example, Unocal, mentioned earlier in this chapter, was criticized and later successfully sued for entering into a joint venture with the repressive military government of Myanmar.
- Does a company have a duty to offer its products or services—say, life-saving medication—at a lower price in poor countries like Mali, or to customers who desperately need them?
- If a government fails to provide basic services to its citizens, such as primary education, decent housing, and sanitation services, is it the duty of a company to provide these things for its own employees or for members of the community in which it is located? This question is particularly likely to arise for companies in extractive industries, such as oil, natural gas, and metal mining, where production may be located far from established communities.

Many people believe that when transnational corporations operate according to strong moral principles, they can become a force for positive change in other nations where they operate. This is known as **constructive engagement**. In some situations, however, constructive engagement may not be possible. At what point do violations of political, human, and economic rights become so extreme that companies simply cannot morally justify doing business in a country any more?

The experience of Shell Oil in Nigeria illustrates this dilemma. Shell entered into a joint venture with the Nigerian government, then ruled by a military dictator, to produce and export oil. Citizens of the oil-producing regions organized to

---

[22] Profiles derived from human development statistics published annually by the United Nations Development Programme.

protest Shell's behavior, charging that the company had despoiled the environment, failed to provide services to the community adequately, and not hired enough indigenous people from the local area. In response, the Nigerian government imposed martial law and arrested the leaders of the protest. Civilians were killed, and several leaders of the protest were executed after military tribunals where they were not given the right to defend themselves. Should Shell have intervened? Was Shell responsible for what the government did? Should Shell have provided basic services in the oil-producing regions that the government had not? Should Shell leave Nigeria, or try to work with the government and communities there to improve conditions in the oil-producing regions?

In this situation, Shell decided not to take a public stance against the government's actions, on the grounds that it should "stay out of politics." The company was strenuously criticized for this and later had to rethink its position on political action. Eventually, Shell announced that it had changed its view and was prepared to make known to governments its position on political matters, such as this one, that affected the company or its stakeholders. It also took action to better protect the environment and to train its managers in human rights principles.

Like Shell, many companies face ongoing dilemmas deciding how to respond to conditions in repressive nations. The next chapter discusses a number of codes of conduct that transnational companies have used to help guide their actions.

Collaborative Partnerships for Global Problem Solving

As the preceding section suggested, doing business in a diverse world is exceptionally challenging for businesses. One solution to the challenging questions facing transnational corporations is to approach them collectively, through a collaborative process. An emerging trend is the development of collaborative, multi-sector partnerships focused on particular social issues or problems in the global economy. This final section of Chapter 6 describes this approach.

A Three-Sector World

The term *sector* refers to broad divisions of a whole. In this context, it refers to major parts or spheres of society, such as business (the private sector), government (the public sector), and civil society. **Civil society** comprises nonprofit, educational, religious, community, family, and interest-group organizations—that is, social organizations that do not have a commercial or governmental purpose.

The process of globalization has spurred development of civil society. In recent decades, the world has witnessed the creation and growth of large numbers of **nongovernmental organizations (NGOs)** concerned with such issues as environmental risk, labor practices, worker rights, community development, and human rights. (NGOs are also called *civil society organizations* or *civil sector organizations*.) The number of NGOs accredited by the United Nations has soared in recent years, rising from 1,000 in 1996 to more than 3,000 in 2008. This figure counts just major organizations.[23] Worldwide, the total number of international NGOs is estimated to be around 21,000.[24] (Many more NGOs operate regionally or locally.)

---

[23] Data available at *www.un.org/esa*.

[24] *Global Civil Society 2009* (London: Sage Publications, 2009), Table 9.1.

Experts attribute the growth of NGOs to several factors, including the new architecture of global economic and political relationships. As the Cold War has ended, with democratic governments replacing dictatorships, greater openness has emerged in many societies. More people, with more views, are free to express their pleasure or displeasure with government, business, or one another. NGOs form around specific issues or broad concerns (environment, human rights) and become voices that must be considered in the public policy debates that ensue.

Recent research has recognized that each of the three major sectors—business, government, and civil society—has distinctive resources and competencies, as well as weaknesses. For example, businesses have access to capital, specialized technical knowledge, networks of commercial relationships, and the management skills to get projects completed on time and on budget. On the other hand, businesses tend to disregard the impacts of their actions on others, especially in the long term. For their part, government agencies have knowledge of public policy, an ability to enforce rules, and revenue from taxation, but are often inflexible, slow to mobilize, and poorly coordinated. Finally, NGOs often enjoy strong community knowledge, volunteer assets, and inspirational leaders, but may lack financial resources and technical skill and may suffer from a narrow, parochial focus.[25] One model highlighting various attributes of actors in the business, government, and civil society sectors is presented in Figure 6.3.

Many businesses have realized that these differences across sectors can be a resource to be exploited. In this view, alliances among organizations from the three sectors, **collaborative partnerships**, can draw on the unique capabilities of each and overcome particular weaknesses that each has.

The opening example of this chapter illustrated a failed effort by a transnational corporation to modernize the water utility in a developing country. Contrast that example with the following more successful one, in which a company used a collaborative partnership strategy:

FIGURE 6.3
Distinctive Attributes of the Three Major Sectors

Source: Adapted from Steven Waddell, "Core Competences: A Key Force in Business-Government-Civil Society Collaborations," *Journal of Corporate Citizenship*, Autumn 2002, pp. 43–56, Tables 1 and 2. Used by permission.

	Business	Government	Civil Society
Organizational form	For-profit	Governmental	Nonprofit
Goods produced	Private	Public	Group
Primary control agent	Owners	Voters/rulers	Communities
Primary power form	Money	Laws, police, fines	Traditions, values
Primary goals	Wealth creation	Societal order	Expression of values
Assessment frame	Profitability	Legality	Justice
Resources	Capital assets, technical knowledge, production skills	Tax revenue, policy knowledge, regulatory and enforcement power	Community knowledge, inspirational leadership
Weaknesses	Short-term focus, lack of concern for external impacts	Bureaucratic, slow-moving, poorly coordinated internally	Amateurish, lack of financial resources, parochial perspective

[25] This paragraph draws on Steven Waddell, "Core Competences: A Key Force in Business-Government-Civil Society Collaborations," *Journal of Corporate Citizenship*, Autumn 2002, pp. 43–56. See also Jonathan Cohen, "State of the Union: NGO-Business Partnership Stakeholders," in *Unfolding Stakeholder Thinking II*, ed. Joerg Andriof et al. (Sheffield, UK: Greenleaf Publishing, 2003), pp. 106–27.

A collaborative partnership formed to bring water and sanitation services to some of the poorest regions of South Africa. Ondeo (formerly Suez-Lyonnaise), a French transnational corporation, brought its expertise in designing and managing large-scale water works. Group 5, a local construction company, brought construction know-how. The government agency in charge of water services provided public funding and staff for regulation and monitoring. A local NGO called the Mvula Trust, headed by a former antiapartheid crusader who had turned his attention to economic development after the overthrow of the racist regime, mobilized the community to define what services were needed and later to help maintain the system. All three groups worked together, drawing on the special talents of each in service of a single goal. This successful collaboration has brought running water and sanitation to many rural communities.[26]

Collaborative partnerships, like this one, carry a number of important advantages for transnational companies. They can enlist the special skills of governments and communities, educate the company about stakeholder expectations, and ensure that a particular project is consistent with local norms and values. Other applications of the principle of cross-sector collaborations are explored in Chapters 11 and 18.

The process of globalization presents today's business leaders with both great promise and great challenge. Despite the global economic downturn and the ever-present threat of war and terrorism, the world's economy continues to become more integrated and interdependent. Transnational corporations, with their financial assets and technical and managerial skills, have a great contribution to make to human betterment. Yet, they must operate in a world of great diversity, and in which their presence is often distrusted or feared. Often, they must confront situations in which political and economic freedoms are lacking and human rights are routinely violated. The challenge facing forward-looking companies today is how to work collaboratively with stakeholders to promote social and economic justice, while still achieving strong bottom-line results.

Summary

- Globalization refers to the increasing movement of goods, services, and capital across national borders. Firms can enter and compete in the global marketplace by exporting products and services; locating operations in another country; or buying raw materials, components, or supplies from sellers abroad.

- The process of globalization is driven by technological innovation, improvements in transportation, the rise of major multinational corporations, and social and political reforms.

- Globalization brings both benefits and costs. On one hand, it has the potential to pull nations out of poverty, spread innovation, and reduce prices for consumers. On the other hand, it may also produce job loss, reduce environmental and labor standards, and erode national cultures. An ongoing challenge is to extend the benefits of globalization to all, while mitigating its adverse effects.

- Multinational corporations operate in nations that vary greatly in their political, social, and economic systems. They face the challenge of deciding how to do business in other nations, while remaining true to their values.

- Businesses can work with governments and civil society organizations around the world in collaborative partnerships that draw on the unique capabilities of each to address common problems.

[26] Business Partnerships for Development, "Flexibility by Design: Lessons from Multi-Sector Partnerships in Water and Sanitation Projects," available at *www.bpd-waterandsanitation.org.*

Key Terms	anti-Americanism, *134*	foreign direct investment	military dictatorships, *135*
	central state control, *137*	(FDI), *126*	nongovernmental
	civil society, *139*	free enterprise system, *136*	organizations
	collaborative	globalization, *125*	(NGOs), *139*
	partnership, *140*	international financial and	transnational corporation
	constructive	trade institution	(TNC), *126*
	engagement, *138*	(IFTI), *128*	World Bank, *128*
	debt relief, *129*	International Monetary	World Trade Organization
	democracy, *135*	Fund (IMF), *128*	(WTO), *129*

Internet Resources	http://en.wordpress.com/tag/globalization	Blogs on globalization and related topics
	www.globalpolicy.org	Global Policy Forum
	www.ifg.org	International Forum on Globalization
	www.imf.org	International Monetary Fund
	www.thomaslfriedman.com	Web site of author and columnist Thomas L. Friedman
	www.unglobalcompact.org/ParticipantsAndStakeholders/civil_society	United Nations Global Compact and Nongovernmental Organizations
	www.un.org/en/civilsociety	United Nations and Civil Society
	www.worldbank.org	World Bank
	www.wto.org	World Trade Organization

Discussion Case: *Conflict Diamonds and the Kimberley Process*

In the 2000s, a common concern emerged among members of an oddly matched group: the diamond industry, the United Nations, several governments, and human rights campaigners. All wished to end the trade in *conflict diamonds*—gemstones that are mined or stolen by rebels fighting internationally recognized governments. To do so, they embarked on an unusual collaboration called the Kimberley Process.

In the 1990s, events in several diamond-rich African nations converged to tarnish the gemstone's carefully cultivated image of love and purity. Combatants in civil wars began to seize control of valuable mineral resources to finance their operations. The situation was particularly gruesome in Sierra Leone, a small nation in West Africa, which was devastated by civil war for much of the 1990s. A journalist who covered the war there described the methods of the Revolutionary United Front (RUF), the rebel force:

> The RUF's whole mode of operation was just to roll into a village that had a diamond mining operation. . . . What made the RUF stand out as a brutal organization was their campaign of amputation. That served no strategic purpose but to terrorize the population. Little children, women, men had their hands and arms chopped off as if they were wood.

By some estimates, the RUF mutilated as many as 20,000 people in Sierra Leone in this manner. Needless to say, the rebels quickly secured control of the mines, and they began selling rough diamonds in exchange for weapons, food, and other supplies.

Similar stories emerged from Angola and the Democratic Republic of the Congo, other African nations with active civil wars and considerable diamond wealth. In Angola alone, the UNITA rebels were reported to have built up a war chest of almost $4 billion during the 1990s from the sale of diamonds, which they used to fund a sophisticated military operation. By some estimates, as many as 6 million civilians were forced from their homes and 3.7 million died in these African conflicts.

By the mid-1990s, several human rights organizations had begun to spread the word about these atrocities. In 1998, Global Witness, a British NGO, issued a report called *A Rough Trade* estimating that up to 8 percent of the world's diamonds were coming from conflict areas. It joined with other NGOs, including Amnesty International and Oxfam, in a campaign to alert the public to the issue of conflict diamonds.

The United Nations also acted; its Security Council passed a resolution in 2000 prohibiting the import of diamonds from Sierra Leone until a process could be set up to certify they did not come from the RUF. The governments of several countries with legitimate diamond industries, including Botswana, South Africa, Namibia, Canada, and Australia, also expressed concern that their economies would be hurt.

Countries with large retail operations were worried about the possible impact of lost sales. The United Kingdom's foreign minister, for example, told the press, "We want to ensure that if somebody goes to buy a diamond from a jeweler's shop, they know that when they put it on the finger of their loved one, they are not pledging a diamond that has cut off the finger of a child in Sierra Leone or Angola."

The De Beers Corporation, the world's leading seller of diamonds, reacted swiftly and decisively to these events. In 1999 the company suspended all buying operations in west and central Africa and, shortly thereafter, stopped buying diamonds from any mines outside its own direct control. In 2000, a De Beers representative appeared before a U.S. Congressional hearing and readily acknowledged that conflict diamonds were a problem: "Having spent hundreds of millions of dollars on advertising its product, De Beers is deeply concerned about anything that could damage the image of diamonds as a symbol of love, beauty, and purity."

Shortly thereafter, the industry association, the World Diamond Congress, passed a resolution banning conflict diamonds. It also took the unusual step of establishing a new organization, called the World Diamond Council, to bring together diamond companies, government representatives, and other interested parties. In 2003, their joint efforts led to the development of what became known as the Kimberley Process (KP) Certification Scheme, a system for tracking diamonds all the way from the mine to the jewelry shop, so that consumers could be assured that their gems were "conflict-free."

Under Kimberley Process rules, every rough (uncut) diamond that crossed an international border had to be sealed in a numbered, tamper-proof container with a government-issued certificate saying it had come from a legitimate source. Diamonds could pass only from one member nation to another. In this way, a chain of custody could be established to keep conflict diamonds out of the market for gemstones. By 2009, 74 diamond-producing countries, accounting for virtually all of the world's rough diamond production, had endorsed the Kimberley Process.

Although human rights activists praised the progress that had been made, some also pointed to possible loopholes. In 2008, Global Witness and Partnership Africa Canada, another NGO, called for the suspension of Zimbabwe, charging that revenue from the diamond trade was helping prop up the violent regime of Robert Mugabe. They also said that the Kimberley Process largely ignored the diamond cutting and polishing industry, providing an entry point for conflict gems. Another problem was that some diamonds were apparently being smuggled from conflict zones into Kimberley member countries, from where they could enter the chain of custody. A particular concern was the border between the Côte d'Ivoire—a known hot spot for conflict diamonds—and Ghana, a Kimberley participant.

Other NGOs called for more direct civil society participation in monitoring the diamond trade. "Many KP member governments are not meaningfully engaging civil society organizations in . . . their home countries," said Alfred Brownell of the organization Green Advocates in Liberia. "We in West Africa are a long haul away from prosperity diamonds."

Sources: Greg Campbell, *Blood Diamonds: Tracing the Deadly Path of the World's Most Precious Stones* (Boulder, CO: Westview Press, 2002); Global Witness, "Loopholes in the Kimberley Process," October 2007; and articles appearing online at: *www.cnn.com, www.nytimes.com, www.salon.com, www.fpa.org, www.worlddiamondcouncil.com, www.diamondfacts.org, www.un.org/peace/africa,* and *www.globalwitness.org.*

Discussion Questions

1. What are conflict diamonds? What groups benefited from the trade in conflict diamonds? What groups were hurt by it?
2. What three sectors were concerned with the problem of conflict diamonds? What was the interest of each, and in what ways did their interests converge?
3. Do you believe that any of these three sectors could have addressed the problem of conflict diamonds unilaterally? Why or why not?
4. What are the possible weaknesses in the Kimberley Process? What role do you think the three sectors will have in addressing these weaknesses?

CHAPTER SEVEN

Global Corporate Citizenship

As businesses have become increasingly global, so have their interactions with society. Global corporate citizenship refers to putting an organization's commitment to social and environmental responsibility into practice worldwide, not only locally or regionally. Like corporate social responsibility, discussed in Chapter 3, global corporate citizenship involves building positive relationships with stakeholders, discovering business opportunities in serving society, and transforming a concern for financial performance into a vision of integrated financial *and* social and environmental performance, but on a much broader scale. Establishing effective structures and processes to meet a company's global corporate citizenship responsibilities, assess results, and report them to the public is an important part of the job of today's managers.

This Chapter Focuses on These Key Learning Objectives:

- Defining global corporate citizenship.
- Understanding how the multiple dimensions of corporate citizenship progress through a series of stages.
- Assessing how corporate citizenship differs among various countries and regions of the world.
- Understanding how business or social groups can audit corporate citizenship activities and report their findings to stakeholders.
- Recognizing how an organization communicates its corporate citizenship practices and manifests its attention to the balanced scorecard and triple bottom line approaches.

Novo Nordisk is a multinational health care company, based in Denmark, dedicated to the treatment of diabetes. It conducts research and markets a range of products, including synthetic insulin and delivery devices—such as a "pen" that diabetics can use to inject medicine more comfortably. Novo Nordisk has publicly committed "to conduct its activities in a financially, environmentally, and socially responsible way." The company is publicly owned, and it seeks to produce high returns for investors. But it is equally committed to social and environmental responsibility. Many of the company's citizenship initiatives are linked to its core mission of fighting diabetes. For example, as part of its "Take Action!" project, Novo Nordisk employees visit schools around the world to work with teachers to promote exercise and healthful eating—practices that can cut down the incidence of adult-onset diabetes. The company constantly monitors its environmental impacts; for example, an initiative was designed to reduce the adverse effects of pharmaceuticals excreted in the urine—potentially a danger to aquatic life when these chemicals enter the sewage system and are eventually discharged into waterways. The company calls its holistic approach the "Novo Nordisk Way of Management."[1]

CEMEX, founded in Mexico in 1906, is a growing global building materials company that provides high-quality products and reliable service to customers and communities throughout the Americas, Europe, Africa, the Middle East, Asia, and Australia, maintaining trade relationships with more than 100 countries. Embedded in its mission is a commitment to be an exemplary global citizen by advancing the quality of life of those served through its efforts. CEMEX was concerned that many Mexican citizens work temporarily in the United States to earn money they hope to use to build a home for the benefit of their families in Mexico. However, these immigrants face a catch-22. The problem is that most U.S. banks will not lend money for home construction outside the United States, while most Mexican banks will not lend money to people who are not living in Mexico. CEMEX addressed this problem through a program called Construmex, which offers home construction loans of up to $50,000, under flexible terms, to Mexicans in the United States for home construction in their homeland—enough money, in most cases, to build a dwelling comfortable by local standards. In Mexico, the company developed an initiative called *Patrimonio Hoy* that organizes low-income families into self-financing units to promote self-construction in Mexico's disadvantaged areas through micro-credit and technical assistance. "We are granting credit to those who apparently are not creditworthy," said Luis Enrique Martinez, a CEMEX representative. "But the most important thing is that we are providing people an opportunity to start building some wealth, to participate in the formal economy and, of course, to help make their dreams a reality."[2] CEMEX hopes that the program can spread into U.S. cities with more than 100,000 first-generation Mexicans.

This chapter introduces the concept of global corporate citizenship and explains how companies around the world, such as Novo Nordisk, CEMEX, and others, have organized themselves to carry out their citizenship responsibilities. It provides examples of what leading-edge companies are doing to put social and environmental responsibility into practice. This chapter also addresses the emerging practice of social auditing, a

---

[1] More information about Novo Nordisk's Way of Management is available online at *www.novonordisk.com.*

[2] "CEMEX's Construmex Celebrates Five Years of Service to the Mexican Community in the U.S.," press release, June 6, 2006; "Work in the States, Build a Life in Mexico," *BusinessWeek,* July 18, 2005, p. 64; "Construmex: Constructing Bridges between the United States and Mexico," *ReVista,* Fall 2006, pp. 29–31; and Bryan Husted and David B. Allen, "Creating Competitive Advantage through Corporate Social Strategy," paper presented at the international annual meeting of the Academy of Management, Honolulu, Hawaii, August 2005. We are grateful to Bryan Husted for bringing this example to our attention.

method for measuring and assessing corporate social performance, and reporting these results to the public.

Global Corporate Citizenship

The term **global corporate citizenship** refers to putting an organization's commitment to social and environmental responsibility into practice worldwide, not only locally or regionally. It entails putting corporate social responsibility into practice by proactively building stakeholder partnerships, discovering business opportunities in serving society, and transforming a concern for financial performance into a vision of integrated financial *and* social performance.[3] Corporate citizenship has become increasingly global in scope, reflecting the global nature of commerce and emerging awareness of the worldwide scope of many social issues. Since corporations are not *global* citizens, but citizens of a single country, the notion of citizenship takes on more all-encompassing meanings ranging from indirect involvement in various community or environmental organizations to explicit and aggressive leadership in addressing societal problems on a global scale.[4]

Roberto Civita, chairman and chief executive officer of the Brazilian Abril Group, has defined global corporate citizenship as "capitalism with a social conscience." According to many business leaders, global corporate citizenship used to be simple and optional. Now, a decade into the 21st century, it has become complicated and mandatory. This is because global markets, lightning-quick access to information, and heightened stakeholder expectations have compelled organizations of all sizes to establish an "integrated global corporate citizenship strategy" as part of their overall business plan.[5]

One way that many businesses carry out their citizenship mission is to think creatively about how to develop products and services that meet the needs of the world's poor—sometimes called selling to the **bottom of the pyramid,** as shown in Exhibit 7.A.

A compelling argument in favor of corporate citizenship was made by N. Craig Smith, Chair in Ethics and Social Responsibility at INSEAD, France:

> . . . mounting evidence suggests that good corporate citizenship can pay handsome dividends both in terms of profitability and global reputation. As a specific example, GE has poured vast resources into its "ecomagination" initiative—developing energy-efficient and environmentally friendly products and services—and the push has paid off with revenues of more than $17 billion. More broadly speaking, companies such as Unilever are offering base-of-the-pyramid initiatives that will give the world's poorest people a chance to become both consumers and producers.[6]

---

[3] See Barbara W. Altman and Deborah Vidaver-Cohen, "A Framework for Understanding Corporate Citizenship," *Business and Society Review,* Spring 2000, pp. 1–7. An understanding of corporate citizenship as embedded in a "liberal view of citizenship" is presented by Dirk Matten and Andrew Crane in "Corporate Citizenship: Toward an Extended Theoretical Conceptualization," *Academy of Management Review,* 2005, pp. 166–79. The concept of global citizenship grounded in voluntary codes of conduct is developed by Jeanne M. Logsdon and Donna J. Wood in "Global Business Citizenship and Voluntary Codes of Ethical Conduct," *Journal of Business Ethics,* 2005, pp. 55–67.

[4] See Jeremy Moon, Andrew Crane, and Dirk Matten, "Can Corporations Be Citizens?" *Business Ethics Quarterly,* 2005, pp. 429–53. Also see Donna J. Wood, Jeanne Logsdon, Patsy G. Lewellyn, and Kim Davenport, *Global Business Citizenship: A Transformative Framework for Ethics and Sustainable Capitalism* (Armonk, NY: M.E. Sharpe, 2006).

[5] "Corporate Citizenship on the Rise," New Futures Media, *www.NewFuturesMedia.com.*

[6] N. Craig Smith, "On Ethics and Social Responsibility," *BizEd,* May/June 2008, p. 28.

Exhibit 7.A

Poverty as a Business Opportunity

The term "bottom of the pyramid" refers to the poorest people in the world—the 4 billion or so who earn less than $1,500 a year. C. K. Prahalad argues in his book *The Fortune at the Bottom of the Pyramid* that this group represents an incredible business opportunity. Although the poor earn little individually, collectively they represent a vast market—and they often pay a "poverty premium," creating an opening for companies able to deliver quality products at lower prices. Casas Bahia, a retail chain in Brazil that specializes in durable goods such as refrigerators, televisions, and washing machines, has carved out a profitable business selling to poor residents of urban slums. Buyers are carefully screened, then required to come back monthly to their local store to make cash installment payments. The default rate is low, and Casas Bahia develops fiercely loyal customers who often become repeat buyers. In South Africa, the French food company Group Danone sells individual packages of vitamin-fortified yogurt for about one rand (about 14 cents) through a network of saleswomen—providing low-cost nutrition as well as work opportunities. Hindustan Lever Ltd. (Unilever's Indian subsidiary) sells antibacterial soap, iodized salt, shampoo, and other badly needed products to the rural poor—and educates buyers about health and hygiene. Many businesses are learning that focusing on the bottom of the pyramid can foster social development and provide employment in underserved communities—and reap profits.

Sources: C. K. Prahalad, *The Fortune at the Bottom of the Pyramid: Eradicating Poverty through Profits* (Upper Saddle River, NJ: Pearson Education, 2006); C. K. Prahalad and Stuart L. Hart, "The Fortune at the Bottom of the Pyramid," *Strategy + Business* 26 (2002); C. K. Prahalad and Allen Hammond, "Serving the World's Poor, Profitably," *Harvard Business Review,* September 2002; and "Corporate Giants Aim to Tap Bottom of the Pyramid," *Business Report Online,* June 4, 2007.

A research report from a leading academic center defines global corporate citizenship in these terms:

> Global corporate citizenship is the process of identifying, analyzing, and responding to the company's social, political, and economic responsibilities as defined through law and public policy, stakeholder expectations, and voluntary acts flowing from corporate values and business strategies. Corporate citizenship involves actual results (what corporations do) and the processes through which they are achieved (how they do it).[7]

This definition of global corporate citizenship is consistent with several major themes discussed throughout this book:

- Managers and companies have responsibilities to all of their stakeholders.
- Corporate citizenship or responsibility involves more than just meeting legal requirements.
- Corporate citizenship requires that a company focus on, and respond to, stakeholder expectations and undertake those voluntary acts that are consistent with its values and business mission.
- Corporate citizenship involves both what the corporation does and the processes and structures through which it engages stakeholders and makes decisions, a subject to which this chapter next turns.

[7] James E. Post, "Meeting the Challenge of Global Corporate Citizenship," *Center Research Report* (Chestnut Hill, MA: Boston College Center for Corporate Community Relations, 2000), p. 8. The document is available through the center Web site: *http://www.bc.edu/cccr.*

Good corporate citizens strive to conduct all business dealings in an ethical manner, make a concerned effort to balance the needs of all stakeholders, and work to protect the environment. The principles of corporate citizenship include the following:

Ethical Business Behavior

1. Engages in fair and honest business practices in its relationship with stakeholders.
2. Sets high standards of behavior for all employees.
3. Exercises ethical oversight of the executive and board levels.

Stakeholder Commitment

4. Strives to manage the company for the benefit of all stakeholders.
5. Initiates and engages in genuine dialogue with stakeholders.
6. Values and implements dialogue.

Community

7. Fosters a reciprocal relationship between the corporation and community.
8. Invests in the communities in which the corporation operates.

Consumers

9. Respects the rights of consumers.
10. Offers quality products and services.
11. Provides information that is truthful and useful.

Employees

12. Provides a family-friendly work environment.
13. Engages in responsible human resource management.
14. Provides an equitable reward and wage system for employees.
15. Engages in open and flexible communication with employees.
16. Invests in employee development.

Investors

17. Strives for a competitive return on investment.

Suppliers

18. Engages in fair trading practices with suppliers.

Environment Commitment

19. Demonstrates a commitment to the environment.
20. Demonstrates a commitment to sustainable development.

Source: Kimberly Davenport, "Corporate Citizenship: A Stakeholder Approach for Defining Corporate Social Performance and Identifying Measures for Assessment," 1998, doctoral dissertation, Fielding Graduate University, http://www.fielding.edu/library/dissertations/default.asp. Used by permission.

What are the core elements of global corporate citizenship? One scholar's answer to this question is shown in Exhibit 7.B.

Citizenship Profile

What are the benefits of global corporate citizenship? When businesses invest time, money, and effort in citizenship activities, they often reap rewards in the form of enhanced reputation and legitimacy. Recent research by Naomi A. Gardberg and Charles

J. Fombrun argues that corporate citizenship programs, particularly those of global firms, should be viewed as "strategic investments comparable to R&D [research and development] and advertising." This is because such programs "create intangible assets for companies that help them overcome nationalistic barriers, facilitate globalization, and build local advantage." (A *tangible* asset is something that can be seen and counted, such as machinery, buildings, or money. An *intangible* asset, by contrast, is something that cannot be seen or counted, but that nevertheless has value—such as a good reputation, trusting relationships, or customer loyalty.)

In this respect, global corporate citizenship activities are considered to be important contributors to "a reinforcing cycle through which global companies create legitimacy, reputation, and competitive advantage." Gardberg and Fombrun suggest this effect is most likely where companies choose a configuration of citizenship activities—they call this a **citizenship profile**—that fits the setting in which the company is working. For example, the public's expectations of corporate philanthropy, management of environmental risk, and worker rights vary across nations and regions. Companies whose citizenship profile best matches public expectations are most likely to benefit from strategic investments in corporate citizenship.[8]

> Coop Italia, one of Italy's oldest supermarket chains, has developed a private label called Solidal ("fair trade" in Italian) to market responsibly sourced goods. For example, the retailer contracted with a factory in the community of Madaplathuruth in southern India, which employed 120 women to cut, sew, and package Camicia Solidal ("fair trade shirts") in a safe and friendly work environment. This program was recognized for "giving a group of women, who live in a part of the world with enormous cultural heritage, the opportunity to be the creators of true self-development, gain an awareness of their own self-worth, and create benefits enjoyed by the entire community." Coop Italia also benefits from this project, as its private label products account for 30 percent of all such products sold in Italy and contribute to its growing worldwide reputation for corporate citizenship.[9]

CEOs increasingly have accepted the multiple roles of business that make up the citizenship profile. The McKinsey Group interviewed 400 CEOs and senior executives of companies that participate in the United Nations Global Compact program (discussed later in this chapter), and found that more than 9 out of 10 corporate leaders are "doing more than they did five years ago to incorporate environmental, social, and political issues into their firms' core strategies." Some visionary CEOs see citizenship as an opportunity to apply their creative resources to gain a competitive advantage and to help address some of the world's biggest challenges.[10]

As companies expand their sphere of commercial activity around the world, expectations grow that they will behave in ways that enhance the benefits and minimize the risk to all stakeholders, wherever they are. This is the essence of legitimacy in a global economy. A company must earn—and maintain—its "license to operate" in every country in which it does business through its efforts to meet stakeholder expectations. (This concept is further explained in Chapter 18.)

[8] Naomi A. Gardberg and Charles Fombrun, "Corporate Citizenship: Creating Intangible Assets across Institutional Environments," *Academy of Management Review* 31, no. 2 (2006), pp. 329–46.

[9] "Coop Italia Wins 2006 Ethics Award," *Social Accountability International Newsletter,* March 2007, available through the SAI Web site at *www.sa-intl.org.*

[10] "Shaping the New Rules of Competition: UN Global Compact Participant Mirror," McKinsey & Company, July 2007, *www.unglobalcompact.org/docs.*

Management Systems for Global Corporate Citizenship

Global corporate citizenship is more than espoused values; it requires action. In order to become leading citizens of the world, companies must establish management processes and structures to carry out their citizenship commitments. This section describes some of the ways forward-thinking companies are changing to improve their ability to act as responsible citizens.

Business for Social Responsibility, representing more than 250 member companies seeking to develop sustainable business strategies, surveyed how companies had organized to carry out their citizenship functions. They observed great variation in what they termed corporate social responsibility (CSR) or corporate citizenship management systems:

> The goal of a CSR management system is to integrate corporate responsibility concerns into a company's values, culture, operations, and business decisions at all levels of the organization. Many companies have taken steps to create such a system by assigning responsibility to a committee of the board, an executive level committee, or a single executive or group of executives who can identify key CSR issues and evaluate and develop a structure for long-term integration of social values throughout the organization. One important observation is that there is no single universally accepted method for designing a CSR management structure. This is definitely not a "one-size-fits all" exercise.[11]

Corporate citizenship, as this study recognized, is a rapidly evolving area of managerial practice in many organizations. In some cases companies have broadened the job of the public relations office to include a wider range of tasks, discussed in Chapter 19. Others have created a **department of corporate citizenship** to centralize under common leadership wide-ranging corporate citizenship functions.

> Pfizer, the New York–based pharmaceutical company with 120,000 employees in more than 100 countries, created a Corporate Citizenship Department shortly after adopting the United Nations' Global Compact Principles, presented later in this chapter. The first action of the department was to create a global, cross-functional team of 25 managers to actively involve all operating and support divisions throughout Pfizer. The department and team members aligned the new focus on corporate citizenship with the company's mission, purpose, and values and inventoried all corporate citizenship activities across the business system: research, development, manufacturing, marketing, sales, policy, and corporate support functions. Pfizer also benchmarked its performance against the nine Global Compact principles, giving the department and team a functional framework to understand corporate citizenship and how this notion could be operationalized across the company.[12]

An emerging trend is the consolidation of corporate citizenship efforts, like the ones at Pfizer, into a single office that may encompass community relations, philanthropy, stakeholder engagement, social auditing and reporting, and other functions. According to a recent study, in 2008 almost all—94 percent—of *Fortune* 250 companies (the largest corporations in the United States, published annually in *Fortune* magazine) had a department of corporate citizenship, global citizenship, corporate social responsibility, or a similar name. Many of

---

[11] Business for Social Responsibility, *Issue Brief: Overview of Corporate Social Responsibility,* available online at *www.bsr.org.* See also *Designing a CSR Structure: A Step-by-Step Guide Including Leadership Examples and Decision-Making Tools* (San Francisco: Business for Social Responsibility, 2002).

[12] "Participants and Stakeholders—Case Story Details," *United Nations Global Compact,* n.d., *www.unglobalcompact.org.*

As the practice of corporate citizenship has spread, so have professional associations and consultancies serving managers active in this arena. Among the leading organizations are these:

- In the United States, *Business for Social Responsibility*, based in San Francisco, functions as a membership organization for companies and provides consulting services to its members and others. The organization, which was founded in 1992, describes itself as a "global resource for companies seeking to sustain their commercial success in ways that demonstrate respect for ethical values, people, communities, and the environment." The organization provides hands-on guidance in setting up social programs, as well as providing useful research and best-practices examples for its member organizations.

- *Canadian Business for Social Responsibility* is seeking to change the way that business does business by supporting Canadian companies to advance their social, environmental, and financial performance. Founded in 1995, CBSR addresses issues of poverty, climate change, and related issues to promote business performance and contribute to a better world.

- *Corporate Social Responsibility Europe*'s mission is to promote the integration of corporate social responsibility into the mainstream of European business. Based in Brussels, Belgium, the organization's Web site provides a database of best practices in the areas of human rights, cause-related marketing, ethical principles, and community involvement. CSR Europe was founded in 1996 by former European Commission president Jacques Delors.

- In Spain, the *Fundacion Empresa y Sociedad*, founded in 1995, is a nonprofit organization directing a network of businesses seeking to inspire and facilitate actions helping to improve social cohesion and business competitiveness simultaneously. The foundation is engaged in four areas: inspiring senior management, involving business lines, having an impact by way of results, and influencing within the sphere.

- *Asian Forum on Corporate Social Responsibility,* based in the Philippines, sponsors conferences to provide CSR practitioners in Asia an opportunity to learn, collaborate, and share insights. The organization also gives awards for excellence in environmental management, education, poverty alleviation, workplace practices, and health care.

Source: More information about these organizations is available online at *www.bsr.org, www.cbsr.ca, www.csreurope.org, www.empresaysociedad.org,* and *www.asianforumcsr.com.*

these departments had been recently established. The heads of many of them were senior vice presidents or vice presidents. Some reported directly to the CEO, while others were one level below this in the organizational hierarchy. A number of companies supported the work of these officers by appointing a committee of board members and a steering committee of top managers to direct and monitor the firms' citizenship efforts.[13]

As businesses have become more committed to citizenship, specialized consultancies and professional associations for managers with responsibility in this area have emerged. Many of these organizations, including Business for Social Responsibility, whose study is cited above, are profiled in Exhibit 7.C.

Stages of Corporate Citizenship

Companies do not become good corporate citizens overnight. The process takes time. New attitudes have to be developed, new routines learned, new policies and action programs designed, and new relationships formed. Many obstacles must be overcome. What

---

[13] Anne T. Lawrence, Gordon Rands, and Mark Starik, "The Role, Career Path, Skill Set, and Reporting Relationships of the Corporate Social Responsibility/Citizenship/Sustainability Officer in *Fortune* 250 Firms," presented at the annual meeting of the International Association for Business and Society, June 20, 2009.

FIGURE 7.1   **The Stages of Global Corporate Citizenship**

	Citizenship Content	Strategic Intent	Leadership	Structure	Issues Management	Stakeholder Relationships	Transparency
Stage 5: Trans-forming	Change the game	Market creation or social change	Visionary, ahead of the pack	Mainstream: business driven	Defining	Multi-organization	Full disclosure
Stage 4: Integrated	Sustainability or triple bottom line	Value proposition	Champion, in front of it	Organizational alignment	Proactive, systems	Partnership alliance	Assurance
Stage 3: Innovative	Stakeholder management	Business case	Steward, on top of it	Cross-functional coordination	Responsive, programs	Mutual influence	Public reporting
Stage 2: Engaged	Philanthropy, environmental protection	License to operate	Supporter, in the loop	Functional ownership	Reactive, policies	Interactive	Public relations
Stage 1: Elementary	Jobs, profits, and taxes	Legal compliance	Lip service, out of touch	Marginal, staff-driven	Defensive	Unilateral	Flank protection

Source: Philip H. Mirvis and Bradley K. Googins, *Stages of Corporate Citizenship: A Developmental Framework,* Center for Corporate Citizenship at Boston College Monograph (Chestnut Hill, MA: Boston College, 2006). Adapted from material on pp. 3–5. Used by permission.

process do companies go through as they proceed down this path? What factors push and pull them along?

In 2006, Philip H. Mirvis and Bradley K. Googins of the Center for Global Citizenship at Boston College proposed a five-stage model of global corporate citizenship, based on their work with hundreds of practitioners in a wide range of companies.[14] In their view, firms typically pass through a sequence of five stages as they develop as corporate citizens. Each stage is characterized by a distinctive pattern of concepts, strategic intent, leadership, structure, issues management, stakeholder relationships, and transparency, as illustrated in Figure 7.1.

Elementary Stage. At this stage, citizenship is undeveloped. Managers are uninterested and uninvolved in social issues. Although companies at this stage obey the law, they do not move beyond compliance. Companies tend to be defensive; they react only when threatened. Communication with stakeholders is one-way: from the company to the stakeholder.

Engaged Stage. At this second stage, companies typically become aware of changing public expectations and see the need to maintain their license to operate. Engaged companies may adopt formal policies, such as governing labor standards or human rights. They begin to interact with and listen to stakeholders, although engagement occurs mainly through established departments. Top managers become involved. Often, a company at this stage will step up its philanthropic giving or commit to specific environmental objectives. When Home Depot announced that it would sell only environmentally certified wood products, this was an example of a company at the engaged stage of corporate citizenship.

Innovative Stage. At this third stage, organizations may become aware that they lack the capacity to carry out new commitments, prompting a wave of structural innovation.

---

[14] Philip H. Mirvis and Bradley K. Googins, *Stages of Corporate Citizenship: A Developmental Framework* (Chestnut Hill, MA: Center for Corporate Citizenship at Boston College, 2006). For a contrasting stage model, based on the experience of Nike, see Simon Zadek, "The Path to Corporate Responsibility," *Harvard Business Review,* December 2004, pp. 125–32.

Departments begin to coordinate, new programs are launched, and many companies begin reporting their efforts to stakeholders. (Social auditing and reporting are further discussed later in this chapter.) External groups become more influential. Companies begin to understand more fully the business reasons for engaging in citizenship. The actions taken by Pfizer, described earlier in this chapter, illustrate a company at this stage.

Integrated Stage. As they move into the fourth stage, companies see the need to build more coherent initiatives. Mirvis and Googins cite the example of Asea Brown Boveri (ABB), a Switzerland-based multinational producer of power plants and automation systems, which carefully coordinates its many sustainability programs from the CEO level down to line officers in more than 50 countries where the company has a presence. Integrated companies may adopt triple bottom line measures (explained later in this chapter), turn to external audits, and enter into ongoing partnerships with stakeholders.

Transforming Stage. This is the fifth and highest stage in the model. Companies at this stage have visionary leaders and are motivated by a higher sense of corporate purpose. They partner extensively with other organizations and individuals across business, industry, and national borders to address broad social problems and reach underserved markets.

Marks & Spencer, a British retail company led by CEO Stuart Rose, exemplifies a firm at the transforming stage of global citizenship. Rather than the common practice of increasing market share by cutting the bottom line or smearing a competitor's image, in 2007, Rose unleashed a new tactic: corporate social responsibility. Each point in Rose's 100-point plan, to be accomplished by 2012, tackles a different challenge to make the company more eco-friendly, intended to drastically cut the firm's energy use, eliminate waste sent to landfills, acquire raw materials from sustainable sources, and enhance the lifestyle of the firm's suppliers, employees, and customers. This approach changed how Marks & Spencer decided to "play the game," characteristic of a company at the transforming stage. The firm was committed to engage with multiple stakeholders and provide full disclosure.[15]

The model's authors emphasize that individual companies can be at more than one stage at once, if their development progresses faster in some areas than in others. For example, a company might audit its activities and disclose the findings to the public in social reports (transparency, stage 5), but still be interacting with stakeholders in a pattern of mutual influence (stakeholder relationships, stage 3). This is normal, the authors point out, because each organization evolves in a way that reflects the particular challenges it faces. Nevertheless, because the dimensions of global corporate citizenship are linked, they tend to become more closely aligned over time.

As corporate citizenship commitments have become more widespread in the global business community, they have attracted critics as well as admirers. Citizenship initiatives have been challenged on the grounds either that they represent superficial attempts to enhance reputation, without real substance, or that they are inherently limited by the corporation's profit-maximizing imperative, or both.

Some allege that companies may be involved in corporate citizenship to distract the public from ethical questions posed by their core operations. The Ronald

[15] "Strictly Business: Marks & Spencer's 100-Point Plan," *Ethisphere Magazine*, March 27, 2008, *ethisphere.com*.

McDonald House charity, operated by McDonald's, provides homes-away-from home for the families of seriously ill children being treated in hospitals. Many view the initiative as a wonderful social gesture by the company and its franchisees. Others, though, have criticized it as a diversion from other aspects of McDonald's operations that may be less praiseworthy—such as the company's contributions to the nation's obesity epidemic, its treatment of animals slaughtered for food, or the low wages of its employees. Yet, McDonald's defends its actions and offers a long list of socially minded programs.[16]

Whether firms embrace corporate citizenship for altruistic reasons or simply to deflect negative publicity remains a lively debate.

Corporate Citizenship in Comparative Perspective

Businesses in many different countries now practice active citizenship. Corporate citizenship programs and partnerships have spread to every corner of the world map. At the same time, however, how businesses interpret and act on their global citizenship commitments varies in important ways among and within regions. Consider the following research findings:

- A survey of companies in 15 countries in Europe, North America, and Asia found significant variations among regions, reflecting differences in laws, public expectation, and local practices. Companies in North America and Europe were more likely than ones in Asia to have written policies on most aspects of corporate citizenship (including human rights, freedom of association, and equal opportunity). However, Asian companies were more likely to have written policies on ethics (bribery and corruption), inspection of suppliers, and labor standards than were countries in the other two regions surveyed. This may reflect the fact that these are issues that many Asian companies experience directly and therefore identify as problems that need to be addressed.[17]

- However, corporate citizenship varied considerably among Asian countries. For example, according to a study of Asian firms, Indian firms were three times more likely to engage in and report their social programs than firms in Indonesia, 72 to 24 percent. Rather than attributing numerous variations to economic development factors, the researchers found that national factors, such as government public policies supporting corporate social action or public assistance replacing the need for private corporate programs, account for the variations across Asia.[18]

- A comparative study of corporate citizenship in Latin America and the Caribbean found what the author called "a huge gap" between the practices of companies in Canada and the United States and those elsewhere in the Americas. The study found four levels of citizenship activity, which it characterized as "running" (Canada and the United States), "catching up" (most developed Latin American countries, including Chile, Argentina, and Mexico), "walking" (the rest of South America), and "stalled" (Central America and the Caribbean). A standout in South America was Brazil, where

[16] See "McDonald's Corporate Responsibility: Values in Practice" at *www.crmcdonalds.com*.

[17] Richard Welford, "Corporate Social Responsibility in Europe, North America, and Asia: 2004 Survey Results," *Journal of Corporate Citizenship* 17 (Spring 2005), pp. 33–52.

[18] Wendy Chapple and Jeremy Moon, "Corporate Social Responsibility (CSR) in Asia," *Business & Society* 44, no. 4 (December 2005), pp. 415–41. Also see Kyoko Fukukawa and Yoshiya Teramoto, "Understanding Japanese CSR: The Reflections of Managers in the Field of Global Operations," *Journal of Business Ethics* 85 (2009), pp. 133–46.

companies such as Petrobras, the state-run oil company, had exemplary citizenship practices.[19]

- Overall, corporate citizenship initiatives are more advanced in northern than in southern Europe. The idea of corporate responsibility has been slow to gain a foothold in the former communist nations of eastern and central Europe, where it is often associated with the paternalistic practices of discredited state-owned enterprises. In Hungary, for example, most major companies report regularly to shareholders but rarely provide public information about human rights, codes of conduct, social responsibilities, or compliance.[20]

- A comparison of company behavior in the United States and Europe found that governments in Europe played a much more important role in promoting social responsibility and corporate citizenship than in the United States, where citizenship activities were mostly voluntary (that is, not mandated by law). The European Commission, the executive body of the European Union, has strongly encouraged businesses to adopt CSR (although it has rejected mandatory rules). Shareholder activism was more pronounced in the United States; consumer activism was more pronounced in Europe.[21]

These studies suggest that corporate citizenship, while worldwide, varies across nations and regions.[22] These differences are driven by variations in regulatory requirements, governmental involvement, stakeholder activism, and cultural traditions.

Social Performance Auditing

As companies around the world expand their commitment to corporate citizenship, they have also improved their capacity to measure performance and assess results. A **social performance audit** is a systematic evaluation of an organization's social, ethical, and environmental performance. Typically, it examines the impact of a business against two benchmarks: a company's own mission statement or policies and the behavior of other organizations and social norms often taking the form of global standards.[23]

Many businesses assess the social benefits and costs through their social performance audit to determine the **social equity** emerging from their actions. In a world where the use of company resources must be justified, the greater the social equity documented, the stronger the argument that a business is meeting its social goals in contributing to society and addressing the social ills it has committed to combat. Other organizations have utilized their social audit results to minimize any risks that emerge from this assessment, or to capitalize on opportunities. They see the process as fostering innovation within the

[19] Paul Alexander Haslam, *The CSR System in Latin America and the Caribbean* (Ottawa, Ontario: Canadian Foundation for the Americas, March 2004). Also see Gladys Torres-Baumgarten and Veysel Yucetepe, "Multinational Firms' Leadership Role in Corporate Social Responsibility in Latin America," *Journal of Business Ethics* 85 (2009), pp. 217–24.

[20] East-West Management Institute, "Report on a Survey of Corporate Social Responsibility of the Largest Listed Companies in Hungary," Budapest, Hungary, March 2004.

[21] David J. Vogel, "Corporate Social Responsibility: A European Perspective," presentation to the Business and Organizational Ethics Partnership, Santa Clara University, July 22, 2003.

[22] Scholars analyzing perspectives of corporate citizenship found few differences when focusing on managers working in Lebanon, Syria, and Jordan, indicating that within geographic regions views of corporate citizenship may be shared or similar. See Dima Jamali, Yusuf Sidani, and Khalil El-Asmar, "A Three Country Comparative Analysis of Managerial CSR Perspectives: Insights from Lebanon, Syria, and Jordan," *Journal of Business Ethics* 85 (2009), pp. 173–92.

[23] The concept of a social audit was first introduced in Howard R. Bowen, *Social Responsibilities of the Businessman* (New York: Harper, 1953).

company. Some believe that to communicate with the organization's stakeholders in a transparent manner is simply the ethical thing to do.

Over the past decade, the demand for social auditing has gained momentum in Europe as well as in the United States. In Europe, auditing is in some cases required by law. In the Netherlands, for example, about 250 companies considered to have serious environmental impacts have been required since 1999 to conduct public environmental studies. In 2001, the French Parliament passed the "new economic regulations" law, which mandated that all French companies listed on the French stock exchange assess the sustainability impact of their social and environmental performance. The law divides social auditing into three categories: human resources (including employment indicators, remuneration, equity, and diversity); community (including the impact on and engagement with local populations and stakeholders); and labor standards (including respect for and promotion of International Labour Organization conventions). Belgium's Social Label Law, passed in 2003, requires corporate annual reporting to include corporate social activities. In Norway and Sweden, since 1999, all business organizations have been required to publish annual environmental reports; and since 2009, all state-owned Swedish companies, an annual sustainability report in conformance with international reporting standards. Social and environmental accounting has been required of businesses in the United Kingdom since 2005 under new regulations passed in response to corporate scandals in the United States.[24]

In the United States, attention to social auditing lags behind Europe, but the gap may diminish soon. Although not legally mandated to do so, many U.S.-based companies now carry out social and environmental audits and report on their findings to the public. In 2008, 161 of the *Fortune* 250 firms (64 percent) had issued at least one corporate social responsibility or citizenship report. (A 2002 survey by PricewaterhouseCoopers found that just 32 percent of large firms had done so, so the proportion issuing such reports had approximately doubled in just six years.)[25]

A few countries in Asia have passed social reporting legislation. In Japan, the mandated reporting of financial and business risks was extended in 2003 to include matters involving corporate reputation and conspicuous deterioration of brand image. China's Asset Supervision and Administration Commission issued a directive in 2008 urging state-owned enterprises to establish a corporate citizenship reporting system.

In response to the emerging interest shown by corporate executives, researchers have developed various ideal corporate citizenship scales against which a firm's citizenship activities can be compared. (One such list of principles appears in Exhibit 7.B, presented earlier in this chapter.) Social performance audits look not only at what an organization does, but also at the results of these actions. For example, if a company supports a tutorial program at a local school, the performance audit might not only look at the number of hours of employee volunteerism, but also assess changes in student test scores as an indicator of the program's social impact. One company that has raised the bar for social auditing is Freeport-McMoran Copper and Gold, one of the world's largest metal mining companies.

In Indonesia, Freeport-McMoran operates the largest gold mine and the third-largest copper mine in the world. The company's mines there have long been criticized by human rights, shareholder, and environmental activists for abuses ranging from cooperation with the repressive military government to dumping toxic mining

---

[24] "New French Law Mandates Corporate Social and Environmental Reporting," SocialFunds.com, *www.socialfunds com/news;* "Environmental, Social Policies Pierce Companies," *The Wall Street Journal,* August 28, 2002, p. A5; and "Mandated Risk Reporting Begins in UK," *Business-Ethics.com magazine,* Spring 2005, p. 13.

[25] Anne T. Lawrence, Gordon Rands, and Mark Starik, private data.

waste into rivers. In the early 2000s, the company responded by developing social and human rights policies and hiring an independent organization, the International Center for Corporate Accountability (ICCA), to carry out an audit of its Indonesian operations. ICCA's report, issued in 2005, revealed many problems, including some that surprised the company, such as the fact that its security personnel were serving as drivers for the Indonesian military. What shocked many observers then was that the company, instead of hiding the auditor's report, posted it to the Web for all to see. Commented *BusinessWeek,* "The company's willingness to open up so wide is a major development in the corporate responsibility movement. Certainly, no other global mining or oil company has come close to such transparency, long a key demand by human rights groups."[26]

Freeport's auditing efforts suffered a setback in 2006, however, when protests broke out after people living nearby were prevented from panning for gold in rivers carrying the mine's waste. Company officials put the audit on hold until order could be restored. This incident served as a reminder that the ultimate purpose of audits is to change company behavior toward stakeholders, not just measure and report it.[27]

Some companies' social audits have met with harsh criticism from critics who have charged them with being deceptive efforts to enhance a company's reputation, without real substance. The Body Shop, a beauty products retailer, commissioned a social audit to provide an independent assessment of the company's social and ethical achievements, in response to concerns raised by some stakeholders. In the report, high marks were given to the Body Shop in areas such as the quality of its mission statement, corporate philanthropy, and environmental and animal welfare. But according to Kirk Hanson, who conducted the audit, the company was resistant to outside criticism and had a poor relationship with the public and the media.

Simon Zadek identified six benefits resulting from businesses following various social audit standards. He argued that businesses need to know what is happening within their firm, to understand what stakeholders think about and want from the business, to tell stakeholders what the business has achieved, to strengthen the loyalty and commitment with stakeholders, to enhance the organization's decision making that comes from conducting an audit, and to improve the business's overall performance.[28]

Global Social Audit Standards

A number of organizations have developed standards to judge corporate performance. These include the International Organisation for Standards (ISO 14001, 14063, and 26000), the Global Reporting Initiative, Social Accountability 8000, the Institute of Social and Ethical Accountability (ISEA), AccountAbility (or AA 1000), and the more general guidelines promulgated in the United Nations Global Compact (discussed earlier in this chapter).[29] The major characteristics of these global audit standards are summarized in Figure 7.2.

---

[26] "Freeport's Hard Look at Itself: The Mining Giant's Gutsy Human-Rights Audit May Set a Standard for Multinationals," *BusinessWeek,* October 24, 2005, pp. 108ff. The audit report may be found at ICCA's Web site at *www.icca-corporateaccountability.org.*

[27] "So Much Gold, So Much Risk," *BusinessWeek,* May 29, 2006, pp. 52ff.

[28] Simon Zadek, "Balancing Performance, Ethics, and Accountability," *Journal of Business Ethics* 17 (1998), pp. 1421–42.

[29] Another comprehensive list of major business-related standards is in Sandra Waddock's "Building a New Institutional Infrastructure for Corporate Responsibility," *Academy of Management Perspectives,* 2008, p. 92, Table 2.

FIGURE 7.2   **Summary of Global Social Audit Standards**

	ISO 14001	Global Reporting Initiative	SA 8000
Origin	1996	1997	1997
Scope	Environmental management standards	Economic, environmental, and social performance	Improved labor conditions for verification and public reporting
Governance	ISO council, technical management board, technical committees	Multi-stakeholder board of directors, technical advisers, stakeholder councils	SAI multi-stakeholder advisory board—experts from business, NGOs, government, and trade unions
Participants	ISO member countries, environmental NGOs, technical experts	Businesses; United Nations; human rights, environmental, labor groups; industry associations; governments	Businesses and their suppliers, trade associations, unions, auditing firms, NGOs, government
Funding	ISO member dues, document sales, volunteer efforts	Foundations, companies, Dutch government	Foundations, government grants, income from services and programs

	ISEA AA 1000	United Nations Global Compact	ISO 14063	ISO 26000
Origin	1999	1999	2001	Implementation target: 2010
Scope	Social/ethical accounting, auditing, and reporting	Business operating principles: human rights, labor, environment	Guidance on environmental communication	Social responsibility standards
Governance	ISEA; business members; nonprofits, academic, and consultancy organizations	UN Secretary General, Global Issues Network, ILO, stakeholder groups	ISO technical committee, working group	ISO technical management board, working group
Participants	Multi-stakeholder membership	Businesses, labor organizations, NGOs	ISO member countries experts: business, NGOs, standards organizations, consultants	ISO member countries, public and private sectors
Funding	Membership income, commissioned research, foundations	Voluntary government and foundation contributions	ISO member dues, document sales, volunteer efforts	ISO member dues, document sales, volunteer efforts

Sources: International Organisation for Standards, ISO14001, *http://www.iso.org;* Global Reporting Initiative, *www.globalreporting.org;* Social Accountability International, SA 8000, *www.sa-intl.org;* AccountAbility, AA 1000, *www.accountability.org.uk;* United Nations Global Compact, *www.unglobalcompact.org;* International Organisation for Standards, ISO14063, *www.iso14000.org;* International Organisation for Standards, ISO 26000, *isotc.iso.org.*

Exhibit 7.D

Implementing the Global Compact at Novartis

An early endorser of the United Nations Global Compact was Novartis, a major pharmaceutical firm based in Switzerland.

In 2000, CEO Daniel Vasella publicly signed the Global Compact, saying, "Novartis would like to see [it] become a catalyst for concrete action of enterprises and nations . . . furthering worldwide acceptance of fundamental human rights, labor and environmental standards." The company reworked its own code of conduct to include the Compact's principles. It established a steering committee made up of representatives from its major operating divisions and functional areas. A senior member of the executive committee (board of directors) was put in charge, and the process was named the Novartis Corporate Citizenship Initiative.

One major challenge faced by the committee was to apply the Compact's very general prescriptions to specific business circumstances. For example, Principle 1 calls on companies to "support and respect the protection of international human rights." The committee quickly concluded that some human rights principles, such as protecting people from such acts as murder, arbitrary imprisonment, and torture, had nothing to do with corporate reality and could be dismissed as irrelevant.

Applying other human rights principles, however, proved more complex. The Universal Declaration of Human Rights states that each person has "the right to a standard of living adequate for the health and well-being of himself and of his family." What did this mean for Novartis?

The committee took its job seriously, consulting widely within the company, writing briefs on various topics, engaging in dialogue with stakeholders, and consulting with outside experts. As a result of this process, Novartis undertook several health care initiatives. Among other things, the company agreed to provide antimalarial drugs at cost for use in poor countries, to subsidize research on diseases of poverty such as dengue fever, and to donate thousands of treatments for tuberculosis. It also committed to provide prevention, diagnosis, treatment, and counseling services for its employees and their immediate family members for HIV/AIDS, TB, and malaria in developing countries. Later, the company committed to provide a living wage—sufficient to provide an adequate standard of living—to all employees. By 2006, it had completed wage studies in all countries where it did business and had made adjustments where necessary to bring up worker pay to the living wage standard.

One researcher who examined the process at Novartis concluded, "[Making] the general commitment is probably the easiest part of the Global Compact adventure for a company. The real challenge is to translate the top management's signature into an organizational commitment for concrete action and into the sustained motivation of employees that it is the right thing to do."

Sources: Klaus M. Leisinger, "Opportunities and Risks of the United Nations Global Compact: The Novartis Case Study," *Journal of Corporate Citizenship* 11 (Autumn 2003), pp. 113–31; and Juegen Brotatzky-Geiger et al., "Implementing a Living Wage Globally—The Novartis Approach," April 4, 2007. For a full description of Novartis's corporate citizenship initiatives, see *www.novartis.com/corporate_citizenship*.

The acceptance and use of all of these audit standards by companies have grown since their inception. Each standard recognizes and concentrates on a combination of internally focused economic benefits for the firm, as well as externally focused social benefits for the environment and key stakeholders. The standards utilize a multiple stakeholder governance structure so that the firm interacts with many of the stakeholders it seeks to serve through its multiple performance targets. Many companies committed to socially responsive practices have used these and other standards and have made their reports available online for their stakeholders and the general public. While most of the standards are voluntary, some businesses have incorporated the standards into their strategic plans, and more stakeholders are expecting firms to adhere to these global standards. The experience of one company that has endorsed the United Nations Global Compact, Novartis, is profiled in Exhibit 7.D.

A discussion case of an innovative corporate social audit is provided at the end of this chapter, featuring Gap, Inc.

FIGURE 7.3
Trend in Corporate Social Reporting, 1993–Present

Source: KPMG's International Survey of Corporate Responsibility Reporting 2008 at *www.kpmg.com*.

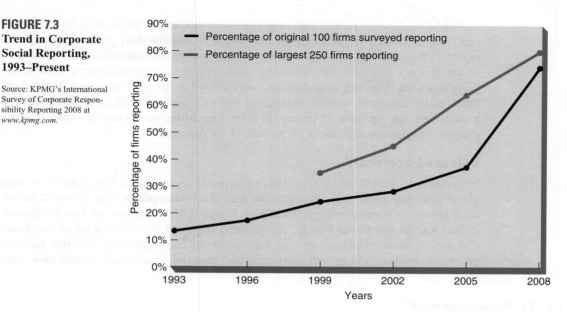

Social and Environmental Reporting

In addition to conducting extensive social performance measurement, some organizations have undertaken the additional action of reporting their efforts through corporate social reports. These reports are on the rise, as reported in an international survey on corporate responsibility in 2008. The report states that corporate responsibility reporting has been steadily rising since 1993 and it has increased substantially in the past six years since 2002, as shown in Figure 7.3.

When we look at social reporting by country, Japan and the United Kingdom top the list of percentage of firms reporting (93 percent and 91 percent). However, the largest increases in reporting from 2005 to 2008 were seen in the United States and in Europe, where Spain, the Netherlands, and Italy all showed dramatic increases, attributed to increased government insistence on reporting as mentioned earlier. In Spain 63 percent of firms now have social reports (up from 25 percent), in the Netherlands reporting increased to 63 percent (up from 29 percent) and in Italy the percentage of firms reporting was 59 percent (up from 31 percent in 2005). In Sweden, where social reporting was mandated in 2009, firms are staying one step ahead of compliance and the percentage of firms engaged in voluntary reporting tripled to 60 percent in 2008. Brazilian firms were analyzed in the report for the first time and showed significant attention to social reporting: 78 percent of Brazilian firms either had stand-alone social reports or integrated social reporting into existing annual reports.[30]

In another study undertaken by the Social Investment Research Analysts Network (SIRAN) in 2006, 79 companies from the Standard and Poor's (S&P) 100 Index had special sections of their Web sites dedicated to sharing information about their social and environmental policies and performance. Over one-third reported that their reports were based on the Global Reporting Initiative Sustainability Reporting guidelines. Forty-three companies in the S&P Index issued corporate social responsibility reports, up from 39 percent in 2005.

---

[30] *KPMG International Survey of Corporate Responsibility Reporting 2008*, KPMG International, *www.us.kpmg.com*.

Why do companies publish these reports? According to one study, most firms (80 percent) are motivated by ethical concerns when publishing their social responsibility reports. Ethical drivers replaced economic considerations (80 percent versus 50 percent) as the primary motivator for publishing these reports, a complete reverse from a few years ago when economic considerations were viewed as the most important. Nearly two-thirds of the 250 firms worldwide reported that they engaged with their stakeholders in a structured way, up from 33 percent in 2005. One of the most pressing issues, climate change, was discussed in about 85 percent of the reports.[31]

Balanced Scorecard

In addition to formal social responsibility reports, organizations have turned to other social reporting methods to communicate with their stakeholders. The **balanced scorecard** system is represented graphically in Figure 7.4. Introduced by two professors, Robert Kaplan and David Norton, the balanced scorecard is a focused set of key financial and nonfinancial indicators, with four quadrants or perspectives—internal business processes, learning and growth, customer, and financial. "Balanced," in this case, does

FIGURE 7.4 **The Balanced Scorecard**[32]

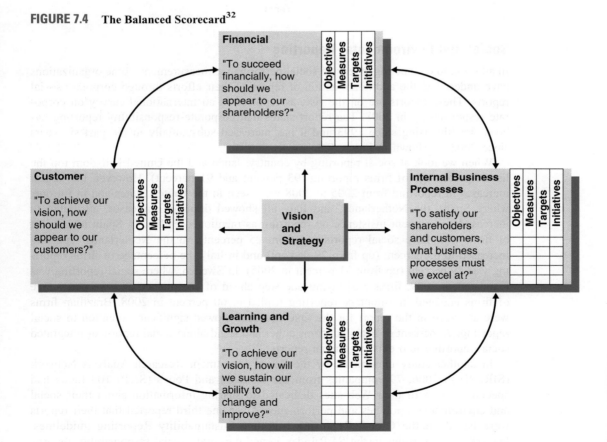

[31] "Socially Responsible Investment Analysts Find More Large U.S. Companies Reporting on Social and Environmental Issues," Social Investment Research Analysts Network report, *www.kld.com.*

[32] Adapted from the Balanced Scorecard Institute Web site at *www.balancedscorecard.org.*

not necessarily mean equal; rather, it is a tool to encourage managers to develop and use performance metrics that cover all aspects of performance.

According to Kaplan and Norton, traditional financial measures are necessary, but no longer sufficient, indicators of business success. Financial measures tell the story of past events, an adequate story for industrial-age companies for which investments in long-term capabilities and customer relations were not critical for success. These measures are inadequate, however, for guiding and evaluating the journey that information-age companies must take to create future value through investment in customers, suppliers, employees, processes, technology, and innovation.

Organizations report several motivations for adopting a balanced scorecard approach. These include economic considerations, ethical considerations, innovation and learning, employee motivation, risk management or risk reduction, access to capital or increased shareholder value, reputation or brand, market position or share, strengthened supplier relationships, and cost savings. In a survey of nearly 200 firms that use the balanced scorecard system, four primary reasons were cited for adopting this system: the need to track progress toward achieving organizational goals, the need to align employee behavior with an organization's strategic objectives, the need to communicate strategy to everyone in a clear and simple manner, and the need to measure performance at different levels in an organization's strategies.[33]

Triple Bottom Line

Another approach to reporting corporate social performance is captured by the term **triple bottom line**.[34] Bottom line refers, of course, to the figure at the end of a company's financial statement that summarizes its earnings, after expenses. Triple bottom line reporting occurs when companies report to stakeholders not just their financial results—as in the traditional annual report to shareholders—but also their environmental and social impacts. Financial, social, and environmental results, taken together as an integrated whole, constitute a company's *triple* bottom line. Novo Nordisk, described in an opening example in this chapter, is one company that has adopted this approach.

As in the trend toward social reporting, firms in Europe have more quickly accepted triple bottom line than have those in the United States. European executives have seized on this notion as both a proactive way to provide stakeholders with increased transparency and a broader framework for decision making. A few American executives have also begun to see the appeal of the idea. "Triple bottom line reporting as it currently stands has its limitations, but it's a great way for companies to disclose meaningful nonfinancial information that impacts their financial results," said Sunny Misser, global and U.S. leader of PricewaterhouseCoopers' sustainability practice. "This is the time for companies, especially in the U.S., to seize the opportunity."[35]

What factors influence the use of triple bottom line (TBL) reporting? In a 2007 study of American and Japanese firms, scholars found that companies "with larger size, lower profitability . . . [and] membership in the manufacturing industry" were more likely to emphasize the combination of economic, social, and

[33] Raef Lawson, William Stratton, and Toby Hatch, "Scorecard Goes Global," *Strategic Finance*, March 2006, pp. 34–41.

[34] One of the more popular books on this topic is John Elkington, *Cannibals with Forks: The Triple Bottom Line of 21st Century Business—Conscientious Commerce* (Gabriola Island, British Columbia: New Society Publishers, 1998). For a critique of triple bottom line accounting, see Wayne Norman and Chris MacDonald, "Getting to the Bottom of 'Triple Bottom Line,'" *Business Ethics Quarterly*, 2004, pp. 243–62.

[35] "Europe Leads International Trend in 'Triple Bottom Line' Reporting," *Ethics Newsline*, Institute for Global Ethics, October 7, 2002, www.globalethics.org.

Exhibit 7.E

"We believe the real success of a business enterprise is measured by a 'triple bottom line': its impact on people, profits, and the planet," according to Rolltronics' annual triple bottom line report. Rolltronics, a Silicon Valley technology company, uses many innovative approaches to produce profits while protecting the environment. For example, an innovative manufacturing process enabled the firm to produce more electronic devices with less expensive equipment, while simultaneously saving on materials, energy, and labor costs.

"Our people create our success. Accordingly, all who work in our company share in our success," the company reported. Rolltronics includes those who live in the local communities and the global community in its quest to serve "its people." The concern for "the planet" is demonstrated in the firm's focus on sustainability, referring to the firm's ability to meet the needs of the current generation without compromising the ability of future generations to meet their needs. "Rolltronics will be one of the leaders in the transition to more sustainable industry. We believe that this is both good citizenship and good business practice."

Traveling halfway around the globe, we discover Sanford Limited, a large and long-established fishing company devoted to the harvesting, farming, processing, storage, and marketing of quality New Zealand seafood. Although Sanford Limited may be miles away from Rolltronics, it shares the same triple bottom line considerations and reporting practices.

Sanford's first triple bottom line report made the following commitments: "to ensure that our operations are sustainable, to maximize positive social outcomes from both the employee and general community perspectives, and to maximize the economic growth and prosperity of the company for the benefits of shareholders, staff, customers, suppliers, and the general community." To further elaborate, Sanford provides an extensive performance scorecard emphasizing its commitments to areas of corporate governance, shareholder value, stakeholder satisfaction, employee orientation, and environmental performance. Sanford has "adopted a wider meaning to the term sustainability—achieving economic growth in an environmentally and socially responsible manner."

Both Rolltronics and Sanford Limited acknowledge and practice the interconnection between a concern for people, a pursuit of profitability, and sensitivity to the natural environment and report on their performance in the quest to balance these three business objectives.

Source: All quotations and other information are taken from the firms' respective Web sites at *www.rolltronics.com* and *www.sanford.co.nz.*

environmental disclosure.[36] (These results do not show that TBL was unprofitable; rather, firms with lower profits used TBL reporting to bolster the public's or financial analysts' confidence.) The authors report that TBL disclosure is primarily driven by noneconomic drivers, and triple bottom line reporting was more frequently found in Japan than in the United States.

Two examples of small firms embracing the triple bottom line approach to business operations and disclosure to the public are shown in Exhibit 7.E.

Businesses have recognized, either through adherence to their values and mission or from externally imposed pressures, that stakeholders demand greater **transparency**—that is, clear public reporting of an organization's performance to various stakeholders, and full reporting of not only financial but also social and environmental data. As firms accept the importance of stakeholders in their quest for financial viability, companies have discovered and welcomed new approaches for disclosure of information such as social auditing, use of the balanced scorecard, and triple bottom line reporting.

[36] Li-Chin Jennifer Ho and Martin E. Taylor, "An Empirical Analysis of Triple Bottom-Line Reporting and Its Determinants: Evidence from the United States and Japan," *Journal of International Financial Management and Accounting,* 2007, pp. 123–52.

Summary

- Global corporate citizenship refers to putting a commitment to serving various stakeholders into practice by building stakeholder partnerships, discovering business opportunities in serving society, and transforming a concern for financial performance into a vision of integrated financial *and* social performance worldwide. Global corporate citizenship programs can be considered a strategic investment by the firm.

- Companies progress through five distinct stages as they develop as global corporate citizens; these are termed the elementary, engaged, innovative, integrated, and transforming stages. A particular company may be at more than one stage at once, as it may be progressing more quickly on some dimensions than on others.

- Corporate citizenship differs among various countries and regions of the world, according to variations in regulatory requirements, stakeholder expectations, and historical and cultural patterns of behavior.

- Many companies have experimented with systemic audits of their social, ethical, and environmental performance, measured against company policies as well as auditing standards developed by global standard-setting organizations.

- An emerging trend is the practice of communicating social, environmental, and financial results to stakeholders through a balanced scorecard system or in an integrated, triple bottom line report.

Key Terms

balanced scorecard, *162*
bottom of the pyramid, *147*
citizenship profile, *150*
department of corporate citizenship, *151*

global corporate citizenship, *147*
social equity, *156*
social performance audit, *156*

transparency, *164*
triple bottom line, *163*

Internet Resources

www.accountability.org.uk	AccountAbility: Institute for Social and Ethical Accountability
www.bsr.org	Businesses for Social Responsibility
www.corporate-registry.com	The Corporate Registry
www.corporateresponsibility.net	Corporate Responsibility.Net
www.thecro.com	The Corporate Responsibility Officer
www.globalreporting.org	Global Reporting Initiative
www.iso.org	International Organization for Standardization
www.sa-intl.org	Social Accountability International
www.unglobalcompact.org	United Nations Global Compact

Discussion Case: *The Gap Inc.'s Social Responsibility Report*

Gap Inc. is widely recognized as an innovator in social auditing and reporting. Beginning in 2004, when it issued a social responsibility report that many activists viewed as pioneering, the company has published three reports to its stakeholders. These documents have posed—and tried to answer—big and important questions: "What is a company's role in society?"; "Can business and human rights go hand in hand?"; "Can business have a positive impact on the planet?" These are not questions that most businesses even ask, let alone use to frame a report to the public.

In 2009, Gap Inc., based in San Francisco, was one of the world's largest specialty retailers of clothing, accessories, and personal care products. Under the brands Gap, Banana Republic, Old Navy, Piperlime, and Athleta, the company operated more than 3,100 stores in the United States, the United Kingdom, Canada, France, and Japan, earning revenue of $14.5 billion in 2008 (down from $16 billion in 2004). The company employed 134,000 people directly, and many more indirectly through its supply chain.

In the 1990s and early 2000s, the company became the target of repeated protests by human rights groups, charging that Gap products were often made in sweatshops—factories where underage, underpaid workers toiled for long hours in abhorrent, unsafe conditions. Activist investors filed a shareholder resolution demanding greater transparency. United Students Against Sweatshops organized rallies at colleges and universities, claiming that Gap was more concerned about profits than the well-being of workers.

Rather than deny these allegations, Gap stepped up by developing one of the most comprehensive factory-monitoring programs in the apparel industry. The company pledged to undertake a thorough assessment of its operations around the world. Gap turned to Social Accountability International (SAI), discussed earlier in this chapter, to help it develop a Code of Vendor Conduct. The company pledged to do business only with vendors (contractors) that agreed to a high set of standards, including the following:

- No discrimination in employment.
- Support for internationally recognized human rights.
- Protection of freedom of association and the right to collective bargaining.
- No child labor.
- No forced or compulsory labor.
- No corruption, including extortion and bribery.

In 2008, the company updated its code by including an explicit reference to the Universal Declaration of Human Rights and the ILO's Core Conventions, and by expanding the discrimination section to include indigenous status, social origin, disability, sexual orientation, union membership and political affiliation. It also required that factories not interfere with workers' rights to organize and bargain collectively.

To assure that contractors were abiding by the code, the company hired dozens of vendor compliance officers, or VCOs. These individuals came from the communities where they worked, so they would be able to communicate well and understand the culture of the contractors they visited. In 2008, these VCOs audited 1,016 factories that made Gap garments in more than 50 countries—99 percent of the total.

When compliance officers found a problem, Gap moved promptly to correct it. For example, in 2007 auditors found an unauthorized, makeshift facility, operated by a subcontractor in India, where children were embroidering a product for GapKids. The company immediately canceled the order, banned the subcontractor from any future Gap work, and cooperated with a child welfare organization to care for the children and reunite them with their families. In other cases, the company has worked with contractors to remediate problems.

But Gap also sought to move from what it called a "fix and fix" mentality to one focused on "find, fix, and prevent." In its 2009 report (which was published entirely online to conserve resources), the company reported on new initiatives to train contractors in modern human resource management systems, facilitate dialogue between managers and unions, and provide classes in life skills to female garment workers.

The company has also worked closely with other organizations. Through its Public Reporting Working Group, Gap has communicated regularly with the Ethical Trading Initiative, Social Accountability International, the United Nations Global Compact, and various social investment organizations. It also partnered with the Global Reporting Initiative and other companies in the apparel and footwear industries to develop a reporting framework specific to that sector.

Claiming that Gap has completely turned the corner, and activists should look elsewhere for targets for their concerns, may be premature. But there certainly appears to be a new way of doing business at the company. Even financial setbacks and declining sales revenue from 2004 through 2008 have not deterred Gap's focus on corporate citizenship. "We know there is still more work ahead of us," commented chairman and CEO Glenn Murphy. Even so, he said, "As I travel around the world to our stores and the factories where our products are made, there's a sense of pride in knowing that we take our commitment to social responsibility seriously."

Source: Gap Inc. 2004, 2005–2006, and 2007–2008 Social Responsibility Reports may be found at *www.gapinc.com*. All quotations are from these documents.

Discussion Questions

1. Do you think Gap has demonstrated global corporate citizenship, as defined in this chapter? Why or why not?
2. In its response to problems in its contractor factories, do you think Gap moved through the stages of corporate citizenship presented in this chapter? Why or why not?
3. Compare Gap Inc.'s social audit and reporting practices with those of other companies described in this chapter. In what ways is Gap's effort different, and in what ways is it similar? Do you think Gap's social auditing and reporting is better or worse than those of other companies, and why?
4. Will Gap Inc. maintain its strong social program focus even as the company experiences financial challenges and declining sales? Why or why not?

PART FOUR

Business and Public Policy

Business–Government Relations

Governments seek to protect and promote the public good and in these roles establish rules under which business operates in society. Therefore, a government's influence on business through public policy and regulation is a vital concern for managers. Government's relationship with business can be either cooperative or adversarial. Various economic or social assistance policies significantly affect society, in which businesses must operate. Many government regulations also impact business directly. Managers must understand the objectives and effects of government policy and regulation, both at home and abroad, in order to conduct business in an ethical and legal manner.

This Chapter Focuses on These Key Learning Objectives:

- Understanding why sometimes governments and business collaborate and other times work at arm's length from each other.
- Defining public policy and the elements of the public policy process.
- Explaining the reasons for regulation.
- Knowing the major types of government regulation of business.
- Identifying the purpose of antitrust laws and the remedies that may be imposed.
- Comparing the costs and benefits of regulation for business and society.
- Examining the conditions that affect the regulation of business in a global context.

In early 2009, the International Monetary Fund and the World Bank projected that the global economic crisis would lead to losses of more than $4.1 trillion in the value of stock and other assets. This number indicated the unprecedented depth of the worldwide economic recession and the challenge facing governments, businesses, and other global institutions. Governments did respond and in ways that significantly affected, and possibly will forever affect, the business–government relationship and the involvement of government in free market systems. Some of the actions taken by governments around the world in response to the global recession are described next:

- The European Commission announced, in November 2008, a €200 billion (euros) stimulus package, or $256.22 billion, to bolster growth and employment across the EU's 27 member countries. The package was equal to 1.5 percent of the EU's gross domestic product.

- The Argentine government nationalized billions of dollars of private pension funds in December 2008 and planned to use some of these assets to help farmers weather the global economic downturn. The country's $3.8 billion stimulus package provided low-cost loans to farmers, automakers, and other expert businesses.

- In February 2009 Australia announced a $26.5 billion stimulus plan and cut interest rates by a full percentage point to 3.25 percent. The stimulus plan targeted infrastructure, schools, and housing.

- In October 2008 British banks received an unprecedented lifeline of funding from the government as a quick solution to the pending credit crisis seen in the United States and spreading around the world. A month later the British government took majority control of the Royal Bank of Scotland by investing in the failing financial institution. Another bailout plan was announced in January 2009 as the government sought to shore up the British financial system. It raised its control of the Royal Bank of Scotland to a 70 percent share of ownership. The latest step would cost British taxpayers another £100 billion (or $147 billion), on top of the £57 billion stimulus committed the previous year.

- The Canadian government offered its country's automakers $4 billion in emergency loans in December 2008, influenced by the pending automobile industry bailout in the United States. The government also extended insurance to auto parts makers and developed a consumer financing loan program for new car purchases.

- China unveiled a $586 billion stimulus package, in November 2008, to bolster its weakening economy and help fight off the effects of the global recession. The money would be spent on a wide array of infrastructure and social welfare projects, including the construction of new railways, subways, and airports and rebuilding depressed communities.

- Even as the German economy slowed to a crawl, the government resisted pressure for a stimulus package, but the outcry was too loud. Senior government members agreed, in January 2009, to raise government spending by €50 billion (or $66.9 billion). The German government also established a fund of €100 billion to help private businesses obtain loans.

- Ireland pumped €5.5 billion (or $7.7 billion) into its three largest banks in December 2008 and took control of Anglo Irish Bank Corporation to protect the nation's financial services industry from collapse.

- Japan's prime minister announced an emergency stimulus plan, in December 2008, hoping to bolster the world's second largest economy by spending ¥23 trillion (yen, or about $250 billion) to create jobs, increase business loans, and help laid-off workers. Two months later the Japanese government purchased shares in Japanese banks, at a cost of ¥1 trillion (or $11.1 billion), to shore up the banks' capital and reduce their exposure to stock market declines and in July 2009 made available ¥180 billion (or $1.7 billion) in funds to shore up the financially troubled computer chip manufacturer Elpida Memory.

- Capitalizing on the economic crisis, in December 2008, Russian government officials announced a widespread plan to exert more control over financially weakened industries by infusing capital into the firms and by overseeing production and other operating systems at the plants. For example, the government assumed greater influence over Norilsk Nickel, the world's biggest nickel producer, since its largest shareholders were experiencing ailing finances.

- Spain's government leaders announced that they would purchase failing bank assets at a cost of €30 billion but argued that it would not cost the taxpayers since the government's plan focused only on quality assets that could be resold once the financial markets settled down and the economy rebounded. The Spanish cabinet also approved a €50 billion fund (about $68 billion) to provide liquidity to banks to stimulate loans to businesses and consumers.

- The largest bailout program was disclosed by the United States in February 2009—a $2.5 trillion plan to prop up the stock market and the ailing banking system and generally stimulate the economy. The bailout was designed to provide banks with more capital to make more student, housing, and other consumer loans to boost the economy. Included in the plan was a proposal to purchase the banks' toxic (bad) assets. A month later, the Federal Reserve pumped another $1 trillion into the financial system by purchasing government-backed treasury bonds and mortgage securities.

In addition to a variety of national governments' actions, the "Group of 20" leaders, representing the largest 20 national economies around the world, met in April 2009 to address the global economic crisis. The leaders of these countries committed $1.1 trillion in new funds to increase capital to the International Monetary Fund, enabling this institution to provide loans and other incentives to countries in desperate need of financial assistance.[1]

What prompted or compelled governments to become more involved in their nations' free market systems and heighten the level of government participation in the economy? How do these government actions affect businesses, and what they are permitted to do? Were these efforts by the governments necessary and effective, or can this be answered only in time?

Governments create the conditions that make it possible for businesses to compete in the modern economy. As shown in the opening examples, governments around the

---

[1] All information is from *The New York Times*, www.nytimes.com: "I.M.F. Puts Bank Losses from Global Financial Crisis at $4.1 Trillion," April 22, 2009; "Giant Stimulus Plan Proposed for Europe," November 27, 2008; "Argentina Announces $3.8 Billion in Stimulus," December 6, 2008; "Canada Agrees to Its Own Auto Bailout," December 21, 2008; "China Unveils $586 Billion Economic Stimulus Plan," November 10, 2008; "China's Route Forward," January 23, 2009; "Germany Is Planning a Bigger Stimulus Package," January 13, 2009; "Britain Takes a Different Route to Rescue Its Banks," October 9, 2008; "U.K. Takes Majority Stake in RBS," November 29, 2008; "Britain Announces New Bank Bailout," January 20, 2009; "Ireland Props Up Three Banks and Takes Control of One," December 22, 2008; "Australia and Japan Offer New Stimulus Plans," February 4, 2009; "Japanese Leader Offers a Vast Stimulus Package," December 13, 2008; "Japan Bails Out Struggling Chipmaker with $1.7 Billion," July 1, 2009; "In Hard Times, Russia Moves In to Reclaim Private Industries," December 8, 2008; "Spain: Plan to Help Banks Will Cost Taxpayers Zero," October 10, 2008; "Bailout Plan: $2.5 Trillion and a Strong U.S. Hand," February 11, 2009; "Fed Plans to Inject Another $1 Trillion to Aid the Economy," March 19, 2009; and "World Leaders Pledge $1.1 Trillion for Crisis," April 3, 2009.

world acted dramatically to prevent the failure of banks, stimulate job creation, and promote lending, in an effort to halt further deepening of the global economic crisis. In good times and bad, government's role is to create and enforce the laws that *balance* the relationship between business and society. Governments become involved when unintended costs of manufacturing a product are imposed on others and government is needed to control or redirect these costs, or when the confidence in the country's stock market or financial services industry drops to the point where a recession impedes productivity and economic growth. Governments also hold the power to grant or refuse permission for many types of business activity. Even the largest multinational companies that operate in dozens of countries must obey the laws and public policies of national governments.

This chapter considers the ways in which government actions impact business through the powerful twin mechanisms of public policy and regulation. The next chapter addresses the related question of actions business may take to influence the political process.

How Business and Government Relate

The relationship between business and government is dynamic and complex. The stability of a government can be shaky or solid. Even within a stable government, different individuals or groups can acquire or lose power through elections, the natural death of a public official, or other means. Understanding the government's authority and its relationship with business is essential for managers in developing their strategies and achieving their organization's goals.

Seeking a Collaborative Partnership

In some situations, government may work closely with business to build a collaborative partnership and seek mutually beneficial goals. They see each other as key partners in the relationship and work openly to achieve common objectives.

The basis for this cooperation may be at the core of the nation's societal values and customs. In some Asian countries, society is viewed as a collective family that includes both government and business. Thus, working together as a family leads these two powers to seek results that benefit both society and business. In Europe, the relationship between government and business often has been collaborative. European culture includes a sense of teamwork and mutual aid. Unions, for example, are often included on administrative boards with managers to lead the organization toward mutual goals through interactive strategies.

During the economic crisis, discussed at the opening of this chapter, the United States government faced a dire situation—the potential collapse of the automobile industry. Believing that such a collapse could send disastrous ripple effects throughout the nation, and likely the world, the government embarked on a collaborative partnership to bolster the financial health of the industry as well as protect the nation's economy, as discussed next.

The saga began in November 2008, when the leader of General Motors, at the time the world's largest automobile manufacturer in terms of revenues and the sixth largest company in the world, stated before the U.S. Congress that the company would not survive without a government-supported bailout. G.M.'s stock was at the lowest point in 65 years, at $2.92 a share, and the company was perilously close to not being able to pay its suppliers, meet its loans, and cover its health care obligations in its labor contracts. During the next few months, the

U.S. government came to G.M.'s rescue, requiring the firm to develop a plan that would ensure its financial stability into the future and to enter into "controlled bankruptcy." Its creditors were encouraged by government-backed assurances and the articulation of specific financial targets that must be met by the firm. Some raised concern over the business–government partnership, calling the new firm "Government Motors," but in general, many businesses dependent upon G.M. and the automobile industry's survival breathed a sigh a relief that the crisis of a G.M. collapse had been avoided. "I am confident that the steps I'm announcing today," said President Obama on June 2, 2009, "will mark the end of the old G.M., and the beginning of a new G.M."[2]

Collaboration between business and government, as shown in this example, often occurs when a situation becomes so severe or widespread that joining of forces becomes necessary. Even traditional adversaries can find grounds for collaboration and support when the need presents itself.

Working at Arm's Length

In other situations, government's goals and business's objectives are at odds, and these conflicts result in an adversarial relationship where business and government tend to work at arm's length from each other.[3] While General Motors was seeking government support, as discussed earlier, other businesses and industries were rejecting offers of government intervention and assistance, believing that they could weather the financial storm themselves and operate quite well without government meddling.

> The nine biggest participants in the derivatives market (where companies seek to minimize potential economic loss due to changes in the value of things, such as assets, loans, exchange rates, etc.), including JPMorgan Chase, Goldman Sachs, Citigroup, and Bank of America, met and created a lobbying group, the CDS Dealers Consortium, to fend off government efforts to regulate their market. The consortium wanted to retain greater control over how derivatives were managed and traded, preferring to use clearinghouses that these firms generally controlled for derivative trading. The derivatives market was a $592 billion industry in 2009 and a valuable prize for the firms engaged in derivate trading. JPMorgan alone earned $5 billion trading derivatives in 2008, making them one of the most profitable businesses. In 2009, Congress debated whether or not to extend government regulation over the derivatives market, despite the industry's opposition.[4]

Why do businesses sometimes welcome government regulation, and other times oppose it? Companies often prefer to operate without government constraints, which can be costly or restrict innovation. But regulations can also help business, by setting minimum standards that all firms must meet, building public confidence in the safety of a product, creating a fair playing field for competition, or creating barriers to entry to maintain a business's competitive advantage. How a specific company reacts to a specific

---

[2] "G.M., Once a Powerhouse, Pleads for Bailout," *The New York Times*, November 12, 2008, *www.nytimes.com;* "Bush Aids Detroit, but Hard Choices Wait for Obama," *The New York Times*, December 20, 2008, *www.nytimes.com;* "U.S. Hopes to Ease G.M. to Bankruptcy," *The New York Times*, April 1, 2009, *www.nytimes.com;* and "Obama Is Upbeat for G.M.'s Future," *The New York Times*, June 2, 2009, *www.nytimes.com.*

[3] The "collaborative partnership" and "at arm's length" models for business–government relations are discussed in "Managing Regulation in a New Era," *McKinsey Quarterly*, December 2008, *www.mckinseyquarterly.com.*

[4] "Even in Crisis, Banks Dig In for Fight against Rules," *The New York Times*, June 1, 2009, *www.nytimes.com.*

government policy often depends on its assessment of whether it would be helped or hurt by that rule.

In short, the relationship between government and business can range from one of cooperation to one of conflict, with various stages in between. Moreover, this relationship is constantly changing. A cooperative relationship on one issue does not guarantee cooperation on another issue. The stability of a particular form of government in some countries may be quite shaky, while in other countries the form of government is static but those in power can change unexpectedly or government rulers can change on a regular basis. The business–government relationship is one that requires managers to keep a careful eye trained toward significant forces that might alter this relationship or to promote forces that may encourage a positive business–government relationship.[5]

Legitimacy Issues

When dealing with a global economy, business may encounter governments whose authority or right to be in power is questioned. Political leaders may illegally assume lawmaking or legislative power, which can become economic power over business. Elections can be rigged, or military force can be used to acquire governmental control.

Business managers may be challenged with the dilemma of doing business in such a country where their business dealings would support this illegitimate power. Sometimes, they may choose to become politically active, or refuse to do business in this country until a legitimate government is installed. The military dictatorship in Myanmar (Burma) is one example of an illegitimate government, as discussed in Chapter 6.

The ability of a government leader or group of leaders to maintain political power can be influenced by businesses' actions. Businesses may boycott economic relations with a country or decide to withdraw operations from that country, as many U.S. firms did in South Africa to protest the practice of apartheid in the 1970s. Some businesses have been ordered by their country to not conduct business with another country due to war or in protest of an illegitimate government, such as the U.S. boycott of Iraq in the 1990s. The United States has imposed economic sanctions on nearly 30 countries because of political and human rights concerns.

Government's Public Policy Role

Government performs a vital and important role in modern society. Although vigorous debates occur about the proper size of programs government should undertake, most people agree that a society cannot function properly without some government activities. Citizens look to government to meet important basic needs. Foremost among these are safety and protection provided by homeland security, police, and fire departments. These are collective or public goods, which are most efficiently provided by government for everyone in a community. In today's world, governments are also expected to provide economic security and essential social services, and to deal with the most pressing social problems that require collective action, or public policy.

Public policy is a plan of action undertaken by government officials to achieve some broad purpose affecting a substantial segment of a nation's citizens. Or as the late U.S. Senator Patrick Moynihan said, "Public policy is what a government chooses to do or not to do." In general, these ideas are consistent. Public policy, while differing in each nation, is the basic set of goals, plans, and actions that each national government follows

---

[5] See George Lodge, *Comparative Business–Government Relations* (Englewood Cliffs, NJ: Prentice Hall, 1990).

in achieving its purposes. Governments generally do not choose to act unless a substantial segment of the public is affected and some public purpose is to be achieved. This is the essence of the concept of governments acting in the public interest.

The basic power to make public policy comes from a nation's political system. In democratic societies, citizens elect political leaders who can appoint others to fulfill defined public functions ranging from municipal services (e.g., water supplies, fire protection) to national services, such as public education or homeland security. Democratic nations typically spell out the powers of government in the country's constitution.

Another source of authority is *common law,* or past decisions of the courts, the original basis of the U.S. legal system. In nondemocratic societies, the power of government may derive from a monarchy (e.g., Saudi Arabia), a military dictatorship (e.g., Myanmar, also known as Burma), or religious authority (e.g., the mullahs in Iran). These sources of power may interact, creating a mixture of civilian and military authority. The political systems in Russia, South Africa, and other nations have undergone profound changes in recent times. And democratic nations can also face the pressures of regions that seek to become independent nations exercising the powers of a sovereign state, as does Canada with Quebec.

Elements of Public Policy

The actions of government in any nation can be understood in terms of several basic elements of public policy. These are inputs, goals, tools, and effects.

Public policy inputs are external pressures that shape a government's policy decisions and strategies to address problems. Economic and foreign policy concerns, domestic political pressure from constituents and interest groups, technical information, and media attention all play a role in shaping national political decisions. For example, many state and local governments have been asked to ban or regulate the use of cell phones by drivers.

> According to the National Highway Traffic Safety Administration, at any given time, more than 10 million drivers in the United States are talking on their cell phones. Specifically, the National Safety Council cited that drivers' use of cell phones played a role in 6 percent of all vehicle crashes—636,000 crashes—leading to 12,000 serious injuries and 2,600 deaths annually. Other research reported that drivers using cell phones are 4 times as likely to cause a crash as other drivers, and the likelihood that they will crash is equal to that of someone with a .08 percent blood alcohol level, the point at which drivers are considered legally drunk.
>
> The practice of texting on cellphones creates an even greater risk to drivers and others. Senator Charles Schumer of New York explained, "Studies show [texting while driving] is far more dangerous than talking on a phone while driving or driving while drunk, which is astounding." The issue of cell phone distraction received fresh attention in 2008 when the engineer of commuter train near Chatsworth, California, allegedly missed a red traffic light while texting a message to a teenage train enthusiast. The resulting crash with a freight train led to 25 deaths, with another 135 passengers injured.[6]

Government bodies—legislatures, town councils, regulatory agencies—need to consider all relevant inputs in deciding whether or not to take action, and if so, what kind of action.

---

[6] "Drivers and Legislators Dismiss Cellphone Risks," *The New York Times*, July 19, 2009, *www.nytimes.com*; "Ban on Texting While Driving Sought," *The New York Times*, July 30, 2009, *www.nytimes.com*; "Complete Ban on Cell Phone Use While Driving Sought," *InformationWeek*, January 12, 2009, *www.informationweek.com*; and "Commuters Killed in Head-on Train Crash," KABC-TV, September 12, 2008, *abclocal.go.com*.

Public policy goals can be broad (e.g., full employment) and high-minded (equal opportunity for all) or narrow and self-serving. National values, such as freedom, democracy, and a fair chance for all citizens to share in economic prosperity, have led to the adoption of civil rights laws and economic assistance programs for those in need. Narrow goals that serve special interests are more apparent when nations decide how tax legislation will allocate the burden of taxes among various interests and income groups, or when public resources, such as oil exploration rights or timber cutting privileges, are given to one group or another. Whether the goals are broad or narrow, for the benefit of some or the benefit of all, most governments should ask, "What public goals are being served by this action?" For example, the rationale for a government policy to regulate cell phone usage while driving has to be based on some definition of public interest, such as preventing harm to others, including innocent drivers, passengers, and pedestrians.

> The goal of cell phone regulations is to prevent deaths and serious injuries resulting from calling or text messaging while driving. However, some members of the public have insisted on their right to use their phones in their vehicles. Traveling salespersons, for example, depend on their phones as an important tool of the job. Some regulations have addressed this by permitting drivers to use hands-free devices that permit them to keep their hands on the wheel. But some government safety experts have disagreed, saying, "When you are on a call, even if both hands are on the wheel, your head is in the call, and not your driving."

The issue of banning the use of cell phones, hand-held or hands-free, for the sake of making our roads a little safer for all, remains at the forefront. The goals of saving lives and reducing injuries and health care costs might justify some form of cell phone regulation. The policy decision would depend, in part, on whether the benefits of the regulation are greater or less than the costs that would be imposed on the public.

Governments use different *public policy tools* to achieve policy goals. The tools of public policy involve combinations of incentives and penalties that government uses to prompt citizens, including businesses, to act in ways that achieve policy goals. Governmental regulatory powers are broad and constitute one of the most formidable instruments for accomplishing public purposes.

> After federal action limiting cell phone use in the United States stalled, the public looked to state and local governments to ban the use of cell phones by drivers while operating their vehicles. The state of New York passed the first law banning cell phone use while driving in 2001. Since then California, Connecticut, the District of Columbia, New Jersey, and Washington have completely banned the use of cell phones while driving without a hands-free device, and another 18 states have partial bans prohibiting the use of cell phones while driving. In California, drivers under the age of 18 cannot use any type of communication device while driving. Washington and New Jersey went a bit further and banned text messaging for all drivers. The Cleveland suburb of Brooklyn, Ohio, became the first city in the United States to ban using a cell phone while driving. Since then dozens of towns have passed cell phone restriction laws. And this is not just a public policy issue for Americans. More than 40 nations, including Australia, Israel, Great Britain, Russia, and Japan, ban calling while driving.[7]

---

[7] For a complete listing of states and countries that have regulated cell phone use while driving see *www.cellular-news.com/car_bans.*

Public policy effects are the outcomes arising from government regulation. Some are intended; others are unintended. Because public policies affect many people, organizations, and other interests, it is almost inevitable that such actions will please some and displease others. Regulations may cause businesses to improve the way toxic substances are used in the workplace, thus reducing health risks to employees. Yet other goals may be obstructed as an unintended effect of compliance with such regulations. For example, when health risks to pregnant women were associated with exposure to lead in the workplace, some companies removed women from those jobs. This action was seen as a form of discrimination against women that conflicted with the goal of equal employment opportunity. The unintended effect (discrimination) of one policy action (protecting employees) conflicted head-on with the public policy goal of equal opportunity.

> The debate over cell phone legislation was filled with conflicting predicted effects. The proponents obviously argued that the ban on cell phone use reduced accidents and saved lives. Opponents of such legislation pointed to numerous other distractions that were not banned, such as drivers reading the newspaper, eating, putting on makeup, or shaving. Cell phone owners cited benefits such as security and peace of mind, increased productivity, privacy, and quicker crime and accident reporting to justify the use of cell phones. A study funded by AT&T found that the cost of lives saved by banning cell phones while driving was estimated to be about $2 billion, compared with about $25 billion in benefits lost, meaning a cell phone ban would cost society about $23 billion.[8]

As the cell phone safety examples illustrate, managers must try to be aware of the public policy inputs, goals, tools, and effects relevant to regulation affecting their business.

Types of Public Policy

Public policies created by governments are of two major types: economic and social. Sometimes these types of regulation are distinct from each another and at other times they are intertwined. In 2009, with the new Obama administration in the White House, the United States was posed for a new era of regulation, both economic and social. This was a significant change from the previous administration, where limited or reduced government involvement through regulation was the norm.

> With many describing the economic crisis born in 2008 as the worst recession since the Great Depression of the 1930s, it was not surprising that numerous policies were proposed and debated by Congress to stimulate the U.S. economy. Economic analysts at the McKinsey & Company, a management consulting firm, said, "For the past generation, free markets have enjoyed a remarkable intellectual and political ascendancy, championed by academics and governments alike as the best way to promote continuing growth and stability. Now the world suddenly appears to think that some problems are too big and threatening to be solved by free-wheeling businesses. Politicians and commentators of every stripe are calling for greater regulation."[9]

Economic Policies

One important kind of public policy directly concerns the economy. The term **fiscal policy** refers to patterns of government taxing and spending that are intended to stimulate

---

[8] "Hello? Cell Phones Cause Crashes," *Wired News*, December 2, 2002, *www.wired.com/news/wireless*.

[9] "Managing Regulation in a New Era," *McKinsey Quarterly*, December 2008, *www.mckinseyquarterly.com*.

or support the economy. The recent stimulus packages adopted in the United States and many other nations are examples of fiscal policies. Governments spend money on many different activities. Local governments employ teachers, trash collectors, police, and firefighters. State governments typically spend large amounts of money on roads, social services, and park lands. National governments spend large sums on military defense, international relationships, and hundreds of public works projects. During the Great Depression of the 1930s, public works projects employed large numbers of people, put money in their hands, and stimulated consumption of goods and services. Today, fiscal policy remains a basic tool to achieve prosperity. Public works projects (e.g., roads, airports) remain among the most popular means of creating employment while achieving other public goals.

By contrast, the term **monetary policy** refers to policies that affect the supply, demand, and value of a nation's currency. The worth, or worthlessness, of a nation's currency has serious effects on business and society. It affects the buying power of money, the stability and value of savings, and the confidence of citizens and investors about the nation's future. This, in turn, affects the country's ability to borrow money from other nations and to attract private capital. In the United States, the Federal Reserve Bank— known as the Fed—plays the role of other nations' central banks. By raising and lowering the interest rates at which private banks borrow money from the government, the Fed influences the size of the nation's money supply and the value of the dollar. During the recent economic downturn, the Fed's action to lower interest rates nearly to zero—an example of a monetary policy—was intended to stimulate borrowing and help the economy get moving again.

Other forms of economic policy include *taxation policy* (raising or lowering taxes on business or individuals), *industrial policy* (directing economic resources toward the development of specific industries), and *trade policy* (encouraging or discouraging trade with other countries).

Social Assistance Policies

The last century produced many advances in the well-being of people across the globe. The advanced industrial nations have developed elaborate systems of social services for their citizens. Developing economies have improved key areas of social assistance (such as health care and education) and will continue to do so as their economies grow. International standards and best practices have supported these trends. Many of the **social assistance policies** that affect particular stakeholders are discussed in subsequent chapters of this book.

One particularly important social assistance policy—health care—has been the focus for concern on the international front and for national and state lawmakers. As discussed later, the United States government has wrestled with the need for better health care for its citizens and the challenge of how to pay for this care. The public also turned to businesses to support health care for their employees and harshly criticized firms that did not take this responsibility seriously enough.

Walmart found itself in the middle of a health care coverage controversy in 2005, when a social watchdog group named WakeUpWalmart reported that 57 percent of the company's 1.39 million workers and their families had no company-paid health insurance. The group estimated that the cost to the U.S. taxpayers to provide health care to Walmart employees and their families, through Medicare and various state public assistance programs, was $1.37 billion annually and would rise to $9.1 billion over the next five years. *The Washington Post* reported in 2009 that as a result of Walmart's aggressive efforts, only

5.5 percent of its workers remained without health care coverage, far below the national average of 18 percent. Health care experts noted that Walmart had introduced many innovations that would lead to higher quality and more efficient care for their workers.[10]

Clearly, the challenges governments and businesses face in providing social assistance, such as in the area of health care, are costly and complex.

Government Regulation of Business

Societies rely on government to establish rules of conduct for citizens and organizations called *regulations*. **Regulation** is a primary way of accomplishing public policy, as described in the previous section. Because government operates at so many levels (federal, state, local), modern businesses face complex webs of regulations. Companies often require lawyers, public affairs specialists, and experts to monitor and manage the interaction with government. Why do societies turn to more regulation as a way to solve problems? Why not just let the free market allocate resources, set prices, and constrain socially irresponsible behavior by companies? There are a variety of reasons.

Market Failure

One reason is what economists call **market failure**—that is, the marketplace fails to adjust prices for the true costs of a firm's behavior. For example, a company normally has no incentive to spend money on pollution control equipment if customers do not demand it. The market fails to incorporate the cost of environmental harm into the business's economic equation, because the costs are borne by someone else. In this situation, government can use regulation to force all competitors in the industry to adopt a minimum antipollution standard. The companies will then incorporate the extra cost of compliance into the product price. Companies that want to act responsibly often welcome carefully crafted regulations, because they force competitors to bear the same costs.

> The issue of global warming, caused in part by greenhouse gas emissions, is such a big issue that no single firm or industry can afford to take the first step and try to control it in order to minimize the harm to our planet and environment. Therefore, in 2009, the U.S. Congress, at the insistence of President Obama, began the long and difficult task of drafting federal regulation that would create a path for businesses to follow to improve the health of our planet and encourage the use of alternative fuels to run our businesses. While people may disagree on how to accomplish this important goal, the challenge is beyond what the marketplace can tackle and it requires some form of government intervention.

Negative Externalities

Governments also may act to regulate business to prevent unintended adverse effects on others. **Negative externalities**, or spillover effects, result when the manufacture or distribution of a product gives rise to unplanned or unintended costs (economic, physical, or psychological) borne by consumers, competitors, neighboring communities, or other business stakeholders. To control or reverse these costs, government may step in to regulate business action.

---

[10] "Stop the Walmart Health Care Crisis," *www.wakeupwalmart.com;* and "At Walmart, a Health Care Turnaround," *The Washington Post*, February 13, 2009, *www.washingtonpost.com.*

As further described in a case study at the end of the book, patients taking Vioxx, a prescription pain medication made by Merck, became deeply concerned when evidence emerged of cardiovascular risk. The Drug Safety Oversight Board was established in 2005 to monitor Food and Drug Administration–approved medicines once they were on the market and to update physicians and patients with pertinent and emerging information on possible risks and benefits.[11]

Natural Monopolies

In some industries, **natural monopolies** occur. The electric utility industry provides an example. Once one company has built a system of poles and wires or laid miles of underground cable to supply local customers with electricity, it would be inefficient for a second company to build another system alongside the first. But once the first company has established its natural monopoly, it can then raise prices as much as it wishes, because there is no competition. In such a situation, government often comes in and regulates prices and access. Other industries that sometimes develop natural monopolies include cable TV, broadband Internet service, software, and railroads.

Ethical Arguments

There is often an ethical rationale for regulation as well. As discussed in Chapter 4, for example, there is a utilitarian ethical argument in support of safe working conditions: It is costly to train and educate employees only to lose their services because of preventable accidents. There are also fairness and justice arguments for government to set standards and develop regulations to protect employees, consumers, and other stakeholders. In debates about regulation, advocates for and against regulatory proposals often use both economic and ethical arguments to support their views. Sometimes firms will agree to self-regulate their actions to head off more costly government-imposed regulatory reform, as shown in the following example:

> Consumer advocates took their battle directly to the food and beverage companies themselves since consumers were having great difficulty in determining which products were, in fact, healthful and which were not. The confusion occurred due to inconsistent labels and language used by the food and beverage companies to note the nutritional elements of their products. Some of the largest companies, such as Coca-Cola, General Mills, Kellogg, Kraft Foods, and Unilever, agreed to use common nutritional standards and the same logo on their packages to denote which items qualified as health products. The "Smart Choices Program" was a collaboration of food producers, scientists, retailers, and academics seeking to better inform the public and consumers about their options to eat healthfully.[12]

Types of Regulation

Government regulations come in different forms. Some are directly imposed; others are more indirect. Some are aimed at a specific industry (e.g., banking); others, such as those dealing with job discrimination or pollution, apply to all industries. Some have been in existence for a long time—for example, the Food and Drug Administration was formed in 1906—whereas others, such as those governing state lotteries and other forms of legalized

---

[11] "FDA to Establish New Drug Oversight Board," *SFGate*, February 15, 2005, *www.sfgate.com*.
[12] "Some Big Food Companies Adopt Nutritional Standards," *The New York Times*, October 28, 2008, *www.nytimes.com*.

Exhibit 8.A

Auctioning Off the Airwaves

After 261 rounds of bidding, in 2008, the Federal Communications Commission completed auctioning off all available airwaves, opening up new opportunities for businesses to create wireless networks for the next-generation phones and other devices. "This auction not only doubled the amount of money Congress anticipated we'd raise, exceeding expectations, [but] . . . we were able to have open access, which I think will be a real win for consumers," explained FCC chairman Kevin Martin. Two of the largest cell phone companies were the biggest winners—Verizon Wireless, which bid $9.4 billion, and AT&T, which bid $6.6 billion to acquire new airwaves for their businesses. Some warned of lessened competition. But Martin pointed out that "a bidder other than a nationwide incumbent [such as Verizon Wireless and AT&T] won a license in every market." For example, Frontier Wireless, owned by EchoStar, a direct broadcast satellite television company, won nearly enough licenses in its $712 million bid to create a national footprint. Some believed that the wireless network could emerge as a third platform creating competition for the telecommunications and cable industries dominated by a few large firms. Whatever the outcome, the government firmly believed that auctioning off the available airwaves to the highest bidders was a fair and equitable way of allocating access in this industry.

Source: "FCC Airwaves Auction Sets Record," *The Wall Street Journal*, March 19, 2008, *online.wsj.com;* and "Winners Named in FCC Airwave Auction," *Seattle Post-Intelligence* March 20, 2008, *www.seattlepi.com.*

gambling, are of recent vintage in many states. As shown in Exhibit 8.A, regulatory agencies have the challenge of setting rules that are fair and effective in achieving public policy goals.

Just as public policy can be classified as either economic or social, so regulations can be classified in the same fashion.

Economic Regulations

The oldest form of regulation is primarily economic in nature. **Economic regulations** aim to modify the normal operation of the free market and the forces of supply and demand. Such modification may come about because the free market is distorted by the size or monopoly power of companies, or because the consequences of actions in the marketplace are thought to be undesirable. Economic regulations include those that control prices or wages, allocate public resources, establish service territories, set the number of participants, and ration resources. The decisions of the Federal Communications Commission (FCC) about how to allocate portions of the electromagnetic spectrum, described in Exhibit 8.A, illustrate one kind of economic regulation.

The U.S. government responded to the global recession, in part, by strengthening some forms of economic regulation, as Exhibit 8.B illustrates.

Antitrust: A Special Kind of Economic Regulation

One important kind of economic regulation occurs when government acts to preserve competition in the marketplace, thereby protecting consumers. **Antitrust laws** prohibit unfair, anticompetitive practices by business. (The term *antitrust law* is used in the United States; most other countries use the term *competition law*.) For example, if a group of companies agreed among themselves to set prices at a particular level, this would generally be an antitrust violation. In addition, a firm may not engage in **predatory pricing**, the practice of selling below cost to drive rivals out of business. If a company uses its market dominance to restrain commerce, compete unfairly, or hurt consumers, then it may be found guilty of violating antitrust laws.

Led by President Obama's efforts to respond to the economic recession, Congress debated a number of new regulatory proposals that involved a greater role for agencies overseeing businesses and their transactions. These included

- Preventing a collapse of the financial system by having the Federal Reserve take the lead in monitoring the risk confronting large financial services firms, given their significant impacts on the overall economy. The Federal Deposit Insurance Corporation would play a key role in cleaning up shaky financial services companies.

- Protecting consumers from financial harm by creating a new agency, the Consumer Financial Protection Agency, empowered to regulate credit cards, mortgages, and other financial products aimed at consumers.

- Regulating the previously largely unregulated market for credit-default swaps and other complex financial products. This also required hedge funds to register with and make financial disclosure to the Securities and Exchange Commission.

- Shoring up the banks, including imposing more stringent capital requirements that could effectively limit the debt they could take on, preventing highly leveraged banks from causing financial instability.

- Making lenders more fiscally responsible, through new regulations requiring originators and sellers of mortgage-backed securities or asset-backed debt to assume a 5 percent stake in the financial instrument. This effort was meant to ensure that these financial companies would have a greater interest in maintaining high lending standards if they were also assuming some level of risk.

Source: Much of this regulatory reform is summarized in "Financial Rules: What Obama Wants," *BusinessWeek,* June 29, 2009, p. 23.

For example, in 2009 the European Commission's antitrust regulators fined Intel, the computer chip manufacturer, €1.06 billion (equivalent to $1.45 billion), a record high fine in Europe, for excluding its only serious competitive rival, Advanced Micro Devices, by paying computer makers and retailers to postpone, cancel, or avoid AMD products entirely, thus denying customers a choice for the chips they wanted in their computers. In a separate case in 2009, the European Commission fined the German utility company, E.On, and its French rival, GDF Suez, €553 million (more than $1.53 billion) each for refusing to sell imported Russian natural gas to each other's home markets after jointly building a gas pipeline from Russia to Western Europe.[13]

The two main antitrust enforcement agencies are the Antitrust Division of the U.S. Department of Justice and the Federal Trade Commission. Both agencies may bring suits against companies they believe to be guilty of violating antitrust laws. They also may investigate possible violations, issue guidelines and advisory opinions for firms planning mergers or acquisitions, identify specific practices considered to be illegal, and negotiate informal settlements out of court. Antitrust regulators have been active in prosecuting price fixing, blocking anticompetitive mergers, and dealing with foreign companies that have violated U.S. laws on fair competition.

The Justice Department's head, Christine A. Varney, publicly stated in 2009 that she would restore an aggressive enforcement policy against corporations that use

[13] "Europe Fines Intel a Record $1.45 Billion in Antitrust Case," *The New York Times,* May 14, 2009, *www.nytimes.com;* and "E.U. Issues Big Antitrust Fines to E.On and GDF Suez," *The New York Times*, July 9, 2009, *www.nytimes.com.*

their market dominance to elbow out competitors or to keep them from gaining market share, a significant turnaround from the tone set during the Bush administration during the mid-2000s. Varney warned that severe recessions can provide dangerous incentives for large and dominating companies to engage in predatory behavior that harms consumers and weakens competition.[14]

If a company is found guilty of antitrust violations, what are the penalties? The government may levy a fine—sometimes a large one, such as the $100 million penalty paid by Archer Daniels Midland for fixing the price of lysine and citric acid. In the case of private lawsuits, companies may also be required to pay damages to firms or individuals they have harmed. In addition, regulators may impose other, nonmonetary remedies. A *structural remedy* may require the breakup of a monopolistic firm; this occurred when AT&T was broken up by government order in 1984. A *conduct remedy,* more commonly used, involves an agreement that the offending firm will change its conduct, often under government supervision. For example, a company might agree to stop certain anticompetitive practices. Finally, an *intellectual property remedy* is used in some kinds of high-technology businesses; it involves disclosure of information to competitors. All these are part of the regulator's arsenal.

Antitrust regulations cut across industry lines and apply generally to all enterprises. Other economic regulations, such as those governing stock exchanges, may be confined to specific industries and companies.

Social Regulations

Social regulations are aimed at such important social goals as protecting consumers and the environment and providing workers with safe and healthy working conditions. Equal employment opportunity, protection of pension benefits, and health care for employees are other important areas of social regulation. Unlike the economic regulations mentioned above, social regulations are not limited to one type of business or industry. Laws concerning pollution, safety and health, and job discrimination apply to all businesses; consumer protection laws apply to all relevant businesses producing and selling consumer goods.

> An example of a social regulation is federal rules for automobile emissions and mileage standards. In 2009, President Obama announced new fuel efficiency standards for cars and trucks, to take effect in 2012. To be overseen by the Environmental Protection Agency, the standards set the first-ever limits on climate-altering gases from cars and trucks, and required vehicles to be 40 percent cleaner by 2016 than in 2009 and to meet a 35.5 miles per gallon fuel efficiency standard.[15]

Another example of a recent social regulation—the Family Smoking Prevention and Tobacco Control Act of 2009, designed to oversee the tobacco industry—is profiled in a discussion case at the end of this chapter.

Other concerns expressed by the new administration have focused on the need for an overhaul of the current health care system in the United States, which is plagued by increasing costs and incomplete coverage. Various controversies have stood in the way of comprehensive health care reform, such as how the program would be funded, what would be the quality of care, how many would be covered by the new system, and whether people would have an option to retain their current health care provider.

Who regulates? Normally, for both economic and social regulation, specific rules are set by agencies of government and by the executive branch, and may be further interpreted

---

[14] "Administration Plans to Strengthen Antitrust Rulers," *The New York Times*, May 11, 2009, *www.nytimes.com*; and "Antitrust Chief Hits Resistance in Crackdown," *The New York Times*, July 26, 2009, *www.nytimes.com.*

[15] "Obama to Toughen Rules on Emissions and Mileage," *The New York Times*, May 19, 2009, *www.nytimes.com.*

by the courts. Many kinds of business behavior are also regulated at the state level. Government regulators and the courts have the challenging job of applying the broad mandates of public policy.

Figure 8.1 depicts these two types of regulation—economic and social—along with the major regulatory agencies responsible for enforcing the rules at the federal level in the United States. Only the most prominent federal agencies are included in the chart.

FIGURE 8.1 **Types of Regulation and Regulatory Agencies**

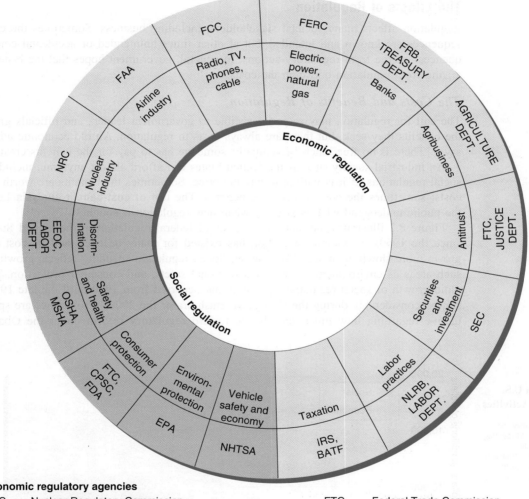

Economic regulatory agencies

NRC	Nuclear Regulatory Commission
FAA	Federal Aviation Administration
FCC	Federal Communications Commission
FERC	Federal Energy Regulatory Commission
FRB	Federal Reserve Board

FTC	Federal Trade Commission
SEC	Securities and Exchange Commission
NLRB	National Labor Relations Board
IRS	Internal Revenue Service
BATF	Bureau of Alcohol, Tobacco, and Firearms

Social regulatory agencies

EEOC	Equal Employment Opportunity Commission
OSHA	Occupational Safety and Health Administration
MSHA	Mine Safety and Health Administration
FTC	Federal Trade Commission

CPSC	Consumer Product Safety Commission
FDA	Food and Drug Administration
EPA	Environmental Protection Agency
NHTSA	National Highway Traffic Safety Administration

Individual states, some cities, and other national governments have their own array of agencies to implement regulatory policy.

There is a legitimate need for government regulation in modern economies, but regulation also has problems. Businesses feel these problems firsthand, often because the regulations directly affect the cost of products and the freedom of managers to design their business operations. In the modern economy, the costs and effectiveness of regulation, as well as its unintended consequences, are serious issues that cannot be overlooked. Each is discussed below.

The Effects of Regulation

Regulation affects many societal stakeholders, including business. Sometimes the consequences are known and intended, but at other times unintended or accidental consequences emerge from regulatory actions. In general, government hopes that the benefits arising from regulation outweigh the costs.

The Costs and Benefits of Regulation

The call for regulation may seem irresistible to government leaders and officials given the benefits they seek, but there are always costs to regulation. An old economic adage says, "There is no free lunch." Eventually, someone has to pay for the benefits created.

An industrial society such as the United States can afford almost anything, including social regulations, if it is willing to pay the price. Sometimes the benefits are worth the costs; sometimes the costs exceed the benefits. The test of **cost-benefit analysis** helps the public understand what is at stake when new regulation is sought.

Figure 8.2 illustrates the increase in costs of federal regulation in the United States since the 1960s. Economic regulation has existed for many decades, and its cost has grown more slowly than social regulation. Social regulation spending reflects growth in such areas as environmental health, occupational safety, and consumer protection. The rapid growth of social regulation spending that occurred from 1970 until the late 1990s slowed considerably during the George W. Bush era of the 2000s. Projections are speculative regarding how much the change toward regulatory reform under the Obama

FIGURE 8.2
Spending on U.S. Regulatory Activities

Source: Susan Dudley and Melinda Warren, "Moderating Regulatory Growth: An Analysis of the U.S. Budget for Fiscal Years 2006 and 2007," *Regulatory Budget Report 28*, Mercatus Center, *www.mercatus.org*.

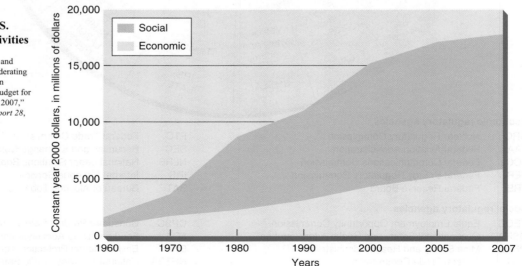

FIGURE 8.3

Staffing of U.S. Regulatory Activities

Source: Susan Dudley and Melinda Warren, "Moderating Regulatory Growth: An Analysis of the U.S. Budget for Fiscal Years 2006 and 2007," *Regulatory Budget Report 28*, Mercatus Center, *www.mercatus.org.*

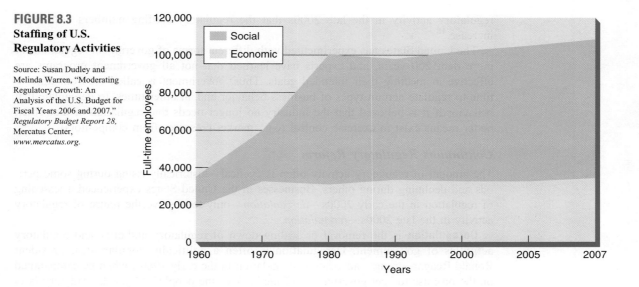

administration will cost, especially if a new health care system is enacted. But one thing that most experts can agree about is that the costs will continue to rise.

> Blogger Michael Hodges, a known critic of government spending in the United States, reported that compliance with federal, state, and local government regulations consumed $1.4 trillion, or nearly 15 percent of the economy, or almost $5,000 per man, woman, and child in the United States. He noted that compliance costs small businesses more per employee than big business.[16]

Yet, the government countered this criticism by noting that there are huge benefits from government regulation. In the annual report to Congress by the federal government's Office of Budget and Management, the estimated annual benefits of major federal regulations from 1997 to 2007 ranged from $122 billion to $656 billion, while the estimated annual costs ranged from $46 billion to $54 billion. The report went on to say that the annual average cost of regulation from 2000 to 2007 was about 24 percent less than the annual average cost over the previous 20 years, claiming that regulatory costs have been controlled to some extent.[17]

In addition to paying for regulatory program, it takes people to administer, monitor, and enforce these regulations. Scholars at the Center for the Study of American Business have documented staffing regulatory activities in the United States since the 1960s, as shown in Figure 8.3. In 1960, fewer than 40,000 federal employees monitored and enforced government regulations. Two decades later, in 1980, nearly 100,000 federal regulatory employees did so. In the early 1980s, President Reagan led a campaign to cut government regulation. This campaign continued during both of the Bush presidencies, and the number of full-time federal employees dedicated to regulatory activities has modestly increased since the 1990s. As noted earlier, it is expected with the increased

---

[16] "Government Regulatory Compliance Report," *Grandfather Economic Report series*, September 2005, *mwhodges.hone.att.net.*

[17] "Draft 2008 Report to Congress on the Benefits and Costs of Federal Regulations," *OIRA Report to Congress*, Office of Budget and Management, September 24, 2008, *www.whitehouse.gov/omb.*

regulatory activity in the late 2000s that the regulatory staffing numbers will likely increase.[18]

The United States has experimented with different forms of government regulation for more than 200 years, and experts have learned that not all government programs are effective in meeting their intended goals. Thus, government is called on from time to time to regulate certain types of business behavior and, at other times, to deregulate that behavior if it is believed that the industry no longer needs that regulation or that other, better means exist to exercise control (e.g., market pressures from competitors).

Continuous Regulatory Reform

The amount of regulatory activity often is cyclical—historically rising during some periods and declining during others. Businesses in the United States experienced a lessening of regulation in the early 2000s—*deregulation*—only to observe the return of regulatory activity in the late 2000s—*reregulation.*

Deregulation is the removal or scaling down of regulatory authority and regulatory activities of government. Deregulation is often a politically popular idea. President Ronald Reagan strongly advocated deregulation in the early 1980s, when he campaigned on the promise to "get government off the back of the people." Major deregulatory laws were enacted beginning in 1975 when Gerald Ford was president and continued through the administrations of Jimmy Carter, Ronald Reagan, and George H.W. Bush, and returned during George W. Bush's administration. Deregulation has occurred in the following industries, among others:

- *Commercial airlines:* removed government-set rates and allowed domestic airlines to compete and more easily make mergers and acquisitions.
- *Interstate trucking companies:* permitted to charge lower prices and provide services over a wider area.
- *Railroads:* given the freedom to set rates in some parts of their business and to compete in new ways.
- *Financial institutions:* allowed to be more flexible in setting interest rates on loans and to compete across state lines.

Deregulation has also occurred in Europe, especially in the arena of social regulation. In the United Kingdom, for example, the Approved Code of Practice (ACoP) governing various employee safety and health issues was downgraded to a "Guidance," a weaker form of regulatory control. In the Netherlands, the Ministry of Social Affairs proposed the deregulation of the Work Environment Act.[19]

Proponents of deregulation often challenge the public's desire to see government solve problems. This generates situations in which government is trying to deregulate in some areas while at the same time creating new regulation in others. **Reregulation** is the increase or expansion of government regulation, especially in areas where the regulatory activities had previously been reduced. The scandals that rocked corporate America in the 2000s—and the failure or near-failure of a number of big commercial and investment banks in the late 2000s—brought cries from many stakeholder groups for reregulation of the securities and financial services industries. Clearly, businesses had not effectively regulated themselves, and the market had not deterred business misdeeds. A flood

---

[18] See Susan Dudley and Melinda Warren, "Regulatory Response: An Analysis of the U.S. Budget for Fiscal Years 2005 and 2006," *Regulatory Budget Report 27,* Mercatus Center, *www.mercatus.org/pdf/materials/1246.pdf.*

[19] From the Sixth European Work Hazards Conference, the Netherlands, *www.geocities.com/rainforest/8803/dereg1.html.*

of regulatory reforms were proposed and began to be passed in 2009 to an extent unseen in the United States for decades. The economic think tank McKinsey & Company described the return to regulation, or *reregulation,* in these words:

> Since September 2008, governments have assumed a dramatically expanded role in financial markets. Policy makers have gone to great lengths to stabilize them, to support individual companies whose failure might pose systemic risks, and to prevent a deep economic downturn. . . . In short, governments will have their hand in industry to an extent few imagined possible only recently.”[20]

Regulation in a Global Context

International commerce unites people and businesses in new and complicated ways, as described in Chapter 6. U.S. consumers routinely buy food, automobiles, and clothing from companies located in Europe, Canada, Latin America, Australia, Africa, and Asia. Citizens of other nations do the same. As these patterns of international commerce grow more complicated, governments recognize the need to establish rules that protect the interests of their own citizens. No nation wants to accept dangerous products manufactured elsewhere that will injure its citizens, and no government wants to see its economy damaged by unfair competition from foreign competitors. These concerns provide the rationale for international regulatory agreements and cooperation.

International regulation in general occurs when there is a growth of existing, yet often conflicting, national regulations of a product, or the product itself is global in nature, thus requiring international oversight and control. Sometimes national leaders resist the notion of international regulation, seeking to control matters of commerce themselves within their own countries, such as the policy approach taken by President Bush in late 2008 in response to the growing global financial crisis.

> Ten days before the leaders of the world's 20 largest economies met for an emergency summit to discuss the emerging financial crisis, Bush discouraged suggestions that this gathering would decide to create a new international market regulator with cross-national authority. “This meeting is not about discarding market principles or about moving to a single global market regulator,” said a senior administration official. “There is very little support for that.” Although rejecting a global regulator solution to the financial crisis, the leaders did acknowledge that a coordinated effort by each country was necessary to prevent devastating global damage in the world economy and stock markets.[21]

Yet, at other times, international regulation is welcomed or at least accepted as necessary. The United Nations monitors international use of nuclear power due to the great potential for harm to those living near nuclear power plants and based on the threat of converting this technology into nuclear weapons. The World Forum for Harmonization of Vehicle Regulations adopted in 2008 two new global regulations to reduce injuries from accidents by better safety glazing of windows and mandating more geometrically fitting head restraints in all vehicles.[22]

---

[20] “Leading through Uncertainty,” *McKinsey Quarterly*, December 2008, *www.mckinseyquarterly.com.*

[21] “U.S. Does Not Support a Global Crisis Regulator,” *The New York Times*, November 6, 2008, *www.nytimes.com.*

[22] “New Global Regulations for Safer Vehicles,” *United Nations Economic Commission for Europe*, press release, March 31, 2008, *www.unece.org.*

In other cases, countries or NGOs call for international regulation, as these examples illustrate:

- The European Commission called for the international regulation of the growth and sale of genetically modified foods, given its serious concerns over the negative health impact these foods may have on humans (this issue is discussed further in Chapter 13).
- The chairman of the International Chamber of Shipping called on the United Nations to enforce global emission regulations for all vessels, particularly a complete ban on high-sulfur marine fuels in favor of running the world's merchant fleet on cleaner-burning distillate fuels.
- Cosmetic companies from around the world met to discuss the global regulation of cosmetic products, citing increasing concerns over the use of potentially toxic materials in cosmetic products. While many countries have such restrictions, the global industry is without such oversight and vulnerable to companies from countries without these regulations flooding the marketplace with potentially harmful products.

Whether at the local, state, federal, or international levels, governments exert their control seeking to protect society through regulation. The significant challenge involves balancing the costs of this form of governance against the benefits received or the prevention of the harms that might occur if the regulation is not in place and enforced. Businesses have long understood that managing and, if possible, cooperating with the government regarding regulation generally leads to a more productive economic environment and financial health of the firm.

Summary

- Government's relationship with business ranges from collaborative to working at arm's length. This relationship often is tenuous, and managers must be vigilant to anticipate any change that may affect business and its operations.
- A public policy is an action undertaken by government to achieve a broad public purpose. The public policy process involves inputs, goals, tools or instruments, and effects.
- Regulation is needed to correct for market failure, overcome natural monopoly, and protect stakeholders who might otherwise be hurt by the unrestricted actions of business.
- Regulation can take the form of laws affecting an organization's economic operations (e.g., trade and labor practices, allocation of scarce resources, price controls) or focus on social good (e.g., consumer protection, employee health and safety, environmental protection).
- Antitrust laws seek to preserve competition in the marketplace, thereby protecting consumers. Remedies may involve imposing a fine, breaking up a firm, changing the firm's conduct, or requiring the disclosure of information to competitors.
- Although regulations are often very costly, many believe that these costs are worth the benefits they bring. The ongoing debate over the need for and effectiveness of regulation leads to alternating periods of deregulation and reregulation.
- The global regulation of business often occurs when commerce crosses national borders or the consequences of unregulated business activity by a national government are so large that global regulation is necessary.

Key Terms

antitrust laws, *182*
cost-benefit analysis, *186*
deregulation, *188*
economic regulation, *182*
fiscal policy, *178*
market failure, *180*

monetary policy, *179*
natural monopoly, *181*
negative
externalities, *180*
predatory pricing, *182*
public policy, *175*

regulation, *180*
reregulation, *188*
social assistance
policies, *179*
social regulation, *184*

Internet Resources

www.betterregulation.gov.uk	Better Regulation Executive, United Kingdom
www.business.gov	Business Link to the U.S. Government
www.cato.org	Cato Institute
www.economywatch.com	Economy, Economics and Investing Reports
www.federalreserve.gov	Board of Governors of the Federal Reserve System
www.ftc.gov	U.S. Federal Trade Commission
www.mercatus.org	Mercatus Center, George Mason University
www.ncpa.org	National Center for Policy Analysis
www.reginfo.gov	U.S. Federal Regulation Information
www.regulations.gov	Regulations.gov
www.usa.gov	Government Made Easy

Discussion Case: *Government Regulation of Tobacco Products*

On June 23, 2009, President Barack Obama, an occasional smoker since his teens, signed into law the Family Smoking Prevention and Tobacco Control Act. "I know—I was one of those teenagers," said Obama. "I know how difficult it can be to break this habit when it's been with you for a long time." The new law provided the Food and Drug Administration (FDA) with the power not only to forbid advertising geared toward children but also to regulate what is in cigarettes. This was the first time in U.S. history that tobacco products were under federal control.

The U.S. Surgeon General, the top medical officer in the country, issued his report in 1964 declaring cigarettes a health hazard, yet as late as 2009 one in five people in the United States still smoked and more than 400,000 died each year from smoking-related diseases. An additional 1,000 Americans under the age of 18 became regular smokers each day, according to conservative government estimates.

Congressional efforts to regulate tobacco received stiff opposition, as expected, from the tobacco manufacturing industry. Reynolds America, parent company of the nation's largest tobacco manufacturer, R.J. Reynolds Tobacco Company, attacked the proposal legislation on the grounds that the FDA was incapable of enforcing it. The company ran a series of television advertisements that showed a plate-spinning routine to illustrate its point that the FDA was overwhelmed and already unable to properly oversee its core mission of ensuring food and drug safety. "Their own scientific experts warn that the FDA can't do their job properly and warn that lives could be at risk," the ad said.

In response to these ads, William V. Corr, executive director of the Campaign for Tobacco-Free Kids, an antismoking advocacy group, said it was no surprise that Reynolds was behind these ads because the company had been "the worst offender when it comes to marketing tobacco products to children." In 2008, six states sued R.J. Reynolds contending that a promotion in *Rolling Stone* magazine violated a 1998 agreement not to use cartoons in cigarette advertisements. *Rolling Stone* came to R.J. Reynolds' defense claiming that the section in the magazine was "editorial content" that just happened to start and end with the Camel logo and health warnings. But a critic of the ad, *Earth Times,* a 24/7 online news source, was far from convinced: "*Rolling Stone* may claim that the four-page cartoon spread is not part of the Camel ad that surrounds it, but the cartoon's content, layout, and placement make it appear to be an integral part of the ad. That can't be an accident. Why would the spread begin and end with a Surgeon General's warning if it wasn't a cigarette ad?"

But not all cigarette manufacturers opposed the new regulation. Breaking ranks with its industry, the Altria Group, parent company of Philip Morris, was a behind-the-scenes supporter of this law as it was debated in Congress. Altria decided to support the legislation since it believed that the law would likely pass anyway, and it wanted a "seat at the table" as the bill was being discussed in Congress. Most important for Altria was to make sure that cigarettes would not be outlawed entirely, which was a provision in an early version of the bill.

Leading the charge as the chief sponsor of the legislation was Massachusetts Senator Edward Kennedy, who said, "This long overdue grant of authority to [the] FDA to regulate tobacco products means that the agency can finally take the actions needed to protect our people from the most deadly of all consumer products." The legislation enabled the FDA to set standards for cigarettes, regulate chemicals in cigarette smoke, and outlaw most tobacco flavorings. Flavorings were seen as a way of luring first-time smokers, usually teenagers, to try cigarettes. The FDA, under this new law, could also study whether to eliminate the use of menthol in cigarettes. Menthol cigarettes were used by three-quarters of all black smokers, who have a disproportionately high incidence of lung cancer.

The new law also targeted advertisements of tobacco products. Colorful advertisements and store displays would be replaced by black-and-white-only text aimed at reducing the appeal of the product to youths. All tobacco advertisements were banned within 1,000 feet of schools and playgrounds and, by 2012, a larger and graphic health warning had to appear on all cigarette packages, occupying 50 percent of the space on each package of cigarettes.

While the FDA was not given the power to ban nicotine from cigarettes, it could mandate a reduction in the levels of this addictive chemical. Health advocates predicted that the new FDA standards could eventually reduce some of the 60 cancer-causing carcinogens and 4,000 harmful toxins in cigarette smoke or make cigarettes taste so bad they deterred users.

The tobacco industry warned that the new law could expose the industry to increased financial risks through lower sales and might violate the companies' first amendment rights to free speech to advertise their products, an issue that is likely to be tested in the courts.

During the signing of the bill into law, Obama said, "Kids today don't just start smoking for no reason. They're aggressively targeted as customers by the tobacco industry.

They're exposed to a constant and insidious barrage of advertising where they live, where they learn, and where they play."

Sources: "Camel Cigarette Cartoon Capers," *Forbidden Planet International Blog Log*, November 27, 2007, *forbiddenplanet.co.uk;* "Reynolds Ads Oppose Move to Regulate Tobacco," *The New York Times*, April 1, 2008, *www.nytimes.com;* "Senate Votes to Impose U.S. Regulation on Tobacco," *The New York Times*, June 12, 2009, *www.nytimes;* "Congress Passes Measure on Tobacco Regulation," *The New York Times*, June 13, 2009, *www.nytimes.com;* "Unlikely Partners in a Cause," *The New York Times*, June 20, 2009, w*ww.nytimes.com;* and "Occasional Smoker, 47, Signs Tobacco Bill," *The New York Times*, June 23, 2009, *www.nytimes.com.*

Discussion Questions

1. Of the various reasons for regulation presented in this chapter, which apply to the regulation of tobacco, and why?
2. Would you describe the orientation of Reynolds toward tobacco regulation as cooperative or at arm's length? How about the attitude of Altria? What do you think explains the differences between the two companies' positions?
3. What public policy inputs, goals, tools, and effects can be found in this discussion case?
4. Do you think the new tobacco control law will be effective in protecting American youth from smoking? Why or why not?

Influencing the Political Environment

Businesses face complicated issues in managing their relationships with politicians and government regulators. Managers must understand the political environment and be active and effective participants in the public policy process. They need to ensure that their company is seen as a relevant stakeholder when government officials make public policy decisions and must be familiar with the many ways that business can influence these decisions. The opportunities afforded businesses to participate in the public policy process differ from nation to nation. Sound business strategies depend on an understanding of these differences, enabling businesses to manage worldwide business–government relations effectively.

This Chapter Focuses on These Key Learning Objectives:

- Understanding the arguments for and against business participation in the political process.
- Knowing the types of corporate political strategies and the influences on an organization's development of a particular strategy.
- Assessing the tactics businesses can use to be involved in the political process.
- Examining the role of the public affairs department and its staff.
- Analyzing how the problem of money and campaign financing in the American political system affects business.
- Recognizing the challenges business faces in managing business–government relations in different countries.

In 2008, Google and Yahoo! announced an advertising partnership that would allow Google to sell ads alongside some search results in Yahoo! It seemed like a natural alliance, yet consumer groups, advertising associations, and some firms, including Microsoft, strongly objected, since Google and Yahoo! already held first and second place in the market for search advertising. Opponents argued that the partnership would create a monopoly and push up advertising prices.

The opposition turned for help to some surprising allies—several farm groups, including the National Association of Farmer Elected Committees and the National Latino Farmers and Ranchers Trade Association. These groups said that this was an important issue for them because farmers use the Internet for advertising and e-business transactions and therefore they were worried about a Google–Yahoo! monopoly. Supported by a $30,000 contribution from Microsoft, the farm groups used their significant political clout to lobby Washington regulators. Google, by contrast, was less skillful in its attempts to build political leverage in Washington. One lobbyist said, "[Google] is known in this town [Washington] for not returning phone calls and not showing up to political events." A few weeks later, citing the possibility of protracted scrutiny by federal regulators, Google announced that it was abandoning its plans for the partnership with Yahoo!.

In another case, Merck, a global pharmaceutical company, turned to lobbying to convince states to pass legislation requiring girls as young as 11 or 12 to receive the drug maker's new vaccine, Gardasil, to protect them against the sexually transmitted cervical cancer virus. Despite opposition from conservatives and parents' rights groups, who believed that the policy requiring vaccination would encourage premarital sex and interfere with how parents wanted to raise their children, nearly half of the states began to debate Merck's request.

Merck funneled (an undisclosed amount of) money through the Women in Government organization, an advocacy group made up of female state legislators around the country. A senior official from Merck sat on the Women in Government's business council, adding to the company's potential political influence. Gardasil was approved for use by the Food and Drug Administration (FDA) in 2007 and was being sold in Canada, Australia, and New Zealand. Despite some reports of serious side effects, even death, attributed to Gardasil, the FDA maintained that Gardasil was a safe and effective vaccine. By 2009 three states, Massachusetts, New Jersey, and Virginia, had passed legislation requiring girls entering the sixth grade to receive the vaccine, and many more states were considering such a measure.

Another industry that has been active in the political arena is solar power. Because solar energy has historically been more expensive to produce than fossil fuel energy, the industry has relied heavily on government incentives and subsidies to level the playing field. Although some major energy companies have entered the solar business, most of the 3,400 solar companies in the United States are small, such as Namaste Solar, a Boulder, Colorado, firm of 60 employees that installs solar energy systems for commercial and residential customers. The solar industry's trade association, the Solar Energy Industries Association, has been very active in government affairs and advocacy, winning a number of policy victories. The federal stimulus bills of 2008 and 2009 provided tax credits and grants for solar installations. States—such as Hawaii, which required all new construction to have solar water heaters by 2010—and cities—such as Berkeley, California, which lends money to residents to install solar panels—have also helped the industry with friendly policies.[1]

---

[1] "Google Learns Lessons in the Ways of Washington," *The New York Times*, October 20, 2008, *www.nytimes.com;* "Merck Lobbying States to Require Its Vaccine for Cervical Cancer Virus," *Pittsburgh Post-Gazette*, January 31, 2007, p. A3; "Expansive Impact of Government Regulation and Legislation," Lori Byrd's Blog, *American Issues Project*, June 25, 2009, *www.americanissuesproject.org/blog;* "U.S. Solar Industry Year in Review 2008," *Solar Energy Industries Association, www.seia.org;* and "Namaste Solar Becomes Poster Child for Economic Recovery," *Greentech Innovations Report*, February 17, 2009, *www.greentechmedia.com.*

As these examples demonstrate, many businesses—big and small—have become active participants in the political process to promote a variety of goals, from protecting themselves from unwanted competition to promoting beneficial legislation. They do not always do so successfully, however. Which political tactics are the most effective may depend on the situation. In general, business recognizes the necessity of understanding the political environment and of addressing political issues as they arise. This is a constant challenge for business and mangers entrusted with managing the political environment.

This chapter focuses on managing business–government relations and political issues. Businesses do not have an absolute right to exist and pursue profits. The right to conduct commerce depends on compliance with appropriate laws and public policy. As discussed in Chapter 8, public policies and government regulations are shaped by many actors, including business, special interest groups, and government officials. The emergence of public issues often encourages companies to monitor public concerns, respond to government proposals, and participate in the political process. This chapter discusses how managers can ethically and practically meet the challenge of managing the business government relationship.

Participants in the Political Environment

In many countries the political environment features numerous participants. These participants may have differing objectives and goals, varying access to political tools, and disparate levels of power or influence. The outcomes sought by businesses may be consistent, or at odds, with the results desired by interest groups. Participants may argue that their needs are greater than the needs of other political actors, or that one group or another group does not have the right to be involved in the public policy process. To better understand the dynamic nature of the political environment, it is important to explore who participates in the political process and their claims of legitimacy.

Business as a Political Participant

There is a serious debate between those who favor and those who oppose business involvement in governmental affairs. This debate involves the question of whether, and to what extent, business should legitimately participate in the political process. As shown in Figure 9.1, some people believe business should stay out of politics, while others argue that business has a right to be involved.

Proponents of business involvement in the political process often argue that since other affected groups (such as special interest groups) are permitted to be involved, it is only fair that business should be, too. This justice and fairness argument becomes even

FIGURE 9.1
The Arguments for and against Political Involvement by Business

Why Business Should Be Involved	Why Business Should Not Be Involved
A pluralistic system invites many participants.	Managers are not qualified to engage in political debate.
Economic stakes are high for firms.	Business is too big, too powerful—an elephant dancing among chickens.
Business counterbalances other social interests.	Business is too selfish to care about the common good.
Business is a vital stakeholder of government.	Business risks its credibility by engaging in partisan politics.

stronger when one considers the significant financial consequences that government actions may have on business.

An Irishman walks into a bar. This may sound like the opening line of a joke, but it actually is the beginning of a television advertisement about responsible drinking, developed by British beverage maker Diageo. The company-sponsored ads promoting moderation in drinking, the first of their kind in the United Kingdom, were aired during prime time to maximize their impact. A Diageo spokesperson admitted that while the company wanted to discourage binge drinking by young people, a growing concern, it also hoped its campaign would help Diageo avoid possible governmental regulation of its product and its advertisements.[2]

Businesses see themselves as countervailing forces in the political arena and believe that their progress, and possibly survival, depends on influencing government policy and regulations. But others are not as confident that the presence of business enhances the political process. In this view, business has disproportionate influence, based on its great power and financial resources.

In a 2009 Harris poll, a large majority of those polled believed that big companies had too much political power (85 percent). Political action committees, a favorite political instrument for businesses, were seen as too powerful by 85 percent of the public, as were political lobbyists (by 81 percent). What is the group perceived as having the least amount of power in politics? The answer is small businesses; only 5 percent of those surveyed felt that they had too much political power. In the 15 years that the Harris Poll has been asking these questions, people have been very consistent in their belief that big companies have too much political power, with only a 1 percent change since 1994.[3]

Although the debate over whether businesses should be involved in the political environment rages on, the facts are that in many countries businesses are permitted to engage in political discussions, influence political races, and introduce or contribute to the drafting of laws and regulations. But businesses do not act alone in these activities. Other stakeholders also are active participants in the political environment.

Stakeholder Groups in Politics

Various stakeholder groups, representing many varied concerns and populations, have a voice in politics and the public policy process. These groups often use the same tactics as businesses to influence government officials, elections, and regulation.

Labor unions have been involved in U.S. politics for decades. The AFL-CIO launched a heavily funded attack on 2008 Republican presidential candidate John McCain's economic platform, called "McCain Revealed." Other unions have also been involved in politics, and as expected, have been heavily supportive of Democratic candidates and issues. The Service Employees International Union, a former member of the AFL-CIO, gave 94 percent of its total $1.9 million in campaign contributions to Democrats in the 2008 election cycle. The United Auto Workers gave all of its $1.1 million in contributions

[2] "Promoting Moderation," *Ethical Performance Best Practices*, Winter 2007/2008, p. 8.

[3] "Very Large Majority of Americans Believe Big Companies, PACs, Political Lobbyists, and the News Media Have Too Much Power and Influence in D.C.," *HarrisInteractive*, March 12, 2009, *www.harrisinteractive.com*.

to Democrats, as did the United Food and Commercial Workers Union, contributing $1.4 million in the 2008 election cycle.[4]

Coalition Political Activity

Business organizations and stakeholder groups do not always act alone in the political process; often two or more participants join together to act in concert. Such **ad hoc coalitions** bring diverse groups together to organize for or against particular legislation or regulation. Politics can create unusual alliances and curious conflicts, as the following example illustrates:

> Daylight saving time involves setting clocks forward in specific areas of the country to increase the amount of daylight that falls later in the day. At various times, different industries have lobbied for or against extending these adjustments. For example, the barbecue industry has argued that an extra few weeks of daylight saving would boost the sale of grills, charcoal, and utensils, which are usually used in the evening. The candy industry said that if daylight saving was not extended past Halloween, candy sales would decline as fewer children went out to trick or treat. The Air Transport Association, representing major U.S. airlines, argued that daylight saving time placed U.S. international flight schedules out of sync with European schedules. The National Parent Teacher Association also was opposed, claiming children would be going to school in the dark morning hours, increasing the potential for more accidents and abductions. In 2006, President Bush signed into law a National Energy Plan that, among other energy initiatives, extended daylight saving time four weeks. The major reason was to conserve electricity by having most work activity fall within daylight hours.[5]

Influencing the Business–Government Relationship

Most scholars and businesspeople agree: Business must participate in politics. Why? Quite simply, the stakes are too high for business not to be involved. Government must and will act upon many issues, and these issues affect the basic operations of business and its pursuit of economic stability and growth. Therefore, businesses must develop a corporate political strategy.

Corporate Political Strategy

A **corporate political strategy** involves the "activities taken by organizations to acquire, develop, and use power to obtain an advantage."[6] This advantage may involve, for example, changing or not changing a particular allocation of resources, such as government

---

[4] "AFL-CIO Plans to Target McCain," *USA Today*, March 12, 2008, *www.usatoday.com;* and "Labor Day Kicks Off GOP Convention, but Unions Back Democrats," *Capital Eye Blog*, August 30, 2008, *www.opensecrets.org.*

[5] "Daylight Savings Extension Draws Heat over Safety, Cost; PTA, Airlines Fight 4-Week Proposal," *USA Today*, July 22, 2005, p. A1; and "President Bush Signs into Law a National Energy Plan," White House Press Release, August 8, 2005, *www.whitehouse.gov.*

[6] The quotation is from John F. Mahon and Richard McGowan, *Industry as a Player in the Political and Social Arena* (Westport, CT: Quorum Press, 1996), p. 29. Also see Jean-Philippe Bonardi, Amy J. Hillman, and Gerald D. Keim, "The Attractiveness of Political Markets: Implications for Firm Strategy," *Academy of Management Review* 30 (2005), pp. 397–413, for a thorough discussion of this concept.

support for a project supported by business. These strategies might be used to further a firm's economic survival or growth. Alternatively, a corporate political strategy might target limiting a competitor's progress or ability to compete. Strategies also may be developed to simply exercise the business's right to a voice in government affairs. Organizations differ in how actively they are involved in politics on an ongoing basis. Some companies essentially wait for a public policy issue to emerge before building a strategy to address that issue. This is likely when they believe the threat posed by unexpected public issues is relatively small.

On the other hand, other companies develop an ongoing political strategy, so that they are ready when various public issues arise. Such was the case for Merck, as described at the beginning of this chapter. Firms are most likely to have a long-term political strategy if they believe the risks of harm from unexpected public issues are great, or when the firm is a frequent target of public attention. For example, firms in the chemical industry, which must contend with frequently changing environmental regulations and the risk of dangerous accidents, usually have a sophisticated political strategy. The same may be true for firms in the entertainment industry, which must often contend with policy issues such as intellectual property rights, public standards of decency, and licensing rights to new technologies.

Political actions by businesses often take the form of one of the following three strategic types, also shown in Figure 9.2:

- *Information strategy* (where businesses seek to provide government policymakers with information to influence their actions, such as lobbying).
- *Financial incentives strategy* (where businesses provide incentives to influence government policymakers to act in a certain way, such as making a contribution to a political action committee that supports the policymaker).

FIGURE 9.2
Business Strategies for Influencing Government

Source: Adapted from Amy J. Hillman and Michael A. Hitt, "Corporate Political Strategy Formulation: A Model of Approach, Participation, and Strategy Decisions," *Academy of Management Review* 24 (1999), Table 1, p. 835. Used by permission.

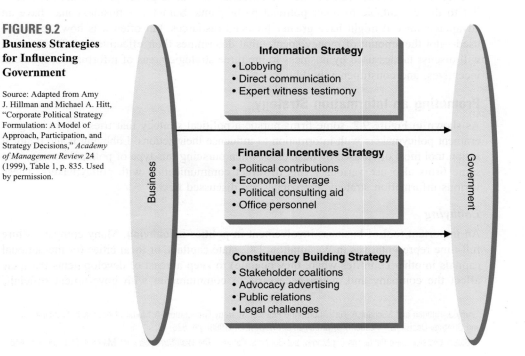

Business

Information Strategy
- Lobbying
- Direct communication
- Expert witness testimony

Financial Incentives Strategy
- Political contributions
- Economic leverage
- Political consulting aid
- Office personnel

Constituency Building Strategy
- Stakeholder coalitions
- Advocacy advertising
- Public relations
- Legal challenges

Government

- *Constituency-building strategy* (where businesses seek to gain support from other affected organizations to better influence government policymakers to act in a way that helps them).[7]

The various tactics used by businesses when adopting each of these political strategies are discussed next in this chapter.

Most companies understand the importance of having a corporate political strategy. Whether a firm has the substantial resources to employ permanent lobbyists in the nation's capital or simply tries to meet local politicians at community gatherings, all companies need to have a clear purpose, message, and plan for engaging in the political environment. Yet, sometimes even the best strategy can fail.

> Global Crossing's founder Gary Winnick set out to sell high-speed fiber networks. Central to his plan was a high-powered political strategy. He placed a top Democratic fund-raiser and a former Republican senator on Global Crossing's board of directors. He hired lobbyists to target both the executive and legislative branches of government. The company and its employees flooded Washington with donations, surpassing even Enron Corporation in the amount of contributions to election campaigns. Yet Global Crossing repeatedly failed to persuade members of the Federal Communications Commission, the Pentagon, and Congress. Winnick discovered that writing big checks gained access to some individuals, but it also brought about greater scrutiny from others. A well-funded political strategy could not mask the weakness of Global Crossing's business plan and could not rescue the firm when its business eventually failed.[8]

Political Action Tactics

The tactics or tools used by business to influence the public policy process are often similar to those available to other political participants. Sometimes business may have an advantage since it might have greater financial resources, but often it is how tactics are used—not the amount of money spent—that determines their effectiveness. This section will discuss tactics used by business in the three strategic areas of information, financial incentives, and constituency building.

Promoting an Information Strategy

As shown in Figure 9.2, some firms pursue a political strategy that tries to provide government policymakers with information to influence their actions. Lobbying is the political action tool most often used by businesses when pursuing this type of political strategy, but some firms also use various forms of direct communication with policymakers. These various information strategy approaches are discussed next.

Lobbying

An important tool of business involvement in politics is **lobbying**. Many companies hire full-time representatives in Washington, DC, state capitals, or local cities (or the national capitals in other countries where they operate) to keep abreast of developments that may affect the company and, when necessary, to communicate with government officials.

---

[7] Amy J. Hillman and Michael A. Hitt, "Corporate Political Strategy Formulation: A Model of Approach, Participation, and Strategy Decisions," *Academy of Management Review* 24 (1999), pp. 825–42.

[8] "Global Crossing Gave Politicians Big Money, but Got Little Return," *The Wall Street Journal*, March 4, 2002, pp. A1, A10.

FIGURE 9.3
Total Federal Lobbying Spending and Number of Lobbyists, 1998–2008, by U.S. Business

Sources: Center for Responsive Politics at *www.opensecrets.org*. Used with permission.

Total Lobbying Spending ($ in billions)		Number of Lobbyists
$1.44	1998	10,684
$1.44	1999	13,316
$1.56	2000	12,743
$1.64	2001	12,069
$1.81	2002	12,346
$2.04	2003	13,157
$2.18	2004	13,396
$2.42	2005	14,427
$2.61	2006	14,838
$2.85	2007	15,384
$3.27	2008	15,223

These individuals are called lobbyists. Their job is to represent the business before the people and agencies involved in determining legislative and regulatory outcomes. Lobbying involves direct contact with a government official to influence the thinking or actions of that person on an issue or public policy. Lobbyists communicate with and try to persuade others to support an organization's interest or stake as they consider a particular law, policy, or regulation.

Businesses, trade associations, and other groups spend a great deal on lobbying. Figure 9.3 shows the total number of lobbyists and the amount spent on lobbying activity from 1998 to 2008. As illustrated, the number of lobbyists has risen about 42 percent since 1998, while the amount of spending on lobbying has grown by 127 percent. Some of the organizations spending the most on lobbying in 2008 were the U.S. Chamber of Commerce, which spent more than $90 million that year, and Exxon Mobil, the AARP (a nonprofit organization helping people 50 years and older), and PG&E Corporation (a utility company), each of which spent about $25 million. Industry associations also hire lobbyists. For example, the pharmaceutical and health products industry spent nearly $250 million on lobbying in 2008, followed by the electrical utilities industry (about $160 million) and the insurance industry (about $155 million).[9]

Under U.S. law, lobbying activities must be disclosed publicly. Lobbying firms and organizations employing in-house lobbyists must register with the government. They must also file regular reports on their earnings (lobbyists) or expenses (organizations), and indicate the issues and legislation that were the focus of their efforts. Lobbyists have also historically provided politicians with various perks and gifts, creating the potential for inappropriately influencing policy. One of the most high-profile cases was that of Jack Abramoff.

In 2006, well-known lobbyist Jack Abramoff received the minimum sentence of six years in prison after he pleaded guilty to charges of fraud, conspiracy, and tax evasion. The light sentence was attributed to Abramoff's cooperation with

[9] For a complete listing of lobbyists and their expenses by organization and by industry, see *www.opensecrets.org/lobby*.

Exhibit 9.A

Under the new "temptation rules," lawmakers and their aides are barred from accepting any gifts, meals, or trips from lobbyists, with penalties up to $200,000 and five years in prison for violating these new rules. "You are basically asking people to certify, with big penalties, that nobody has lied on their expense accounts," said one of the biggest lobbyists in Washington. Yet, the lobbyist also shared his skepticism about the impact of these rules since "these are people [lobbyists and government employees] who are sharing apartments together, playing on the same softball teams, dating each other—young people with active social lives."

Once Congress reconvened after the passage of the "temptation rules," it did not take long to discover how these rules could be circumvented. Lawmakers invited lobbyists to pay for a variety of lavish outings: birthday parties in a lawmaker's honor ($1,000 per lobbyist), a California wine-tasting tour (all donors were welcomed), hunting and fishing trips (typically $5,000), rock concerts by The Who or Bob Seger ($2,500 for two seats), and many more. Instead of directly paying the lawmaker, lobbyists made a contribution to a political fund-raising committee set up by the lawmaker. The committee, in turn, paid the lawmaker's way to these events, not banned by the new rules. Some lobbyists argued that the new rules might even increase the volume of contributions flowing to Congress from lobbyists. Others admitted that the new rules needed a quick review and that enforcement would always be difficult, especially at first.

Sources: "Tougher Rules Change Game for Lobbyists," *The New York Times*, August 7, 2007, *www.nytimes.com;* and "Congress Finds Ways to Avoid Lobbyist Limits," *The New York Times*, February 11, 2007, *www.nytimes.com.*

investigations of bribery and political corruption involving numerous members of Congress. Federal records showed that 220 members of Congress received more than $1.7 million in political contributions from Abramoff and his associates and clients, as well as enjoying the benefits of lavish trips, free meals, and entertainment.[10]

Partially in response to the Abramoff scandal and conviction, Congress passed sweeping new legislation in 2007 directed at lobbyists and attempting to bring ethics back into the political process, as described in Exhibit 9.A.

Businesses sometimes hire former government officials as lobbyists and political advisers. These individuals bring with them their personal connections and detailed knowledge of the public policy process. This circulation of individuals between business and government is often referred to as the **revolving door**. One study by the Project on Government Oversight showed that three of the most powerful committees in the House of Representatives—Energy and Commerce, Ways and Means, and Appropriations— had the greatest number of staffers-turned-lobbyists or lobbyists-turned-staffers of all of the Congressional committees. One hundred thirty-three people had either served as aides to the Energy and Commerce Committee and were now lobbyists or vice versa, with 85 such cases for the Ways and Means Committee and 82 cases for the Appropriations Committee. The report concluded, "The revolving door has become such an accepted part of federal contracting in recent years that it is frequently difficult to determine where the government stops and the private sector begins."

While it is perfectly legal for government officials to seek employment in industry, and vice versa, the revolving door carries potential for abuse. Although it may be praised

[10] "Guilty Plea by Lobbyist Raises Prospect of Wider Investigation," *The Wall Street Journal Online*, January 4, 2006, *online.wsj.com;* "Abramoff Pleads Guilty, Agrees to Cooperate in Sprawling Probe," Institute for Global Ethics, *Ethics Newsline*, January 9, 2006, *www.globalethics.com;* and "Jack Abramoff Gets Nearly Six Years for Fraud in Miami Scam," Institute for Global Ethics, *Ethics Newsline*, April 3, 2006, *www.globalethics.com.*

as an act of public service when a business executive leaves a corporate position to work for a regulatory agency, that executive may be inclined to act favorably toward his or her former employer. Such favoritism would not be fair to other firms also regulated by the agency. Businesses can also seek to influence public policy by offering jobs to regulators in exchange for favors, a practice that is considered highly unethical, as shown in the following example:

> In the final days before leaving their government offices, two administrators quietly reversed the findings of the Interior Department staff historians, resulting in the recognition of three groups as Indian tribes. This recognition gave the three groups the right to open gaming casinos, which could provide the groups with the opportunity to make millions of dollars. According to a *Boston Globe* article, the two officials, Bureau of Indian Affairs head Kevin Gover and his deputy Michael J. Anderson, immediately left government service and became executives representing the now-recognized Indian tribes.[11]

In general, lobbying—as well as hiring former government officials for positions in the corporate world—is normally legal, but great care must be exercised to act ethically.

Direct Communications

Businesses can also promote an information strategy through direct communication with policymakers.

Democracy requires citizen access and communication with political leaders. Businesses often invite government officials to visit local plant facilities, give speeches to employees, attend awards ceremonies, and participate in activities that will improve the officials' understanding of management and employee concerns. These activities help to humanize the distant relationship that can otherwise develop between government officials and the public.

One of the most effective organizations promoting direct communications between business and policymakers is the **Business Roundtable**. Founded in 1972, the Roundtable is an organization of chief executive officers (CEOs) of leading corporations. The organization studies various public policy issues and advocates for laws that it believes "foster vigorous economic growth and a dynamic global economy." Some issues the Roundtable has taken a position on in recent years include corporate governance, education, health care, and civil justice reform. One of the most distinctive aspects of the Roundtable's work is that CEOs are directly involved. Once the Roundtable has formulated a position on a matter of public policy, CEOs go to Washington, DC, to talk personally with lawmakers. The organization has found that this direct approach works very well.[12]

Expert Witness Testimony

A common method of providing information to legislators is for CEOs and other executives to give testimony in various public forums. Businesses may want to provide facts, anecdotes, or data to educate and influence government leaders. One way that government officials collect information in the United States is through public congressional hearings, where business leaders may be invited to speak. These hearings may influence whether legislation is introduced in Congress, or change the language or funding of a

---

[11] "Aides OK Casinos, Get Jobs," *Boston Globe*, March 25, 2001, p. A11.

[12] More information about the Business Roundtable is available at *www.brtable.org*.

proposed piece of legislation, or shape how regulation is implemented. In some cases, the very future of the industry may be at stake.

> On two occasions in 2008 the CEOs of the "Big Three" American automakers— General Motors, Ford, and Chrysler—testified before Congress to persuade law- makers to provide bailout funds to save the U.S. automobile industry. General Motors and Chrysler indicated that without financial assistance, the companies would be below the minimum cash requirements needed to continue by March 2009. Ford said it could last until 2010 but worried that a General Motors or Chrysler failure would have devastating effects on Ford. CEOs Wagoner (General Motors), Mulally (Ford), and Nardelli (Chrysler) also provided their plans to turn around their firms if given the government support they requested. The Senate committee members hearing this testimony were impressed. "There is no doubt," said Christopher Dodd (Democrat–Connecticut), "that the automobile companies have done far more, far more, I would suggest, than the financial companies to show that they deserve taxpayer support." Congress did authorize bailout funds for the automakers, along with strict rules and performance goals to be met. Ford declined the funds since the firm believed it could survive without the assistance.[13]

Promoting a Financial Incentive Strategy

Businesses may wish to influence government policymakers by providing financial incen- tives in the hope that the legislator will be persuaded to act in a certain way or cast a vote favorable to the business's interests. Political action committees and economic lever- age are the two most common political action tools when pursuing this strategy.

Political Action Committees

One of the most common political action tools used by business is to form and contribute to a political action committee. By law, corporations are not permitted to make direct con- tributions to political candidates for national and most state offices. That is, companies cannot simply write a check from their own corporate treasuries to support a candidate, say, for president. Since the mid-1970s, however, companies have been permitted to spend company funds to organize and administer **political action committees (PACs)**. PACs are independently incorporated organizations that can solicit contributions and then channel those funds to candidates seeking political office. Companies that have organized PACs are not permitted to donate corporate funds to the PAC or to any political candidate; all donations to company-organized PACs must come from individuals, such as business executives, company employees or stockholders, or other interested individuals.

Individuals can also contribute to political campaigns. For the 2010 election cycle, the limits for campaign contributions changed for individuals but not for political action committees. Under the new law, an individual could directly contribute up to $2,400 to any candidate per election. Individuals can give up to $115,500 in total when combining contributions to political action committees, political parties, and individ- ual candidates. However, the contribution limits for PACs remained the same under the new law: $5,000 per candidate per election, $15,000 to any national committee per year, and $5,000 to any state or local party per year. PACs have no aggregate total

---

[13] "Auto Execs in the Hot Seat," *BusinessWeek*, November 19, 2008, *www.businessweek.com;* and "Auto CEOs Return to Capitol Hill," *ABC News*, December 4, 2008, *www.abcnews.com.*

Exhibit 9.B

The Cost of Running for the Presidency

In 2008, for the first time ever, candidates for the presidency of the United States raised more than $1 billion. Leading the way were Democrat Barack Obama and Republican John McCain, but even Bob Barr, the Libertarian Party candidate, and Independent Ralph Nader found that raising big money was necessary to gain recognition and to get their message out to the American people. Obama chose not to receive any funding from political action committees and declined any public (federal) funds, which would impose spending limits on his campaign. McCain, alternatively, did accept federal funding, and thus was limited to spending only $84 million on his campaign. Like Obama, Nader refused contributions from political action committees. Shown below are the amounts that each candidate raised and the sources of the funding.

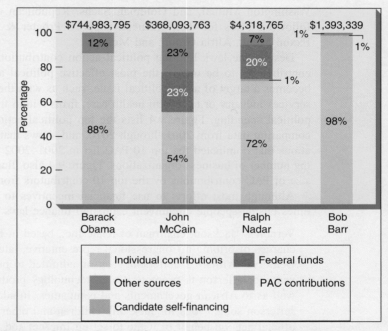

Sources: "Banking on Becoming President," Center for Responsive Politics," n.d., *www.opensecrets.org.*

limit. Some issues generate significant political interest and subsequently massive amounts of political contributions. Consider the lively debate over national health care coverage in 2009.

In preparation for the 2009 health care debate in Congress, business organizations and industries started early in their efforts to contribute to key policymakers. Since 2005, health insurers, legally through PACs, and their employees contributed $2.2 million to 10 key House and Senate lawmakers. In addition, drug makers, also using PACs, and their employees, gave more than $3.3 million to key congressional members. President Obama received more than $2 million from individuals with ties to the insurance and pharmaceutical industries during his record-breaking presidential campaign (see Exhibit 9.B). Other key politicians, who were positioned to take an active role in shaping the pending health care reform legislation, were likewise a big target for political contributions. Senator John McCain received more than $500,000 in contributions from health-related company PACs, with Senate Minority Leader Mitch McConnell accepting

$425,000 and Max Baucus, chair of the influential Senate Finance Committee, 413,000.[14]

Extensive fund-raising—whether from individual contributions, political action committee contributions, federal finding, or other sources—is essential for any politician seeking to be elected. Exhibit 9.B shows the amount of funding needed for a candidate to compete for the United States presidency. But other political offices also require support, and business can play a large role in this quest. Business organizations have been somewhat balanced in their support of Democrat versus Republican candidates through various PACs. For example, the following companies, through political action committee contributions, have generally supported Democratic candidates: Apple, Cisco Systems, Washington Mutual, and Goldman Sachs. Republican candidates could count on the following firms for their financial support: Procter & Gamble, Berkshire Hathaway, Exxon Mobil, Altria Group, and Merck.[15]

Despite the laws limiting political action contributions, businesses have found PAC contributions to be one of the most effective political action tools. When an industry becomes a target of a hot political issue, such as with the effort to regulate the financial services industry or to reform health care, firms within that industry often increase their political spending. Figure 9.4 lists the top political action committees by contribution, comparing data from 2001 through 2010, and shows that labor unions and trade associations that dominated the top 10 PAC list in 2001–2002 have been replaced by a growing number of business organizations. Figure 9.4 also illustrates the overall growth in the size of PAC contributions by the top 10 contributors from 2001–2002 to 2007–2008.

Although most efforts to use financial incentives to influence politics are legal, at times businesspeople circumvent campaign finance laws and regulations.

Vernon L. Jackson, chairman of iGate Inc., based in Kentucky, pleaded guilty to charges of bribing a Congressional representative, later identified as Louisiana Democrat William J. Jefferson. Jackson admitted to paying $367,500 over four years to Jefferson to promote iGate's technology products to federal agencies, as well as to African governments and companies. In addition, it was reported that Jefferson sought jobs for Jackson's children and other favors in exchange for official acts on behalf of iGate to set up Internet and cable television services in Nigeria. Jefferson was found guilty of 11 counts of bribery, racketeering, and money laundering in 2009 for his role in seeking bribes from 2000 to 2005 from dozens of companies including Jackson's.[16]

Economic Leverage

Another political action tool often used by businesses when pursuing a financial incentive strategy is to use their economic leverage to influence public policymakers. **Economic leverage** occurs when a business uses its economic power to threaten to leave a city, state, or country unless a desired political action is taken. Economic leverage also can be used to persuade a government body to act in a certain way that would favor the business, as seen in the following story.

[14] "Donations Underscore Health Care Debate," *Pittsburgh Post-Gazette*, March 9, 2009, *www.post-gazette.com.*

[15] For a more comprehensive listing of business contributions by political party, see "Partisan Portfolios," *Miller-McCune Magazine*, 2009, *www.miller-mccune.com.*

[16] "Businessman Pleads Guilty to Bribing a Representative," *The New York Times*, May 4, 2006, *www.nytimes.com;* "F.B.I. Contends Lawmaker Hid Bribe in Freezer," *The New York Times*, May 22, 2006, *www.nytimes.com;* and "Ex-Rep. Jefferson Convicted in Bribery Scheme," *The New York Times*, August 6, 2009, *www.nytimes.com.*

FIGURE 9.4 **Political Action Committee Activity**

PAC Name	2001–2002	PAC Name	2007–2008	PAC Name	2009–2010*
1 National Association of Realtors	$3,648,526	National Association of Realtors	$4,020,900	Operating Engineers Union	$1,945,000
2 Laborers Union	$2,814,200	International Brotherhood of Electrical Workers	$3,344,650	National Community Pharmacists Association	$952,000
3 Association of Trial Lawyers of America	$2,813,753	AT&T, Inc.	$3,108,200	International Brotherhood of Electrical Workers	$828,650
4 National Auto Dealers Association	$2,578,750	American Bankers Association	$2,918,143	AT&T, Inc.	$624,775
5 American Medical Association	$2,480,972	National Beer Wholesalers Association	$2,869,000	American Crystal Sugar	$519,000
6 American Federation of State/County/Municipal Employees	$2,423,500	National Auto Dealers Association	$2,864,000	National Beer Wholesalers Association	$508,000
7 Teamsters Union	$2,390,003	International Association of Fire Fighters	$2,734,900	Carpenters & Joiners Union	$500,000
8 United Auto Workers	$2,339,000	Operating Engineers Union	$2,704,067	Honeywell International	$465,000
9 International Brotherhood of Electrical Workers	$2,249,300	American Association for Justice	$2,700,500	American Bankers Association	$441,500
10 Carpenters & Joiners Union	$2,243,000	Laborers Union	$2,555,850	American Association for Justice	$439,000

* 2009–2010 = incomplete election cycle; data as of June 1, 2009.

Sources: "Top PACs" for 2001–2002, 2007–2008, and 2009–2010, Center for Responsive Politics, *www.opensecrets.org.*

When the state of Pennsylvania was considering legalizing slot machines at racetracks, the owners of a National Hockey League team located in the state, the Pittsburgh Penguins, were lobbying for a new ice hockey arena to be built with public funds. Government leaders were hesitant to use public funds for a new arena unless substantial private funds were also available. Ted Arneault, owner of the Mountaineer Racetrack and Gaming Resort and part owner of the Pittsburgh Penguins, offered a deal. He said his company would contribute $60 million to build the new ice hockey arena if the state would approve the use of slot machines at Pennsylvania racetracks, including his proposed racetrack facility near Pittsburgh. Legislators agreed.[17]

[17] "Penguins, Arneault Make $107 Million Private Funding Proposal for New Arena Project," *Pittsburgh Post-Gazette,* June 24, 2003, p. A1.

In this example, the business owner successfully used economic leverage. By committing his own private money to help support the construction of a new ice hockey arena, he was able to persuade politicians to vote in favor of legislation to approve the use of slot machines at racetracks in the state.

Promoting a Constituency-Building Strategy

The final strategy used by business to influence the political environment is to seek support from organizations or people who are also affected by the public policy or who are sympathetic to business's political position. This approach is sometimes called a *grassroots strategy*, because its objective is to shape policy by mobilizing the broad public in support of a business organization's position, or a *grasstops strategy,* because its objective is to influence local opinion leaders. Firms use several methods to build support among constituents. These include advocacy advertising, public relations, and building coalitions with other affected stakeholders.

Stakeholder Coalitions

Businesses may try to influence politics by mobilizing various organizational stakeholders—employees, stockholders, customers, and the local community—to support their political agenda. If a political issue can negatively affect a business, it is likely that it also will negatively affect that business's stakeholders. If pending regulation will impose substantial costs on the business, these costs may result in employee layoffs, or a drop in the firm's stock value, or higher prices for the firm's customers. Often, businesses organize programs to get organizational stakeholders, acting as lobbyists or voters, to influence government officials to vote or act in a favorable way. For example, some companies have asked their shareholders to participate in grassroots efforts to persuade their congressional representatives to reduce capital gains taxes and thereby make stock purchases and other investments more lucrative. These programs send strong messages to elected officials that voters support the desired action.

Advocacy Advertising

A common method of influencing constituents is **advocacy advertising**. Advocacy ads focus not on a particular product or service, like most ads, but rather on a company's views on controversial political issues. Advocacy ads, also called *issue advertisements,* can appear in newspapers, on television, or in other media outlets. They have been legal in the United States since 1978. Mobil (now ExxonMobil) pioneered the use of advocacy advertising, focusing on issues such as gasoline price controls and environmental regulations at a time when such advertising was largely unknown. Supporters of advocacy advertisements believe that they identify a company as an interested and active stakeholder and can help mold public opinion on a particular policy issue.

More recent examples of advocacy advertisements, also discussed in Chapter 19, include organizations seeking to promote their political position with regard to the federal energy policy in the United States. The oil and gas industry took to the nation's newspapers to promote their investment in and support of a federal energy policy that included a greater dependence on U.S. natural gas and refined oil. They showed a dollar bill cut into pieces to indicate how much was spent for the crude oil ($.56), for refining, distribution, and service stations ($.26), and taxes ($.18). This informed the public that the cost of the crude oil, mostly imported, was the single most expensive cost for the gas they were getting at the pump. They also directed readers of their advocacy ads to their Web site, *www.api.org.*

Trade Associations

Many businesses work through **trade associations**—coalitions of companies in the same or related industries—to coordinate their grassroots mobilization campaigns. Examples of trade associations include the National Realtors Association (real estate brokers), National Federation of Independent Businesses (small businesses), the National Association of Manufacturers (manufacturers only), or the U.S. Chamber of Commerce (broad, diverse membership).[18]

The U.S. Chamber of Commerce has a membership of more than 200,000 companies. The chamber has a multimillion-dollar budget, publishes a widely circulated magazine, and operates a satellite television network to broadcast its political messages. The Chamber of Commerce takes positions on a wide range of political, economic, and regulatory questions and actively works to promote its members' views of what conditions are necessary for them to effectively compete in a free marketplace.

Activities of trade associations may include letters, faxes, telegrams, telephone calls, and Internet communications to register approval or disapproval of a government official's position on an important issue.

Legal Challenges

A political tactic available to businesses (and other political participants) is the use of legal challenges. In this approach, business seeks to overturn a law after it has been passed or threatens to challenge the legal legitimacy of the new regulation in the courts. Such an approach is shown in the following example:

> The passage of the Family Smoking Prevention and Tobacco Act of 2009, Chapter 8's discussion case, sparked numerous legal challenges from marketing, advertisement, and tobacco manufacturing firms. The ban on outdoor advertisement of any tobacco product within 1,000 feet of schools and playgrounds effectively outlawed legal advertising in many cities. In addition, according to the opponents of the bill, which included the Association of National Advertisers and the American Civil Liberties Union, the new rule was a violation of free speech, a right protected under the First Amendment of the U.S. Constitution. They also contended that restricting many forms of print advertising to black-and-white text interfered with legitimate communication to adults of the tobacco products. In 2001, the U.S. Supreme Court struck down a Massachusetts ban on tobacco ads, including outdoor billboards and signs that could be seen within 1,000 feet of any public playground and elementary or secondary school, stating that the law was an unconstitutional limit of the First Amendment's right to free speech because it was too broad.[19]

Levels of Political Involvement

Business executives must decide on the appropriate level of political involvement for their company. As shown in Figure 9.5, there are multiple levels of involvement and many ways to participate. To be successful, a business must think strategically about objectives and how specific political issues and opportunities relate to those objectives.

---

[18] The classic discussion of corporate political action can be found in Edwin Epstein, *The Corporation in American Politics* (Englewood Cliffs, NJ: Prentice Hall, 1969). An up-to-date discussion of current trends in American political and civic life is in Robert D. Putnam, *Bowling Alone* (New York: Simon and Schuster, 2000), especially ch. 4.

[19] "Tobacco Firms Sue to Block Marketing Law," *The New York Times*, September 1, 2009, *www.nytimes.com*; and "Tobacco Regulation Is Expected to Face a Free-Speech Challenge," *The New York Times*, June 16, 2009, *www.nytimes.com*.

FIGURE 9.5
Levels of Business Political Involvement

> ↑ *Level 3   Aggressive Organizational Involvement—direct and personal*
>
> - Executive participation
> - Involvement with industry working groups and task forces
> - Public policy development
>
> *Level 2   Moderate Organizational Involvement—indirect yet personal*
>
> - Organizational lobbyist
> - Employee grassroots involvement
> - Stockholders and customers encouraged to become involved
>
> *Level 1   Limited Organizational Involvement—indirect and impersonal*
>
> - Contribution to political action committee
> - Support of a trade association or industry activities

Organizations often begin at the lowest level of political participation, *limited organizational involvement.* Here managers of the organization are not ready or willing to become politically involved by giving their own time or getting their stakeholders involved, but they want to do something to influence the political environment. Organizations at this level may show their political interest, for example, by writing out a check to a trade association to support an industry-backed political action, such as hiring a lobbyist on a specific issue.

When the organization is ready for *moderate political involvement,* managers might directly employ a lobbyist to represent the company's political strategy in Washington or the state capital to push the firm's political agenda. This is a more active form of political involvement since the lobbyist is an employee of the organization. Getting the organization's stakeholders involved is another way a firm can increase its political involvement. Employees can write letters to their congressperson or become involved in a political campaign. Senior executives might communicate with stockholders or customers on particular issues that might affect the firm and its stakeholders and encourage them to write letters or otherwise voice their concerns. Some firms have sent letters to their stockholders soliciting their political contributions for a particular candidate or group of candidates but have asked that the contributions be sent to the company. Then the company takes all of the contributions to the candidate or candidates, clearly indicating that the contributions are from the firm's stockholders. This technique is called **bundling**.

The most direct and personal involvement in the political environment is achieved at the third level—*aggressive organizational involvement*—where managers become personally involved in developing public policy. Some executives are asked to sit on important task forces charged with writing legislation that will affect the firm or the firm's industry. When state legislatures were writing laws limiting the opportunities for corporate raiders to acquire unwilling companies in their states, the legislators turned to corporate general counsels, the company attorneys, to help draft the law. Another example of aggressive organizational involvement is provided by the Business Roundtable, described earlier in this chapter.

Managing the Political Environment

In many organizations, the task of managing political activity falls to the department of public affairs or government relations. The role of the **public affairs department** is to manage the firm's interactions with governments at all levels and to promote the firm's

Exhibit 9.C

Corporate Public Affairs Activities

Activities Conducted within the Public Affairs Department	Percentage of Companies, 2005	Percentage of Companies, 2008
Federal government relations	95%	95%
State government relations	85	91
Issues management	82	84
Business/trade association oversight	75	81
Political action committee	83	80
Coalitions	71	78
Local government relations	79	76
Grassroots/grasstops	75	74
Community relations	58	57

Source: Foundation for Public Affairs, *The State of Corporate Public Affairs, 2008–2009* (2008), p. 9. Based on a survey of 130 companies. Used by permission.

interests in the political process. (*Public relations,* discussed in Chapter 19, has a different business function.) The creation of public affairs units is a global trend, with many companies in Canada, Australia, and Europe developing sophisticated public affairs operations.[20] As shown in Exhibit 9.C, eight of the 10 most frequently performed activities by public affairs officers or departments involve a political action tactic, and attention has increased for most of these political activities during the past few years.

Most companies have a senior manager or executive to lead the public affairs department. This manager is often a member of the company's senior management committee, providing expertise about the company's major strategy and policy decisions. The size of the department and the support staff varies widely among companies. Many companies assign employees from other parts of the business to work on public affairs issues and to help plan, coordinate, and execute public affairs activities. In this way, the formulation and implementation of the policies and programs developed by a company's public affairs unit are closely linked to the primary business activities of the firm.

> Eaton Corporation, a diversified power management company with annual revenues of $80 billion and more than 40,000 employees, chose to combine its public affairs and corporate communications functions into one department. According to Barry Doggett, Eaton's vice president for public and community affairs, "two things make this structure effective for us. First, Don McGrath, our vice president for communications, and I both report directly to the CEO. Second, the two of us have a great relationship. We stay on the same page. As a result, we now have two voices, and not one, at the table." Doggett is responsible for Eaton's federal, state, and local government relations activities, as well as the company's charitable and community relations initiatives.[21]

[20] The global patterns of public affairs practice are documented in *Journal of Public Affairs,* published by Henry Stewart Publishing beginning in 2001. For an excellent review of public affairs development around the world, see Craig S. Fleisher and Natasha Blair, "Surveying the Field: Status and Trends Affecting Public Affairs across Australia, Canada, EU and the U.S.," in *Assessing, Managing and Maximizing Public Affairs Performance,* Management Handbook series, ed. Craig S. Fleisher (Washington, DC: Public Affairs Council, 1997).

[21] "Six Thousand Stores, One Voice, How Is That Possible?" *Public Affairs Council,* n.d., *pac.org.* Also see Eaton Corporation's Web site at *www.Eaton.com.*

The heads of most public affairs departments are senior vice president or vice president positions; some report directly to the CEO, as at Eaton Corporation, while others are one level below this in the organizational hierarchy. Most work out of company headquarters; most of the rest—particularly those whose work focuses on government relations—work in Washington, DC. More than half of the senior public affairs executives, 55 percent, sit on the corporation's strategic planning committee.[22]

Campaign Finance Reform: A Special Issue

During the 1990s, it became clear to Americans that the cost of running for political office was rising at an unbelievable rate and was only getting worse. Critics feared that the growing amount of money pouring into elections would become a corrupting influence on politics. Politicians would become more and more beholden to the interest groups, individuals, and businesses that had supported their expensive campaigns.

The Bipartisan Campaign Reform Act of 2002, initiated by senators John McCain (Republican–Arizona) and Russell Feingold (Democrat–Wisconsin), imposed a ban on **soft money**—unlimited contributions to the national political parties by individuals or organizations for party-building activities. As an alternative, the act permitted contributors to give their money to so-called **527 organizations**, named after their provision in the tax code. These organizations provide potential contributors with a new and legal way to influence the election of a candidate or bring attention to a political issue. An example of a 527 organization is Emily's List, an organization committed to electing pro-choice Democratic women, recruiting and funding viable women candidates, helping them build and run effective campaign organizations, and mobilizing women voters to help elect progressive candidates across the nation.[23]

What was anticipated as a revolutionary change in American campaign financing quickly turned into a legal nightmare. On the day after the McCain–Feingold proposal became law, an extraordinary cross-section of American politics formed an unexpected coalition. The National Rifle Association, the American Civil Liberties Union, antiabortion groups, the U.S. Chamber of Commerce, and the Republican and Democratic National Committees joined together in filing a lawsuit arguing that the law was unconstitutional. Some of these groups were concerned about possible violations of free speech; others were simply concerned that their rights to donate money and influence policy would be restricted.

In 2003, the U.S. Supreme Court upheld key provisions of the law, stating that while the law may step lightly on the toes of free-speech rights, it more importantly restricts a large source of likely government corruption: soft money.

The immediate reactions to the new campaign reforms were mixed. Some companies were relieved to be free of pressure to contribute large amounts of money indirectly to campaigns. Verizon, International Paper, and several other companies that had poured unprecedented amounts of cash into the political system in the 1990s reported that they were largely dropping out of the political money race. "It was an opportunity to draw the line in the sand and say no," said Kristin Krouse, FedEx Corporation spokesperson.[24]

[22] Foundation for Public Affairs, *The State of Corporate Public Affairs, 2008–2009* (Washington, DC: Foundation for Public Affairs, 2008), pp. 23–25.

[23] See Emily's List Web site at *emilyslist.org*.

[24] "In New Law's Wave, Companies Slash Their Political Donations," *The Wall Street Journal*, September 3, 2004, pp. A1, A4.

Yet other firms learned how to work within the new rules by channeling their contributions through the 527 organizations. By 2008, some of the largest 527 organizations included America Votes (which coordinates activities of more than 20 Democratic interest groups, with expenditures of nearly $23 million in 2008) and American Solutions Winning the Future (created by former House Speaker and Republican Newt Gingrich, with expenditures of nearly $23 million). Individuals also found that contributing to 527 organizations enabled them to be politically active. Fred Eschelman, a pharmaceutical executive and primary supporter of the conservative-leaning Rightchange.com, contributed nearly $5.5 million to attempt to block Barack Obama from winning the presidential election. The second largest 527 contributor, financial investor George Soros, gave $5 million to 527 organizations that were sympathetic to Democratic Party issues.[25]

Business Political Action: A Global Challenge

Most of the discussion so far in the chapter has focused on business political activity in the United States. As more companies conduct business abroad, it is critical that managers be aware of the opportunities for and restrictions on business involvement in the political processes in other countries. Other societies and governments also struggle with issues of participation in the political environment, campaign financing, and maintaining a fair ethical climate throughout the public policy process. One example is Japan.

In Japan, a pluralistic political environment characterizes the public policy process. The major actors are members of big business, agriculture, and labor. These special interest groups are quite powerful and influential. Some of the largest interest groups support more than a few hundred candidates in each important election and provide them with large financial contributions. The *Kiedanren,* or federation of economic organizations, is mostly concerned with Japanese big business, but other interest groups promote the concerns of small and medium-sized businesses, such as barbers, cosmeticians, dry cleaners, innkeepers, and theater owners. Some political influence is in the hands of smaller groups such as the teachers union (*Nikkyoso*), Japan Medical Association, employers association (*Nikkeiren*), and a labor union (*Rengo*).[26]

A different political system is in place in China, a one-party communist state. This has important implications for political strategies used by businesses there. Direct political participation by businesses in China occurs in one of three ways. First, a firm's leader can be elected as a congressman to the National People's Congress in China. Second, the firm's leader can be elected as a member of the National Political Consultation Conference, an organization somewhat like the U.S. Congress but that offers advice rather than formulates laws. Third, the firm can become a member of groups organized to prepare industrial policy or standards for government (similar to the third level of political involvement described earlier in the chapter). Businesses in China also may become involved through information strategy tactics, such as lobbying or mobilizing support for legislative issues. But before lobbying can occur, the firm must build *guanxi*, a relationship, with government officials first. Financial strategies also occur in the Chinese political system even though there is no political campaigning. Businesses use gift giving,

---

[25] See "Top 50 Federally Focused Organizations," *Center for Responsive Politics, www.opensecrets.org.*

[26] Ryan Beaupre and Patricia Malone, "Interest Groups and Politics in Japan," *alpha.fdu.edu/~woolley/JAPANpolitics/Beaupre.htm.*

charity and education contributions, honoraria for speaking engagements, and other personal services as ways to financially influence the political system.[27]

Controlling Corruption in Politics

Despite efforts to maintain an ethical political environment, political corruption is common in many countries around the world. Consider the case of Lebanon.

> In the 2009 parliamentary elections, hundreds of millions of dollars streamed into the small nation from around the globe. Seen as a key player in the hotly contested Middle East, voters were given cash or in-kind services presumably paid for by political candidates. Candidates offered their competitors huge sums to withdraw from the race. Thousands of Lebanese citizens flew back to their native country with the expectation they would vote for the candidate that paid for the trip. Surprisingly, Lebanon was the first Arab country to impose campaign spending limits, although analysts admitted that the monitoring was very loose and applied only to the last two months before the election. The laws were laughably easy to circumvent, according to Lebanese election monitors.[28]

According to a report developed by Transparency International, a German-based international organization that studies bribery and corruption, Mohammed Suharto, Ferdinand Marcos, and Mobutu Sese Seko, the leaders of Indonesia, the Philippines, and Zaire, respectively, combined to personally take more than $50 billion from their impoverished nations and people. According to Transparency International's chairman, Peter Eigen, "The abuse of political power for private gain deprives the most needy of vital public services, creating a level of despair that breed conflicts and violence."[29] More than any other cause, political scandals have given rise to efforts to develop fairer and less corrupt political processes for electing government officials around the world.

Campaign Financing Reform Abroad

In general, efforts to reform campaign financing in countries have focused on the following themes:

- Limits on expenditures—for example, ceilings on permitted spending by each candidate or political party.
- Contribution limits—restricting the amount an individual or organization is permitted to donate.
- Disclosure regulations—mandating the reporting of the names of campaign contributors and the amount contributed.
- Bans against certain types of contributions—for example, the prohibition or restriction of payments by businesses, unions, or foreign organizations and foreign citizens.
- Bans against certain types of expenditures—for example, bans on bribes to individual electors, on entertainment, or on the purchasing of advertising time.
- Measures designed to encourage donations—providing tax relief or tax credits for political donations.

[27] Yongquiang Gao and Zhilong Tian, "A Comparative Study of Corporate Political Action in China," *Journal of American Academy of Business* 8 (2006), pp. 67–72.

[28] "Foreign Money Seeks to Buy Lebanese Votes," *The New York Times*, April 23, 2009, *www.nytimes.com.*

[29] "Suharto, Marcos, and Mobutu Head Corruption Table with $50 Billion Scams," *Political Corruption: A Collection of Links on Politics and Political Corruption in Relation to Financial Scandals*, March 26, 2004, *www.ex.ac.uk/~RDavies/arian/scandals/political.html.*

- Subsidies in kind—where candidates are provided with free postage for election literature or free television airtime.
- Public subsidies—providing financial payments to political parties or candidates from public funds.[30]

Underlying these themes are attempts to minimize political corruption, promote fairness in the electoral process, control the rapid rise in the costs of campaigning, enhance the role of political parties in elections, and encourage grassroots participation by various societal groups.

> At the 2007 Global Electoral Organization Conference, more than 200 of the world's top election officials and democracy advocates met to celebrate "transparency in the election process." Delegates from Eastern Europe, Central Asia, the Middle East, and Africa discussed the most critical issues in election administration, including how to resolve election disputes, the role of the media in elections, and tracking money in political campaigns. This was the fourth global conference on this theme and indicated the growing importance of cleaning up political elections worldwide. One conference delegate explained, "I think standards are changing and politicians will have to recognize this—that as we are now in the 21st century, public opinion is applying different standards to politics, to politicians, to political parties. They're not allowed to do things they were doing in the 19th and 20th centuries. People have high expectations, high demands, and they will keep politicians accountable."[31]

Political action by business—whether to influence government policy or the outcome of an election—is natural in a democratic, pluralistic society. In the United States, business has a legitimate right to participate in the political process, just as consumers, labor unions, environmentalists, and others do. One danger arising from corporate political activity is that corporations may wield too much power. As businesses operate in different communities and countries, it is important that ethical norms and standards guide managers as they deal with political issues. If corporate power tips the scales against other interests in society, both business and society may lose. Whether it is in the media-rich arena of electoral politics or the corridors of Congress where more traditional lobbying prevails, business leaders must address the issues of how to manage relationships with government and special interests in society in ethically sound ways. Ultimately, business has an important long-term stake in a healthy, honest political system.

Summary

- Some believe that businesses should be involved in politics because their economic stake in government decisions is great and they have a right to participate, just as do other stakeholders in a pluralistic political system. But others believe that businesses are too big, powerful, and selfish, and that they wield too much influence in the political arena.

---

[30] "Party and Campaign Financing," ACE Web site, *www.aceproject.org/main/english/pc.*

[31] "World: Campaign Finance Seen as Central to Fair Elections," *RadioFreeEurope*, April 3, 2007, *www.rferl.org.*

- There are three political strategies: information, financial incentives, and constituency-building. Some firms implement strategies as needed, on an issue-by-issue basis, while other firms have a long-term, ongoing political strategy approach.
- Some of the political action tactics available for business include lobbying, direct communications, expert witness testimony, political action committee contributions, economic leverage, advocacy advertising, trade association involvement, legal challenges, and encouraging the involvement of other stakeholders.
- Businesses manage their government interactions through a public affairs department. Most public affairs officers report to the CEO or some high-level official, although how these departments are structured is widely varied.
- Businesses are a major contributor to campaigns, although the U.S. government and other countries have limited the kinds and amounts of contributions.
- The differing national rules and practices governing political activity make business's political involvement complex in the global environment. Many governments, like the United States, are trying to restrict political contributions or make campaign financing more transparent.

Key Terms

ad hoc coalitions, *198*
advocacy advertising, *208*
bundling, *210*
Business Roundtable, *203*
corporate political strategy, *198*

economic leverage, *206*
527 organizations, *212*
lobbying, *200*
political action committees (PACs), *204*

public affairs departments, *210*
revolving door, *202*
soft money, *212*
trade associations, *209*

Internet Resources

www.businessroundtable.org	The Business Roundtable
www.campaignfinancesite.org	Hoover Institution, Campaign Finance
www.commoncause.org	Common Cause
www.consumeraction.gov/trade	Consumer Action Web site, Trade Associations
www.fec.gov	U.S. Federal Election Commission
lobbyingdisclosure.house.gov	Lobbying Disclosure, U.S. House of Representatives
www.ncpa.org	National Center for Policy Analysis
www.nfib.com	National Federation of Independent Businesses
www.opensecrets.org	Opensecrets.org
www.politicsonline.com	PoliticsOnline: News, Tools & Strategies
pac.org	Public Affairs Council
www.pdc.wa.gov	Public Disclosure Commission

Discussion Case: *Ex-Senator, Now Business Lobbyist—Ethical Questions of Use of Campaign Funds*

New Jersey Senator Robert G. Torricelli ran for reelection in 2002, raising millions of dollars in campaign contributions from loyal supporters, as one must do to be elected to the U.S. Senate. Then, abruptly, Torricelli quit the race amid allegations of ethical misconduct. (Several weeks later, the Senate Ethics Committee issued a letter "severely admonishing" Torricelli for accepting campaign gifts from a contributor.) Two months after quitting the race, Torricelli founded a lobbying practice, Rosemont Associates, with clients in Taiwan, Puerto Rico, and the United States. But the critical issue was, what should Torricelli do with the $2.9 million in campaign funds, more than any other senator who retired from the Senate in the past 20 years but one?

His decision on how to spend the campaign funds surprised some and irritated others. Torricelli gave $10,000 to Illinois Governor Rod Blagojevich, and more than $40,000 to Nevada Democratic Party organizations and candidates linked to the Senate majority leader, Harry Reid. All of these politicians had one thing in common—they all had some influence over Torricelli or his clients' business interests.

But Torricelli did not violate any federal campaign financing rules. The federal government permits retired officials to give leftover campaign funds to charities, candidates, and political parties. Torricelli's campaign treasurer and a partner in his lobbying firm said that any suggestion that the contributions were tied to his business interests was "ridiculous." He said that Torricelli simply contributed to people he knew or with whom he shared policy goals.

But others pointed to these contributions as particularly troubling. Shortly after Torricelli's political gift to Nevada Senator Harry Reid, he reached out to Reid on behalf of a Taiwanese client, setting up a meeting between Reid and the client to discuss Taiwan's opposition to a new Chinese law that authorized the use of force if Taiwan declared independence. Similarly, Torricelli had a private meeting with Governor Blagojevich and Leonard Barrack, head of Barrack, Rodos & Bacine, a law firm hired by Torricelli as a consultant. Five days after the meeting, Torricelli gave a $10,000 contribution to Blagojevich's reelection campaign. Shortly thereafter, Barrack, Rodos & Bacine was placed on the Illinois State Teachers Retirement System's list of preferred outside attorneys. While the retirement system's board of trustees decides who is placed on the list, the governor appoints 4 of the 11 board members.

Torricelli also used his excess campaign funds to influence other issues linked to his business. In 2002 CSC Holdings, operator of Cablevision, made a $162,000 contribution to Torricelli's senatorial campaign. Later, as a lobbyist, Torricelli took on Cablevision as a client and attempted to lobby the New Jersey State Senate to change the wording of a bill in a way that would favor Cablevision. Torricelli used $5,000 from his own Senate campaign fund to support a slate of municipal candidates in New Jersey. This influence from various cities helped the New Jersey State Senate pass a cable television bill that included the weakened provisions sought by Cablevision.

Campaign finance watchdogs said that former officials are prohibited from using leftover funds for personal expenses. They admit that Torricelli had not violated the rules, but acknowledged that he may have found a legal loophole to spend funds in a way that would support his private business. According to Massie Ritsch of the Center for Responsive Politics, a nonprofit campaign oversight organization, "Contributors should reasonably expect that their money will go for campaigning and not that it will sit in an account for years and be doled out to build someone's personal business."

Sources: "Now a Lobbyist, an Ex-Senator Uses Campaign Money," *The New York Times,* August 24, 2007, *www.nytimes.com.*

Discussion Questions

1. Has Torricelli violated the intentions of his campaign contributors, even though he may not have violated specific campaign financing laws?

2. Should there be additional and more severe limits on how retired politicians can use leftover campaign finances? If so, how should these leftover funds be used?

3. Is the Torricelli case another example of the problem of the "revolving door" between politics and business, a senator-turned-lobbyist? How can government place better controls to guard against the problems that emerge from the revolving door?

4. Should those that received political contributions from Torricelli, the lobbyist, refused his contributions? Why or why not?

5. Should Torricelli's business clients be concerned about his use of leftover campaign funds on their behalf?

PART FIVE

Business and the Natural Environment

CHAPTER TEN

Ecology and Sustainable Development in Global Business

The world community faces unprecedented ecological challenges in the 21st century. Many political and business leaders have embraced the idea of sustainable development, calling for economic development without destroying the natural environment or depleting the resources on which future generations depend. Yet the concept has remained controversial, and implementation has been difficult. The task for government policymakers and corporate leaders will be to find ways to meet both economic and environmental goals in the coming decades.

This Chapter Focuses on These Key Learning Objectives:

- Defining sustainable development.
- Understanding the obstacles to developing the world's economy to meet the needs of the present without hurting future generations.
- Assessing the major threats to the Earth's ecosystem.
- Recognizing the ways in which population growth, inequality, and economic development have accelerated the world's ecological crisis.
- Examining common environmental issues that are shared by all nations.
- Analyzing the steps the global business community can take to reduce ecological damage and promote sustainable development.

In 1992, representatives of the world's nations gathered in Rio de Janeiro, Brazil, for a groundbreaking event, the first World Summit on Sustainable Development. In a series of contentious sessions, delegates considered, on the one hand, the growing dangers of environmental degradation and, on the other hand, the urgent need for economic development in poorer nations. Would it be possible, they asked, to foster economic growth sufficient to lift the majority of the world's people out of poverty without compromising the ability of future generations to meet their own needs?

Now, almost two decades later, progress toward achieving these goals has been in many respects disappointing. Consider that at the 1992 gathering

- Delegates had pledged to attack the problem of global warming, increases in the Earth's temperature caused in part by carbon dioxide emissions from the world's factories, utilities, and vehicles. The conference had called on developed countries to cut back to 1990 levels by the year 2000. But only half the developed countries met this target, and annual emissions of carbon dioxide have reached new highs, threatening disruption of the world's climate. China, with its rapid economic growth and heavy reliance on coal-fueled power plants, has surpassed the United States to become the world's largest emitter of greenhouse gases.[1]

- Delegates had committed to a framework Convention on Biological Diversity, dedicated to conserving the Earth's biological resources, particularly in species-rich tropical forests. But many plants and animals remain endangered. Vast stretches of rain forest have been cut down. In Indonesia, for example, home to large numbers of endangered birds, mammals, and reptiles, tropical forest is being logged for timber and burned to clear land at an astonishing rate, destroying habitat and, not incidentally, causing serious air pollution throughout Southeast Asia.[2]

- Many developed nations had pledged to increase foreign aid to 0.7 percent of their gross national income (GNI) to help poorer countries develop their economies in an environmentally sustainable way. But during the intervening years, aid has actually fallen to just 0.3 percent of GNI, lower than it was in 1992.[3] Now the question is just as urgent as it was before: Who will pay for the costs of clean development in the poorer countries?

However, important progress has been made. Although the world population is still growing, the rate of growth has dropped somewhat. An international treaty on global warming has gone into effect, and negotiations to strengthen it continue. The World Bank, an important lender to developing countries, has instituted a strict environmental review process, refusing to fund ecologically destructive projects. Important gains have been made in efforts to restore the health of the ozone layer. Many nations, notably in Europe, have made progress on energy conservation. And possibly most promisingly, many segments of the global business community have become increasingly active in promoting environmentally sound management practices. Can the world's governments, businesses, nongovernmental organizations, and individuals, working together, meet the ecological challenges of the 21st century and put the global economy on a more sustainable course?[4]

[1] The Web site for the United Nations Framework Convention on Climate Change is available at *http://unfccc.int*.

[2] The Web site for the Convention on Biological Diversity is available at *www.biodiv.org*.

[3] Data on percentages of GNI devoted to development assistance by industrialized nations are available at the Web site of the Organization for Economic Cooperation and Development, Development Assistance Committee, at *www.oecd.org/dac*.

[4] For current data, including the biannual report *Global Environmental Outlook*, see the Web site of the United Nations Environment Programme at *www.unep.org*.

Ecological Challenges

Humankind is now altering the face of the planet, rivaling the forces of nature herself—glaciers, volcanoes, asteroids, and earthquakes—in impact. Human beings have literally rerouted rivers, moved mountains, and burned vast forests. By the beginning of the 21st century, human society had transformed about half of the earth's ice-free surface and made a major impact on most of the rest. In many areas, as much land was used by transportation systems as by agriculture. Although significant natural resources—fossil fuels, fresh water, fertile land, and forest—remained, exploding populations and rapid economic development had reached the point where, by some measures, the demands of human society had already exceeded the carrying capacity of the Earth's ecosystem.

Ecology is the study of how living things—plants and animals—interact with one another in the Earth's unified natural system, or ecosystem. Damage to the ecosystem in one part of the world often affects people in other locations. Depletion of the ozone layer, destruction of the rain forests, and species extinctions have an impact on all of society, not just particular regions or nations.

The Global Commons

Throughout history, communities of people have created *commons*. A **commons** is a shared resource, such as land, air, or water, that a group of people use collectively. The *paradox of the commons* is that if all individuals attempt to maximize their own private advantage in the short term, the commons may be destroyed, and all users, present and future, lose. The only solution is restraint, either voluntary or through mutual agreement.[5] The *tragedy of the commons*—that freedom in a commons brings ruin to all—is illustrated by the following parable.

> There was once a village on the shore of a great ocean. Its people made a good living from the rich fishing grounds that lay offshore, the bounty of which seemed inexhaustible. Some of the cleverest fishermen began to experiment with new ways to catch more fish, borrowing money to buy bigger and better-equipped boats. Since it was hard to argue with success, others copied their new techniques. Soon fish began to be harder to find, and their average size began to decline. Eventually, the fishery collapsed, bringing economic calamity to the village. A wise elder commented, "You see, the fish were not free after all. It was our folly to act as if they were."[6]

In a sense, we live today in a global commons, in which many natural resources, like the fishing grounds in this parable, are used collectively. The image of the Earth as seen from space, a blue-and-green globe, girdled by white clouds, floating in blackness, dramatically shows us that we share a single, unified ecosystem. Preserving our common ecosystem and assuring its continued use is a new imperative for governments, business, and society. As Maurice Strong, the first executive director of the United Nations Environmental Program, stated, "We now face the ultimate management challenge, that of managing our own future as a species."

---

[5] Garrett Hardin, "Tragedy of the Commons," *Science* 162 (December 1968), pp. 1243–48.

[6] Abridgment of "The Story of a Fishing Village," from *1994 Information Please Environmental Almanac.* Copyright © 1993 by World Resources Institute. Reprinted by permission of Houghton Mifflin Co. All rights reserved.

Sustainable Development

The need for balance between economic and environmental considerations is captured in the concept of **sustainable development**. This term refers to development that "meets the needs of the present without compromising the ability of future generations to meet their own needs."[7] The concept includes two core ideas:

- Protecting the environment will require economic development. Poverty is an underlying cause of environmental degradation. People who lack food, shelter, and basic amenities misuse resources just to survive. For this reason, environmental protection will require providing a decent standard of living for all the world's citizens.

- But economic development must be accomplished sustainably—that is, in a way that conserves the Earth's resources for future generations. Development cannot occur at the expense of degrading the forests, farmland, water, and air that must continue to support life on this planet. We must leave the Earth in as good shape—or better shape—than we found it.

In short, the idea of sustainable development encompasses a kind of puzzle. It challenges government and business leaders to eradicate poverty and develop the world economy but to do so in a way that does not degrade the environment or plunder natural resources.

Sustainable development is an appealing idea but also a controversial one. For sustainable development to work, rich nations such as the United States and Japan would have to consume fewer resources and dramatically cut pollution, without simply exporting environmental stresses to other countries. Developing nations, such as Brazil or Pakistan, for their part, would have to use less destructive agricultural practices, cut birthrates, and industrialize more cleanly. This would be possible only with the aid of money, technology, and skills from the developed nations.

What would the idea of sustainable development mean for business? One attempt to apply this concept to business operations has been an initiative in Sweden called The Natural Step, described in Exhibit 10.A. Other voluntary efforts by the global business community to operate with less harm to the environment are addressed in the last section of this chapter and in Chapter 11.

Threats to the Earth's Ecosystem

Sustainable development requires that human society use natural resources at a rate that can be continued over an indefinite period. Human activity affects three major forms of natural resources: water, air, and land. Biologists distinguish between *renewable* resources, such as fresh water or forests, that can be naturally replenished and *nonrenewable* resources, such as fossil fuels (oil, gas, and coal), that once used are gone forever. Many natural resources, renewable and nonrenewable, are now being depleted or polluted at well above sustainable rates. Consider the following examples.

Water Resources

Only 3 percent of the water on the Earth is fresh, and most of this is underground or locked up in ice and snow. Only about one-tenth of 1 percent of the Earth's water is in lakes, rivers, and accessible underground supplies, and thus available for human use. Water is, of course, renewable: Moisture evaporates from the oceans and returns to Earth

---

[7] World Commission on Environment and Development, *Our Common Future* (Oxford: Oxford University Press, 1987), p. 8.

The Natural Step (TNS) was founded in 1989 by a prominent Swedish physician, Karl-Henrik Robert. Dr. Robert joined other leading scientists in Sweden to develop a consensus document on how businesses, governments, and individuals could act in a way that was consistent with the principle of sustainable development. Their report was endorsed by the King of Sweden, and a summary was distributed to all households in the country.

The Natural Step encouraged businesses to act voluntarily to cut back on the use of synthetics and nonrenewable resources, minimize their consumption of energy, and preserve natural diversity and ecosystems. Within a decade, more than 300 companies and half the cities in Sweden had adopted TNS principles, and by the late 2000s the movement had spread to 11 countries and hundreds of businesses. An example of a company that has followed The Natural Step is IKEA, the Swedish-based global home furnishings retailer. IKEA signed on, committing itself to the use of materials, technologies, and transportation methods that had the least possible damaging effect on the environment. For example, the company switched from truck to rail shipping where possible to conserve fuel and introduced a new line of furnishings, called the Eco-Line, that used only recycled materials or wood and fibers that had been sustainably harvested. The company said the initiative not only had enabled it to protect the environment and attract "green" customers; it had also actually helped the bottom line by avoiding waste and saving on energy and materials.

Sources: Karl-Henrik Robert, *The Natural Step Story: Seeding a Quiet Revolution* (Gabriola Island, BC: New Catalyst Books, 2008). IKEA's corporate Web site, including material on the company's environmental policies, is available at *www.ikea-group.ikea.com.* The Web site of The Natural Step is at *www.naturalstep.org.*

as freshwater precipitation, replenishing used stocks. But in many areas, humans are using up or polluting water faster than it can be replaced or naturally purified, threatening people and businesses that depend on it.

> The Ganges River supports more than 400 million Indians, providing water for drinking, irrigation, fishing, transportation, and trade along its 1,500-mile course from high in the Himalayan mountains to the coastal city of Kolkata (Calcutta). Hindus believe the river to be holy, and it is the site of many religious observances. But the Ganges is increasingly polluted, choked with raw sewage, industrial waste, animal carcasses, and even human remains. "The [river] is the silken thread which binds this country together. What will happen if it breaks?" asked one Indian.[8]

By one estimate, if society were able to eliminate all pollution, capture all available fresh water, and distribute it equitably—all of which are unlikely—demand would exceed the supply within a hundred years. By the late 2000s, water shortages had already caused the decline of local economies and in some cases had contributed to regional conflicts. In Africa, for example, water disputes had flared among Egypt, Ethiopia, and Sudan, the three countries traversed by the world's longest river, the Nile. In the Middle East, disagreement over access to water from the River Jordan had exacerbated conflict between Israel and Palestine.[9] According to a United Nations study, one-third of the world's population lives in countries experiencing moderate to high water stress.[10]

[8] "India's Sullied River Goddess," *Christian Science Monitor,* January 5, 2007.

[9] "Water Wars: Climate Change May Spark Conflict," *The Independent,* February 28, 2006.

[10] A report on world water resources may be found at *www.wri.org/wri/trends/water.html.* For a projection of water stress levels in 2025, see the United Nations Environmental Program, *Global Environmental Outlook* at *www.unep.org/geo2000/english/i42a.htm.*

Fossil Fuels

Fossil fuels, unlike water, are nonrenewable. Human society used 60 times as much energy in the late 20th century as it did in 1860, when industrialization was in its early stages. Most of this came from the burning of fossil fuels; 85 percent of energy used in the United States, for example, comes from the combustion of coal, oil, and natural gas.[11] The amount of fossil fuel burned by the world economy in one year took about a million years to form, and only one barrel is discovered for every three or four consumed. No one knows how much longer it will be possible to produce oil economically. However, some estimates suggest that oil production will peak sometime between 2010 and 2020.[12] Coal reserves are plentiful and could last three to four more centuries, although coal is more polluting than either oil or natural gas. Eventually, however, many fossil fuel reserves will be depleted, and the world economy will need to become much more energy efficient and switch to renewable energy sources, such as those based on water, wind, and sunshine.

Arable Land

Arable (fertile) land is necessary to grow crops to feed the world's people. Land, if properly cared for, is a renewable resource. Although the productivity of land increased through much of the 20th century, by the late 2000s much of the world's arable land was threatened with decline from soil erosion, loss of nutrients, and water scarcity. Worldwide, a fifth of irrigated land required reclamation because of salinization (excess salt) or poor drainage.[13] In many areas, overly intensive farming practices had caused previously arable land to turn into desert. In 2001, a massive dust storm caused by overgrazed grasslands in China blew all the way across the Pacific, darkening skies over North America.[14] The United Nations has estimated that 10 million hectares of arable land are lost every year to desertification (one hectare equals about two and a half acres).[15]

Forces of Change

Pressure on the Earth's resource base is becoming increasingly severe. Three critical factors have combined to accelerate the ecological crisis facing the world community and to make sustainable development more difficult. These are population growth, world income inequality, and the rapid industrialization of many developing nations.

The Population Explosion

A major driver of environmental degradation is the exponential growth of the world's population. A population that doubled every 50 years, for example, would be said to be growing exponentially. Many more people would be added during the second 50 years than during the first, even though the rate of growth would stay the same. Just 10,000 years ago, the Earth was home to no more than 10 million humans, scattered in small settlements. For many thousands of years, population growth was gradual. Around 1950, as

---

[11] U.S. Energy Information Administration, "Greenhouse Gases, Climate Change, and Energy," May 2008, *www.eia.doe.gov*.

[12] "Peak Oil Forum," *World Watch*, January/February 2006, *www.worldwatch.org*. The Web site of the Association for the Study of Peak Oil and Gas may be found at *www.peakoil.net*.

[13] United Nations Environmental Program, *Global Environmental Outlook* (2007), at *www.unep.org/geo/geo4/report/GEO-4_Report_Full_en.pdf*.

[14] This dust storm was tracked by NASA; see *http://science.nasa.gov*.

[15] "Implementation of Desertification Convention Seen as Key to Promoting Sustainable Development, Fighting Poverty in Drylands," *www.johannesburgsummit.org/html/whats_new/otherstories_desertification.htm*.

FIGURE 10.1
World Population Growth

Source: United Nations Population Division, "World Population Prospects: The 2008 Revision Highlights," 2009, and "Long-Range World Population Projections," November 23, 2005. These figures represent the medium-range scenario. Other estimates are higher and lower. All estimates are available at *www.un.org/esa/population*.

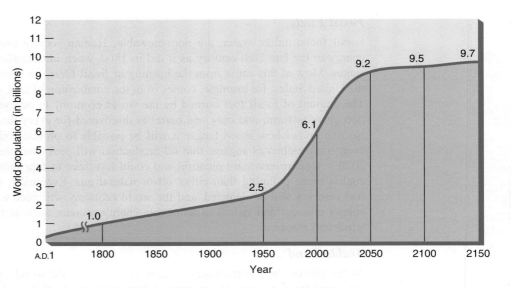

shown in Figure 10.1, the world population reached 2.5 billion. World population crossed the 6 billion mark in 1999 and is expected to cross the 7 billion mark in 2012. The United Nations estimates that the population will eventually level out at just under 10 billion around 2150. To gain some perspective on these figures, consider that someone born in 1950 who lives to be 75 years old will have seen the world's population increase by more than 5 billion people.

This growth will not be distributed equally. In the industrialized countries, especially in Europe, population growth has already slowed. Almost all of the world's population growth over the next 40 years is predicted to be in less developed countries, especially in Africa.

The world's burgeoning population will put increasing strain on the Earth's resources. Each additional person uses raw materials and adds pollutants to the land, air, and water. The world's total industrial production would have to quintuple over the next 40 years just to maintain the same standard of living that people have now. Protecting the environment in the face of rapid population growth is very difficult. For example, in some parts of western Africa, population growth has put great pressure on available farmland, which is not allowed to lie fallow. Because much of the available firewood has already been cut, people use livestock dung for fuel instead of fertilizer. The result has been a deepening cycle of poverty, as more and more people try to live off less and less productive land.

World Income Inequality

A second important cause of environmental degradation is the inequality between rich and poor. Although economic development has raised living standards for many, large numbers of the world's people continue to live in severe poverty. According to the most recent estimates, around 2.6 billion people (about 40 percent of the world's population) had incomes below the international poverty line of $2 a day. These people, most of them in sub-Saharan Africa, South Asia, East Asia, and the Pacific, lived very near the margin of subsistence. They had only a tiny fraction of the goods and services enjoyed by those in the industrialized nations.[16]

---

[16] *World Bank Development Indicators, 2008,* at *www.worldbank.org* and *www.globalissues.org*.

Some of the most extreme poverty is found on the outskirts of rapidly growing cities in developing countries. In many parts of the world, people have moved to urban areas in search of work. Often, they must live in slums, in makeshift dwellings without sanitation or running water. In Manila in the Philippines, a sprawling city of 12 million people, more than a third of the inhabitants live in such shantytowns. Hundreds died when a garbage dump nearby shifted, burying scores of people. By 2008, half of all humans lived in cities—many recent migrants to so-called megacities of 10 million or more—that lacked adequate housing or infrastructure to support them.[17]

The world's income is not distributed equally. The gap between people in the richest and poorest countries is large and getting larger. In 2008, the income of the average American, for example, was 45 times the income of the average Vietnamese and 90 times that of the average Tanzanian.[18] Figure 10.2 illustrates just how inequitably the world's income is distributed. The figure shows that the top 20 percent of the world's people had 73 percent of the income; the poorest 20 percent had just 2 percent.

Inequality is an environmental problem because countries (and people) at either extreme of income tend to behave in more environmentally destructive ways than those in the middle. People in the richest countries consume far more fossil fuels, wood, and meat, for example. People in the poorest countries, for their part, often misuse natural resources just to survive—for example, cutting down trees for fuel to cook food and keep warm.

Parts of the Third World are developing at a rapid pace. This is positive because it holds out the promise of reducing poverty and slowing population growth. But economic development has also contributed to the growing ecological crisis. Industry requires energy, much of which comes from burning fossil fuels, releasing pollutants of various

FIGURE 10.2

World Income Distributed by Deciles (Tenths) of the Population, 2000

Source: Yuri Dikhanov, "Trends in Global Income Distribution, 1970–2000, and Scenarios for 2015," United Nations Development Programme, Human Development Report Office Occasional Paper, 2005, p. 12.

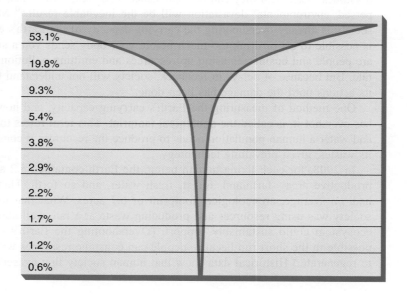

| 53.1% |
| 19.8% |
| 9.3% |
| 5.4% |
| 3.8% |
| 2.9% |
| 2.2% |
| 1.7% |
| 1.2% |
| 0.6% |

[17] "Half of Humanity Will Live in Cities by Year's End," March 13, 2008, *www.nationalgeographicnews.com,* and "The Urban Housing Issues of Metro Manila," January 19, 2007, *www.associatedcontent.com.*

[18] International Monetary Fund, "World Economic Outlook Database" (2008 data), at *www.imf.org.*

types. The complex chemical processes of industry produce undesirable by-products and wastes that pollute land, water, and air. Its mechanical processes often create dust, grime, and unsightly refuse. The agricultural "green" revolution, although greatly increasing crop yields in many parts of the world, has caused contamination by pesticides, herbicides, and chemical fertilizers. Industrialization is also often accompanied by rising incomes, bringing higher rates of both consumption and waste.

China dramatically illustrates the tight connection between economic development and environmental risk. China is one of the fastest-growing economies in the world, expanding at a rate approaching 10 percent annually. The evidence of industrialization is everywhere, from skyscrapers under construction, to cars crowding the streets, to factories operating 24/7 to produce goods for export. Yet a major consequence has been increased pollution. Fifty-eight percent of China's main rivers are too dirty for human consumption. In Beijing, residents can rarely see nearby mountains because of bad air. The country has some of the world's worst acid rain, and 30 percent of its agricultural land is acidified, according to the Worldwatch Institute. China and other fast-growing developing nations challenge business and society to "leapfrog" stages and move directly to cleaner technologies and methods of production.[19]

The Earth's Carrying Capacity

Some observers believe that the Earth's rapid population growth, people's rising expectations, and the rapid rise of developing countries are on a collision course with a fixed barrier: the limited **carrying capacity** of the Earth's ecosystem. In this view, the world's resource base, the air, water, soil, minerals, and so forth, is essentially finite, or bounded. We have only one Earth; the ecosystem itself is not growing. If human societies use up resources faster than they can be replenished, and create waste faster than it can be dispersed, environmental devastation will be the inevitable result.[20] Many believe human society is already overshooting the carrying capacity of the Earth's ecosystem. Just as it is possible to eat or drink too much before your body sends you a signal to stop, so too are people and businesses using up resources and emitting pollution at an unsustainable rate. But because of delays in feedback, society will not understand the consequences of its actions until the damage has been done.

One method of measuring the Earth's carrying capacity, and how far human society has overshot it, is called the **ecological footprint**. This term refers to the amount of land and water a human population needs to produce the resources it consumes and to absorb its wastes, given prevailing technology.

In 2008, for each living human being, the Earth contained 5.2 acres of biologically productive area—farmland, forest, fresh water, and so forth. That year, each person had, on average, an ecological footprint of 6.7 acres. What that means is that human society was using resources and producing waste at a rate well above what the Earth's ecosystem could sustainably support. (Overshooting the Earth's carrying capacity is possible in the short run because people can consume resources without allowing them to regenerate.) Historical data show that human society first exceeded world ecological

[19] Worldwatch Institute, *State of the World 2006: Special Focus—China and India* (New York: W.W. Norton, 2006).

[20] James Gustave Speth, *The Bridge at the Edge of the World* (New Haven: Yale University Press, 2008); Herman E. Daly, *Beyond Growth: The Economics of Sustainable Development* (Boston: Beacon Press, 1996); Paul Hawken, Amory Lovins, and L. Hunter Lovins, *Natural Capitalism: Creating the Next Industrial Revolution* (Boston: Little, Brown, 1999).

capacity in the late 1980s, and the gap between the two has been widening steadily since then.

Not surprisingly, some nations and individuals have bigger ecological footprints than others. For example, in the United States the average citizen has an ecological footprint of 23 acres, more than four times their share of the world's resources. By comparison, in Panama the average citizen's ecological footprint is 8 acres, and in Tanzania it is less than 3 acres. (The only nation with a bigger per capita footprint than the United States is the United Arab Emirates.) In part, a nation's footprint size is a function of affluence: rich societies tend to use more resources per person. But footprint size also reflects national policy and individual choices. The Netherlands, for example, is a relatively affluent nation, but has a footprint of 10.9 acres per person, less than half that of the United States, because of a strong public commitment to sustainability.[21]

How can human society bring the Earth's carrying capacity—and the demands placed on it—back into balance? This is without a doubt one of the great challenges now facing the world's people. Any solution will require change on many fronts:

- *Technological innovation.* One approach is to develop new technologies to produce energy, food, and other necessities of human life more efficiently and with less waste. Vast solar arrays in the desert, offshore wind turbines, or state-of-the-art utility plants that pump carbon dioxide deep into the Earth could power homes and businesses. Genetic engineering could create more nutritious and productive crops. (Some concerns about genetic engineering are explored in Chapter 13.) Energy-efficient homes and commercial buildings could allow people to go about their lives while using fewer of the Earth's resources.[22]

- *Changing patterns of consumption.* Individuals and organizations concerned about environmental impact could decide to consume less or choose less harmful products and services. In a consumer society, when many people decide to reduce their personal footprints, society's footprint becomes smaller. Homes, workplaces, and places of entertainment could be built closer to each other and to public transit, so people could get where they needed to go with less wasted energy.[23]

- *"Getting the prices right."* Some economists have called for public policies that impose taxes on environmentally harmful products or activities. For example, when individuals bought gasoline—or a utility burned coal to make electricity—they would be charged an added carbon tax. Because prices would reflect true environmental costs, individuals and firms would have an incentive to make less harmful choices.[24]

Some contemporary thinkers have gone even further and suggested that what is needed is nothing less than a completely new set of values about what is truly important. In this view, society needs a new "sustainability consciousness" that views the quality of life—not

---

[21] Global Footprint Network, at *www.footprintnetwork.org*. Individuals can estimate their own ecological footprint by taking a quiz available at *www.myfootprint.org*.

[22] A number of technological approaches to reducing the adverse impact of human society on the ecosystem are explored in *2009 State of the World: Into a Warming World* (New York: W.W. Norton, 2009).

[23] A discussion of sustainable urban planning and design may be found in Jonathan Barnett et al., *Smart Growth in a Changing World* (Washington DC: American Planning Association, 2007).

[24] A Web site that advocates for a carbon tax is *www.carbontax.org*.

Exhibit 10.B

Voices Calling for a New Sustainability Consciousness

"The emergence of a new suite of values is the foundation of the entire edifice of our planetary society. Consumerism, individualism, and domination of nature—the dominant values of yesteryear—have given way to a new triad: quality of life, human solidarity, and ecological sensibility." —Paul D. Raskin, *The Great Transition Today: A Report from the Future* (Boston: Tellus Institute: 2006).

"What could change the direction of today's civilization? It is my deep conviction that the only option is a change in the sphere of the spirit, in the sphere of human conscience. It's not enough to invent new machines, new regulations, new institutions. We must develop a new understanding of the true purpose of our existence on this Earth. Only by making such a fundamental shift will we be able to create new models of behavior and a new set of values for the planet." —Vaclav Havel, "Spirit of the Earth," *Resurgence,* November–December, 1998.

"The Great Turning begins with a cultural and spiritual awakening—a turning in cultural values from money and material excess to life and spiritual fulfillment, from a belief in our limitations to a belief in our possibilities, and from fearing our differences to rejoicing in our diversity. . . . The values shift of the cultural turning leads us to redefine wealth—to measure it by the health of our families, communities, and natural environment." —David Korten, *The Great Turning* (San Francisco: Berrett Kohler, 2006).

the quantity of things—as the goal most worthy of human aspiration. Quotations from some of these writers are presented in Exhibit 10.B.

Global Environmental Issues

Some environmental problems are inherently global in scope and require international cooperation. Typically these are issues pertaining to the *global commons*—that is, resources shared by all nations. Four global problems that will have major consequences for business and society are ozone depletion, global warming, decline of biodiversity, and threats to the world's oceans.

Ozone Depletion

Ozone is a bluish gas, composed of three bonded oxygen atoms, that floats in a thin layer in the stratosphere between 9 and 28 miles above the planet. Although poisonous to humans in the lower atmosphere, ozone in the stratosphere is critical to life on Earth because 18 absorbs dangerous ultraviolet light from the sun. Too much ultraviolet light can cause skin cancer and damage the eyes and immune systems of humans and other species.

In 1974, scientists first hypothesized that chlorofluorocarbons (CFCs), manufactured chemicals widely used as refrigerants, insulation, solvents, and propellants in spray cans, could react with and destroy ozone. Little evidence existed of actual ozone depletion, however, until 1985, when scientists discovered a thin spot, or hole, in the ozone layer over Antarctica. Studies showed that in the upper atmosphere, intense solar rays had split CFC molecules, releasing chlorine atoms that had reacted with and destroyed ozone. Scientists later found evidence of ozone depletion in the northern latitudes over Europe and North America during the summer, when the sun's ultraviolet rays are the strongest and pose the greatest danger.

World political leaders moved quickly in response to scientific evidence that CFCs posed a threat to the Earth's protective ozone shield. In 1987, a group of nations negotiated the **Montreal Protocol**, agreeing to cut CFC production; the agreement was later amended to ban CFCs, along with several other ozone-depleting chemicals. Developing countries were given until 2010 to phase out CFCs completely. As of 2009, 195 countries, all but a tiny handful, had signed the protocol.[25]

> By the turn of the century, most businesses in the developed world had completed the transition to CFC substitutes, and many had made money by doing so. Du Pont, Allied Signal, Elf-Altochem, and several other chemical companies had developed profitable substitutes for banned ozone-depleting chemicals. All the major appliance manufacturers, such as Electrolux in Sweden and Whirlpool in the United States, had brought out successful new lines of CFC-free refrigerators and freezers, and carmakers had developed air conditioners that operated without the dangerous coolant.

Have the Montreal Protocol and business efforts to respond to it been successful? By 2005, the world's production of ozone-depleting substances had fallen 95 percent from its peak, and scientists estimated that the protective layer would gradually recover over the following century, provided that regulations continued to be effective.[26] The world community still faces the challenge of restricting the manufacture of other ozone-depleting substances not yet fully regulated by treaty. But overall, this is an example of world governments working together effectively to address a global environmental threat.

Global Warming

Another difficult problem facing the world community is the gradual warming of the Earth's atmosphere. In the face of a growing scientific consensus on the threat of **global warming**, many businesses and governments are responding assertively to the issue.

The Earth's atmosphere contains carbon dioxide and other trace gases that, like the glass panels in a greenhouse, prevent some of the heat reflected from the Earth's surface from escaping into space, as illustrated in Figure 10.3. Without this so-called greenhouse effect, the Earth would be too cold to support life. Since the Industrial Revolution, which began in the late 1700s, the amount of greenhouse gases in the atmosphere has increased by as much as 25 percent, largely due to the burning of fossil fuels such as oil and natural gas. According to the Intergovernmental Panel on Climate Change (IPCC), a group of the world's leading atmospheric scientists, the Earth has already warmed by between 0.6 and 0.9 degrees Celsius over the past century. (One degree Celsius equals 1.8 degrees Fahrenheit, the unit commonly used in the United States.) The IPCC found that most of the increase was "very likely" due to human-generated greenhouse gases. Depending on whether or not society curbs greenhouse gas emissions, the Earth could warm by as much as 6.4 degrees Celsius (11.5 degrees Fahrenheit) more by 2100.[27]

The possible causes of global warming are numerous. The burning of fossil fuels, which releases carbon dioxide, is the leading contributor. But consider the following additional causes:

[25] The text of the Montreal Protocol and its various amendments and a list of signatories may be found at *http://ozone.unep.org.*

[26] U.S. Climate Change Program, "The Ozone Layer: Ozone Depletion, Recovery in a Changing Climate, and the 'World Avoided,'" November 2008, at *www.climatescience.gov.*

[27] These estimates are from "Climate Change 2007: Synthesis Report—Summary for Policymakers," November 2007. The next full IPCC report is due in 2014. A complete set of materials may be found at IPCC's Web site, *www.ipcc.ch.*

FIGURE 10.3
Global Warming

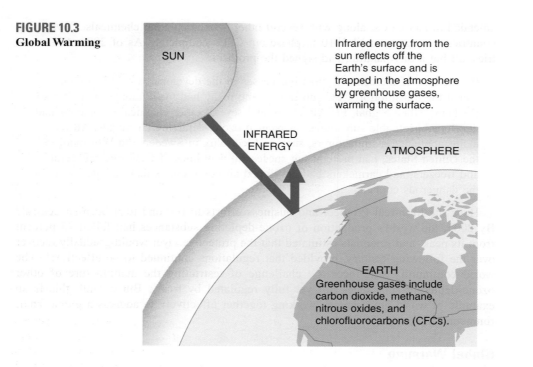

- *Black carbon.* Recent scientific research has shown that black carbon—the sooty smoke that is created by the incomplete combustion of diesel engines, wildfires, and cookstoves fueled by dung and twigs—is the second largest contributor to climate change, responsible for as much as 18 percent of global warming. Black carbon, which can travel thousands of miles in the atmosphere, absorbs heat and settles on glaciers, speeding up melting.[28]

- *Deforestation.* Trees and other plants absorb carbon dioxide, removing it from the atmosphere. Deforestation—cutting down and not replacing trees—thus contributes to higher levels of carbon dioxide. Burning forests to clear land for grazing or agriculture also releases carbon directly into the atmosphere as a component of smoke. And when trees are removed, their leaves do not shade the ground, leading to still more warming. Large-scale deforestation thus contributes in several ways to climate change.[29]

- *Beef production.* Methane, a potent greenhouse gas, is produced as a by-product of the digestion of some animals, including cows. Cattle ranching therefore contributes to global warming. According to the Food and Agriculture Organization of the United Nations, livestock are responsible for 18 percent of greenhouse gas emissions, measured in carbon equivalents. As the world's economies develop, people tend to eat more meat; the world's meat consumption is projected to double between 2000 and 2050.[30]

[28] "Third-World Stove Soot Is Targeted in Climate Fight," *The New York Times,* April 16, 2009; and "Hearing Examines Black Carbon and Global Warming," U.S. House of Representatives, Committee on Oversight and Government Reform, October 18, 2007.

[29] "Deforestation: The Hidden Cause of Global Warming," *The Independent (U.K.,)*, May 14, 2007.

[30] "Humans' Beef with Livestock: A Warmer Planet," *Christian Science Monitor,* February 20, 2007. The report cited is *Livestock's Long Shadow: Environmental Issues and Options* (Rome: United Nations Food and Agriculture Organization, 2006).

- *CFCs.* In addition to destroying the ozone, these are also greenhouse gases. The Montreal Protocol, discussed earlier in this chapter, will have the unintended beneficial consequence of slowing global warming. An ongoing problem, however, is that the chemicals now used as substitutes for CFCs (including hydrofluorocarbons, or HCFCs) are themselves powerful greenhouse gases. (In fact, one pound of HCFC released into the atmosphere has more than 3,000 times the warming impact as the same amount of carbon dioxide.)[31]

If global warming continues, the world may experience extreme heat waves, air pollution crises, violent storms, damaging wildfires, and even epidemics of tropical diseases in the 21st century. The polar ice caps may partially melt, raising sea levels and causing flooding in low-lying coastal areas such as Florida, Bangladesh, and the Netherlands. It may become as difficult to grow wheat in Iowa as it is now in arid Utah. Such climate change could devastate many of the world's economies and destroy the habitats of many species.[32]

In 1997, representatives of many of the world's nations gathered in Kyoto, Japan, to consider amendments to the Convention on Climate Change, an international treaty on global warming. In difficult negotiations, the parties hammered out an agreement called the **Kyoto Protocol** that would require industrial countries to reduce greenhouse gas emissions more than 5 percent below 1990 levels, over a period of several years. The Kyoto Protocol went into effect in 2005, after countries representing 55 percent of the world's carbon emissions had ratified it. The European Union took an immediate lead, restricting the amount of carbon that could be emitted by power, steel, paper, cement, and glass plants. An official there commented that although compliance with Kyoto would cost money in the short run, energy conservation would cause European firms to become "leaner and more efficient, and that could turn into a long-term business advantage."[33] By 2009, 183 nations, representing 64 percent of the world's carbon emissions, had ratified.[34] Although the United States had still not joined them, President Obama had committed to participate in negotiations for a new global warming treaty and to seek U.S. legislation to curb carbon emissions. At a summit meeting that year, the G-8 (the world's leading industrial countries) agreed to reduce their emissions of greenhouse gases by 80 percent by 2050. But the emerging nations of India, China, Brazil, South Africa, and Mexico—where most future increases in emissions were expected—refused to go along until the G-8 had agreed to medium-term targets.[35]

Addressing the challenge of climate change will require action not only by governments, but also by the world corporate community. The efforts of several business organizations to reduce their carbon emissions are profiled in Exhibit 10.C.

[31] Janos Mate, Kert Davies, and David Kanter, "The Risks of Other Greenhouse Gases," in *2009 State of the World: Into a Warming World* (New York: W.W. Norton, 2009).

[32] Photographs of observable evidence of global warming may be found on the Web site of *National Geographic* at *http://environment.nationalgeographic.com/environment/global-warming*.

[33] "New Limits on Pollution Herald Change in Europe," *The New York Times*, January 1, 2005.

[34] The Web site of the U.N. Framework Convention on Climate Change and a list of countries that have ratified the protocol is at *http://unfccc.int*.

[35] "Obama's Backing Raises Hopes for Climate Pact," *The New York Times*, March 1, 2009; "G-8 Climate-Change Agreement Falls Short," *The Wall Street Journal*, July 9, 2009; and "Developing Giants Make Weight Felt as G8 Mutates," *The Wall Street Journal*, July 10, 2009.

Unlike other trading exchanges operating out of the Windy City, the Chicago Climate Exchange (CCX) does not trade pork bellies or soybean futures but something even more exotic—carbon emissions credits.

In 2003, a group of large American companies, including Ford, DuPont, International Paper, and BP America, came together to launch the project. The participating companies agreed to reduce their overall carbon emissions—a major cause of global warming—by 2 percent from their 1999 levels in the first year, and then another 1 percent a year thereafter. Companies that did not meet these goals would have to buy credits from other companies that had earned them by exceeding their goals. Participants could also earn credits by supporting projects that removed carbon from the atmosphere, such as reforestation or energy efficiency. By 2009, the exchange had more than 350 members, including companies, municipalities, and even some universities, and had branched out to trading carbon futures and options as well. What was remarkable about the whole experiment was that it was entirely voluntary, since the United States had not ratified the Kyoto Protocol, and no U.S. law required companies to cut their carbon emissions.

Source: The Web site of the Chicago Climate Exchange is at *www.chicagoclimatex.com*.

Decline of Biodiversity

Biodiversity refers to the number and variety of species and the range of their genetic makeup. To date, approximately 1.7 million species of plants and animals have been named and described. Many scientists believe these are but a fraction of the total. The Earth contains at least 10 million species and possibly more than 100 million. Scientists estimate that species extinction is now occurring at 100 to 1,000 times the normal, background rate, mainly because of pollution and the destruction of habitat by human society. Biological diversity is now at its lowest level since the disappearance of the dinosaurs some 65 million years ago. The eminent biologist Edward O. Wilson has eloquently stated the costs of this loss:

> Every species extinction diminishes humanity. Every microorganism, animal, and plant contains on the order of from 1 million to 10 billion bits of information in its genetic code, hammered into existence by an astronomical number of mutations and episodes of natural selection over the course of thousands or even millions of years of evolution. . . . Species diversity—the world's available gene pool—is one of our planet's most important and irreplaceable resources. . . . As species are exterminated, largely as the result of habitat destruction, the capacity for natural genetic regeneration is greatly reduced. In Norman Myers' phrase, we are causing the death of birth.[36]

Genetic diversity is vital to each species' ability to adapt and survive and has many benefits for human society as well. By destroying this biological diversity, we are actually undermining our survivability as a species.

A major reason for the decline in the Earth's biodiversity is the destruction of rain forests, particularly in the tropics. Rain forests are woodlands that receive at least 100 inches of rain a year. They are the planet's richest areas in terms of biological diversity. Rain forests cover only about 7 percent of the Earth's surface but account for somewhere

[36] Edward O. Wilson, "Threats to Biodiversity," in *Managing Planet Earth: Readings from Scientific American Magazine* (New York: W. H. Freeman, 1990), pp. 57–58. This article originally appeared in *Scientific American*, September 1989. Used by permission.

between 40 and 75 percent of the Earth's species. Only about half of the original tropical rain forests still stand, and at the rate they are currently being cut, all will be gone or severely depleted within 30 years. The reasons for destruction of rain forests include commercial logging, cattle ranching, and conversion of forest to plantations to produce cash crops for export. Overpopulation also plays a part, as landless people clear forest to grow crops and cut trees for firewood.

The destruction is ironic because rain forests may have more economic value standing than cut. Rain forests are the source of many valuable products, including foods, medicines, and fibers. The pharmaceutical industry, for example, each year develops new medicines based on newly discovered plants from tropical areas. The U.S. National Cancer Institute has identified 1,400 tropical forest plants with cancer-fighting properties. As rain forests are destroyed, so too is this potential for new medicines. The Convention on Biological Diversity, an international treaty first negotiated in 1992, addresses many of these issues. By 2009 it had been ratified by 191 countries. (The United States was not among them; it declined to ratify, citing concerns with provisions on intellectual property rights and financial assistance to developing countries.) The treaty commits these countries to draw up national strategies for conservation, to protect ecosystems and individual species, and to take steps to restore degraded areas. It also allows countries to share in the profits from sales of products derived from their biological resources.

Threats to Marine Ecosystems

An additional issue of concern is threats to the world's **marine ecosystems**. This term refers broadly to oceans and the salt marshes, lagoons, and tidal zones that border them, as well as the diverse communities of life that they support. Salt water covers 70 percent of the Earth's surface and is home to a great variety of species, from tiny plankton to the giant blue whale, from kelp beds to mangrove forests. Marine ecosystems are important to human society in many ways. Fish, marine mammals, and sea plants provide food and other useful products such as fertilizer, animal feed, cooking and heating oil, medicines, clothing, and jewelry. Healthy coastal zones protect coastlines from erosion and filter runoff from the land. Many communities have survived for centuries off the bounty of the sea.

Today, the health of these ecosystems is increasingly threatened. Some of the key issues include the following:

Fish populations. Oceans provide 90 percent of the world's fish catch. The United Nations has estimated that of the world's commercial fish species, almost one-fourth are overexploited or depleted, and some fisheries—such as those for cod off the Grand Banks (eastern United States and Canada) and for anchovies off Peru—have probably been permanently destroyed by overfishing. Active management, such as limiting the number of fishing boats, establishing fish quotas, or banning fishing for periods of time, has allowed fish to regenerate in some areas.

Coral reefs. Coral reefs are limestone structures that develop from the skeletons of aquatic life and are host to great biological diversity. Today, however, they are in decline from pollution, oceanic warming, damage from ships, and cyanide and dynamite fishing. The Nature Conservancy estimates that at their current rate of decline, 70 percent of coral reefs will be gone within 50 years.

Coastal development. Much of the world's population growth is now concentrated in coastal areas, often in ecologically fragile areas. In the United States, for example, 50 percent of the population lives in counties bordering the ocean—which comprise just 17 percent of the land. Inappropriate development can put pressure on ecologically fragile areas.[37]

One group of businesses whose actions directly affect the health of the oceans is the cruise ship industry.

More than 200 cruise ships, many carrying 5,000 or more passengers and crew members, ply the world's seas, taking some 14 million people a year on a cruise vacation. Cruise ships are literally floating cities, producing on average 30,000 gallons of human waste and seven tons of garbage and solid waste a day. Under international agreements, beyond 12 miles from shore, cruise ships are permitted to discharge untreated sewage, gray water (from kitchens, baths, and laundries), and garbage (except plastic) directly into the ocean. Cruise ships also produce large amounts of oily bilge water, toxic chemicals, and diesel pollution, and carry invasive species in their ballast water. These impacts are especially worrisome because 70 percent of cruise ship destinations are considered biodiversity "hot spots."[38]

In a voluntary effort to address these issues, the International Council of Cruise Lines, a trade association, entered into a partnership with Conservation International in 2003 to promote responsible practices. Individual cruise operators also took action. Celebrity Cruises, for example, began outfitting its ships with smokeless gas engines. Carnival Cruises began an onboard recycling program, and Royal Caribbean decided not to discharge any wastewater while cruising near Australia's Great Barrier Reef.[39]

Response of the International Business Community

Since so many ecological challenges cross national boundaries, the international business community has a critical role to play in addressing them. This section describes some of the important initiatives undertaken by companies around the world to put the principle of sustainable development into practice.

World Business Council for Sustainable Development

One of the leaders in the global effort to promote sustainable business practices is the World Business Council for Sustainable Development (WBCSD). In 2009, the council was made up of about 200 companies drawn from more than 35 countries and 20 industries, among them such major transnational corporations as IBM, Nokia, Deutsche Bank, Honda, Infosys, and Cemex. The WBCSD's goals were to encourage high standards of environmental management and to promote closer cooperation among businesses, governments, and other organizations concerned with sustainable development.[40]

The WBCSD called for businesses to manufacture and distribute products more efficiently, to consider their lifelong impact, and to recycle components. In a series of publications,

[37] Pew Charitable Trusts, "Coastal Sprawl: The Effects of Urban Development on Aquatic Ecosystems in the United States," *www.pewtrusts.org.*

[38] "Cruise Ship Pollution: Background, Laws and Regulations, and Key Issues," CRS Report for Congress, February 6, 2008; The Ocean Conservancy, "Cruise Control: A Report on How Cruise Ships Affect the Marine Environment," *www.oceanconservancy.org;* and "Protect Our Oceans: Stop Cruise Ship Pollution," *www.oceana.org.*

[39] Center for Environmental Leadership in Business, "A Shifting Tide: Environmental Challenges and Cruise Industry Responses," *www.celb.org.*

[40] The WBCSD's agenda is described in Charles O. Holliday, Jr., Stephan Schmidheiny, and Philip Watts, *Walking the Talk: The Business Case for Sustainable Development* (San Francisco: Berrett-Koehler, 2002).

the group set forth the view that the most eco-efficient companies—those that added the most value with the least use of resources and pollution—were more competitive and more environmentally sound.

Eco-efficiency was possible only, the council concluded, in the presence of open, competitive markets in which prices reflected the true cost of environmental and other resources. In the past, environmental costs have not been fully accounted—for example, in calculating measures of production such as the gross domestic product. The WBCSD recommended revising systems of national accounting to include the costs of environmental damage and pricing products to reflect their full environmental costs.[41]

Many individual businesses and industry groups have also undertaken voluntary initiatives to improve their environmental performance. These are discussed next.

Voluntary Business Initiatives

Many firms around the world have tried to determine how sustainable development translates into actual business practice. Some of the more important voluntary initiatives undertaken by businesses include the following.

Life-cycle analysis involves collecting information on the lifelong environmental impact of a product, all the way from extraction of raw material to manufacturing to its distribution, use, and ultimate disposal. The aim of life-cycle analysis is to minimize the adverse impact of a particular product at all stages. For example, Dell Computer has designed its personal computers with many recyclable parts and offers free recycling to its customers. Many old computers are taken apart, rebuilt, and sold as refurbished machines. These actions have greatly reduced waste from discarded PCs.[42]

Industrial ecology refers to designing factories and distribution systems as if they were self-contained ecosystems. For example, businesses can save materials through closed-loop recycling, use wastes from one process as raw material for others, and make use of energy generated as a by-product of production.

> An example of industrial ecology may be found in the town of Kalundborg, Denmark, where several companies have formed a cooperative relationship that produces both economic and environmental benefits. The local utility company sells excess process steam, which had previously been released into a local fjord (waterway), to a local pharmaceutical plant and oil refinery. Excess fly ash (fine particles produced when fuel is burned) is sold to nearby businesses for use in cement making and road building. Meanwhile, the oil refinery removes sulfur in the natural gas it produces to make it cleaner burning and sells the sulfur to a sulfuric acid plant. Calcium sulfate, produced as a residue of a process to cut smoke emissions, is sold to a gypsum manufacturer for making wallboard. The entire cycle both saves money and reduces pollution.[43]

Extended product responsibility refers to the idea that companies have a continuing responsibility for the environmental impact of their products or services, even after they are sold. This implies, for example, that firms pay close attention to the energy efficiency of their products when used by the consumer. It also implies that companies design products for disassembly—that is, so that at the end of their useful life they can be disassembled and recycled. At Volkswagen, the German carmaker, engineers design cars for

---

[41] A full set of learning materials on the subject of eco-efficiency is available at *www.wbcsd.org.*

[42] Dell's design and recycling initiatives are described at *www.dell.com/content/topics/global.aspx/about_dell/values/sustainability/environment.*

[43] This case is described in *Business and Sustainable Development: A Global Guide,* at *www.bsdglobal.com.*

eventual disassembly and reuse. At the company's specialized auto recycling plant in Leer, old cars can be taken apart in just three minutes. Plastics, steel, precious metals, oil, acid, and glass are separated and processed. Many materials are used again in new Volkswagens.

Carbon neutrality occurs when an organization or individual produces net zero emissions of greenhouse gases. Since virtually all activity produces some atmospheric warming, this is usually accomplished by a combination of energy efficiencies (to reduce their own emissions) and carbon offsets (to reduce others' emissions). **Carbon offsets** (sometimes called carbon credits) are investments in projects that remove carbon dioxide (or its equivalent in other greenhouse gases) from the atmosphere. This can be done, for example, by paying others to plant trees, produce clean energy, or sequester (bury underground) earth-warming gases. A number of organizations now broker carbon offsets to businesses and individuals wishing to reduce their climate impact.

> In 2008, Dell Computer announced that it had met its goal to become carbon neutral. The company started by measuring its own emissions of greenhouse gases—for example, from heating and cooling its factories and offices, operating company cars, and sending employees on airplane trips. It then reduced its carbon footprint by cutting electricity use and reducing business travel. Dell offset the remainder of its carbon emissions by funding a forest restoration project in Madagascar and wind farms in the United States. Some criticized Dell for not including in its calculations the climate change impact of its suppliers and customers, but others thought that the company had taken an important first step.[44]

Other companies that have achieved—or pledged to achieve—carbon neutrality include Google, the News Corporation, Timberland, Barclays UK, and Van City.[45]

Sustainable development will require **technology cooperation** through long-term partnerships between companies in developed and developing countries to transfer environmental technologies, as shown in the following example:

> In South Africa, Shell entered into a partnership with Eskom, a local utility company, to provide electricity to 50,000 homes in isolated rural communities not served by the national power grid. The two firms cooperated to set up technologically advanced solar panels and metering units measuring power flow to individual homes. People could pay for the amount of electricity they actually used, without any up-front investment. The cost to customers, averaging about $8 a month, was comparable to the amount they had been spending on candles, paraffin, and other less efficient fuels.[46]

The idea of sustainable development is increasingly accepted in the business community. A survey of business leaders in 50 countries, for example, reported that 9 in 10 executives said sustainable development was accepted as a desirable goal in their companies. Six in 10 said that the benefits of working toward this goal outweighed the costs, and 7 in 10 regularly reported on their environmental performance to stakeholders.[47]

---

[44] "Green Goal of 'Carbon Neutrality' Hits Limit," *The Wall Street Journal,* December 30, 2008.

[45] A list of companies that have pledged or achieved carbon neutrality may be found in "Who's Going 'Carbon Neutral,'" at *www.bsr.org.*

[46] *Building A Better Future: Industry, Technology, and Sustainable Development: A Progress Report* (World Business Council on Sustainable Development, June 2000), p. 19.

[47] "GlobalScan Survey of Business Leaders on Sustainable Development," *www.environicsinternational.com/specialreport/GlobeScan_Biz/survey.pdf.*

Codes of Environmental Conduct

Earlier chapters of this text have discussed the emergence of codes of conduct in the areas of ethics and global corporate citizenship. Similarly, a number of national and international organizations have developed *codes of environmental conduct*. Recent years have seen a proliferation of such codes at many levels. Some are designed to be universally applicable, while others are tailored to particular industries. All, however, share the characteristic that they are *voluntary:* corporations choose to comply with these codes to show customers, investors, regulators, and others that they have met certain environmental standards in their operations.

Some of the leading universal codes include the following:

- The International Chamber of Commerce has developed the *Business Charter for Sustainable Development,* 16 principles that identify key elements of environmental leadership and call on companies to recognize environmental management as among their highest corporate priorities.[48]

- The *CERES Principles,* 10 voluntary principles developed by the Coalition for Environmentally Responsible Economies (CERES), commit signatory firms to protection of the biosphere, sustainable use of natural resources, energy conservation, risk reduction, and other environmental goals.[49]

- *ISO 14000* is a series of voluntary standards developed by the ISO, an international group based in Geneva, Switzerland, that permit companies to be certified as meeting global environmental performance standards.[50]

An emerging trend is codes of environmental conduct developed by and for specific industries.

A prominent example is the Equator Principles, a set of environmental standards for the financial services industry. Their focus is specific to banking: they commit signatories to determine, assess, and manage environmental risk in project financing. In other words, when a bank considers whether or not to lend money, for example, for the construction of an oil pipeline, it must examine the environmental impact of the project and whether or not its sponsors have systems in place to mitigate adverse impacts. Where borrowers are unable to comply, the bank will not lend them money. The Equator Principles, launched in 2003 and strengthened in 2006, have spread widely in the financial industry. By 2009, 70 banks around the world had signed on, ranging from huge institutions such as Citigroup to regional banks such as Egypt's Arab African International Bank, China's Industrial Bank Company, and Uruguay's Banco de la Republica Oriental.[51]

Other industry-specific standards include the Forest Stewardship Council Principles in the forest products industry, the Marine Stewardship Council in the fishing industry, and the U.S. Green Building Code standards for the commercial and residential construction industry.

Protecting the environment and the well-being of future generations is, as a founder of the WBCSD put it, "fast becoming a business necessity and even an opportunity."[52] Environmental regulations are getting tougher, consumers want cleaner products, and

---

[48] *www.iccwbo.org/policy/environment.*

[49] *www.ceres.org.*

[50] *www.iso.org.*

[51] The Web site of the Equator Principles is *www.equator-principles.com.*

[52] Stephan Schmidheiny, "The Business Logic of Sustainable Development," *Columbia Journal of World Business* 27, nos. 3–4 (1992), pp. 19–23.

employees want to work for environmentally conscious companies. Finding ways to reduce or recycle waste saves money. Many executives are championing the idea that corporations have moral obligations to future generations. The most successful global businesses in coming years may be those, like the ones profiled in this chapter, that recognize the imperative for sustainable development as an opportunity both for competitive advantage and ethical action.

Summary

- Many world leaders have supported the idea of sustainable development—economic growth without depleting the resources on which future generations will depend. But achieving sustainable development remains a challenge, and the community of nations has not yet worked out who will pay.

- Major threats to the Earth's ecosystem include depletion of nonrenewable resources such as oil and coal, air and water pollution, and the degradation of arable land.

- Population growth, income inequality, and rapid economic development in many parts of the world have contributed to these ecological problems. Human society is now using resources and producing waste at a rate well above what the Earth's ecosystem can sustainably support.

- Four environmental issues—ozone depletion, global warming, declining biodiversity, and threats to the marine ecosystem—are shared by all nations. International agreements are addressing these issues, although more remains to be done.

- Global businesses have begun to put the principles of sustainable development into action through such innovative actions as life-cycle analysis, industrial ecology, extended product responsibility, technology cooperation, carbon neutrality, and compliance with various voluntary codes.

Key Terms

biodiversity, *234*
carbon neutrality, *238*
carbon offset, *238*
carrying capacity, *228*
commons, *222*
eco-efficiency, *237*
ecological footprint, *228*

ecology, *222*
extended product responsibility, *237*
global warming, *231*
industrial ecology, *237*
Kyoto Protocol, *233*
life-cycle analysis, *237*

marine ecosystems, *235*
Montreal Protocol, *230*
ozone, *230*
sustainable development, *223*
technology cooperation, *238*

Internet Resources

www.earthcharterinaction.org	The Earth Charter Initiative
www.epa.gov/docs/ozone	Environmental Protection Agency ozone site
www.iclei.org	International Council for Local Environmental Initiatives (ICLEI)
www.ipcc.ch	Intergovernmental Panel on Climate Change
www.unep.org	United Nations Environmental Program
unfccc.int	United Nations Framework Convention on Climate Change
www.wbcsd.ch	World Business Council on Sustainable Development
www.worldwatch.org	The Worldwatch Institute
www.wri.org	World Resources Institute

Discussion Case: *The Three Gorges Dam*

When completed in 2008, the Three Gorges Dam on the Yangtze River in central China was the largest hydroelectric project in the world. One of only a handful of manmade structures big enough to be visible from space, the massive dam stretched one-and-a-half-miles from one end to the other. The lake created behind the dam extended for more than 400 miles and covered an area bigger than Switzerland.

When fully operational in 2011, the Three Gorges Dam was expected to have the capacity to generate 22,500 megawatts of electricity, about 22 times as much as a standard nuclear power plant. This energy would be crucial to the fast-developing Chinese economy, where demand for electricity was projected to double every 15 years. "The dam will make life better for our children," said one construction worker. "They'll have electric lights, TV, be able to study their lessons. With luck they'll go to the university."

Locks and ship lifts adjacent to the dam permitted oceangoing ships to navigate 1,500 miles inland to the city of Chongqing, opening markets in the vast interior of China. Many hoped that the dam would end the disastrous floods that had inundated the region every five or so years throughout history. In the 20th century alone, 300,000 lives had been lost and millions of homes destroyed. In 1998, a flood on the river had killed 3,656 people and cost the nation $38 billion.

But some, both inside and outside China, criticized the project. To create the reservoir, a quarter-million acres of fertile farmland were flooded. At least 1.3 million Chinese, mostly in rural towns and villages along the river, were forcibly resettled to higher ground. A study by Chinese researchers found that most were worse off after the move. "When I had land I could grow my own food and was free to work when I wanted. I was happy then," said one resettled farmer.

As it filled, the water inundated the string of gorges after which the dam was named, thought by many to be among the most starkly beautiful scenery in the world. At this point in its course, the Yangtze had formerly passed through a narrow passage, with dramatic limestone walls towering as high as 3,000 feet above the river. The reservoir also covered many unexcavated archaeological sites, destroying irreplaceable ancient heritage.

The Three Gorges Dam radically transformed the ecology of the river. Some environmentalists pointed out that migrating fish would be blocked, and plants and animals adapted to the river habitat would die out. Moreover, some thought that provisions to treat the billions of tons of industrial and municipal sewage expected to flow into the reservoir were inadequate. (In the past, the fast-moving river had carried untreated waste to the sea.) A related concern was the long-term effect on water quality of existing factories, landfills, and dumps—many containing toxic waste—that had been flooded by the reservoir.

But other environmentalists thought the project had merit. Hydroelectric power, of the sort generated by the Three Gorges Dam, was nonpolluting. Coal-fired power plants were the main source of power in China, supplying more than 80 percent of the nation's energy. Coal combustion produced sulfur dioxide, a cause of acid rain, and carbon dioxide, a major contributor to global warming. The air in much of China was fouled by coal dust and smoke, and one-fourth of all deaths were caused by lung disease.

Sources: "China Increases Lead as Biggest Carbon Dioxide Emitter," *The New York Times,* June 14, 2008; "China's Environmental Challenges: Three Gorges Dam: Into the Unknown," *Science Magazine,* August 1, 2008; "Chinese Dam Projects Criticized for their Human Cost," *The New York Times,* November 19, 2007; "Three Gorges Dam: The Cost of Power," *www.internationalrivers.org.* Dramatic photographs of the Three Gorges before the dam and of the construction process may be found in Arthur Zich, "China's Three Gorges: Before the Flood," *National Geographic* 92, no. 3 (September 1997).

Discussion Questions

1. What stakeholders have been helped by the Three Gorges Dam? What stakeholders have been hurt by it?

2. How does the Three Gorges Dam relate to the issues of global warming, biodiversity, and water pollution discussed in this chapter?

3. Do you agree with the decision of the Chinese government to construct the Three Gorges Dam? Why or why not?

4. Going forward, what strategies do you believe would best promote economic development in China without destroying the ecological resources on which future generations depend?

CHAPTER ELEVEN

Managing Environmental Issues

Growing public concern about the health of the Earth's ecosystems has prompted political, corporate, and civil society leaders to become increasingly responsive to environmental issues. In the United States and other nations, government policymakers have moved toward greater reliance on economic incentives, rather than command and control regulations, to achieve environmental goals. At the same time, many businesses have become increasingly proactive and have pioneered new approaches to effective environmental management, sometimes in partnership with advocacy organizations. These actions have often given firms a competitive advantage by cutting costs, gaining public support, and spurring innovation.

This Chapter Focuses on These Key Learning Objectives:

- Knowing the main features of environmental laws in the United States and other nations.
- Understanding the advantages and disadvantages of different regulatory approaches.
- Assessing the costs and benefits of environmental regulation.
- Defining an ecologically sustainable organization and the stages through which firms progress as they become more sustainable.
- Understanding how businesses can best manage environmental issues.
- Analyzing how effective environmental management makes firms more competitive.

A sprawling factory just off Interstate 65 in Lafayette, Indiana, produces around 800 Subaru cars a day. The plant, which is owned by Fuji Industries of Japan, is one of the most environmentally responsible in the world. Since 2000, the factory has slashed its waste per vehicle almost in half, and now sends no waste at all to landfills. The company returns packaging materials—including the styrofoam used to protect engines in transit—to suppliers, to be used again. Cafeteria scraps go to a nearby waste-to-energy power plant. The company processes and reuses solvent and oil. Dried paint sludge is shipped to other companies that use it to make railroad ties, parking lot bumpers, and bicycle helmets. Leftover metal slag goes to a company that extracts the copper it contains. These initiatives not only reduce the plant's environmental impact, they also save the company more than $2 million a year.[1]

The European Union (EU) has adopted an innovative policy to curb global warming—a system of tradable permits for carbon dioxide emissions. Opting for a flexible, market-based approach, the European Commission (the EU's governing body) allocates permits, or quotas, for carbon dioxide emissions to the 27 member governments. They, in turn, distribute them to thousands of plants, including power generators, chemical factories, and pulp and paper mills. Companies that are able to cut their emissions of the greenhouse gases can sell their permits to others that have exceeded their quota, providing an incentive to reduce their pollution. Over time, the European Commission is ratcheting down the number of permits in circulation, driving down overall carbon dioxide emissions. In 2008—the policy's third year of operation—discharges fell by 4 to 6 percent. "The constraints on emissions are tightening," said a French energy analyst. In 2009, the United States and a number of other nations were considering adopting similar policies to curb global warming.[2]

The Environmental Defense Fund (EDF), a leading environmental advocacy organization, has formed partnerships with a number of companies, including McDonald's, DuPont, Wegmans Food Stores, and Starbucks, to improve their environmental performance. In one such partnership, it worked with FedEx, the world's largest express transportation company, to develop a more environmentally friendly delivery truck. The organization's scientists worked with FedEx and with Eaton, a truck manufacturer, to design a new hybrid vehicle, powered by both a conventional combustion engine and an electric motor that burned 50 percent less fuel and decreased emissions by more than 75 percent. FedEx rolled out its first hybrid truck in 2004. By 2009, Fed Ex operated the largest fleet of commercial hybrid vehicles in North America and was experimenting with other technologies, including fuel cell and biodiesel-powered engines.[3]

In the early years of the 21st century, many businesses, governments, and environmental advocacy organizations became increasingly concerned that old strategies for promoting environmental protection were failing and new approaches were necessary. Government policymakers moved toward greater reliance on economic incentives to achieve environmental goals. Environmentalists engaged in greater dialogue and cooperation with industry leaders. Many businesses pioneered new approaches to effective environmental management, such as using waste from one process as input for another.

The challenge facing government, industry, and environmental advocates alike, as they tried out new approaches and improved on old ones, was how to promote ecologically sound business practices in an increasingly competitive and integrated world economy.

---

[1] "Greener and Cheaper: The Conventional Wisdom Is That a Company's Costs Rise as Its Environmental Impact Falls; Think Again," *The Wall Street Journal,* March 23, 2009; "The Many Shades of Green," *Mechanical Engineering,* January 2009; and "How Subaru's Going Green," *Science Friday* (National Public Radio), April 9, 2008.

[2] "E.U. Carbon Trading System Shows Signs of Working," *The New York Times,* April 2, 2009. Information about the EU Emissions Trading Scheme is available at *www.euractiv.com.*

[3] "Cleaner Vehicles," *http://about.fedex.designcdt.com.* More information about EDF's corporate partnerships is available at *www.edf.org.*

Role of Government

In many nations, government is actively involved in regulating business activities in order to protect the environment. Business firms have few incentives to minimize pollution if their competitors do not. A single firm acting on its own to reduce discharges into a river, for example, would incur extra costs. If its competitors did not do the same, the firm might not be able to compete effectively and could go out of business. Government, by setting a common standard for all firms, can take the cost of pollution control out of competition. It also can provide economic incentives to encourage businesses, communities, and regions to reduce pollution, and it can offer legal and administrative systems for resolving disputes.

In the United States, government has been involved in environmental regulation at least since the late 19th century, when the first federal laws were passed protecting navigable waterways. The government's role began to increase dramatically, however, around 1970. Figure 11.1 summarizes the major federal environmental laws enacted by the U.S. Congress in the modern environmental era. The nation's main pollution control agency is the **Environmental Protection Agency (EPA)**, which was created in 1970 to coordinate most of the government's efforts to protect the environment. Other government agencies involved in enforcing the nation's environmental laws include the Nuclear Regulatory Commission (NRC), the Occupational Safety and Health Administration (OSHA), and various regional, state, and local agencies.

Major Areas of Environmental Regulation

In the United States, the federal government regulates in three major areas of environmental protection: air pollution, water pollution, and land pollution (solid and hazardous waste). This section will review the major ecological issues and the U.S. laws pertaining to each, with comparative references to similar initiatives in other nations.

Air Pollution

Air pollution occurs when more pollutants are emitted into the atmosphere than can be safely absorbed and diluted by natural processes. Some pollution occurs naturally, such as smoke and ash from volcanoes and forest fires. But most air pollution today results from human activity, especially industrial processes and motor vehicle emissions. Air pollution degrades buildings, reduces crop yields, mars the beauty of natural landscapes, and harms people's health.

> The American Lung Association (ALA) estimated in 2008 that 125 million Americans, 42 percent of the population, were breathing unsafe air for at least part of each year. Of particular concern to the ALA was diesel exhaust from trucks, farm and construction equipment, marine vessels, and electric generators. Fully 70 percent of the cancer risk from air pollution, it reported, was due to diesel exhaust.[4]

The EPA has identified six criteria pollutants, relatively common harmful substances that serve as indicators of overall levels of air pollution. These are lead, carbon monoxide, particulate matter, sulfur dioxide, nitrogen dioxide, and ozone. (Ozone at ground level is a particularly unhealthful component of smog.) In addition, the agency also has identified a list of toxic air pollutants that are considered hazardous even in relatively small concentrations. These include asbestos, benzene, chloroform, dioxin, vinyl chloride, and radioactive materials. Emissions of toxic pollutants are strictly controlled. In 2009, for the first time, the

[4] American Lung Association, "State of the Air: 2008," and "Diesel Exhaust and Air Pollution," both at *www.lungusa.org;* and National Resources Defense Council, "Exhausted by Diesel: How America's Dependence on Diesel Engines Threatens Our Health," *www.nrdc.org.*

FIGURE 11.1
Leading U.S.
Environmental
Protection Laws

1969	National Environmental Policy Act	Created Council on Environmental Quality to oversee quality of the nation's environment.
1970	Clean Air Act	Established national air quality standards and timetables.
1972	Water Pollution Control Act	Established national goals and timetables for clean waterways.
1972	Pesticide Control Act	Required registration of and restrictions on pesticide use.
1973	Endangered Species Act	Conserved species of animals and plants whose survival was threatened or endangered.
1974 & 1996	Safe Drinking Water Act	Authorized national standards for drinking water.
1974	Hazardous Materials Transport Act	Regulated shipment of hazardous materials.
1976	Resource Conservation and Recovery Act	Regulated hazardous materials from production to disposal.
1976	Toxic Substances Control Act	Established national policy to regulate, restrict, and, if necessary, ban toxic chemicals.
1977	Clean Air Act amendments	Revised air standards.
1980	Comprehensive Environmental Response Compensation and Liability Act (Superfund)	Established Superfund and procedures to clean up hazardous waste sites.
1986	Superfund Amendments and Reauthorization Act (SARA)	Established toxics release inventory.
1987	Clean Water Act amendments	Authorized funds for sewage treatment plants and waterways cleanup.
1990	Clean Air Act amendments	Required cuts in urban smog, acid rain, and greenhouse gas emissions; promoted alternative fuels.
1990	Pollution Prevention Act	Provided guidelines, training, and incentives to prevent or reduce pollution at the source.
1990	Oil Pollution Act	Strengthened EPA's ability to prevent and respond to catastrophic oil spills.
1999	Chemical Safety Information, Site Security, and Fuels Regulatory Relief Act	Set standards for the storage of flammable chemicals and fuels.

EPA classified carbon dioxide and several other greenhouse gases as pollutants, and thus subject to regulation, because of the potential hazards of global warming to human health.[5]

Failure to comply with clean air laws can be very expensive for business. In 2009, BP agreed to pay nearly $180 million to settle government charges of

[5] "How Carbon Dioxide Became a Pollutant," *The Wall Street Journal*, April 18, 2009.

As part of its efforts to control acid rain, the U.S. government in 1990 initiated new restrictions on the emission of sulfur dioxide by utilities. Many electric companies complied with the law by switching from high-sulfur coal, which produces more sulfur dioxide when burned, to low-sulfur coal, which produces less. This action had the beneficial effect of reducing acid rain.

But the law had some environmentally destructive results that had been unintended by regulators. Much of the highest-quality low-sulfur coal in the United States lies in horizontal layers near the tops of rugged mountains in Appalachia, including parts of West Virginia, Kentucky, Tennessee, and Virginia. Some coal companies discovered that the cheapest way to extract this coal was through what came to be known as mountaintop removal. Explosives were used to blast away up to 500 feet of mountaintop. Massive machines called draglines, 20 stories tall and costing $100 million each, were then used to remove the debris to get at buried seams of coal. By 2009, almost 450,000 acres had been ravaged in this manner by surface mining.

Although coal operators were required to reclaim the land afterward—by filling in adjacent valleys with debris and planting grass and shrubs—many environmentalists believed the damage caused by mountaintop removal was severe. Many rivers and creeks were contaminated, and much habitat was destroyed. Aquifers dried up, and the entire region became vulnerable to devastating floods. Many felt it was deeply ironic that a law that was designed to benefit the environment in one way had indirectly harmed it in another.

Source: "The High Cost of Cheap Coal: When Mountains Move," *National Geographic,* March 2006, pp. 105–23. Aerial maps showing the location and extent of surface mines may be found at *www.skytruth.org.*

violations of environmental laws at its Texas City, Texas, refinery. The EPA found that the company had illegally discharged ozone-depleting chemicals, asbestos-contaminated waste, diesel exhaust, and other pollutants into the air. Of particular concern were emissions of benzene, a toxic chemical known to cause cancer, nerve damage, and reproductive harm. Regulators ordered the company to clean up its refining processes and improve management oversight. "BP failed its obligation under the law," said a representative of the Justice Department, which had worked with the EPA. "Today's settlement will improve air quality for the people living in and around Texas City, many of whom come from minority and low-income backgrounds."[6]

A special problem of air pollution is **acid rain**. Acid rain is formed when emissions of sulfur dioxide and nitrogen oxides, by-products of the burning of fossil fuels by utilities, manufacturers, and motor vehicles, combine with natural water vapor in the air and fall to Earth as rain or snow that is more acidic than normal. Acid rain can damage the ecosystems of lakes and rivers, reduce crop yields, and degrade forests. Structures, such as buildings and monuments, are also harmed. Within North America, acid rain is most prevalent in New England and eastern Canada, regions that are downwind of coal-burning utilities in the Midwestern states.[7] Acid rain is especially difficult to regulate because adverse consequences often occur far—often hundreds of miles—from the source of the pollution, sometimes across international borders. The major law governing air pollution is the Clean Air Act, passed in 1970 and amended in 1990. The 1990 Clean Air Act toughened standards in a number of areas, including stronger restrictions on emissions of acid rain–causing chemicals.

The efforts of the U.S. government to reduce acid rain illustrate some of the difficult trade-offs involved in environmental policy. These are described in Exhibit 11.A.

[6] "BP Products to Pay Nearly $180 Million to Settle Clean Air Violations at Texas City Refinery," U.S. Environmental Protection Agency press release, February 19, 2009.

[7] More information about acid rain may be found at *www.epa.gov/acidrain.*

Water Pollution

Water pollution, like air pollution, occurs when more wastes are dumped into waterways than can be naturally diluted and carried away. Water can be polluted by organic wastes (untreated sewage or manure), by the chemical by-products of industrial processes, and by the disposal of nonbiodegradable products (which do not naturally decay). Heavy metals and toxic chemicals, including some used as pesticides and herbicides, can be particularly persistent. Like poor air, poor water quality can decrease crop yields, threaten human health, and degrade the quality of life.

In 2000, more than 2,000 people in Walkerton, Ontario, a small farming community, became ill with severe diarrhea. About 1 in 10 had to be hospitalized, and 7 people died. The mass outbreak had been caused by *E. coli* bacteria in the municipal water supply. Investigators found that manure contaminated by the dangerous bacteria had washed into a public well during a heavy rainstorm, and the water company had failed to disinfect the water as required by law. One of its managers was later convicted and served a prison term in connection with the incident.[8]

In the United States, regulations address both the pollution of rivers, lakes, and other surface bodies of water and the quality of drinking water. The main U.S. law governing water pollution is the Water Pollution Control Act, also known as the Clean Water Act. This law aims to restore or maintain the integrity of all surface water in the United States. It requires permits for most *point* sources of pollution, such as industrial emissions, and mandates that local and state governments develop plans for *nonpoint* sources, such as agricultural runoff or urban storm water. The Pesticide Control Act specifically restricts the use of dangerous pesticides, which can pollute groundwater.

The quality of drinking water is regulated by another law, the Safe Drinking Water Act of 1974, amended in 1996. This law sets minimum standards for various contaminants in both public water systems and aquifers that supply drinking wells.

Land Pollution

The third major focus of environmental regulation is the contamination of land by both solid and hazardous waste. The United States produces an astonishing amount of solid waste, adding up to almost five pounds per person per day. Of this, 46 percent is recycled, composted, or incinerated, and the rest ends up in municipal landfills.[9] Many businesses and communities have tried to reduce the solid waste stream by establishing recycling programs. The special case of recycling electronic products is described in Exhibit 11.B.

Of all the world's nations, Germany has made probably the greatest progress in reducing its solid waste stream. Two decades ago, faced with overflowing landfills and not enough space for new ones, the German government passed a series of strict recycling laws. Manufacturers and retailers were required to take back almost all packaging waste, from aluminum cans, to plastic CD wrappers, to cardboard shipping boxes. Packaging material was labeled with a green dot, indicating that it could be disposed of in special containers, from which it would be whisked to processing centers for recycling and reuse, at the manufacturer's expense. The incentive was that Germans had to pay for trash pickup—but not

[8] "Waterworks Manager Jailed," *Montreal Gazette,* December 21, 2004; and "Few Left Untouched after Deadly E. Coli Flows through an Ontario Town's Water," *The New York Times,* July 10, 2000.

[9] Environmental Protection Agency, "Municipal Solid Waste in the United States: 2007 Facts and Figures," *www.epa.gov/epawaste.*

What happens to old personal computers (PCs), printers, MP3 players, cell phones, televisions, VCRs, and other electronic equipment when they are no longer wanted? The dimensions of the problem are huge. In the United States alone, more than 300 million electronic devices become obsolete every year, making this the fastest-growing part of the waste stream. (The switch from analog to digital television broadcasting in 2009 compounded the problem, as many people upgraded their TV sets and threw out their old ones.) About 80 percent of discarded electronics, sometimes called e-waste, ends up in municipal landfills, according to EPA. This is a problem because e-waste is not only bulky, but is also loaded with toxic metals like lead, zinc, mercury, and cadmium.

Is recycling the answer? Potentially, yes. Unfortunately, most recycled e-waste from the United States is shipped overseas—westward to China, India, Pakistan, and the Philippines and, more recently, eastward to Ghana, Nigeria, and the Ivory Coast. There, workers who disassemble and burn old equipment to recover valuable metals are exposed to toxic, sometimes deadly, chemicals, which then spread to nearby land, water, and air. In response, some forward-looking companies are taking action. Dell and IBM both take back used equipment for a small fee. Sony, Panasonic, and Toshiba now offer lead-free monitors. After an internal investigation showed that "a lot of the leftover guts" of its machines were being sent to China, Hewlett-Packard opened its own facilities in California and Tennessee where it works to safely recycle obsolete equipment. "We don't hurt the environment or the people in any place our products are made, used, or disposed of," said the company's product recycling manager. "It's not good for the bottom line, and it's not good for HP's image."

Sources: "E-Waste Not," *Time Magazine,* January 8, 2009; "High Tech Trash," *National Geographic,* January 2008; and EPA, "Fact Sheet: Management of Electronic Waste in the United States," July 2008. EPA statistics on e-waste are at *www.epa.gov/waste/conserve/materials/ecycling/manage.* Information on HP's program is available at *www.hp.com/recycle.*

for recycling. By the late 2000s, Germany was recycling around two-thirds of its packaging waste and had become a model for the rest of Europe.[10]

The safe disposal of hazardous waste is a special concern. Several U.S. laws address the problem of land contamination by hazardous waste. The Toxic Substances Control Act of 1976 requires the EPA to inventory the thousands of chemicals in commercial use, identify which are most dangerous, and, if necessary, ban them or restrict their use. For example, polychlorinated biphenyls (PCBs), dangerous chemicals formerly used in electrical transformers, were banned under this law. The Resource Conservation and Recovery Act of 1976 (amended in 1984) regulates hazardous materials from "cradle to grave." Toxic waste generators must have permits, transporters must maintain careful records, and disposal facilities must conform to detailed regulations. All hazardous waste must be treated before disposal in landfills.

Some studies have suggested that hazardous waste sites are most often located near economically disadvantaged African-American and Hispanic communities. Since 1994, the EPA has investigated whether state permits for hazardous waste sites violate civil rights laws and has blocked permits that appear to discriminate against minorities. The effort to prevent inequitable exposure to risk, such as from hazardous waste, is sometimes referred to as the movement for **environmental justice**.[11]

[10] "Recycling: German Style," *Globe and Mail,* April 22, 2008.

[11] Robert D. Bullard, "Environmental Justice in the 21st Century," Environmental Justice Resource Center, available at *www.ejrc.cau.edu/ejinthe21century.htm;* Christopher H. Foreman, Jr., *The Promise and Perils of Environmental Justice* (Washington, DC: Brookings Institution, 2000); and Bunyan Bryant, ed., *Environmental Justice: Issues, Policies, and Solutions* (Washington, DC: Island Press, 1995).

A promising regulatory approach to waste management, sometimes called **source reduction**, was taken in the Pollution Prevention Act of 1990. This law aims to reduce pollution at the source, rather than treat and dispose of waste at the end of the pipe. Pollution can be prevented, for example, by using less chemically intensive manufacturing processes, recycling, and better housekeeping and maintenance. Source reduction often saves money, protects worker health, and requires less abatement and disposal technology. The law provides guidelines, training, and incentives for companies to reduce waste.

The major U.S. law governing the cleanup of existing hazardous waste sites is the Comprehensive Environmental Response, Compensation, and Liability Act, or **CERCLA**, popularly known as **Superfund**, passed in 1980. This law established a fund, supported primarily by a tax on petroleum and chemical companies that were presumed to have created a disproportionate share of toxic wastes. EPA was charged with establishing a National Priority List of the most dangerous toxic sites. Where the original polluters could be identified, they would be required to pay for the cleanup; where they could not be identified or had gone out of business, the Superfund would pay.

One of the largest hazardous waste sites on the Superfund list is an almost 200-mile long stretch of the Hudson River, extending from Hudson Falls, New York, to Manhattan. Over a period of three decades until the late 1970s, General Electric (GE) factories discharged an estimated 1.3 million pounds of PCBs, cancer-causing chemicals formerly used in electrical equipment, into the river. After years of legal wrangling, in 2009 GE finally started dredging the riverbed to remove PCB-contaminated sediment. Since the company was responsible, it was required to supervise and pay for the job—at an estimated cost of $750 million.[12]

Remarkably, one in four U.S. residents now lives within four miles of a Superfund site. The 1,200 or so sites originally placed on the National Priority List may be just the tip of the iceberg. Congressional researchers have said that as many as 10,000 other sites may need to be cleaned up.

Although Superfund's goals were laudable, it has been widely regarded as a public policy failure. Although cleanup was well under way at almost all sites by the end of 2008, just 332 sites—about a quarter of the total—had been removed from the list, indicating that no further actions were required to protect human health or the environment. (A number of Superfund cleanups got extra money as part of the 2009 federal economic stimulus, promising quicker progress at these sites.) Some analysts estimated that the entire cleanup could cost as much as $1 trillion and take half a century to complete.

Alternative Policy Approaches

Governments can use a variety of policy approaches to control air, water, and land pollution. The most widely used method of regulation historically has been to impose environmental standards. Increasingly, however, government policymakers have relied more on market-based and voluntary approaches, rather than command and control regulations, to achieve environmental goals. These different approaches are discussed next.

Environmental Standards

The traditional method of pollution control is through **environmental standards**. Standard allowable levels of various pollutants are established by legislation or regulatory action and applied by administrative agencies and courts. This approach is also called

---

[12] "Dredging of Pollutants Begins in Hudson," *The New York Times,* May 16, 2009.

command and control regulation, because the government commands business firms to comply with certain standards and often directly controls their choice of technology.

One type of standard is an *environmental quality standard*. In this approach a given geographical area is permitted to have no more than a certain amount or proportion of a pollutant, such as sulfur dioxide, in the air. Polluters are required to control their emissions to maintain the area's standard of air quality. A second type is an *emission standard*. For example, the law might specify that manufacturers could release into the air no more than 1 percent of the ash (a pollutant) they generated. Emission standards, with some exceptions, are usually set by state and local regulators who are familiar with local industry and special problems caused by local topography and weather conditions. Sometimes the EPA mandates that companies use the *best available technology*, meaning a particular process that the agency determines is the best economically achievable way to reduce negative impacts on the environment.

Market-Based Mechanisms

In recent years, regulators have begun to move away from command and control regulation, favoring increased use of **market-based mechanisms**. This approach is based on the idea that the market is a better control than extensive standards that specify precisely what companies must do.

One approach that has become more widely used is to allow businesses to buy and sell the right to pollute, in a process known as **cap-and-trade**. The European Union's *tradable permit* program for carbon emissions, described in one of the opening examples of this chapter, illustrates this approach. The U.S. Clean Air Act of 1990 also incorporated the concept of tradable permits as part of its approach to pollution reduction. The law established emission levels (called "caps") and permitted companies with emissions *below* the cap to sell ("trade") their rights to the remaining permissible amount to firms that faced penalties because their emissions were above the cap. Over time, the government would reduce the cap, thus gradually reducing overall emissions, even though individual companies might continue to pollute above the cap. Companies could choose whether to reduce their emissions—for example, by installing pollution abatement equipment—or to buy permits from others. One study showed that the tradable permit program for acid rain may have saved companies as much as $3 billion per year, by allowing them the flexibility to choose the most cost-effective methods of complying with the law.[13]

In 2009, the United States House of Representatives for the first time adopted global warming legislation establishing such a cap-and-trade system for emissions of greenhouse gases, including carbon dioxide. The goal of the law was to reduce U.S. greenhouse gas emissions by 17 percent by 2020 and 83 percent by 2050 (from a baseline of 2005 levels). The Senate continued to debate the issue, however, and legislative action remained uncertain.[14]

Another market-based type of pollution control is establishment of *emissions charges* or *fees*. Each business is charged for the undesirable waste that it emits, with the fee varying according to the amount of waste released. The result is, "The more you pollute, the more you pay." In this approach, polluting is not illegal, but it is expensive, creating an incentive for companies to clean up. In recent years, both federal and state governments have experimented with a variety of so-called *green taxes* or *eco-taxes* that levy a fee on various kinds of environmentally destructive behavior. In addition to taxing bad behavior, the government

[13] For more on the tradable permit system for acid rain, see *www.epa.gov/acidrain.*

[14] "House Passes Bill to Address Threat of Climate Change," *The New York Times*, June 27, 2009.

may also offer various types of positive incentives to firms that improve their environmental performance. For example, the government may decide to purchase only from those firms that meet a certain pollution standard, or it may offer aid to those that install pollution control equipment. Tax incentives, such as faster depreciation for pollution control equipment, also may be used. Governments may also levy eco-taxes on individuals.

> In 2008, for instance, Ireland introduced auto registration fees based on the greenhouse gas emissions of the vehicle. New car buyers would pay between €100 and €2,000, depending on how polluting the vehicle was. Lawmakers hoped that the eco-tax would encourage people to buy cleaner cars. Other countries with similar programs include the Netherlands, Portugal, Spain, and Finland. Germany has enacted eco-taxes on gasoline and electricity, with the intention of promoting energy efficiency.[15]

In short, the trend has been for governments to use more flexible, market-oriented approaches—tradable allowances, pollution fees and taxes, and incentives—to achieve environmental objectives where possible.

Information Disclosure

Another approach to reducing pollution is popularly known as *regulation by publicity*, or *regulation by embarrassment*. The government encourages companies to pollute less by publishing information about the amount of pollutants individual companies emit each year. In many cases, companies voluntarily reduce their emissions to avoid public embarrassment.

The major experiment in regulation by publicity has occurred in the area of toxic emissions to the air and water. The 1986 amendments to the Superfund law, called SARA, included a provision called the Community Right-to-Know Law, which required manufacturing firms to report, for about 300 toxic chemicals, the amount on site, the number of pounds released, and how (if at all) these chemicals were treated or disposed of. EPA makes this information available to the public in the *Toxics Release Inventory,* or *TRI,* published annually and posted on the Internet.

From 1988 to 2007, reporting manufacturers in the United States cut their releases and disposal of these chemicals to the air, water, and land overall by 61 percent, according to TRI data.[16] Some of the biggest cuts were made by the worst polluters. These dramatic results were especially surprising to regulators, because many of the hazardous chemicals were not covered under clean air and water regulations at the time. The improvements, in many instances, had been completely voluntary. Apparently, fear of negative publicity had compelled many companies to act. "We knew the numbers were high, and we knew the public wasn't going to like it," one chemical industry executive explained.

The advantages and disadvantages of alternative policy approaches to reducing pollution are summarized in Figure 11.2.

Civil and Criminal Enforcement

Companies that violate environmental laws are subject to stiff civil penalties and fines, and their managers can face prison if they knowingly or negligently endanger people or the environment. Proponents of this approach argue that the threat of fines and even imprisonment can be an effective deterrent to corporate outlaws who would otherwise degrade the air, water, or land. Since 1989, about 100 individuals and companies have been found guilty of environmental crimes each year.

---

[15] "Ireland Goes Green with Light Bulb Rules and Car Tax," *Reuters,* December 6, 2007.

[16] Data released by EPA in March, 2009, available at *www.epa.gov/TRI.* The Right-to-Know Network provides a searchable database with information on releases by specific companies at *www.rtk.net.*

FIGURE 11.2
Advantages and Disadvantages of Alternative Policy Approaches to Reducing Pollution

Policy Approach	Advantages	Disadvantages
Environmental standards	• Enforceable in the courts. • Compliance mandatory.	• Across-the-board standards not equally relevant to all businesses. • Requires large regulatory apparatus. • Older, less efficient plants may be forced to close. • Can retard innovation. • Fines may be cheaper than compliance. • Does not improve compliance once compliance is achieved.
Market-based mechanisms		
Cap-and-trade systems	• Gives businesses more flexibility. • Achieves goals at lower overall cost. • Saves jobs by allowing some less efficient plants to stay open. • Permits the government and private organizations to buy allowances to take them off the market. • Encourages continued improvement.	• Gives business a license to pollute. • Permit levels are hard to set. • May cause regional imbalances in pollution levels. • Enforcement is difficult.
Emissions fees and taxes	• Taxes bad behavior (pollution) rather than good behavior (profits).	• Fees are hard to set. • Taxes may be too low to curb pollution.
Government incentives	• Rewards environmentally responsible behavior. • Encourages companies to exceed minimum standards.	• Incentives may not be strong enough to curb pollution.
Information disclosure	• Government spends little on enforcement. • Companies able to reduce pollution in the most cost-effective way.	• Does not motivate all companies.
Civil and criminal enforcement	• May deter wrongdoing by firms and individuals.	• May not deter wrongdoing if penalties and enforcement efforts are perceived as weak.

For example, in 2008 Massey Energy, one of the nation's largest coal companies, paid $20 million to settle charges it had violated the Clean Water Act. Regulators found that for years Massey had illegally dumped metals, sediment, and acid mine drainage into nearby waterways, polluting hundreds of rivers and streams in West Virginia and Kentucky. Besides the fine, Massey was required to spend $10 million on new procedures and employee training, set aside land for conservation, and undertake water cleanup projects downstream from its mines.[17]

---

[17] "Massey Energy to Pay Largest Civil Penalty Ever for Water Permit Violations," EPA press release, January 17, 2008.

European regulators and prosecutors have also actively pursued corporate environmental criminals. For example, the EU standardized its laws against marine pollution and raised maximum penalties to $1.8 million after a series of oil tanker wrecks fouled the coasts of France, Spain, and Portugal. Europe is the world's largest importer of oil, and 90 percent is transported to the continent by seagoing ships.[18]

The U.S. Sentencing Commission, a government agency responsible for setting uniform penalties for violations of federal law, has established guidelines for sentencing environmental wrongdoers. Under these rules, penalties would reflect not only the severity of the offense but also a company's demonstrated environmental commitment. Businesses that have an active compliance program, cooperate with government investigators, and promptly assist any victims would receive lighter sentences than others with no environmental programs or that knowingly violate the law. These guidelines provide an incentive for businesses to develop active compliance programs to protect themselves and their officers from high fines or even prison if a violation should occur.[19]

Costs and Benefits of Environmental Regulation

One central issue of environmental protection is how costs are balanced by benefits. In the quarter century or so since the modern environmental era began, the nation has spent a great deal to clean up the environment and keep it clean. Some have questioned the value choices underlying these expenditures, suggesting that the costs—lost jobs, reduced capital investment, and lowered productivity—exceeded the benefits. Others, in contrast, point to significant gains in the quality of life and to the economic payoff of a cleaner environment.

As a nation, the United States has invested heavily in environmental cleanup. According to the EPA, by 1990 environmental spending exceeded $100 billion a year, about 2 percent of the nation's gross national product, and reached around $160 billion annually by 2000. Business spending to comply with environmental regulation has diverted funds that might otherwise have been invested in new plants and equipment or in research and development. Sometimes, strict rules have led to plant shutdowns and loss of jobs. Some regions and industries, in particular, have been hard hit by environmental regulation, especially those with high abatement costs, such as paper and wood products, chemicals, petroleum and coal, and primary metals. Economists often find it difficult, however, to sort out what proportion of job loss in an industry is attributable to environmental regulation and what proportion is attributable to other causes.

In many areas, the United States has made great progress in cleaning up the environment. The benefits of this progress have often been greater than the costs, as these figures show:

- Although problems remain, as noted earlier in this chapter, overall emissions of nearly all major air pollutants in the United States have dropped substantially since 1990, the date of the Clean Air Act amendments. By 2008, levels of volatile organic compounds had dropped by 31 percent, nitrous oxides by 35 percent, sulfur dioxide by 50 percent, and lead by 60 percent. A study done for the EPA showed that by the year

---

[18] "The Community Framework for Cooperation in the Field of Accidental or Deliberate Marine Pollution," *http://ec.europa.eu/environment;* and "Europe Unites against Marine Polluters," *Environmental News Service,* June 11, 2005, *www.ens-newswire.com.*

[19] For a discussion of criminal liability in environmental law, and how to avoid it, see Frank B. Friedman, *Practical Guide to Environmental Management,* 10th ed. (Washington, DC: Environmental Law Institute, 2006).

2010, the Clean Air Act amendments will have prevented 23,000 premature deaths from air pollution, averted almost 2 million asthma attacks, and prevented 4 million lost workdays, among other gains. The cost of compliance was estimated at $27 billion, about one-fourth of the economic value of the act's benefits.[20]

- Water quality has also improved. Since the Water Pollution Control Act went into effect in 1972, many lakes and waterways have been restored to ecological health. The Cuyahoga River in Ohio, for example, which at one time was so badly polluted by industrial waste that it actually caught on fire, has been restored to the point where residents can fish and even swim in the river. By one estimate, 33,000 more miles of rivers and streams were swimmable in 2000 than would have been the case without the Clean Water Act.[21] The cumulative cost to industry and the public of compliance with the act was estimated at $14 billion in 1997; this was much less than the estimated benefits of clean water of $11 billion *a year*.[22]

Environmental regulations also stimulate some sectors of the economy. The environmental services and products industry, for example, has grown dramatically. While jobs are being lost in industries such as forest products and high-sulfur coal mining, others are being created in areas like recycling, environmental consulting, wind turbine and solar panel production and installation, waste management equipment, and air pollution control.[23] In 2008, more than 3 million Americans worked in such "green" jobs. The economic stimulus legislation of 2009 provided funds for renewable energy, transportation infrastructure, and alternative-fuel vehicles—promising further growth in these sectors of the economy.[24] Jobs are saved or created in industries such as fishing and tourism when natural areas are protected or restored. Moreover, environmental regulations can stimulate the economy by compelling businesses to become more efficient by conserving energy, and less money is spent on treating health problems caused by pollution.

Because of the complexity of these issues, economists differ on the net costs and benefits of environmental regulation. In some respects, government controls hurt the economy, and in other ways they help, as summarized in Figure 11.3. An analysis of data from several studies found that, on balance, U.S. environmental regulations did not have a large overall effect on economic competitiveness because losses in one area tended to balance gains in another.[25] What is clear is that choices in the area of environmental regulation reflect underlying values, expressed in a democratic society through an open political process. Just how much a society is prepared to pay and how "clean" it wants to be are political choices, reflecting the give and take of diverse interests in a pluralistic society.

[20] "Air Quality Trends," *www.epa.gov/airtrends;* and "The Benefits and Costs of the Clean Air Act 1990 to 2010," *www.epa.gov/air.* The latter study is ongoing and periodically updated; the most recent data may be found at the EPA's Web site.

[21] "A Benefits Assessment of Water Pollution Control Programs Since 1972," prepared for the U.S. Environmental Protection Agency, January 2000.

[22] "A Retrospective Assessment of the Costs of the Clean Water Act: 1972 to 1997," prepared for the U.S. Environmental Protection Agency, October 2000; and "A Benefits Assessment of Water Pollution Control Programs Since 1972," prepared for the U.S. Environmental Protection Agency, January 2000.

[23] For a study of the economic impact of the recycling and reuse industries, see National Recycling Coalition, Inc., *U.S. Recycling Economic Information Study*, prepared by R.W. Beck, Inc., July 2001.

[24] "Can Obama's Stimulus Plan Spur Green Jobs in the U.S.?" *BusinessWeek*, November 26, 2008; and "Green-Collar Jobs Generated by the Senate Stimulus Plan," *http://apolloalliance.org*, February 24, 2009.

[25] Adam B. Jaffe, Steven R. Peterson, Paul R. Portney, and Robert N. Stavins, "Environmental Regulations and the Competitiveness of U.S. Industry," prepared for the U.S. Department of Commerce, July 1993. For another summary of the evidence that comes to a similar conclusion, see Steven Peterson, Barry Galef, and Kenneth Grant, "Do Environmental Regulations Impair Competitiveness?" prepared for the U.S. EPA, September 1995.

FIGURE 11.3
Costs and Benefits of Environmental Regulations

Costs	Benefits
• $160 billion a year spent by business and individuals in the United States by 2000.	• Emissions of nearly all pollutants have dropped since 1970.
• Job loss in some particularly polluting industries.	• Air and water quality improved, some toxic-waste sites cleaned; improved health; natural beauty preserved or enhanced.
• Competitiveness of some capital-intensive, "dirty" industries impaired.	• Growth of other industries, such as environmental products and services, tourism, and fishing.

The Greening of Management

Environmental regulations, such as the laws governing clean air, water, and land described in this chapter, establish minimum legal standards that businesses must meet. Most companies try to comply with these regulations, if only to avoid litigation, fines, and, in the most extreme cases, criminal penalties. But many firms are now voluntarily moving beyond compliance to improve their environmental performance in all areas of their operations. Researchers have sometimes referred to the process of moving toward more proactive environmental management as the **greening of management**. This section describes the stages of the greening process and discusses what organizational approaches companies have used to manage environmental issues effectively. The following section explains why green management can improve a company's strategic competitiveness.

Stages of Corporate Environmental Responsibility

Although environmental issues are forcing all businesses to manage in new ways, not all companies are equally green, meaning proactive in their response to environmental issues. One widely used model identifies three main stages of corporate environmental responsibility.

According to this model, companies pass through three distinct stages in the development of green management practices.[26] The first stage is *pollution prevention,* which focuses on "minimizing or eliminating waste before it is created." Subaru Automotive of America's effort to minimize waste, mentioned earlier in this chapter, is an example of pollution prevention. The second stage is *product stewardship.* In this stage, managers focus on "all environmental impacts associated with the full life cycle of a product," from the design of a product to its eventual use and disposal. Hewlett-Packard, for example, has designed its laser printer ink cartridges so they can be refurbished and reused, and provides a mailing label for customers to return them free of charge. Finally, the third and most advanced stage is *clean technology,* in which businesses develop innovative new technologies that support sustainability.

General Electric, a company long associated with pollution, from building coal-fired power plants to dumping toxic chemicals in the Hudson River, took a dramatic turn

---

[26] Stuart Hart, "Beyond Greening: Strategies for a Sustainable World," *Harvard Business Review,* January–February 1997. All quotes in this paragraph are taken from this article. An alternative stage model may be found in Dexter Dunphy, Suzanne Benn, and Andrew Griffiths, *Organisational Change for Corporate Sustainability* (New York: Routledge, 2003).

in 2005. Jeffrey Immelt, the company's new CEO, announced a new strategy he dubbed "ecomagination." He pledged to double GE's investment in developing renewable energy, fuel cells, efficient lighting, water filtration systems, and cleaner jet engines, with the aim of growing revenue from these products to $20 billion by 2010. Immelt's reason was that clean technologies represented a huge commercial opportunity. "Increasingly for business," he said, "green is green." In 2008, the company reached $17 billion in revenues from the ecomagination initiative, well on its way to meeting its goal.[27]

Where are most companies on this continuum of environmental responsibility? A 2008 worldwide survey of more than 1,200 senior executives by the Economist Intelligence Unit found that 53 percent of companies had a coherent strategy for sustainability for the entire business, and an additional 23 percent were in the process of developing one. Around a third reported their intention to develop new products to reduce or prevent social or environmental problems in the next five years (a possible indicator of the *clean technology* stage). In short, most big companies appear to be addressing sustainability issues. Many are still at an early stage in the developmental sequence, but a substantial minority has begun development of environmental products and technologies.[28]

Researchers have discovered that several factors push companies along the continuum from lower to higher levels of corporate environmental responsiveness. One study of firms in the United Kingdom and Japan found three main motivations for "going green": the chance to gain a *competitive advantage,* a desire to gain *legitimacy* (approval of the public or regulators), and a moral commitment to *ecological responsibility.*[29] Other research has cited a desire to avoid the risks associated with environmental harm.

The Ecologically Sustainable Organization

An **ecologically sustainable organization (ESO)** is a business that operates in a way that is consistent with the principle of sustainable development, as presented in Chapter 10. In other words, an ESO could continue its activities indefinitely, without altering the carrying capacity of the Earth's ecosystem. Such businesses would not use up natural resources any faster than they could be replenished or substitutes found. They would make and transport products efficiently, with minimal use of energy. They would design products that would last a long time and that, when worn out, could be disassembled and recycled. They would not produce waste any faster than natural systems could absorb and disperse it. They would work with other businesses, governments, and organizations to meet these goals.[30]

Of course, no existing business completely fits the definition of an ecologically sustainable organization. The concept is what social scientists call an ideal type—that is, a kind of absolute standard against which real organizations can be measured. A few

[27] "A Clean, Lean Electric Machine," *The Economist,* December 10, 2005, pp. 77–79; "GE Turns Green," *Forbes.com,* August 15, 2005; and "Enhancing Our Commitment to a Sustainable Future: 2009 Progress Report," Business Roundtable, 2009.

[28] Economist Intelligence Unit, "Doing Good: Business and the Sustainability Challenge," February 2008, *www.eu.com.*

[29] Pratima Bansal and Kendall Roth, "Why Companies Go Green: A Model of Ecological Responsiveness," *Academy of Management Journal,* August 2000.

[30] Mark Starik and Gordon P. Rands, "Weaving an Integrated Web: Multilevel and Multisystem Perspectives of Ecologically Sustainable Organizations," *Academy of Management Review,* October 1995.

visionary businesses, however, have embraced the concept and begun to try to live up to this ideal.

> One such business is Interface, a $1 billion company based in Atlanta, Georgia, that makes 40 percent of the world's commercial carpet tiles. In 1994, CEO Ray C. Anderson announced, to many people's surprise, that Interface would seek to become "the first sustainable corporation in the world." Anderson and his managers undertook hundreds of initiatives. For example, the company started a program by which customers could *lease,* rather than *purchase,* carpet tile. When tile wore out in high-traffic areas, Interface technicians would replace just the worn units, reducing waste. Old tiles would be recycled, creating a closed loop. In 2009, Interface reported that in 15 years it had saved $405 million by cutting waste, and revenues and profits had soared. But Anderson said it was "just a start. It's daunting, trying to climb a mountain taller than Everest."[31]

No companies, including Interface, have yet become truly sustainable businesses, and it will probably be impossible for any single firm to become an ESO in the absence of supportive government policies and a widespread movement among many businesses and other social institutions.

Environmental Partnerships

Many businesses that are seeking to become more sustainable have formed voluntary, collaborative partnerships with environmental organizations and regulators to achieve specific objectives, as illustrated by the FedEx example at the beginning of this chapter. These collaborations, called **environmental partnerships**, draw on the unique strengths of the different partners to improve environmental quality or conserve resources.[32]

> Unilever, the Anglo-Dutch consumer goods company, is the largest buyer of seafood in the world. Concerned about the rapidly declining stocks of many species of fish used in its frozen food products, Unilever entered into a partnership with the World Wildlife Fund, a conservation organization. Together, they formed the nonprofit Marine Stewardship Council to set standards for sustainable fisheries, educate suppliers, and certify harvested catch, and Unilever committed to eventually buying all of its fish from sustainable sources. Unfortunately, this partnership collapsed when Permira, a European private equity group, bought Unilever's frozen foods business in 2006, without committing to Unilever's sustainability goals. The Marine Stewardship Council carried on, however, and by the late 2000s was working with hundreds of fisheries, seafood processors, retailers, and food service establishments to realize its vision of "the world's oceans teeming with life, and seafood supplies safeguarded for this and future generations."[33]

[31] "Interface Reports Annual Ecometrics," April 22, 2009, *www.interfaceglobal.com;* and Ray C. Anderson, *Mid-Course Correction: Toward a Sustainable Enterprise—The Interface Model* (Atlanta, GA: The Peregrinzilla Press, 1998). Interface's sustainability initiatives are described at *www.interfaceglobal.com/sustainability.*

[32] Dennis A. Rondinelli and Ted London, "How Corporations and Environmental Groups Cooperate," *Academy of Management Executive* 17, no. 1 (2003); and Frederick J. Long and Matthew B. Arnold, *The Power of Environmental Partnerships* (Fort Worth, TX: Dryden Press, 1995).

[33] "Fishing for the Future: Unilever's Sustainable Fisheries Initiative," *http://www.unilever.com/Images/ 2002%20Fishing%20for%20the%20Future%20%20Unilever%27s%20Sustainable%20Fisheries%20Initiative_tcm13-5306.pdf;* and "Private Equity Firm Acquires Iglo, Birds Eye," *IntraFish,* September 2006. The Web site of the Marine Stewardship Council is *www.msc.org.*

Environmental Management in Practice

Companies that have begun to move toward environmental sustainability have learned that new structures, processes, and incentives are often needed. Some of the organizational elements that many proactive green companies share are the following:[34]

Top management with a commitment to sustainability. The most environmentally proactive companies almost all have CEOs and other top leaders with a strong espoused commitment to sustainability. Most also give their environmental managers greater authority and access to top levels of the corporation. Many leading firms now have a **sustainability officer**, often with a direct reporting relationship with the CEO. These individuals often supervise extensive staffs of specialists and coordinate the work of managers in many areas, including research and development, marketing, and operations, whose work is related to a firm's sustainability mission. The role of top-level managers in setting the tone at the top for environmental excellence is illustrated in the case "Kimpton Hotels' EarthCare Program" that appears at the end of this book.

Line manager involvement. Environmental staff experts and specialized departments are most effective when they work closely with the people who carry out the company's daily operations. For this reason, many green companies involve line managers and workers directly in the process of change. At the Park Plaza Hotel in Boston, green teams of employees make suggestions ranging from energy-efficient windows to refillable bottles of soap and shampoo.

Codes of environmental conduct. Environmentally proactive companies put their commitment in writing, often in the form of a code of conduct or charter that spells out the firm's environmental goals. A study of a group of European companies found, perhaps not surprisingly, that employees at firms with a well-communicated environmental policy were much more likely to come up with creative proposals for helping the environment.[35]

Cross-functional teams. Another organizational element is the use of ad hoc, cross-functional teams to solve environmental problems, including individuals from different departments. For example, when Siemens Building Technologies, a provider of fire safety, security, and control systems, undertook a comprehensive effort to green the organization in 2007, it created a cross-functional team drawn from marketing, product design, procurement, manufacturing, facilities, and human resources. Its goal was to pull together key players with the skills and resources to get the job done, wherever they were located in the corporate structure.[36]

Rewards and incentives. Businesspeople are most likely to consider the environmental impacts of their actions when their organizations acknowledge and reward this behavior. The greenest organizations tie the compensation of their managers, including line managers, to environmental achievement and take steps to recognize these achievements publicly. At Xcel Energy, a utility that is a leading supplier of wind

---

[34] Anne T. Lawrence and David Morell, "Leading-Edge Environmental Management: Motivation, Opportunity, Resources, and Processes," *Research in Corporate Social Performance and Policy*, supp. 1 (1995), pp. 99–127; and James Maxwell, Sandra Rothenberg, Forrest Briscoe, and Alfred Marcus, "Green Schemes: Corporate Environmental Strategies and Their Implementation," *California Management Review* 39, no. 3 (March 22, 1997), pp. 118 ff.

[35] Catherine A. Ramus and Ulrich Steger, "The Roles of Supervisory Support Behaviors and Environmental Policy in Employee Ecoinitiatives at Leading European Companies," *Academy of Management Review*, August, 2000, pp. 605–26.

[36] "Siemens Building Technologies: Committed to a Greener, Sustainable Future," *CSRwire.com*, April 30, 2009.

power, one-third of the CEO's bonus is linked to meeting specific sustainability goals set annually by the board.[37]

Environmental Audits

Green companies not only organize themselves to achieve environmental goals; they also closely track their progress toward meeting them. Chapter 7 introduced the concept of social performance auditing and presented recent evidence on what proportion of companies report results to their stakeholders. In the 1990s, in a parallel development, many companies began to audit their environmental performance. More recently, many firms have moved to integrate their social and environmental reporting into a single **sustainability report**. In 2008, 79 percent of the world's top 250 companies issued such an integrated report, up from just 14 percent in 2002. A much smaller proportion, 8 percent of these firms, integrate social, environmental, *and* financial data in a single document.[38]

> An example of a company that has undertaken a fully audited, integrated report is Novosymes, a Danish biotechnology firm. The company produced its first environmental report in 1993 and its first combined social and environmental report six years later. Since 2002, it has produced a single report to stakeholders that integrates its financial, social, and environmental results. The company acknowledges the challenge of preparing a single report "in accordance with more than one set of rules and guidelines," but says that the process improves transparency and accurately reflects its commitment to sustainability.[39]

As discussed earlier in Chapter 7, the movement to audit and report on social and environmental performance has gained momentum in recent years in many regions of the world.

Environmental Management as a Competitive Advantage

Some researchers believe that by moving toward ecological sustainability, business firms gain a competitive advantage. That is, relative to other firms in the same industry, companies that proactively manage environmental issues will tend to be more successful than those that do not.[40]

> When General Motors emerged from bankruptcy in mid-2009, it committed itself to a new vision of sustainability. On her blog, Beth Lowery, the company's vice president for environment, energy, and safety policy, suggested that "GM" also stood for "Green Motors." She cited the company's development of the advanced hybrid Volt, improved fuel economy vehicles, and its sponsorship of the EcoCAR challenge, in which student teams competed to transform a Saturn Vue into a zero-emission vehicle.[41]

---

[37] "Comp Committees Link Incentive Pay [to] Environmental Goals," *www.compensationresources.com*, no date, appears to be 2007.

[38] *KPMG International Survey of Corporate Responsibility Reporting 2008*, at *www.kpmg.com*. Toyota's social and environmental reports are available at *www.toyota.co.jp/en/csr*.

[39] "Integrated Reporting," *www.csreurope.org* [no date]. Novozymes' Web site is at *www.novozymes.com/en*.

[40] For a full elaboration of this argument, see Forest L. Reinhardt, "Bringing the Environment Down to Earth," *Harvard Business Review*, July–August 1999.

[41] Beth Lowery, "GM = Green Motors?" *http://fastlane.gmblogs.com/archives/2009/06/gm_green_motors.html*.

Effective environmental management confers a competitive advantage in four different ways, as follows.

Cost Savings

Companies that reduce pollution and hazardous waste, reuse or recycle materials, and operate with greater energy efficiency can reap significant cost savings. An example is Herman Miller, the office furniture company.

> Herman Miller goes to great lengths to avoid wasting materials. The company sells fabric scraps to the auto industry for use as car linings; leather trim to luggage makers for attaché cases; and vinyl to the supplier to be re-extruded into new edging. Burnable solid waste is used as fuel for a specialized boiler that generates all the heating and cooling for the company's main complex in Zeeland, Michigan. The result is that the company actually makes money from materials that, in the past, it would have had to pay to have hauled away and dumped.[42]

Product Differentiation

Companies that develop a reputation for environmental excellence and that produce and deliver products and services with concern for their sustainability can attract environmentally aware customers.

> In 2009, Motorola released a new product, called the "Renew," that it dubbed the world's first carbon-free cell phone. Packaged in recycled paper and made from recycled water bottles, the phone came with a prepaid shipping envelope so customers could return it to the company at the end of its life. Motorola also said it would offset carbon emissions produced during the manufacture and distribution of the Renew by contributing to a methane gas recapture project. (Methane is also a greenhouse gas.) The company said the product was aimed at "our eco-conscious customers."[43]

Creating "green" products and services—and pitching them to environmentally aware customers—is sometimes called **green marketing**. The size of the green market is difficult to estimate. Consumer survey data released in 2009 showed that 36 percent of Americans said they "almost always" or "regularly" bought green products, but most were willing to pay only "a little more" for them. Another study found, though, that a quarter of American consumers felt they had "no way of knowing" if environmental claims were true, indicating some skepticism about green marketing.[44] Companies are said to be guilty of **greenwashing** (formed from the words "green" and "whitewash") when they mislead consumers regarding the environmental benefits of a product or service.

> The rate of green advertising tripled between 2006 and 2009. According to TerraChoice, an environmental marketing firm, many green ads are suspect, particularly those for children's toys, cosmetics, and cleaning supplies. These run the gamut from ads that offer no proof for their claims, to ones that are

---

[42] Herman Miller's sustainability initiatives are described at *www.hermanmiller.com.*

[43] "Cellphone Makers Start Offering 'Green' Models," *The New York Times,* February 16, 2009; and *www.motorola.com.*

[44] Joel Makower, "Earth Day, Green Marketing, and the Polling of America, 2009" [blog], *http://www.makower.typepad.com,* April 12, 2009.

simply vague ("all natural"), to ones that are irrelevant ("CFC-free," even though CFCs have been illegal for years). An example is Poland Spring plastic water bottles, touted as "purposely designed with an average of 30% less plastic to be easier on the environment." Commented an environmental journal, "The label on the bottle neglects to mention that . . . water bottles are one of the most detrimental products [in] the world, even if they have less plastic than their competitors."[45]

In short, green marketing can provide a competitive edge, but only if it is honest.

Environmental excellence may also attract business customers, a trend that has emerged in the gold mining industry, as illustrated in the discussion case at the end of this chapter.

Technological Innovation

Environmentally proactive companies are often technological leaders, as they seek imaginative new methods for reducing pollution and increasing efficiency. In many cases, they produce innovations that can win new customers, penetrate new markets, or even be marketed to other firms as new regulations spur their adoption.

> Nikon, a Japanese firm that makes cameras and other optical products, became concerned about use of environmentally harmful materials in the production of optical glass. The company invested several years of effort and millions of yen to develop a new product, dubbed "eco-glass," that equaled the performance of other optical glass but was made entirely without lead or arsenic. By 2005, Nikon had switched to eco-glass in all the consumer products it shipped. The company's innovation attracted customers such as environmentally aware bird-watchers who were impressed with eco-glass binoculars.[46]

In Europe, new rules that went into effect in 2006 banned all electronics products that used six toxic substances, including lead, cadmium, and mercury. Companies that had learned how to make their products free of these substances suddenly had a big advantage in winning European accounts.[47]

Strategic Planning

Companies that cultivate a vision of sustainability must adopt sophisticated strategic planning techniques to allow their top managers to assess the full range of the firm's effects on the environment. The complex auditing and forecasting techniques used by these firms help them anticipate a wide range of external influences on the firm, not just ecological influences. Wide-angle planning helps these companies foresee new markets, materials, technologies, and products.

> In 2009, Toyota Motor Corporation was named to the "Global 100 Most Sustainable Corporations" list, announced annually at the World Economic Forum in Davos, Switzerland. It was the fifth year in a row the company had been so honored. The winners were selected based on their "exceptional capacity to

---

[45] TerraChoice, "The Seven Sins of Greenwashing," 2009, *http://terrachoice.com;* and "Greenwashing Water Bottles," *On Earth* (Natural Resources Defense Council), February 6, 2009.

[46] "Environmental Report 2005," *www.nikon.co.jp.*

[47] "Europe Says: Let's Get the Lead Out," *BusinessWeek,* February 7, 2005, p. 12.

address their sector-specific environmental, social, and governance risks and opportunities." Toyota, well known for its ability to anticipate market trends, had been among the first to produce a commercially successful hybrid vehicle, the Prius, and had pledged to adapt hybrid technology in all its vehicles by the mid-2020s. As U.S. carmakers struggled—and some went into bankruptcy—in the deep recession of the late 2000s, Toyota fared relatively well, for the first time surpassing General Motors in 2009 as the world's largest carmaker. The same sophisticated planning that enabled Toyota to weather the recession had also contributed to its ability to meet the public's increased interest in less polluting, more efficient transportation.[48]

In short, proactive environmental management may help businesses not only promote sustainability but also become more competitive in the global marketplace by reducing costs, attracting environmentally aware customers, spurring innovation, and encouraging long-range strategic planning that anticipates external change.[49]

Summary

- Government environmental regulations focus on protecting the ecological health of the air, water, and land. Environmental laws are designed to limit the amount of pollution that companies may emit.

- Environmental laws have traditionally been of the command and control type, specifying standards and results. New laws, in both the United States and Europe, have added market incentives to induce environmentally sound behavior and have encouraged companies to reduce pollution at the source.

- Environmental laws have brought many benefits. Air, water, and land pollution levels are in many cases lower than in 1970. But some improvements have come at a high cost. A continuing challenge is to find ways to promote a clean environment and sustainable business practices without impairing the competitiveness of the U.S. economy.

- Companies pass through three distinct stages in the development of green management practices. Many businesses are now moving from lower to higher stages. An ecologically sustainable organization is one that operates in a way that is consistent with the principle of sustainable development.

- Effective environmental management requires an integrated approach that involves all parts of the business organization, including top leadership, line managers, and production teams, as well as strong partnerships with stakeholders and effective auditing.

- Many companies have found that proactive environmental management can confer a competitive advantage by saving money, attracting green customers, promoting innovation, and developing skills in strategic planning.

---

[48] A list of the Global 100 most sustainable corporations is available at *www.global100.org.* Information on Toyota's sustainability initiatives is at *www.toyota.co.jp/en/environment.*

[49] For a collection of articles by leading scholars, see Sanjay Sharma and J. Alberto Aragon-Correa, eds., *Corporate Environmental Strategy and Competitive Advantage* (Northampton, MA: Edgar Elgar Academic Publishing, 2005). For a general statement of the argument that environmental management confers a competitive advantage, see Michael E. Porter and Claas van der Linde, "Green and Competitive: Beyond the Stalemate," *Harvard Business Review,* September–October 1995, pp. 120 ff; Stuart L. Hart, "Beyond Greening: Strategies for a Sustainable World," *Harvard Business Review,* January–February 1997, pp. 66–76; and Renato J. Orsato, "Competitive Environmental Strategies: When Does It Pay to Be Green?" *California Management Review* 48, no. 2 (Winter 2006), pp. 127–43.

Key Terms

acid rain, *247*
cap-and-trade, *251*
command and control
regulation, *251*
ecologically sustainable
organization
(ESO), *257*
environmental
justice, *249*

environmental
partnerships, *258*
Environmental Protection
Agency (EPA), *245*
environmental
standards, *250*
greening of
management, *256*
green marketing, *261*

greenwashing, *261*
market-based
mechanisms, *251*
source reduction, *250*
Superfund (CERCLA), *250*
sustainability officer, *259*
sustainability report, *260*

Internet Resources

www.envirolink.org
www.environmentalleader.com
www.epa.gov
www.GreenBiz.com
www.sustainablebusiness.com
www.sustainability.com
www.sustainablog.org

Environmental organizations and news
Briefing for executives
Environmental Protection Agency
Green Business Network
Site for green businesses
SustainAbility (consultancy)
Blogs on green and sustainable businesses

Discussion Case: *Digging Gold*

Gold mining is one of the most environmentally destructive industries in the world. Most gold today is extracted using a technique called cyanide heap-leaching. Workers dig and blast the earth in open-pit mines so massive that astronauts can see them from space. Using huge earth-moving machines, they pile the gold-bearing ore into mounds the size of pyramids, then spray them with a solution of cyanide to leach out the gold. In a series of steps, gold is then removed from the drainage at the bottom of the heap and is further refined in smelters into pure bars of the precious metal.

Heap-leaching enables the economic extraction of gold from low-grade ores; some modern mines use as much as 30 tons of rock to produce a single ounce of precious metal. But this process can be highly damaging to the environment. Cyanide is one of the most potent poisons known; a pellet the size of a grain of rice can kill a person. Most spent cyanide solution is stored in reservoirs, where it gradually breaks down. But these reservoirs are prone to accidents. In 2000, at a gold mine in Romania operated by the Australian firm Esmeralda Exploration, 100,000 tons of wastewater laced with cyanide spilled into a tributary of the Danube River. The toxic plume washed all the way to the Black Sea, causing a massive kill of fish and birds and contaminating the drinking water of 2.5 million people.

After this incident, a Romanian citizen's group called Alburnus Maior organized to block construction of a new gold mine by the Canadian firm Gabriel Resources at Rosia Montana. "We have to decide whether we want [these] mountains to become a no-man's land," said Eugen David, a local farmer and activist.

Transportation of materials to and from mines, which are often located in remote areas, poses additional risks. A truck carrying containers of mercury (a by-product of gold extraction) from the Yanacocha Mine in Peru, owned by U.S.-based Newmont Mining, spilled its load on a rural road. Villagers from the area, not understanding the danger, collected the hazar   d metal. More than 1,000 people became ill, some permanently, a lawsuit la   n their behalf charged.

In most develope   environmental laws prohibit the discharge of mining waste directly into waterv   elsewhere in the world, laws are often weaker and regulations poorly enforced. In Indonesia, U.S.-based Freeport McMoran's Grasberg operation, the largest gold mine in the world, dumped its waste directly into local rivers, badly damaging downstream rain forests and wetlands. An official of the Environment Ministry said that the agency's regulatory tools were so weak that it was like "painting on clouds" to get the company even to follow the law.

Gold mining also pollutes the air. The entire process of metal extraction—from diesel-powered earth-moving equipment to oil- and coal-burning smelters—consumes large quantities of fuel, contributing to global warming. Smelters produce oxides of nitrogen and sulfur, components of acid rain, as well as traces of toxic metals such as lead, arsenic, and cadmium.

Another environmental hazard of gold extraction is acid mine drainage. Often, the rock that harbors gold also contains sulfide minerals. When this rock is crushed and exposed to air and water, these minerals form sulfuric acid. As this acid drains from mine debris, it picks up other metals, such as arsenic, mercury, and lead, creating a toxic brew that can drain into groundwater and waterways. This process can go on for decades, long after a mine has shut down.

In the United States, although mining companies have to follow environmental laws, no law specifically ensures that a mine will not create acid runoff. Sixty-three Superfund sites are abandoned mines; the EPA has estimated their cleanup cost at $7.8 billion. In a study for Congress in 2005, the General Accounting Office called for new rules to require mining companies to post adequate surety bonds (a kind of insurance) to cover the costs of remediation if they went out of business.

Pegasus Gold, a Canadian company, declared bankruptcy in 1998 and abruptly shut down its Zortman-Landusky mine in Montana, once the largest gold mine in the United States, sticking the state's taxpayers with a $33 million bill for ongoing water treatment and cleanup. The citizens of Montana subsequently voted to ban cyanide heap-leach mining completely anywhere in the state. After an effort to overturn this initiative failed, Canyon Resources, a company that held the rights to a valuable Montana deposit, said it was looking into other ways to extract gold, including an innovative new technology that used bacteria instead of cyanide.

In 2004, Earthworks, an environmental NGO based in the United States, launched a campaign called "No Dirty Gold" and called on jewelry retailers to support the Golden Rules, agreeing to source only from responsibly operated mines. Many retailers—from Tiffany & Co. and Cartier to Walmart and JC Penney—signed on. In 2007, Earthworks joined with mining companies, retailers, and jewelers in the Madison Dialogue, an ongoing conversation about how best to encourage best environmental practices in their industry. A manager from Cartier, the jewelry retailer, said, "It is our duty to provide our clients with creations that are beautiful, desirable . . . and responsibly made. As times change, so do society's expectations."

Sources: "The New Gold Standard," *Time,* February 6, 2009; "Dirty Metals: Mining, Communities, and the Environment," a Report by Earthworks and Oxfam America, *www.nodirtygold.org;* "Beyond Gold's Glitter: Torn Lands and Pointed Questions," *The New York Times,* October 24, 2005, pp. A1, A10; "Tangled Strands in Fight over Peru Gold Mine," *The New York Times,* October 25, 2005, pp. A1, A14; "Hardrock Mining: BLM Needs to Better Manage Financial Assurances to Guarantee Reclamation Costs," GAO Report to the Ranking Minority Member, Committee on Homeland Security and Governmental Affairs, U.S. Senate, June 2005; Jared Diamond, *Collapse: How Societies Choose to Fail or Succeed* (New York: Viking, 2005), ch. 15, "Big Business and the Environment: Different Conditions, Different Outcomes"; Web sites of Westerners for Responsible Mining, *www.bettermines.org,* and Alburnus Maior, *www.rosiamontana.org;* and additional articles in the Northwest Mining Association Bulletin, *High Country News,* and *Billings Gazette.* The Web site of the Madison Dialogue is at *www.madisondialogue.org.*

Discussion Questions

1. Using the classification system presented in the chapter section "Major Areas of Environmental Regulation," explain what type(s) of pollution is (are) generated by gold mining. Which of these do you think is (are) most damaging to the environment, and why?

2. Using the classification system presented in the section "Alternative Policy Approaches," explain what type(s) of government regulation would most effectively address the concerns you identified in question 1.

3. In your view, what role should nongovernmental organizations (NGOs) and citizen movements play in reducing the adverse environmental impacts of gold mining?

4. Which of the gold mining companies mentioned in this case are more—or less—environmentally responsible? What factors, in your view, might cause these differences?

PART SIX

Business and Technology

CHAPTER TWELVE

Technology, Organizations, and Society

Technology is an unmistakable economic and social force in both business and the world where we live. Global communications, business exchanges, and the simple tasks that make up our daily lives are all significantly influenced by technology. Whether we are at home, in school, or in the workplace, emerging technological innovations have dramatically changed how we live, play, learn, work, and interact with others, raising important social and ethical questions.

This Chapter Focuses on These Key Learning Objectives:

- Defining technology and its characteristics.
- Recognizing the evolving phases of technology throughout history and what fuels technological innovation today.
- Examining how the Internet and other technological innovations have changed the way organizations operate and interact with their stakeholders around the world.
- Analyzing new uses of the Internet—social networking, blogs, vlogs, spam, phishing, and pharming—and the challenges they create for businesses and government policymakers.
- Recognizing socially beneficial uses of technology in education and medicine.
- Evaluating recent efforts to address and narrow the digital divide.

AT&T, sponsors of the television hit series *American Idol,* reached out to 75 million customers through text messages urging people to tune in to the 2009 season. The response from AT&T customers was not what the company had hoped for. Many of them believed that this was a breach of cell phone etiquette. "AT&T just sent me a text message advertisement about *American Idol.* [This is] Evil," wrote Joe Brockmeier. Another user, Nick Dawson, wrote, "Seriously AT&T? Did you just text me twice during a meeting to tell me about *American Idol*? Very unprofessional."

An AT&T spokesperson said that the messages were meant as a friendly reminder and thought they were appropriate, since AT&T customers often used their cell phones to vote for their favorite performers on the show. He also pointed out that AT&T customers had been clearly asked if they wanted to receive messages of this sort and could have easily declined them. But Richard Cox, the chief information officer for Spamhaus, a nonprofit anti-spam organization based in Britain, countered, "It's absolutely spam. It's an unsolicited text message. People who received it didn't ask for it. That's the universal definition of spam."

Joseph Calderaro is a health care success story, and he owes much of his good health to the Marshfield Clinic's innovative health information strategy. The Marshfield Clinic, located in Wisconsin, created a regimen of diet, exercise, and medication for Calderaro that enabled him to manage his diabetes and lower his blood sugar, blood pressure, and cholesterol. These good results may not be unusual, but the strategy used by his health care provider was. The Marshfield Clinic had digitized all of Calderaro's medical records, including his health history, medications, laboratory test results, and notes from his doctors and nurses. The medical staff at the clinic used these records to coordinate and prescribe his treatment and to guard against harmful drug interactions. According to a hospital administrator, "this procedure was effective and cost efficient. It resulted in fewer unnecessary medical tests, reduced medical errors, and better care so the patient is less likely to require costly treatment in hospitals."[1]

Technology is a major factor in our lives, helping us communicate with others around the world, providing new opportunities for business to promote its activities, and improving the quality of our lives. But what are the consequences of the emergence of technology? Has technology replaced human contact and, if so, what are the consequences of this change in how we relate to others? Should businesses be allowed to use technology freely, or should there be some constraints on its use by business? Who should determine what these constraints are?

Technology Defined

Technology is a broad term referring to the practical applications of science and knowledge to commercial and organizational activities. The dominant feature of technology is *change and then more change.* For example, nanotechnology, discussed later in the chapter, has brought so much change that some speak of it in terms of the latest *future shock,* in which change comes so fast and furiously that it approaches the limits of human tolerance and people lose their ability to cope with it successfully. Although technology is not the only cause of change in society, it is a primary cause. It is either directly or indirectly involved in most changes that occur in society.

Another feature of technology is that *its effects are widespread,* reaching far beyond the immediate point of technological impact in unpredictable ways. Technology ripples

---

[1] "A Text Arrives, Oh, It's Just an 'Idol' Ad," *The New York Times,* January 14, 2009, *www.nytimes.com;* and "Health Care That Puts a Computer on the Team," *The New York Times,* December 27, 2008, *www.nytimes.com.*

through society until every community is affected by it. An example of a technology with widespread effects is cloud computing—the use of publicly accessible servers to store users' text, photos, videos, and other data at remote sites, rather than on their own computers.[2]

Cloud computing led to fundamental changes in several industries and markets. It helped create a market for netbooks, small, inexpensive personal computers that had wireless connectivity but usually lacked the large amounts of local storage provided by a hard drive or optical drive. In 2009, consumers purchased more netbooks than ever before, as they realized they did not need as much storage capability. This trend created profits for manufacturers and retailers of netbooks, but created problems for others. Cable and satellite television providers, for example, began losing revenue as consumers realized they could watch programs and videos on their netbooks instead of their televisions. And the storage of personal information on remote sites created the potential for a greater invasion of individual privacy and the use of personal information to target marketing, as shown later in Chapter 13.[3]

A final feature of technology is that it is *self-reinforcing*. As stated by Alvin Toffler, "Technology feeds on itself. Technology makes more technology possible."[4] This self-reinforcing feature means that technology acts as a multiplier to encourage its own faster development. It acts with other parts of society so that an invention in one place leads to a sequence of inventions in other places. Thus, invention of the microprocessor led rather quickly to successful generations of the modern computer, which led to new banking methods, electronic mail, bar-code systems, global tracking systems, and so on.

Phases of Technology in Society

Six broad phases of technology have developed, as shown in Figure 12.1. As shown, societies have tended to move sequentially through each phase, beginning with the lowest technology and moving higher with each step, so the six phases roughly represent the progress of civilization throughout history. The first phase was the nomadic-agrarian, in which people hunted wild animals for meat and gathered wild plants for food. The second was the agrarian, corresponding with the domestication of animals and plants. The

FIGURE 12.1   **Phases in the Development of Technology**

Technology Level	Phases in the Development of Technology	Approximate Period	Activity	Primary Skill Used
1	Nomadic-agrarian	Until 1650	Harvesting	Manual
2	Agrarian	1650–1900	Planting and harvesting	Manual
3	Industrial	1900–1960	Building material goods	Manual and machine
4	Service	1960–1975	Providing services	Manual and intellectual
5	Information	1975–2000	Thinking and designing	Intellectual and electronic
6	Semantic	2000–today	Relevance and context	Intellectual and networking

[2] For a contrarian view of the explosion of technology in our society, see Michael Mandel, "Innovation Interrupted," *BusinessWeek,* June 15, 2009, pp. 34–40.

[3] "Asus T91 Netbook Battery Not Replaceable," *Boingboing blog,* May 17, 2009, *gadgets.boingboing.net;* and "$200 Laptops Break a Business Model," *The New York Times,* January 26, 2009, *www.nytimes.com.* Also see "Cloud Computing's Big Bang for Business," *BusinessWeek,* June 15, 2009, pp. 42–48.

[4] Alvin Toffler, *Future Shock* (New York: Bantam, 1971), p. 26.

first two used manual labor exclusively. The third phase was the industrial, characterized by the development of powered machinery, first in the textile industry and later in many other forms of manufacturing. The fourth was the service phase, marked by the rise of service industries and intellectual labor. The fifth was the **information phase**. This phase emphasized the use and transfer of knowledge and information rather than manual skill. Businesses of all sizes, including the smallest firms, explored the benefits of the information age through the availability of nanotechnology and similar inventions. These inventions catapulted societies into **cyberspace**, where information is stored, ideas are described, and communication takes place in and through an electronic network of linked systems. The technology developed in this age provided the mechanisms for more information to be produced in a decade than in the previous 1,000 years.

The **semantic phase**, which began around 2000, saw the development of processes and systems to enable organizations and people to navigate through the expanding amount of links and information available on the Internet. Networked services analyzed user requests and made assumptions based on context, location, the user's history, and other factors. Search engines, such as Google, employed massive clusters of computers to analyze the *metadata* or descriptive information embedded within Web pages, documents, and files. A Google search for a specific airline flight, for example, might return links to a flight tracking Web site, an estimated time of departure or arrival for that day's flight, weather forecasts, and airport maps. A blog article might be automatically linked to popular or recent articles in other blogs with similar keywords or tags. Social interaction is an important part of the semantic phase. Services such as Facebook, Twitter, LinkedIn, and MySpace, discussed later, analyzed the transactions and metadata from each user's activity to suggest new contacts, entertainment, and links.[5]

Where will technology head next? Some observers have suggested that society is now at the beginning of a new phase dominated by *biotechnology*. As discussed in more detail in Chapter 13, **biotechnology** is a technological application that uses biological systems or living organisms to make or modify products or processes for specific use. Its applications are common in agriculture, food science, and medicine. This emerging phase of technology extends beyond the design and analysis of information to the manipulation of organisms that produce fabricated products or act as components within a computer network.

Fueling Technological Growth

As Figure 12.1 demonstrates, in recent decades the pace of technological change has accelerated, and the time lapse between phases has dramatically shortened. Several factors have fueled these developments:

Government: Government investment has helped launch many new technologies, including the Internet, and these trends continue. For 2010, the U.S. federal government pledged $147.6 billion to support technological innovation in the areas of basic sciences, clean energy, biomedical and health research, and high-tech safety and security—slightly more than in 2009. "These investments in science and technology pay dividends for the nation," said Congressman Bart Gordon, chairman of the House Committee on Science and Technology. "Roughly half of the growth in GDP [gross domestic product] over the past 50 years came from development and adoption of new technologies. Innovation—especially new energy

[5] Tim Berners-Lee, James Hendler and Ora Lassila, "The Semantic Web," *Scientific America*, May 2001, *www.scientificamerican.com.*

technologies—is the path to reinvigorating our economy and ensuring our competitiveness over the next 50 years."[6]

Private investment: Venture capitalists are investors who provide capital to start-up companies that do not have access to public funding. They have long targeted technological innovation, with the aim of making outsized returns. When Google was first created in1998, two venture capital firms invested $25 million in the fledgling search engine company. A decade later, Google's sales approached $11 million annually, with assets of $33.5 million. Facebook started with $500,000 from "super venture capitalist angel" Peter Thiel; after Microsoft acquired the company, it was worth $15 billion. Similarly, Sequoia Capital took a chance on YouTube with a $3.5 million initial investment, and a year later Google acquired the online video service site for $1.65 billion in stock.[7]

Business investment: Business firms have also invested directly in technology through their research and development (R&D) operations. These investments have often benefited the business, as well as produced innovations that have moved their industries forward.

For example, Google relies heavily on data centers to provide search services and cloud-based applications to individual and corporate users. Its innovations in this area have given it a competitive edge over its rivals. Google has invested billions of dollars in developing highly modular data centers that house the company's servers and networking equipment in shipping containers. These data centers were designed to use electricity, water, and other resources in a highly efficient manner. Google opened its data center in The Dalles, Oregon, in 2007, becoming a leading customer of the Grand Coulee Dam's inexpensive electric power. Computer equipment, especially hard disk drives, is highly sensitive to temperature, humidity, and airborne pollution. Data centers require massive heating and air conditioning facilities. Google's network is highly distributed and redundant, so a single Google search may require servers that are spread across a continent to deliver relevant results in less than a second.[8]

The combination of government, private investor, and business investment in technology has continued to drive innovation forward. But ultimately, technology continues to evolve because of people's insatiable desire for it. They forever seek to expand the use of technology in their lives, probably because of the excitement in having new things and their belief that these new things may help them better adapt to their environment. As Bill Joy, Sun Microsystems' chief scientist, explained,

By 2030, we are likely to be able to build machines, in quantity, a million times as powerful as the personal computer of today. As this enormous computing power is combined with the manipulative advances of the physical sciences and the new, deep understanding in genetics, enormous transformative power is being unleashed. These combinations open up the opportunity to completely redesign the world, for better or worse: The replicating and evolving processes that have been confined to the natural world are about to become realms of human endeavor.[9]

[6] "U.S. Government Spending $147.6 Billion for R&D Next Year," *InformationWeek,* May 14, 2009, *www.informationweek.com.*

[7] "These Angels Go Where Others Fear to Tread," *BusinessWeek,* June 1, 2009, pp. 44–48.

[8] Bobbie Johnson, "Google's Power Hungry Data Centers," *The Guardian,"* May 3, 2009, *www.guardian.co.uk.*

[9] Bill Joy, "Why the Future Doesn't Need Us," *Wired,* April 2000, *www.wired.com/wired/archive/8.04/joy.*

Technology as a Powerful Force in Business

Technology and business have been intertwined since the Industrial Revolution. The connection between the two became even stronger in the information and semantic phases. Today, technology influences every aspect of the global marketplace—driving innovation, affecting partnerships, and changing business–stakeholder relationships. It has created great opportunities for business—but also serious ethical and social challenges. This section will explore some ways in which three technologies—the Internet, e-business, and m-commerce—have presented both opportunities and challenges for business.

The Internet

More people have more access to technology than ever before. Residents of developing countries increasingly enjoy energy-powered appliances, entertainment devices, and communications equipment. Individuals and businesses in developed countries in North America, Europe, and portions of Asia more than ever are dependent on electronic communication devices for access to information and for conducting business transactions. In today's workplace environment, nearly every North American manager has a desktop or laptop computer, fax machine, voice mail, mobile phone, PDA, and a host of other electronic devices to connect the manager to other employees, customers, suppliers, and information. These technology devices have become common tools.

The Emergence of the Internet

One of the most visible and widely used technological innovations over the past decade has been the Internet. The **Internet** is a global network of interconnected computers, enabling users to share information along multiple channels linking individuals and organizations. Springing to life in 1994, this conduit of information revolutionized how business was conducted, students learned, and households operated.

Any estimate of the number of Internet users is clearly only an estimate. In 2008, China surpassed the United States with the most Internet users by country. China claimed to have nearly 300 million Internet users, compared to the United States' 220 million, about 70 percent of the U.S. population, as shown in Figure 12.2. China's Internet population has surged since 2005, particularly among teenagers. But Internet users represent only 19 percent of the Chinese population, indicating a huge potential for even greater growth in that country.[10]

While opportunities to use the Internet are growing quickly, some limitations have appeared, such as in China when the government attempted to convert all identification records to its digital database systems.

> Ma Cheng was told by the Chinese government that she must change her given name from "Cheng" to an approved name that can be recorded in a modernized version of the country's identity database. The database would not accommodate handwritten characters as names, and "Cheng" was one of over 22,000 characters that was not included in the system's 32,252 Chinese character set. Sixty million Chinese citizens were in a similar predicament as the government completed a long-delayed conversion from handwritten identity cards to computer readable cards with embedded microchips and digital color photographs. From a systems perspective, the government's decision was logical and highly efficient. Eighty-five percent of China's population used one of a hundred common surnames; the remaining 15 percent were told that they had to conform to the new system.

[10] "China Surpasses U.S. in Number of Internet Users," *The New York Times*, July 26, 2008, *www.nytimes.com*.

FIGURE 12.2   **Top 20 Internet Users by Country, 2008**

Source: Internet World Stats, March 31, 2009, *www.internetworldstats.com.*

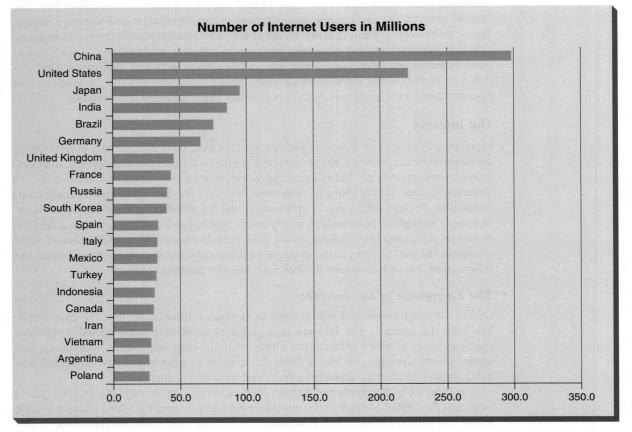

Number of Internet Users in Millions

The United Nations recognizes a personal name as a basic human right, but researcher Andrea DiMaio noted that "different identity credentials are being used for different government services[, a]nd emerging forms of personal identity, through mobile devices or social media, will challenge the status quo." While a minority of Chinese citizens fought to keep their names through temporary cards and political influence, many Chinese decided to conform to their government's wishes and selected new names from an approved list.[11]

New ways of going online are contributing to the growing use of the Internet. Digital music players and game consoles from Apple, Microsoft, Sony, and Nintendo now include Web browsers, e-mail and messaging capability, and wireless Internet access. These small, handheld devices are popular among young adults and mobile professionals who have come to expect easy, pervasive Internet access wherever they go. Some smartphones, including models from RIM and Apple, include WiFi connectivity to provide users with faster data transfer speeds than mobile phone carriers can provide. When device manufacturers add features such as digital cameras, video recording, and GPS,

[11] "Name Not On Our List? Change It," *The New York Times,* April 21, 2009, *www.nytimes.com;* and "Even Chinese Struggle with Smart ID Cards," *The Gartner Blog Network,* April 21, 2009, *blog.gartner.com.*

these portable devices become useful tools for collecting and distributing information. Technologies, such as mesh networks and WiMAX, can provide wireless Internet access over larger areas than WiFi.

Thousands of new Internet users each day demonstrate the power of this technology as a force in our lives. The Internet also has been adopted by businesses to create new opportunities for commerce, as described in the following sections.

E-Business

During the information and semantic phases of technological development, shown in Figure 12.1, electronic business exchanges between businesses and between businesses and their customers emerged. These electronic exchanges, generally referred to as **e-business**, consist of buying and selling goods and services between businesses, organizations, and individuals electronically—that is, via Internet-based systems such as XML and TCP/IP. During the past few years, e-business revenue has increased at a faster pace than that of traditional, or nonelectronic, business. E-business sales in 2006 topped $3 trillion, led primarily by business-to-business (B2B) sales in the manufacturing and wholesale business sectors.[12]

Yet, business-to-consumer sales were quickly growing as well. Most businesses created a multitude of Web pages to advertise and sell their products and services over the Internet. By 2009 a record number of Americans were turning to online shopping as an important way of buying products and services. Internet users in the United States spent more than 14 hours per week online. From a global perspective the numbers were even more staggering.

> More than 875 million people had shopped online by 2008, according to a Nielsen Global Online Survey, up from about 627 million two years earlier. Among Internet shoppers, South Korea accounted for the highest percentage (99 percent) of those with Internet access who used the Internet to shop, followed by the United Kingdom, Germany, and Japan (all at 97 percent). From books to electronic entertainment products to clothing, online shopping had firmly entrenched itself as a critical means of consumer purchasing and reinforced the necessity of e-business for global business organizations seeking to reach consumers.[13]

E-commerce had become a way of life, from large companies and smaller start-up businesses to individuals interested in shopping online. As technology became more affordable and easier to use, small and medium-sized businesses committed investment dollars to e-commerce and technology systems. These businesses discovered that the adoption of technology was a money-saver rather than an expense in the long run and that it gave the businesses a competitive edge over rivals by enabling them to add new services and operate more efficiently.

> When a computer programmer offered to create a custom package for Top Dog Daycare, owners Joelle and Tom Hilfers were shocked but agreed to take the plunge, on a payment plan. Three years and nearly $30,000 in technology investments later, the Hilfers do not know how they ever survived without the company's K-9 Connect software, which allows dog owners to book appointments

---

[12] "E-Stats," *United States Census Bureau,* May 16, 2008, *www.census.gov/estats.*

[13] "Four Out of Five Adults Now Use the Internet," *Harris Interactive,* November 17, 2008, *www.harrisinteractive.com;* and "Number of Internet Shoppers Up 40% in Two Years," *Internet Retailing,* January 29, 2008, *www.internetretailing.net.*

online, view their accounts, post photos of their pets, and look in on them during the day through a live Web cam. K-9 Connect also stores the pets' vaccination records, meal plans, and special requirements and has pages on e-commerce, dog training, and dog grooming. Business at Top Dog Daycare has tripled since the computerized system was adopted.[14]

E-commerce is undoubtedly here to stay, and new applications appear inevitable. One controversial area where e-business has made a significant impact is online gambling. Some of the world's largest gaming companies opened up new business opportunities by developing mobile gaming systems that allowed guest in their hotels to place wagers on the casino floor without ever leaving their rooms. Using handheld PDA-type devices, individuals can make wagers on sporting or other events. This generated an even greater revenue pool for the gaming companies but raised an important ethical question—is it good that people can place their bets anywhere in the hotel–casino building? What if children of the hotel guests get these devices? On the casino floor, drunken guests can be spotted and steered away from the tables, but remote betting circumvents this control.

With each new innovation comes this important ethical question: *Should* we develop and offer the new application? At present, many inventors, computer programmers, and business managers appear only to be asking, *Can* we develop and offer the new application? Both questions are paramount as technology and e-commerce continue to influence individual, business, and society interactions in the world in which we live.

M-Commerce

Cellular telephones, or cell phones, use radio technology to enable users to place calls from a mobile device, with transmission over a service area divided into small "cells," each with its own low-power radio transmitter. The first generation of cell phones, introduced in the 1980s, were clumsy analog devices; today's digital "smartphones" provide a range of applications, including e-mail and Internet access, in addition to voice communications. In North America, cell phones are used mainly as a communications tool. But many Europeans and Asians have embraced what they call a "mobile phone" in a different way—as a method of conducting commerce. **M-commerce**, commerce conducted via mobile or cell phones, provides consumers with an electronic wallet when using their mobile phones. People can trade stocks or make consumer purchases of everything from hot dogs to washing machines and countless other products. France Telecom has marketed a mobile phone with a built-in credit card slot for easy wireless payments.

On a hot and humid Tokyo summer day, a Coca-Cola manager sent an e-mail to several thousand mobile phone customers. The message urged them to buy a drink from one of the hundreds of high-tech vending machines in their area. The m-commerce machines enabled customers to use their mobile phones, rather than cash, to purchase products. Those who bought a Coca-Cola product from one of these machines would get a free download of a company ad jingle for their mobile phones. Sales jumped 50 percent among those who received the message. This was an effort by Coca-Cola to tap into the Japanese obsession with mobile phones and introduce them to the world of m-commerce.[15]

---

[14] "High Tech Isn't Just for the Big Guys," *The New York Times,* January 20, 2005, *www.nytimes.com.*
[15] "Coke Lures Japanese Customers with Cellphone Come-Ons," *The Wall Street Journal,* September 8, 2003, pp. B1, B4.

Exhibit 12.A

Too Much of a Good Thing? Wireless Dependence

Robert Bornstein, a psychologist at Adelphia University, says, "The superconnected may develop a dual dependence. They're not only counting on other people too much, they're also hooked on the devices themselves, sometimes to the point where they feel utterly disconnected, isolated, and detached without them." Exactly how bad is the dependence on technology, specifically wireless devices? Some experts have warned that handheld e-mailing devices are so addictive that soon compulsive users will need to be weaned off them using treatment programs like the ones used by drug addicts. This overreliance on technology can also cause physical problems, such as

- BlackBerry thumb—a pain or numbness in your thumbs caused by constant e-mailing, messaging, or Internet surfing on handheld devices.
- Cell phone elbow—arthritic pain and swelling in the elbow from constantly holding a cell phone to the ear, which in some severe cases may cause nerve damage.
- PDA (personal data assistant) hunch—neck pain caused by looking straight down at your PDA mini-monitor.

Source: "Wireless Dependence," *The New York Times,* February 17, 2007, *www.nytimes.com.*

By the mid-2000s, the trend toward m-commerce via mobile or cell phones had quickly spread across Europe and Asia. What was the roadblock in the United States? According to experts, the reason why American consumers had not been introduced to m-commerce was that the multitude of companies involved could not agree how to split the anticipated revenues from m-commerce sales. According to a Nokia executive, "In Japan it was easier. It was just the major guys saying, 'This is how it will be.'" A single carrier, NTT DoCoMo, accounted for more than half of the Japanese m-commerce market. In the United States, cell phone manufacturers, carriers, financial institutions, and retailers all potentially played a role in m-commerce and wanted their share of the proceeds. Some experts predicted that by 2012 most of the problems would be worked out and Americans would join other developed nations in the world of m-commerce.[16]

But with the potential for greater m-commerce activity in the United States, some stakeholder groups warned that accompanying the increased usage would be increased frustration. Critics predicted more unwanted and unsolicited mobile text messages and incidents of malware and spyware. The spread of smartphones also raised privacy concerns, especially regarding children. In response, the Federal Trade Commission promised to undertake a review of the Children's Online Privacy Protection Act in 2010, five years earlier than originally scheduled, to ensure that protections extended to include the mobile marketplace as well.[17] (The Children's Online Privacy Protection Act is discussed in Chapter 13.)

Some unexpected consequences of mobile technology are described in Exhibit 12.A.

Social Networking

Social networking, a system using technology to enable people to connect, explore interests, and share activities around the world, exploded onto the technology scene in the 2000s, altering many social and human interactions. Exhibit 12.B describes some of the more popular social networking sites on the Internet and some of the ethical challenges they face.

[16] "Cellphones as Credit Cards? Americans Must Wait," *The New York Times,* January 25, 2009, *www.nytimes.com.*
[17] "FTC Issues Staff Report on Mobile Commerce Marketplace," Federal Trade Commission, April 22, 2009, *www.ftc.gov.*

Exhibit 12.D

Sites and Their Challenges

Facebook began in 2005 in a Harvard University dormitory room as a way for college students to become or stay connected. Four years later, Facebook registered its 200 millionth user, doubling in size from 2008 to 2009, with more than 70 percent of users living outside the United States. Facebook has become the Internet's dominant social ecosystem and an essential personal and business networking tool, allowing people to connect with old friends, begin new friendships, or establish business relationships. But ethical and legal privacy and pornography challenges arose over the content on Facebook pages, causing the company to adopt new procedures in a government settlement as the social network learned that it needed to better police the content on its service. The company pledged to respond to user complaints about nudity, pornography, or harassment within 24 hours. Facebook executives also agreed to a court-appointed examiner to review all Facebook procedures for two years to ensure compliance with the government settlement.

MySpace, an online community that "lets you meet your friend's friends," began in 2003 and registered its 100 millionth user in 2006. Some businesses have become increasingly concerned over MySpace content, as employees or former employees have posted information about the company, managers, or fellow employees. Sites critical of business—such as Best Buy Losers Club, the Disneyland Bitterness Convention, T.J. Maxx Needs to Die, and the Abercrombie Is Evil Awareness Foundation—have caused businesses to be more aggressive in learning what is being posted on MySpace and to respond to negative, especially factually untrue, company information.

YouTube was launched in 2005 to serve a different social networking segment: video news and entertainment. After only one year of operations, the YouTube founders sold their company to Google for $1.65 billion in stock. By 2009, YouTube regularly claimed that tens of millions of viewers watched exciting or unusual videos posted to the site. Ranging from the "Britain's Got Talent" singing sensation Susan Boyle to two employees of Domino's Pizza filming their disgusting prank of sabotaging food (discussed in Chapter 19), YouTube quickly became the Internet's go-to platform for music videos and a wide variety of professional and homemade video clips. YouTube has continuously been accused of allowing copyrighted material to be uploaded for public viewing on its site, despite efforts by the company to warn against this practice. YouTube argued that it is the copyright holder's responsibility to challenge the illegal posting of legally protected material. Like the other social networking companies, YouTube also faced serious challenges regarding questionable content and flags a variety of questionable material to warn viewers of controversial content.

Twitter exploded on the social networking scene in 2009 and within a few months had 14 million unique viewers, compared to 8 million only a month earlier. Boosted by a special appearance on the *Oprah Winfrey* show, Twitter allowed users to broadcast messages of 140 characters or less. Like other social networking options, Twitter quickly learned that messages on its system that might be offensive or inaccurate could result in liability for the company and that the protection of information was of the utmost importance. For example, 33 high-profile Twitter accounts, including that of then President-elect Obama, were breached with sexually explicit and drug-related messages after someone was able to guess a Twitter administrator's password. The company quickly shut down the sender's accounts and installed new security measures. In another case, an administrative employee's e-mail account was breached, giving the hacker access to spreadsheets and documents about company plans, confidential contracts, and financial details. This information was sent to two tech blogs in the United States and France. Personal information about Twitter employees, including credit card information, was also accessed.

Sources: "Is Facebook Growing Up Too Fast?" *The New York Times,* March 29, 2009, *www.nytimes.com;* "As Facebook Settles Case, Sites Moves on Child Safety," *The Wall Street Journal,* October 17, 2007, *online.wsj.com;* "The Young and the Vicious," *BusinessWeek,* July 31, 2006, p. 34; "In 4 Years, YouTube Succeeded in Catching World's Eye," *Pittsburgh Post-Gazette,* April 20, 2009, *www.post-gazette.com;* "With Oprah Onboard, Twitter Grows," *The New York Times,* April 28, 2009, *www.nytimes.com;* "Obama's Twitter Site Hacked?" *Washington Times,* January 5, 2009, *www.washingtontimes.com;* and "Twitter Hack Raises Flags on Security," *The New York Times,* July 16, 2009, *www.nytimes.com.*

Social networking has also ventured into the workplace. Some businesses have questioned their employees' use of these services or banned them altogether, while others have seen their potential value to the employer.

A 2006 Forrester Research study estimated that 4 of every 10 adults in North America played online games. Most game playing occurred around 1 p.m. each day and significantly dropped off after 5 p.m. "We don't know for certain that all of those people are at work, but most people work between the hours of 9 a.m. and 5 p.m., [so] you do the math," said Jim Greer, founder of Kongregate, an online game company in California. Some employers forbid workers from game playing on the job or ignore the practice. Yet, others have welcomed the trend and set up separate game areas on the company's intranet system. "It's the modern-day spin on the ordinary break room," explained Simon Spearman, analyst at Social Technologies, a Washington consulting firm. "The idea is to develop a place where employees can interact with their coworkers, compete, and have a short little spurt of excitement during the workday."[18]

IBM researchers developed Beehive, a social network available only to IBM employees on the company's intranet. IBM has thousands of employees in locations all over the world, providing the opportunity for a large semantic web. Beehive was designed to help foster personal connections, to improve career opprtunities within the company, and to promote new projects and proposals.[19] This company felt that social networking technology could be a boon for business, rather than a distraction for employees.

Blogs and Vlogs

A **blog** is a Web-based journal or log maintained by an individual with regular entries of commentary, descriptions, or accounts of events or other material such as graphics or video. The blogging revolution began in the early 2000s. Just a few years later, it was widely popular, and many believed already out of control. Technorati, Inc., a company that tracks and analyzes blogging activity, reported that by 2008, 184 million people worldwide had started a blog. Bloggers ranged widely in their age and occupation, with 95 percent of the top 100 U.S. newspapers having reporter blogs.[20] Blogging about politics is big business too, as politicians have learned. Politicians and political parties, in the United States and across Europe, regularly hire bloggers to promote their issues or candidates, as discussed in Chapter 9.

As blogging spread into all areas of our lives, ethical questions about blogs emerged. According to a *Los Angeles Times* report, thousands of bloggers were being paid by marketing firms to promote or attack various products on the market. Critics argue that this blurred the ethical line between what was honest opinion or helpful information and what was an advertisement paid for by companies to influence individuals' purchasing decisions. Medical professionals also weighed in on the blogging controversy, claiming that patients were posting unfounded and damaging reports on a doctor's performance. While some doctors admitted that blogs provided many patients with useful information, medical misinformation from uncensored blogs was far more harmful.[21]

---

[18] "It's Only a Game, but It's Played at Work," *The New York Times*, September 30, 2007, *www.nytimes.com*.

[19] "Project Beehive," *IBM Watson Research Center*, IBM Web site, *domino.watson.ibm.com*.

[20] For more information on blogs and bloggers see Technorati's Web site at *technorati.com*.

[21] "Questions about Blogging Chart New Ethical Territory in Cyberspace," Institute for Global Ethics, *Ethics Newsline*, March 19, 2007, *www.globalethics.org*.

A new generation of blogs appeared in the mid-2000s, called **vlogs**, or video Web logs. All that was needed was access to a digital camera that could capture moving images and high-speed Internet access.

Viewers of Beth Agnew's Web site could watch videos of her laughing while looking at an oak leaf, while wearing a pirate's patch, and while pretending someone had dropped an ice cube down her back. The vlog, *laughpractice. blogspot.com,* promoted finding hilarity in the mundane and spreading goodwill through laughter. "Anyone anywhere in the world can log into the blog and have a laugh along with me," said Agnew, a college professor in Toronto and self-described certified laugh leader.

The emerging vlog medium attracted thousands of aspiring video producers. The number of vlogs mushroomed due to improved streaming video technology, faster Internet speeds, new Web sites that would host the video free of charge, and new cell phones and other devices designed to play videos. Videos produced by individuals and small companies found their way to on-demand services offered by cable companies and new networks that solicit user content. While most viewers stumbled across vlogs while Web surfing, others found them on Apple Computer's iTunes directory, which listed some vlogs, calling them video podcasts. The vlog mode became a social voice for actress Mia Farrow during her eight-day hunger strike to protest the genocide in Darfur, as well as an opportunity for unemployed individuals to describe their value to potential employers during the economic recession of 2008–2009.

Threats from Technology

Spam and Unsolicited Commercial E-Mail

The emergence of the Internet launched not only the blog and vlog avalanche but also the onslaught of *spam,* as the opening example describing AT&T's 75 million e-mails to its customers to promote the *American Idol* show demonstrated. **Spam** refers to **unsolicited commercial e-mails** (also called UCE or junk e-mail) sent in bulk to valid e-mail accounts. These messages can vary from harmless advertisements for commercial products to offensive material and finance scams. Spam has created problems for e-mail users as it has caused extra network traffic and wasted time spent sorting through the irrelevant or unwanted e-mails to access desired messages. The impact of spam on consumers is discussed in Chapter 15.

Spamming was big business and a big headache for business. Internet watchdogs reported that the number of malicious Web sites blocked for hosting malware, software designed to infiltrate and damage a computer, tripled in 2009, with nearly 3,000 potentially harmful Web sites being intercepted daily. That year, the percentage of e-mail–borne malware containing links to malicious sites reached its highest level, 20.3 percent. The global ratio of spam in e-mail traffic was 1 in every 1.32 e-mails.[22]

To combat spam, organizations turned to software, hardware, and services that filter, classify, and categorize incoming e-mail messages. While generally effective, there were problems making sure the bad e-mails were blocked and the desired e-mails got through. Google and other Web mail providers used a variety of systems to identify and mark spam e-mails, relying on their users to help. Real-time blacklists (RTBLs) played an important

---

[22] "Infected Websites Increase Three-fold, and Email-borne Malicious Links Reaches Nine Month High," *MessageLabs Press Releases,* March 31, 2009, *www.messagelabs.co.uk.*

role as major filtering devices reporting Internet provider addresses and servers that were identified as chronic gateways and sources of malicious spam e-mail. Companies used these RTBLs to block traffic from these sites. But the systems were not foolproof, as Olga Ocon discovered.

> An employment recruiter, Olga Ocon, decided to sift through an e-mail folder containing messages identified by her company's computer system as spam. Embedded in the 756 e-mail advertisements for Viagra, cell phones, and loan refinancing offers, all ready to be deleted in a few days, were eight résumés from prospective job applicants. Ocon suspected that since some of the résumés contained phrases such as "four-time winner of sales awards" and "oversaw in excess of $40 million in sales," the company's spam filter caught these messages and determined they were e-mails containing money-making offers.[23]

Governments have stepped in to monitor, control, and prosecute spammers who use the Internet for illegal activity. The United Kingdom has passed anti-spam legislation making it a crime to send unsolicited e-mail messages to people's private e-mail addresses or cell phones. The government believed that the threat of $8,000 for a conviction and limitless fines if the case made its way to a jury would deter the growing spam problem. The United Kingdom was following Italy's lead, which made spam a crime with punishments ranging from $108,000 in fines to three years in prison. "These regulations will help combat the global nuisance of unsolicited e-mails and texts by enshrining in law rights that give consumers more say over who can use their personal details," said U.K. communications minister Stephen Timms.[24]

Phishing

Compounding the problem of spam or unsolicited commercial e-mail is **phishing**, the practice of duping computer users into revealing their passwords or other private data under false pretenses. The Anti-Phishing Working Group, a U.S. industry association, reported in 2008 an 827 percent increase in password stealing, from 3,362 cases in January 2008 to 31,173 cases in December 2008.

Businesses have not sat idly by while con artists have gone phishing. Some companies, such as the antivirus software maker Symantec, created a task force to respond to the steep rise in malicious phishing efforts. Combating phishing became a growth industry, as numerous companies offered protection from phishing efforts through filters, features embedded in browsers, extensions or toolbars for browsers, or as part of Web site login procedures at a nominal cost to the users. Other companies were focusing on user education, believing that if the user became more aware of phishing, then he or she would be on guard against these attacks.

In 2009, about 1 in 300 e-mails contained some form of a phishing attack, an increase of more than 30 percent from the previous year. "The economy and other seasonal happenings, such as St. Patrick's Day and the U.S. March Madness basketball tournament, remain predictable avenues for spammers, phishers, and fraudsters to exploit," said a senior intelligence analyst. "It is not likely that these tactics will go away, but in the coming months we may see more nontraditional techniques, like those from cash-strapped individuals seeking charity, begin to take hold."[25]

[23] "Stringent Spam Filters Mistakenly Block E-Mailed Resumes," *The Wall Street Journal,* April 13, 2004, pp. B1, B4.
[24] "Britain Makes It a Crime to Send Spam," Institute for Global Ethics, *Ethics Newsline,* September 22, 2003, *www.globalethics.org.*
[25] *MessageLabs Press Releases,* op cit., *www.messagelabs.co.uk.*

Pharming

Pharming, or domain name system (DNS) poisoning, is a hacking technique that redirects a user's computer from a legitimate Web site to another site by altering the user's computer or router. Every computer attached to the Internet has a numeric Internet Protocol (IP) address. Pharming changes the IP address for one or more Web sites. Another popular pharming attack is to force a router to use a rogue server. A router sits between one or more computers and an Internet connection. Most WiFi access points also act as routers, to allow two or more simultaneous users on the WiFi connection. These wireless routers are especially vulnerable to pharming attacks, as many users keep their router's factory default password and username after installation, and share their unencrypted WiFi signal with neighbors and friends.

Pharming attacks were first reported in the 1990s, but e-mail and wireless computing have provided hackers and criminals with many more opportunities. All a user has to do is click the links or view the message to activate the pharming attack on their computer or router.[26]

A new safeguard from pharming attacks emerged—OpenDNS.com. This system was made up of a free network of DNS servers that can block entire categories of domain names, including sites most commonly associated with phishing, gambling, and adult sites. Specific Web sites or entire categories can also be allowed on the user's network, if selected. The OpenDNS system can also alert administrators when users are accessing sites that are associated with phishing and pharming attacks. OpenDNS.com earns revenue through advertisements that are displayed when users enter a partial or misspelled domain name.

Internet Censorship

Many people believe that information on the Internet should be universally accessible. Some believe that restrictions should be placed on some categories of information, such as sexually explicit material, gambling, or Nazi or racist propaganda. Some countries, however, have gone much further, imposing censorship on broad categories of online information.

The Chinese government operates one of the most sophisticated systems of Internet censorship in the world. It requires all China-based Web sites and blogs to register with the government and blocks access to many kinds of information, including material critical of the government. In 2009, Chinese government officials censored a YouTube video, which it said was fabricated, that showed Chinese police brutally beating Tibetans after riots in Lhasa, the Tibetan capital.[27] (A case at the end of the book, "Google in China," further discusses Chinese Internet censorship and its implications for U.S. companies doing business there.)

Other governments have also tried to control Internet access to controversial information. In 2006, Thailand announced it was blocking access to YouTube for anyone with a Thai Internet address and then identified 20 offensive videos for Google, the owner of YouTube, to remove as a condition for unblocking the site.

[26] "Pharming Out-scams Phishing," *Wired*, March 14, 2005, *www.wired.com;* "Drive-by Pharming Attack Hits Home," *Cnet News*, January 22, 2008, *news.cnet.com;* and "Hosts File Pharming and Other Botnet Recruitment Methods," *ZDNet Asia*, February 17, 2009, *www.zdnetasia.com.*

[27] "China Orders Web Sites, Blogs to Register with Government," *The Wall Street Journal*, June 7, 2005, *online.wsj.com;* and "YouTube Blocked in China, Google Says," *The New York Times*, March 25, 2009, *www.nytimes.com.*

The next year Thailand's military government blocked access to YouTube and other Internet sites, claiming that the information defamed the country's monarch. "We have blocked YouTube because it contains a video insulting to our king," said the head of Thailand's Ministry of Communication and Information Technology.[28]

The Thai crackdown followed a similar action taken by Turkish government officials who cut off access to YouTube for several days after a video was considered insulting to Mustafa Kemal Ataturk, the founder of modern Turkey. Insulting Ataturk was a crime in Turkey. Similarly, a Brazilian judge ordered access to YouTube blocked after clips of a prominent model cavorting in the sea with her lover kept reappearing on the site.

Socially Beneficial Uses of Technology

Despite all the abuses of technology documented above—the challenges of social networking; the misuse of blogs and vlogs; the intrusions of spam, phishing, and pharming; and censorship of the Internet—technology clearly can be used to improve the quality of our lives. How we communicate with others, conduct business, learn new things, and acquire information is enhanced by technology.

Technology and Education

Technology has democratized education by enabling students in the some of the poorest and most remote communities to access the world's best libraries, instructors, and courses available through the Internet. (The status of the digital divide and the issue of who has access and who does not have access to technology are discussed later in the chapter.) A digital learning environment provides students with skills to rapidly discover and access information needed to solve complex problems. By 2008, the ratio of computers to students in the United States was one to one. Technology was no longer off in a computer lab but was in most classrooms, always at the ready. Web-based education software enables an emphasis on project-based learning, a break from an overreliance on the textbook-and-lecture model of education. Project-based learning encourages active learning and produces better performance in class and on standardized tests.[29] Yet, some educators, parents, and technology advocates wonder if technology may be crossing over the line, as discussed in Exhibit 12.C.

Technology has also brought education online. In the United States, online enrollment continued to grow faster than conventional enrollment. By 2007, more than 3.9 million postsecondary students were taking at least one online course, a 12 percent increase over the previous year.[30] The University of Phoenix, the world's largest for-profit education provider, offered associate, bachelor, master, and doctoral degrees in such diverse fields as business, criminal justice, education, nursing, health care, and technology. Other institutions, such as AIU Online, Capella University, Walden University, Kaplan University, and DeVry University, allowed stay-at-home students or students who frequently traveled to complete their certificate or degree programs. Traditional colleges and universities also offered online courses or programs to reach out to nontraditional students. Businesses joined the

[28] "Thailand Bans YouTube," *The New York Times,* April 5, 2007, *www.nytimes.com;* and "Google's Gatekeepers," *The New York Times,* November 30, 2008, *www.nytimes.com.*

[29] "At School, Technology Starts to Turn a Corner," *The New York Times,* August 17, 2008, *www.nytimes.com.*

[30] I. Elaine Allen and Jeff Seaman, *Staying the Course: Online Education in the United States, 2008* (Needham, MA: Babson Survey Research Group/Sloan Consortium).

Exhibit 12.C

Are Cell Phones in the Classroom a Good Thing?

Cell phone manufacturers and service providers believe the key to improving the math skills of students is for them to spend more time on their cell phones in the classroom. At the Mobile Learning 09 conference in Washington, DC, CTIA, a wireless industry trade group, announced its campaign for more cell phones in schools. According to research funded by Qualcomm, a maker of cell phone chips, "smartphones can make students smarter." The trade industry responded to criticism that this was simply a self-promotional ploy by saying that smartphones would bring many of the capabilities of computers into the classroom—and they were smaller, cheaper, and more popular with students.

In trial projects in Chicago, San Diego, and Florida, students used cell phones to record themselves solving problems and posted the videos to a private social networking site where classmates could watch. The studies showed that students with the phones performed 25 percent better on an end-of-the-year algebra exam than did students without the devices in similar classes. After experimenting with cell phones in the classroom in North Carolina, one teacher said, "[the cell phones] took average-level kids and made them into honors-level kids."

Source: "Industry Makes Pitch That Smartphones Belong in Classroom," *The New York Times,* February 16, 2009, *www.nytimes.com.*

---

online education movement by offering many employee training programs online. This was especially beneficial for global companies that wanted to standardize their training but did not want to send their trainers around the world. Seemingly everywhere we turn, including schools, technology is all around us.

Medical Information via the Internet

The explosion of medical information on the Internet has dramatically affected people's lives. How people are examined, diagnosed, and treated; how health-related information is collected and stored; and the time and costs associated with health care have all been changed by technological innovations, as described at the beginning of this chapter.

> By 2009, the Internet had become the primary source for health information for 70 percent of Americans, with most traffic on sites offered by WebMD, Google, Yahoo!, and Microsoft. But the most heavily trafficked health destination was one that most people had not heard of—Everyday Health. Started in the kitchen of the cofounder's apartment, Benjamin Wolin, Everyday Health linked information from a broad array of other Web sites, including South Beach Diet, alternative medicine guru Dr. Andrew Weil, and What to Expect, based on the popular pregnancy book read by 93 percent of first-time mothers in the United States. Everyday Health boasted of having nearly 25 million unique visitors a month to its Web site, with plans to continue to acquire additional smaller health sites to extend its network of information.[31]

While the abundance of medical information available on the Internet was welcomed by medical practitioners and the public in general, some warned that this easily available information may create a group of **cyberchondriacs**, a term referring to people who leap to the most dreadful conclusions while researching health matters online. In a study conducted by Microsoft researchers, they found that self-diagnosis, enabled by easy-to-use medical search engines, led Web browsers to conclude the worst about what ailed them. People searching medical Web sites often focused on the most sensational or worst

---

[31] "Why This Web Site Looks So Healthy," *BusinessWeek,* March 23 and 30, 2009, p. 73.

possible diagnosis; for example, if suffering from a headache, the cyberchondriac might conclude the cause was a brain tumor, even though a much more likely reason might be something as benign as caffeine withdrawal.[32]

Another emerging issue within the arena of medical care and technology focused on **digital medical records,** or how a patient's medical records should be stored and linked to other health care providers. National and local regulations and practice, along with language issues and privacy concerns, were frequent obstacles to the implementation of these systems. Insurers, medical equipment companies, and pharmaceutical companies each have their own concerns regarding electronic records. In 2009 the U.S. government announced plans to spend $19 billion to spur the use of digital or electronic patient records, as part of a national effort to reduce medical costs. Included in this funding was more than $1 billion in grants to help hospitals transition to digital medical records.[33]

However, as appealing as the government's plan to bring technology to enhance patient medical record keeping might be, some medical personnel were doubtful of the wisdom of this strategy.

In an article published in the *New England Journal of Medicine* in 2009, based on a survey of 3,000 hospitals, only 9 percent of the nation's medical care facilities were found to have digital or electronic health records. The lead author of the article said, "We have a long way to go and we did not measure effective use. Even if a hospital does have [digital or] electronic health records, it does not mean it is sharing information with other hospitals and doctors down the road." In another article in the same journal, doctors warned that the current health record suppliers were offering costly and outdated pre-Internet era software, making it difficult to switch vendors and for outside programmers to make upgrades and improvements.[34]

While generally seen as a good idea, the digitalization of patient health records and the sharing of that information to enhance medical care in the United States appear to have a rocky and long road ahead.

Special Issue: The Digital Divide

Some people were concerned that the phenomenal development and use of technology were greater in developed than developing countries or among some segments of the population than others. This gap between those who have access to technology and those who do not has been called the **digital divide.**[35]

Recently, some evidence has suggested that the digital divide in the United States is becoming smaller. The falling prices of laptops, more computers in public schools and libraries, and the newest generation of cell phones and Internet-enabled handheld devices have all combined to narrow the digital divide. Studies and mounting anecdotal evidence suggest that blacks in America, even those at the lower end of the economic scale, are making significant gains in access to the Internet. As a result, organizations that serve

---

[32] "Microsoft Examines Causes of 'Cyberchondria,'" *The New York Times,* November 25, 2008, *www.nytimes.com.*

[33] "Microsoft, Google in Healthy Competition," *Cnet,* May 18, 2009, *news.cnet.com;* and "On Talk Radio, Obama Stands by Health-Care Plan," *Pittsburgh Post-Gazette,* August 20, 2009, *www.post-gazette.com.*

[34] "Doctors Raise Doubts on Digital Health Data," *The New York Times,* March 26, 2009, *www.nytimes.com.*

[35] For a contrarian's viewpoint, see Walter Block,"The 'Digital Divide' Is Not a Problem in Need of Rectifying," *Journal of Business Ethics* 53 (2004), pp. 393–406.

African-Americans, as well as companies seeking their business, are increasingly turning to the Internet to reach out to this group.

Progress in narrowing the digital divide in developing countries has been slower, but still evident, as illustrated by the following example:

> Entasopia, Kenya, is a remote village with about 4,000 inhabitants. The village has a single dirt path winding over hills and through the desert to arrive at the outpost that has no bank, no post office, few cars, and little infrastructure. Newspapers arrive every three to four weeks. Kerosene lamps and candles light the huts. But in 2008 three engineers from the University of Michigan, with financial support from Google, arrived and installed a small satellite dish powered by a solar panel to connect a few computers in the Entasopia community center to the rest of the world. Although cell phone use in Africa grew tenfold from 2002 to 2007, satellite connections were faster and more stable and offered a way to connect 95 percent of Africans who until recently had no access.[36]

Other programs were developed to narrow the global digital divide. Nicholas Negroponte and the MIT Media Lab developed a program called One Laptop per Child (OLPC) to design, build, and market an ultralightweight, durable netbook computer for children aged 6 through 12 throughout the world. The target price for the computer was $100 (U.S.), to be achieved through economies of scale, industry partnerships, government purchases, and open-source software. The computer used a touchpad and water-resistant keyboard to control highly graphical applications running on an inexpensive starter version of Microsoft Windows XP or on Fedora, a free version of the Red Hat Linux operating system. Files were stored on an internal 1 gigabyte flash drive, on external USB devices, and through cloud computing services.

OLPC allowed consumers in the United States and Canada to purchase an OLPC through a "give one, get one" program. Consumers paid $399 for two OLPCs and received one network-ready computer for their own use. The other computer was donated to an OLPC project in a participating country. At least 1.3 million OLPCs were ordered for almost 40 countries by 2009.[37]

As some businesses, government bodies, and nonprofit organizations met the digital divide challenge by providing computers, another approach was to connect everyone around the world with mobile phones. The United Nations' Human Settlements Program forecast that by the year 2020, 25 percent of the world's population would live in poverty. Mobile phone service helped developing countries leapfrog older landline technologies to provide cheap, reliable phone service to rural and urban areas. A 2005 study by London Business School researchers concluded that a country's gross domestic product (GDP) could rise as much as 0.5 percent when there were an additional 10 mobile phones per 100 people.

> In 2008, there were 3.3 billion mobile phone subscriptions worldwide, a number that was barely half of the world's total population. Nokia and its competitive rivals were faced with flattening growth curves in developed countries. Adapting mobile phone design and marketing processes to high-volume, low-margin markets required an in-depth knowledge of local markets. In many areas of the world, communities shared a mobile phone, relying on small phone kiosks that sold calls by the minute. One prototype phone concept that

---

[36] "Bringing the Internet to Remote African Villages," *The New York Times,* February 2, 2009, *www.nytimes.com.*

[37] "One Laptop Meets Big Business," *BusinessWeek,* June 5, 2008, *www.businessweek.com.*

Nokia developed had a target price of $5. Mobile manufacturers had problems reducing their current prices to $25. There were plenty of challenges; for example, in some communities, electricity was unreliable. Mobile phones sold in these markets had to be able to charge their batteries from two or more power sources, such as diesel generators, community storage batteries, bicycles, or solar power.

Governments saw opportunities and challenges in the rapid adoption of mobile phones. Public health workers in Kenya and South Africa used text messaging to deploy anonymous surveys about tuberculosis, breast cancer, AIDS, and sexually transmitted diseases. Vodafone delivered mobile banking services to almost 2 million Kenyan customers. Mobile phone users there turned to text messaging to spread information, news, and rumors after a postelection media blackout in December 2007.[38]

Clearly, high-technology businesses, governments, and community groups acting together appear to be winning the battle of making technology more accessible to all people regardless of their race, income, education, age, or residence.

The unmistakable economic and social force of technology is evident in every part of the world, in every industry, and in every aspect of our lives. The technologically driven semantic phase has changed how businesses operate and the quality of our lives, regardless of where we live or what we do. These profound changes give rise to important, and possibly perplexing, questions about whether technology should be controlled or who should manage technology and its growth. These issues are discussed in the following chapter.

Summary

- Technology is the practical application of science and knowledge that is rapidly changing and spreading across societies.

- Six phases of technology represent the progress of civilization throughout history fueled by economic growth and research and development.

- Technology has changed how businesses offer, sell, and account for their goods and services in the global marketplace and their interactions with their stakeholders around the world through e-business and m-commerce. Individuals are investing and buying goods and services online at an astonishing rate.

- Technology has exponentially increased our ability to communicate with others around the world through e-mail and social networking, yet some technological innovations also provide significant threats to our privacy and safety. Some national governments have taken steps to censor the Internet.

- Socially beneficial uses of technology in education and medicine have opened up new learning opportunities, significantly changed medical record keeping, and offered new sources for acquiring medical information.

- Recently, collaborative initiatives by businesses, governments, and nonprofit organizations addressing Internet and mobile phone access around the world appear to have significantly closed differences in access to technology according to age, income, and ethnicity or nationality that are referred to as a "digital divide."

[38] "Can the Cellphone Help End Global Poverty?" *The New York Times*, April 13, 2008, *www.nytimes.com*.

Key Terms

biotechnology, *271*	e-business, *275*	social networking, *277*
blog, *279*	information phase, *271*	spam, *280*
cellular telephones, *276*	Internet, *273*	technology, *269*
cyberchondriacs, *284*	m-commerce, *276*	unsolicited commercial
cyberspace, *271*	pharming, *282*	e-mails, *280*
digital divide, *285*	phishing, *281*	vlog, *280*
digital medical records, *285*	semantic phase, *271*	

Internet Resources

www.antiphishing.org	Anti-Phishing Working Group
www.bio.org	Biotechnology Industry Organization
www.digitaldividenetwork.org	Digital Divide Network
www.ecommercetimes.com	E-Commerce Times
www.foresight.org	Foresight Institute
www.isoc.org	Internet Society
laptop.org	One Laptop Per Child
www.onguardonline.gov	OnGuard Online
www.pewinternet.org	Pew Internet and American Life Project
www.pharming.org	Yahoo!-sponsored site on pharming attacks
www.spamtrackers.eu	Spam Trackers
technorati.com	Technorati

Discussion Case: *Teen Suicide Viewed Online*

In November 2008, a 19-year-old community college student living in Pembroke Pines, Florida, committed suicide by taking a lethal drug overdose in front of a live webcam. Some computer viewers urged him on by texting messages that encouraged the teen to swallow the antidepressant pills that eventually killed him. Others used the message board to try to talk him out of committing suicide. Online communities "are like the crowd outside the building with the guy on the ledge," said a university professor who studies the effects of technology on society. "Sometimes there is someone who gets involved and tries to talk him down. Often the crowd chants, 'jump, jump.' They can enable suicide or help prevent it." Some viewers did contact the police but only after the teen had lapsed into unconsciousness, so the emergency crew arrived at the student's home too late to save him. Their arrival was also captured on the live webcam, as hundreds of people continued to watch the tragedy play out. In the chat room, users typed acronyms for "oh my God" and "laughing out loud" before the police covered the webcam, ending the show.

The student, who suffered from bipolar disorder, had announced his plans to kill himself on a bodybuilder's Web site, but many viewers did not take his threats seriously since he had threatened suicide on the site before. During the past year, the student had posted more than 2,300 messages to the bodybuilder's Web site and wrote that online forums had "become like a family to me." "I know it is kind [of] sad" that he chose to talk about his troubles online because he did not want to talk about them to anyone in person, the student wrote. His real family was appalled by the reaction of others to the broadcast suicide. "As a human being, you don't watch someone in trouble and sit back and just watch," said the teen's father. "Some kind of regulation is necessary."

Unfortunately, this was not the first time someone had used the Web in this way. In 2003, an Arizona man overdosed on drugs while writing about his actions in a chat room. In Britain a year earlier, a man hung himself while chatting online and webcasting the scene. In both cases, other users encouraged the individuals with their online messages.

Message boards and blog sites are generally unmonitored, one of the attractions to using this site for many young people. Some site providers do attempt to supervise what is posted, however. After the Florida teen's suicide, BodyBuilding.com and Justin.tv removed much of the evidence of the suicide and many users' reactions to it because they were deemed distasteful or provided information that would enable someone else to recreate the suicide.

Most Internet service providers, such as Facebook and MySpace, have taken actions to try to monitor the activity on their sites after strong public outcry to a specific incident. Much of this effort has targeted instances of piracy or nudity. One child protection group, WiredSafety.org, scans Web sites for inappropriate content and notifies the Web site hosts, but the organization admits that surveillance is challenging. "The only thing you get from the combination of Web cams and young people are problems," said the organization's executive director. It is extremely difficult to monitor unexpected video-casting of suicides.

Despite some efforts to restrain Web content, new Web sites pop up that appear to be without any controls. Stickam.com built its following by going where other sites feared—into the realm of unfiltered live broadcasts from Web cameras. Basically, Stickam offers a free service for anyone to post anything they wish; all you need is "an Internet connection and a browser with the most recent version of Macromedia Flash Player installed." The 35-employee staff of Stickam reportedly does not monitor any of the content. "Letting people do whatever they want is one way for these sites to differentiate themselves," said Josh Bernoff, a Forrester Research analyst. "It is a race to the bottom."

So, what is the answer? Does the type of action showing a teen committing suicide become part of our technology-based culture, or should there be controls? Who should be responsible, and what should be controlled? These questions have plagued individuals and organizations involved with the Internet for decades and have become more complex and serious as technology has developed and become more pervasive in our society.

Since its inception in 2005, YouTube has banned nudity and taken down copyrighted material when right holders file specific complaints. Under additional pressure from copyright holders, YouTube placed a 10-minute limit on all clips. But new start-up sites are under pressure to compete with the larger sites and typically do not screen or restrict content. Dailymotion users posted 9,000 new videos a day to the emerging site, which had more than 1.3 million visitors in one month, an increase of 100 percent from six months earlier. Dailymotion, which is based in Paris, had entire episodes of television shows and recording of music without copyright permission or payment of copyright fees. Yet, even this focus on copyrighted material begs the question: Should Web sites seek to control the webcasting of suicides?

The police in Broward County, Florida, where the teen who committed suicide lived, promised to launch an investigation to determine if any criminal wrongdoing was committed. "If somebody threatens suicide or attempts suicide, it's never a joke," said the Broward County chief medical examiner. "It always requires attention. It's basically a cry for help."

Sources: "Web Suicide Viewed Live and Reaction Spur a Debate," *The New York Times,* November 25, 2008, *www.nytimes.com;* and "Young Turn to Web Sites without Rules," *The New York Times,* January 7, 2007, *www.nytimes.com.*

Discussion Questions

1. Should government weigh in and control what is posted to the Internet for the sake of public good, or does an individual's right to free speech trump government intervention?

2. What is the responsibility of the Web site provider in monitoring content? Is it enough to control for pirated material and nudity? Should Web hosts be held responsible for webcasts of suicides or criminal activity on their sites once they are aware of them?

3. What is your responsibility as an individual when viewing a webcast? If you witness a suicide or read of someone talking about suicide, should you do something? If so, what should you try to do?

CHAPTER THIRTEEN

Managing Technology and Innovation

Technology through innovation fosters change and more change. Technological change has raised ethical and social questions of privacy, security, ownership, health, and safety. What are the implications of this fast-paced change and attention to innovation for our society and those who live in it? Moreover, who is responsible for determining how much technological change should occur or how fast things should change? Should technology be controlled, and if so, who should be in charge of managing technology and innovation and the challenges they pose for our global community?

This Chapter Focuses on These Key Learning Objectives:

- Evaluating potential breaches of privacy and initiatives taken by business to manage stakeholders' privacy.
- Assessing how secure information is in a free-access information society given the vulnerability to zombies, computer viruses and worms, and hackers.
- Understanding the role and responsibilities of the organization's chief information officer.
- Analyzing threats from and safeguards implemented in response to the Internet pornography industry.
- Examining violations of intellectual property through the piracy of software, music, movies, and books, and how business and government attempt to prevent these illegal actions.
- Recognizing the ethical and social challenges that arise from technological breakthroughs in science and medicine.

Technology raises serious ethical questions regarding our privacy, ownership of intellectual property, and rights to scientific research, as shown by the following examples:

Alex Rodriguez, the all-star third baseman for the New York Yankees, was outraged when he found that the results from his positive drug test for steroid use were publicly available for viewing on the Internet. Rodriguez had participated in a survey on steroid use among major league baseball players, which included taking blood samples from the players. The players were promised that all information would remain anonymous, samples would be destroyed after analysis, and no individual information would be released. Yet, Rodriguez's personal information was not destroyed. His drug test results were compared with other survey information by an undisclosed third party, who traced this information back to Rodriguez and posted the results on the Internet. As Rodriguez's friend said in an e-mail, "Privacy is serious. It is serious the moment the data gets collected, not the moment it is released."

The National Broadcasting Company (NBC) owned the rights to the 2008 Beijing Summer Olympics, but ran into huge problems controlling their property. The company decided to delay broadcasting the opening ceremonies by 12 hours to take advantage of prime viewing time in heavily populated countries. But people around the world went to their computers and were able to watch the events in real time by finding foreign broadcasters' newsfeeds posted to YouTube and other sites. More than 100 video clips of the opening ceremonies were available on YouTube, even though Google, the owner of this site, attempted to remove as many of the clips as it could. NBC spent hours asking that Web sites stop allowing people to view the ceremonies, but could not keep up with bloggers who were sharing new links to new sources every minute. "We have a billion dollars worth of revenue here," said Gary Zenkel, president of NBC Olympics, "so that means we're not public television, for better or worse." Even though more Americans watched the tape-delayed ceremonies than watched live Internet streams, this experience showed television network executives that the time-delayed broadcasts might be uncontrollable.

In 2008 the British Parliament approved the Human Fertilisation and Embryology Act, giving approval to researchers to fuse human DNA with cow eggs to produce embryos to extract stem cells. These embryos, called cytoplasmic hybrids or cybrids, are arguably a more effective and ethical way to obtain stem cells, because they do not require the harvesting and destruction of human eggs. Sixty-one percent of the British public approved of interspecies embryonic research if it would lead to improved understanding of disease. Opponents of the practice, though, expressed ethical and religious objections to the creation of an animal–human hybrid. The Lawyers' Christian Fellowship and Comment on Reproductive Ethics launched a legal challenge to the bill, but their efforts were unsuccessful.[1]

Are individuals' rights to privacy at the mercy of those with the technological ability to expose facts about individuals without their permission? Do companies no longer have the right to control their own property, such as when it will be broadcast? Is all information public information? Does the technological question "Can it

[1] "As Data Collecting Grows, Privacy Erodes," *The New York Times,* February 16, 2009, *www.nytimes.com;* "Tape Delay by NBC Faces End Run by Online Fans," *The New York Times,* August 9, 2008; and The Human Fertilisation and Embryology Act 2008 at *www.dh.gov.uk.*

be done?" become the only question asked regarding scientific research? Should the ethical question be asked: "Should it be done?" Who should decide the answer to this question? Issues of privacy, security, ownership, health, and safety abound in our age of innovation.

Bill Joy, Sun Microsystems' chief scientist, warned of the dangers of rapid advances in technology:

> The experiences of the atomic scientists clearly show the need to take personal responsibility, the danger that things will move too fast, and the way in which a process can take on a life of its own. We can, as they did, create insurmountable problems in almost no time flat. We must do more thinking up front if we are not to be similarly surprised and shocked by the consequences of our inventions.[2]

As this quotation implies, technology and innovation pose numerous challenges for society. If these important questions are not discussed and answered for the betterment of all members of society and in ways that protects our personal rights, what will be the ethical consequences?

Protecting Privacy

The potential for breaches of privacy, such as when the results of Alex Rodriguez's drug test were announced to the public without his consent, are everywhere. Employers can use new sophisticated technology to monitor employees' movements, computer usage, and personal and work interactions. Businesses can learn more about their customers' preferences or shopping habits. (Many of these issues are discussed in Chapters 15 and 16.) In response to employees' and consumers' complaints that these practices are invasions of their privacy, many businesses have developed a **privacy policy**, which explains what use of the company's technology is permissible. HCA (Hospital Corporation of America) Healthcare, for example, issued an "electronic communication policy" to its employees warning them that it might be necessary for authorized personnel to access and monitor the contents of their computer's hard drive. However, some consumers have been reluctant to acceptance company privacy policies, as discussed later.

Issues of privacy also spill over into the business–consumer relationship. Most Americans mistakenly believe that when they see a privacy policy on popular Web sites, then those sites are not collecting or selling their personal information and online activities to others. According to a Minnesota Department of Public Safety report, more than 800 companies took advantage of an opportunity to purchase the personal data information of all Minnesota driver's license holders for $1,500. Despite efforts by companies to help consumers feel more secure about their personal information, consumer mistrust persists, as discussed in Exhibit 13.A.

More aggressive efforts by cyber criminals resulted in a steep rise of attacks on information security. In 1988 there were 1,738 attacks, by 1998 this number skyrocketed to 177,615, and it reached 20 million by the end of 2008.[3] Recent technological advancements have increased the number of ways that privacy violations may occur. For example, Radio Frequency Identification (RFID) technology was featured in a

---

[2] Bill Joy, "Why the Future Doesn't Need Us," *Wired*, April 2000, *www.wired.com/wired/archive/8.04/joy*.

[3] Enterprise Data Exposed," *BusinessWeek*, June 22, 2009, p. 14.

Exhibit 13.A
Consumers' Discomfort with Use of Personal Information

In a 2008 survey directed by Dr. Alan Westin of Columbia University, 59 percent of American adults said they were uncomfortable when Web sites like Google and Yahoo! used personal information to tailor advertisements based on their hobbies or interests. Dr. Westin observed, "Web sites pursuing customized or behavioral marketing maintain that the benefits to online users that advertising revenues make possible . . . should persuade most online users that this is a good trade-off. . . . 59 percent of current online users clearly do not accept it."

After the survey participants viewed a series of four potential company privacy policies, the percentage saying they would be uncomfortable dropped to 45. For Echo Boomers, individuals aged 18 to 31, the discomfort level dropped from 51 to 38 percent after privacy policies were introduced. Only the Matures, adults aged 63 or older, were not reassured by the use of privacy policies. Dr. Westin commented, "The failure of a larger percentage of respondents to express comfort after four privacy policies were specified may have two bases—concern that Web companies would actually follow voluntary guidelines, even if they espoused them, and the absence of any regulatory or enforcement mechanisms in the privacy policy steps outlined in the question."

Source: "Majority Uncomfortable with Websites Customizing Content Based Visitors Personal Profiles," *The Harris Poll,* April 10, 2008, *www.harrisinteractive.com.*

clever television commercial where "the packages knew the truck was lost" before the driver did. Yet, many experts have raised ethical questions about the ways RFID technology enables businesses, governments, and criminals to gather information about presale, sales transaction, and postsale activities. The RFID tags could continue to record information long after the sale was made, possibly providing information on future purchases, or personal travel.[4] The increase in the number of cell phones enabling users to take clearer pictures of what is happening around them has raised various privacy objections. Sometimes this technology has aided law enforcement in capturing criminals, who were caught breaking into an automobile or store. But in other cases, people felt that their privacy was violated when they were caught in a romantic or embarrassing situation.

Managing the Protection of Privacy

Businesses have gone to great lengths to build strong defenses to protect information and ensure stakeholder privacy. In 2002, the Platform for Privacy Preference Project (P3P)[5] allowed Web sites to tell the user's Web browser about the site's data privacy policies. During the standard's development, advocacy groups such as the Electronic Privacy Information Center (EPIC) criticized the P3P concept as too difficult for users to understand or use properly. (Chapter 15 provides additional discussion of consumer Internet privacy issues.)

Although some companies have addressed the issue of Internet privacy, some skeptics believe international government coordination is necessary. Since 2008, representatives from the United States and 27 European countries have gathered annually for Data Privacy Day. This event, which brings together privacy professionals, government leaders, academics and students, and business executives, was designed to raise awareness and generate discussion about data privacy practices and rights. Supporting events are

---

[4] For an excellent discussion of the ethical issues surrounding RFID technology, see Alan R. Peslak, "An Ethical Exploration of Privacy and Radio Frequency Identification," *Journal of Business Ethics* 59 (2005), pp. 327–45.

[5] See the P3P Web site at *www.w3.org/P3P.*

held in Canada, Europe, and the United States throughout the year. These include the Privacy Day Cocktail Event in Brussels, Belgium, on January 28, 2009, sponsored by the European Privacy Officers Forum and International Association of Privacy Professionals, or the "Surf the Net—Think Privacy" video competition for 15- to 19-year-olds, organized by the European Schoolnet with support from Microsoft.[6]

Children are exceptionally vulnerable to invasions of privacy. The Children's Online Privacy Protection Act of 1998, also known as COPPA, requires commercial Web sites to collect a verifiable form of consent from the parent or guardian of any user below the age of 13. Web site operators must post user privacy policies and adhere to federal marketing restrictions, even if the Web site is operated from outside the United States. Canada and Australia have enacted similar legislation.

Nevertheless, it will be difficult to achieve international government control of privacy, especially as it pertains to the Internet. The management of privacy may need to come from the Internet companies themselves.[7]

The Management of Information Security

Businesses have become acutely aware of the importance of maintaining information in a secure location and guarding this valuable resource. In a 2007 survey of more than 800 North American privacy and security professionals, 85 percent acknowledged having at least one reportable data breach of personally identifiable information within their organizations during the past 12 months. Even more startling is the fact that 63 percent of those surveyed said that their firms had experienced multiple data breaches. Information security and various computer-related crimes cost U.S. businesses an estimated $67 billion annual, according to an FBI study.[8] How best to manage information security remains a major challenge for businesses.

> In 2005, Time Warner reported that a cooler-sized container of computer tapes containing personal information on 600,000 current and former employees had been lost, apparently during transfer to a storage facility. A month later, Citigroup informed its customers that computer tapes containing personal information on nearly 3.9 million customers were lost by the United Parcel Service while in transit to a credit reporting bureau. Between 2005 and 2007, information from nearly 46 million credit and debit cards was stolen by hackers who gained access to TJX Companies, parent company of retailer T.J. Maxx. The company did not discover the breach until nearly two years later. And in 2009, the largest data breach to date occurred when Heartland Payment Systems announced the potential exposure of tens of millions of credit and debit cardholder information—card numbers, expiration dates, and cardholder names.[9]

---

[6] "Data Privacy Day 2009," Intel Web site, *www.intel.com/policy/dataprivacy.htm.*

[7] For a discussion of Internet regulation see Norman E. Bowie and Karim Jamal, "Privacy Rights of the Internet: Self-Regulation or Government Regulation," *Business Ethics Quarterly* 16, no. 3 (2006), pp. 323–42.

[8] "Reportable and Multiple Privacy Breaches Rising at Alarming Rate," Deloitte Web site, December 11, 2007, *www.deloitte.com;* and "Computer Crime Costs $67 Billion," FBI Says," *CNET News.com,* January 19, 2006, *www.cnetnews.com.*

[9] "Time Warner Alerts Staff to Lost Data," *The Wall Street Journal,* May 3, 2005, *online.wsj.com;* "Citigroup Says Data Lost on 3.9 Million Customers," *The Wall Street Journal,* June 6, 2005, *online.wsj.com;* "TJX Says Theft of Credit Data Involved 45.7 Million Cards," *The New York Times,* March 30, 2007, *www.nytimes.com;* and "Credit Card Processor Says Some Data Was Stolen," *The New York Times,* January 21, 2009, *www.nytimes.com.*

In these incidents, human error and poor organizational security systems placed personal information at risk. Sometimes, threats to privacy come from criminals. One of the most harmful forms of criminal activity involving computers is a zombie. A **zombie** is a hijacked computer that can be remote-controlled by the attacker to respond to the attacker's commands. According to a study by the security firm McAfee, there was a 50 percent increase in zombie computers infiltrating the Internet in 2008 compared to 2007. The report also stated that 18 percent of all computers in the United States are infected by malicious programs that trick users into installing or running these virus-laden programs and then continuously run the programs in the background, often without the user's knowledge, responding to signals sent out by zombie attackers.[10]

Most computer viruses are carried in file attachments and are activated when users click to open them. A newer kind of virus, called a computer worm, does not require human intervention to activate. Instead, worms slip into a computer connected to the Internet and silently scan a network for other machines and try to infect them.

Attackers set on shutting down large Web sites have armed themselves with the ability to hijack computer networks to form *botnets* that spray random packets of data in huge streams over the Internet. The deluge of data is meant to clog Web sites and entire corporate networks. These attacks are called D.D.O.S., distributed denial of service attacks, and they are often used in military conflicts. The largest of these attacks grew to over 40 gigabits, from less than half a megabit, in the past few years. Since most network connections carry 10 gigabits of data, these attacks easily overwhelm the systems targeted. "We're definitely seeing more targeted attacks toward e-commerce sites," said Danny McPherson, chief security officer at Arbor Networks. "Most enterprises are connected to the Internet with a one-gigabit connection or less. Even a two-gigabit D.D.O.S. attack will take them offline."[11]

The corporate nemesis responsible for creating and spreading computer zombies, viruses, and worms is called a computer hacker. **Computer hackers** are individuals, often with advanced technology training, who, for thrill or profit, breach a business's information security system. Businesses are not the only organizations vulnerable to the predatory practices of hackers, as some prestigious universities found out in 2005. This incident is described in Exhibit 13.B.

Although businesses are spending millions of dollars to protect the information they store from hackers and other criminals, some organizations have discovered that their own employees can be their worst security leak. To avoid the cumbersome multiple layers of often-changing password security, employees forward their e-mail to free Web-accessible personal accounts offered by Google, Yahoo!, and other companies. Company security experts fear that corporate secrets are circumventing the otherwise well-protected computer networks and leaking out the back of the company. "If employees are just forwarding to their Web e-mail, we have no way to know what they are doing on the other end. They could do anything they want. They could be giving secrets to the K.G.B. [a former secret service agency in Communist Russia]," said an information security executive.[12]

Businesses' Responses to Invasions of Information Security

To address the number, severity, and ease of hacker attacks on businesses, firms began to see the necessity of investing more resources in protecting their information. The

---

[10] "Computer Hijackings Increase by 50% in 2008," and "New Worm Targets Cell Phones, Turns Them to Zombies," *Switched*, May 29, 2009, *www.switched.com*.

[11] "Internet Attacks Grow More Potent," *The New York Times*, November 10, 2008, *www.nytimes.com*.

[12] "Firms Fret as Office E-Mail Jumps Security Walls," *The New York Times*, January 11, 2007, *www.nytimes.com*.

In 2005, about 150 business school applicants took advantage of a 10-hour security vulnerability on a site maintained by ApplyYourself, Inc., a Virginia-based company that manages admissions data for dozens of elite business schools. A hacker was able to post instructions to a bulletin board belonging to a *BusinessWeek* online forum enabling individuals to access their own admissions files. Since most of the schools had not made final admissions decisions on the applicants, the individuals saw only preliminary evaluations or data, and some accessed only blank screens.

Nonetheless, many of the universities affected took the breach of security very seriously. "This behavior is unethical at best—a serious breach of trust that cannot be countered by rationalization," said Kim Clark, dean of the Harvard Business School. Most schools—including Carnegie Mellon, Harvard, Duke, and MIT—decided to deny admission to the prospective students who had accessed the ApplyYourself site. Stanford officials decided to review each hacker's case individually before making a final decision, but added, "Our mission statement talks about principled, innovative leaders and we take the principled part seriously."

A few days after the incident occurred, Dartmouth broke rank from the other universities and announced that it would admit some of the 17 business school applicants who had hacked into its computerized database. After lengthy discussions among Dartmouth faculty and staff, the university decided that the action should be a major strike against the prospective students but was not enough, by itself, to disqualify them. Dartmouth's dean, Paul Danos, said, "Their curiosity got the best of them. All of them expressed some remorse. Some were admitted. Some were rejected."

Sources: "Business Schools Bar Applicants Who Hacked Admissions Web Site," Institute for Global Ethics, *Ethics Newsline,* March 14, 2005, *www.globalethics.org;* and "Dartmouth Swims against Tide, Will Admit Some of Hackers," *Pittsburgh Post-Gazette,* March 18, 2005, p. B6.

Federal Trade Commission (FTC) began a series of workshops offered to businesses, such as "Protecting Personal Information: Best Practices for Businesses." The simple five key principles advocated by the FTC were these: take stock (know what personal information you have in your files and on your computers), scale down (keep only what you need for your business), lock it (protect the information in your care), pitch it (properly dispose of what you no longer need), and plan ahead (create a plan to respond to security incidents).[13]

When a group of suspected hackers broke into a U.S.-based computer system, they thought they had successfully penetrated the security system guarding an important Web site. Rather, they had technologically walked into a *honeypot,* a system used by security professionals to lure hackers to a fabricated Web site where the hacker's every move can be tracked. Lance Spitzner, creator of numerous honeypot traps, posted his findings of hacker activities on the Internet for the security community to see and learn from these discoveries.[14] Another method some businesses have used to reduce criminal intrusion of their sites is to pay hackers for their proprietary methods—so others will not use them.

A Russian hacker, simply known as "Bit," spotted a defect in Microsoft's Internet Explorer Web browser that made it vulnerable to attack. Bit simply had to go to Web-hack.ru, a Russian Internet storefront, to offer to sell his discovery to the highest bidder. Organized crime reportedly would pay top dollar for information that would break into corporate databases and pilfer people's identities. Typically efforts were made to detect these actions and prosecute the offenders.

[13] See other information security tips at *www.ftc.gov/infosecurity.*
[14] "Around the World, Hackers Get Stuck in 'Honeypots,'" *The Wall Street Journal,* December 19, 2000, p. A18; and see Spitzner's Web site at *http://project.honeynet.org.*

But computer security firms decided on a different approach and created legitimate markets for hacker intelligence. The firms offered to purchase tips from some of the very people they were trying to arrest. Critics said that this was akin to rewarding hackers for uncovering computer loopholes, but security firms retorted that this free market approach would give them critical information so they could boost their protection for their clients.[15]

The Chief Information, Security, or Technology Officer

The responsibility of managing technology with its many privacy and security issues for business organizations is entrusted to the **chief information officer (CIO)** or individuals with other similar titles such as *chief security officer* or *chief technology officer*. Many firms have elevated the role of their data processing managers by giving them the title of chief information officer.

> According to one security expert, "The CIO is a 'general.' Generals are not concerned with how the weapons function or how the rank and file are performing. This is the job of the lieutenants. The general focuses on the strategic application of resources on the battlefield. It is his/her duty to bring the plans of the sovereign (e.g. the CEO, the board of directors) to fruition."[16]

More CIOs report directly to the company's CEO (42 percent) than to the CFO (23 percent). Primarily the CIO is expected to reduce costs through efficiency and productivity, enable or drive business innovation, and create or enable a competitive advantage for the company. "It's the sharp edge of the business, a tool for revenue generation," explained William E. Kelvie, former CIO of Fannie Mae. "Every business needs an executive who can harness the latest technology to reach out to customers and suppliers with seamless, up-to-the-minute data communications."

> The benefits of having an innovative CIO were clear to most businesses. Peter Solvik, CIO at Cisco Systems, was credited with slashing $1.5 billion in costs by using Internet technologies for everything from human resources to manufacturing. At General Electric, CIO Gary Reiner was responsible for moving $5 billion in goods and services through the Internet, which helped improve the company's operating margins. Dawn Lepore, CIO at Charles Schwab, discovered that online trading cost only 20 percent as much as conventional trading and helped boost the firm's gross operating margin. The job of implementing these fundamental changes in business operations increasingly was entrusted to the company's CIO, whose duties now involved much more than keeping the computers properly functioning.[17]

CIOs increasingly must see the big corporate picture. The CIO must set, align, and integrate an information technology vision with the company's overall business objectives. The CIO serves as the "coach" in guiding the information technology resources of the firm toward the long-term business goals. In addition, CIOs are also responsible for information breaches when they occur, as described next.

---

[15] "From Black Market to Free Market," *BusinessWeek*, August 22/29, 2005, pp. 28–32.

[16] Steven Fox, "The Art of CIO Success," *CSO Security and Risk*, June 29, 2009, *blogs.csoonline.com*.

[17] Edward Prewitt and Lorraine Cosgrove Ware, "The State of the CIO '06: A Report," *CIO Research*, at *www.cio.com/state*; and "From Gearhead to Grand High Pooh-Bah," *BusinessWeek*, August 28, 2000, pp. 129–30. Also see "Focus On: The Chief Information Officer," *BusinessWeek*, December 16, 2002, pp. 24–25; and "Chief Privacy Officers: Real Change or Window Dressing," *Business Ethics*, September–October 2001, pp. 8–9.

Maureen Govern, the chief technology officer at American Online (AOL), and two other AOL employees, were fired after a release of Web-search data. The data detailed more than 20 million queries made by 650,000 AOL users and were posted to a new AOL research Web site. The data were intended to be used by other search technology researchers, but bloggers gained access to the site and began sending the information out widely across the Internet. The data were downloaded by hundreds of unintended users before the problem was identified and the site could be shut down.[18]

Special Issue: Internet Pornography

Many believe that the Internet pornography industry, containing sexually explicit writing or images intended to arouse sexual desire, is the most active and lucrative area of e-business. Estimates claimed that there were more than 4 million pornography Web sites, nearly 400 million Web pages, and approximately 2.5 billion daily pornography e-mails worldwide. Pornography accounted for 35 percent of all Internet downloads. Experts estimated the annual revenues of the pornography industry at $57 billion worldwide and $12 billion in the United States alone. Every second more than $3,000 is being spent on porn and nearly 30,000 Internet users are viewing pornography. Every 39 minutes a new pornographic video is being created in the United States. Porn revenue is greater than the combined revenues of all professional football, baseball, and basketball teams.[19] The popularity of adult-oriented Web sites was seen when Victoria's Secret, a maker of women's lingerie, launched a fashion show on the Internet. The company reported that 1.5 million viewers logged on to see its merchandise.

Some countries aggressively monitor and try to control activities associated with these porn Web sites. Yahoo! Japan, Japan's most popular Web site, had its Tokyo offices raided by police investigating the possible sale of illegal pornographic material on its auction site. Later, Yahoo! removed all adult-related advertising and products, such as videos, from its Japanese Web sites.[20]

China attempted to enforce new regulation in 2009 that required that all personal computers sold in the country include software that filtered out pornography and other Internet content considered to be vulgar by Chinese government officials. The backlash was quick and expected. "Mandatory installation of filtering software is simply acting blindly," said an editorial appearing in the *Wuhan Evening News* in China. Other critics worried that the Chinese government would use these filters to block more than porn, such as material critical of the government and its policies. The government ordered patches to fix potential security breaches in the software in response to these critics, indicating the government's steadfastness toward implementing this regulation.

Computer manufacturers in the United States said that it was impossible to fulfill the requirements within the time period required by the legislation and asked the Chinese government to reconsider its new law. The Chinese government initially did not back down, stating, "If you have children or are expecting

---

[18] "AOL Fires Technology Chief after Web-Search Data Scandal," *The Wall Street Journal*, August 21, 2006, *online.wsj.com.*

[19] Jerry Ropelato, "Pornography Industry Revenue Statistics," 2006, *www.TopTenREVIEWS.com.*

[20] "Police Raid Yahoo! Japan Office in Pornography Probe," *The Wall Street Journal*, November 28, 2000, p. A23; "Yahoo! Ordered to Bar the French from Nazi Items," *The Wall Street Journal*, November 21, 2000, pp. B1, B4; and "Yahoo! Plans to Remove Adult Content," *The Wall Street Journal*, April 16, 2001, p. B6.

children you could understand the concerns of parents over unhealthy online content." However, eventually the Chinese government modified its position and announced that the anti-pornography software must be on all computers used in Internet cafés, schools, and other public places but individual consumers are exempt.[21]

Elsewhere around the world, many adult Web sites asked users to verify that they were of legal age, often by requiring the user to supply valid debit or credit card information. This control is easily circumvented. As discussed in Chapter 12, the OpenDNS.com system provides a solid level of protection; however, other options are available. For example, several major Internet companies launched a site called Get-NetWise.[22] It provides parents with information on adult-oriented Web sites, including reading material and downloadable software that could safeguard their children when they are online. Other commercial porn-blocking software includes Cyber Sitter, Cyber Patrol, Net Nanny, Cyber Sentinel, Norton Parental Controls, Cyber Snoop, and Child Safe. These programs work with the Internet browser to block out violent or X-rated Web pages.

Companies such as Verizon, Sprint, and Time Warner Cable have begun to help parents control their children's access to pornography by agreeing to block access to Internet bulletin boards and Web sites nationwide that disseminate child pornography.

In a similar effort, MySpace adopted technologies to identify known sex offenders by name, date of birth, height, weight, and zip code. The information was used to deny known sex offenders access to MySpace and, depending on the circumstances, turn the individuals over to law enforcement agencies. News Corp., owner of MySpace, offered free notification software, named Zephyr, to parents to upload to their home computers. Zephyr allowed parents to learn the name, age, and location that their children were using to represent themselves on MySpace. These actions were taken in cooperation with state legal officials who were seeking greater controls for online networking sites to prevent sexual predators from using those sites to contact children. "We thank the Attorneys General for a thoughtful and constructive conversation on Internet safety," said MySpace's chief security officer. "This is an industrywide challenge and we must all work together to create a safer Internet."[23]

In 1998, President Clinton signed into law the Child Online Privacy Protection Act (COPA) (not to be confused with the COPPA discussed earlier). The primary goal of the COPA is to give parents control over what information is collected from their children online and how such information may be used. The act specifically applies to children under 13 years of age. However, in 2007, a federal judge struck down the law, stating that parents can protect their children through software filters and other less restrictive means, discussed earlier, that do not limit the rights of adults to free speech.[24]

---

[21] "China Faces Criticism over New Software Censor," *The New York Times,* June 11, 2009, *www.nytimes.com;* "China Orders Patches to Planned Web Filter," *The New York Times,* June 16, 2009, *www.nytimes.com;* "A Breach in the Green Dam," *The Wall Street Journal,* July 1, 2009, *online.wsj.com;* and "China Scales Back Software Filter Plan," *The New York Times,* August 14, 2009, *www.nytimes.com.*

[22] See GetNetWise's Web site at *www.GetNetWise.org.*

[23] "MySpace.com Moves to Keep Sex Offenders Off of Its Site," *The New York Times,* December 6, 2006, *www.nytimes.com;* "MySpace Moves to Give Parents More Information," *The Wall Street Journal,* January 17, 2007, *online.wsj.com;* and "MySpace, States Reach Deal On New Security Measures," *The Wall Street Journal,* January 14, 2008, *online.wsj.com.*

[24] "Judge Blocks 1998 Law Criminalizing Web Porn," *The Wall Street Journal,* March 22, 2007, *online.wsj.com.*

Protecting Intellectual Property

With advances in technology, protecting the ownership of intellectual property has become more challenging than ever, as described earlier in the example of the early release of the 2008 Beijing Olympics' opening ceremony. The ideas, concepts, and other symbolic creations of the human mind are often referred to as **intellectual property**. In the United States, intellectual property is protected through a number of special laws and public policies, including copyrights, patents, and trademark laws. Not all nations have policies similar to those in the United States.

With the ease of accessing information through technology, especially the Internet, have come serious questions regarding protecting intellectual property. From software and video game piracy to downloading copyrighted music, movies, and books for free, many new means for using others' intellectual property have unlawfully emerged.

Violations of Property—Piracy of Software, Music, Movies, Books

Theft of intellectual property, artistic performance, or copyrighted material exploded with the entrance of the Internet and global connectivity. Whether it is computer-based software, musical recordings, video movie productions, or lately electronic versions of books, piracy is on the rise and victims are retaliating, turning to governments for enforcement and protection of their rights, or seeking collaborative solutions to this ethical challenge.

The illegal copying of copyrighted software, or **software piracy**, is a global problem. According to the Business Software Alliance, global software piracy accounted for 41 percent of all software installed on personal computers and resulted in $53 billion in losses worldwide in 2009, despite efforts to fight piracy in India and China, two of the largest strongholds for software piracy. For every $100 of legitimate software sold, another $69 was pirated.[25] Software companies predicted these losses would continue to rise as Third World countries became more involved in the global marketplace.

Technology now enables individuals to download music from the Internet at a faster pace than ever before, and to store the music for repeated listening. Individuals have downloaded millions of songs onto their iPods or burned them onto CDs and had their favorite collections of songs available for their listening pleasure whenever they wanted—all without the cost of purchasing the music. This process denied legitimate compensation to the artists who created the music and to the companies that manufactured or distributed these artists' CDs.

The pirating of copyrighted music is a growing and widespread epidemic. According to the International Intellectual Property Alliance, in 2008 piracy of music and records cost the industry nearly $2 billion in lost sales. Nine out of 10 recordings in China were pirated, and 75 percent of Singaporeans surveyed said they had no personal objection to using pirated material.[26]

With advances in technology, movies can be downloaded from the Internet to CDs or DVDs more easily than ever. BitTorrent is one of the most common protocols for sharing large files and enables movies to be downloaded easily. By some estimates BitTorrent

---

[25] "Study Finds Software Piracy Growing," Yahoo! Tech, May 12, 2009, *tech.yahoo.com*; and "Sixth Annual BSA-IDC Global Software–08 Piracy Study," *Business Software Alliance*, May 2009, *global.bsa.org*.

[26] "Free Downloads—After this Message," *BusinessWeek*, October 9, 2006, p. 95; "U.S. Is Only the Tip of Pirated Music Iceberg," *The New York Times*, September 26, 2003, *www.nytimes.com*; and "International Intellectual Property Alliance Submits to U.S. Trade Representatives Its Report on Copyright Piracy in 48 Countries," *International Intellectual Property Alliance*, February 19, 2009, *www.iipa.com*. Also see *The Recording Industry 2006 Piracy Report: Protecting Creativity in Music* at *www.ifpi.com*.

accounted for 35 percent of all traffic on the Internet, and a large portion of this may be the illegal transfer of copyrighted files such as movies. Virtually all of the movie theater blockbusters were also on the top 10 list of pirated and downloaded movies.[27]

Much of the blame is leveled at college students and young adults. The Motion Picture Association of America claimed that 44 percent of the industry's domestic losses came from illegal downloading of movies by college students or recent graduates. Verifying these figures is difficult, since many people download from their homes or Internet cafés, not college dormitories or on-campus computer labs. Nonetheless, the U.S. motion picture industry reportedly lost $6.1 billion to piracy worldwide, with most of the losses outside the United States. And piracy was spreading to new forms of entertainment.[28]

Ursula LeGuin, a science fiction writer, was shocked when she came across digital copies of books that seemed familiar to her. No surprise, since the work was her own—and neither she nor her publisher had authorized electronic editions of her work. "I thought, who do these people think they are? Why do they think they can violate my copyright and get away with it?" said LeGuin.

The printed word now faces the same test of intellectual property and copyright protection as music and movies have for more than a decade.

John Wiley & Sons, a textbook publisher, employed three full-time staff members to search for unauthorized copies of its books. In April 2009, the company uncovered 5,000 titles—five times more than a year ago—and sent notices to various site managers to take down the digital versions of Wiley's books. "It's a game of Whac-a-Mole," said the president of the Science Fiction and Fantasy Writers of America. "You knock one down and five more pop up." Sites like Scribd and Wattpad, which invite users to upload documents such as college theses and self-published novels, were primary targets as illegal reproductions of popular titles have appeared on their sites. Both sites reportedly remove copyrighted material immediately upon notification by the publisher.[29]

Government and Industry Efforts to Combat Piracy

Companies have sought assistance on the issue of software piracy from governmental agencies and the courts both inside and outside the United States. For example, the Argentinean Supreme Court upheld a lower court ruling that the country's antiquated copyright laws did not cover software, thus denying software manufacturers any legal basis to attack those with pirated materials in Argentina. However, the outcry from U.S. software makers and vendors was so strong that within months the Argentinean Chamber of Deputies made software piracy a crime punishable by fines or imprisonment or both. In 1998, the United States passed the **Digital Millennium Copyright Act**, making it a crime to circumvent antipiracy measures built into most commercial software agreements between the manufacturers and their users. In China, where experts estimate that 90 percent of all software in use is unlicensed, government officials took steps to curb piracy.

The Chinese government announced that computer makers must ship all their products with licensed operating systems preinstalled and inspected all government computer systems for licensed software. "This is good news, marking a clear step in the right direction

[27] "The Music Streams That Soothe an Industry," *The New York Times*, July 26, 2009, *www.nytimes.com*.

[28] "Piracy Figures Are Restated," *The Wall Street Journal*, January 23, 2008, *online.wsj.com*.

[29] "Print Books Are Target of Pirates on the Web," *The New York Times*, May 12, 2009, *www.nytimes.com*.

to reverse the serious problem of software piracy that frustrates the development in China for both foreign and domestic vendors," explained the president of the Beijing-based United States Industry Technology Office. In 2009, China sent 11 people to prison for manufacturing and distributing pirated Microsoft software throughout the world. Microsoft called the group part of "the biggest software counterfeiting organization we have ever seen, by far" and estimated its global sales at more than $2 billion.[30] Other governments joined the crackdown on piracy.

In 2009, a Swedish court convicted four men of violating the copyright law after it was proven that these men created and supported an extensive Internet file-sharing service that provides thousands of songs, films, video games, and other material and helped users download the copyrighted material. In addition to the one-year sentence, each man was ordered to pay 30 million kronor, or about $3.6 million, in damages to the entertainment companies affected. The French National Assembly sought to join the anti-piracy movement by passing a law that would suspend the Internet connection of anyone found guilty of piracy. The Culture Ministry hailed the action as an important step toward "preserving cultural diversity and the industries threatened by piracy." But a month later, the French Constitutional Council, the country's highest governing body, rejected the core portion of the measure, saying that the law was contrary to core constitutional provisions, such as the presumption of innocence and freedom of speech.[31]

Recently, some companies seriously affected by piracy negotiated a compromise solution to the increasing threat of piracy.

In 2008, a group of Internet, media, and technology companies, led by Walt Disney and Microsoft, announced a set of rules that would be followed when pursuing legal challenges of copyright violations. Joined by General Electric, Viacom, CBS, News Corp (owner of Fox Broadcasting and MySpace), and others, the alliance of companies agreed to not pursue Internet companies for infringement claims if their sites adhered to certain principles. The principles included eliminating copyright-infringing content uploaded by users to Web sites and blocking infringing material before it became publicly accessible. Unfortunately the pact was not legally binding, and significantly missing from the alliance was the Internet giant Google. But the companies involved were in agreement that something had to be done and felt optimistic that this was a promising start.[32]

Other user-friendly efforts were seen as compromise actions to address the piracy issue. In 2007, Amazon.com began selling music on the EMI label, one of the country's largest music labels. The music was free to be copied to any computer, cell phone, or music player, including the iPod from Apple. "We are offering a great selection of music that our customers love in a way they clearly desire, which is D.R.M.-free [a digital rights management software system], so they can play it on any device they own today or in the future," said Bill Carr, Amazon.com vice president. Two years later, Apple, which controlled 85 percent of the American market for music downloads, announced that it

---

[30] "China Begins Effort to Curb Piracy of Computer Software," *The New York Times,* May 30, 2006, *www.nytimes.com;* and "Chinese Court Jails 11 in Microsoft Piracy Ring," *The New York Times,* January 1, 2009, *www.nytimes.com.*

[31] "Court Says File-Sharing Site Violated Copyright," *The New York Times,* April 18, 2009, *www.nytimes.com;* "France Approves Crackdown on Internet Piracy," *The New York Times,* May 13, 2009, *www.nytimes.com;* and "French Court Defangs Plan to Crack Down on Internet Piracy," *The New York Times,* June 11, 2009, *www.nytimes.com.*

[32] "Disney, Microsoft Lead Copyright Pact," *The Wall Street Journal,* October 19, 2007, *online.wsj.com.*

was removing anti-copying restrictions on all songs in its iTunes Store and would allow record companies to set a range of prices for the download of the songs. Universal Music also reached an agreement with Virgin Media, offering Universal's entire music catalog to Virgin Media customers for a monthly subscription.[33]

Another approach businesses have tried to protect music copyrights involves **streaming**. Streaming refers to a customized, on-demand radio or video service and has become more accessible for users with the advent of technology that allows the user to download the material to a computer and save it on a hard drive. Streaming provides music distributors with new revenues from selling subscriptions to the music for which they hold the copyright. The benefits of this were seen almost immediately. When a court ordered San Diego–based MP3.com to pay $10 million for creating a database of more than 45,000 CDs without copyright permission, the company agreed to a licensing fee. MP3.com agreed to pay 1.5 cents each time it copied a track of music and about 0.3 cents when a customer downloaded the song.[34] Another firm, MP3tunes.com, permits users to store and stream their digital files in a cloud-based service—without sharing the music with other users.

Because the ability to download digital music, television shows, and movies is here to stay, the music industry has changed how it manages users' access to its products. iTunes was very successful with season pass subscriptions that allowed users to pay in advance for an entire run of television episodes, and this model was extended to music recordings that include remixes, videos, and additional content. As the music industry accepted that strict control over copyrighted material was impossible to achieve, it turned to methods that seek to compensate those who are entitled to benefits for their work, yet acknowledge the ease of access to this form of entertainment.

Managing Scientific Breakthroughs

Dramatic advances in the biological sciences also have propelled the impact of technology on our lives and business practices. As explained in Chapter 12, biotechnology refers to a technological application that uses biological systems or living organisms to make or modify products or processes for specific use. Recent unprecedented applications of biological science to industry have made possible new, improved methods of health care and agriculture, but they have also posed numerous ethical challenges regarding safety and the quality of life.

As Bill Joy of Sun Microsystems warns, speaking of biotechnology as well as other innovative applications of science, "21st century technologies . . . are so powerful that they can spawn whole new classes of accidents and abuses. Most dangerously, for the first time, these accidents and abuses are widely within the reach of individuals or small groups. They will not require large facilities or rare raw materials. Knowledge alone will enable the use of them."[35]

[33] "Amazon to Sell Music without Copy Protection," *The New York Times,* May 17, 2007, *www.nytimes.com;* "Want to Copy iTunes Music? Go Ahead, Apple Says," *The New York Times,* January 7, 2009, *www.nytimes.com;* and "Universal Music and Virgin Reach a Download Deal," *The New York Times,* June 16,m 2009, *www.nytimes.com.*

[34] "If You Can't Lick 'Em, License 'Em," *BusinessWeek,* June 26, 2000, p. 46.

[35] Joy, "Why the Future Doesn't Need Us."

Nanotechnology

One of the most significant technology changes affecting business is the emergence of **nanotechnology**, the application of engineering to create materials on a molecular or atomic scale. Because these small particles, just a few billionths of a meter in size, have a relatively large surface area, nanomaterials exhibit physical properties that are markedly different from their normal scale equivalents. Applications of nanotechnology spread through the scientific and business communities like wildfire in the 2000s, giving rise to some remarkable products, as illustrated by the following examples:

Nanoscale silver particles can be mixed into molten plastic to create containers that retard food spoilage—or even purify contaminated water. Under Armour has added nanoparticles to athletic clothing to inhibit the growth of odor-causing bacteria. There are "nano-pants," stain-resistant chinos and jeans whose fabric contain nano-sized whiskers that repel dirt and oil. Nanocycles made from carbon nanotubes are stronger and lighter than standard steel bicycles. Nanoscale materials have also been used in consumer electronics. Apple's iPod Nano uses a flash storage system that includes nanomaterials.

By 2008, almost 800 products that used some form of nanotechnology were on the market. Yet, as the use of nanotechnology invaded many aspects of our lives, concerns arose. For example, nanoscale materials can be used to create very small containers for use in cosmetics and medicine. The small size of these nanoparticles may create unforeseen problems when a person touches, breathes, or swallows a substance that is coated with or contains nanoparticles. Medical researchers have determined that nanoparticles can penetrate human skin and enter the bloodstream, but further research is needed to determine whether nanomaterials can be toxic to humans and other life forms. Dr. Adnan Nasir, a professor of dermatology at the University of North Carolina, explained, "The smaller the particle, the further it can travel through tissue, along airways, or in blood vessels, especially if the nanoparticles are indestructible and accumulate and are not metabolized; if you accumulate them in the organs, the organs could fail."[36] So far, at least, the U.S. government has not regulated the use of nanomaterials and nanoparticles in consumer products.

Human Genome

When Celera Genomics Group announced that it had finished the first sequencing of a **human genome**, the achievement was hailed as the most significant scientific breakthrough since landing a man on the moon. Strands of human deoxyribonucleic acid, or DNA, are arrayed across 23 chromosomes in the nucleus of every human cell, forming a unique pattern for every human. These strands are composed of four chemical units, or letters, used over and over in varying sequences. These replicated letters total 3 billion and form the words, or genes—our unique human signature—that instruct cells to manufacture the proteins that carry out all of the functions of human life.[37] The identification of human genes is critical to the early diagnosis of life-threatening diseases, the invention of new ways to prevent illnesses, and the development of drug therapies to treat a person's unique genetic profile. A new era of medicine, as well as great opportunity for biotechnology companies, appeared to be born with the decoding of the human genome.

---

[36] "New Products Bring Side Effect: Nanophobia," *The New York Times,* December 4, 2008, *www.nytimes.com;* and "The Smaller, the Better? Consumer Groups Sound the Alarm over Nanotechnology, *PalmBeachPost.com,* May 17, 2009, *www.palmbeachpost.com.*

[37] "Genetic Secrets of Malaria Bug Cracked at Last," *The Wall Street Journal,* January 18, 2002, pp. B1, B6.

However, while advances in understanding DNA were exalted as one of humanity's greatest achievements, ethical challenges emerged in private and public research focusing on genetics.

One family, afflicted by a rare genetic heart disease called Brugada syndrome, wondered how others might react if they learned of the family's medical condition. Would employers want to hire someone who might die prematurely or require an expensive implantable defibrillator? Would they be eligible for individual health care coverage or be able to afford life insurance if their condition were known? The underlying fear for this family and others with genetic conditions was whether they would be treated fairly if their genetic fingerprints became public.

The debate over whether advances in human genome sequencing and genetic research outweigh the risks or harms will continue for years. What is clear is that our scientific understanding of the human body and its makeup has changed, and significant technological innovations are on the horizon. What is not clear is who, if anyone, can manage these changes to better ensure the improvement of the quality of our lives and society.

Biotechnology and Stem Cell Research

Complementing the discovery of DNA sequencing were numerous medical breakthroughs in the area of regenerative medicine, as described in the opening example of this chapter. **Tissue engineering**, the growth of tissue in a laboratory dish for experimental research, and **stem cell research**, research on nonspecialized cells that have the capacity to self-renew and to differentiate into more mature cells, were two such breakthroughs. Both offered the promise that failing human organs and aging cells could be rejuvenated or replaced with healthy cells or tissues grown anew. While the promise of immortality may be overstated, regenerative medicine provided a revolutionary technological breakthrough for the field of medicine.

Stem cell research spilled over from the laboratories into government arenas as politicians weighed in on the ethical controversy. In 2009, a majority of Americans, 52 percent, supported easing or removing entirely the restrictions on stem cell research imposed by former President Bush. (Exhibit 13.C explores the position of the Obama administration on stem cell research.) Support for stem cell research was evident in California, where nearly 60 percent of voters supported Proposition 71, which set aside $350 million annually for a decade or a total of more than $3 billion, dwarfing the $25 million the National Institutes of Health had allocated to embryonic stem cell research. The European Parliament encouraged the financial units of the EU nations to free up nearly $5 billion in research to be used specifically to study the potential windfall of medical advances reaped from stem cell research.[38]

Supported by private and government funding, hundreds of biotechnology companies and university laboratories were actively pursuing new approaches to replace or regenerate failed body parts. Research included efforts to insert bone growth factors or stem cells into a porous material cut to a specific shape, creating new jaws or limbs. Genetically engineered proteins were successfully used to regrow blood vessels that might repair

[38] "Bush to Allow Funds for Study of Stem Cells," *The Wall Street Journal*, August 10, 2001, pp. A3, A4; "California Vote Brings Windfall for Stem Cells," *The Wall Street Journal*, November 4, 2004, pp. B1, B7; and "European Parliament Urges Resumption of Stem-Cell Research," Institute for Global Ethics, *Ethics Newsline*, November 24, 2003, *www.globalethics.org*.

Coinciding with the inauguration of President Barack Obama, on January 23, 2009, the Food and Drug Administration approved the world's first test of a therapy from human embryonic stem cells on humans. Although federal regulators stated that political considerations had no role in the decision, it was clear to others that the new administration was taking a new approach to stem cell research.

Two months later, Obama reversed the Bush administration limits on federal funding for embryonic stem cell research, as part of a pledge to separate science and politics. Advocates of unfettered stem cell research and 30 Democratic and Republican lawmakers were invited to the White House for the president's announcement. The administration also asked the National Institutes of Health to develop new guidelines for this type of research. By lifting funding restrictions, Obama avoided one of the most controversial issues surrounding stem cell research—whether taxpayer money should be used to experiment on embryos themselves. The president left it to Congress to decide whether the long-standing ban on federal financing for human embryo experiments should be overturned. This ban, called the Dickey-Wicker amendment, was passed in 1996, and Congress had renewed the amendment every year since. Yet, analysts agreed that Obama's executive order made it clear that "the government intends to support human embryonic stem cell research," said a science adviser to the president.

Sources: "F.D.A. Approves a Stem Cell Trial," *The New York Times*, January 23, 2009, *www.nytimes.com*; "Obama Set to Reverse Bush's Stem-Cell Restrictions," *The New York Times*, March 7, 2009, *www.nytimes.com*; and "Obama Is Leaving Some Stem Cell Issues to Congress," *The New York Times*, March 9, 2009, *www.nytimes.com*.

or replace heart values, arteries, and veins. The process to regrow cartilage was used to grow a new chest for a boy, and a human ear was grown on a mouse.

In addition, the Food and Drug Administration (FDA) laid the early groundwork for generic versions of biotechnology medicines, an effort that could transform the market for some of the most innovative and expensive new treatments for cancer and other diseases. This effort was particularly important as some of the oldest biotech drugs, such as Eli Lilly's bioengineered insulin Humulin and Genetech's Nutropin growth hormone, were about to lose patent protection. "We are concerned about finding safe ways to lower drug costs for Americans," said FDA Commissioner Mark McClellan. "If we can find a safe plan to produce generic or follow-up products for biologics, that can be an important step." According to medical drug market experts, the biotech market is growing more rapidly than the pharmaceutical drug market. By 2007, revenues for the U.S. biotech market were an estimated $37 million and projected to be $8.5 billion by 2016. This market segment grew 20 percent in 2006, while pharmaceutical company drug sales grew 8 percent during the same period.[39]

Cloning

In 1986, a Danish scientist announced the first successful cloning of a sheep from fetal cells. Another significant breakthrough occurred in 1997, when Ian Wilmut of the Roslin Institute unveiled Dolly, the first mammal to be cloned from adult cells. In 2003 doctors in China reported they had become the first to make an infertile woman pregnant with an experimental technique devised in the United States for women who have healthy genes but defects in their eggs that prevent embryos from developing. Critics argued that this technique came perilously close to human cloning.[40]

[39] "Big Pharma Blurring the Lines with Big Biotech," *CNNMoney.com*, May 29, 2007, *money.cnn.com;* and "Stem Cell Market Analysis Fact Sheet," *4th Annual Stem Cell Summit*, February 17, 2009, *www.stemcellsummit.com*.

[40] "Pregnancy Created Using Infertile Woman's Egg Nucleus," *The New York Times*, October 14, 2003, *www.nytimes.com*.

As each new announcement of a more advanced and successful cloning experiment was announced to the public, more fears arose. Whether it was a vision of Jurassic Park dinosaurs running loose in a metropolitan downtown area or the eerie absurdity of cloning multiple Adolf Hitlers in the film *The Boys of Brazil,* fears of cloning living tissue invaded our lives.

In 1997, when Dolly appeared on the cloning scene, there were no laws on record that prevented scientists from attempting human cloning. Experts recognized that the technique used in Scotland to clone a sheep was so simple and required so little high-tech equipment that most biology laboratories with a budget of a few hundred thousand dollars could attempt it.

In response to a growing concern over unrestricted or unsupervised cloning on a global scale, in 2005 the United Nations approved (by a vote of 84 in favor, 34 against, and 37 abstentions) a declaration that prohibited all forms of human cloning "inasmuch as cloning is incompatible with human dignity and the protection of human life." Proponents of the declaration saw this as a first step toward the promotion of human rights and a complete ban on all human cloning. Although difficult to enforce, this action was intended to discourage cloning efforts.[41]

Cloning of animals was beyond the focus of the United Nations ban and continued to thrive. Although a fraction of the total number of cattle or pigs in the United States, the presence of cloned dairy animals increased at a fast pace and received positive support from the FDA. In 2008 the F.D.A. declared that food from cloned animals and their offspring was safe to eat, clearing the way for milk and meat derived from genetic copies of prized dairy cows, steers, and hogs to be sold at the grocery store. Farmers welcomed this action as support for the less expensive method of replenishing their herds, yet the U.S. Department of Agriculture asked farmers to withhold cloned products voluntarily from the market to allow time to calm fears among retailers and overseas trading partners.[42]

The concerns from Europe were voiced by the European Group on Ethics in Science and New Technologies. They said that "the risk of negative effects [of consuming food from cloned animals] were grave enough to keep cloned products off the European market." This caution came even though the European Food Safety Authority, which advises the European Commission and governments, said that "cloned products appear to be safe for consumption." "Both studies are important," said a European Commission spokesperson, "and you can't say we will favor either one of them."[43]

Clearly stem cell research leading to the possibility of human cloning and the human consumption of food from cloned animals are important issues and will likely increase in prominence in the near future. What must also be clear is the need for specific and binding ethical guidelines for scientists engaging in this volatile field. The debate over how to govern this scientific community and its work inevitably will continue for years.

Bioterrorism

An emerging yet tragic outcome of scientific breakthroughs in bioengineering is the potential for **bioterrorism**. Terrorist groups see the use of deadly bioengineered diseases

---

[41] "General Assembly Adopts United Nations Declaration on Human Cloning by Vote of 84–34–37," *United Nations press release GA/10333,* August 3, 2005, *www.un.org.*

[42] "Animal Clones' Offspring Are in Food Supply," *The Wall Street Journal,* September 2, 2008, *online.wsj.com;* and "F.D.A. Says Food From Cloned Animals Is Safe," *The New York Times,* January 16, 2008, *www.nytimes.com.*

[43] "Europe's Ethics Panel Says Cloning Harms Animals," *The New York Times,* January 18, 2008, *www.nytimes.com.*

and poisons, such as smallpox, anthrax, and bubonic plague, as effective tools since they are more difficult to detect when transported than guns or bombs. Germs are more effective as a terrorist tool because tens of thousands of people easily can be affected. Oklahoma Governor Frank Keating said, "It not only stunned me how horrific a biological attack could be, but also how woefully unprepared we are."[44]

President Bush announced in 2003 Project BioShield, a 10-year government program to spur pharmaceutical companies to research, develop, and produce medical countermeasures to respond to the adverse effects of public health emergencies involving chemical, biological, radiological, and nuclear threats. By 2005, the annual budget for civilian biodefense funding was more than $8 billion, although it had been lowered to around $5.5 billion by 2008. As a medical bioterrorist expert explained, "improving public health preparedness is an ongoing process as science advances, innovations mature, and the threat scope changes."[45]

Genetically Engineered Foods

The biotechnological revolution targeting improvements in health care was also adapted for use by the agricultural industry. Technological advances in genetics and biology led to an unprecedented number of innovations. **Genetic engineering**, altering the natural makeup of a living organism, allowed scientists to insert virtually any gene into a plant and create a new crop or a new species. The economic force of this technological revolution was immediately apparent. Venture capitalists injected $750 million into the agricultural industry in the 2000s, an area generally ignored by venture capitalists for decades.

In Europe, a severe backlash emerged to **genetically modified foods**, or GM foods—that is, food processed from genetically engineered crops. Protesters there called GM foods "Frankenstein foods."

In 2008, a French court upheld the country's ban on a kind of corn grown from genetically modified seeds produced by Monsanto. The plant had been modified to resist pests that commonly attacked corn in the field. Despite French farmers' protests that the ban would inflict great economic harm on them and the country's economy, the court cited the call from French specialists in the area for continued studies of the food's safety issues, especially regarding human consumption. A year later Germany announced a ban on the only genetically modified strain of corn grown in Europe, which reinforced the ban on the Monsanto crops. The German agriculture minister said, "The decision is not a political decision, it's a decision based on the facts." He affirmed the government's commitment to protect the safety of consumers and the environment. In 2009, the European Union delivered another blow to the biotechnology industry by allowing Austria and Hungary to maintain their national bans on growing genetically modified crops. Despite the European Commission's interests in calming fears over GM foods and a desire to work with the United States regarding better trade relations involving GM foods, the Austrian and Hungarian national governments

---

[44] "The Next Phase: Bioterrorism?" *BusinessWeek,* October 1, 2001, pp. 58–61.

[45] For a thorough discussion of Project BioShield see Crystal Franco and Shana Deitch, "Billions for Biodefense: Federal Agency Biodefense Funding, FY 2007–FY2008," *Biosecurity and Bioterrorism: Biodefense Strategy, Practice and Science 5,* no. 2, pp. 117–33; and "HHS Releases Project BioShield Annual Report to Congress," *U.S. Department of Health and Human Services News Release,* July 9, 2008, *www.hhs.gov.*

were firm in their resistance and pressured the European Commission to support them on the issue.[46]

Despite bans on the selling of GM food products directly to the consumer throughout Europe, these altered products have found their way into the foods we buy at the grocery stores in the United States. Most genetically modified corn grown in the United States is made into animal feed or ethanol. Yet, it is also processed into food industry staples such as corn syrup or tortilla chips. Monsanto breeds a soybean seed that yields oil used as a substitute for trans-fat oils at many fast-food restaurants. Biotech cotton supplies the food industry but also ends up in the food chain as cottonseed oil for mayonnaise or margarine. Biotech canola, important for Canadian farmers, makes animal feed but also is included in canola oil sold in U.S. grocery stores. According to Monsanto, more than half of the crops grown in the United States, including nearly all the soybeans and 70 percent of the corn, are genetically modified. And this trend of turning to genetically altered crops is growing outside the United States as well.

In some economically developed countries and most developing countries around the world, genetically modified food was welcomed and seen as a boost to the often lagging agricultural industry. By 2007, developing countries planting genetically modified seeds outnumbered developed countries, according to a report from the International Service for the Acquisition of Agri-biotech Applications. The organization reported in 2007 that 282.3 million acres of the world's cropland were planted with soybeans, corn, cotton, and other crops genetically altered to resist pests and herbicides, an increase of 12 percent from the previous year.[47] Countries' biotech crop production levels are shown in Figure 13.1. Increasingly farmers around the world were seeing the importance and even necessity of genetically engineered seeds or crops.

China's leaders made genetic research a top scientific priority, funneling billions of government dollars into research on modifying the genes of crops and vegetables. Government leaders saw genetic crop production as a source of stable food supplies and the

FIGURE 13.1
Commitment to Biotechnology Crop Planting by Country

Source: "Monsanto: Winning the Ground War," *Businessweek*, December 17, 2007, pp. 35–41.

Country	Millions of Seeds Planted, 2006	Percentage Increase, 2002–2006
United States	54.6	40%
Argentina	18.0	33%
Brazil	11.5	None in 2002
Canada	6.1	74%
India	3.8	None in 2002
China	3.5	67%
Paraguay	2.0	None in 2002
South Africa	1.4	366%

[46] "French Court Says Ban on Gene-Altered Corn Seed Will Remain, Pending Study," *The New York Times*, March 20, 2008, www.nytimes.com; "Germany Bars Genetically Modified Corn," *The New York Times*, April 15, 2009, www.nytimes.com; and, "Europe to Allow Two Bans on Genetically Altered Crops," *The New York Times*, March 3, 2009, www.nytimes.com.

[47] "Developing Countries Grew More Biotech Crops in '07," *The New York Times*, February 14, 2008, www.nytimes.com.

path to a national presence in the agricultural import–export arena. Professor Zhangliang Chen estimated that within 5 to 10 years, half of the country's fields would be planted with GM rice, potatoes, and other crops.

Another application of biotechnology—genetically engineering plants to grow medicines—is explored in the case "Ventria Bioscience and the Controversy over Plant-Made Medicines" at the end of this book.

The controversies over genetic engineering, stem cell research, cloning, and genetically modified food production raise serious ethical and social issues. The questions concerning the role of businesses, social activist groups, or governments in overseeing these technological developments must continue to be addressed, as new innovations appear on the horizon.

Summary

- Many stakeholders, especially employees and customers, are vulnerable to breaches of personal information privacy. Some businesses and governments have taken steps to better protect stakeholder privacy.

- Acts of sabotage by computer hackers threaten companies' control of information, causing businesses to develop elaborate information security systems to more quickly detect hacking efforts and to patch systems targeted by zombie, virus, or worm attacks.

- Businesses have entrusted the management of technology to their chief information (or security or technology) officers. These managers often report to the company's CEO or CFO and are entrusted with setting, aligning, and integrating the information technology strategy with the company's overall business objectives.

- Company and industry initiatives have been joined by governmental action to better shield children from the growing and lucrative Internet pornography industry.

- Threats of software, music, movie, and book piracy challenge businesses' ownership of their property, prompting industry and international governmental responses to these ethical violations. Recently, the entertainment industry has adopted a more cooperative approach, moving away from an earlier litigation strategy.

- Nanotechnology, human genetic research, stem cell research, human cloning, and genetically modified foods carry great promise for society, but have also raised serious concerns. Businesses and governments have attempted to address the objections of activists, while promoting the benefits of these scientific technological breakthroughs.

Key Terms

bioterrorism, *308*	genetically modified foods, *309*	privacy policy, *293*
chief information officer (CIO), *298*	genetic engineering, *309*	software piracy, *301*
computer hackers, *296*	human genome, *305*	stem cell research, *306*
Digital Millennium Copyright Act, *302*	intellectual property, *301*	streaming, *304*
	nanotechnology, *305*	tissue engineering, *306*
		zombie, *296*

Internet Resources

www.bioportfolio.com	Bioterrorism Biodefense
www.bsa.org	Business Software Alliance
www.buzzle.com/articles/ pros-and-cons-of-cloning	Buzzle.com site, pros and cons of cloning
www.cio.com	Chief information officer professional Web site
www.coppa.org	Children's Online Privacy Protection Act
www.ftc.gov/infosecurity	U.S. Federal Trade Commission Web site on information security
genomics.energy.gov	Genome Projects of the U.S. Department of Energy, Office of Science
www.getnetwise.org	GetNetWise
www.iipa.com	International Intellectual Property Alliance
isscr.org	International Society for Stem Cell Research
www.monsanto.com/biotech-gmo	Monsanto's biotechnology Web page
www.nano.gov	National Nanotechnology Initiative
www.privacyalliance.com	Online Privacy Alliance
www.projecthoneypot.org	Project Honey Pot
www.w3.org/P3P	Platform for Privacy Preference Project

Discussion Case: *Vidding—Free Expression or Copyright Piracy?*

"It's on the Internet, publically available, so it must be free to be used." "It is simply a way for me to express myself." "It is totally different than what they created, it is mine now." And so go the arguments to justify, ethically or legally, the increasing practice of vidding among young and old alike. This issue was so controversial that National Public Radio aired a one-hour feature on its show *All Things Considered* on February 25, 2009, to bring the differing opinions on vidding to light.

Vidding is the practice of creating new videos, sometimes called songvids or fanvids, which takes existing clips, usually from popular television shows, anime series, or music videos, and blends them with a song. It is a mix of narrative story telling and visual poetry. These new forms of entertainment or self-expression can be transferred to different formats and made accessible on the computer and the Internet. While blossoming at a rapid pace, vidding raises serious ethical and legal questions regarding copyright protection versus free speech.

The first songvid is attributed to Kathy Fong, who at a Star Trek convention in 1975 showed a slide show of Leonard Nimoy (Dr. Spock on Star Trek, who often repressed his half-human side) singing a Joni Mitchell song. Fong said that she wanted to show Spock's dual nature. More recently, vids often compile dozens of clips from various episodes of a television show or movie set to music. The band Good Charlotte, for example, edited gritty crime scenes from *CSI: New York* with their own mournful songover, saying they wanted to show the dangers faced by police on the show.

Some argue that vidding is really just free expression. "The media seem to think they own the things they've pumped into my brain in 27 years," said British vidder Lim. "It seems to me ludicrous that television spends so much time and so much money carefully colonizing my mind. But it is my mind."

"Vidding is a way of seeing," explained vidder Francesca Coppa, who is a professor at Muhlenberg College and author of scholarly papers about vids. "This is our place to talk [referring to the Internet]," said Coppa. She believes that YouTube serves as a public square for opinions and conversation in this technologically wired world. Georgetown University law professor Rebecca Tushnet, also an occasional vidder, agrees: "Viddeers should not be treated like pirates. They're people responding to culture in noncommercial ways."

Yet, the space and material being used for vids is owned, raising serious legal questions concerning intellectual property. Like people who download music without paying a fee to those that created the music and hold the copyright, vidders are using material owned by others without compensating them for their intellectual property. However, Henry Jenkins, a leading academic in popular culture studies and author, argues that while vidding does use previously copyrighted material, it does so in a way that would hardly be recognized by the original artists. Vidders "are not simply trying to recover what the original producers meant. They are trying to entertain hypotheticals, address what-if questions, and propose alternative realities." Since only small snippets of video images are used and no profit is made, some vidders and lawyers argue that vidding should fall under the Fair Use exception to copyright laws.

Nevertheless, vidders' use of copyrighted material, such as clips from television scenes or movies and copyrighted music, appears to be in violation of the law. Web sites, such as YouTube, caution against the uploading of copyrighted material, even though thousands of vids have been uploaded there. As a matter of policy, YouTube will remove illegal material, such as vids containing unapproved copyrighted material, if informed of the violation of copyright laws.

Others wonder if vidders (or lawyers for that matter) would be so tolerant if they discovered vids contained their own original (and copyrighted) work or images but presented in an unflattering way. Just as musical artists believe that their work and creativity should earn them royalties, so do the creators of television clips or video images. In addition, beyond expressions of creativity, vids can be used as propaganda or in ways that may be viewed as slanderous or in bad taste. People whose images are used in these objectionable vids may want to seek legal recourse. These ethical and legal issues have become more prominent as vids have proliferated on the Internet.

Sources: "Vidders Talk Back to Their Pop-Culture Muses," National Public Radio, May 30, 2009, *www.npr.org;* "Best Practices in Fair Use in Online Video," Center for Social Media, *www.centerforsocialmedia.org;* and "Remixing Television: Francesca Coppa on the Vidding Underground," *Reason Magazine*, August/September 2008, *www.reason.com.*

Discussion Questions

1. Using the ethical criteria introduced in Chapter 4 (utilitarianism, rights, and justice), is the creating and uploading of vids to the Internet simply an ethical expression of one's free speech, or is it an infringement of intellectual property?

2. Where do you draw the line when using material found on the Internet, but trying to respect the artists' intellectual property and rights to royalties from their creations? How different should a vid be from the original source to justify that it is no longer the same material as the original artist created and thus not covered under the copyright laws?

3. Should there be a place in this technology-laden world for people to express themselves freely in a public forum, without restrictive oversight? Should people be able to say or show anything they wish, or should there be limits? If so, what should the limits be, and who should set them?

PART SEVEN

Business and Its Stakeholders

CHAPTER FOURTEEN

Stockholder Rights and Corporate Governance

Stockholders occupy a position of central importance in the corporation because they are the company's owners. As owners, they pursue both financial and nonfinancial goals. How are stockholders' rights best protected? What are the appropriate roles of top managers and boards of directors in the governance of the corporation? How can their incentives be aligned with the interests of the company's stockholders? And how can government regulators best protect the rights of investors? In the stock market turmoil of the late 2000s, these questions seemed more urgent than ever.

This Chapter Focuses on These Key Learning Objectives:

- Identifying different kinds of stockholders and understanding their objectives and legal rights.
- Knowing how corporations are governed and explaining the role of the board of directors in protecting the interests of owners.
- Analyzing the function of executive compensation and debating if top managers are paid too much.
- Evaluating various ways stockholders can promote their economic and social objectives.
- Understanding how the government protects against stock market abuses, such as fraudulent accounting and insider trading.

AIG International was one of the largest insurance companies in the world—an organization that for decades had insured individuals and organizations against all manner of hazards. In late 2008, investors—and those holdings its policies—were shocked to learn that the firm was on the verge of collapse. It turned out that the company had written large numbers of insurance contracts (called "credit default swaps") on complex financial instruments, including mortgage-backed securities. For a time, these contracts had been big moneymakers for AIG. But as housing prices fell and the value of securities backed by their mortgages plunged, the insurance company was forced to put up collateral—money it did not have. Alarmed at the effect AIG's collapse might have on the financial system, the U.S. government stepped in with a $150 *billion* bailout—the largest of a private firm in history—becoming, in the process, AIG's majority shareholder.

The near-collapse of AIG was, without a doubt, a disaster for the company's stockholders; in a single year, the share price fell from around $50 to mere pennies. Why did the board of directors and top executives fail to manage the apparently excessive risk taken on by the firm? Why didn't government regulators do a better job of protecting stockholders' interests? What role did compensation and reward systems play in the firm's behavior? Why didn't stockholders themselves figure out what was going on and sell their shares before it was too late? And once the government held a majority stake, how could it best use its new ownership role?

Stockholders are the legal owners of corporations. But as the debacle at AIG so vividly illustrates, their rights are not always protected. In the middle to late 2000s, in the wake of major losses by stockholders at AIG and other firms, many groups took steps to improve the overall system of corporate governance. This chapter will address the important legal rights of stockholders and how corporate boards, government regulators, managers, and activist shareholders can protect them. It will also discuss recent changes in corporate practice and government oversight designed to better guard stockholder interests, in both the United States and other nations, and some of the proposals now under debate that would strengthen regulation of the financial markets.

Stockholders

Stockholders (or shareholders, as they also are called) are the legal owners of business corporations. By purchasing shares of a company's stock, they become part owners. For this reason, stockholders have a big stake in how well their company performs. They are considered one of the market stakeholders of the firm, as explained in Chapter 1. The firm's managers must pay close attention to stockholders' needs and assign a high priority to their interests in the company.[1]

Who Are Stockholders?

Two types of stockholders own shares of stock in corporations: individual and institutional.

- *Individual stockholders* are people who directly own shares of stock issued by companies. These shares are usually purchased through a stockbroker and are held in brokerage accounts. For example, a person might buy 100 shares of Intel Corporation for

---

[1] The following discussion refers to publicly held corporations—that is, ones whose shares of stock are owned by the public and traded on the various stock exchanges. U.S. laws permit a number of other ownership forms, including sole proprietorships, partnerships, and mutual companies. The term *private equity* refers to shares in companies that are not publicly traded.

his or her portfolio. Such stockholders are sometimes called "Main Street" investors, because they come from all walks of life.

- *Institutions,* such as pensions, mutual funds, insurance companies, and university endowments, also own stock. For example, mutual funds such as Fidelity Magellan and pensions such as the California Public Employees Retirement System (CalPERS) buy stock on behalf of their investors or members. These institutions are sometimes called "Wall Street" investors. For obvious reasons, institutions usually have more money to invest and buy more shares than individual investors.

Since the 1960s, growth in the numbers of such **institutional investors** has been phenomenal. Studies by the securities industry showed that in 2007, institutions accounted for 75 percent of the value of all equities (stocks) owned in the United States, worth a total of $16 *trillion*—about two-and-a-half times the value of institutional holdings a decade earlier.[2] In an unprecedented twist, the U.S. government itself became a major institutional shareholder in 2008 and 2009 as it acquired ownership in a number of firms, including AIG, Citigroup, and General Motors, which it bailed out with taxpayers' money.

In 2008, nearly one-half of all U.S. households owned stocks or bonds, either directly or indirectly through holdings in mutual funds. This proportion had dropped somewhat since the early 2000s, as market turbulence had reduced some investors' willingness to take risks. Stockholders are a diverse group. People from practically every occupational group own stock. Although older people are more likely to own stock, slightly over 40 percent of young households (with a decision maker born between 1970 and 1979) do so. At all ages, equity ownership is higher as income and education rise.[3]

Do racial groups have different rates of stock ownership? A recent study based on Federal Reserve data shows that around 57 percent of white households own stock, compared with 23 percent of African-American households and 19 percent of Hispanic households. One possible explanation for these disparities, the researchers concluded, was different attitudes toward risk. Fifty-seven percent of African-Americans, for example, said they were "unwilling to take risks with their investments," compared with 36 percent of whites. (Stocks are riskier, but also have a higher potential for gain than many other kinds of investments.) Another factor, said the researchers, was that "white investors are more experienced with the stock market, so that they are prepared for the inevitable drops."[4]

Figure 14.1 shows the relative stock holdings of individual and institutional investors from the 1960s through the late 2000s. It shows the growing influence of the institutional sector of the market over the past four decades. (Because the data series ends in 2007, the total market value shown does not reflect the sharp decline in the value of equities that resulted from the credit crisis that began in 2008.)

---

[2] "Holdings of U.S. Equities Outstanding," *Fact Book 2008* (New York: Securities Industry Association, 2008). These data are based on analysis of the Federal Reserve Bank's flow of funds accounts. It should be noted that these figures precede the stock market downturn that began in 2008.

[3] "Equity and Bond Ownership in America, 2008," Investment Company Institute and the Securities Industry Association, 2008. A bond is a debt instrument that allows corporations (and other organizations, such as government entities) to raise capital by borrowing. Typically, bonds promise to repay principal and interest on a specific date.

[4] "Minority Stock Ownership Continues to Fall in Market Downturn," press release, Ohio State University, at *http://researchnews.osu.edu/archiver/minoritystock.htm.* The study summarized in the press release is S.D. Hanna and S. Lindamood, "The Decrease in Stock Ownership by Minority Households" (2008), *Financial Counseling and Planning* 19, no. 2, 46–58.

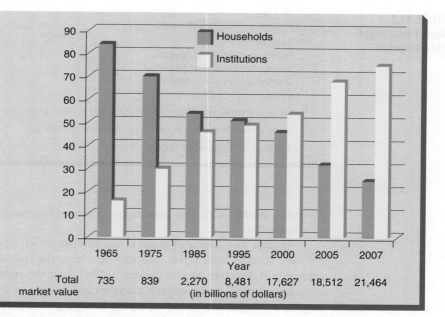

FIGURE 14.1
Household versus Institutional Ownership in the United States, 1965–2007, by Market Value

Source: Securities Industry Association, *Securities Industry Fact Book* (New York: Securities Industry Association, 2008). Household sector includes nonprofit organizations. Based on Federal Reserve Flow of Funds Accounts (revised). Used by permission.

Total market value	735	839	2,270	8,481	17,627	18,512	21,464

(in billions of dollars)

Objectives of Stock Ownership

Individuals and institutions own corporate stock for a number of reasons. Foremost among them is to make money. People buy stocks because they believe stocks will produce a return greater than they could receive from alternative investments. Stockholders make money when the price of the stock rises (this is called *capital appreciation*) and when they receive their share of the company's earnings (called *dividends*). Most companies pay dividends, but some—particularly new companies with good prospects for rapid growth—do not. In this case, investors buy the stock with the goal of capital appreciation only.

Stock prices rise and fall over time, affected both by the performance of the company and by the overall movement of the stock market. In the middle to late 1990s, a *bull market* (in which share prices rise overall) produced large gains for many investors; this was followed from 2000 to 2002 by a *bear market* (in which share prices fall overall), in which many investors lost money. After a period when the markets rose again, share values declined sharply in 2008 and early 2009, as the global economy fell into a severe recession. Typically, bull and bear markets alternate, driven by the health of the economy, interest rates, world events, and other factors that are often difficult to predict. Although stock prices are sometimes volatile, stocks historically have produced a higher return over the long run than investments in bonds, bank certificates of deposit, or money markets.

Although the primary motivation of most stockholders is to make money from their investments, some have other motivations as well. Some investors use stock ownership to achieve social or ethical objectives, a trend that is discussed later in this chapter in the section on social investment. Investors may also buy stock in order to take control of a company in a hostile takeover bid. Some investors have mixed objectives; for example, they wish to make a reasonable return on their investment but also to advance social or ethical goals.

Stockholders' Legal Rights and Safeguards

As explained in Chapter 1, managers have a duty to all stakeholders, not just to those who own shares in their company. Nevertheless, in the United States and most other

FIGURE 14.2
Major Legal Rights of Stockholders

- To receive dividends, if declared
- To vote on
  - Members of board of directors
  - Major mergers and acquisitions
  - Charter and bylaw changes
  - Proposals by stockholders
- To receive annual reports on the company's financial condition
- To bring shareholder suits against the company and officers
- To sell their own shares of stock to others

countries, stockholders have legal rights that are often more extensive than those of other stakeholders.

To protect their financial stake in the companies whose stocks they hold, stockholders have specific legal rights. Stockholders have the right to share in the profits of the enterprise if directors declare dividends. They have the right to receive annual reports of company earnings and company activities and to inspect the corporate books, provided they have a legitimate business purpose for doing so and that it will not disrupt business operations. They have the right to elect members of the board of directors, usually on a "one share equals one vote" basis. They have the right to hold the directors and officers of the corporation responsible for their acts, by lawsuit if they want to go that far. Furthermore, they usually have the right to vote on mergers, some acquisitions, and changes in the charter and bylaws, and to bring other business-related proposals before the stockholders. And finally, they have the right to sell their stock. Figure 14.2 summarizes the major legal rights of stockholders.

Many of these rights are exercised at the annual stockholders' meeting, where directors and managers present an annual report and shareholders have an opportunity to approve or disapprove management's plans. Because most corporations today are large, typically only a small portion of stockholders vote in person. Those not attending are given an opportunity to vote by absentee ballot, called a **proxy**. The use of proxy elections by stockholders to influence corporate policy is discussed later in this chapter.

How are these rights of stockholders best protected? Within a publicly held company, the board of directors bears a major share of the responsibility for making sure that the firm is run with the shareholders' interests in mind. We turn next, therefore, to a consideration of the role of the board in the system of corporate governance.

Corporate Governance

The term **corporate governance** refers to the process by which a company is controlled, or governed. Just as nations have governments that respond to the needs of citizens and establish policy, so do corporations have systems of internal governance that determine overall strategic direction and balance sometimes divergent interests. The collapse of Enron and WorldCom in the early 2000s—and more recently of Lehman Brothers and other investment banks—has focused renewed attention on corporate governance, because at times the control systems in place have not effectively protected stockholders and others with a stake in the company's performance.

The Board of Directors

The **board of directors** plays a central role in corporate governance. The board of directors is an elected group of individuals who have a legal duty to establish corporate objectives, develop broad policies, and select top-level personnel to carry out these objectives and policies. The board also reviews management's performance to be sure the company is well run and stockholders' interests are protected. Boards typically meet in full session around six times a year.

Corporate boards vary in size, composition, and structure to best serve the interests of the corporation and the shareholders. A number of patterns do exist, however. According to a survey of governance practices in leading firms in North America, Europe, and Asia Pacific, corporate boards average 10 members. Most typically, 8 of the 10 are *outside* directors (not managers of the company, who are known as *inside* directors when they serve on the board). (In the United States, the New York Stock Exchange now requires listed companies to have boards with a majority of outsiders.) Board members may include chief executives of other companies, major shareholders, bankers, former government officials, academics, representatives of the community, or retired executives from other firms. Eighty-five percent all companies have at least one woman on the board, and 78 percent have at least one member of an ethnic minority.[5]

Corporate directors are typically well paid. Compensation for board members is composed of a complex mix of retainer fees, meeting fees, grants of stock and stock options, pensions, and various perks. In 2007, the median compensation for directors at the largest U.S. corporations was $205,759, an increase of almost 60 percent since 2001. (Of this compensation, 41 percent was paid in cash and 59 percent in stock or stock options.)

According to a study by compensation specialists Pearl Meyers and Associates, the highest-paid directors in 2007 were in the securities industry—that is, Wall Street's leading investment banks. They were paid, on average, $341,500. Ironically, by the end of 2008 all five of the securities industry firms surveyed by Meyers—Lehman Brothers, Bear Stearns, Merrill Lynch, Morgan Stanley, and Goldman Sachs—had either collapsed, been acquired, or been converted into a commercial bank.[6]

Some critics believe that board compensation is excessive, and that high pay contributes to complacency by some directors who do not want to jeopardize their positions by challenging the policies of management.

Most corporate boards perform their work through committees as well as in general sessions. The compensation committee (present in 100 percent of corporate boards), normally staffed by outside directors, administers and approves salaries and other benefits of high-level managers in the company. The nominating committee (97 percent) is charged with finding and recommending candidates for officers and directors, especially those to be elected at the annual stockholders' meeting. The executive committee (42 percent) works closely with top managers on important business matters. A significant minority of corporations (17 percent) now have a special committee devoted to issues of corporate responsibility.[7]

---

[5] Korn/Ferry International, *34th Annual Board of Directors Study.* Data are for 2007.
[6] Pearl Meyer & Partners, *2007 Director Compensation,* at *www.execpay.com.*
[7] Korn/Ferry International, *34th Annual Board of Directors Study.*

One of the most important committees of the board is the audit committee. Present in virtually all boards, the audit committee is required by U.S. law to be composed entirely of outside directors and to be "financially literate." It reviews the company's financial reports, recommends the appointment of outside auditors (accountants), and oversees the integrity of internal financial controls.

At Enron Corporation, further described in a case at the end of this book, lax oversight by the six-person audit committee was a major contributor to the collapse of the firm. In the five years leading up to the company's 2001 bankruptcy, Enron executives carried out a series of complex financial transactions designed to remove debt from the balance sheet and artificially inflate revenue. These transactions were later found to be illegal, and Enron was forced to drastically restate its earnings. A subsequent investigation found that although the audit committee had reviewed these transactions, "these reviews appear to have been too brief, too limited in scope, and too superficial to serve their intended function." In short, the audit committee, which typically met with the company's outside accountants for only an hour or two before regular board meetings, had simply missed one of the biggest accounting frauds in U.S. history.

Directors who fail to detect and stop accounting fraud, as in this example, may be liable for damages. At WorldCom—a leading telecommunications company that collapsed in 2002 in the wake of a major accounting fraud—investors successfully sued former members of the board of directors for $55 million.[8] Because of tighter regulations and increased risk, audit committees now meet more frequently than they used to, on average nine times a year.

How are directors selected? Board members are elected by shareholders at the annual meeting, where absent owners may vote by proxy, as explained earlier. Thus, the system is formally democratic. However, as a practical matter, shareholders often have little choice in the matter. Typically, the nominating committee, working with the CEO and chairman, develops a list of possible candidates and presents these to the board for consideration. When a final selection is made, the names of these individuals are placed on the proxy ballot. Shareholders may vote to approve or disapprove the nominees, but because alternative candidates are often not presented, the vote has little significance. Moreover, many institutional investors routinely turn their proxies over to management. The selection process therefore tends to produce a kind of self-perpetuating system.

Because boards typically meet behind closed doors, scholars know less about the kinds of *processes* that lead to effective decision making by directors than they do about board composition and structure.

In their book *Back to the Drawing Board,* Colin Carter and Jay Lorsch observe, based on their extensive consulting experience, that boards develop their own norms that define what is—and is not—appropriate behavior. For example, *pilot boards* see their role as actively guiding the company's strategic direction. *Watchdog boards,* by contrast, see their role as assuring compliance with the law—and intervening in management decisions only if something is clearly wrong. These norms are often powerfully influenced by the chairman. Boards that share a

[8] "Judge Approves $3.65 Billion Settlement for WorldCom Investors," *The New York Times,* September 22, 2005.

consensus on behavioral norms tend to function more effectively as a group than those that do not.[9]

An example of a situation where the board disagreed fundamentally over the roles and duties of directors is presented in the case "Hewlett-Packard's Secret Surveillance of Directors and Journalists" at the end of this book.

Principles of Good Governance

In the wake of the corporate scandals of the early 2000s and the financial crisis later in the decade, many sought to define the core principles of good corporate governance. What kinds of boards were most effective? During the 2000s, public agencies, investor groups, and stock exchanges all struggled to determine what reforms might be necessary. By the late 2000s, a broad consensus had emerged about some key features of effective boards. These included the following:

- *Select outside directors to fill most positions.* Normally, no more than two or three members of the board should be current managers. Moreover, the outside members should be truly independent—that is, should have no connection to the corporation other than serving as a director. This would exclude, for example, directors who themselves performed consulting services for the company on whose board they served, or who were officers of other firms that had a business relationship with it. The audit, compensation, and nominating committees should be composed *solely* of outsiders. By the late 2000s, virtually all major companies were following these practices.

- *Hold open elections for members of the board.* Some groups favored a proposal under which dissident shareholders, under certain conditions, could put their own candidates for the board on the proxy ballot. Another idea was that candidates would have to get at least 50 percent of votes to be elected (many companies required only a plurality). Some thought that directors should stand for election every year; others thought that staggered terms were a better idea (for example, on a nine-person board, three individuals would stand for election each year for a three-year term). In any event, the idea was to give shareholders more control over the selection of directors.

- *Appoint an independent lead director (chairman of the board) and hold regular meetings without the CEO present.* Many experts in corporate governance also believed that boards should separate the duties of the chief executive and the board chairman, rather than combining the two in one person as is done in many corporations. The independent chairman would then hold meetings without management present, improving the board's chances of having completely candid discussions about a company's affairs. For example, in 2008 Samuel J. Palmisano was elected by Exxon's independent directors to preside over regular separate sessions.[10] Eighty-four percent of large company boards now have an independent lead director—a sharp increase in the past decade.[11]

- *Align director compensation with corporate performance.* Like top executives, directors should be paid based, at least in part, on how well the company does. For example,

[9] Colin B. Carter and Jay W. Lorsch, *Back to the Drawing Boards: Designing Corporate Boards for a Complex World* (Boston: Harvard Business School Press, 2003).

[10] "Additional Governance Developments at Exxon," GovernanceMetrics International, *In Focus*, January 22, 2009.

[11] Korn-Ferry International, *34th Board of Directors Study*. (Data are for 2007.)

Coca-Cola announced in 2006 that it would change the way its directors were compensated. Members of the board would be paid only if the company met its earnings-per-share target of at least 8 percent annual compound growth over a three-year period. If the company did not, directors would get nothing.[12]

- *Evaluate the board's own performance on a regular basis.* Directors themselves should be assessed on how competent they were and how diligently they performed their duties. Normally, this would be the responsibility of the governance committee of the board. In the wake of the corporate scandals of the early 2000s, many companies made dramatic improvements in this area; between 2002 and 2004, the proportion of global companies that formally evaluated their board members rose from 35 to 90 percent, according to a survey by Governance Metrics International.[13]

The discussion case at the end of this chapter describes the functioning of the board of directors and top managers at Citigroup and their role in the bank's failure to rein in the excessive risk taking that brought it to the brink of collapse in 2009.

The movement to improve corporate governance has been active in other nations and regions, as well as the United States. The Organization for Economic Cooperation and Development (OECD), representing 30 nations, issued a revised set of principles of corporate governance in 2004 to serve as a benchmark for companies and policymakers worldwide. In 2009, OECD issued a report that concluded that the financial crisis affecting many of its member states had been caused, to an important extent, by failures of corporate governance, and it called for a reexamination of the adequacy of these principles.[14] For its part, the European Union has worked hard to modernize corporate governance practices and harmonize them across its member states. Corporate governance reforms have also taken hold in South Africa, India, and many other nations. But progress had been slow in many emerging market countries.

According to GovernanceMetrics International (GMI), governance practices in emerging market (EM) companies are very different from those in the United States, Canada, the United Kingdom, and Australia. Only 35 percent of boards in EM countries have a majority of independent directors (compared with 93 percent in the latter group of countries). Only 50 percent have a compensation committee (compared with 98 percent). As an example of poor governance, GMI cited a Brazilian steel company where one man served as chairman, CEO, and chief financial officer, and a bank he controlled managed transactions for the firm. In another example, a South Korean securities firm had only one independent director (among 10).[15]

In short, by the late 2000s the movement to make boards more responsive to shareholders was an international one, although much work remained to be done, especially in emerging market countries.[16]

---

[12] "Coke Directors Agree to Give Up Pay If Company Misses Earnings Goals," *The Wall Street Journal,* April 6, 2006, p. A1.

[13] "GMI Releases New Global Governance Ratings," press release, September 7, 2004, *www.gmiratings.com.*

[14] Grant Kirkpatrick, "The Corporate Governance Lessons from the Financial Crisis," OECD, February 2009. For the complete principles, see *www.oecd.org.* Information about recent changes in corporate governance practices in Europe is available at the Web site of the European Corporate Governance Institute, *www.ecgi.org.*

[15] "GovernanceMetrics International Releases Ratings on 3800 Global Companies," press release, February 28, 2006, *www.gmiratings.com.*

[16] The Corporate Library, *www.thecorporatelibrary.org,* routinely posts news stories from all over the world on current developments in corporate governance reform.

Special Issue: Executive Compensation

Setting **executive compensation** is one of the most important functions of the board of directors. The emergence of the modern, publicly held corporation in the late 1800s effectively separated ownership and control. That is, owners of the firm no longer managed it on a day-to-day basis; this task fell to hired professionals. This development gave rise to what theorists call the *agency problem.* If managers are merely hired agents, what will guarantee that they act in the interests of shareholders rather than simply helping themselves? The problem is a serious one, because shareholders are often geographically dispersed, and government rules make it difficult for them to contact each other and to organize on behalf of their collective interests. Boards meet just four or five times a year. Who, then, is watching the managers?

An important mechanism for aligning the interests of the corporation and its stockholders with those of its top managers is executive compensation. But recent events suggest the system is not always doing its job.

In the late 2000s, a number of top executives made out handsomely, even as their companies were spiraling toward collapse. At Merrill Lynch, Stanley O'Neal earned $70 million in compensation over his four years as CEO—and then an additional $161 million in severance pay when the board fired him in 2007. Just a year later, Merrill went under. Angelo Mozilo, the CEO of the disgraced subprime mortgage lender Countrywide, was paid $125 million in the year before his company collapsed and was taken over by the Bank of America. In response to these and other similar cases, some legislators called for "clawback"—a process by which executives of failed firms would have to pay back some of their earnings. "There is a line that separates fair compensation from stealing from shareholders," said the founder of Investors for Director Accountability. "When managements ignore that line . . . then, . . . yes, they should be required to give the money back."[17]

Many critics feel that executive pay has become excessive—not just at companies accused of fraud but in fact at most companies—reflecting aggressive self-dealing by managers without regard for the interests of others.

Executive compensation in the United States, by international standards, is very high. In 2008, the median total compensation of chief executives of the largest corporations in the United States was $8.4 million, including salaries, bonuses, and the present value of retirement benefits, incentive plans, and **stock options**, according to the compensation firm Equilar.[18] (Stock options and the controversy surrounding this form of compensation are further explained in Exhibit 14.A.) This amount represented a 9 percent decrease from the prior year, the first such downturn in five years, reflecting the depth of the recession that hit that year. (The all-time peak median pay, about $13 million, occurred in 2000, at the height of the stock market boom of the late 1990s.) The top-paid executive in 2008 was Sanjay Jha of Motorola, who earned $104 million.[19]

---

[17] "Gimme Your Paycheck," *The New York Times,* February 22, 2009; "How the Thundering Herd Faltered and Fell," *The New York Times,* November 9, 2008; and "The Compensation Question," *Boston Globe,* November 9, 2008.

[18] "Who Moved My Bonus? Executive Pay Makes a U-Turn," *The New York Times,* April 5, 2009.

[19] "Motorola CEO Tops Pay Survey," *The Wall Street Journal,* April 3, 2009.

Exhibit 14.A

Stock Options: A Controversial Form of Compensation

An important component of compensation at many companies is stock options. These represent the right (but not obligation) to buy a company's stock at a set price (called the strike price) for a certain period. The option becomes valuable when, and if, the stock price rises above this amount. For example, an executive might receive an option to buy 100,000 shares at $30. The stock is currently selling at $25. If the stock price rises to, say, $35 before the option expires, the executive can exercise the option by buying 100,000 shares at $30, for $3 million, and then turning around and selling them for $3.5 million, pocketing $500,000 in profit, less taxes. Stock options became very popular during the 1990s, particularly in high-tech and other fast-growing companies, because they were seen as a way to align executives' interests with those of shareholders. The idea was that executives would work hard to improve the company's performance, because this would lift the stock and increase the value of their options.

But in the wake of WorldCom and other corporate scandals, many began to reconsider this form of compensation. The danger was that unscrupulous executives might become so fixated on the value of their options that they would do anything to increase the stock price, even if this involved unethical accounting practices. One study seemed to confirm this, reporting that the higher the proportion of executive compensation in stock options, the more likely the firm was later to have to restate its profits. Another problem with stock options was that because companies were not required to report them as an expense (even though they cost the company money when exercised), they tended to skew the company's books, misleading investors. In a bear market, options were less attractive to holders, because they often expired without ever reaching the exercise price.

In 2005, the Securities and Exchange Commission approved new rules that for the first time required companies to deduct the cost of stock options from their earnings. Some companies responded by phasing out or reducing their use of options. In 2008 and 2009, many options were "under water" because their underlying stocks were trading below their exercise price.

Sources: "Options Expensing Is Here to Stay," *BusinessWeek,* January 20, 2005; "Stock Options: Old Game, New Tricks," *BusinessWeek,* December 19, 2005; and "Do Options Breed Fraud at the Top?" *International Herald Tribune,* August 5, 2005.

By contrast, top managers in other countries earned much less. Although the pay of top executives elsewhere was catching up, it was still generally well below what comparable managers in the United States earned. Figure 14.3 represents graphically the gap between executive pay in the United States and Europe.

These disparities caused friction in some international mergers. For instance, shareholders at GlaxoSmithKline, a pharmaceutical company formed through a merger of British and American firms, complained loudly when the board proposed a $28 million benefits package for CEO Jean-Pierre Garnier. Garnier, who was born in France but had moved to the United States to head the merged company, said he needed more pay to "stay motivated." But this level of compensation seemed out of line to many European shareholders, and it was later reduced.[20]

Another way to look at executive compensation is to compare the pay of top managers with that of average employees. In the United States, CEOs in 2007 made 344 times what the average worker did. Figure 14.4 shows that the ratio of average executive to average worker pay has increased markedly over the past decade and a half, with the exception of periods of stock market downturn such as the early 2000s.

Why are American executives paid so much? Corporate politics play an important role. In their book *Pay without Performance: The Unfulfilled Promise of Executive*

[20] "Mad about Money: The Outrage over CEO Pay Isn't Only a U.S. Phenomenon; Just Ask Shareholders in Europe," *The Wall Street Journal,* April 14, 2003.

FIGURE 14.3   Relative Executive Compensation in the United States and Europe

Source: "U.S. CEOs May Face Euro-Style Pay Packages," *Global Finance,* March 2008. Data are from the Hay Group. See also "Business: Pay Attention; Executive Pay in Europe," *The Economist,* June 14, 2008.

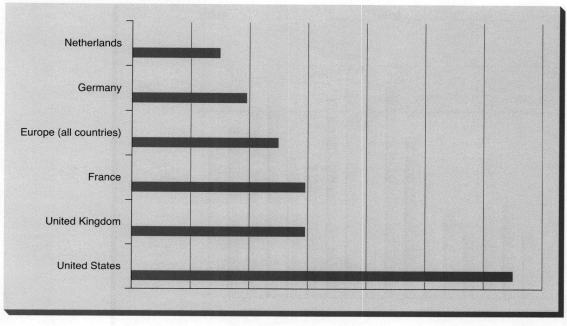

Compensation, Lucian A. Bebchuk and Jesse M. Fried argue that one reason salaries are so high is that top managers have so much influence over the pay-setting process. Compensation committees are made up of individuals who are selected for board membership by the CEO, and they are often linked by ties of friendship and personal loyalty. Many are CEOs themselves and sensitive to the indirect impact of their decisions on their own salaries. Moreover, compensation committees rely on surveys of similar firms and usually want to pay their own executives above the industry average, over time ratcheting up pay for all.[21]

Some observers say that the comparatively high compensation of top U.S. executives is justified. In this view, well-paid managers are simply being rewarded for outstanding performance.

For example, Lee Raymond, who retired in 2005, earned $686 million during his 13 years at the helm of Exxon Mobil. During this period, the company's market value quadrupled, and the company paid out $67 billion in dividends.[22] To at least some shareholders, his eye-popping pay was clearly worth it. A major share of the increase in executive compensation in the late 1990s resulted from the exercise of stock options, reflecting the bull market of that era, a development that benefited shareholders as well as executives.

[21] Lucian A. Bebchuk and Jesse M. Fried, *Pay without Performance: The Unfulfilled Promise of Executive Compensation* (Cambridge, MA: Harvard University Press, 2004); their argument is summarized in "Pay without Performance: Overview of the Issues," *Academy of Management Perspectives,* February 2006.

[22] "For Leading Exxon to Its Riches, $144,573 a Day," *The New York Times,* April 15, 2006.

FIGURE 14.4 **Ratio of Average CEO Pay to Average Production Worker Pay, 1990–2007**

Source: Institute for Policy Studies and United for a Fair Economy, *Annual CEO Compensation Surveys,* at *www.faireconomy.org.* Used by permission.

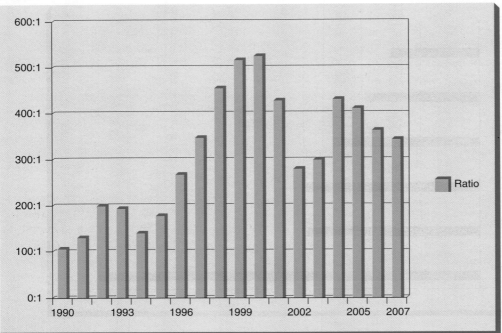

Supporters also argue that high salaries provide an incentive for innovation and risk taking. In an era of intense global competition, restructuring, and downsizing, the job of CEO of large U.S. corporations has never been more challenging, and the tenure in the top job has become shorter. Another argument for high compensation is a shortage of labor. In this view, not many individuals are capable of running today's large, complex organizations, so the few that have the necessary skills and experience can command a premium. Today's high salaries are necessary for companies to attract or retain top talent. Why shouldn't the most successful business executives make as much as top athletes and entertainers?

On the other hand, critics argue that inflated executive pay hurts the ability of U.S. firms to compete with foreign rivals. High executive compensation diverts financial resources that could be used to invest in the business, increase stockholder dividends, or pay average workers more. Multimillion-dollar salaries cause resentment and sap the commitment—and sometimes lead to the exodus of—hard-working lower- and mid-level employees who feel they are not receiving their fair share. As for the performance issue, critics suggest that as many extravagantly compensated executives preside over failure as they do over success. Many executives get outsized salaries despite their companies' dismal performance—a reality that sometimes prompts shareholder activism.

At the 2009 annual meeting, held in The Hague, shareholders of Royal Dutch Shell lashed out at the board for handsomely rewarding executives even though they had not achieved their performance targets. "The gravy train has got to stop," said one retiree. Fifty-nine percent of shareholders voted against the pay proposal. Although the vote was only advisory, Shell's chairman said the board would "take the outcome of this vote very seriously."[23]

Executive compensation has also been the subject of government regulations. Under U.S. government rules, companies must clearly disclose what their five top executives are paid, and lay out a rationale for their compensation. Companies must also report the value of various perks, from the personal use of corporate aircraft to free tickets to sporting events, which had previously escaped investor scrutiny. The U.S. government also allows shareholder votes on executive and director compensation, and the government of the United Kingdom *requires* such votes. Although in both cases these votes are not binding, they provide a mechanism for shareholders to voice displeasure over excessive compensation, as shown in the preceding example about Royal Dutch Shell. In 2009, President Obama called the big bonuses of executives at some of the banks that had failed "shameful." Later, he appointed a "special master for compensation," who was given broad authority over executive pay at companies that had received government bailout money.[24]

For their part, many companies have responded to stakeholder pressure by changing the process by which they set executive pay. Most boards now staff their compensation committees exclusively with outside directors and permit them to hire their own consultants. Many firms have sought to restructure compensation to tie top executives' pay more closely to performance. A few top managers have even taken pay cuts—such as AIG's CEO Edward Liddy, who worked for an annual salary of $1 in 2008, as the company received billions of dollars of government bailout money.[25] A tiny handful of companies have said that top executives cannot earn more than a certain multiple of others' pay. Whole Foods Market, for example, has a rule that no executive's salary and bonus can be more than 14 times what the average worker makes. "We have a philosophy of shared fate, that we're in this together," said John Mackey, the company's cofounder and CEO.[26]

How to structure executive compensation to best align managers' interests with those of stockholders and other stakeholders will remain a core challenge of corporate governance.

Shareholder Activism

Shareholders do not have to rely exclusively on the board of directors. Many owners, both individual and institutional, have also taken action directly to protect their own interests, as they define them. This section will describe the increased activism of three shareholder groups: large institutions, social investors, and owners seeking redress through the courts.

The Rise of Institutional Investors

As shown earlier, institutional investors—pensions, mutual funds, endowment funds, and the like—have enlarged their stockholdings significantly over the past two decades and have become more assertive in promoting the interests of their members.

---

[23] "Shell Investors Revolt over Executive Pay Plan," *The Wall Street Journal,* May 20, 2009.

[24] "Obama Lays Out Limits on Executive Pay," *The Wall Street Journal,* February 5, 2009; and "Pay Czar Gets Broad Authority over Executive Compensation," *The Wall Street Journal,* June 11, 2009.

[25] "AIG Says Liddy Took a $1 Salary," *The Wall Street Journal,* May 1, 2009.

[26] "Putting a Ceiling on Pay," *The Wall Street Journal,* April 12, 2004. Whole Foods' measure of executive pay does not include the value of stock options.

One reason institutions have become more active is that it is more difficult for them to sell their holdings if they become dissatisfied with management performance. Large institutions have less flexibility than individual shareholders, because selling a large block of stock could seriously depress its price, and therefore the value of the institution's holdings. Accordingly, institutional investors have a strong incentive to hold their shares and organize to change management policy.

The Council of Institutional Investors (CII) is an organization that represents institutions and pension funds with investments collectively exceeding $3 trillion. The council has developed a Shareholder Bill of Rights and has urged its members to view their proxies as assets, voting them on behalf of shareholders rather than automatically with management. The activism of institutional shareholders has often improved company performance. One study showed that in the five years before and after a major pension fund became actively involved in the governance of companies whose shares it owned, stock performance improved dramatically, relative to the overall market.[27]

In late 2008, a group of leading state pension funds and staff members of the CII gathered to consider possible regulatory reforms to prevent future financial crises. Among the group were the two big California pension funds, CalPERS and CalSTRS, which had together lost about a third of their value in the sharp market downturn. "There is a shared belief that institutional investors need to have a unified posture going into the supercharged environment for change and reform that presently exists," said a report from the meeting. The group later produced a set of principles for regulatory reform and committed to push for their adoption.[28]

The activism of institutional investors has begun to spread to other countries. In many cases, U.S.-based pension and mutual funds that have acquired large stakes in foreign companies have spearheaded these efforts. In 2007, U.S. investors owned more than $6 trillion worth of foreign securities.[29] To protect their globalized investments, fund managers have become active in proxy battles in Japan, Britain, Hong Kong, and many other countries. In addition, sovereign wealth funds operated by the governments of Singapore, Abu Dhabi, and China have recently become more active as institutional investors. The movement for the rights of shareholders—like the investments they hold—is becoming increasingly globalized.

Social Investment

Another movement of growing importance among activist shareholders is **social investment**, sometimes also called *social responsibility investment*. This refers to the use of stock ownership as a strategy for promoting social objectives. This can be done in two ways: through selecting stocks according to various social criteria, and by using the corporate governance process to raise issues of concern.

Stock Screening

Shareholders wishing to choose stocks based on social or environmental criteria often turn to screened funds. A growing number of mutual funds and pension funds use *social screens*

[27] "The 'CalPERS Effect' on Targeted Company Share Price," July 31, 2008, at *www.calpers-governance.org.*

[28] Ed Mendel, "CalPERS and CalSTRS: New Sheriff on Wall Street?" January 19, 2009, at *http://calpensions.com.* The group's "Principles of Financial Regulation Reform" are available at *www.calpers-governance.org.*

[29] "U.S. Holdings of Foreign Securities," *Securities Industry Factbook 2008,* p. 88.

to select companies in which to invest, weeding out ones that pollute the environment, discriminate against employees, make dangerous products like tobacco or weapons, or do business in countries with poor human rights records. In 2007, according to the Social Investment Forum, $2.7 trillion in the United States was invested in mutual funds or pensions using social responsibility as an investment criterion, accounting for about one in every nine investment dollars. Between 2005 and 2007, socially responsible investment grew more than 18 percent, while all assets under professional management grew less than 3 percent.[30]

In recent years, socially responsible investing also has grown rapidly in Europe and beyond. In Europe, $3.9 trillion (about one-fifth of all assets under management) were invested using social criteria, according to the European Social Investment Forum.[31] Growth has been particularly rapid in the United Kingdom, where government rules require pension funds to disclose the extent to which they use social, environmental, or ethical criteria in selecting investments. Most evidence shows that socially screened portfolios provide returns that are competitive with the broad market.[32]

Social criteria may also be used when selling stocks. For example, some have at various times called for divestment (sale of stock) from companies that had operations in China, where some products were made by forced labor, and in Nigeria, Myanmar (Burma), and Sudan, where repressive regimes had been accused of human rights abuses.

Social Responsibility Shareholder Resolutions

Another important way in which shareholders have been active is by sponsoring **social responsibility shareholder resolutions**. This is a resolution on an issue of corporate social responsibility placed before stockholders for a vote at the company's annual meeting.

The Securities and Exchange Commission (SEC), a government regulatory agency that is further described later in this chapter, allows stockholders to place resolutions concerning appropriate social issues, such as environmental responsibility or alcohol and tobacco advertising, in proxy statements sent out by companies. The SEC has tried to minimize harassment by requiring a resolution to receive minimum support to be resubmitted—3 percent of votes cast the first time, 6 percent the second time, and 10 percent the third time it is submitted within a five-year period. Resolutions cannot deal with a company's ordinary business, such as employee wages or the content of advertising, since that would constitute unjustified interference with management's decisions.[33]

In 2007, shareholder activists sponsored around 650 resolutions dealing with major social issues. Backers included church groups, individual shareholders, unions, environmental groups, socially responsible mutual funds, and public pension funds. Many of these groups were members of a coalition, the Interfaith Center on Corporate Responsibility (ICCR), which coordinated the activities of the social responsibility shareholder movement. Some key issues raised in these resolutions included executive compensation, environmental responsibility, anti-bias policies, and corporate governance.[34] In 2009, as concern about management pay mounted, many shareholder proposals called

---

[30] Social Investment Forum, "2007 Report on Socially Responsible Investing Trends in the United States," *www.socialinvest.org.*

[31] Data are as of December 31, 2007. Annual surveys of socially responsible investment in Europe are available on the Web site of the European Social Investment Forum at *www.eurosif.org.*

[32] References to this literature may be found in Donald H. Schepers and S. Prakash Sethi, "Do Socially Responsible Funds Actually Deliver What They Promise?" *Business and Society Review* 108, no. 1 (Spring 2003), pp. 11–32.

[33] Current SEC rules on shareholder proposals may be found at *www.sec.gov/rules/final.*

[34] Data on shareholder resolutions are available at *www.riskmetrics.com.*

for the right to vote in nonbinding elections on executive compensation—so-called "say on pay" provisions.[35]

In 2009, shareholders at Pfizer, the pharmaceutical company, voted to give themselves an advisory vote on executive compensation. The vote was 52 percent in favor of the "say on pay" provision, even though the company's board had recommended a "no" vote. In 2008, Pfizer's CEO's pay was $16 million. Of the first 29 "say on pay" proposals considered in 2009, 10 received a majority of votes cast. "Shareholders are urging boards to provide a platform to send feedback on executive compensation policies and practices," said Timothy Smith, a longtime shareholder activist.[36]

Some shareholder activists viewed the financial crisis as a "once in a lifetime" opportunity to push for reforms, said an attorney for a proxy advisory group.[37]

Social responsibility shareholder resolutions usually do not pass; they garner, on average, about 15 percent of votes.[38] This figure does not capture their full influence, however. In recent years, managers have often acted on an issue before the election so shareholder activists will withdraw their resolutions. For example, in 2008 the Connecticut State Treasurer's Office and the Sisters of St. Dominic withdrew their resolution after Ford Motor Company agreed to provide details of how it planned to reduce greenhouse gas emissions from its vehicles by 30 percent by 2020.[39] According to a recent study, 20 percent of companies always work with shareholders to resolve their concerns, and 59 percent sometimes do so. Companies that rank high on various measures of corporate social responsibility, not surprisingly, are more likely to try to address shareholder concerns than those that do not.[40]

Stockholder Lawsuits

Another way in which stockholders can seek to advance their interests is by suing the company. If owners think that they or their company have been damaged by actions of company officers or directors, they have the right to bring lawsuits in the courts, either on behalf of themselves or on behalf of the company (the latter is called a *derivative* lawsuit). **Shareholder lawsuits** may be initiated to check many abuses, including insider trading, an inadequate price obtained for the company's stock in a buyout (or a good price rejected), or lush executive pension benefits. The outcome can be very expensive for companies, as illustrated by the following example involving accounting fraud:

In 2006, Nortel Networks, a maker of telecommunications equipment, offered $2.4 billion (about 15 percent of the value of the company) to settle two lawsuits

[35] "Shareholders Renew Push to Regulate Executive Pay," *The Wall Street Journal,* February 13, 2009. A list of currently active proposals may be found at *www.iccr.org.*

[36] "Say on Pay Wins at Pfizer, Loses at J&J," *The Wall Street Journal,* April 24, 2009; and "Say on Pay Shareholder Proposals Garner Record Support during Tumultuous Shareholder Season," press release, American Federation of State, County, and Municipal Employees, May 4, 2009.

[37] "Theory and Practice: Shareholders to Focus on Executive Compensation," *The Wall Street Journal,* January 12, 2009.

[38] Riskmetrics Group, "2008 Postseason Report Summary," p. 10, *www.riskmetrics.com.*

[39] "Investors Achieve Major Company Commitments on Climate Change," CERES press release, August 20, 2008, *www.ceres.org.*

[40] Kathleen Rehbein, Stephen Brammer, Jeanne Logsdon, and Harry J. Van Buren III, "Understanding Corporate Responses to Shareholder Activists: Uniform or Heterogeneous?" *International Association for Business and Society Proceedings,* 2009.

brought by shareholders. The plaintiffs charged that the company had reported sales it had not made, defrauding investors who thought the company was performing better than it was and leading to big stock market losses.[41]

The late 2000s witnessed another wave of shareholder lawsuits, as individual and institutional investors responded to rapidly falling stock values.[42]

In many ways—whether through their collective organization, the selection of stocks, the shareholder resolution process, or the courts—shareholder activists can and do protect their economic and social rights.

Government Protection of Stockholder Interests

The government also plays an important role in protecting stockholder interests. This role has expanded, as legislators have responded to the corporate scandals of the early 2000s and the business failures later in the decade.

Securities and Exchange Commission

The major government agency protecting stockholders' interests is the **Securities and Exchange Commission (SEC)**. Established in 1934 in the wake of the stock market crash and the Great Depression, its mission is to protect stockholders' rights by making sure that stock markets are run fairly and that investment information is fully disclosed. The agency, unlike most in government, generates revenue to pay for its own operations. (The revenue comes from fees paid by companies listed on the major stock exchanges.)

Government regulation is needed because stockholders can be damaged by abusive practices. Two areas calling for regulatory attention are protecting stockholders from fraudulent financial accounting and from unfair trading by insiders.

Information Transparency and Disclosure

Giving stockholders more and better company information is one of the best ways to safeguard their interests, and this is a primary mission of the SEC. The stockholder should be as fully informed as possible in order to make sound investments. By law, stockholders have a right to know about the affairs of the corporations in which they hold ownership shares. Those who attend annual meetings learn about past performance and future goals through speeches made by corporate officers and documents such as the company's annual report. Those who do not attend meetings must depend primarily on annual reports issued by the company and the opinions of independent financial analysts.

In recent years, management has tended to disclose more information than ever before to stockholders and other interested people. Prompted by the SEC, professional accounting groups, and individual investors, companies now disclose a great deal about their financial affairs, with much information readily available on investor relations sections of company Web pages. Stockholders can learn about sales and earnings, assets, capital expenditures and depreciation by line of business, details of foreign operations, and many other financial matters. Corporations also are required to disclose detailed information about directors and top executives and their compensation. In addition, many companies

---

[41] "Nortel Offers $2.4 Billion to Settle Lawsuits," *The New York Times,* February 9, 2006.

[42] "If Everyone's Finger-Pointing, Who's to Blame?" *The New York Times,* January 22, 2008.

have begun reporting detailed information about social and environmental, as well as financial, performance, as discussed in Chapter 7.

Although the overall trend has been toward greater transparency, some observers felt that a lack of disclosure about complex financial instruments, such as mortgage-backed securities, that became common in the mid-2000s, may have led investors to underestimate their risk.

In March 2008, Bear Stearns, an investment banking firm that had been a fixture on Wall Street for almost a century, abruptly collapsed and was sold to JP Morgan Chase. Bear Stearns was an early pioneer in the business of securities backed by subprime mortgages and other risky collateral. When investors began to suspect that the firm's assets were worth much less than they had thought, and that it might not be able to meet its obligations, the Federal Reserve and Treasury stepped in and forced a quick sale to JP Morgan Chase. The firm's sale price was just $10 a share, a shocking drop from a share value of $172 just over a year earlier. Various institutional shareholders later sued Bear Stearns executives, saying they had been misled about extreme risk taken by the company.[43]

Some have called for new rules requiring greater disclosure by issuers and holders of complex securities. The role of credit rating agencies in evaluating risk is explored in the case "Moody's Credit Ratings and the Subprime Mortgage Meltdown" at the end of this book.

Information is useful to investors only if it is accurate. Fraudulent financial statements filed by WorldCom, Enron, and Adelphia in the early 2000s misled investors and led to billions of dollars of losses in the stock market. The reasons for these accounting scandals were complex. They included lax oversight by audit committees, self-dealing by managers, and shareholders who were not sufficiently vigilant. Another problem was that some accounting firms had begun to make more money from consulting and other services than they did from providing routine financial audits. Often, accounting firms provided both consulting and audit services to the same company, creating a potential conflict of interest. Arguably, some accountants were afraid to blow the whistle on questionable financial transactions, out of fear of losing a valuable consulting client.

In 2002, in response to concerns about the lack of transparency in financial accounting, Congress passed an important new law that greatly expanded the powers of the SEC to regulate information disclosure in the financial markets. The law, called the Sarbanes-Oxley Act (for its congressional sponsors), had strong bipartisan support and was signed into law by President George W. Bush. The accounting firm PricewaterhouseCoopers, echoing a common sentiment, called it "the single most important piece of legislation affecting corporate governance, financial disclosure, and the practice of public accounting since the U.S. securities laws of the early 1930s."[44] The major provisions of the Sarbanes-Oxley Act are summarized in Chapter 5.

Insider Trading

Another area the SEC regulates is stock trading by insiders. **Insider trading** occurs when a person gains access to confidential information about a company's financial condition

---

[43] The story of the collapse of Bear Stearns is told in William D. Cohan, *House of Cards: A Tale of Hubris and Wretched Excess on Wall Street* (New York: Doubleday, 2009).

[44] PricewaterhouseCoopers, "The Sarbanes-Oxley Act of 2002," *www.pwcglobal.com.*

and then uses that information, before it becomes public knowledge, to buy or sell the company's stock. Since others do not know what an inside trader does, the insider has an unfair advantage.

> Joe Nacchio, the former CEO of Qwest Communications, a regional phone company based in Denver, was sentenced to six years in prison for illegal insider trading. He was also ordered to forfeit $52 million in ill-gotten gains and pay a $19 million fine. The court found that in early 2001, while he was CEO, Nacchio had sold $100 million worth of Qwest stock after insiders warned him that the company's financial situation was rapidly deteriorating. Even as he was selling his own holdings, he continued publicly to reassure investors about the company's prospects. Qwest's stock later collapsed in value, and the company narrowly avoided bankruptcy. The board ousted Nacchio the following year. "Insider trading is not a victimless crime," said the lead prosecutor. "There are victims here, a lot of whom lost their hopes and dreams." In 2009, an appeals court ordered Nacchio to begin serving his sentence at a prison camp in Pennsylvania.[45]

Insider trading is illegal under the Securities and Exchange Act of 1934, which outlaws "any manipulative or deceptive device." The courts have generally interpreted this to mean that it is against the law to

- Misappropriate (steal) nonpublic information and use it to trade a stock.
- Trade a stock based on a tip from someone who had an obligation to keep quiet (for example, a man would be guilty of insider trading if he bought stock after his sister, who was on the board of directors, told him of a pending offer to buy the company).
- Pass information to others with an expectation of direct or indirect gain, even if the individual did not trade the stock for his or her own account.

In an important legal case, *U.S. vs. O'Hagen*, the Supreme Court clarified insider trading law. The court ruled that someone who traded on the basis of inside information when he or she *knew* the information was supposed to remain confidential was guilty of misappropriation, whether or not the trader was directly connected to the company whose shares were purchased. Under the new court interpretation, insider trading rules would cover a wide range of people—from lawyers, to secretaries, to printers—who learned of and traded on information they knew was confidential. They would not, however, cover people who came across information by chance, for example, by overhearing a conversation in a bar.[46]

The best-known kind of insider trading occurs when people improperly acquire confidential information about forthcoming mergers of large corporations in order to buy and sell stocks before the mergers are announced to the public. More recently, another kind of insider trading, called front-running, has become more common. Front-runners place buy and sell orders for stock in advance of the moves of big institutional investors, such as mutual funds, based on tips from informants. This form of insider trading is often harder for regulators to detect and prosecute.

Insider trading is contrary to the logic underlying the stock markets: All stockholders ought to have access to the same information about companies. In the Qwest case

---

[45] "Nacchio Must Report to PA Prison," *Denver Post*, March 4, 2009; and "Nacchio Convicted on 19 Counts," *Denver Post*, April 20, 2007.

[46] "Supreme Court Upholds S.E.C.'s Theory of Insider Trading," *The New York Times*, June 26, 1997, pp. C1, C23.

described above, the CEO had insider information that ordinary investors did not—information that he used to give himself an unfair advantage over others. If ordinary investors think that insiders can use what they know for personal gain, the system of stock trading could break down from lack of trust. Insider trading laws are important in order for investors to have full confidence in the fundamental fairness of the stock markets.

Another responsibility of the SEC is to protect investors against fraud. One situation where they apparently failed to guard against a massive scheme to cheat investors was the fraud perpetrated by Bernard Madoff. (This case is also discussed in Chapter 4.)

The victims of Madoff's fraud—including prominent universities, charities, and cultural institutions, as well as individual investors—lost as much as $65 *billion.* Where were the government regulators in all of this? In congressional hearings, SEC chairman Christopher Cox admitted that his agency had missed repeated warnings, dating back to 1999, that things might be amiss at Madoff's firm. "I am gravely concerned by the apparent multiple failures over at least a decade to thoroughly investigate these allegations or at any point to seek formal authority to pursue them," said Cox. *The New York Times* wrote in a harsh editorial that the agency's failure to uncover the Madoff fraud "exemplifies its lackadaisical approach to enforcing the law on Wall Street."[47]

Researchers at the Syracuse University reported in 2008 that the Bush administration had cut staffing and loosened enforcement at the SEC, leading to a significant drop in investigations for securities fraud in the 2000s.[48]

As the governments of the United States and other nations around the world struggled to confront the financial crisis that began in 2008, many debated what changes in the regulation of the securities industry might be necessary going forward to protect the interests of shareholders and the public. Some called for greater oversight by the SEC and other government agencies of risk taking by financial institutions. For example, in 2004 the SEC had decided to allow investment banks to develop their own models for determining how much money they could borrow, relative to their capital reserves. Some thought that excessive borrowing (called "leverage") had been a major cause of these institutions' troubles, and said that the government—not the banks themselves—should set capital requirements.[49] In June 2009, the Obama administration proposed a series of reforms of the financial regulatory system. These included broad new authority for the SEC, Federal Reserve, Treasury Department, and Commodities Futures Exchange Commission to oversee hedge funds, derivatives markets, insurance companies, credit ratings firms, and other parts of the financial industry. These proposals are further discussed in Chapter 8.[50]

[47] "Standing Accused: A Pillar of Finance and Charity," *The New York Times,* December 13, 2008; "SEC Issues Mea Culpa on Madoff," *The New York Times,* December 17, 2008; "SEC Knew Him as a Friend and Foe," *The New York Times,* December 18, 2008; and "You Mean That Bernie Madoff?" *The New York Times* [editorial], December 19, 2008.

[48] "Federal Cases of Stock Fraud Drop Sharply," *The New York Times,* December 25, 2008. The Syracuse University studies are available at *http://trac.syr.edu.*

[49] "How Bad Regulation Created the Crisis: Former FDIC Chief Laments Wrongheaded Moves by SEC," *The Wall Street Journal,* December 15, 2008.

[50] "The Financial Regulation Plan: Relief and Resignation Spread across Wall Street," and "The Financial Regulation Plan: Key Points," *The Wall Street Journal,* June 18, 2009.

Stockholders and the Corporation

Stockholders have become an increasingly powerful and vocal stakeholder group in corporations. Boards of directors, under intense scrutiny after the recent wave of corporate scandals and business failures, are giving close attention to their duty to protect owners' interests. Reforms in the corporate governance process are under way that will make it easier for them to do so. Owners themselves, especially institutional investors, are pressing directors and management more forcefully to serve stockholder interests. The government, through the Securities and Exchange Commission, has taken important new steps to protect investors and promote fairness and transparency in the financial marketplace.

Clearly, stockholders are a critically important stakeholder group. By providing capital, monitoring corporate performance, assuring the effective operation of stock markets, and bringing new issues to the attention of management, stockholders play a very important role in making the business system work. A major theme of this book is that the relationship between the modern corporation and *all* stakeholders is changing. Corporate leaders have an obligation to manage their companies in ways that attempt to align stockholder interests with those of employees, customers, communities, and others. Balancing these various interests is a prime requirement of modern management. While stockholders are no longer considered the only important stakeholder group, their interests and needs remain central to the successful operation of corporate business.

Summary

- Individuals and institutions own shares of corporations primarily to earn dividends and receive capital gains, although some have social objectives as well. Shareholders are entitled to vote, receive information, select directors, and attempt to shape corporate policies and action.

- In the modern system of corporate governance, boards of directors are responsible for setting overall objectives, selecting and supervising top management, and assuring the integrity of financial accounting. The job of corporate boards has become increasingly difficult and challenging, as directors seek to balance the interests of shareholders, managers, and other stakeholders. Reforms have been proposed to make boards more responsive to shareholders and more independent of management.

- Some observers argue that the compensation of top U.S. executives is justified by performance, and that high salaries provide a necessary incentive for innovation and risk taking in a demanding position. Critics, however, believe that it is too high. In this view, high pay hurts firm competitiveness and undermines employee commitment.

- Shareholders have influenced corporate actions by forming organizations to promote their interests and by filing lawsuits when they feel they have been wronged. They have also organized under the banner of social investment. These efforts have included screening stocks according to social and ethical criteria, and using the voting process to promote shareholder proposals focused on issues of social responsibility.

- Recent enforcement efforts by the Securities and Exchange Corporation have focused on improving the accuracy and transparency of financial information provided to investors. They have also focused on curbing insider trading, which undermines fairness in the marketplace by benefiting those with illicitly acquired information at the expense of those who do not have it. Some believed that the SEC had not acted vigorously enough to prevent the financial crisis, however, and said that new regulations were needed.

Key Terms	board of directors, *321*	institutional investors, *318*	social investment, *330*
	corporate governance, *320*	proxy, *320*	social responsibility
	executive	Securities and Exchange	shareholder resolutions, *331*
	compensation, *325*	Commission (SEC), *333*	stockholders, *317*
	insider trading, *334*	shareholder lawsuits, *332*	stock option, *325*

Internet Resources	www.cii.org	Council of Institutional Investors
	www.ecgi.org	European Corporate Governance Institute
	www.gmiratings.com	GovernanceMetrics International
	www.irrc.org	Investor Responsibility Research Center
	www.nyse.com	New York Stock Exchange
	www.socialfunds.com	Site for socially responsible individual investors
	www.socialinvest.org	Social Investment Forum
	www.thecorporatelibrary.com	The Corporate Library

Discussion Case: *Living Richly*

In late 2008 and early 2009, Citigroup received a series of multibillion-dollar cash infusions from the U.S. government in an effort to stave off total collapse of the bank. By March 2009, the government owned 36 percent of the company and had become its largest shareholder. The question weighing on the minds of both regulators and shareholders was how the world's leading financial institution had gotten into such dire straits—and what it could possibly do to extricate itself.

Before the crisis, Citigroup Inc., often called simply Citi, ranked eighth on the list of *Fortune* 500 corporations—higher than any other bank. Citi had been formed from a series of megamergers, culminating with one with Travelers Group in 1998. At its core was a bank that served retail customers at 2,500 branches in the United States and thousands more around the world. Citigroup also included a consumer finance division; a credit card operation; a brokerage and investment bank; and a unit that handled "alternative" investments in private equity, hedge funds, real estate, and complex asset-backed securities.

In 2001, Citigroup launched a major rebranding campaign under the new slogan, "Live Richly." Television, billboard, and print ads displayed the word "citi" in lowercase blue type, with an eyebrow connecting the two i's, against a plain white background. Each ad presented a quirky aphorism, such as "Holding shares shouldn't be your only form of affection," "A sure way to get rich quick: Count your blessings," and "He who dies with the most toys is still dead." Each was followed with the tag line, "Live Richly." The ads seemed to imply that money couldn't buy love, health, or happiness—while slyly implying that Citi could help you get the things that money *could* buy.

In 2003, newly appointed CEO Charles Prince, with the support of the board of directors, began pushing into riskier activities in an effort to improve Citi's earnings. Like a number of other financial institutions at the time, Citi began buying mortgages and other consumer debt and repackaging them into securities called collateralized debt obligations, or CDOs. It both sold these to investors and also traded them for its own accounts—eventually acquiring over $40 billion worth of the risky instruments. Initially, the strategy was highly successful: Citi earned $500 million in fees from issuing CDOs in 2005 alone.

Citi's managers and traders were handsomely rewarded as the revenues rolled in. "Management and traders are compensated on booking profits," explained a finance professor. "It didn't take a long time [for them] to figure out if you undertake very risky activities, you get higher bonuses." In 2006, CEO Prince earned $24 million. Top producers were rewarded with bonuses that could reach even higher than the CEO's. "I just think senior managers got addicted to the revenues and arrogant about the risks they were running," said a person who had worked in the CDO group.

Where was the board of directors as Citi plunged into increasingly risky activities? Some thought that Citigroup's 15-person board—a number of whom were CEOs of other firms—just did not have enough time to manage such a complex business. Others said that the directors were simply going along with how many financial institutions were operating at the time—a strategy that seemed to be working. "The universe of people who misread the risks . . . is very broad. You could extend it to the rating agencies, to managements, to regulators," said a representative of the U.S. Chamber of Commerce.

In 2007, the game began to unravel as the value of the CDOs on Citi's books began to fall, and the firm was forced to announce billions of dollars of write-downs on bad assets. In November, Prince resigned—walking away with a bonus of $12 million and stock then valued at $68 million. As the company's stock price fell precipitously, angry institutional shareholders demanded changes. The AFL-CIO (a labor union federation) and other shareholders pushed for the removal of director Michael Armstrong, former CEO of AT&T, who had headed the risk and audit committees of the board. Armstrong stepped down shortly afterward. At the 2008 annual meeting, the California State Teachers' Retirement System and other institutional investors withheld votes from eight directors, saying they had failed to manage risk and excessive pay at the company.

As the U.S. government poured money into Citi to keep it solvent, it strengthened its regulatory control. The government permanently stationed examiners at the bank and became actively involved in strategic discussions. Regulators urged managers to reduce risk and increase capital reserves, and demanded veto power over executive compensation. In February 2009, Vikram Pandit, who had succeeded Prince as CEO, said he would take a salary of $1 a year, with no bonus, until the bank became profitable again.

In 2008, Citi got a new ad agency and returned to its slogan from the late 1970s: "The Citi never sleeps."

Sources: "Citigroup Saw No Red Flags Even as It Made Bolder Bets," *The New York Times,* November 23, 2008; "SEC to Examine Boards' Role in Financial Crisis," *Washington Post,* February 20, 2009; "Citigroup: Marketing Campaign Case Studies," *http://marketing-case-studies.blogspot.com;* "Wake up and Smell the Subterfuge," Salon.com, February 4, 2002; "Citigroup Board Revamp Signals Heavy U.S. Hand," Bloomberg.com, March 2, 2009; "We're Buying Citi, but What Has It Been Selling Us?" *Washington Post,* March 1, 2009; "U.S. Rachets Up Citi Oversight," *The Wall Street Journal,* December 17, 2008; "Credit Crisis: Citigroup Board Re-Elected Amid Protest," *The Wall Street Journal,* April 23, 2008.

Discussion Questions

1. Did the size and structure of compensation received by the CEO and other top managers contribute to the problems at Citigroup? What reforms of the compensation system would you recommend, and why?

2. Did the actions or inactions of the board of directors contribute to the problems at Citigroup? What changes in governance would you recommend, and why?

3. Do you feel that institutional shareholders took adequate steps to protect their interests? What more, if anything, could they have done?

4. What is the appropriate role, if any, of the government in the management of a financial institution at risk of failure? What steps should government regulators take now?

CHAPTER FIFTEEN

Consumer Protection

Safeguarding consumers while continuing to supply them with the goods and services they want, at the prices they want, is a prime social responsibility of business. Many companies recognize that providing customers with excellent service and product quality is an effective, as well as ethical, business strategy. Consumers, through their organizations, have advocated for their rights to safety, to be informed, to choose, to be heard, and to privacy. Government agencies serve as watchdogs for consumers, supplementing the actions taken by consumers to protect themselves and the actions of socially responsible corporations.

This Chapter Focuses on These Key Learning Objectives:

- Analyzing the reasons for consumer advocacy and the methods consumer organizations use to advance their interests.
- Knowing the five major rights of consumers.
- Assessing the ways in which government regulatory agencies protect consumers and what kinds of products are most likely to be regulated.
- Determining how consumer privacy online can best be protected.
- Examining how the courts protect consumers and efforts by businesses to change product liability laws.
- Evaluating how socially responsible corporations can proactively respond to consumer needs.

In January 2009, the Food and Drug Administration and the Justice Department opened a criminal investigation into the actions of the Peanut Corporation of America (PCA). In one of the worst food contamination cases in U.S. history, 19,000 people in 43 states (half of them children) had become ill—and nine had died—after eating salmonella-tainted peanut butter. Public health investigators traced the suspect peanut butter to PCA's processing plant in Blakely, Georgia, where they found rodents, a leaking roof, roasting machines that were not hot enough to kill germs, and demoralized temporary workers earning the minimum wage. Salmonella, a potentially deadly bacterium found in human and animal feces, was growing on the plant's floors. It turned out that the company itself—in its own internal tests—had found salmonella in its peanut butter no fewer than 12 times since 2007, but had continued to ship its tainted products. The president's press secretary called these revelations "beyond disturbing for millions of parents," and many called for stronger food safety regulations.[1]

Users of Facebook, the popular social networking site, were startled to learn in early 2009 that the site's administrators had changed their "terms of service." Under the old rules, when one of Facebook's 175 million users closed his or her account, the site's rights to any content the person had uploaded would expire. Under the new rules, users could shut down their own pages, but any content they had posted on another user's site— say, a photo or video sent to a friend—would remain. Many users immediately expressed their displeasure. "Make sure you never upload anything you don't feel comfortable giving away forever, because it's Facebook's now," said a writer for the blog "The Consumerist." Thousands joined online groups to protest the rules, claiming that Facebook had violated their privacy and rights to their own words and images. Just a few days later, Mark Zuckerberg, Facebook's young cofounder and CEO, announced that the company had gone back to the old rules, and promised that the site's users would have "a lot of input" in crafting any future changes.[2]

What would happen if businesses could literally read your mind to determine why you choose to buy some products or services, but not others? A new field, called *neuromarketing,* does just that. Scientists scan the brains of volunteers, using functional magnetic resonance imaging (fMRI) machines, while asking questions, showing them images and videos, and allowing them to examine products. As the volunteers respond, the fMRI records how the parts of their brains associated with pleasurable feelings, memory, and comprehension react. One such study showed, for example, that product placements integrated into a television program were more effective than stand-alone ads, because viewers were paying more attention at the time. Many leading firms—including Unilever, Intel, McDonald's, Procter & Gamble, and MTV—already use this technology to understand better how to boost the effectiveness of advertising. But some consumer activists sounded a warning. "We already have an epidemic of marketing-related diseases," said the director of an advertising watchdog group.[3]

These three examples demonstrate some of the complexities of serving consumers today. Companies face challenging—and often conflicting—demands to produce a safe and high-quality product or service, keep prices down, protect privacy, prevent fraud

---

[1] "Peanut Plant Recall Leads to Criminal Investigation," *The New York Times,* January 31, 2009; "Peanut Case Shows Holes in Food Safety Net," *The New York Times,* February 9, 2009; "Dangerous Food" [editorial], *The New York Times,* February 17, 2009.

[2] This controversy can be followed on *http://blog.facebook.com* and *www.consumerist.org.*

[3] "Why Buy? The Role of Neuromarketing in Understanding Consumer Behavior," *Marketing Matters,* February 27, 2009; "Brain Sells," *Time,* September 10, 2006; and "Marketing to Your Mind," *Time,* January 19, 2007. CBS's *Sixty Minutes* aired a feature on neuromarketing under the title "Tech Reads Your Mind" on January 5, 2009.

and manipulation, and meet the changing expectations of diverse customers around the world. This chapter examines these issues and the various ways that consumers and their advocates, government regulators, the courts, and proactive business firms have dealt with them.

Advocacy for Consumer Interests

As long as business has existed—since the ancient beginnings of commerce and trade—consumers have tried to protect their interests when they go to the marketplace to buy goods and services. They have haggled over prices, taken a careful look at the goods they were buying, compared the quality and prices of products offered by other sellers, and complained loudly when they felt cheated by shoddy products. So consumer self-reliance—best summed up by the Latin phrase *caveat emptor,* meaning "let the buyer beware"—has always been one form of consumer protection and is still practiced today.

However, the increasing complexity of economic life has led to organized, collective efforts by consumers to safeguard their own rights in many nations. These organized activities are usually called consumerism or the **consumer movement**.

Today, many organized groups actively promote and speak for the interests of millions of consumers. In the United States, one organization alone, the Consumer Federation of America, brings together 300 nonprofit groups to espouse the consumer viewpoint; they represent more than 50 million Americans. Other active U.S. consumer advocacy organizations include Public Citizen, the National Consumers League, the Public Interest Research Group (PIRG), and the consumer protection unit of the American Association for Retired People (AARP).

Many other nations have also experienced movements for consumer rights, as illustrated by the following example:

> In central Europe, a consumer movement blossomed after the fall of communism. In Latvia, for instance, activists formed a national federation of consumer clubs, joining groups that had sprung up independently in many cities and towns. By the late 2000s, the Latvian Consumers Protection Federation was handling consumer complaints, publishing a consumer guide, and lobbying for better consumer protection legislation.[4]

Consumers International is an international nongovernmental organization that represents more than 220 consumer groups in 115 nations. Headquartered in London, it has offices in Asia, Latin America, and Africa. Its growth since 1960 has paralleled the expansion of global trade and the integration of many developing nations into the world economy, as discussed in Chapter 6.

> The most effective consumer advocacy organizations today harness a wide range of technologies to get the word out to their constituents. One such organization is Consumers Union (CU), which conducts extensive tests on selected consumer products and services. CU publishes the results of its tests, with ratings on a brand-name basis, online at *www.consumerreports.org,* which is supported through subscriptions. In addition, the organization's extensive Web site provides a great deal of free information. Consumers Union also hosts online chats on a

---

[4] Online at *www.pateretaja-celvedis.lv/english/club.htm*

range of consumer rights topics. In a recent forum, a participant named Bob complained, "Why is my car's hands-free phone shackled to Verizon? I love the built-in, hands-free cell phone in my Saturn Vue, but Saturn did me wrong by making Verizon the only wireless carrier I can use with it. It's time for all such exclusive deals between wireless carriers and cell phone makers to be banned." His comment provoked a lively online conversation. Consumers Union also offers RSS feeds on various topics and a service that alerts supporters by e-mail so they can make their voices heard electronically on various legislative issues relevant to consumer rights.[5]

Reasons for the Consumer Movement

The consumer movement exists because consumers want to be treated fairly and honestly in the marketplace. Some business practices do not meet this standard. Consumers may be harmed by abuses such as unfairly high prices, unreliable and unsafe products, excessive or deceptive advertising claims, and the promotion of products known to be harmful to human health.

Additional reasons for the existence of the consumer movement are the following:

- *Complex products have enormously complicated the choices consumers need to make when they go shopping.* For this reason, consumers today are more dependent on business for product quality than ever before. Because many products, from smart phones to hybrid automobiles, are so complex, most consumers have no way to judge at the time of purchase whether their quality is satisfactory. In these circumstances, unscrupulous business firms can take advantage of customers.

- *Services, as well as products, have become more specialized and difficult to judge.* When choosing health plans, Internet service providers, credit cards, or colleges, most consumers do not have adequate guides for evaluating whether they are good or bad. They can rely on word-of-mouth experiences of others, but this information may not be entirely reliable. Or the consumer may not be told that service will be expensive or hard to obtain.

- *When businesses try to sell either products or services through advertising, claims may be inflated or they may appeal to emotions.* Abercrombie & Fitch, the fashion retailer, for example, has been criticized for promoting its clothing to teens in magazine-style catalogs that are packed with sexual imagery, like scantily clad young men playing with water hoses. In the process, consumers do not always receive reliable and relevant information about products and services.

- *Some businesses have ignored product safety.* Business has not always given sufficient attention to product safety. Certain products, such as automobiles, pharmaceutical drugs, medical devices, processed foods, and children's toys, may be particularly susceptible to causing harm. The case of tainted peanut butter, mentioned in the opening example of this chapter, is just one of the latest incidents of unsafe food.

The Rights of Consumers

The central purpose of the consumer movement around the world is to protect the rights of consumers in the marketplace. It aims to make consumer power an effective counterbalance to the power of business firms that sell goods and services.

---

[5] See *www.consumersunion.org.*

As business firms grow in size and market power, they increasingly acquire the ability to dominate marketplace transactions with their customers. As online shopping has become ubiquitous, moreover, they can entice customers at almost any time and any place. Frequently, they can dictate prices. Typically, their advertisements sway consumers to buy one product or service rather than another. If large enough, they may share the market with only a few other large companies, thereby weakening some of the competitive protections enjoyed by consumers if business firms are smaller and more numerous. The economic influence and power of business firms may therefore become a problem for consumers unless ways can be found to promote an equivalent consumer power.

Consumer advocates argue that consumers are entitled to five core rights:

1. *The right to be informed:* to be protected against fraudulent, deceitful, or grossly misleading information, advertising, and labeling, and to be given the facts to make an informed purchasing decision.

2. *The right to safety:* to be protected against the marketing of goods that are hazardous to health or life.

3. *The right to choose:* to be assured, wherever possible, of access to a variety of products and services at competitive prices; and in those industries in which competition is not workable and government regulation is substituted, to be assured of satisfactory quality and service at fair prices.

4. *The right to be heard:* to be assured that consumer interests will receive full and sympathetic consideration in the formulation of government policy and fair and expeditious treatment in the courts.

5. *The right to privacy:* to be assured that information disclosed in the course of a commercial transaction, such as health conditions, financial status, or identity, is not shared with others unless authorized.

Consumers' efforts to protect their own rights, through direct advocacy, are complemented by the actions of government regulators, the courts, and businesses themselves.

How Government Protects Consumers

The role of government in protecting consumers is extensive in many nations. This section will describe legal protections afforded consumers in the United States and offer some comparisons with other countries.

Goals of Consumer Laws

Figure 15.1 lists some of the safeguards provided by U.S. **consumer protection laws**. Taken together, these safeguards reflect the goals of government policymakers and regulators in the context of the five rights of consumers outlined above. Many of these safeguards are also embedded in the laws of other nations.

First, some laws are intended to provide consumers with better information when making purchases. Consumers can make more rational choices when they have accurate information about the product. For example, the laws requiring health warnings on cigarettes and alcoholic beverages broaden the information consumers have about these items. Manufacturers, retailers, and importers must spell out warranties (a guarantee or assurance by the seller) in clear language and give consumers the right to sue if they are not honored. The Truth in Lending Act requires lenders to inform borrowers of the annual rate of interest to be charged, plus related fees and service charges. A recent case

FIGURE 15.1
Major Consumer Protections Specified by Consumer Laws

Information protections

Hazardous home appliances must carry a warning label.

Home products must carry a label detailing contents.

Automobiles must carry a label showing detailed breakdown of price and all related costs.

Credit loans require lenders to disclose all relevant credit information about rate of interest, penalties, and so forth.

Tobacco advertisements and products must carry a health warning label.

Alcoholic beverages must carry a health warning label.

All costs related to real estate transactions must be disclosed.

Warranties must specify the terms of the guarantee and the buyer's rights.

False and deceptive advertising can be prohibited.

Food and beverage labels must show complete information.

Food advertising must not make false claims about nutrition.

Direct hazard protections

Hazardous toys and games for children are banned from sale.

Safety standards for motor vehicles are required.

National and state speed limits are specified.

Hazardous, defective, and ineffective products can be recalled under pressure from the EPA, CPSC, NHTSA, and FDA.

Pesticide residue in food is allowed only if it poses a negligible risk.

Pricing protections

Unfair pricing, monopolistic practices, and noncompetitive acts are regulated by the FTC and Justice Department and by states.

Liability protections

When injured by a product, consumers can seek legal redress.

Privacy protections

Limited collection of information online from and about children is allowed.

Other protections

No discrimination in the extension of credit is allowed.

in which mortgage lenders were accused of violating truth in lending rules is presented in Exhibit 15.A.

Deceptive advertising is illegal in most countries. Manufacturers may not make false or misleading claims about their own product or a competitor's product, withhold relevant information, or create unreasonable expectations. In the United States, the Federal Trade Commission (FTC) enforces the laws prohibiting deceptive advertising.

For example, in 2008 Airborne Health Inc.—the maker of the Airborne dietary supplement, which claimed to protect against colds and germs on airplanes— paid around $30 million in refunds to customers and attorneys' fees to settle charges brought by the FTC. Regulators found that "there [was] no credible evidence that Airborne products . . . [would] reduce the severity or duration of colds, or provide any tangible benefit for people who are exposed to germs in crowded places," said the director of the FTC's bureau of consumer protection.[6]

[6] "Airborne Settles with FTC over Supplement," *The Wall Street Journal*, August 15, 2008.

Did Countrywide—the largest mortgage lender in the United States until its collapse in July 2008—defraud and deceive its customers during the housing bubble of the mid-2000s?

In late 2008, the attorneys general of 11 states settled with Countrywide in the largest predatory lending case in U.S. history. Predatory lending—which is prohibited under federal and many state laws—occurs when a lender, such as a bank or mortgage company, uses unfair, deceptive, or fraudulent practices when making a loan. The states' lawsuit charged that Countrywide had misled its customers about the terms of their home loans, pushing them into loans they could not afford. For example, it had used "bait and switch" tactics to put borrowers who thought they were getting fixed-rate loans into riskier payment-optional loans (in which the amount owed could increase over time) or ones with initially low "teaser" rates that later jumped much higher.

As part of the settlement, Countrywide—which had been acquired by Bank of America in July 2008—was required to modify the terms of many of the loans it made between 2004 and 2007, at a cost of over $8 billion. Nearly 400,000 mortgage holders were expected to benefit. "Countrywide must now bail out homeowners it recklessly misled into mortgages doomed to fail," said one of the state attorneys general who had brought the suit.

Sources: "Countrywide Settles Fraud Cases for $8.4 Billion," Bloomberg.com, October 6, 2008; and "Bank of America in Settlement Worth over $8 Billion: Up to 390,000 Borrowers Covered in Deal with State Attorneys General over Risky Loans Originated by Countrywide Financial," *The Wall Street Journal,* October 6, 2008.

Deceptive advertising is also illegal in Europe, where, for example, U.K. regulators recently slapped a huge fine on the French insurance company AXA Sun Life for misleading promotion of various life insurance products.[7]

U.S. law also requires food manufacturers to adopt a uniform nutrition label, specifying the amount of calories, fat, salt, and other nutrients contained in packaged, canned, and bottled foods. Labels must list the amount of trans fat—partially hydrogenated vegetable oils believed to contribute to heart disease—in cakes, cookies, and snack foods. Nutritional information about fresh fruits and vegetables, as well as fish, must be posted in supermarkets. Strict rules also define what can properly be labeled "organic."

A second aim of consumer legislation is to protect consumers against possible hazards. As the opening example about contaminated peanut butter showed, consumers can be injured—and even killed—by dangerous products. U.S. laws seek to safeguard consumers in many ways, such as requiring warnings about possible side effects of pharmaceutical drugs, placing limits on flammable fabrics, restricting pesticide residues in fresh and processed foods, banning lead-based paints, and requiring regular inspections to eliminate contaminated meats. In 2008, following a major recall of toys contaminated with lead paint, Congress passed the Consumer Product Safety Improvement Act, which required that toys and infant products be tested before sale and gave regulators more resources to work with.[8]

The third and fourth goals of consumer laws are to promote competitive pricing and consumer choice. When competitors secretly agree to divide up markets among themselves, or when a single company dominates a market, this artificially raises prices and limits consumer choice. Both federal and state antitrust laws forbid these practices, as discussed in Chapter 8. Competitive pricing also was promoted by the deregulation of the railroad, airline, trucking, telecommunications, banking, and other industries in the 1970s and 1980s and of the telecommunications, ocean shipping, and parts of the financial services industries in the late 1990s. Before deregulation, government agencies frequently

[7] "U.K. Fines AXA Unit for Misleading Advertising," *Asian Wall Street Journal,* December 22, 2004.

[8] "Consumer Groups Applaud President for Signing Strong Product Safety Bill into Law," August 14, 2008, *www.uspirg.org.*

held prices artificially high and, by limiting the number of new competitors, shielded existing businesses from competition.

A fifth and final goal of consumer laws is to protect privacy. This issue has recently received heightened regulatory attention, as discussed later in this chapter. The Children's Online Privacy Protection Act, which took effect in 2000, limits the collection of information online from and about children under the age of 13. In 2003, the Federal Trade Commission established a "do not call" list to protect individuals from unwanted telemarketing calls at home. Such calls to a person's mobile phone are also illegal. Other threats to privacy caused by the emergence of new technologies are discussed later in this chapter and in Chapter 12.

Major Consumer Protection Agencies

Figure 15.2 depicts the principal consumer protection agencies that operate at the federal level of the U.S. government, along with their major areas of responsibility. The oldest of the six is the Department of Justice, whose Antitrust Division dates to the end of the 19th century. The Food and Drug Administration was founded in the first decade of the 20th century. The Federal Trade Commission was established in 1914 and has been given additional powers to protect consumers over the years, including in the area of online privacy. Three of the agencies—the Consumer Product Safety Commission, the National Highway Traffic Safety Administration, and the National Transportation Safety Board—were created during the great wave of consumer regulations in the 1960s and early 1970s. Not included in Figure 15.2 are the Department of Agriculture, which has specific responsibility for the

FIGURE 15.2 **Major Federal Consumer Protection Agencies and Their Main Responsibilities**

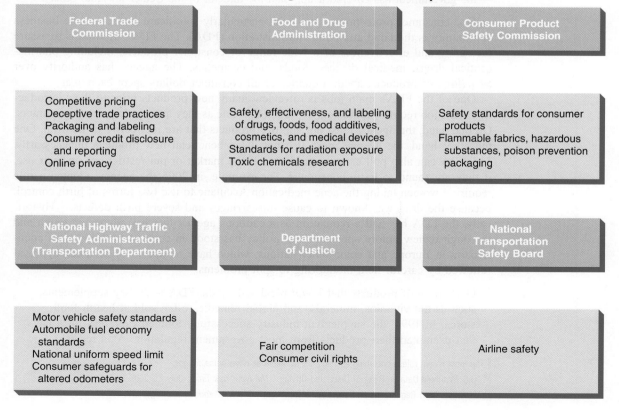

inspection of meat and poultry, and the Environmental Protection Agency, which has authority over genetically modified food and some chemicals that may affect consumers.

The Civil Rights Division of the Department of Justice enforces the provisions of the Civil Rights Act that prohibit discrimination against consumers. For example, in 2000, Adam's Mark settled a class-action lawsuit, brought by the U.S. Justice Department, charging that the upscale hotel chain had systematically discriminated against African-American customers. Although admitting no wrongdoing, Adam's Mark agreed to pay $8 million.

The National Highway Traffic Safety Administration (NHTSA) affects many consumers directly through its authority over automobile safety. For example, the agency develops regulations for car air bags, devices that inflate rapidly during a collision, preventing the occupant from striking the steering wheel or dashboard. Driver and passenger-side air bags have long been required as standard equipment on most cars. In 2007, the agency adopted new rules requiring all new cars also to have side air bags by 2012. Eventually, the NHTSA said it would require so-called "smart" air bags that would adjust the force of deployment according to the weight of the occupant.[9]

> In 2009, two consumer advocacy groups—the Center for Auto Safety and Public Citizen—filed a Freedom of Information Act lawsuit against the NHTSA to obtain hundreds of pages of research on the dangers of using cell phones while driving. The former NHTSA director said he had been pressured to withhold the documents to avoid angering members of Congress, who thought the agency should stay out of issues covered by state legislation. The agency's research showed that drivers distracted by their cell phones had caused 955 fatalities and 240,000 accidents in a single year. "We're looking at a problem that could be as bad as drunk driving and the government has covered it up," said the director of the Center for Auto Safety.[10]

One consumer protection agency with particularly significant impact on the business community is the Food and Drug Administration (FDA). The FDA's mission is to assure the safety and effectiveness of a wide range of consumer products, including pharmaceutical drugs, medical devices, foods, and cosmetics. The agency has authority over *$1 trillion* of products, about a quarter of all consumer dollars spent each year.

One of the FDA's main jobs is to review many new products prior to their introduction. This job requires regulators to walk a thin line as they attempt to protect consumers. On one hand, the agency must not approve products that are ineffective or harmful. One the other hand, the agency must also not delay beneficial new products unnecessarily. The FDA can also pull existing products off the market or put restrictions on their use, if they are found to harm consumers. For example, in 2005 the agency adopted a rule requiring women taking the acne medication Accutane to use two forms of birth control, because the drug was known to cause miscarriages and severe birth defects.[11] Historically, the FDA has had a reputation as a cautious agency that has advocated tough and thorough review before approval. This policy has stood in contrast to those of its counterparts in Europe and some other nations, which have tended to favor quick approval followed by careful field monitoring to spot problems.

> One group of products that is *not* regulated by the FDA is dietary supplements, such as the vitamins, minerals, and herbal remedies often sold at health food stores. In 1994, the supplement industry successfully lobbied Congress for a law that exempted their products from most government regulation. As a result,

---

[9] The most recent rules concerning air bags are available at *www.nhtsa.dot.gov.*

[10] "U.S. Withheld Data on Risks of Distracted Driving," *The New York Times,* July 21, 2009.

[11] "FDA Puts New Regulations on Severe Acne Treatment," *The New York Times,* August 13, 2005.

Exhibit 15.B

The Debate over a New Consumer Protection Agency

In June 2009, the president proposed the creation of a new Consumer Financial Protection Agency (CFPA) to regulate financial products such as mortgages, home equity loans, credit cards, and payday loans. The proposal immediately attracted a great deal of attention—both positive and negative.

The new agency was originally the idea of Elizabeth Warren, a professor at the Harvard Law School. Warren's research focused on the devastating effects of credit card and other abusive lending practices on ordinary people. She argued that the government agencies in charge of regulating banks—such as the Federal Reserve and the Comptroller of the Currency—had a conflict of interest, because they were responsible *both* for the soundness of the banks and for protecting their customers. (Actions that would help the banks' bottom lines might not be best for borrowers.) The proposed agency would be solely responsible for protecting consumers.

Backers of the CFPA said it would shield consumers from predatory mortgages, sky-high credit card fees, and other abusive practices by financial institutions. It would also protect the economy as a whole, by restraining banks from making the kind of risky loans that had contributed to the crash of 2008–2009. "It's obvious from the history of the last 20 years that the regulators never understood that protecting consumers is also a way of ensuring the safety and soundness of financial institutions," said the president of the national Community Reinvestment Coalition.

But others were vigorously opposed. The Chamber of Commerce, many banks (including JP Morgan Chase and Wells Fargo), and the Securities Industry and Financial Markets Association (a trade group) all geared up to lobby against the bill. One member of Congress said he found it "offensive" that consumers were considered so "intellectually deficient" that they could not judge for themselves if a loan was risky or not. Another Congress member said the legislation would create a "fractured system [of regulation] where everybody can point fingers and nobody gets the job done."

Sources: "Banks Brace for Fight over an Agency Meant to Bolster Consumer Protection," June 18, 2009; "Banks Balk at Agency Meant to Aid Consumers," July 1, 2009; "Office of Aid to Consumers Draws Fire and Support," July 15, 2009; "Financial Invention vs. Consumer Protection," July 19, 2009; "Sharks Circle in Congress," July 20, 2009,—all *The New York Times;* and "Financial Regulation: Industry Objections Increasing," *BusinessWeek,* June 26, 2009.

unlike pharmaceutical drugs, supplements do not have to be proven safe or effective before being brought to market. This issue received fresh attention after several people, including a professional athlete, died after taking ephedra, an herbal stimulant. Saying that ephedra "appears not to be safe," the editor of the *Journal of the American Medical Association* called for regulation of all supplements claiming a biological function.[12]

The FDA's role in the approval and subsequent review of Vioxx, a pain medication withdrawn from the market by its manufacturer after it was associated with heart attacks and strokes, is discussed in a case at the end of this textbook.

All six government regulatory agencies shown in Figure 15.2 are authorized by law to intervene directly into the very center of free market activities, if that is considered necessary to protect consumers. In other words, consumer protection laws and agencies substitute government-mandated standards and the decisions of government officials for decision making by private buyers and sellers.

In 2009, Congress debated a proposal by President Obama to create a powerful new consumer regulatory body, to be called the Consumer Financial Protection Agency. Some of the diverse views on this proposal are presented in Exhibit 15.B. The debate over whether government should become involved in protecting consumer privacy is discussed in the next section of this chapter.

[12] Marion Nestle, *Food Politics: How the Food Industry Influences Nutrition and Health* (Berkeley: University of California Press, 2002), Part IV, "Deregulating Dietary Supplements"; and "Ephedra under Siege from New Quarters," *San Francisco Chronicle,* March 11, 2003.

Consumer Privacy in the Digital Age

In the early 21st century, rapidly evolving information technologies have given new urgency to the broad issue of **consumer privacy**. Shoppers have always been concerned that information they reveal in the course of a sales transaction—for example, their credit card or driver's license numbers—might be misused. But in recent years, new technologies have increasingly enabled businesses to collect and use vast amounts of personal data about their customers and potential customers. The danger is not only that this information might rarely be used fraudulently, but also that its collection represents an unwarranted incursion into personal privacy.

Smart phones, such as Apple's iPhone and RIM's Blackberry, enable people on the move to do everything from check their e-mail, to make a bid on eBay, to search for local eateries. These services offer great convenience, but also risk an invasion of privacy. Each time people use an application on their smart phones, the provider learns something about their state of mind. This has the potential to lead to directed marketing, such as a list of restaurant deals in the vicinity around lunch or dinnertime. So far, this happens only when a user agrees—as they might to an iPhone application offered by Amazon that searches for the nearest location and lowest price for an item of the person's choice. But what if applications developers did this without the user's permission? Most marketers believe that people will not tolerate targeted ads on their mobile phones unless they have asked for them.[13]

Businesses can also collect a great deal of information about individuals when they shop or surf for information online. Many Web sites use *cookies,* identifying markers placed on a user's computer hard drive, to identify the user during each subsequent visit and to build profiles of users' behavior over time. If sold to advertisers, this information can be used to target online solicitations. Cloud computing—applications such as e-mail, photo or video storage, or data backup, where both the software and data are stored centrally on the provider's servers rather than the user's computer—also presents privacy concerns. A 2008 study by the Pew Internet and American Life Project found that while users liked the ease and convenience of cloud computing, most were very concerned that data they stored online might be sold or used for targeted ads.[14]

The dilemma of how best to protect consumer privacy in the digital age, while still fostering legitimate commerce, has generated a wide-ranging debate. Three major solutions have been proposed: consumer self-help, industry self-regulation, and privacy legislation.

- *Consumer self-help.* In this view, the best solution is for users to employ technologies that enable them to protect their own privacy. For example, special software can help manage cookies, encryption can protect e-mail messages, and surfing through intermediary sites can provide user anonymity. "We have to develop mechanisms that allow consumers to control information about themselves," commented a representative of the Center for Democracy and Technology, a civil liberties group.[15] Critics of this approach argue that many unsophisticated Web surfers are unaware of these

[13] "Next Net," *BusinessWeek,* March 9, 2009.

[14] Pew Internet and American Life Project, "Use of Cloud Computing and Services," September 2008. A summary of polling data on online privacy may be found at the Web site of the Electronic Privacy Information Center, *http://epic.org/privacy/survey.*

[15] More information about privacy protection for consumers is available at *www.cdt.org* (Center for Democracy and Technology) and *www.epic.org/privacy* (Electronic Privacy Information Center).

technologies, or even of the need for them. Moreover, tools for protecting privacy can always be defeated by even more powerful technologies.

- *Industry self-regulation.* Many Internet-related businesses have argued that they should be allowed to regulate themselves. In their view, the best approach would be for businesses to adopt voluntary policies for protecting the privacy of individuals' information disclosed during electronic transactions. One advantage of the self-regulation approach is that companies, presumably sophisticated about their own technology, might do the best job of defining technical standards. Critics of this approach feel, however, that industry rules would inevitably be too weak. One survey found that although most large companies operating online had some kind of voluntary privacy policy, only 17 percent of Web sites were rated "excellent" overall, and nearly three-quarters were rated "poor" on reusing personal data for marketing purposes.[16]

- *Privacy legislation.* Some favor new government regulations protecting consumer privacy online. In 2009, the Federal Trade Commission issued new guidelines that would give consumers more information about how advertisers collect and use data about their online activity. Among other things, the guidelines would allow consumers to *opt out* of ads tailored to their own Web searches—a practice known as behavioral targeting. The agency said that it might later push for new laws on online privacy. Consumer privacy protections are generally stronger in the European Union than in the United States; in the EU, the right to privacy is strongly ingrained in both law and culture.[17]

Any approach to online privacy would face the challenge of how best to balance the legitimate interests of consumers—to protect their privacy—and of business—to deliver increasingly customized products and services in the digital age.

A related issue—protecting Internet users from e-mail spam—is profiled in Exhibit 15.C.

Special Issue: Product Liability

Who is at fault when a consumer is harmed by a product or service? This is a complex legal and ethical issue. The term **product liability** refers to the legal responsibility of a firm for injuries caused by something it made or sold. Under laws in the United States and some other countries, consumers have the right to sue and to collect damages if harmed by an unsafe product. Consumer advocates and trial attorneys have generally supported these legal protections, saying they are necessary both to compensate injured victims and to deter irresponsible behavior by companies in the first place. Some in the business community, by contrast, have argued that courts and juries have unfairly favored plaintiffs, and they have called for reforms of product liability laws. This section describes this debate and recent changes in relevant U.S. law. The special issue of whether or not food companies and restaurants should be held liable for obesity is profiled in the discussion case at the end of this chapter.

Strict Liability

In the United States, the legal system has generally looked favorably on consumer claims. Under the doctrine of **strict liability**, courts have held that manufacturers are responsible for injuries resulting from use of their products, whether or not the manufacturers were negligent or breached a warranty. That is, they may be found to be liable, whether

---

[16] The Customer Respect Group, "2005 Privacy Research Report."

[17] "FTC Online Privacy Guidelines Faulted," *BusinessWeek*, February 13, 2009.

By the late 2000s, the amount of "spam" cluttering electronic mailboxes—and even cell phones—had reached unprecedented proportions. Spam has been defined as unsolicited bulk e-mail or text messages, where the sender has no relationship to the recipient. By 2008, spammers were sending 164 billion unsolicited e-mails *a month*—97 percent of the total, according to research by Cisco. Much of it was offensive, ranging from sex ads to fraudulent business offers—and some was downright dangerous, such as invitations to Web sites that would infect the visitor's computer with malicious code. Spam was often disguised with a subject line like "order confirmation" so that people would open the message before realizing it was unwanted. "Spam is now totally out of control," said an anti-spam engineer for Symantec.

What should be done about all this spam? In 2004, a new federal law called the CAN-SPAM Act went into effect. (It is also discussed in Chapter 12.) The law banned deceptive subject lines and routing information, required that commercial e-mail be identified as an advertisement, and ordered senders to give recipients a way to opt out of future e-mails. It also permitted the government to prosecute spammers and gave ISPs such as America Online and Yahoo! the right to sue. The law led to some high-profile convictions—such as that of Adam Vitale, who was sent to jail for two and a half years for spamming millions of AOL users. But some said the law was too weak, and should be amended to allow recipients to opt in (rather than opt out) to commercial messages. Others said that even strict laws would never be enough. "[Legislation] is rather futile anyways, because the attackers are so advanced in their threats, and it's so hard to detect where they're coming from," said one chief technology officer. Many thought that nothing could substitute for powerful anti-spam filters—and users vigilant about what mail they did, and did not, respond to.

Sources: "CAN-SPAM: What Went Wrong?" *Network World,* October 6, 2008; and "Some Federal Cybercrime Crackdowns in 2008," *USA Today,* November 17, 2008. The Federal Trade Commission's Web site on spam may be found at *www.ftc.gov/spam.*

or not they knowingly did anything wrong. Consumers can also prevail in court even if they were partly at fault for their injuries. The following well-publicized case illustrates the extent to which businesses can be held responsible under this strict standard.

An 81-year-old woman was awarded $2.9 million by a jury in Albuquerque, New Mexico, for burns suffered when she spilled a cup of hot coffee in her lap. The woman, who had purchased the coffee at a McDonald's drive-through window, was burned when she tried to open the lid as she sat in her car. In the 1994 case, McDonald's argued that customers like their coffee steaming, that its cups warned drinkers that the contents are hot, and that the woman was to blame for spilling the coffee herself. But jurors disagreed, apparently swayed by arguments that the woman's burns were severe—requiring skin grafts and a seven-day hospital stay—and by evidence that McDonald's had not cooled down its coffee even after receiving many earlier complaints. McDonald's appealed the jury's verdict and later settled the case with the woman for an undisclosed amount.[18]

In this case, McDonald's was held liable for damages even though it provided a warning and the customer's actions contributed to her burns.

Huge product liability settlements, like the McDonald's case, are well publicized, but they remain the exception. According to the U.S. Department of Justice, one in five noncriminal cases was a tort (liability) case, and plaintiffs (the people suing companies) won

[18] "How a Jury Decided that a Coffee Spill Is Worth $2.9 Million," *The Wall Street Journal,* September 1, 1994; and "McDonald's Settles Lawsuit over Burn from Coffee," *The Wall Street Journal,* December 2, 1994.

34 percent of product liability cases filed. The average settlement in all tort cases was $201,000, although a few settlements were much higher.[19]

The product liability systems of other nations differ significantly from that of the United States. In Europe, for example, judges, not juries, hear cases. Awards are usually smaller, partly because the medical expenses of victims are already covered under national health insurance, and partly because punitive damages are not allowed. In a few cases, however, companies have faced tough penalties. Baxter International, the health care company, was forced to pay over $250,000 each to the families of 10 kidney patients in Spain. They had died after receiving dialysis on machines equipped with Baxter filters that caused lethal gas bubbles to form in their blood.[20]

> Historically, product liability cases have been exceedingly rare in China. But that began to change in 2009, in the wake of China's tainted-milk scandal. The previous year, almost 300,000 children became ill—and at least six died—after drinking baby formula contaminated by the industrial chemical melamine. Milk producers had apparently knowingly added the chemical to boost the formula's protein content. More than 200 families brought suit against the formula companies, even thought the government had sought to keep the case out of the courts.[21]

Should guns be subject to product liability laws, or are they a special case? This issue is profiled in Exhibit 15.D.

Business Efforts to Reform the Product Liability Laws

Many businesses have argued that the evolution of strict liability has unfairly burdened them with excess costs. Liability insurance rates have gone up significantly, especially for small businesses, as have the costs of defending against liability lawsuits and paying large settlements to injured parties. Moreover, businesses argue that it is unfair to hold them financially responsible in situations where they were not negligent.

Businesses have also argued that concerns about liability exposure sometimes slow research and innovation. For example, many pharmaceutical companies halted work on new contraceptive methods because of the risk of being sued. Despite the need for new contraceptives that would be more effective and also provide protection against viral diseases, such as herpes and AIDS, research had virtually come to a halt by the late 1990s, according to some public health groups.[22]

In 2005, Congress passed the Class Action Fairness Act, the first significant reform of product liability laws in many years. The two key elements of this legislation were these:

- *Most large class-action lawsuits were moved from state to federal courts.* This provision applied to cases involving $5 million or more and that included plaintiffs from more than one state. Supporters of the law said this would prevent lawyers from shopping for friendly local venues in which to try interstate cases.

- *Attorneys in some kinds of cases were paid based on how much plaintiffs actually received, or on how much time the attorney spent on the case.* Under the old system, attorneys were often paid a percentage of the settlement amount. This sometimes led to excessive compensation for the lawyers.

---

[19] U.S. Department of Justice, Office of Justice Programs, Bureau of Justice Statistics, "Federal Tort Trials and Verdicts, 2002–03," August 2005, *www.ojp.gov/bjs.*

[20] "Baxter Will Settle with Families of 10 Dialysis Patients Who Died," *The Wall Street Journal,* November 29, 2001.

[21] "Tainted-Milk Victims File Lawsuit in China's Highest Court," *The Wall Street Journal,* January 20, 2009; and "Chinese Parents File Milk Lawsuit," *The Wall Street Journal,* October 1, 2008.

[22] "Birth Control: Scared to a Standstill," *BusinessWeek,* June 16, 1997.

Two hundred million guns are in circulation in the United States, and a third of all households own at least one. In 2005, more than 30,000 Americans died, and many more were injured, from gun violence.

In the late 1990s, a number of cities and counties brought suit against the firearms industry, demanding compensation for the medical and law enforcement costs of gun violence. The governments argued that gun manufacturers were liable because they had failed to apply common-sense consumer product safety standards to firearms. So-called Saturday night specials—cheap, easily hidden handguns—for example, lacked locks or other protective devices and sometimes misfired, causing unintentional injury. Some guns, such as automatic assault rifles, seemed to have been customized for killing. Moreover, gun makers knowingly made large shipments to regions that had lax gun laws, looking the other way while weapons fell into the hands of criminals.

Most manufacturers, however, disputed these arguments. They pointed out that guns are legal; in fact, they are the only consumer products that the U.S. Constitution (in the Second Amendment) guarantees the right to own. No one, least of all gun manufacturers, has ever claimed that guns do not kill. Guns have a legitimate, even beneficial, purpose in hunting, self-defense, and law enforcement.

The gun liability lawsuits did not fare well in the courts. In a series of decisions in favor of manufacturers, judges and juries seemed to be saying that criminals, not gun makers, were the real killers. In 2005, Congress passed the Protection of Lawful Commerce in Arms Act, which barred lawsuits against gun makers and dealers, with certain narrow exceptions—seemingly putting an end to these liability cases. However, in a major setback to the industry, in 2009 the Supreme Court of Indiana ruled in a case brought against gun manufacturers by the city of Gary that federal law did not shield these companies from liability for sales practices that put guns in the hands of criminals.

Sources: "Indiana Supreme Court Denies Gun Manufacturers' Appeal of Gary, Indiana, Lawsuit," *PR Newswire,* January 13, 2009; "Jury Decides Gun Makers Aren't Liable for Violence," *The Wall Street Journal,* May 15, 2003; and "High Noon in Gun Valley," *Newsweek,* March 27, 2000. Statistics on deaths due to firearms are available at *www.cdc.gov/nchs.*

Although most businesses welcomed these changes, many called for further reforms, such as the following:

- *Set up uniform federal standards for determining liability.* Companies would not have to go through repeated trials on the same charges in different states, which would lower costs for companies and help them develop a uniform legal strategy for confronting liability charges.

- *Shift the burden of proving liability to consumers.* Consumers would have to prove that a manufacturer knew or should have known that a product design was defective. Under present law and judicial interpretations, a company is considered to be at fault if a product injures the user, whether or not the company was negligent.

- *Require the loser to pay the legal costs of the winner.* If a plaintiff (consumer) refused an out-of-court settlement offer from the company and then received less in trial, he or she would have to pay the company's legal fees up to the amount of his or her own fees. This would discourage many plaintiffs from proceeding to trial.

- *Limit punitive damages.* (Punitive damages punish the manufacturer for wrongdoing, rather than compensate the victim for actual losses.) Although many punitive damage awards are small, some multimillion-dollar awards have been reached.

- *Establish liability shields for certain kinds of products.* For example, consumers could be barred from receiving punitive damages in cases involving products, such as pharmaceutical drugs, that had been approved by regulators.

Although supported by many business groups, product liability reform proposals such as these have faced vigorous opposition from consumers' organizations and from the American Trial Lawyers Association, representing plaintiffs' attorneys. These groups have defended the existing product liability system, saying it puts needed pressure on companies to make and keep products safe.

Plaintiffs scored a legal victory in 2009 when the U.S. Supreme Court decided an important case called *Wyeth v. Levine.* Diana Levine, a musician, was injected with an anti-nausea drug made by Wyeth after complaining of migraines. The drug's label said that "extreme care" should be used to avoid hitting an artery, which could lead to "gangrene requiring amputation." Unfortunately, this happened to the musician, whose right arm had to be amputated. In the ensuing lawsuit, Wyeth defended itself on the grounds that because the FDA had approved the warning label, the company was shielded from the lawsuit. The Supreme Court disagreed and said the suit could go forward—federal regulatory approval had not preempted the company's liability under state laws.[23]

A promising approach to resolving product liability conflicts without going to court is called **alternative dispute resolution**. In ADR, a professional mediator works with both sides to negotiate a settlement. Generally, if this process fails, the parties can still proceed to trial. Supporters of ADR say it saves money that would be spent on lawyers' fees, so that more can go to plaintiffs in a settlement. Cases can be resolved quickly, rather than waiting for an opening on a busy judge's calendar. Some businesses feel that such a process would enable them to better predict, and budget for, future liabilities. Eventually, ADR may be widely used to settle individual complaints brought under mass torts, such as those involving injuries from asbestos, tobacco, or defective medical devices. In this situation, a court would set up a procedure and a set of rules by which individuals could negotiate a settlement tailored to the facts of their own cases.[24]

Positive Business Responses to Consumerism

The consumer movement has demonstrated that business is expected to perform at high levels of efficiency, reliability, and fairness in order to satisfy the consuming public. Because business has not always responded quickly or fully enough, consumer advocates and their organizations have turned to government for protection. On the other hand, much effort has been devoted by individual business firms and by entire industries to encourage voluntary responses to consumer demands. Some of the more prominent positive responses are discussed next.

Quality Management

One way that many businesses address consumer interests is to manage quality in a highly proactive way. Quality has been defined by the International Organization for Standardization (ISO) as "a composite of all the characteristics, including performance, of an item, product, or service that bear on its ability to satisfy stated or implied needs." **Quality management**, by extension, refers to "all the measures an organization takes to assure quality." These might include, for example, defining the customer's needs, monitoring whether or not a product or service consistently meets these needs, analyzing the quality of finished products to ensure that they are free of defects, and continually improving processes to eliminate quality problems. Taking steps at all stages of the production process to ensure consistently high quality has many benefits. Responsible businesses know that building products right the first time reduces the risk of liability lawsuits and builds brand loyalty.

[23] "High Court Eases Way to Liability Lawsuits," *The Wall Street Journal,* March 5, 2009.

[24] John Gibeaut, "At the Crossroads," *American Bar Association Journal,* March 1998.

Toyota Motor Corporation, a Japanese car company with factories around the globe, earned 10 of the 25 top model awards for quality in the annual J. D. Power survey in 2009. Its Lexus models ranked highest in the entry premium, midsized premium, and large premium segments, and had the fewest problems per 100 new cars sold of any model. The company credited a relentless emphasis on worker training. "We strive to get better by reducing variation in our manufacturing," explained the general manager of the quality division of the company's North American operations. "Everyone can screw in a bolt, but we teach people to recognize when it's misthreaded . . . to recognize a fault and keep the problem from ever leaving the factory."[25]

Managing for product quality is an attempt by business to address its customers' needs. It is an example of the interactive strategy discussed in Chapter 2, where companies try to anticipate and respond to emerging stakeholder expectations.

Fortune magazine publishes an annual list of the "world's most admired companies." Firms are rated by executives, directors, and securities analysts according to nine criteria, one of which is the quality of their product or service. In 2009, high-ranking companies in this category were a diverse group; they included The New York Times Company (news, information, and media); Graybar Electric (supply chain management and distribution services in the telecommunications industry); Anheuser-Busch (beer); Sysco (food service for institutions); and Walt Disney (resorts, entertainment, and media). Clearly, positive relationships with customers know no industry boundaries.[26]

The challenging issue of business's responsibility for products that are safe and of high quality—but used by others in illegal or dangerous ways—is profiled in Exhibit 15.E.

Voluntary Industry Codes of Conduct

In another positive response, businesses in some industries have banded together to agree on voluntary codes of conduct, spelling out how they will treat their customers. Often, this action is taken to forestall even stricter regulation by the government. One such voluntary code is described in the following example:

In 2007, the Western Growers Association, a trade association of farmers, adopted voluntary guidelines for growers and handlers of leafy green vegetables. The move followed an outbreak of E. coli poisoning, in which three people died and hundreds were sickened. Public health investigators traced the rash of illnesses to spinach grown on a California farm that had become contaminated with infected wild pig feces. Over 100 farm companies subsequently signed on to the new standards in an effort to alleviate customer concerns—and to reduce pressure for mandatory government rules.[27]

Consumer Affairs Departments

Many large corporations operate consumer affairs departments, often placing a vice president in charge. The **consumer affairs officer** typically manages a complex network of

---

[25] J. D. Powers and Associates, "While Quality Gap Continues to Narrow, Import Nameplates Capture 15 of 22 Segment Awards," press release, June 22, 2009; and "GM's Quality Quandary," *Detroit Free Press,* April 10, 2006.

[26] "World's Most Admired Companies," *Fortune,* March 16, 2009.

[27] "Government Hails Produce Handling Rules," *San Francisco Chronicle,* March 24, 2007; and "E. Coli Outbreak from Fresh Spinach Has USDA Mulling New Leafy Green Regulations," *NEWSInferno.com,* November 30, 2007.

What should a company do when a legitimate product it makes is used for an illegal or unethical purpose? This problem confronted the drug company Pfizer, Inc., maker of Sudafed. This over-the-counter decongestant, commonly used to treat colds and allergies, includes pseudoephedrine, a key ingredient in the illegal drug methamphetamine. Commonly known as "meth" or "crystal," methamphetamine is a highly addictive synthetic stimulant that eventually destroys the user's capacity to experience pleasure and causes permanent brain damage, heart attacks, and psychosis. Traffickers manufacture the drug in labs where they cook pseudoephedrine with other ingredients, including ammonia and lye. In 2006, meth was the most abused drug in the world, according to the United Nations, with 26 million addicts. In the United States, 58 percent of law enforcement officials said meth was their most serious drug problem.

What, if anything, could or should Pfizer do to keep pseudoephedrine out of the hands of drug traffickers? In the mid-1990s, the company began experimenting with versions of the chemical that could not be converted into methamphetamine. Pfizer gave up, however, when it discovered that whatever they came up with criminals could find a way around. "The tough lesson we learned," said a company spokesperson, "is, as fast as we could do things, . . . the meth cooks could move a lot more quickly." Instead, in 2004 the company introduced a version of its medicine, Sudafed PE, which did not include pseudoephedrine. Some critics, however, faulted Pfizer for continuing to sell the old version and for opposing some efforts to restrict the sale of pseudoephedrine-based products.

Sources: The quotation is from an interview with Steven Robins, a representative of Pfizer, Inc., conducted September 14, 2005, *www.pbs.org/wgbh/frontline/meth/interviews/robins.html*. More information about the methamphetamine epidemic and business's response may be found at *www.pbs.org/wgbh/frontline/meth* and in a series of articles appearing in *The Oregonian* under the title, "Unnecessary Epidemic," October 2004, *www.oregonlive.com*.

contacts with customers. The contact infrastructure usually includes a Web site with a self-service component; many sites are interactive, allowing customers to post comments or questions that are answered electronically by customer relations staff. Most companies also host a call center, using an interactive voice response system that leads callers to an appropriately trained customer service representative. Sophisticated software underpins all levels of the infrastructure, to help resolve customer complaints and inquiries efficiently and satisfactorily.[28]

Cutting-edge consumer affairs offices also proactively monitor customer reactions to their products and advertising, using a wide range of social media. Doing so can help companies avoid costly gaffes.

In 2008, Johnson & Johnson posted a promotion for its pain reliever, Motrin, on its Web site. The ad showed a mother who was suffering from back and neck pain from wearing a baby carrier, and referred to mothers who "wear their babies." Many mothers who saw the ad were annoyed, and they started messaging, blogging, and twittering. "A baby will never be a fashion statement," said one. Fortunately, Johnson & Johnson actively monitored its brand in the social media, and within 24 hours had taken down the ads and issued an apology to its customers. What could have been a public relations nightmare was quickly averted.[29]

Experienced companies are aware that consumer complaints and concerns can be handled more quickly, at lower cost, and with less risk of losing goodwill by a consumer affairs department than if customers take a legal route or if their complaints receive widespread publicity.

[28] "2009 Service Leaders," *Customer Relationship Management,* April, 2009.
[29] "Strategy and Social Media: Everything's Social Now," *Customer Relationship Management,* June 2009.

Product Recalls

Companies also deal with consumer dissatisfaction by recalling faulty products. A **product recall** occurs when a company, either voluntarily or under an agreement with a government agency, takes back all items found to be dangerously defective. Sometimes these products are in the hands of consumers; at other times they may be in the factory, in wholesale warehouses, or on the shelves of retail stores. Wherever they are in the chain of distribution or use, the manufacturer tries to notify consumers or potential users about the defect. The case "Mattel and Toy Safety," which appears at the end of this textbook, describes a recall carried out by Mattel after discovering that some of its toys had been contaminated by dangerous lead paint.

One problem with recalls is that the public may not be aware of them, so dangerous products continue to be used. For example, several babies were killed when Playskool Travel-Lite portable cribs unexpectedly collapsed, strangling them. Although the Consumer Product Safety Commission (CPSC) ordered an immediate recall, not all parents and child care providers heard about it, and additional deaths occurred.[30] Some consumer organizations advocated a system that would require manufacturers of certain products—such as cribs—to include purchaser identification cards so users could be quickly traced in the event of a recall.[31]

The four major government agencies responsible for most mandatory recalls are the Food and Drug Administration, the National Highway Traffic Safety Administration, the Environmental Protection Agency (which can recall polluting motor vehicles), and the Consumer Product Safety Commission.

Consumerism's Achievements

The leaders of the consumer movement can point to important gains in both the United States and other nations. Consumers today are better informed about the goods and services they purchase, are more aware of their rights when something goes wrong, and are better protected against inflated advertising claims, hazardous or ineffective products, and unfair pricing. Several consumer organizations serve as watchdogs of buyers' interests, and a network of government regulatory agencies act for the consuming public.

Some businesses, too, have heard the consumer message and have reacted positively. They have learned to assign high priority to the things consumers expect: high-quality goods and services, reliable and effective products, safety in the items they buy, fair prices, and marketing practices that do not threaten important human and social values.

All of these achievements, in spite of negative episodes that occasionally occur, bring the consuming public closer to realizing the key consumer rights: to be safe, to be informed, to have choices, to be heard, and to privacy.

Summary

- The consumer movement represents an attempt to promote the interests of consumers by balancing the amount of market power held by sellers and buyers.
- The five key consumer rights are the rights to safety, to be informed, to choose, to be heard, and to privacy.

---

[30] David Zivan, "The Playskool Travel-Lite Crib (A), (B), and (C)," Center for Decision Research, University of Chicago, November 5, 2002.

[31] For information on initiatives to protect children from dangerous products, see *www.kidsindanger.org.*

- Consumer protection laws and regulatory agencies attempt to ensure that consumers are treated fairly, receive adequate information, are protected against potential hazards, have free choices in the market, and have legal recourse when problems develop. They also protect children's privacy online.

- Rapidly evolving information technologies have given new urgency to the issue of consumer privacy. Three approaches to safeguarding online privacy are consumer self-help, industry self-regulation, and protective legislation.

- Business has complained about the number of product liability lawsuits and the high cost of insuring against them. Although consumer groups and trial attorneys have opposed efforts to change product liability laws, modest tort reforms have recently been legislated.

- Socially responsible companies have responded to the consumer movement by giving serious consideration to consumer problems, increasing channels of communication with customers, instituting arbitration procedures to resolve complaints, and recalling defective products. They have also pursued voluntary codes of conduct and quality management in an effort to meet, and even anticipate, consumers' needs.

Key Terms	alternative dispute resolution, *355*	consumer privacy, *350*	product recall, *358*
	consumer affairs officer, *356*	consumer protection laws, *344*	quality management, *355*
	consumer movement, *342*	deceptive advertising, *345*	strict liability, *351*
		product liability, *351*	

Internet Resources	www.bbb.org	Better Business Bureau
	www.consumeraction.gov	Consumer action Web site (federal government)
	www.consumeraffairs.com	Consumer news and resource center
	www.consumerfed.org	Consumer Federation of America
	www.consumersinternational.org	Consumers International
	www.cpsc.gov	U.S. Consumer Product Safety Commission
	www.ftc.gov	U.S. Federal Trade Commission
	www.socap.org	Society of Consumer Affairs Professionals

Discussion Case: *Big Fat Liability*

In 2003, a judge in New York dismissed a lawsuit filed on behalf of two obese teenage girls against McDonald's. The lawsuit alleged that the fast-food giant had "negligently, recklessly, carelessly, and/or intentionally" marketed products to children—such as burgers, chicken nuggets, fries, and sodas—that were "high in fat, salt, sugar, and cholesterol." And it had done so without warning customers of the risks of "obesity, diabetes, coronary heart disease, high blood pressure, strokes, elevated cholesterol intake, [and] related conditions" associated with such foods and beverages.

In his decision, the judge noted that the plaintiffs had failed to show that the girls had no way of knowing the risks of fast food. Moreover, the judge pointed out, "Nobody is forced to eat at McDonald's."

A spokesperson for McDonald's expressed relief, saying, "Common sense has prevailed." But many in the food and restaurant industries were worried that this lawsuit was just an opening salvo in a long battle. Potentially, liability for the health effects of fast food could become the next mass tort, rivaling the huge lawsuits against the cigarette companies of the 1990s. "It has gotten everyone's attention," said the president of the National Restaurant Association.

The problem of obesity and its health effects was growing. In 2001, the U.S. Surgeon General released a report called "The Surgeon General's Call to Action to Prevent and Decrease Overweight and Obesity."[32] The report called overweight and obesity "among the most pressing health challenges we face today." Among the report's startling findings were these:

- Six out of 10 American adults and 13 percent of children and adolescents were overweight or obese—that is, with a body mass index (BMI) of 25 or more.[33] Only 3 percent of Americans met the government's dietary recommendations, and fewer than a third exercised enough.

- Obesity in the United States among adults had doubled, and among adolescents had tripled, since 1980. Although these increases cut across all ages, genders, ethnic groups, and social classes, obesity was a particular problem for people from lower-income families.

- Obesity was a major cause of asthma, diabetes, heart disease, arthritis, infertility, and some kinds of cancer. In the United States, around 300,000 premature deaths a year were associated with being overweight—approaching the 400,000 deaths associated with cigarettes. The direct and indirect costs of being overweight and obese were $117 billion a year (compared with $140 billion for smoking).

The immediate cause for this epidemic of obesity was that people were simply eating too much. Americans consumed, on average, around 2,750 calories a day, well above the healthy amount for most people. The critical question, of course, was to what extent, if at all, the food industry could be held responsible for the fattening of America. Many felt that food and lifestyle choices were an individual responsibility. Unlike cigarettes, food products were not normally addictive. Moreover, the rising level of obesity had many causes, and the exact role of particular companies was unclear. As one legal analysis asked, "How would any court determine . . . whether a given class action member's obesity was caused by eating one of the defendant's products as opposed to eating some other food, overeating generally, a sedentary lifestyle, or genetic predisposition?"

Others, however, thought the food industry was at least partially at fault. Fast food had become a big part of Americans' diets. In 1970, they spent $6 billion a year on it; 30 years later, they spent $110 billion. This trend seemed to parallel the obesity epidemic. The problem was not just the relatively high fat and sugar content of fast foods, but the super-sizing of portions. When fast-food restaurants increasingly began to compete on the basis of value—more for less—customers simply ate more.

---

[32] A summary is available online at *www.surgeongeneral.gov/topics/obesity/calltoaction.*

[33] Body mass index is calculated as a person's weight in pounds divided by the square of that person's height in inches, multiplied by 703. For example, a person who was 66 inches tall and weighed 140 pounds would have a BMI of 22.59 (140 divided by 66 times 66 times 703). "Overweight" is defined as a BMI of 25–29.9 and "obese" as a BMI of 30 or higher. A chart showing BMIs for various weights and heights is available online at *www.surgeongeneral.gov/topics/obesity/calltoaction/1_1.htm.*

For their part, food companies had concentrated on developing processed products, such as candy, gum, snacks, and bakery goods, that carried high profit margins along with excessive calories. They had introduced many more new products in these categories than entrées, fruits, and vegetables since the early 1980s, data showed. Moreover, both restaurants and food processors, in their critics' view, had failed to communicate adequately the health risks of some foods and had inappropriately marketed their products to children.

In 2005, the U.S. House of Representatives, acting to block what some feared might become a flood of liability lawsuits, voted for a law popularly known as the Cheeseburger Bill, which would shield both producers and retailers of food from lawsuits by obese consumers. The bill did not become law, because the Senate did not act on the issue. Several states, however, enacted similar legislation. The National Restaurant Associated strongly supported these initiatives.

Faced with an uncertain legal landscape, some companies took voluntary steps to reduce their exposure to liability. Saying that "the rise in obesity is a complex public health challenge of global proportions," Kraft announced it would change the recipes for some products. The company also said it would label products that were high in beneficial nutrients or low in calories, fat, sugar, and salt. It also pledged to stop advertising to children products, such as Oreo cookies, that did not qualify for its "sensible solutions" label. McDonald's introduced entrée-size salads with low-fat dressing, and PepsiCo switched to nonhydrogenated cooking oils for some snacks.

Sources: "Kraft to Curb Ads of Snack Foods," *The Wall Street Journal,* January 12, 2005; "The Food Industry Empire Strikes Back," *The New York Times,* July 7, 2005; "Judge Dismisses Obesity Suit by 2 Girls against McDonald's," *The Wall Street Journal,* January 23, 2003, p. D3; "Is Fat the Next Tobacco?" *Fortune,* February 3, 2003, pp. 51–54; "Kraft Promises to Take Healthier Approach to Food," *San Francisco Chronicle,* July 2, 2003, p. A1; Eric Schlosser, *Fast Food Nation: The Dark Side of the All-American Meal* (New York: Perennial, 2002); and Greg Cristser, *Fat Land: How Americans Became the Fattest People in the World* (New York: Houghton Mifflin, 2003), ch. 2. A summary of the Surgeon General's "Call to Action" is available online at *www.surgeongeneral.gov/topics/obesity/calltoaction.*

Discussion Questions

1. What are the arguments for and against the proposition that the food and restaurant industries should be held liable for the rise of obesity in the United States?

2. In your opinion, should the food and restaurant industries be held liable for the rise of obesity, or not? That is, which side do you support, and why?

3. If you were a manager for a fast-food chain or food company, what actions would you take with respect to obesity, if any?

4. What do you think is the best solution to the obesity epidemic? What roles can the food and restaurant industries, trial attorneys, government policymakers and regulators, and individual consumers play in a solution, if any?

Employees and the Corporation

Employees and employers are engaged in a critical relationship affecting the corporation's performance. There is a basic economic aspect to their association: Employees provide labor for the firm, and employers compensate workers for their contributions of skill and productivity. Yet, also present in the employee–employer exchange are numerous social, ethical, legal, and public policy issues. Attention to the rights and duties of both parties in this relationship can benefit the firm, its workers, and society.

This Chapter Focuses on These Key Learning Objectives:

- Understanding workers' rights to organize unions and bargain collectively.
- Knowing how government regulations ensure occupational safety and health and what business must do to protect workers.
- Evaluating the limits of employers' duty to provide job security to their workers.
- Appraising the extent of employees' right to privacy, when businesses monitor employee communications, police romance in the office, test for drugs or alcohol, or subject employees to honesty tests.
- Debating if employees have a duty to blow the whistle on corporate misconduct, or if employees should always be loyal to their employer.
- Assessing the obligations of transnational corporations to their employees around the world.

A worker at the Lincoln Financial Stadium in Philadelphia, where the Eagles play, was fired two days after he posted an angry message on his Facebook page. The stadium worker, who was upset that the Eagles had just traded his favorite player, Brian Dawkins, to the Denver Broncos, said he was "[expletive] devastated" and called the franchise "retarded" [sic]. "I shouldn't have put it up there," the worker later said. "I was ticked off, and I let my emotions go." Increasingly, managers are watching what employees say about their companies on their blogs or in the social media. The result is sometimes an unintended disclosure of behavior and opinions that can damage careers.[1]

Should employees, like this stadium worker, have a right to criticize their employers online in the social media? Is a manager justified in using an Internet search engine to find information about employees that they, or others, have posted? Were the Eagles justified in terminating this employee?

Fourteen people died and dozens more were seriously injured in a fiery explosion at Imperial Sugar's refinery in Port Wentworth, Georgia, in 2008. Government investigators found that dangerous levels of highly combustible sugar dust had built up in the plant and had been ignited by a spark thrown off by metal machinery. A company manager later told Congress that he had warned his bosses that conditions at the plant were "shocking" and "disgraceful" and that a fatal disaster was likely—but was told to back off. But company representatives said that the government did not have specific standards for combustible dust to guide their actions.[2]

Who is responsible for the deaths and injuries of these refinery workers? What roles should government regulators, managers, and workers and their unions play in ensuring the safety and health of people on the job?

Across the southeast coast of China, dozens of manufacturing plants produce shoes for Nike Corporation. Working conditions at the contractor factories, which are bound by Nike's code of conduct, have improved markedly, and workers there now make at least $1.35 an hour—a significant raise from the early 2000s. But many of them, mostly young women, are separated from their families in rural areas for months at a time, and a recent audit found continuing problems with excessive overtime and underage workers.[3]

What wages and hours are fair in this case? Should multinational companies pay their overseas workers enough to enjoy a decent family standard of living, even if this is well above the legally mandated wage or above wages common in the area for similar kinds of work? Should extra be paid for overtime work, even if not required by law?

All of these difficult questions will be addressed later in this chapter. As the situations giving rise to them suggest, the rights and duties of employers and employees in the modern workplace are incredibly complex—and have become more so as business has become increasingly global.

The Employment Relationship

As noted in Chapter 1, employees are a market stakeholder of business—and a critically important one. Businesses cannot operate without employees to make products, provide services, market to customers, run the organization internally, and plan for the future. At

---

[1] "Cold Eagles Sure Are Thin-Skinned," Philly.com, March 9, 2009.

[2] "Explosion Injures Dozens at Georgia Sugar Refinery," *The New York Times*, February 8, 2008; "Death Toll Rises from Explosion," *The New York Times*, April 24, 2008; "OSHA Seeks $8.7 Million Fine against Sugar Company," *The New York Times*, July 26, 2008; and "Executive Said He Warned of Conditions at Refinery," *The New York Times*, July 30, 2008.

[3] "Nike Report Cites Continuing Problems in China," *The Wall Street Journal*, March 15, 2008; and *Innovate for a Better World: Nike China 2008 Corporate Responsibility Reporting Supplement* (online at *www.nikebiz.com*).

FIGURE 16.1
Rights and Duties of Employees and Employers

Employee Rights/Employer Duties	Employee Duties/Employer Rights
• Right to organize and bargain	• No drug or alcohol abuse
• Right to a safe and healthy workplace	• No actions that would endanger others
• Right to privacy	• Treat others with respect and without harassment of any kind
• Duty to discipline fairly and justly	
• Right to blow the whistle	• Honesty; appropriate disclosure
• Right to equal employment opportunity	• Loyalty and commitment
• Right to be treated with respect for fundamental human rights	• Respect for employer's property and intellectual capital

the same time, employees are dependent on their employers for their livelihood—and often much more, including friendship networks, recreational opportunities, health care, retirement savings, even their very sense of self. Because of the importance of the relationship to both parties, it must be carefully managed, with consideration for both legal and ethical obligations.

The employment relationship confers rights and duties on both sides. (As further explained in Chapter 4, a *right* means someone is entitled to be treated a certain way; rights often confer *duties* on others.) Some of these responsibilities are legal or contractual; others are social or ethical in nature. For their part, employers have an obligation to provide some measure of job security, a safe and healthy workplace, and equal opportunity for all. They are obliged to pay a decent wage and to respect workers' rights to organize and bargain collectively, as guaranteed by U.S. law (and the laws of many other nations). Employers must also respect employees' rights to privacy and—to some extent at least—their rights to free speech and to do what they want outside the workplace.

But employees also have a duty to behave in acceptable ways. For example, most would agree that employees should not abuse drugs or alcohol in a way that impairs their work performance, use company e-mail to send offensive messages, or take the employer's property for their own personal use. Employees should deal with customers and coworkers in an honest, fair, and nondiscriminatory way. They should not reveal proprietary information to others outside the company, unless there is compelling reason to do so—such as an imminent threat to the public's safety. Some main rights and duties of employers and employees are summarized in Figure 16.1. How to balance these sometimes conflicting obligations poses an ongoing, and frequently perplexing, challenge to business.

This chapter considers the rights and duties—both legal and ethical—of both parties in the employment relationship. The following chapter explores the related issue of workforce diversity and discusses the specific legal and ethical obligations of employers with respect to equal employment opportunity.

Workplace Rights

Employees in the United States enjoy several important legal guarantees. They have the right to *organize and bargain collectively*, to have a *safe and healthy workplace*, and, to some degree, to have *job security*. This section will explore these three rights, emphasizing U.S. laws and regulation, but with comparative references to policies in other nations.

The Right to Organize and Bargain Collectively

In the United States, and in most other nations, employees have a fundamental legal right to organize **labor unions** and to bargain collectively with their employers. The exceptions are some communist countries (such as China, Vietnam, Cuba, and the People's

Democratic Republic of Korea) and some military dictatorships (such as Myanmar, also known as Burma), where workers are not permitted to form independent unions. Labor unions are organizations, such as the Service Employees International Union or the Teamsters, that represent workers on the job. Under U.S. laws, most private and public workers have the right to hold an election to choose what union they want to represent them, if any. Unions negotiate with employers over wages, working conditions, and other terms of employment. Employers are not required by law to agree to the union's demands, but they are required to bargain in good faith. Sometimes, if the two sides cannot reach agreement, a strike occurs, or employees apply pressure in other ways, such as appealing to politicians or refusing to work overtime.

The influence of labor unions in the United States has waxed and waned over the years. During the New Deal period in the 1930s, many workers, particularly in manufacturing industries such as automobiles and steel, joined unions, and the ranks of organized labor grew rapidly. Unions negotiated with employers for better wages, benefits such as pensions and health insurance, and improved job safety—significantly improving the lot of many workers. Studies show that union workers make, on average, 20 percent more than nonunion workers, and 28 percent more, when benefits are added. (All workers, whether or not they are members of unions, are protected by wage and hour laws that require employers to pay at least a minimum wage and extra pay for certain kinds of overtime work.) Since the mid-1950s, the proportion of American workers represented by unions has declined. In 2008, only about 12 percent of all employees were union members. (The percentage was higher—37 percent—in government employment.)[4]

Some observers, however, believed that unions in the United States might be poised for recovery. Survey data showed that more than half of nonunion, nonsupervisory workers said they would join a union if they could.

In 2006, the Service Employees International Union (SEIU) succeeded in organizing more than 5,000 commercial building janitors in Houston, many of them Latino immigrants, in a campaign that *The New York Times* labor reporter Steven Greenhouse concluded "did everything right." The SEIU, which invested $1 million in the effort, won the support of the mayor, half the city council, and the city's Roman Catholic archbishop. The union used multiple tactics, including staging protest marches, forming alliances with pension funds with large real estate holdings, and mounting a strike against one of the city's largest cleaning contractors. Eventually the campaign won a 48 percent pay increase, better hours, and—for the first time—health insurance coverage for Houston's janitors.[5]

Other significant recent union organizing wins occurred at Smithfield Pork in North Carolina, the world's largest pork slaughterhouse, and Delta Pride, a catfish processor in Mississippi that employed mainly African-American women.[6]

Labor union power was evident in other ways in the 2000s. Unions organized in the political arena, using political action committees (PACs) and other methods (discussed in Chapter 9), and voted shares of stock in which their pension funds were invested (discussed in Chapter 14) to pursue their institutional objectives. A major legislative goal of unions was labor law reform.

[4] U.S. Bureau of Labor Statistics, "Union Members in 2008," *www.bls.gov.*

[5] The SEIU's Justice for Janitors campaign in Houston is described in Steven Greenhouse, *The Big Squeeze: Tough Times for the American Worker* (New York: Anchor Books, 2009), ch. 13, "The State of the Unions."

[6] "Victory at Smithfield: Union Scores Big Win in North Carolina," *Facing South,* Institute of Southern Studies, December 12, 2008; and Phil M. Dine, *State of the Unions* (New York: McGraw-Hill, 2008), ch. 2.

In 2009, unions mobilized to pass a law called the Employee Free Choice Act (EFCA). Its purpose was to help make it easier for workers to organize. When first drafted, the bill included a provision, known as "card check," that would require employers to recognize and bargain with a union if a majority of workers signed cards saying they wanted that union to represent them. But backers withdrew this language after many businesses complained, saying it would take away workers' right to a secret ballot election on union representation. In a later version of the bill, EFCA shortened the time workers would have to wait for an election and stiffened penalties on employers who intervened unfairly in the process. The proposed law also said that if the employer and union could not negotiate a contract within six months, they would have to call in a neutral arbitrator.[7]

Some labor unions departed from their traditional adversarial approach to work cooperatively with employers for their mutual benefit. At Kaiser Permanente (a large health maintenance organization), for example, management and unions forged a collaborative partnership aimed both at giving workers a greater say in the business and improving quality and productivity.[8] However, in some industries, old-line labor-management conflict predominated. Walmart, the world's largest private employer, has aggressively opposed efforts to organize its workers—going so far as to shut down one store in Quebec, Canada, where employees had voted to join a union.[9] And in the "new economy" sector, Amazon.com used its internal Web site to distribute anti-union materials to its managers in an effort to block organizing efforts among its employees.[10]

One issue that unions and others have been concerned with is job safety and health. It is discussed next.

The Right to a Safe and Healthy Workplace

Many jobs are potentially hazardous to workers' safety and health. In some industries, the use of high-speed and noisy machinery, high-voltage electricity, extreme temperatures, or hazardous gases or chemicals poses risks. Careful precautions, extensive training, strict regulations, and tough enforcement are necessary to avoid accidents, injuries, illnesses, and even deaths on the job.

A worker at an industrial laundry in Tulsa, Oklahoma, was gruesomely killed when a conveyor belt pulled him into a large dryer as he was trying to clear a jam. Investigators found that the employer, Cintas Corporation, the largest U.S. supplier of uniforms, had failed to safeguard and train its workers properly. "Plant management . . . could have prevented the death of this employee," said an assistant secretary of labor.[11]

Over the past few decades, new categories of accidents or illnesses have emerged, including the fast-growing job safety problem of repetitive motion disorders, such as the wrist pain sometimes experienced by supermarket checkers, meat cutters, or keyboard operators. In response, many businesses have given greater attention to **ergonomics**, adapting the job to the worker, rather than forcing the worker to adapt to the job. For

[7] "Card Check Is Dead," *The New York Times,* July 16, 2009.

[8] Thomas A. Kochan, Adrienne E. Eaton, and Robert B. McKersie, *Healing Together: The Labor–Management Partnership at Kaiser Permanente* (Ithaca: Cornell University Press, 2009).

[9] "Walmart to Close Store in Canada with a Union," *The New York Times,* February 10, 2005.

[10] "Amazon.com Is Using the Web to Block Unions' Efforts to Organize," *The New York Times,* November 29, 2000.

[11] "U.S. Proposes $2.78 Million Fine in Worker's Death," *The New York Times,* August 18, 2007.

Stories of angry or distraught employees, ex-employees, or associates of employees attacking workers, coworkers, or superiors at work have become more frequent. For example, there is a growing trend for workers who have lost their jobs—or who face some other financial threat—to seek vengeance, often in calculated and cold-blooded fashion. In other cases, seemingly trivial events can provoke an assault. In one recent incident, a long-time mechanic at a bus maintenance depot in San Diego, California, entered his workplace in the early morning and announced, "Nobody's going to leave." He then retrieved a gun and shot and killed two coworkers, before he was himself killed by police who had been called to the scene. Although authorities were unsure of his motive, the mechanic's marriage had recently ended, and he had lost his home.[12]

Homicide is the third leading cause of death on the job (only vehicle accidents and falls kill more). Every year, around 600 workers are murdered, and as many as 2 million are assaulted at work in the United States. Police officers, prison guards, and taxi drivers are most at risk. Although workplace violence is often considered an American problem, a survey by the International Labor Organization found that workplace assaults were actually more common in several other industrial nations, including France, England, and Argentina, than in the United States. Four percent of workers in the European Union said they had been subjected to physical violence in the past year.

OSHA has developed recommendations to help employers reduce the risk of violence. Employers should try to reduce high-risk situations, for example, by installing alarm systems, convex mirrors, and pass-through windows. They should train employees in what to do in an emergency situation. Unfortunately, many companies are poorly prepared to deal with these situations. Only 24 percent of employers offer any type of formal training to their employees in coping with workplace violence.

Sources: "Census of Occupational Injuries, 2007," August 20, 2008, *www.bls.org;* and "Violence on the Job: A Global Problem," *www.ilo.org.* Current statistics are available at *www.cdc.gov/niosh/topics/violence.*

example, ergonomically designed office chairs that conform to the shape of the worker's spine may help prevent low productivity and lost time due to back injuries.

Annually, more than 4 million workers in private industry are injured or become ill while on the job, according to the U.S. Department of Labor. This amounts to about four hurt or sick workers out of every hundred. Some of the highest rates are found in the primary and fabricated metals; lumber; warehousing; and food, beverage, and tobacco processing industries. In general, manufacturing and construction jobs are riskier than service jobs—although couriers and workers in nursing homes suffer relatively high rates of injury.[13] Teenagers are twice as likely to be hurt on the job as adults. Young workers are often inexperienced, have less training, and are more reluctant to challenge the boss over a dangerous task.

Workplace violence—a particular threat to employee safety—is profiled in Exhibit 16.A.

In the United States, the Occupational Safety and Health Act, passed in 1970 during the great wave of social legislation discussed in Chapter 8, gives workers the right to a job "free from recognized hazards that are causing or likely to cause death or serious physical harm." This law is administered by the **Occupational Safety and Health Administration (OSHA).** Congress gave OSHA important powers to set and enforce safety and health standards. Employers found in violation can be fined and, in the case of willful violation causing the death of an employee, jailed as well. In 2005, for example, BP paid $21 million in fines for safety violations linked to an explosion of a refinery in Texas that killed 15 workers and injured 170.[14]

OSHA has had considerable success in improving worker safety and health. Although workers—such as the victims of the Imperial Sugar and BP refinery explosions—continue

[12] "3 Killed in Shooting at San Diego Transit Facility," *(San Diego) Union Tribune,* March 24, 2009.

[13] U.S. Bureau of Labor Statistics data, *www.bls.gov.* These data are for 2007.

[14] "BP Agrees to Penalties Totaling $21.4 Million for Fatal Texas Blast," *The Wall Street Journal,* September 23, 2005.

to die on the job, since OSHA's creation in 1970 the overall workplace death rate has been halved. Very serious occupational illnesses, such as brown lung (caused when textile workers inhale cotton dust) and black lung (caused when coal miners inhale coal dust), have been significantly reduced. The rate of lead poisoning, suffered by workers in smelters and battery plants, among other workplaces, has been cut by two-thirds. Deaths from trench cave-ins have been reduced by 35 percent, to cite several examples.

Although many businesses have credited OSHA with helping reduce lost workdays and worker compensation costs, others have criticized the agency's rules as being too costly to implement and administer. For example, when OSHA proposed new rules designed to prevent worker injuries in nursing homes by eliminating the manual lifting of residents, many nursing home operators attacked the proposal, charging that it was based on "junk science."[15] In part in response to employer criticisms, OSHA has entered into cooperative partnerships with employers, aimed at improving occupational safety and health for the benefit of both companies and their workers.

Although problems remain, three decades of occupational safety and health regulation in the United States and efforts by businesses and unions have significantly lowered deaths and injuries on the job. In many developing nations, however, conditions remain brutally dangerous.

In Bangladesh, a fast-growing garment and textile industry—mostly sourcing apparel to Western companies—has been the site of numerous tragedies. In 2006, an electrical fire at the KTS Textile Industries factory in the port city of Chittagong killed 54 workers, mostly women and girls as young as 12, and injured close to 100 more. Managers had intentionally locked exits to prevent theft and had no fire safety equipment on site. This was only the most recent in a series of fires and building collapses that have killed or seriously injured more than 2,800 Bangladeshi workers since 1990. In response, garment workers organized a national half-day strike to demand tougher health and safety standards and compensation for victims and their families. They also called on international buyers to adopt and enforce codes of conduct for their Bangladeshi suppliers.[16]

Efforts by governments, businesses, and unions to improve conditions of workers in overseas factories are further discussed later in this chapter.

The special problem of smoking in the workplace—a safety and health threat to both smokers and nonsmokers—is addressed in the discussion case at the end of this chapter.

The Right to a Secure Job

Do employers have an obligation to provide their workers with job security? Once someone is hired, under what circumstances is it legal—or fair—to let him or her go? In recent years, the expectations underlying this most basic aspect of the employment relationship have changed, both in the United States and in other countries around the globe.

In the United States, since the late 1800s, the legal basis for the employment relationship has been **employment-at-will**. Employment-at-will is a legal doctrine that means that employees are hired and retain their jobs "at the will of"—that is, at the sole discretion of—the employer. However, over time, this doctrine has been eroded by a number

---

[15] "Business Flexes Muscles over Ergonomics, Again," *The Wall Street Journal,* December 26, 2003.

[16] "Bangladesh Factory Fire Toll 54: Official," *Reuters News Service,* February 24, 2006; and "425 Garment Workers Killed in Incidents Since 1990," *United News of Bangladesh,* April 10, 2006. More information on efforts to improve conditions in the Bangladeshi garment and textile industry is available online at *www.cleanclothes.org.*

of laws and court decisions that have dramatically curtailed U.S. employers' freedom to terminate workers. Some of the restrictions on employers include the following:

- An employer may not fire a worker because of race, gender, religion, national origin, age, or disability. The equal employment and other laws that prevent such discriminatory terminations are further described in Chapter 17.

- An employer may not fire a worker if this would constitute a violation of public policy, as determined by the courts. For example, if a company fired an employee just because he or she cooperated with authorities in the investigation of a crime, this would be illegal.

- An employer may not fire a worker if, in doing so, it would violate the Worker Adjustment Retraining Notification Act (WARN). This law, passed in 1988, requires most big employers to provide 60 days' advance notice whenever they lay off a third or more (or 500 or more, whichever is less) of their workers at a work site. If they do not, they must pay workers for any days of advance notice that were missed.

  In 2008, workers at Republic Window and Doors in Chicago occupied their factory after the owner shut it down with only three days' notice. The workers, who were represented by the United Electrical Workers union, said that the abrupt plant closure violated the terms of WARN. After five days of tense negotiations, the sit-in ended when Bank of America agreed to lend the owner enough money to meet his financial obligations to the employees. Serious Materials, a California-based maker of energy-efficient windows, later bought the plant and pledged to rehire the laid-off workers.[17]

- An employer may not fire a worker simply because the individual was involved in a union organizing drive or other union activity.

- An employer may not fire a worker if this would violate an implied contract, such as a verbal promise, or basic rules of "fair dealing." For example, an employer could not legally fire a salesperson just because he or she had earned a bigger bonus under an incentive program than the employer wanted to pay.

Of course, if workers are covered by a collective bargaining agreement, it may impose additional restrictions on an employer's right to terminate. Many union contracts say employees can be fired only "for just cause," and workers have a right to appeal the employer's decision through the union grievance procedure. Many European countries and Japan have laws that extend "just cause" protections to all workers, whether or not they are covered by a union contract.

The commitments that employers and employees make to each other go beyond mere legal obligations, however. Cultural values, traditions, and norms of behavior also play important roles. Some have used the term **social contract** to refer to the *implied understanding* (not a legal contract, but rather a set of shared expectations) between an organization and its stakeholders. This concept includes, perhaps most significantly, the understanding between businesses and their employees.

Research suggests that the social contract governing the employment relationship has varied across cultures, and also across time. For example, in Europe, employers have historically given workers and their unions a greater role in determining company policy than do most U.S. employers. Employee representatives are often included on boards of

[17] "In Factory Sit-In, An Anger Spread Wide," *The New York Times,* December 8, 2008; and "New Owners to Reopen Window Plant, Site of a Sit-In in Chicago," *The New York Times,* February 27, 2009. The full provisions of the Worker Adjustment Retraining Notification Act are available at *www.doleta.gov/programs.*

directors in a practice sometimes called *codetermination.* For many years, big Japanese companies offered a core group of senior workers lifelong employment; in exchange, these workers felt great loyalty to the company. This practice declined in the 1990s and 2000s, as the Japanese economy stagnated.

When the global recession hit Japan in 2008–2009, many employees found themselves without job security or a social safety net. By then, more than a third of the nation's workers were so-called nonregulars, hired on short-term contracts with fewer benefits and no protections against layoffs. In Japan, where workers must be employed for at least a year to get jobless benefits, many nonregulars who lost their jobs in the recession had nothing to fall back on. Said one worker who had been laid off from a Canon digital camera factory, "We did our best, so Canon should have taken care of us. That is the Japanese way. But this isn't Japan anymore."[18]

In the former Soviet Union, many enterprises felt an obligation to provide social benefits, such as housing and child care, to their workers. These benefits declined with the advent of privatization in these formerly state-run economies.

Fierce global competition and greater attention to improving the bottom line have resulted in significant corporate restructuring and downsizing (termination) of employees in many countries. This trend has led some researchers to describe a *new social contract.* Increasingly, bonds between employers and employees have weakened. Companies aim to attract and retain employees not by offering long-term job security, but rather by emphasizing interesting and challenging work, performance-based compensation, and ongoing professional training. For their part, employees are expected to contribute by making a strong commitment to the job task and work team and to assume a share of responsibility for the company's success. But they cannot count on a guaranteed job.[19]

The social contract between employers and workers was further weakened when several prominent companies cut or eliminated long-standing pension benefits. In 2008, for example, IBM froze its pension plan for current U.S. employees, meaning workers would no longer build up benefits with additional years of service, and shifted instead to a 401(k) plan. Other companies cutting defined benefit pensions, or eliminating them altogether, included such major firms as Verizon, Lockheed Martin, Motorola, and General Motors. (Defined benefit pensions provide a predictable payout each month, usually based on a combination of an employee's age at retirement, years of service, and average pay.) "People just have to deal with a lot more risk in their lives, because all of these things that used to be more or less assured—a job, health care, a pension—are now variable," said one expert.[20]

Should companies have strong or weak bonds with their employees? When businesses invest in their employees by providing a well-structured career, job security, and benefits including pensions, they reap the rewards of enhanced loyalty, productivity, and commitment. But such investments are expensive, and long-term commitments make it hard for companies to adjust to the ups and downs of the business cycle. Some firms resolve this dilemma by employing two classes of employees: permanent workers, who enjoy stable

---

[18] "In Japan, New Jobless May Lack Safety Net," *The New York Times,* February 8, 2009.

[19] James E. Post, "The New Social Contract," in Oliver Williams and John Houck, eds., *The Global Challenge to Corporate Social Responsibility* (New York: Oxford University Press, 1995).

[20] "More Companies Ending Promises for Retirement," *The New York Times,* January 9, 2006; "IBM to Freeze Pension Plans to Trim Costs," *The New York Times,* January 6, 2006; and "GM to Freeze Pension Plans of White-Collar Workers," *The New York Times,* March 8, 2006.

In 2009, CEO Paul Levy of the Beth Israel Deaconess Medical Center in Boston faced a grim situation. Beth Israel, a major medical center, served three-quarters of a million people annually and employed 6,200 people in a wide range of professional and support roles. Like many businesses in the worst economic slump since the Great Depression, Beth Israel faced hard times. Reductions in government reimbursements, decisions by families to defer medical care, and a slowdown in research funding had combined to produce a $20 million budget shortfall for the fiscal year. The medical center faced the imminent prospect of laying off as many as 600 workers—adding yet another notch to the nation's unemployment rate, then 8.5 percent, the highest in a quarter-century.

Levy wanted to try a different approach. He called a series of town meetings, in which he asked for employees' support for an unusual initiative. "I'd like to do what we can to protect the low-wage earners—the transporters, the housekeepers, the food service people," he told his staff. "A lot of these people work really hard, and I don't want to put an additional burden on them. Now, if we protect these people, it means the rest of us will have to make a bigger sacrifice." He asked for their ideas.

Over the following days, Levy received thousands of e-mails, with suggestions for how the medical center could avoid layoffs. A week later, thanking the staff for their "generosity of spirit," Levy announced a series of steps—including pay cuts for top administrators, wage freezes for mid-level employees, and temporary elimination of the employer match for retirement savings plans. In addition, the heads of 13 medical departments voluntarily donated $350,000 and invited their colleagues to give more. The result was that the layoffs were pared to just 150, saving the jobs of 450 workers. Said a nurse coordinator, "Most people are willing to make a sacrifice so that our colleagues won't have to lose their jobs . . . [It] makes me glad to work here."

Sources: "How a Hospital Braces for a $20 Million Operating Loss," *The Wall Street Journal,* March 6, 2009; "A Head with a Heart," *Boston Globe,* March 12, 2009; "Sparing 450 Jobs at Beth Israel," *Boston Globe,* March 19, 2009; "Beth Israel Finds Cure for Layoffs," *Boston Globe,* March 20, 2009. Paul Levy's reflections are available on his blog, *http://www.runningahospital.blogspot.com.* Unemployment statistics are available at *www.bls.gov.*

employment and full benefits, and temporary workers and independent contractors, who do not. The U.S. Labor Department estimates that about 10 million Americans on the job, about 1 in every 14, are independent contractors. About 6 million, or 1 in every 24, are contingent workers who do not expect their jobs to last. On university campuses, to cite one example, many faculty members are part-timers who are not on a tenure (career) track and are often paid much less per course and receive fewer, if any, benefits.

Sara Horowitz, a labor lawyer, founded the Freelancers Union to serve the needs of independent workers—freelancers, consultants, temps, contingent workers, and the self-employed. This unusual labor organization grew very rapidly in the late 2000s, attracting members by offering group health and disability insurance and other services to workers who would otherwise be on their own. "I started Freelancers Union because I believe in the radical notion of fairness," said Horowitz. "We should all have access to the social safety net, regardless of how we work."[21]

In general, during periods of economic expansion, employers are usually more willing to offer long-term commitments to workers and during periods of economic downturn are less likely to do so. In the severe recession of the late 2000s, for instance, many workers were laid off, severing sometimes long-term employment relationships. However, this is not always the case. Exhibit 16.B describes a medical center that worked hard to avoid layoffs, even during a severe economic downturn. In any case, finding the right balance

[21] *www.freelancersunion.org.*

in the employment relationship between commitment and flexibility—within a basic context of fair dealing—remains a challenge to socially responsible companies.

Privacy in the Workplace

An important right in the workplace, as elsewhere, is privacy. Privacy can be most simply understood as the right to be left alone. In the business context, **privacy rights** refer primarily to protecting an individual's personal life from unwarranted intrusion by the employer. Many people believe, for example, that their religious and political views, their health conditions, their credit history, and what they do and say off the job are private matters and should be safe from snooping by the boss. Exceptions are permissible only when the employer's interests are clearly affected. For example, it may be appropriate for the boss to know that an employee is discussing with a competitor, through e-mail messages, the specifications of a newly developed product not yet on the market.

But other areas are not so clear-cut. For example, should a job applicant who is experiencing severe financial problems be denied employment out of fear that he may be more inclined to steal from the company? Should an employee be terminated after the firm discovers that she has a serious medical problem, although it does not affect her job performance, since the company's health insurance premiums may dramatically increase? At what point do company interests weigh more heavily than an employee's right to privacy? This section will address several key workplace issues where these privacy dilemmas often emerge: electronic monitoring, office romance, drug and alcohol abuse, and honesty testing.

Electronic Monitoring

As discussed in Chapters 12 and 13, changing technologies have brought many ethical issues to the forefront. One such issue is employee **electronic monitoring**. New technologies—e-mail and messaging, voice mail, wi-fi enabled cell phones, GPS satellite tracking, Internet browsing, and digitally stored video—enable companies to gather, store, and monitor information about employees' activities. A company's need for information, particularly about its workers, may be at odds with an employee's right to privacy. Even senior executives may not be immune, as shown in the following example:

> Henry Stonecipher was fired from his job as CEO of Boeing Co. after directors learned about a sexually explicit e-mail he had sent to a female company executive with whom he was having an affair. The board determined that the CEO had violated Boeing's code of ethical conduct, which prohibited employees from engaging in conduct that would embarrass the company. The CEO's "poor judgment . . . impaired his ability to lead," said Boeing's nonexecutive board chairman.[22]

Employee monitoring has exploded in recent years, reflecting technological advances that make surveillance of employees easier and more affordable. A 2007 survey found that two-thirds of U.S. firms monitored workers' Internet usage and used software to block their access to inappropriate sites, such as ones used for social networking, shopping, or entertainment. About half stored and reviewed employees' e-mail messages and computer files. Smaller proportions used GPS technology to track company vehicles (8 percent) and cell phones (3 percent). "Workers' e-mail and other electronically stored information create written business records that are the electronic equivalent of DNA evidence," said the

---

[22] "Extramarital Affair Topples Boeing CEO," *USA Today,* March 8, 2005.

executive director of the ePolicy Institute.[23] These programs can be customized to the industry; for example, a hospital might scan for "patient info"; a high-tech company with proprietary technology might scan for a competitor's name or phone number.[24]

Management justifies the increase in employee monitoring for a number of reasons. Employers have an interest in efficiency. When employees log onto the Internet at work to trade stocks, plan their vacations, or chat with friends, this is not a productive use of their time. Employers also fear lawsuits if employees act in inappropriate ways. An employee who views pornographic pictures on a computer at work, for example, might leave the company open to a charge of sexual harassment—if other workers observed this behavior and were offended by it. (Sexual harassment is further discussed in the following chapter.) The employer also needs to make sure that employees do not disclose confidential information to competitors or make statements that would publicly embarrass the company or its officers.

> Is electronic monitoring by employers legal? For the most part, yes. The Electronic Communications Privacy Act (1986) exempts employers. In general, the courts have found that privacy rights apply to personal, but not business, information, and that employers have a right to monitor job-related communication. In an important 1996 case, an employee sued his employer after he was fired for deriding the sales team in an internal e-mail, referring to them as "back-stabbing bastards." The court sided with the company, saying it owned the e-mail system and had a right to examine its contents. Yet some have criticized recent court decisions like this one, saying public policy should do a better job of protecting employees from unwarranted secret surveillance.[25]

In seeking to balance their employees' concerns about privacy with their own concerns about productivity, liability, and security, businesses face a difficult challenge. One approach is to monitor employee communication only when there is a specific reason to do so, such as poor productivity or suspicion of theft. For example, the chipmaker Intel Corporation chose not to check its employees' e-mail routinely, feeling this would undermine trust. Most management experts recommend that employers, at the very least, clearly define their monitoring policies, let employees know what behavior is expected, and apply any sanctions in a fair and even-handed way.

Romance in the Workplace

Another issue that requires careful balancing between legitimate employer concerns and employee privacy is romance in the workplace. People have always dated others at work. In fact, one study showed that one-third of all long-term relationships began on the job, and 30 percent of all managers said they had had one or more romantic relationships at work during their careers.[26] In fact, workplace dating has probably become more common as the average age of marriage has risen. (For women, that age is now around 26; for men, around 27.) Said one human resources director, "It's a reality that work is where people meet these days. When you don't meet at college, that's a pool of people that's taken away from you."[27] Yet office romance poses problems for employers. If the

---

[23] American Management Association, "2007 Electronic Monitoring & Surveillance Survey," *www.amanet.org*.

[24] "Snooping by E-Mail Is Now a Workplace Norm," *The Wall Street Journal*, March 9, 2005.

[25] For example, see the position of the American Civil Liberties Union, *www.aclu.org*.

[26] Dennis M. Powers, *The Office Romance* (New York: Amacom Books, 1998); and "AMA's 2003 Survey on Workplace Dating," *www.amanet.org*.

[27] "Love on the Job: Breaking the Taboo at Bay Area Companies," *San Francisco Chronicle*, November 11, 2007.

relationship goes sour, one of the people may sue, charging sexual harassment—that is, that he or she was coerced into the relationship. When one person in a relationship is in a position of authority, he or she may be biased in an evaluation of the other's work, or others may perceive it to be so.

For many years, most businesses had a strict policy of forbidding relationships in the workplace, especially those between managers and those reporting to them. They assumed that if romance blossomed, one person—usually the subordinate—would have to find another job. Today, however, most companies try to manage office relationships, rather than ban them outright. Southwest Airlines, for example, does not allow workers to report directly to someone with whom they are romantically involved. If a relationship develops, it is up to the people involved to come forward and to change assignments if necessary.[28] A few companies require their managers to sign a document, sometimes called a *consensual* relationship agreement, stipulating that an office relationship is welcome and voluntary—to protect against possible harassment lawsuits if the people involved later break up.

Employee Drug Use and Testing

Abuse of drugs, both illegal drugs such as heroin and methamphetamine and legal drugs such as Oxycontin when used inappropriately, can be a serious problem for employers. Only a small fraction of employees abuse illegal or prescription drugs. But those who do can cause serious harm. They are much more likely than others to produce poor-quality work, have accidents that hurt themselves and others, and steal from their employers. Some break the law by selling drugs at work to support their habits. Drug abuse costs U.S. industry and taxpayers an estimated $181 billion a year. This figure includes the cost of lost productivity, medical claims, rehabilitation services, and crime and accidents caused by drugs.[29]

One way business has protected itself from these risks is through **drug testing**. More than three-fifths of companies test employees or job applicants for illegal substances, according to a study by the American Management Association.[30] Significant drug testing first began in the United States following passage of the Drug-Free Workplace Act of 1988, which required federal contractors to establish and maintain a workplace free of drugs. At that time, many companies and public agencies initiated drug testing to comply with government rules.

Typically, drug testing is used on three different occasions:

- *Preemployment screening.* Some companies test all job applicants or selected applicants before hiring, usually as part of a physical examination, often informing the applicant ahead of time that there will be a drug screening.
- *Random testing of employees.* This type of screening may occur at various times throughout the year. In many companies, workers in particular job categories (e.g., operators of heavy machinery) or levels (e.g., supervisors) are eligible for screening at any time.
- *Testing for cause.* This test occurs when an employee is believed to be impaired by drugs and unfit for work. It is commonly used after an accident or some observable change in behavior.

---

[28] "Theory and Practice: Firms Confront Boss–Subordinate Love Affairs," *The Wall Street Journal,* October 27, 2008.

[29] "The Economic Costs of Drug Abuse in the United States 1992–2002," *www.whitehousedrugpolicy.gov.*

[30] American Management Association survey data on workplace medical testing are available at *www.amanet.org;* this figure is from the 2004 survey.

FIGURE 16.2

Pros and Cons of Employee Drug Testing

Arguments Favoring Employee Drug Testing	Arguments Opposing Employee Drug Testing
• Supports U.S. policy to reduce illegal drug use and availability	• Invades an employee's privacy
• Improves employee productivity	• Violates an employee's right to due process
• Promotes safety in the workplace	• May be unrelated to job performance
• Decreases employee theft and absenteeism	• May be used as a method of employee discrimination
• Reduces health and insurance costs	• Lowers employee morale
	• Conflicts with company values of honesty and trust
	• May yield unreliable test results
	• Ignores effects of prescription drugs, alcohol, and over-the-counter drugs
	• Drug use an insignificant problem for some companies

Employee drug testing is controversial. Although businesses have an interest in not hiring, or getting rid of, people who abuse drugs, many job applicants and employees who have never used drugs feel that testing is unnecessary and violates their privacy and due process rights. The debate over employee drug testing is summarized in Figure 16.2. In general, proponents of testing emphasize the need to reduce potential harm to other people and the cost to business and society of drug use on the job. Opponents challenge the benefits of drug testing and emphasize its intrusion on individual privacy.

Alcohol Abuse at Work

Another form of employee substance abuse—which causes twice the problems of all illegal drugs combined—is alcohol use and addiction. About 6 percent of full-time employees are heavy drinkers—that is, they had five or more drinks on five or more occasions in the past month. Like drug abusers, they can be dangerous to themselves and others. Studies show that up to 40 percent of all industrial fatalities and 47 percent of industrial injuries are linked to alcohol. The problem is not just hard-core alcoholics, however. Most alcohol-related problems in the workplace, one study found, were caused by people who occasionally drank too much after work and came in the next day with a hangover, or who went out for a drink on their lunch break. U.S. businesses lose an estimated $70 billion per year in reduced productivity directly related to alcohol abuse.[31]

Company programs for drug abusers and alcohol abusers are often combined. Many firms recognize that they have a role to play in helping alcoholic employees. As with drug rehabilitation programs, most alcoholism programs work through **employee assistance programs (EAPs)** that offer counseling and follow-up. Roughly 90 percent of *Fortune* 500 companies provide EAPs for alcohol and drug abusers. (The figure is much lower for small companies though, only 1 in 10 of which have such programs.) In general, EAPs have been very cost-effective. General Motors, for example, estimated that it had saved $3,700 for each of the employees enrolled in its EAP.

---

[31] The statistics reported in this paragraph are available at the Web site of the Working Partners for an Alcohol- and Drug-Free Workplace, *www.dol.gov/asp/programs/drugs/workingpartners.*

Employee Theft and Honesty Testing

Employees can irresponsibly damage themselves, their coworkers, and their employer by stealing from the company. Employee theft has emerged as a significant economic, social, and ethical problem in the workplace. A 2007 survey of large retail stores in the United States showed that 44 percent of all inventory losses were due to employee theft (shoplifting, administrative error, and vendor fraud accounted for the rest). The value of goods stolen by employees was more than $15 billion.[32]

> Employee theft is also a problem in other parts of the world, as well. According to the Global Retail Theft Barometer, so-called retail crime (employee theft, shoplifting, and customer, supplier, and vendor fraud) costs European, North American, and Asian-Pacific businesses around $98 billion annually, or about 1.4 percent of sales. Expensive branded products such as cosmetics, alcohol, fragrances, accessories, and designer wear were the items most commonly stolen.[33]

Many companies in the past used polygraph testing (lie detectors) as a preemployment screening procedure or on discovery of employee theft. In 1988, the Employee Polygraph Protection Act became law. This law severely limited polygraph testing by employers and prohibited approximately 85 percent of all such tests previously administered in the United States. In response to the federal ban on polygraphs, many corporations have switched to written psychological tests that seek to predict employee honesty on the job by asking questions designed to identify desirable or undesirable qualities. When a British chain of home improvement centers used such tests to screen more than 4,000 applicants, theft dropped from 4 percent to 2.5 percent, and actual losses from theft were reduced from £3.75 million to £2.62 million.

The use of **honesty tests**, however, like polygraphs, is controversial. The American Psychological Association noted there is a significant potential for these tests to generate false positives, indicating the employee probably would or did steal from the company even though this is not true. Critics also argue that the tests intrude on a person's privacy and discriminate disproportionately against minorities.[34]

In all these areas—monitoring employees electronically, policing office romance, testing for drugs, and conducting psychological tests—businesses must balance their needs to operate safely, ethically, and efficiently with their employees' right to privacy.

Whistle-Blowing and Free Speech in the Workplace

Another area where employer and employee rights and duties frequently conflict involves free speech. Do employees have the right to openly express their opinions about their company and its actions? If so, under what conditions do they have this right?

The U.S. Constitution protects the right to free speech. This means the government cannot take away this right. For example, the legislature cannot shut down a newspaper that editorializes against its actions or those of its members. However, the Constitution does not explicitly protect freedom of expression in the workplace. Generally, employees are not free to speak out against their employers, since companies have a legitimate

---

[32] Richard C. Hollinger and Amanda Adams, *2007 National Retail Security Survey* (Gainesville, FL: University of Florida, 2008).

[33] These data are for 2007. The Global Retail Theft Barometer is available online at *www.retailresearch.org/theft_barometer.*

[34] Dan R. Dalton and Michael B. Metzger, "Integrity Testing for Personnel Selection: An Unsparing Perspective," *Journal of Business Ethics,* February 1993. The position of the American Civil Liberties Union on honesty testing is available at *www.workrights.org.*

interest in operating without harassment from insiders. Company information is generally considered to be proprietary and private. If employees, based on their personal points of view, were freely allowed to expose issues to the public and allege misconduct, a company might be thrown into turmoil and be unable to operate effectively.

On the other hand, there may be situations in which society's interests override those of the company, so an employee may feel an obligation to speak out. When an employee believes his or her employer has done something that is wrong or harmful to the public, and he or she reports alleged organizational misconduct to the media, government, or high-level company officials, **whistle-blowing** has occurred.

> One of the most publicized whistle-blowers of recent years was Dr. Jeffrey Wigand, whose dramatic story was later portrayed in the movie *The Insider*. Dr. Wigand, a scientist and chief of research for cigarette maker Brown & Williamson, came forward with inside information that his employer had known that nicotine was addictive and had actively manipulated its level in cigarettes. His allegations, made under oath, made an important contribution to the success of litigation against the tobacco industry.[35]

Speaking out against an employer can be risky; many whistle-blowers find their charges ignored—or worse, find themselves ostracized, demoted, or even fired for daring to go public with their criticisms. Whistle-blowers in the United States have some legal protection against retaliation by their employers, though. As noted earlier in this chapter, most workers are employed *at will*, meaning they can be fired for any reason. However, most states now recognize a public policy exception to this rule. Employees who are discharged in retaliation for blowing the whistle, in a situation that affects public welfare, may sue for reinstatement and in some cases may even be entitled to punitive damages. The federal Sarbanes-Oxley Act, passed in 2002 (and described more fully in Chapters 4 and 14), makes it illegal for employers to retaliate in any way against whistle-blowers who report information that could have an impact on the value of a company's shares. It also requires boards of directors to establish procedures for hearing employee complaints.

Moreover, whistle-blowers sometimes benefit from their actions. The U.S. False Claims Act, as amended in 1986, allows individuals who sue federal contractors for fraud to receive up to 30 percent of any amount recovered by the government. In the past decade, the number of whistle-blower lawsuits—perhaps spurred by this incentive—increased significantly, exposing fraud in the country's defense, health care, municipal bond, and pharmaceutical industries. A case in which whistle-blowers and their attorneys used this law to launch a major case against Eli Lilly for illegal drug marketing is described in Exhibit 16.C.

Whistle-blowing has both defenders and detractors. Those defending whistle-blowing point to the successful detection and prosecution of fraudulent activities. Under the False Claims Act, through 2008 almost $22 billion had been recovered that would otherwise have been lost to fraud.[36] Situations dangerous to the public or the environment have been exposed and corrected because insiders have spoken out. Yet opponents cite hundreds of unsubstantiated cases, often involving disgruntled workers seeking to blackmail or discredit their employers.

---

[35] Dr. Wigand's story is told in Philip J. Hilts, *Smoke Screen: The Truth Behind the Tobacco Industry Cover-Up* (Reading, MA: Addison-Wesley, 1996).

[36] U.S. Department of Justice statistics, summarized at the Web site of Taxpayers against Fraud, *www.taf.org*.

In 2009, Eli Lilly, a leading pharmaceutical company, paid $1.4 billion to settle charges that it had illegally marketed its drug Zyprexa—the biggest amount ever in a case arising from allegations made by company whistle-blowers.

Zyprexa was one of a class of drugs known as atypical antipsychotics. The Food and Drug Administration (FDA) first approved Zyprexa in 1996 for the treatment of psychosis and later for schizophrenia and bipolar disorder—all serious psychiatric illnesses—in adults. Government scientists also found that the drug had potentially dangerous side effects, including weight gain, metabolic disorders, and heart failure. Under U.S. law, doctors may prescribe a medication in any way they choose, but drug makers are explicitly prohibited from marketing their products for any uses that have not been approved by the FDA.

In the early 2000s, several Lilly sales representatives came forward, charging that the company had organized an illegal nationwide campaign to convince doctors to prescribe Zyprexa for unapproved uses, particularly for the elderly in long-term care facilities. Under the slogan "5 at 5," the marketing campaign suggested that 5 mg of the drug (which was known to have a sedating effect) be given at 5 p.m. to control agitation, anxiety, and insomnia in older patients, particularly those with Alzheimer's or other forms of dementia. Explained the whistle-blowers' lawyer, "this potent antipsychotic was essentially used as a 'chemical restraint' for the elderly for whom [it] had no other health benefit." The company also promoted the drug for treating disruptive children.

Lilly's strategy was very effective. Since the drug's introduction, the company had sold $39 billion worth of Zyprexa, which cost as much as $25 for a daily pill. Forty percent of these sales were for off-label uses, investigators found. The company's illegal marketing, the government concluded, had generated hundreds of millions of dollars in profit, much of it paid for by taxpayers in the form of Medicare and Medicaid reimbursements. The government did not estimate the number of children, elders, and others who were harmed by dangerous or inappropriate medication. Nine whistle-blowers—several of whom had been fired by Lilly after complaining—shared $79 million of the settlement.

Sources: "Eli Lilly Pays a Record $1.4 Billion to Settle Federal and State Fraud Investigations into Illegal Zyprexa Off-Label Marketing Practices," *Biotech Business Week,* January 26, 2009; "Settlement Called Near on Zyprexa," *The New York Times,* January 15, 2009; and "Justice Department Beats Chest over Zyprexa Settlement," *The Wall Street Journal Health Blog,* January 15, 2009. Many of the legal documents from the case are available at *www.usdoj.gov/usao/pae/eli_lilly.html.*

When is an employee morally justified in blowing the whistle on his or her employer? According to one expert, four main conditions must be satisfied to justify informing the media or government officials about a corporation's actions.

- The organization is doing (or will do) something that seriously harms others.
- The employee has tried and failed to resolve the problem internally.
- Reporting the problem publicly will probably stop or prevent the harm.
- The harm is serious enough to justify the probable costs of disclosure to the whistle-blower and others.[37]

Only after each of these conditions has been met should the whistle-blower go public.

Working Conditions around the World

Much of this chapter has focused on the employment relationship, and the legal and ethical norms governing it, in the United States. Workplace institutions differ dramatically around the world. Laws and practices that establish fair wages, acceptable working conditions, and employee rights vary greatly from region to region. As illustrated by the

[37] Manuel G. Velasquez, *Business Ethics: Concepts and Cases,* 6th ed. (Upper Saddle River, NJ: 2006), p. 379.

opening example of this chapter that described a Nike contract factory in China, these differences pose a challenge to multinational corporations. By whose standards should these companies operate?

Recent headlines have turned the public's attention to the problem of **sweatshops**, factories where employees, sometimes including children, are forced to work long hours at low wages, often under unsafe ˊworking conditions. Several well-known companies in addition to Nike, including Walmart, Disney, and McDonald's, have been criticized for tolerating abhorrent working conditions in their overseas factories or those of their contractors. In recent years, student groups have pressured companies by rallying to prevent their colleges and universities from buying school-logo athletic gear, clothing, and other products made under sweatshop conditions.

Fair Labor Standards

The term *labor standards* refers to the conditions under which a company's employees—or the employees of its suppliers, subcontractors, or others in its commercial chain—work. Some believe that labor standards should be universal; that is, companies should conform to common norms across all their operations worldwide. Such universal rules are sometimes called **fair labor standards**. For example, such standards might include a ban on all child labor, establishment of maximum work hours per week, or a commitment to pay a wage above a certain level. Others think that what is fair varies across cultures and economies, and it is often difficult to set standards that are workable in all settings. For example, in some cultures child labor is more acceptable (or economically necessary) than in others. A wage that would be utterly inadequate in one economic setting might seem princely in another. In some countries, unions are legal and common; in others, they are illegal or actively discouraged.

In the face of growing concerns over working conditions overseas, a debate has developed over how best to establish fair labor standards for multinational corporations. Several approaches have emerged.

Voluntary *corporate codes of conduct,* described in detail in Chapters 5 and 6, can include labor standards that companies expect their own plants and those of their contractors to follow. One of the first companies to develop such standards was Levi Strauss, a U.S. apparel maker. After the company was accused of using an unethical contractor in Saipan, the company reviewed its procedures and adopted a wide-ranging set of guidelines for its overseas manufacturing. Reebok, Boeing, DaimlerChrysler, and other companies have followed suit.

Nongovernmental organization (NGO) labor codes have also been attempted. For example, the Council on Economic Priorities has developed a set of workplace rules called Social Accountability 8000, or SA 8000. Modeled after the quality initiative of the International Organization for Standardization, ISO 9000, SA 8000 establishes criteria for companies to meet in order to receive a "good working condition" certification. Other groups, including the International Labour Organization, the Caux Roundtable, and the United Nations, have also worked to define common standards to which companies can voluntarily subscribe. Some of these efforts are further described in Chapter 7.

Yet a third approach is *industrywide labor codes.* Groups of companies, sometimes with participation of government officials, NGOs, and worker and consumer representatives, define industrywide standards that they can all agree to. In 2004, for instance, three leading high-tech companies—HP, IBM, and Dell—released a common Electronic Industry Code of Conduct, establishing a uniform set of labor, health and safety, and

The Ethical Trading Initiative (ETI), an alliance of companies, nongovernmental organizations, and unions, has defined a living wage as "a wage that allows a worker to provide for him or herself and family, to buy essential medicines, to send children to school, and to save for the future." ETI has called on companies around the world, big and small, to commit to paying all employees a living wage. The following are among those that have done so.

The White Dog Café in Philadelphia, founded in 1983 by Judy Wicks, is a popular restaurant near the University of Pennsylvania that offers fresh, locally grown food served in an old Victorian brownstone. Wicks decided early on that the minimum wage set by the federal government was not enough to live on. In 2009, the entry wage at the restaurant was $8 an hour, with a raise to $9 an hour after a year; most White Dog Café employees earned much more. "The traditional value system in the restaurant business of running people into the ground needs to change in order to create a more fulfilling workplace for everyone," Wicks said.

When *Novartis,* a major multinational pharmaceutical firm, committed to pay a living wage to all its employees around the world, it faced the daunting task of figuring out what exactly that would mean. The company brought in outside NGOs to help it estimate a "basic needs basket" of goods and services in the many nations where it operated. By 2006, it had met its goal of paying living wages to all 93,000 employees. "No other companies are doing this locally," said a company manager in Pakistan. "I can proudly say . . . that we are not just a profit-making business."

New Look, a fashion retailer based in the United Kingdom, partnered with its suppliers in Bangladesh to raise wages as part of a project sponsored by the ETI. In the first year, wages for machine operators went up 24 percent. This made a huge difference in the lives of the Bangladeshi workers, many of whom had had to pay up to 70 percent of their pay for rice and other basic foodstuffs.

Sources: "Living Wage: Make It a Reality," workshop report, Ethical Trading Initiative Conference 2008; "Implementing a Living Wage Globally—The Novartis Approach," April 7, 2007, *www.corporatecitizenship.novartis.co;* Responsible Wealth, *Choosing the High Road: Businesses That Pay a Living Wage and Prosper,* 2000, *www.responsiblewealth.org;* and *www.whitedog.com.*

environmental standards for their global supply chains.[38] Cisco Systems, Microsoft, and several other companies later endorsed the effort. Supporters said a common code would likely improve supplier compliance and lower the costs of training and monitoring.

Whatever the approach, certain common questions emerge in any attempt to define and enforce fair labor standards. These questions include the following:

- *What wage level is fair?* Some argue that market forces should set wages, as long as they do not fall below the level established by local minimum wage laws. Others feel that they should pay workers a fair share of the sale price of the product or of the company's profit. Still others argue that companies have a moral obligation to pay workers enough to achieve a decent family standard of living; this is called a **living wage**. Exhibit 16.D further explains this concept and profiles several businesses that share a commitment to paying their employees a living wage.

- *Should standards apply just to the firm's own employees, or to all workers who have a hand in making its products?* Some say that while the responsibility of a firm to its own employees is clear, its responsibility to the employees of its subcontractors is indirect and therefore of lower importance. Other firms have embraced their responsibility for standards through the supply chain. The Gap, for example, requires factories

[38] "HP, Dell, IBM and Leading Suppliers Release Electronics Industry Code of Conduct," press release, October 21, 2004, *www.hp.com.*

that produce its branded apparel to pledge in writing to follow labor standards outlined in the company's code of vendor conduct.

- *How should fair labor standards best be enforced?* Adherence to fair labor standards, unlike national labor laws, for example, is strictly voluntary. Companies can adopt their own code, or agree to one of the NGO or industry codes. But who is to say that they, and their contractors, are actually living up to these rules? In response to this concern, a debate has emerged over how best to monitor and enforce fair labor standards. Some have advocated hiring outside accounting firms, academic experts, or advocacy organizations to conduct independent audits to determine if a code's standards are being met.

As businesses have become more and more global, as shown in Chapter 6, companies have faced the challenge of operating simultaneously in many countries that differ widely in their working conditions. For these companies, abiding by government regulations and local cultural traditions in their overseas manufacturing may not be enough. Many business leaders have realized that subscribing to fair labor standards that commit to common norms of fairness, respect, and dignity for all their workers is an effective strategy for enhancing their corporate reputations, as well as meeting the complex global challenges of corporate social responsibility.

Employees as Corporate Stakeholders

The issues discussed in this chapter illustrate forcefully that today's business corporation is open to a wide range of social forces. Its borders are very porous, letting in a constant flow of external influences. Many are brought inside by employees, whose personal values, lifestyles, and social attitudes become a vital part of the workplace.

Managers and other business professionals need to be aware of these employee-imported features of today's workforce. The employment relationship is central to getting a corporation's work done and to helping satisfy the wishes of those who contribute their skills and talents to the company. The task of a corporate manager is to reconcile potential clashes between employees' human needs and legal rights and the requirements of corporate economic production.

Summary

- U.S. labor laws give most workers the right to organize unions and to bargain collectively with their employers. Some believe that unions are poised for resurgence after many years of decline.

- Job safety and health concerns have increased as a result of rapidly changing technology in the workplace. U.S. employers must comply with expanding OSHA regulations and respond to the threat of violence at work.

- Employers' right to discharge "at will" has been limited, and employees now have a number of bases for suing for wrongful discharge. The expectations of both sides in the employment relationship have been altered over time by globalization, business cycles, and other factors.

- Employees' privacy rights are frequently challenged by employers' needs to have information about their health, their work activities, and even their off-the-job lifestyles. When these issues arise, management has a responsibility to act ethically toward employees while continuing to work for a high level of economic performance.

- Blowing the whistle on one's employer is often a last resort to protest company actions considered harmful to others. In recent years, U.S. legislation has extended new protections to whistle-blowers.
- The growing globalization of business has challenged companies to adopt fair labor standards to ensure that their products are not manufactured under substandard, sweatshop conditions.

Key Terms

drug testing, *374*	honesty tests, *376*	privacy rights, *372*
electronic monitoring, *372*	labor union, *364*	social contract, *369*
employee assistance programs (EAPs), *375*	living wage, *380*	sweatshops, *379*
employment-at-will, *368*	Occupational Safety and Health Administration (OSHA), *367*	whistle-blowing, *377*
ergonomics, *366*		
fair labor standards, *379*		

Internet Resources

www.aclu.org	American Civil Liberties Union
www.afl-cio.org	American Federation of Labor-Congress of Industrial Organizations
www.business.com/human-resources	Business.com (human resources topics)
www.drugfreeworkplace.org	Institute for a Drug-Free Workplace
www.ethicaltrade.org	Ethical Trading Initiative
www.ilo.org	International Labour Organization (ILO)
www.osha.gov	Occupational Safety and Health Administration
www.state.gov/g/drl/lbr	U.S. State Department, Office of International Labor and Corporate Social Responsibility
www.whistleblowers.org	National Whistleblowers Center
www.workrights.org	National Workrights Institute

Discussion Case: *No Smoking Allowed—On the Job or Off*

Weyco, a benefits management company in Michigan, took an unusual step in 2005: it fired all employees who were smokers, even if they had never lit up on the job. Howard Weyers, president and founder of the privately held company, believed in promoting healthy lifestyles both at his own company and those of his clients. "I spent all my life working with young men, honing them mentally and physically to a high performance," the 70-year-old former college football coach explained. "I think that's what we need to do in the workplace."

About a year earlier, the company had announced that it would no longer hire smokers. To assist its employees who used tobacco, the company offered smoking cessation programs and paid for medication and acupuncture. It also hired a full-time specialist to advise all employees on diet and nutrition and subsidized their health club memberships. Smokers were given 15 months to kick the habit. By the deadline, 20 employees had succeeded in doing so; the 4 who had not were fired.

Weyco employees were of mixed opinion about the tobacco-free policy. One employee who gave up cigarettes commented, "I had to choose between whether I wanted to keep my job and whether I wanted to keep smoking. To me it was a no-brainer." But another, who left the company rather than quit smoking, decried the invasion of privacy. "You feel like you have no rights," she said. "It had to do with my privacy in my own home."

Weyco's decision to prohibit smoking off the job as well as in the workplace was unusual. Most U.S. employers—some acting voluntarily and some because they were forced to by local and state antismoking laws—had banned smoking on the job or restricted it to a few separate areas, but very few had tried to dictate what employees could do on their own time.

Employers cited several reasons for adopting antismoking rules. Secondhand smoke— smoke emitted from a lit cigarette, cigar, or pipe, or exhaled by a smoker—caused nearly 50,000 nonsmoker deaths in the United States each year, according to medical research. Nonsmoking employees could be sickened, or even killed, by exposure to others' tobacco smoke at work, particularly in workplaces where smoking is common, such as bars and restaurants. Moreover, smoking employees were expensive. Smokers, on average, cost their employers $1,800 more per year in health care costs, and lost twice as much production time, as nonsmokers.

For their part, employees who smoke have been divided in their reaction to tobacco restrictions or bans. Some smokers, like many at Weyco, welcomed the opportunity to quit. A study by researchers at the University of California found that employees who were covered by strong workplace smoking policies were more likely to quit the habit than other smokers. Others, however, were incensed at what they perceived as a violation of personal rights and freedoms. They resented having to go outside to smoke, particularly in bad weather. Some even argued that smoking was, in effect, an addiction to nicotine, and so their right to smoke should be protected under the Americans with Disabilities Act (further described in the following chapter).

Lawmakers weighed in on both sides of the issue. Many towns and cities, and 23 states, passed antismoking ordinances or laws that banned smoking in enclosed workplaces. But many states (sometimes the same ones) also passed laws making job discrimination against smokers illegal. Although these laws did not affect smoking bans or restrictions in the workplace, they did prohibit companies from refusing to hire smokers and from firing employees who continued to smoke. (Michigan, where Weyco was located, did not have such a law.)

Many other countries have historically been more tolerant of smoking, both in the workplace and elsewhere, than the United States. By the mid-2000s, however, this had begun to change. In 2005, the World Health Organization's Framework Convention on Tobacco Control took effect, after ratification by many of the world's nations. Among other things, the convention called on governments to protect people from workplace exposure to secondhand smoke.

In 2006, Meritain Health acquired Weyco, but pledged to continue its no-smoking policy.

Sources: "Now, the Stick: Workers Pay for Poor Health Habits," *Washington Post,* November 13, 2007; "Company's Smoking Ban Means Off-Hours, Too," *The New York Times,* February 8, 2005; "Workers Fume as Firms Ban Smoking at Home," *Detroit News,* January 27, 2005; "Effect of Smoking Status on Productivity Loss," *Journal of Occupational and Environmental Medicine,* October 2006; and "UC Study Says Workplace Smoking Ordinances Help Employees Quit," *Cal-OSHA Reporter,* May 5, 2000. The Web site of the Framework Convention on Tobacco Control is at *www.who.int//tobacco/framework.* Other statistics are available at *www.cdc.gov/tobacco; http://no-smoke.org* and *www.tobaccofreekids.org.*

Discussion Questions

1. Should employers have the right to ban or restrict smoking by their employees at the workplace? Why do you think so?

2. Should employers have the right to restrict or ban smoking by the employees off the job, as Weyco did? Why do you think so?

3. Should the government regulate smoking at work? If so, what would be the best public policy? Why do you think so?

4. Should multinational firms have a single corporate policy on smoking in the workplace, or vary their policies depending on local laws and norms of behavior in various countries where they do business?

CHAPTER SEVENTEEN

Managing a Diverse Workforce

The workforce in the United States is more diverse than it has ever been, reflecting the entry of women into the workforce, immigration from other countries, the aging of the population, and shifting patterns of work and retirement. Equal opportunity laws and changing societal expectations have challenged corporations to manage workforce diversity effectively. Full workplace parity for women and persons of color has not yet been reached. However, businesses have made great strides in reforming policies and practices in order to draw on the skills and contributions of their increasingly varied employees.

This Chapter Focuses on These Key Learning Objectives:

- Knowing in what ways the workforce of the United States is diverse, and evaluating how it might change in the future.
- Understanding where women and persons of color work, how much they are paid, and the roles they play as managers and business owners.
- Identifying the role government plays in securing equal employment opportunity for historically disadvantaged groups, and debating whether or not affirmative action is an effective strategy for promoting equal opportunity.
- Assessing the ways diversity confers a competitive advantage.
- Formulating how companies can best manage workforce diversity, making the workplace welcoming, fair, and accommodating to all employees.
- Understanding what policies and practices are most effective in helping today's employees manage the complex, multiple demands of work and family obligations.

Marriott International, the large hospitality chain, employs 146,000 workers in 66 countries, doing jobs ranging from managing vacation resorts, to flipping burgers, to cleaning bathrooms and changing sheets. Their employees speak 50 different languages and represent dozens of distinct cultures. Many of Marriott's employees in the United States are immigrants, some are in welfare-to-work programs, and many are single parents. A large proportion work nights or odd hours. In an effort to address its employees' needs, in 2003 Marriott established a Committee of Excellence—an external board of experts—to set diversity objectives and monitor progress. Among other initiatives, the company provided consultations on a wide range of personal issues, offered child care services, and operated *Sed de Saber* (thirst for knowledge) to teach life skills to Spanish-speaking employees. Marriott credited its innovative programs with helping it attract and retain committed employees from many backgrounds. "In this competitive marketplace, we must continue to embrace the unique talents and experiences of our employees . . . to help us meet the changing needs of our customers," said CEO J.W. Marriott, Jr.[1]

The example of Marriott Corporation demonstrates both the promise and the perils of a workforce that encompasses tremendous diversity on every imaginable dimension. Having many different kinds of workers can be a great benefit to businesses, as it gives them a wider pool from which to recruit talent, many points of view and experiences, and an ability to reach out effectively to a diverse, global customer base. Yet it also poses great challenges, as business must meet the mandates of equal employment laws and help people who differ greatly in their backgrounds, values, and expectations get along—and succeed—in the workplace.

The Changing Face of the Workforce

Human beings differ from each other in many ways. Each person is unique, as is each employee within an organization. Individuals are also similar in many ways, some of which are more readily visible than others. The term **diversity** refers to variation in the important human characteristics that distinguish people from one another. The *primary* dimensions of diversity are age, ethnicity, gender, mental or physical abilities, race, and sexual orientation. The *secondary* dimensions of diversity are many; they include such characteristics as communication style, family status, and first language.[2] Individuals' distinguishing characteristics clearly impact their values, opportunities, and perceptions of themselves and others at work. **Workforce diversity**—diversity among employees—thus represents both a challenge and an opportunity for businesses.

Today, the U.S. workforce is as diverse as it has ever been, and it is becoming even more so. Consider the following major trends:[3]

- *More women are working than ever before.* Married women, those with young children, and older women, in particular, have greatly increased their participation in the workforce. By 2016, the Bureau of Labor Statistics estimates that 47 percent of all workers will be women, nearly equal to their share of the population. One effect of this trend is that more employed men have wives who also work—changing the nature of their responsibilities within the family.

---

[1] "Diversity and Inclusion Global Fact Sheet," 2009. Marriott's Web site is at *www.marriott.com.*

[2] This definition is based on Marilyn Loden, *Implementing Diversity* (New York: McGraw-Hill, 1995), ch. 2.

[3] Except as noted, the figures in the following paragraphs are drawn from "Labor Force Projections to 2016: More Workers in Their Golden Years," *Monthly Labor Review,* November 2007, and *Statistical Abstract of the United States 2009* (Washington DC: U.S. Census Bureau).

Andrés Tapia, chief diversity officer for the Hewitt Associates, a human resources consulting and benefits administration firm, has written compellingly about the ways in which generational identity is itself a dimension of diversity. "As a diversity leader," Tapia writes, "I've seen that a telltale sign of inclusion breakdown is when judgments pop up unchallenged and groupthink sets in about the newcomer. When behaviors by others are different from behaviors we all believe is right, it elicits one of two reactions about the other: They either are incompetent or a bad person. This is now happening in response to the millennials. As in other forms of diversity, this kind of stance not only is exclusionary, it is not helpful in addressing the real issues. Today, generational diversity is as much an issue as gender and racial diversity. . . . Just by the nature of who they are, millennials will transform the workplace."

Millennials, Tapia says, tend to be idealistic, technologically savvy, environmentally conscious, globally networked, and collaborative. In the workplace, they tend to challenge traditional planning, being told what to do, and rigidity in career paths. Corporations will need to change, he argues, to accommodate the talents of these young workers—who bring yet another dimension of diversity into an increasingly diverse workplace.

Source: Andrés Tapia, "The Millennials: Why This Generation Will Challenge the Workplace like No Other," Hewitt Associates, 2008, *www.hewitt.com*.

- *Immigration has profoundly reshaped the workplace.* Between 2000 and 2007, more than 10 million immigrants entered the United States, the largest number in any seven-year period in the nation's history. The leading countries of origin are now Mexico, China, India, the Philippines, Vietnam, El Salvador, Cuba, and the nations comprising the former U.S.S.R. Immigrants now make up about 15 percent of U.S. workers, increasing linguistic and cultural diversity in many workplaces.[4]

- *Ethnic and racial diversity is increasing.* Hispanics (defined by the Census as persons of Spanish or Latin American ancestry), now about 14 percent of U.S. workers, are expected to comprise 16 percent by 2016. Although less numerous overall, Asians are expected to be the fastest-growing segment of the labor force. The proportion of African-Americans is expected to hold steady at around 12 percent. By 2016, the U.S. workforce is projected to be about 35 percent nonwhite (this category includes persons of Hispanic origin). In some states, such as California, these trends will be much more pronounced.

- *The workforce will continue to get older.* As the baby boom generation matures, birthrates drop, and people live longer and healthier lives, the population will age. Many of these older people will continue to work, whether out of choice or necessity. One survey conducted in late 2008 found that 16 percent of people 45 and older had postponed retirement because of the economic downturn. Said one 67-year-old utility company employee, "I felt that I was in a good position to retire until the market kept going down and down . . . [But] there's no point in retiring in this time of uncertainty until I have a better feel for where the economy is going." Employers will have to find new ways to accommodate older workers.[5]

- *Millennials are entering the workforce.* Even as many baby boomers extend their working years, so-called *millennials*—young people born after 1980 or so—are entering the workforce in large numbers, bringing fresh perspectives and practices. The observations of the senior diversity executive at Hewitt Associates on what the influx of millennials will mean for the workplace are presented in Exhibit 17.A.

[4] "Immigrants in the United States, 2007: A Profile of America's Foreign-Born Population," Center for Immigration Studies, November 2007, *www.cis.org.*

[5] "Older Workers, Hurt by Recession, Seek New Jobs," *Associated Press,* March 31, 2009.

Workforce diversity creates many new employee issues and problems. This chapter will consider the changing face of today's workplace, and its implications for management. Laws and regulations clearly require that businesses provide equal opportunity, and avoid discrimination and harassment. How to meet—and exceed—these mandates presents an ongoing challenge to businesses seeking to reap the benefits of a well-integrated, yet culturally diverse work population. We turn first to two important dimensions of workforce diversity: gender and race.

Gender and Race in the Workplace

Gender and race are both important primary dimensions of workforce diversity. Women and persons of color have always worked, contributing both paid and unpaid labor to the economy. Yet the nature of their participation in the labor force has changed, posing new challenges to business.

Women and Minorities at Work

One of the most significant changes in the past half-century has been the growing labor force participation of women. During the period following World War II, the proportion of women working outside the home rose dramatically. In 1950, about a third of adult women were employed. This proportion rose steadily for several decades, leveling off at around 59 percent in the mid-2000s. Participation rates (the proportion of women in the workforce) have risen for all groups of women, but the most dramatic increases have been among married women, mothers of young children, and middle-class women, those who had earlier been most likely to stay at home. Men's participation rates declined somewhat during this period; between 1950 and 2007, the proportion of adult men who worked fell from 86 percent to 73 percent. Figure 17.1 shows the convergence of the labor force participation rates for men and women over the past 60 years or so.

Women have entered the labor force for many of the same reasons men do. They need income to support themselves and their families. Having a job with pay also gives a woman psychological independence and security. The high cost of living puts financial pressure on families, frequently pushing women into the labor force just to sustain an

FIGURE 17.1
Proportion of Women and Men in the Labor Force, 1950–2007

Source: U.S. Bureau of Labor Statistics.

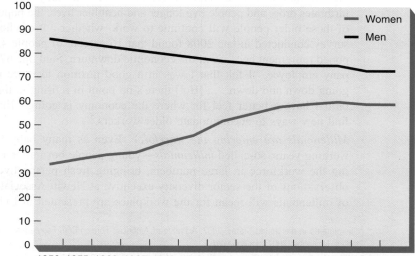

accustomed standard of living or to put children through college or care for aging parents. The inadequacies and uncertainties of retirement plans and health care programs frequently mean that women, as well as men, need to save, invest, and plan for the future. When women divorce, they often can no longer rely on a partner's earnings for support.

The rapid rise of female labor force participation in the postwar years also reflects the expansion of segments of the economy that were major employers of women. In 1940, about one-third of all U.S. jobs were white-collar (not requiring manual labor); by 1980, over half were white-collar. Professional, technical, and service jobs also grew relative to the economy. The creation of many new positions in fields traditionally staffed by women produced what economists call a demand-side pull of women into the labor force. More "women's jobs" meant more women working.

Labor force participation rates for minorities, unlike those of women, have always been high. For example, in 1970 about 62 percent of all African-Americans (men and women combined) worked; the figure is about 64 percent today. Participation rates have also been consistently high for most other minority groups; for Asians, it is 67 percent; for Hispanics, 69 percent. The key change here has been the move of persons of color, in recent decades, into a wider range of jobs as barriers of discrimination and segregation have fallen; minorities have become better represented in the ranks of managers, professionals, and the skilled trades. These trends will be further discussed later in this chapter.

> The face of success in the United States is diverse, just as the workforce is. Consider Jenny Ming, president of the Old Navy division of Gap, Inc., from 1998 to 2006. Ming emigrated with her family from Macao (an island nation off the coast of China) when she was 9 years old. She later recalled in an interview that as a youngster, she loved everything about America, especially Halloween. After completing her education in the public university system, Ming took her first job as an assistant department manager for Mervyn's. She moved up fast in the retail world, becoming a top executive at Old Navy when she was just 39. A profile in *BusinessWeek* attributed Ming's success to her "uncanny knack for predicting which hip-looking clothes of the moment will appeal to the masses, then making big bets on producing the huge quantities needed to assure the chain a continual string of hits." After leaving Old Navy, Ming became a partner in a private equity firm specializing in the retail sector.[6]

The Gender and Racial Pay Gap

One persistent feature of the working world is that women and persons of color on average receive lower pay than white men do. This disparity, called the **pay gap**, narrowed over the past three decades, as Figure 17.2 shows. But in 2007 black men and white women still earned only slightly more than three-quarters of white men's pay; black women earned about 68 percent. (These data are based on full-time workers only.) The pay gap for Hispanic women declined by almost 5 percent since 2000; and that for Hispanic men, 3 percent. A study by two labor economists showed that the gender pay gap, now 80 percent, understates lifetime differences in earnings, because women work fewer hours and are more likely to take time off for child rearing. Over their prime working years, women make only 38 percent of what men earn, the study found.[7]

---

[6] "Jenny Ming Made Operating Partner at Advent International," press release, September 9, 2008; "Old Navy's Jenny Ming Setting Sail," July 11, 2006, *www.brandweek.com;* and "A Savvy Captain for Old Navy: Jenny Ming's Drive and Vision Are Paying Off Big for Parent Gap, Inc.," *BusinessWeek,* November 8, 1999.

[7] Stephen J. Rose and Heidi I. Hartmann, *Still a Man's Labor Market: The Long-Term Earnings Gap* (Washington, DC: Institute for Women's Policy Research, 2004).

FIGURE 17.2   **The Gender and Race Pay Gap, 1990–2007 (median weekly earnings of full-time workers, as a percentage of those of white men)**

Source: U.S. Census Bureau, *Statistical Abstract of the United States 2009,* Table 626; and *Statistical Abstract of the United States 2000,* Table 696.

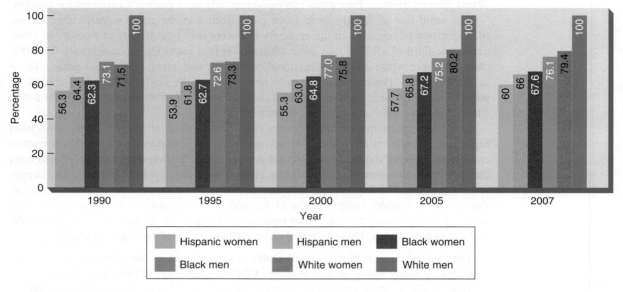

Experts disagree about the cause of the pay gap between women and men. Some believe the continuing gender disparity in pay is evidence of sex discrimination by employers; others believe the gap reflects women's choices to pursue lower-paying jobs or slower advancement because of time off for family responsibilities. Many observers agree, however, that the pay gap persists, in part, because of what is called **occupational segregation**. This term refers to the inequitable concentration of a group, such a minorities or women, in particular job categories. The large pay gap for Hispanic workers, for example, partly reflects their concentration in several low-paid occupations. Fifty-two percent of cement masons, 41 percent of meatpackers, 40 percent of farmworkers, and 40 percent of private household cleaners are of Hispanic origin, according to the Census Bureau, although Hispanics make up only 14 percent of the workforce as a whole. Although women, for their part, have made great strides in entering occupations where they were formerly underrepresented, many remain concentrated in a few sex-typed jobs that some have called the "pink-collar ghetto." Women still make up 97 percent of pre-school and kindergarten teachers, 90 percent of bookkeepers, 99 percent of dental hygienists, and 97 percent of secretaries, for example. Eliminating the pay gap will require, therefore, business programs and government policies that create opportunity for women and people of color to move out of more segregated jobs into ones where the pay and chances for upward mobility are greater.[8]

The most prestigious and highest-paying jobs in a corporation are in top management. Because most corporations are organized hierarchically, management jobs—particularly those at the top—are few. For that reason, only a small fraction of workers, of whatever gender or race, can hope to reach the upper levels in the business world. White men have traditionally filled most of these desirable spots. Business's mandate now is to broaden

[8] The data in this paragraph are drawn from Table 596, "Employed Civilians by Occupation, Sex, Race, and Hispanic Origin," in the U.S. Census Bureau, *Statistical Abstract of the United States 2009.*

these high-level leadership opportunities for women and persons of color, a topic to which we turn next.

Where Women and Persons of Color Manage

Slightly more than 9 million U.S. women were working as managers by the late 2000s. As Figure 17.3 reveals, in 2007 more than 4 out of 10 managers—and a majority of managers in some categories—were women. Clearly, women have broken into management ranks. Women are more likely to be managers, though, in occupational areas where women are more numerous at lower levels, such as health care and education. Grouped by industry, women tend to be concentrated in service industries and in finance, insurance, real estate, and retail businesses. Women managers have also made gains in newer industries, such as biotechnology, where growth has created opportunity.

Where do persons of color manage? As is shown in Figure 17.3, African-Americans, Asians, and Hispanics are underrepresented in management ranks in the United States, making up just 7.5, 5.0, and 7.3 percent of managers, respectively. But they have approached or exceeded parity in a few areas. Blacks make up 12.6 percent of education administrators (more than their 11 percent of the workforce), reflecting less discrimination and more opportunity in public schools. Asians are best represented in the ranks of food service and computer and information systems managers; Hispanics are best represented in food service management. Figure 17.3 shows the continuing underrepresentation of blacks, Asians, and Hispanics in many other management categories.

Breaking the Glass Ceiling

A few exceptional women and persons of color—and some women of color—have reached the pinnacles of power in corporate America.

> In 2009, Ursula Burns was named CEO of Xerox Corporation, the first African-American woman to lead a major U.S. company. (She was also the first woman CEO to succeed another woman, Anne Mulcahy, who stepped down to become the chairman of the board.) Burns, who had been raised in a New York City housing project by a single mother, had gone on to earn a graduate degree in mechanical engineering at Columbia. She was recognized early in her career for extraordinary potential, and had worked her way up at Xerox through a series of increasingly responsible positions. When appointed CEO, Burns commented, "I'm in this job because I believe I earned it through hard work and high performance."[9]

High achievers such as Ursula Burns remain unusual, however. Although women and minorities are as competent as white men in managing people and organizations, they rarely attain the highest positions in corporations. Their ascent seems to be blocked by an invisible barrier, sometimes called a **glass ceiling**. According to Catalyst, an advocacy organization for female executives, in 2008 only 16 percent of the corporate officers of the *Fortune* 500 companies were women (in this context, *corporate officer* refers to a member of the most senior executive group).[10] Only 12 of these companies (2 percent) had women as CEOs, and 19 (4 percent) had persons of color. The latter group included Kenneth Chenault of American Express, Antonio Perez of Eastman Kodak, and

---

[9] "An Historic Succession at Xerox," *BusinessWeek*, June 8, 2009.

[10] "Catalyst 2008 Census of the *Fortune* 500 Reveals Women Gained Little Ground Advancing to Business Leadership Positions," press release, December 10, 2008, *www.catalyst.org.*

FIGURE 17.3
Extent of Diversity in Selected Management Occupations

Source: U.S. Census Bureau, *Statistical Abstract of the United States 2009*, Table 596.

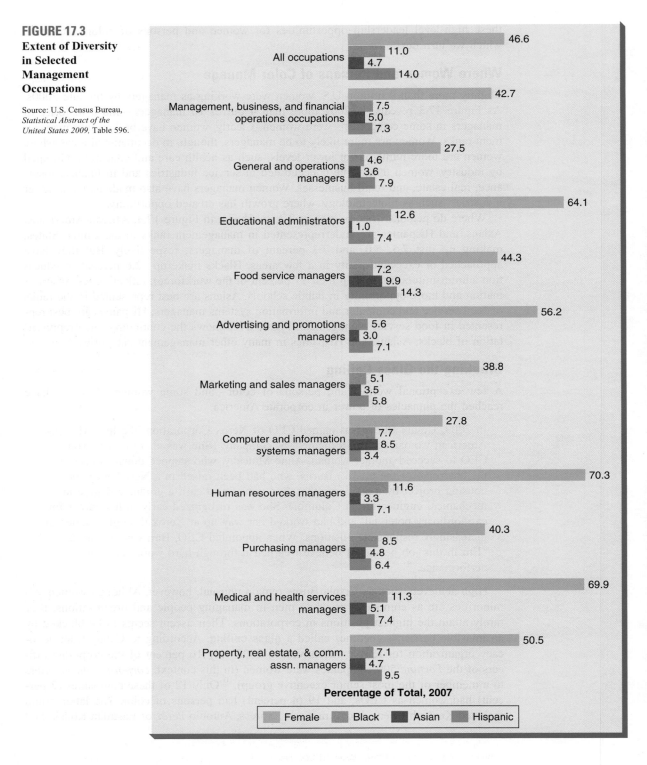

Andrea Jung of Avon Products.[11] In Europe, diversity in the top ranks is also rare. A 2005 study of 360 leading companies in the European Union and Scandinavia found that only one company, Vodafone, had a chief executive from a minority group (he was Arun Sarin, an American citizen born in India); only three companies were headed by a woman.[12]

> Failure to promote women to top-level positions may be hurting companies' financial performance. Studies by faculty members at Pepperdine University, based on data from 2001 to 2007, showed that "companies identified as being the best at promoting women outperformed the industry median" on three different measures of profitability (profit as a percentage of revenue, assets, and equity). The researchers concluded, "Firms exhibit higher profitability when their top executives make smart decisions. One of the smart decisions those executives have consistently made at successful *Fortune* 500 firms is to include women in the executive suite—so that regardless of gender, the best brains are available to continue making smart, and profitable, decisions."[13]

Women and minorities are also scarce on corporate boards. A 2009 study reported that only 15 percent of board members of *Fortune* 500 firms were women; only 3 percent were women of color.[14] Fifteen percent were minorities.[15] Some have cited the lack of board diversity as a contributing factor in the financial crisis that began in 2008. A researcher from the International Centre for Women Business Leaders in the United Kingdom, for example, wryly noted that "had there been a few more Lehman Sisters, it [Lehman Brothers, the investment banking firm that collapsed in 2008] would not have been in the state that it was in."[16]

In 2006, an unusual law promoting boardroom diversity went into effect in Norway. It mandated that, by 2008, 40 percent of corporate directors in large Norwegian companies be women. "Women will have a place where the power is," said Norway's minister of children and equality. "This . . . will set an example for other centers of society." Opponents, including many in the business community, complained that it would force many experienced men off corporate boards and would violate the basic principle that shareholders should be able to vote for anyone they wanted. By the time the law went into effect, 37 percent of board members in Norway were women—almost meeting the quota. In 2007, Spain followed suit—passing a law requiring 40 percent female representation on boards by 2015.[17]

Failure to attain the topmost jobs in some cases is due to lack of experience or inadequate education. Because gender and racial bias has kept women and minorities

---

[11] "*Fortune* 500 Black, Latino, and Asian CEOs," *DiversityINC*, July 22, 2008; and "Wonder Women: Profiles of Leading Female CEOs and Business Executives," *www.infoplease.com.*

[12] "Corporate Europe Ignores Diversity at Its Peril," *Financial Times (London)*, November 30, 2005. Data are from a study conducted by the Aspen Institute Italia.

[13] Roy Douglas Adler, "Profit: Thy Name is . . . Woman?" *Miller-McCune.com*, February 27, 2009.

[14] "2008 Catalyst Census of Women Board Directors of the *Fortune* 500," January 12, 2009, *www.catalyst.org.*

[15] The Alliance for Board Diversity, "Women and Minorities on *Fortune* 100 Boards," 2008, *www.elcinfo.com.* Data on minority board membership are for 2006.

[16] "In a Male Recession, Women Are the First to Quit," *The Times (London)*, April 15, 2009.

[17] "Norway Sets the Pace for Women with Board Quotas," *Financial Times (London)*, June 27, 2008; "Norsk Hydro, Orkla Rush to Add Women Directors under Norway Law," *Bloomberg.com*, December 31, 2007; and "Men Chafe as Norway Ushers Women into Boardroom," *The New York Times*, January 12, 2006.

out of management until recent years, few have had time to acquire the years of experience that are typical of most high-ranking executives. Also, in earlier years women and minorities were discouraged from entering graduate schools of engineering, science, business, and law, the traditional pathways to top corporate management. Even as those barriers have been lowered, though, these groups remain underrepresented at executive levels.

What continues to hold women and minorities back? A study in the *Harvard Business Review* reported that the primary obstacle is **glass walls**: fewer opportunities to move sideways into jobs that lead to the top. Female and minority managers are often found in staff positions, such as public relations or human resources, rather than in line positions in such core areas as marketing, sales, or production where they can acquire the broad management skills necessary for promotion.[18] Another problem is that in filling top positions, recruiters rely on word of mouth—the old boys' network from which women and persons of color are often excluded. Sometimes women voluntarily choose to step off the career track to care for children or elderly relatives.[19] Other causes include a company's lack of commitment to diversity and too little accountability at the top management level for equal employment opportunity. However, recent advances by both women and minorities in the executive suite suggest that the glass ceiling may finally be cracking.

Women and Minority Business Ownership

Some women and minorities have evaded the glass ceiling and risen to the top by founding or taking over their own businesses.

By 2009, over 10 million businesses—40 percent of all privately held firms in the United States—were owned or controlled by women, according to the Center for Women's Business Research. Of these, about one in five was owned by a woman of color.

An example of a successful female entrepreneur is Catherine Hughes, founder and chairperson of Radio One, a company that owns over 50 radio stations, mainly in urban markets. Hughes, who is black, started the business in 1980, when she was general manager at Howard University's FM station, by buying a defunct R&B station. For several years, Hughes slept in the station, ran her own morning talk show, and pounded the pavement in the afternoon looking for advertisers. By the mid-1980s, the station was turning a healthy profit, and Hughes began acquiring other stations. In 2009, the company operated 53 radio stations in 16 urban markets and operated Magazine One and TV One. "I was determined to make this work," Hughes said.[20]

Although most female-headed firms are small, collectively they employ over 13 million people in the United States and generate $1.9 trillion in sales.[21]

Persons of color have also used business ownership as a path to success. According to the Small Business Administration, there were around 4.1 million minority-owned

[18] "What's Holding Women Back?" *Harvard Business Review*, June 1, 2003. The reports of the Glass Ceiling Commission of the U.S. Department of Labor may be accessed at *www.dol.gov/oasam/programs/history/reich/reports/ceiling.pdf*.

[19] "How Women Are Redefining Work and Success," *BusinessWeek*, May 21, 2009.

[20] "Top Ten Black Female Entrepreneurs," *Essence*, October 1999. The Web site for Radio One is *www.radio-one.com*.

[21] These data include privately held businesses in which women own a controlling interest, privately held businesses owned equally by women and men (for example, by a married couple), and publicly traded companies with majority or substantial women's ownership. For current statistics, see the Web site of the Center for Women's Business Research, *www.cfwbr.org*.

businesses in the United States in 2002. Within this group, Hispanic-owned businesses were the most numerous, followed by African-American and Asian-owned businesses.[22] Immigrants were responsible for a good share of the entrepreneurial spirit in the minority community; nearly half of Hispanic business owners and more than two-thirds of Asian business owners were born outside of the United States, according to U.S. Census Bureau figures.

Government's Role in Securing Equal Employment Opportunity

Eliminating workplace discrimination and ensuring equal job opportunity has been a major goal of public policy in the United States for four decades. This section reviews the major laws that govern business practices with respect to equal opportunity, affirmative action, and sexual and racial harassment.

Equal Employment Opportunity

Beginning on a major scale in the 1960s, U.S. presidents issued executive orders and Congress enacted laws intended to promote equal treatment of employees—that is, **equal employment opportunity**. These government rules apply to most businesses in the following ways:

- Discrimination based on race, color, religion, sex, national origin, physical or mental disability, or age is prohibited in all employment practices. This includes hiring, promotion, job classification, and assignment, compensation, and other conditions of work.

- Government contractors must have written affirmative action plans detailing how they are working positively to overcome past and present effects of discrimination in their workforce. However, affirmative action plans must be temporary and flexible, designed to correct past discrimination, and cannot result in reverse discrimination against whites or men.

- Women and men must receive equal pay for performing equal work, and employers may not discriminate on the basis of pregnancy.

In 2009, as one of his first acts in office, President Barack Obama signed into law the Lilly Ledbetter Fair Pay Act. Ledbetter, a supervisor at a Goodyear tire factory in Alabama, had filed a lawsuit shortly before her retirement in 1998, claiming that Goodyear had violated the equal pay laws. Ledbetter said that she had recently learned that for many years the company had been paying her less than men doing the same job. Her case eventually came before the Supreme Court, which ruled against Ledbetter, saying that because the discrimination had started more than 180 days before she filed suit, she had exceeded the time limits. Under the Ledbetter Act, the 180-day time limit would start fresh every time a worker received a discriminatory paycheck. "I will never receive a cent," said Ledbetter. (The law named after her was not retroactive.) "But with the president's signature today I have an even richer reward."[23]

Figure 17.4 outlines the major laws and one executive order that are intended to promote equal opportunity in the workplace. The provisions of one of these, the Americans

---

[22] U.S. Census Bureau, "2002 Survey of Business Owners: Preliminary Estimates of Business Ownership by Gender, Hispanic or Latino Origin, and Race," *www.census.gov.*

[23] "Obama Signs Equal-Pay Legislation," *The New York Times,* January 30, 2009.

FIGURE 17.4
Major Federal Laws and Executive Orders Prohibiting Job Discrimination

Equal Pay Act (1963)—Mandates equal pay for substantially equal work by men and women.
Civil Rights Act (1964; amended 1972, 1991, 2009)—Prohibits discrimination in employment based on race, color, religion, sex, or national origin.
Executive Order 11246 (1965)—Mandates affirmative action for all federal contractors and subcontractors.
Age Discrimination in Employment Act (1967)—Protects individuals who are 40 years of age or older.
Equal Employment Opportunity Act (1972)—Increases power of the Equal Employment Opportunity Commission to combat discrimination.
Pregnancy Discrimination Act (1978)—Forbids employers to discharge, fail to hire, or otherwise discriminate against pregnant women.
Americans with Disabilities Act (1990)—Prohibits discrimination against individuals with disabilities.
Family and Medical Leave Act (1993)—Requires companies with 50 or more employees to provide up to 12 weeks unpaid leave for illness, care of a sick family member, or the birth or adoption of a child.

with Disabilities Act, are further described in Exhibit 17.B. The major agency charged with enforcing equal employment opportunity laws and executive orders in the United States is the **Equal Employment Opportunity Commission (EEOC)**. The EEOC was created in 1964 and given added enforcement powers in 1972 and 1990. In 2008, bias complaints filed with the EEOC surged. Some experts felt that that the reason was the economic downturn. "[T]here's been an extreme recession," said one employment attorney. "People are being let go and are searching for reasons. It may or may not be related to discrimination."[24]

Companies that fail to follow the laws shown in Figure 17.4 often find themselves facing expensive lawsuits. One of the more sensational examples of a suit against racial discrimination in the workplace involved Texaco.

A number of African-American employees sued the big oil company, charging discrimination. In the course of investigating the case, these employees' attorneys obtained a copy of a tape recording, apparently of top Texaco executives at a meeting to discuss how to respond to the lawsuit. The tape seemed to contain offensive racial epithets as well as discussion of destroying evidence that would be harmful to Texaco's position. When a transcript of the tape was published, it was very embarrassing for the company. Texaco settled the lawsuit out of court, agreeing to pay $176.1 million over five years, then the largest settlement in the history of racial discrimination suits in the United States. The company also created organizational programs promoting racial sensitivity at work.[25]

Potentially costly lawsuits can involve other forms of discrimination as well, such as those based on age, gender, or disability. A class-action lawsuit involving alleged discrimination against women at the nation's largest private sector employer, Walmart, is described in the discussion case at the end of this chapter.

Affirmative Action

One way to promote equal opportunity and remedy past discrimination is through **affirmative action**. Since the mid-1960s, major government contractors have been required

---

[24] "Heavy Job Losses Cited in Surge of Bias Allegations," *McClatchy-Tribune Business News*, March 24, 2009.
[25] "Texaco to Pay $176.1 Million in Bias Suit," *The Wall Street Journal*, November 18, 1996.

Exhibit 17.B

Accommodating Persons with Disabilities

The Americans with Disabilities Act (ADA) of 1990 requires employers to make accommodations for disabled workers and job applicants and prohibits employers from discriminating on the basis of a person's disability. A disabled worker is defined by the law as one who can perform the essential functions of a job, with or without reasonable accommodations. (The law was amended in 2008 to make it easier for someone to establish that he or she has a disability under the ADA.) The law prohibits employers from asking in a job interview, for example, about a person's medical history or past treatment for mental illness or alcoholism. And it requires employers to make reasonable accommodations, for example, by modifying work equipment, adjusting work schedules, or making facilities accessible. The courts have interpreted the ADA to cover persons with acquired immunodeficiency syndrome (AIDS). This means that discrimination against persons with AIDS, or who are infected with HIV (the virus that causes AIDS), is prohibited, so long as the person can perform the essential elements of the job. Some businesses have complained about the law, citing its vagueness, the high cost of compliance, and the expense of defending against lawsuits. But the ADA has benefited the nation's disabled, 56 percent of whom are now employed, compared with only about a third when the law was passed.

Source: "Disabled Find Jobs but Face Obstacles," *Orlando Sentinel,* May 12, 2006. Information about the law is available online at *www.eeoc.gov;* the most recent data are available at *www.census.gov.*

by presidential executive order to adopt written affirmative action plans specifying goals, actions, and timetables for promoting greater on-the-job equality. Their purpose is to reduce job discrimination by encouraging companies to take positive (that is, affirmative) steps to overcome past employment practices and traditions that may have been discriminatory.

Affirmative action became increasingly controversial in the 1990s and 2000s. In some states, new laws (such as Proposition 209 in California) were passed banning or limiting affirmative action programs in public hiring and university admissions, and the issue was debated in Congress and in the courts. Backers of affirmative action argued that these programs provided an important tool for achieving equal opportunity. In this view, women and minorities continued to face discriminatory barriers, and affirmative action was necessary to level the playing field. Some large corporations backed affirmative action programs, finding them helpful in monitoring their progress in providing equal job opportunity. General Electric, AT&T, and IBM, for example, have said that they would continue to use affirmative action goals and timetables even if they were not required by law.

Critics, however, argued that affirmative action was inconsistent with the principles of fairness and equality. Some pointed to instances of so-called **reverse discrimination**, which occurs when one group is unintentionally discriminated against in an effort to help another group. For example, if a more qualified white man were passed over for a job as a police officer in favor of a less qualified Hispanic man to remedy past discrimination in a police department, this might be unfair to the white candidate.

In 2009, the Supreme Court heard a case brought by a Frank Ricci, a white firefighter in New Haven, Connecticut. Earlier, Ricci had taken an exam for promotion to lieutenant and had scored sixth among 77 candidates. But the city decided to discard the results, because none of the 19 African-Americans who took the test qualified for promotion. Ricci and 19 other firefighters (one of whom was Hispanic) then sued the city, saying they had been the victims of reverse discrimination. The city defended its action, saying the test was flawed. The Supreme Court ruled in favor of the firefighter plaintiffs, saying they had been subjected to race discrimination "solely because the higher-scoring candidates were white."[26]

Critics of affirmative action also argued that these programs could actually stigmatize or demoralize the very groups they were designed to help. For example, if a company hired a woman for a top management post, other people might think she got the job just because of affirmative action preferences, even if she were truly the best qualified. This might undermine her effectiveness on the job or even cause her to question her own abilities. For this reason, some women and persons of color called for *less* emphasis on affirmative action, preferring to achieve personal success without preferential treatment.[27]

In 1995, the Supreme Court ruled in an important decision that affirmative action plans were legal but only if they were temporary and flexible, were designed to correct past discrimination, and did not result in reverse discrimination. Under this ruling, quotas (for example, a hard-and-fast rule that 50 percent of all new positions would go to women, say, or African-Americans) would no longer be permitted in most situations. The court confirmed this general approach in 2003 when it ruled in a case involving admissions policies at the University of Michigan that a "holistic" approach that took race into consideration along with other factors in the admissions process, without using quotas, was legal. More than 60 corporations, including Boeing, Pfizer, Steelcase, and even MTV, had filed briefs in support of the university's affirmative action program.[28]

Sexual and Racial Harassment

Government regulations ban both sexual and racial harassment. Of the two kinds, sexual harassment cases are more prevalent, and the law covering them is better defined. But racial harassment cases are a growing concern to employers.

Sexual harassment at work occurs when any employee, woman or man, experiences repeated, unwanted sexual attention or when on-the-job conditions are hostile or threatening in a sexual way. It includes both physical conduct—for example, suggestive touching—as well as verbal harassment, such as sexual innuendoes, jokes, or propositions. Sexual harassment is not limited to overt acts of individual coworkers or supervisors; it can also occur if a company's work climate is blatantly and offensively sexual or intimidating to employees. Women are the targets of most sexual harassment. Sexual harassment is illegal, and the U.S. Equal Employment Opportunity Commission (EEOC) is empowered to sue on behalf of victims. Such suits can be very costly to employers who tolerate a hostile work environment, as the following example shows:

North Country, a 2005 film starring Charlize Theron, was based on the true story of the first sexual harassment lawsuit to be certified as a class action. A group of women employed at a mine operated by Eveleth Taconite in northern Minnesota sued, charging they had been victims of brutal harassment. As portrayed in the film, male workers had called the women obscene names, grabbed and threatened them, and even knocked over a portable toilet when one woman was inside. The lawsuit was finally settled in 1998, when the company agreed to pay the

---

[26] "Justices to Hear White Firefighters Bias Claims," *The New York Times*, April 10, 2009; and "Supreme Court Finds Bias against White Firefighters," *The New York Times*, June 30, 2009.

[27] See, for example, Ward Connerly, *Creating Equal: My Fight Against Race Preferences* (San Francisco: Encounter Books, 2000).

[28] "Affirmative Action: A Corporate Diary," *The New York Times*, June 29, 2003; and "Count Business among the Converted," *St. Louis Post-Dispatch*, June 29, 2003.

plaintiffs $3.5 million. The case "put employers on notice that sexual harassment was going to be taken very seriously," said the president of the National Partnership for Women and Families.[29]

Women employees regularly report that sexual harassment is common. From 40 to 70 percent of working women (and from 10 to 20 percent of working men) have told researchers they have been sexually harassed on the job. Managers and supervisors are the most frequent offenders, and female office workers and clerical workers are the main targets. In almost two-thirds of the cases, the individual who was the target did not report the incident.[30] This kind of conduct is most likely to occur where jobs and occupations are (or have been) sex-segregated and where most supervisors and managers are men, as was the case at the mine portrayed in *North Country.*

In 2002, the European Union recognized sexual harassment as a form of gender discrimination and required its member states to bring their laws into compliance by 2005. Evolving norms about appropriate interactions at the workplace came as a shock to many, particularly in Eastern and Central Europe, where obscene jokes, suggestive remarks, and unwelcome advances at work were commonplace. One study found, for example, that 45 percent of Czech women had been sexually harassed, although most did not identify the behavior by this term. "Sexual harassment is something like folklore in the Czech Republic," said one researcher.[31]

Harassment can occur whether or not the targeted employee cooperates. It need not result in the victim's firing, or cause severe psychological distress; the presence of a hostile or abusive workplace can itself be the basis for a successful suit. Moreover, a company can be found guilty as a result of actions by a supervisor, even if the incident is never reported to top management.

Racial harassment is also illegal, under Title VII of the Civil Rights Act. Under EEOC guidelines, ethnic slurs, derogatory comments, or other verbal or physical harassment based on race are against the law, if they create an intimidating, hostile, or offensive working environment or interfere with an individual's work performance. Although fewer racial than sexual harassment charges are filed, their numbers have more than doubled since the early 1990s (to about 7,000 a year in 2007), and employers have been liable for expensive settlements.[32] For example, FedEx was sued by two ground drivers, both of Lebanese descent, who charged the company had created a hostile work environment. The drivers said in their lawsuit they had been called "terrorists," "camel jockeys," and other epithets by their terminal manager. In 2006, a jury awarded the men $61 million. The verdict was later reduced to $12 million on appeal. A number of recent cases have focused on racist graffiti, such as the hangman's noose, long a symbol of violence against blacks.[33]

---

[29] The story of the lawsuit is told in Clara Bingham and Laura Leedy Gansler, *Class Action* (New York: Random House, 2002). The quotation is from "North Country Film Stems from Seattle Lawyer's Work," *Seattle Times*, October 31, 2005.

[30] "Sexual Harassment Statistics in the Workplace," *www.sexualharassmentlawfirms.com;* and "Sexual Harassment in the Workplace," *www.sexualharassmentsupport.org.*

[31] "Sexual Harassment in the European Union: The Dawning of a New Era," *SAM Advanced Management Journal* 69, no. 1 (Winter 2004); and "Sexual Harassment at Work Widespread in Central Europe," *Plain Dealer (Cleveland)*, January 9, 2000.

[32] "Racial Harassment Lawsuits at Work Go Up," *USA Today*, October 25, 2007. Information on the latest government policies on racial and sexual harassment may be found at the Web site of the Equal Employment Opportunity Commission at *www.eeoc.gov.*

[33] "Jury Awards $61 Million to Two FedEx Drivers in Harassment Suit," June 3, 2006, *www.sfgate.com;* and "Calif. Judge Slashes $61 Million FedEx Verdict," *Law.com*, September 14, 2006.

What can companies do to combat sexual and racial harassment—and protect themselves from expensive lawsuits? In two important court cases in 1998, the Supreme Court helped clarify this question. The court said that companies could deflect lawsuits by taking two steps. First, they should develop a zero-tolerance policy on harassment and communicate it clearly to employees. Then they should establish a complaint procedure—including ways to report incidents without retaliation—and act quickly to resolve any problems. Companies that took such steps, the court said, would be protected from suits by employees who claimed harassment but had failed to use the complaint procedure.

Developing mechanisms for preventing sexual and racial harassment is just one important action companies can take. Others positive steps by business are discussed in the following section.

What Business Can Do: Diversity Policies and Practices

All businesses, of course, are required to obey the laws mandating equal employment opportunity and prohibiting sexual and racial harassment; those that fail to do so risk expensive lawsuits and public disapproval. But it is not enough simply to follow the law. The best-managed companies go beyond compliance; they implement a range of policies and practices to make the workplace welcoming, fair, and accommodating to all employees.

Companies that manage diversity effectively take a number of related actions, in addition to obeying all relevant laws. Research shows that these actions include the following.

Articulate a clear diversity mission, set objectives, and hold managers accountable.

An example of a company that has done so is Johnson & Johnson, which ranked number one in *DiversityInc* magazine's "Top 50 Companies for Diversity" in 2009. The company's well-known credo emphasizes the importance of serving all stakeholders fairly and equitably. Six percent of top executive bonuses are tied to meeting diversity goals. Women comprise nearly half of the company's top 10 percent of earners. Commented the chief diversity officer (who reports directly to the CEO), "In the face of current economic conditions, we remain committed . . . to driving our diversity-and-inclusion goals forward."[34]

Three-quarters of *Fortune* 500 companies have diversity programs, mostly training designed to promote sensitivity and awareness. At United Parcel Service, senior-level managers are required to attend a one-month diversity and leadership course. Another important step is to reward managers. At Henry Ford Health System in Detroit, for example, 7 percent of senior executives' bonuses is linked to their effectiveness in meeting diversity goals.[35]

Spread a wide net in recruitment, to find the most diverse possible pool of qualified candidates. Those in charge of both hiring and promotion need to seek all workers who may be qualified—both inside and outside the company. This often involves moving beyond word-of-mouth networks, which may produce a pool of applicants who are similar to people already working for the company or in particular jobs. One company's efforts to promote diversity in its hiring using a range of techniques are described in the following example:

---

[34] "No.1: Johnson & Johnson," *DiversityInc*, May/June 2009, *www.diversityinc.com.*

[35] "Henry Ford Cited as a Top Company for Diversity," April 6, 2009, *www.henryford.com.*

KPMG, a leading provider of audit, tax, and advisory services, works hard to build a diversified workforce. The firm actively recruits at historically black colleges and universities and is a member of INROADS, a program that places minorities in internships with the company. It sponsors the PhD Project, which supports persons of color in doctoral programs that lead to faculty positions in colleges of business—where they can serve as role models for many students. In recent years, KPMG has embraced the use of technology to cast a wider net in hiring. In 2008, the company created a 48-hour "virtual" recruiting fair that enabled 11,000 people in 150 countries to interact with company recruiters online, view three-dimensional renderings of exhibits, learn about job opportunities, and upload their résumés.[36]

Identify promising women and persons of color, and provide them with mentors and other kinds of support. What techniques work to shatter the glass ceiling? One study of a group of highly successful women executives found that most had been helped by top-level supporters and by multiple chances to gain critical skills. Some companies have promoted mobility by assigning mentors—more senior counselors—to promising female and minority managers and by providing opportunities that include wide-ranging line management experience. AFLAC, the insurance company, for example, runs a mentorship program to help prepare its minority sales representatives for successful careers. Alcoa launched a "Women in Line Roles" initiative to provide promising women opportunities to try out production and technical roles.[37]

Set up diversity councils to monitor the company's goals and progress toward them. A **diversity council** is a group of managers and employees responsible for developing and implementing specific action plans to meet an organization's diversity goals. Sometimes, a diversity council will be established for a corporation as a whole; sometimes, it will be established within particular business units. An example of a company that has used diversity councils effectively is Pitney Bowes, a company whose business is mailstream technology. The company adopted a series of diversity strategic plans, each setting specific goals for the next five-year period. Diversity councils were set up in each business unit to implement programs to meet these objectives, and each year progress was assessed. A Corporate Responsibility Committee of the board oversaw the program as a whole. Pitney Bowes has repeatedly been named to lists of the best employers of women and persons of color.[38]

Businesses that manage diversity effectively enjoy a strategic advantage. While fundamental ethical principles, discussed in Chapters 4 and 5, dictate that all employees should be treated fairly and with respect for their basic human rights, there are also bottom-line benefits to doing so:

- Companies that promote equal employment opportunity generally do better at attracting and retaining workers from all backgrounds. This is increasingly important as the pool of skilled labor grows more diverse. Nortel, the telecommunications firm, has attributed its low turnover rates, relative to the industry, in part to its strong diversity policies. The company partners with nonprofit organizations to develop and place

---

[36] "KPMG's Commitment to Diversity," *www.kpmg.com;* and "Virtual Job Fairs Attract Recruiters and Talent Worldwide," *Talent Management Perspectives,* March 2009.

[37] "Stopping the Exodus of Women in Science," *Harvard Business Review,* June 2008. The full report is available at *www.BrainDrain.hbr.org.* AFLAC's diversity programs are described at *www.aflac.com.*

[38] "Pitney Bowes Earns Four Diversity Leadership Awards," press release, June 25, 2008. Information about Pitney Bowes' diversity programs is available at *www.pb.com.*

talented minority students, sponsors networking groups for African-American and Latino employees, and works closely with minority and women-owned suppliers.[39]

- Businesses with employees from varied backgrounds can often more effectively serve customers who are themselves diverse. Explained Steve Reinemund, CEO of PepsiCo, "If we don't have people from the front line up to the boardroom who represent the consumers we sell to, we're not going to be successful." He offered the following example: "We had an urban market where our market share was half of what we had in the suburban market. By changing the sales force for the urban population and changing some products, our market share went up. That demonstration helped us get a lot of traction [for diversity initiatives] within PepsiCo."[40]

- The global marketplace demands a workforce with language skills, cultural sensitivity, and awareness of national and other differences across markets. For example, Maria Elena Lagomasino, senior managing director of Chase Manhattan's Global Private Banking Group, credited her Cuban heritage with helping her do her job more effectively. "When I got into private banking with Latin American customers," she commented, "I found my ability to understand their reality a great advantage."[41]

Finally, companies with effective diversity programs can avoid costly lawsuits and damage to their corporate reputations from charges of discrimination or cultural insensitivity.

Another important step businesses can take to manage diversity effectively is to accommodate the wide range of family and other obligations employees have in their lives outside work. This subject is discussed in the next section.

Balancing Work and Life

The nature of families and family life has changed, both in the United States and in many other countries. The primary groups in which people live are just as diverse as the workforce itself. One of the most prominent of these changes is that dual-income families have become much more common. According to the latest U.S. Census data, in two-thirds of married couples with children at home (66 percent), both parents worked at least part-time. This was up from just a third of such families in 1976. (To round out the picture, in 29 percent of married couples with children, just the father worked; in 3 percent, just the mother worked. In the remainder, both parents were unemployed.)[42] Families have adopted a wide range of strategies for combining full- and part-time work with the care of children, elderly relatives, and other dependents. Commented the president of the Work and Family Institute, speaking of dual-career families, "It's time to move beyond, is it good, is it bad, and get to: how do we make it work?"[43] How to help "make it work" for employees trying to balance the complex, multiple demands of work and family life has became a major challenge for business.

Child Care and Elder Care

One critical issue for business is supporting workers with responsibilities for children and elderly relatives.

---

[39] Nancy R. Lockwood, "Workplace Diversity: Leveraging the Power of Difference for Competitive Advantages," *HR Magazine*, June 2005, p. A1-10; and "Diversity @ Nortel," at *www.nortel.com/employment/life_at_nn/diversity.html*.

[40] "Speaking Out on Diversity," *Fortune*, February 20, 2006.

[41] "Chasing a Global Edge," *Fortune*, July 19, 1999.

[42] The data in this paragraph are drawn from Table 580, "Married Couples by Labor Force Status of Spouse," in the U.S. Census Bureau, *Statistical Abstract of the United States 2009*.

[43] "Dual Income Families Now Most Common," *San Francisco Chronicle*, October 24, 2000.

The demand for **child care** is enormous and growing. Millions of children need daily care, especially the nearly 7 out of every 10 children whose mothers hold jobs. A major source of workplace stress for working parents is concern about their children; and problems with child care are a leading reason why employees fail to show up for work.

Business has found that child care programs, in addition to reducing absenteeism and tardiness, also improve productivity and aid recruiting by improving the company's image and helping to retain talented employees. Ninety-five percent of large U.S. companies provide some type of child care assistance, including referral services, dependent care accounts, and vouchers. One in 10 large companies subsidizes on-site or near-site child care services.[44] An example is S.C. Johnson, a consumer products firm that cares for 500 children in a state-of-the-art center at its Racine, Wisconsin, headquarters. "This isn't a benefit," explained a company spokesperson. "It's a good business decision because we want to attract the best."[45]

In addition to caring for children, many of today's families have responsibilities for **elder care**. Employees' responsibilities for aging parents and other older relatives will become increasingly important to businesses in the coming decade as baby boomers pass through their forties and fifties, the prime years for caring for elderly family members. Thirty-four million adults in the United States now care for an older person. Nearly 60 percent of male caregivers, and 41 percent of female caregivers, work full-time. This is a concern for employers because caregivers often have to go to work late or leave early to attend to these duties, or are distracted or stressed at work by their responsibilities.[46] Almost half of the large corporations surveyed by Hewitt Associates, a benefits company, offer assistance to workers caring for older relatives, as illustrated by the following examples:

> IBM, where 36 percent of employees are affected by elder care issues, offers a Web site and professional counseling for the 36 percent of its employees who are affected by elder care issues. "I was able to read about it and talk to someone," said an IBM business analyst who had been caring for her mother, who had Alzheimer's. Ernst & Young, the accounting firm, provides consultations on available resources, backup emergency adult care services, and seminars on elder care.

Also available at many firms are referral services, dependent care accounts, long-term care insurance, and time off to deal with the often unpredictable crises that occur in families caring for elders.[47]

When a mother or father is granted time off when children are born or adopted and during the important early months of a child's development, this is called a **parental leave**; when the care of elderly relatives is involved, this is called a **family leave**. Under the Family and Medical Leave Act (FMLA), passed in 1993, companies that employ 50 or more people must grant unpaid, job-protected leaves of up to 12 weeks to employees faced with serious family needs, including the birth or adoption of a baby. Smaller companies, not covered by the FMLA, usually do less for expectant and new parents and for those with ill family members.

[44] Sloan Work and Family Research Network, "Questions and Answers about Employer-Supported Child Care," updated March 2009, *www.wfnetwork.bc.edu/pdfs/ESCC.pdf.*

[45] Information about S.C. Johnson's child care center is available at *www.scjohnson.com.*

[46] AARP Public Policy Institute, "Valuing the Invaluable: The Economic Value of Family Caregiving," 2008, *www.aarp.org.*

[47] "Some Firms Offer Help as More Employees Juggle Work, Care for Aging Parent," *USA Today,* June 25, 2007.

Work Flexibility

Companies have also accommodated the changing roles of women and men by offering workers more flexibility through such options as flextime, part-time employment, job sharing, and working from home (sometimes called telecommuting because the employee keeps in touch with coworkers, customers, and others by phone or over the Internet). Abbott Laboratories, a global health care company, demonstrates the benefits of the many kinds of work flexibility for both business and employees.

> Many of Abbott's employees, men and women, work flextime schedules, beginning and quitting at different times of the day. Others share jobs, with each working half a week. Many jobs are held on a part-time basis, leaving the worker time to be at home with children or elderly parents. Other Abbott employees telecommute from their homes. "After my son got sick, I needed to . . . drop down to part time and work from home a few days a week," said one manager. "Abbott gave me the flexibility I needed to take care of my family." The company, whose work/life programs have been widely honored, says that its employees return the investment through their increased productivity, innovative thinking, and loyalty.[48]

Abbott is not the only corporation using these practices. One survey revealed that 79 percent offered some kind of flexible work schedules, such as changing starting or quitting times, working from home, or compressed workweek schedules.[49] These arrangements can benefit employers by attracting and retaining valuable employees, reducing absences, and improving job satisfaction.[50]

However, many observers believe that most careers are still structured for people who are prepared to put in 40 hours a week at the office—or 50 or 60—giving their full and undivided commitment to the organization. Many women and men have been reluctant to take advantage of various flexible work options, fearing that this would put them on a slower track, sometimes disparagingly called the *Mommy track* or *Daddy track*. In this view, businesses will need to undergo a cultural shift, to value the contributions of people who are prepared to make a serious, but less than full-time, commitment to their careers.

> In the United Kingdom, the government's Equal Opportunities Commission publishes an annual update called "Who Runs Britain." Recent reports have shown little progress for women in entering top positions in business, politics, and other areas of public life. The problem, according to the government agency, is employers' failure to accommodate women's need to manage multiple responsibilities at home and work, a phenomenon that in the U.K. is sometimes called the "mummy track." The commission called for adoption of more workplace practices that provided high-quality, highly paid flexible and part-time work to those who have caring responsibilities.[51]

---

[48] "Abbott Named One of the 'Top 10' Innovative Family-Friendly Companies by *Working Mother* Magazine," press release, September 23, 2008, available at *www.abbott.com*.

[49] Sloan Work and Family Research Network, "Questions and Answers about Flexible Work Schedules," updated September 2008, *wfnetwork.bc.edu/pdfs/flexworksched.pdf*.

[50] Workplace Flexibility 2010, "Flexible Work Arrangements: The Fact Sheet," Georgetown University Law Center, *www.law.georgetown.edu/workplaceflexibility2010*.

[51] "Sex and Power: Who Runs Britain?" 2006, *www.eoc.org.uk*.

Working Mother magazine singled out Steve Sanger, CEO of General Mills, for his commitment to building a family-friendly company. The magazine related in an anecdote one of Sanger's own memorable experiences as a working parent:

> Early in his tenure . . . the newly minted CEO was scheduled to appear before a roomful of Wall Street analysts in New York City and decided to bring his family along on the business trip. He was poised to take the podium at 9:00 a.m., but minutes before, his then-toddler daughter inadvertently locked herself in the hotel bathroom. "I was in a suit on my knees talking to a two-year-old through a keyhole—a very comical scene that took my mind off the presentation for the five minutes until we got her out," he recall[ed] . . . "It's funny how your priorities shift when you have children."

General Mills has been an innovator in integrating family considerations into its operations. Some of its programs include

- An on-site infant care center.
- Flexible work arrangements.
- On-site health care services, including mammograms for busy working mothers.
- Emergency child care for parents whose regular arrangements fall through.
- Exercise classes offered at the company's health and fitness center.

In explaining the business benefits of General Mills' family programs, Sanger commented, "You know what's really expensive? Turnover. If we've invested in recruiting and developing good people, then we want them to stay."

Source: "Thinking Outside the [Cereal] Box," *Working Mother,* October 2002.

What would such a cultural shift look like? Some have used the term **family-friendly corporation** to describe firms that would fully support both men and women in their efforts to balance work and family responsibilities. Job advantages would not be granted or denied on the basis of gender. People would be hired, paid, evaluated, promoted, and extended benefits on the basis of their qualifications and ability to do the tasks assigned. The route to the top, or to satisfaction in any occupational category, would be open to anyone with the talent to take it. The company's stakeholders, regardless of their gender, would be treated in a bias-free manner. All laws forbidding sex discrimination would be fully obeyed. Programs to provide leaves or financial support for child care, elder care, and other family responsibilities would support both men and women employees and help promote an equitable division of domestic work. And persons could seek, and achieve, career advancement without committing to a full-time schedule, year after year.[52] An example of an executive who has taken the lead in promoting family-friendly policies is given in Exhibit 17.C.

An important step businesses can take is to recognize, and provide benefits to, nontraditional families. Some firms now offer domestic partner benefits to their gay and lesbian employees, extending health insurance and other benefits to the same-sex partners of employees. Although U.S. law does not explicitly bar discrimination based on sexual orientation, some local laws do; and many firms have found that extending health insurance and other benefits to the same-sex partners of employees is an effective strategy for recruiting and retaining valuable contributors. Domestic partner benefits are further described in Exhibit 17.D.

[52] *Working Mother* magazine publishes an annual list of the "100 Best Companies for Working Mothers." The current year's list may be viewed at *www.workingmother.com.*

Many corporations in the United States now acknowledge differences in employee sexual orientation and gender identity. Gay, lesbian, bisexual, and transgender employees have become a vocal minority, winning important victories in the workplace. By 2008, 286 of the *Fortune* 500 companies provided health benefits to domestic partners and same-sex spouses, according to the Human Rights Campaign Foundation. Lotus Development was the first major employer to offer spousal benefits to same-sex partners; it was followed by many others, including AT&T, Chase Manhattan, Microsoft, United Airlines, and the Big Three automakers. Other steps companies have taken to support their homosexual employees have included written antidiscrimination policies, management training on sexual diversity issues, and visible gay and lesbian advertising.

Source: Human Rights Campaign Foundation, "Domestic Partner Benefits," 2009.

No other area of business illustrates the basic theme of this book better than the close connection between work and life. Our basic theme is that business and society are closely and unavoidably intertwined, so that what affects one also has an impact on the other. As the workforce has become more diverse, business has been challenged to accommodate employees' differences. When people go to work, they do not shed their identities at the office or factory door. When employees come from families where there are young children at home, or where elderly parents require care, companies must learn to support these roles. Businesses that help their employees achieve a balance between work and life and meet their obligations to their families and communities often reap rewards in greater productivity, loyalty, and commitment.

Summary

- The U.S. workforce is as diverse as it has ever been and is becoming more so. More women are working than ever before, many immigrants have entered the labor force, ethnic and racial diversity is increasing, the workforce is aging, and millennials are entering the workplace.

- Women and persons of color have made great strides in entering all occupations, but they continue to be underrepresented in many business management roles, especially at top levels. Both groups face a continuing pay gap. The number of women-owned businesses has increased sharply, and many minorities, especially immigrants, also own their own businesses.

- Under U.S. law, businesses are required to provide equal opportunity to all, without regard to race, color, religion, sex, national origin, disability, or age. Sexual and racial harassment are illegal. Affirmative action plans remain legal, but only if they are temporary and flexible, are designed to correct past discrimination, and do not result in reverse discrimination.

- Companies that manage diversity effectively have a strategic advantage because they are able to attract and retain talented workers from all backgrounds, serve a diverse customer base, and avoid expensive lawsuits and public embarrassment.

- Successful diversity management includes articulating a mission, recruiting widely, mentoring promising women and persons of color, and establishing mechanisms for assessing progress.

- Many businesses have helped employees balance the complex demands of work and family obligations by providing support programs such as child and elder care, flexible work schedules, domestic partner benefits, and telecommuting options.

Key Terms

affirmative action, *396*
child care, *403*
diversity, *386*
diversity council, *401*
elder care, *403*
equal employment
opportunity, *395*
Equal Employment
Opportunity Commission
(EEOC), *396*

family-friendly
corporation, *405*
family leave, *403*
glass ceiling, *391*
glass walls, *394*
occupational
segregation, *390*
parental leave, *403*

pay gap, *389*
racial harassment, *399*
reverse discrimination, *397*
sexual harassment, *398*
workforce diversity, *386*

Internet Resources

www.abcdependentcare.com   American Business Collaboration for Quality Dependent Care

www.catalyst.org   Catalyst—"expanding opportunities for women and business"

www.diversityinc.com   *Diversity Inc.* magazine and other resources

www.eeoc.gov   U.S. Equal Employment Opportunity Commission

www.familiesandwork.org   Families and Work Institute

www.multiculturaladvantage.com   Resources for diversity officers and professionals of diverse backgrounds

www.sba.gov   U.S. Small Business Administration

www.workingmother.com   *Working Mother* magazine and other resources

Discussion Case: *Dukes v. Walmart Stores, Inc.*

In 2009, a panel of 11 federal judges reconsidered an earlier decision that a lawsuit charging Walmart Stores with discrimination against six women, *Dukes v. Walmart Stores, Inc.,* could go forward as a class action. If confirmed, this would mean the lawyers could argue the case on behalf of all female Walmart employees in the United States, not just those who had brought suit. The historic lawsuit was the largest employment discrimination case ever heard in the United States. If the decision ultimately went against Walmart (the case, first filed five years earlier, was expected to take several more years to resolve), the cost to the company could be in the hundreds of millions of dollars.

In 2009, Walmart was the largest private employer in the world. The company operated 7,800 facilities globally and had annual sales of $401 billion. In the United States, Walmart employed 1.4 million people, about 62 percent of them women. The company had become a magnet for both strenuous praise and strenuous criticism. Its hyperefficient supply chain was credited with saving U.S. customers $20 billion annually, suppressing inflation, and spurring productivity gains throughout the economy; and *Fortune* had several times named Walmart its most admired company. Yet Walmart had also been blamed for driving out small businesses, depressing wages, and discriminating against women.

Plaintiffs in *Dukes* charged that female employees at Walmart were paid less than men in comparable positions, in spite of having greater seniority and equal or better qualifications. They also charged that women received fewer promotions to store management positions and waited longer to move up than men did.

Q2 b

The lead plaintiff in the case was Betty Dukes. Dukes had started working at Walmart in 1994. Despite repeated expressions of interest, she was not promoted into the ranks of salaried managers. "I was always told my time would come, that there were no openings available, that I didn't have enough experience to move on. But on a number of occasions men with less experience than me were put in jobs that I desperately wanted and know I could have done well," Dukes explained. In 2000, she approached antidiscrimination attorneys for help.

The other plaintiffs had similar stories to tell. Claudia Renati was denied a promotion after her boss asked her to stack 50-pound bags of dog food. Men were not subject to a lifting requirement. When Christine Kwapnoski, another plaintiff, asked what she needed to do to be promoted, she was told to "doll up and blow the cobwebs off [your] makeup." Stephanie Odle, an assistant store manager, complained to her district manager when she learned that a man in the same position at her store was making $23,000 more. He told her the man had "a family and two children to support." Recalled Odle, "I told him I'm a single mother, and I have a 6-month-old child to support."

In asking that the case be tried as a class action, lawyers argued that these women's experiences were not isolated, but representative of broader patterns. Statistical evidence presented by the plaintiffs showed the following:

- At each successive level of the management ladder at Walmart, women's representation decreased, as shown in Figure 17.5. Women made up nearly 90 percent of customer service managers (supervisors of cashiers), but only 15 percent of store managers.
- Among employees who were promoted to assistant manager (the lowest salaried position), women took longer to reach this milestone: 4.38 years from date of hire to promotion, compared with 2.86 years for men.
- Women made less than men in every job classification examined, from the lowest-ranking hourly jobs to top positions in management, as shown in Figure 17.6. "Women start out being paid less, and the gap just widens," said Brad Seligman, one of the plaintiffs' attorneys.

#4 Performance expectation gap that led to the problem facing firm?

FIGURE 17.5
Approximate Percentages of Women in Salaried Store Management and Hourly Supervisory Positions, 2001
CSM is customer service manager, a supervisor of cashiers. The assistant manager, comanager, and store manager are salaried management positions; the others are hourly supervisory positions.

Source: Richard Drogin, Ph.D., "Statistical Analysis of Gender Patterns in Walmart Workforce," February 2003, p. 15, Table 7.

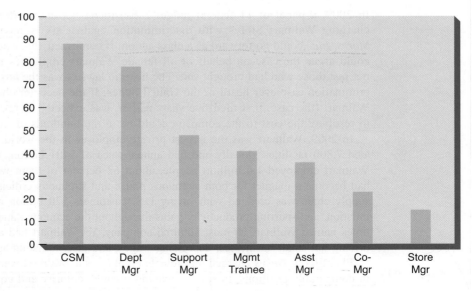

FIGURE 17.6

Average Annual Earnings for Men and Women at Walmart in Selected Jobs, 2001

Source: Richard Drogin, Ph.D., "Statistical Analysis of Gender Patterns in Walmart Workforce," February 2003, p. 17, Tables 9 and 10.

	Men	**Women**
Regional vice president	$419,435	$279,772
District manager	239,519	177,149
Manager	105,682	89,280
Assistant manager	39,790	37,322
Management trainee	23,175	22,371
Department head	23,518	21,709
Sales associate	16,526	15,067
Cashier	14,525	13,831

- These differences in pay and promotion persisted despite similar or better performance. Walmart employees received job ratings ranging from 1 to 7, with 7 the highest. Women hourly employees received, on average, slightly higher ratings than men (3.91 compared with 3.84).

In response, Walmart defended its record on diversity, saying the *Dukes* plaintiffs were not representative of other women working at the company. In a statement on its Web site, the company declared that "Walmart is a great place for women to work, and isolated complaints that arise from its 3,000+ stores do not change this fact." A company spokesperson explained, "Many of these women had the opportunity to go into training to become an assistant manager, but they did not want to work the odd shifts, like working all night long, Saturdays, or Sundays."

Although it continued to contest the lawsuit, Walmart began taking steps to improve the climate for women. In 2003, Walmart established an Office of Diversity and appointed a chief diversity officer. The company also for the first time linked officer bonuses, in part, to their success in meeting diversity goals. It also said it would promote women in proportion to the number that applied. At the 2009 annual shareholders' meeting, the company's new CEO, Mike Duke, announced the formation of a "global women's council," composed of 14 members representing the various markets in which the company operated. Its aim was to increase the proportion of women in management. Saying he was "not satisfied" with the progress that had been made, Duke said he wanted to "move faster."

Sources: "Walmart Vows to Promote Women," *BusinessWeek*, June 5, 2009; Liza Featherstone, *Selling Women Short: The Landmark Battle for Workers' Rights at Walmart* (New York: Basic Books, 2004); "The Women Taking on Walmart," *The Observer*, June 27, 2004; "Walmart Sex Bias Suit Given Class-Action Status," *The New York Times*, June 23, 2004; "Is Walmart Too Powerful?" *BusinessWeek*, October 6, 2003; "Walmart Faces Lawsuit over Sex Discrimination," *The New York Times*, February 16, 2003; "Study Finds Pay Gap at Walmart," *Los Angeles Times*, February 4, 2003; "Order Granting in Part and Denying in Part Motion for Class Certification," June 21, 2004, U.S. Court of Appeals; Richard Drogin, Ph.D., "Statistical Analysis of Gender Patterns in Walmart Workforce," February 2003; Walmart, "Diversity Is a Way of Life at Walmart," March 3, 2006, *www.walmartfacts.com*.

Discussion Questions

1. From the evidence presented in the case, do you think that Walmart violated any U.S. laws, as shown in Figure 17.4? If so, which ones, and why?
2. What actions has Walmart taken before and after the certification of the class action to promote equal opportunity for all employees?
3. If you were an executive of the company, what further steps would you take, if any? How would you communicate your diversity program to your employees and to the public?
4. What do you think would be an appropriate outcome of this case, and why?

The Community and the Corporation

A strong relationship benefits both business and its community. Communities look to businesses for civic leadership and for help in coping with local problems, while businesses expect to be treated in fair and supportive ways by the community. As companies expand their operations, they develop a wider set of community relationships. Community relations programs, including corporate giving, are an important way for a business to express its commitment to corporate citizenship.

This Chapter Focuses on These Key Learning Objectives:

- Defining a community, and understanding the interdependencies between companies and the communities in which they operate.
- Analyzing why it is in the interest of business to respond to community problems and needs.
- Knowing the major responsibilities of community relations managers.
- Examining how different forms of corporate giving contribute to building strong relationships between businesses and communities.
- Evaluating how companies can direct their giving strategically, to further their own business objectives.
- Analyzing how collaborative partnerships between businesses and communities can address today's pressing social problems.

Whole Foods Market is a natural foods retailer with stores in many communities in North America and the United Kingdom. Founded in 1980 in Austin, Texas, the company believes that its business "is intimately tied to the neighborhood and larger community that we serve and in which we live." Whole Foods donates 5 percent of its net profit to charitable causes and operates a foundation that supports rural economic development, as well as projects that support animal welfare, organic production, and healthy nutrition. Each of the company's 270 stores hosts a community giving day three times a year, with 5 percent of the day's total sales revenue contributed to a worthy local nonprofit organization. Whole Foods also encourages its employees to volunteer their time and expertise to the community. Employees have been involved in a wide range of service projects, including organizing blood donation drives, raising money for breast cancer research, developing community gardens, renovating housing, and delivering "meals on wheels."[1]

One of the leading financial institutions in the world, ING has operations in more than 50 countries. Based in the Netherlands, the company provides insurance, banking, and asset management services throughout Europe, with a growing presence in the Americas and Asia. Recognizing that the needs of the many communities where it does business differ, the company has delegated responsibility for corporate citizenship programs to business unit managers, provided their decisions are consistent with the firm's core values. The result has been a remarkable diversity of community initiatives. In India, ING trained secondary school heads; in the United States, it ran financial literacy classes for teens; in Malaysia, it worked on the conservation of rain forests. In 2008, 12,000 ING employees participated in a worldwide fund-raising effort for Chances for Children, the company's partnership with UNICEF.[2]

Hindustan Lever, the Indian subsidiary of the transnational corporation Unilever, faced a problem when a dairy it owned in a rural area in northern India incurred substantial losses. Rather than closing the operation, the company decided to address the underlying cause—inadequate care of dairy cattle by impoverished local villagers. The company gave interest-free loans to farmers and offered classes in animal care. Within a few years, the dairy was making a profit. The program was so successful that the company expanded it to 400 villages and committed to investing 10 percent of its pretax profits in rural development projects, including children's immunizations, water system improvements, and classes in sewing, nutrition, and agriculture. Every year, the company sends 50 of its most promising young managers to live with a rural family and work on development projects, to learn firsthand the value of community involvement.[3]

Why do businesses as diverse as Whole Foods Market, ING, and Hindustan Lever invest in community organizations, projects, and charities? Why do they contribute their money, resources, and time to help others? What benefits do they gain from such activities? This chapter explains why many companies believe that being an involved citizen is part of their basic business mission. The chapter also looks at how companies participate in community life and how they build partnerships with other businesses, government, and community organizations. The core questions that we consider in this chapter are these: What does it mean to be a good corporate neighbor? What is the business case for doing so?

---

[1] See *www.wholefoodsmarket.com/values/giving.*

[2] Information on ING's community initiatives and its latest corporate responsibility reports are available at *www.ing.com.*

[3] "Hindustan Lever in India," *www.business-humanrights.org; www.unilever.com/environmentsociety/community;* and "Unilever in Uttar Pradesh," in McIntosh et al., *Corporate Citizenship: Successful Strategies for Responsible Companies* (London: Financial Times, 1998).

The Business–Community Relationship

The term **community**, as used in this chapter, refers to a company's area of local business influence. Traditionally, the term applied to the city, town, or rural area in which a business's operations, offices, or assets were located. With the rise of large, complex business organizations, the meaning of the term has expanded to include multiple localities. A local merchant's community relationships may involve just the people who live within driving distance of its store. A bank in a large metropolitan area, by contrast, may define its community as both the central city and the suburbs where it does business. And at the far extreme, a large transnational firm such as ING, ExxonMobil, or Nokia has relationships with numerous communities in many countries around the world.

Today the term *community* may also refer not only to a geographical area or areas but to a range of groups that are affected by an organization's actions, whether or not they are in the immediate vicinity. In this broader view, as shown in Figure 18.1, the *geographical* (sometimes called the *site*) community is just one of several different kinds of communities.

Whether a business is small or large, local or global, its relationship with the community or communities with which it interacts is one of mutual interdependence. As shown in Figure 18.2, business and the community each need something from the other. Business depends on the community for education, public services such as police and fire protection, recreational facilities, and transportation systems, among other things. The

FIGURE 18.1
The Firm and Its Communities

Source: Adapted from a discussion in Edmund M. Burke, *Corporate Community Relations: The Principle of Neighbor of Choice* (Westport, CT: Praeger, 1999), ch. 6.

Community	Interest
Site community	Geographical location of a company's operations, offices, or assets
Fence-line community	Immediate neighbors
Virtual communities	People who are connected to the company online
Communities of interest	Groups that share a common interest with the company
Employee community	People who work near the company

FIGURE 18.2
What the Community and Business Want from Each Other

Business Participation Desired by Community	Community Services Desired by Business
• Pays taxes	Schools—a quality educational system
• Provides jobs and training	Recreational opportunities
• Follows laws	Libraries, museums, theaters, and other cultural services and organizations
• Supports schools	Adequate infrastructure, e.g., sewer, water, and electric services
• Supports the arts and cultural activities	Adequate transportation systems, e.g., roads, rail, airport, harbor
• Supports local health care programs	Effective public safety services, e.g., police and fire protection
• Supports parks and recreation	Fair and equitable taxation
• Assists less advantaged people	Streamlined permitting services
• Contributes to public safety	Quality health care services
• Participates in economic development	Cooperative problem-solving approach

The professional sports franchise is one kind of business that has historically been particularly dependent on support from the community. Cities often compete vigorously in bidding wars to attract or keep football, basketball, baseball, hockey, and soccer teams. Communities subsidize professional sports in many ways. Government agencies build stadiums and arenas, sell municipal bonds to pay for construction, give tax breaks to owners, and allow teams to keep revenues from parking, luxury boxes, and food concessions. In the United States, subsidies to pro sports cost taxpayers around $500 million a year, on average. Consider the following taxpayer subsidies to build sports facilities: Scottsdale, $535 million (for the Phoenix Coyotes); Houston, $180 million (for the Houston Astros); Denver, $215 million (for the Colorado Rockies), and Miami, $212 million (for the Florida Panthers). As of 2009, the new ballpark for the New York Yankees had already cost the public $1.2 billion (and was still under construction); the new ballpark for the New York Mets had cost $614 million. Some say that public support is warranted, because high-profile teams and sports facilities spur local economic development, offer wholesome entertainment, and build civic pride. But critics argue that subsidies simply enrich affluent team owners and players at taxpayer expense and shift spending away from other more deserving areas, such as schools, police and fire protection, social services, and the arts. In this view, this is a case in which the relationship between business and the community is deeply out of balance.

Sources: Kevin J. Delaney and Rick Eckstein, *Public Dollars, Private Stadiums* (New Brunswick, NJ: Rutgers University Press, 2003). A Web site critical of public subsidies to sports facilities is *www.fieldofschemes.com*.

community depends on business for support of the arts, schools, health care, and the disadvantaged, and other urgent civic needs, both through taxes and donations of money, goods, and time.

Ideally, community support of business and business support of the community are roughly in balance, so that both parties feel that they have benefited in the relationship. Sometimes, however, a business will invest more in the community than the community seems to provide in return. Conversely, a community sometimes provides more support to a business than the firm contributes to the community. Exhibit 18.A discusses subsidies by communities to professional sports franchises, an instance in which the relationship between business and the community is sometimes perceived as out of balance.

The Business Case for Community Involvement

The term **civic engagement** describes the active involvement of businesses and individuals in changing and improving communities. *Civic* means pertaining to cities or communities, and *engagement* means being committed to or involved with something. Why should businesses be involved with the community? What is the business case for civic engagement?

The ideas of corporate social responsibility and global citizenship, introduced in earlier chapters, refer broadly to businesses acting as citizens of society by behaving responsibly toward all their stakeholders. Civic engagement is a major way in which companies carry out their corporate citizenship mission. As explained in Chapters 3 and 7, business organizations that act in a socially responsible way reap many benefits. These include an enhanced reputation and ability to respond quickly to changing stakeholder demands. By acting responsibly, companies can also avoid or correct problems caused by their operations—a basic duty that comes with their significant power and influence. They can win the loyalty of employees, customers, and neighbors. And by doing the right thing, businesses can often avoid, or at least correctly anticipate, government regulations. All these reasons for social responsibility operate at the level of the community as well, via civic engagement.

Another specific reason for community involvement is to win local support for business activity. Communities do not have to accept a business. They sometimes object to the presence of companies that will create too much traffic, pollute the air or water, or engage in activities that are viewed as offensive or inappropriate. A company must earn its informal **license to operate**—or right to do business—from society. In communities where democratic principles apply, citizens have the right to exercise their voice in determining whether a company will or will not be welcome, and the result is not always positive for business.

> Walmart has encountered serious local objection to its plans to build superstores and distribution centers in a number of local communities. Walmart's founder, Sam Walton, now deceased, was fond of saying he would never try to force a community to accept a Walmart store. "Better to go where we are wanted," he is reported to have said. In recent years, however, Walmart management less often endorses that view. In a series of high-profile local conflicts, Walmart sparked intense local opposition when it tried to move into town. On Lady's Island in South Carolina, for example, local officials blocked the company's plan to build a supercenter after residents expressed concerns it would increase traffic, hurt the environment, and drive out small, neighborhood businesses. The problem of community opposition seems likely to grow more complex for Walmart as it continues its expansion into international markets.[4]

Through positive interactions with the communities in which its stores are located, Walmart is more likely to avoid this kind of local opposition.

Community involvement by business also helps build social capital. **Social capital**, a relatively new theoretical concept, has been defined as the norms and networks that enable collective action. Scholars have also described it as "the goodwill that is engendered by the fabric of social relations."[5] When companies such as Whole Foods Market, described at the beginning of this chapter, work to address community problems such as blood shortages, hunger, and dilapidated housing, their actions help build social capital. The company and groups in the community develop closer relationships, and their people become more committed to each other's welfare. Many experts believe that high levels of social capital enhance a community's quality of life. Dense social networks increase productivity by reducing the costs of doing business, because firms and people are more likely to trust one another. The development of social capital produces a win–win outcome because it enables everyone to be better off.[6]

Community Relations

The organized involvement of business with the community is called **community relations**. The importance of community relations has increased markedly in recent years. According to one expert, "Over the years, community involvement has moved from the margins of the corporation to a position of growing importance. More companies regard

---

[4] "Top Story of 2008: Walmart's Failed Attempt to Build Lady's Island Megastore," *Beaufort (S.C.) Gazette*, December 27, 2008. For the company's perspective on its community relationships, see *www.walmart.com*.

[5] Paul S. Adler and S. W. Kwon, "Social Capital: Prospects for a New Concept," *Academy of Management Review* 27, no. 1 (January/February 2002), pp. 17–40. For a more general discussion, see Robert D. Putnam, *Bowling Alone: The Collapse and Revival of American Community* (New York: Simon and Schuster, 2000).

[6] Some benefits of social capital are described on the World Bank Web site at *www.worldbank.org/prem/poverty/scapital*.

their involvement in the community as a key business strategy and a linchpin in their overall corporate citizenship efforts."[7] The importance of community relations is shown by the following statistics, drawn from a study conducted by the Center for Corporate Citizenship:[8]

- 81 percent of companies now include a statement in their annual report about their commitment to community relations.
- 74 percent of companies have a written mission statement for their community relations program.
- 68 percent of companies factor community involvement into their overall strategic plan.

In support of this commitment, some corporations have established specialized community relations departments; others house this function in a department of public affairs or corporate citizenship. The job of the **community relations manager** (sometimes called the community involvement manager) is to interact with local citizens, develop community programs, manage donations of goods and services, work with local governments, and encourage employee volunteerism. These actions are, in effect, business investments intended to produce more social capital—to build relationships and networks with important groups in the community. Community relations departments typically work closely with other departments that link the company to the outside world, such as external affairs and government relations (discussed in Chapters 2 and 8). All these roles form important bridges between the corporation and the community.

Community relations departments are typically involved with a range of diverse issues. According to a survey of community involvement managers, education (kindergarten through high school) was viewed as the most important issue. Other critical issues included health care, economic development, higher education, and housing. Further down the list of issues, although still important, were literacy, environmental issues, crime, transportation, and job training.[9] (Figure 18.5, which appears later in this chapter, shows the issues to which companies donate the most money.) Although not exhaustive, this list suggests the range of needs that a corporation's community relations professionals are asked to address. These community concerns challenge managers to apply talent, imagination, and resources to develop creative ways to strengthen the community while still managing their businesses as profitable enterprises.

Several specific ways in which businesses and their community relations departments have addressed some critical concerns facing communities are discussed below. The all-important issue of business involvement in education reform is addressed in the final section of the chapter, which discusses collaborative partnerships.

Economic Development

Business leaders and their companies are frequently involved in local or regional economic development that is intended to bring new businesses into an area. Financial institutions, because of their special expertise in lending, have been at the forefront of many recent initiatives to bring development money into needy communities. In the United States, the federal **Community Reinvestment Act** requires banks to demonstrate their

---

[7] Center for Corporate Citizenship, *Community Involvement Index 2005* (Chestnut Hill, MA: Boston College, 2005). For related data, see *www.bcccc.net*.

[8] Ibid.

[9] Ibid., p. 2. Based on an opinion survey of 163 community involvement managers.

Exhibit 18.B

Micro-Credit: A New Model for Economic Development

Grameen Bank (meaning *village bank*), based in Bangladesh, is an internationally recognized innovator in the field of economic development. In 1974, Muhammad Yunus, an economics professor at Chattagong University, took his students on a field trip to a poor rural village. There, they interviewed a woman who supported herself by crafting bamboo stools. The woman had to borrow money for raw materials at the outrageous interest rate of 10 percent *a week,* leaving a profit of only one penny per stool. The professor, shocked by what he saw, began lending his own money to villagers. Finding that small loans helped many people pull themselves out of poverty, Yunus founded Grameen in 1983 to provide *micro-credit* to individual entrepreneurs who would not normally qualify for loans. Today, Grameen serves 7.5 million borrowers in thousands of villages. "These millions of small people with their millions of small pursuits can add up to create the biggest development wonder," Yunus has said. In 2006, Yunus was awarded the Nobel Peace Prize in recognition of his work.

Sources: *www.grameen-info.org;* and Muhammad Yunus, *Banker to the Poor* (South Asia Books, 1998).

commitment to local communities through low-income lending programs and to provide annual reports to the public. This law has led many banks to begin viewing the inner city as an opportunity for business development. Some have even created special subsidiaries that have as their mission the development of new lending and development in needy urban neighborhoods. ShoreBank, for example, has been deeply involved in meeting the housing needs of low-income residents in Chicago, Cleveland, and Detroit. Financial institutions have been active in this area in many other nations, as well. An innovative initiative by a small bank in Bangladesh to provide micro-credit for economic development in rural areas is described in Exhibit 18.B.

Crime Abatement

Many urban areas around the world are forbidding and inhospitable places, fraught with drugs, violence, and high crime rates. Business has an interest in reducing crime, because it hurts the ability to attract workers and customers and threatens property security. Some firms have become actively involved in efforts to reduce crime in their neighborhoods, as the following example illustrates:

In the mid-1990s, the crime rate in the metropolitan area of St. Paul-Minneapolis, Minnesota, had become so bad that out-of-town newspapers disparagingly called the city "Murderopolis." To combat this situation, a collaborative alliance formed called Minnesota HEALS (Hope, Education, and Law and Safety). Sixty companies and other organizations, including Honeywell, General Mills, 3M, and Allina Health Systems, worked closely with police and civic groups to address public safety issues in the community. Among their many initiatives were development of an integrated information system for law enforcement agencies, better housing, job training, and afterschool programs. Crime rates dropped sharply, and the overall climate for business in the city improved. A decade later, HEALS remained an active coalition of more than 60 local companies and government agencies committed to crime prevention.[10]

[10] Ellen Luger and Pat Hoven, "Minnesota HEALS: Creating a Public–Private Partnership," *www.mcf.org;* "Minnesota HEALS Violent Crimes," August 13, 2008, posted to "Crime Prevention" at *www.mncriminals.com.*

Housing

Another community issue in which many firms have become involved is housing. Life and health insurance companies, among others, have taken the lead in programs to revitalize neighborhood housing through organizations such as Neighborhood Housing Services (NHS) of America. NHS, which is locally controlled, locally funded, nonprofit, and tax-exempt, offers housing rehabilitation and financial services to neighborhood residents. Similar efforts are being made to house the homeless. New York City's Coalition for the Homeless includes corporate, nonprofit, and community members. Corporations also often work with nongovernmental organizations (NGOs) such as Habitat for Humanity to build or repair housing. In the wake of Hurricane Katrina, a number of innovative business–nonprofit partnerships arose to help rebuild houses in the devastated city of New Orleans, as shown in the following example:

> Artistic Tile, a New York producer of high-end ceramic, concrete, and porcelain tile for use in homebuilding, often had excess inventory after jobs had been completed. These tiles usually ended up in the dump. In 2008, a New Jersey trucking company (which chose to remain anonymous) volunteered to pick up loads of tiles and drive them to Louisiana, where they could be used by volunteers working to rebuild homes destroyed by Hurricane Katrina. "We donate whatever we can," said Nancy Epstein, CEO of the tile company.[11]

Aid to Minority Enterprises

Private enterprise has also extended assistance to minority-owned small businesses. These businesses often operate at a great economic disadvantage: They do business in economic locations where high crime rates, poor transportation, low-quality public services, and a low-income clientele combine to produce a high rate of business failure. Large corporations, sometimes in cooperation with universities, have provided financial and technical advice and training to minority entrepreneurs. They also have financed the building of minority-managed inner-city plants and sponsored special programs to purchase services and supplies from minority firms.

> Microsoft spends $10 billion annually on procuring supplies and services. About 5 percent of this is directed to minority-owned businesses. "The general rule here," said the company's director of supplier diversity, "is, if all other things are equal, pick the minority company." Microsoft works closely with its minority suppliers to refine their business processes to make them more competitive. An example is Group O Direct, an Illinois-based firm that provides fulfillment services for customer promotions. Group O Direct, which is owned by Mexican-Americans, now has several other high-profile clients in addition to Microsoft, including SBC Communications, and annual revenues of $445 million.[12]

Disaster, Terrorism, and War Relief

One common form of corporate involvement in the community is disaster relief. Throughout the world, companies, like individuals, provide assistance to local citizens and communities when disaster strikes. When floods, fires, earthquakes, ice storms,

---

[11] "From Debris Pile to New Homes," *The New York Times,* November 11, 2008.

[12] "Taking Minority-Owned Businesses under Their Wing," *The New York Times,* September 20, 2005; and private correspondence with Group O.

hurricanes, or terrorist attacks devastate communities, funds pour into affected communities from companies.

Businesses from all over the world responded with great generosity to the communities impacted by the massive earthquake that struck China's Sichuan Province in 2008. Many companies gave cash either directly or through the Red Cross. Others drew on their own special expertise to lend a hand. United Parcel Service mobilized its planes to airlift relief supplies to the region. Pfizer donated medicines. Coca-Cola sent tens of thousands of cases of bottled water. Caterpillar, with several dealerships in China, provided generators, heavy equipment, and operators to run them. Motorola pitched in with mobile phones and network services to help restore communications to the hardest-hit areas.[13]

International relief efforts are becoming more important, as communications improve and people around the world are able to witness the horrors of natural disasters, terrorism, and war. Corporate involvement in such efforts is an extension of the natural tendency of people to help one another when tragedy strikes.

In all these areas of community need—economic development, crime abatement, housing, aid to minority enterprise, and disaster relief—as well as many others, businesses around the world have made and continue to make significant contributions.

Corporate Giving

An important aspect of the business–community relationship is **corporate philanthropy**, or **corporate giving**. Every year, businesses around the world give generously to their communities through various kinds of philanthropic contributions to nonprofit organizations.

America has historically been a generous society. In 2008, individuals, bequests (individual estates), foundations, and corporations collectively gave more than $307 billion to churches, charities, and other nonprofit organizations, as shown in Figure 18.3. Businesses are a small, but important, part of this broad cultural tradition of giving. In 2008, corporate contributions totaled $14.5 billion, or about 5 percent of all charitable giving.

FIGURE 18.3

Philanthropy in the United States, by Source of Contributions, 2008 (in $ billions)

Source: Giving USA Foundation™ (formerly the American Association of Fundraising Counsel Trust for Philanthropy), *Giving USA 2009* (Indianapolis: Center on Philanthropy at Indiana University, 2009), p. 3. Used by permission.

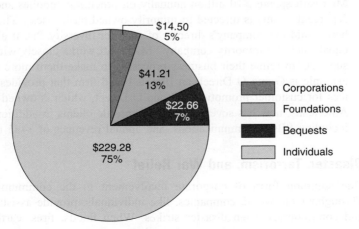

$14.50
5%

$41.21
13%

$22.66
7%

$229.28
75%

Corporations
Foundations
Bequests
Individuals

Total value of contributions was $307.65 billion.

[13] "U.S. China Business Council, U.S. Companies Aid Chinese Earthquake Victims," *BioTech Business Week,* May 26, 2008; and "Multinationals Rev Up Disaster Relief Efforts," *Kiplinger Business Forecasts,* June 2, 2008.

FIGURE 18.4

Corporate Contributions in the United States, as a Percentage of Pretax Corporate Profits, 1968–2008

Source: Giving USA Foundation™ (formerly the American Association of Fundraising Counsel Trust for Philanthropy), *Giving USA 2009* (Indianapolis: Center on Philanthropy at Indiana University, 2009), p. 218. Used by permission.

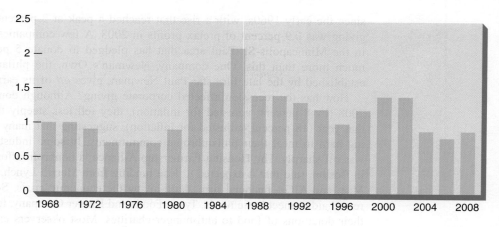

This amount included in-kind gifts claimed as tax deductions and giving by corporate foundations. (This amount represented a drop of 8 percent, adjusted for inflation, from 2007, reflecting the economic recession that began around that time.)

As U.S. firms have become increasingly globalized, as shown in Chapter 6, their international charitable contributions have also grown. A 2008 survey of 197 large U.S. companies and their foundations found that their international giving had increased to 13 percent of all donations. About two-thirds of international gifts were in the form of goods and services; the rest were in the form of cash. Europe received the most (26 percent of international donations), followed by Asia-Pacific excluding China (13 percent), Latin America and the Caribbean (10 percent), Canada (9 percent), China, India, and Africa (4 percent each), and the Middle East (1 percent) (Some contributions were to more than one region.)[14] To cite just one example, the Coca-Cola Foundation has donated millions of dollars to support education around the world. Its contributions have, among other projects, helped build schools in Chile, Egypt, and the Philippines.[15]

In the United States, tax rules have encouraged corporate giving for educational, charitable, scientific, and religious purposes since 1936.[16] Current rules permit corporations to deduct from their taxable income all such gifts that do not exceed 10 percent of the company's before-tax income. In other words, a company with a before-tax income of $1 million might contribute up to $100,000 to nonprofit community organizations devoted to education, charity, science, or religion. The $100,000 in contributions would then reduce the income to be taxed from $1 million to $900,000, thus saving the company money on its tax bill while providing a source of income to community agencies. Of course, nothing prevents a corporation from giving more than 10 percent of its income for philanthropic purposes, but it would not be given a tax break above the 10 percent level.

As shown in Figure 18.4, average corporate giving in the United States is far below the 10 percent deduction now permitted. Though it varies from year to year, corporate giving has generally ranged between one-half of 1 percent and 2 percent of pretax profits

[14] *2008 Corporate Contributions Report* (New York: The Conference Board, 2008), pp. 6 and 28–40; and *Giving USA 2009* (Indianapolis: Center on Philanthropy at Indiana University, 2009), p. 79.

[15] Coca-Cola, "2007–2008 Sustainability Review," *www.thecoca-colacompany.com/citizenship*.

[16] The evolution of corporate philanthropy is summarized in Mark Sharfman, "Changing Institutional Rules: The Evolution of Corporate Philanthropy, 1883–1953," *Business and Society* 33, no. 3 (December 1994).

since the early 1960s, with a rise that reached a peak at 2 percent in 1986. Corporate giving was 0.9 percent of pretax profits in 2008. A few companies, including a cluster in the Minneapolis-St. Paul area that has pledged to donate 5 percent annually, give much more than this. One company, Newman's Own, the philanthropic corporation established by the late film star Paul Newman, gives *all* of its earnings to charity.

How has the recession affected corporate giving? Although donations were down in 2008 (by 8 percent, adjusted for inflation), they fell less steeply than corporate profits that year (18 percent, adjusted for inflation), suggesting that many companies were trying hard to meet their philanthropic commitments. In some industries, however, giving was off sharply. The Housing Partnership Alliance, a nonprofit affordable housing group in Boston, said that it expected to lose funding from Merrill Lynch, Freddie Mac, Fannie Mae, and AIG—financial firms hard-hit by the economic crisis. Some companies redirected aid to meet basic needs. Tyson Foods and Kroger Company, for example, increased their donations of food to anti-hunger charities. Most observers expected business philanthropy to bounce back with the economy. "Corporate giving has weathered economic turbulence year over year," commented the president of the Association of Corporate Contribution Professionals.[17]

> One kind of giving that was hurt by the economic downturn was matching gift programs. Under these programs, companies agree to match voluntary gifts made by their employees to a charity or nonprofit of their choice, up to a certain limit. The idea is that these programs build goodwill in the community and increase participating employees' commitment to the company. In 2007, 88 percent of large U.S. companies had such a program, and the median amount matched per company was around $2 million. During 2008, however, more than a dozen big companies—including Procter & Gamble, Weyerhaeuser, and R.R. Donnelley—shut down their matching programs or significantly cut the amount they contributed. The impact has been particularly severe in communities where recession-hit companies are based. Commented the annual giving coordinator at Michigan Technology University, "We lost Ford in 2006, and this past October [2008] we lost GM, and they were our biggest matching-gift companies." The university had benefited greatly from these programs, because many alumni worked for the auto companies.[18]

The effect of the recession on corporate giving to the arts is explored in the discussion case at the end of this chapter. Exhibit 18.C asks how nonprofit organizations should respond when corporate donors attach conditions to their gifts.

In Europe, corporate philanthropy has lagged behind that in the United States, in part because tax breaks are less generous and differences in the law across countries make cross-border giving difficult. Greater spending on social welfare by governments also reduces incentives and need for private sector philanthropy.[19] Europe-based multinational corporations have become more active, however, as illustrated by the following example:

> The motto of Nokia, the cellular phone company based in Finland, is "connecting people." In partnership with the International Youth Foundation, the company launched a program called "Make A Connection" to help develop life skills

[17] "A Gloomy Giving Outlook," *The Chronicle of Philanthropy,* August 21, 2008; and "Nonprofits Gird for Loss of Funding: Fallout from Collapse of Wall Street Firms," *Boston Globe,* September 22, 2008.

[18] Committee Encouraging Corporate Philanthropy, *Giving in Numbers,* 2008 ed., p. 28, and "Next Benefit to Face the Axe: Matching Gifts," *The Wall Street Journal,* January 14, 2009.

[19] "Understanding Philanthropy," *Financial Times (London),* December 16, 2005.

Exhibit 18.C

Thanks for the Gift, But Are Strings Attached?

Many organizations, including schools and universities, social agencies, arts organizations, and other nonprofits, depend on—and gratefully receive—gifts from corporations, foundations, and individual philanthropists. Without this generosity, many of these organizations would be hard-pressed to survive economically. Yet, what if a gift comes with "strings attached"? Are there circumstances under which an organization should reject a gift, or its conditions?

Bayerische Motoren Werke, the auto company commonly known as BMW, donated $10 million to Clemson University. A major BMW plant is located in Greer, South Carolina, just 50 miles away from the university. In return for the largest gift ever received by the university at that time, BMW management asked for input in creating the curriculum for the automotive and motor sports graduate engineering program. The company also provided Clemson with what it thought was a profile of "the ideal student" and provided the university with a list of engineering professors and specialists to interview to staff the school's program. BMW even asked for approval rights over the school's architectural plans for a new building. The university expressed profound gratitude for the gift, which helped build a major Center for Automotive Research. But some critics expressed concern that the university had given BMW too much control. Said one researcher, "It looks like you've got a profit-making corporation calling the shots in a university setting."

Source: "BMW's Custom-Made University," *The New York Times,* August 29, 2006.

among young people in 25 countries. In 2005, Nokia pledged $23 million to the program over five years, as well as equipment and expertise. In the Philippines, for example, the program's "text2teach" initiative used mobile technology to bring interactive, multimedia learning materials to 80 schools. Said Nokia's vice president for corporate social responsibility, "It's about developing the social glue within a peer group or community."[20]

Although most companies give directly, some large corporations have established nonprofit **corporate foundations** to handle their charitable programs. This permits them to administer contribution programs more uniformly and provides a central group of professionals that handles all grant requests. Ninety-two percent of large U.S.-based corporations have such foundations; collectively, corporate foundations gave $2.1 billion in 2007.[21] Foreign-owned corporations use foundations less frequently, although firms such as Matsushita (Panasonic) and Hitachi use sophisticated corporate foundations to conduct their charitable activities in the United States. As corporations expand to more foreign locations, pressures will grow to expand international corporate giving. Foundations, with their defined mission to benefit the community, can be a useful mechanism to help companies implement philanthropic programs that meet this corporate social responsibility.

Forms of Corporate Giving

Typically, gifts by corporations and their foundations take one of three forms: charitable donations (gifts of money), in-kind contributions (gifts of products or services), and volunteer employee service (gifts of time). Many companies give in all three categories.

An example of a particularly generous cash gift was one made by Intel, the computer chip maker, in 2008. Intel, together with its foundation, pledged $120 million over the next 10 years to the Society for Science & the Public

[20] "Making a Connection to Boost Life Skills," *Financial Times (London),* January 26, 2006; and *Corporate Social Responsibility Report 2007, www.nokia.com.* An analysis of program outcomes is available at *www.iyfnet.org.*
[21] *Giving in Numbers,* 2008 ed., op. cit., p. 18; and *Giving USA 2009,* op. cit., p. 74.

Interest. The purpose of the gift was to support this organization's Science Talent Search, a prestigious science competition for high school seniors. The gift also included funds for outreach to young people and mentoring for program alumni. As part of the competition, every year 40 finalists traveled to Washington, DC, to present their research to members of the scientific community. Awards included college scholarships and computers. Many former winners had gone on to distinguished careers in science and entrepreneurship. "I can't think of a more critical time to invest in math and science education," said Intel's vice president for corporate affairs.[22]

The share of all giving comprising **in-kind contributions** of products or services has been rising steadily for the past decade or so and has now surpassed cash contributions. Of U.S. corporate contributions in 2007, more than half—54 percent—were in the form of in-kind gifts.[23] For example, computer companies have donated computer hardware and software to schools, universities, and public libraries. Grocery retailers have donated food, and Internet service providers have donated time online. Publishers have given books. The most generous industry, in terms of in-kind contributions, is pharmaceuticals, as illustrated by the following example:[24]

In 2007, Pfizer contributed an extraordinary $1.68 *billion* worth of medicines and other products and services, an amount equal to 8.7 percent of that year's profit. Many of these donations were directed to the poorest nations and communities in the world, where the company gave away drugs to treat malaria, HIV/AIDS, trachoma, and many other illnesses. In 2009, Pfizer announced it would give access to its "library" of 200,000 novel chemical compounds to Medicines for Malaria Venture, a nonprofit created to develop safe and effective drugs to treat malaria—a dreadful scourge that killed 881,000 people annually, most of them African children. "People are suffering in developing countries, and we want to help by sharing resources and boosting research against tropical diseases," said a Pfizer executive.[25]

In-kind contributions can be creative—and they need not cost a lot. Frito-Lay, for example, donated publicity to Do Something—a nonprofit whose mission is to encourage young people to improve the world—by featuring photos of the organization's work on 500 million bags of Doritos chips. "It drove fabulous recognition for our organization and helped our Web traffic," said the grateful director.[26] The contribution was a low-cost one for Frito-Lay, which would have had to print its bags anyway.

Under U.S. tax laws, if companies donate new goods, they may deduct their fair market value within the relevant limits. For example, if a computer company donated $10,000 worth of new laptops to a local school, it could take a deduction for this amount on its corporate tax return, provided this amount was less than 10 percent of its pretax income.

[22] "Intel Encourages More Youth to Participate in Math and Science," press release, October 20, 2008, *www.intel.com/pressroom.* The Web site of the Intel Science Talent Search is at *www.societyforscience.org.*
[23] *2008 Corporate Contributions Report* (New York: The Conference Board, 2008), p. 22.
[24] Committee to Encourage Corporate Philanthropy, *Adding It Up 2004: The Corporate Giving Standard* (Chestnut Hill, MA: Center for Corporate Citizenship at Boston College, 2006).
[25] "Pfizer and Medicines for Malaria Venture Advancing International Research Efforts in the Fight against Malaria," press release, April 22, 2009, *http://mediaroom.pfizer.com;* and "A Gloomy Outlook for Giving," *The Chronicle of Philanthropy,* August 21, 2008. Pfizer's philanthropic initiatives are reported at *www.pfizer.com/responsibility.*
[26] "Philanthropy: A Special Report: Firm Decisions: As Companies Become More Involved in Giving, Charities Are Glad to Get Aid Faster and with Less Red Tape," *The Wall Street Journal,* December 10, 2007.

Business leaders and employees also regularly donate their own time—another form of corporate giving. **Volunteerism** involves the efforts of people to assist others in the community through unpaid work. According to a report by the Department of Labor, about 26 percent of Americans ages 16 and older volunteered during the prior year, donating on average 52 hours of their time.[27] Many companies encourage their employees to volunteer by publicizing opportunities, sponsoring specific projects, and offering recognition for service. Some companies partner with a specific agency to provide volunteer support over time, as illustrated by the following example:

> KaBOOM! is a nonprofit organization that builds playgrounds. The group's goal is "to help develop a country in which all children have, within their communities, access to equitable, fun, and healthy play opportunities." Since it was founded in 1996, the organization has maintained a strong partnership with Home Depot, the building supply firm. Home Depot employees in many communities have volunteered their building skills, along with materials, to build KaBOOM! playgrounds in underserved neighborhoods. "Team Depot" volunteers, working alongside people from the community, can build a state-of-the-art playground in a single day. In 2008, Home Depot reached a milestone of 1,000 play spaces built in collaboration with KaBOOM![28]

An important trend is what is known as *skills-based volunteerism,* in which employee skills are matched to specialized needs. For example, Target, the Minneapolis-based retailer, has set up a pilot program under which employees with architectural design and construction skills can volunteer to help renovate public libraries.[29]

Another, less common approach is for companies to provide employees with *paid* time off for volunteer service in the community. For example, Wells Fargo offers a volunteer leave program, under which employees can apply for a fully paid sabbatical of up to four months to work in a nonprofit organization of their choice. In recent years, Wells Fargo employees on paid leave have trained teachers in Afghanistan; built homes in Oaxaca, Mexico; and helped renovate a facility for the mentally ill.[30] The increasing use of technology to help organize and promote employee volunteering is profiled in Exhibit 18.D.

Priorities in Corporate Giving

Overall, what kinds of organizations receive the most corporate philanthropy? The distribution of contributions reflects how businesses view overall community needs, and how this perception has changed over time. As shown in Figure 18.5, the corporate giving "pie" is divided into several main segments. The largest share of corporate philanthropy goes to health and human services; the next largest share goes to education. Civic and community organizations and culture and the arts also receive large shares of business philanthropy. Of course, these percentages are not identical among different companies and industries; some companies tend to favor support for education, for example, whereas others give relatively greater amounts to cultural organizations or community groups.

---

[27] "Volunteering in the United States, 2008," U.S. Department of Labor, press release, January 23, 2009.

[28] "The Home Depot and KaBOOM! Celebrate 1,000th Play Space," press release, April, 10, 2008. The Web site for KaBOOM! is at *www.kaboom.org.*

[29] "A Gloomy Giving Outlook," *The Chronicle of Philanthropy,* August 21, 2008.

[30] Boston College Center for Corporate Citizenship, "Company Example: Wells Fargo," June, 2007.

Exhibit 18.D

Using Technology to Encourage Employee Volunteerism

Many companies have turned to technology to improve the amount and effectiveness of employee volunteerism. "Technology is transforming the landscape," commented the executive director of the Mitsubishi Electric America Foundation. "The speed of communications enables us to quickly get information to and from our employees." Horizon Bank, for example, has linked Volunteer Match, a Web-based service that enables nonprofits to post volunteer opportunities online, to its company intranet. The bank uses the service to track employee volunteer hours and makes a contribution to charities based on the number of hours its employees commit to them. Other providers of volunteer software include AmeriGives, AngelPoints, and JK Group. Some firms—among them, Oracle and IBM—have developed their own computerized systems to oversee their employees' volunteerism. Bank of America has developed a custom-designed Web site to measure and recognize employee volunteerism. BofA gives workers two hours a week of paid time to volunteer, and for every 50 hours contributed gives the organization a $250 contribution on the volunteer's behalf. Whether provided by outside vendors or in-house, software enables companies to better monitor the impact of their employees' work in the community. Commented the national director of community involvement for Deloitte, a large consulting firm, "We can be more strategic and more focused on social outcomes [and can more easily] answer questions about when and how we as a company [become] engaged."

Sources: "Corporate Philanthropy: Striving to Give in Good Times and Bad," *New Jersey Business,* September 2008; "Employee Volunteering/Giving Technology Vendor Survey," 2008, *www.bccc.net;* "Philanthropy: A Special Report: Firm Decisions: As Companies Become More Involved in Giving, Charities Are Glad to Get Aid Faster and with Less Red Tape," *The Wall Street Journal,* December 10, 2007; and "Corporate Volunteerism in the Internet Age," *The CRO,* December 14, 2006, *www.thecro.com.*

Does corporate giving contribute to business success? One study addressed this question directly. The Council on Foundations developed a Corporate Philanthropy Index (CPI) that rated companies from 1.0 to 5.0 on a five-point scale based on their stakeholders' perceptions. Researchers asked employees, customers, and influential members of the community to evaluate companies' contributions to the community and society. The study showed that companies with high CPI scores had better reputations and generated more admiration and goodwill than did others; people were also more willing to give these companies the benefit of the doubt if they received bad publicity.[31] Further research may reveal more about the specific benefits of donations.

FIGURE 18.5

Priorities in Corporate Giving (percentage of corporate cash and in-kind contributions to various sectors)

Source: *2008 Corporate Contributions Report* (New York: The Conference Board, 2008), Tables 19–25. All data are for 2007. Used by permission.

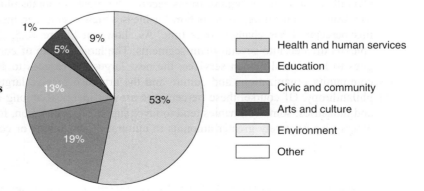

- Health and human services — 53%
- Education — 19%
- Civic and community — 13%
- Arts and culture — 5%
- Environment — 1%
- Other — 9%

[31] "Measuring the Business Value of Corporate Philanthropy," *Research Report Executive Summary,* October 2000 (conducted by Walker Information Inc. for the Council on Foundations). The Web site of the Council on Foundations is *www.cof.org.*

Corporate Giving in a Strategic Context

Communities have social needs requiring far more resources than are normally available, and businesses often face more demands than they can realistically meet. This is particularly true in hard economic times, when funds may be less plentiful. Companies must establish priorities to determine which worthy projects will be funded or supported with the company's in-kind or volunteer contributions and which ones will not. What criteria should community relations departments apply in determining who will receive corporate gifts? These are often difficult choices, both because businesses may want to support more charities than they can afford, and because saying no often produces dissatisfaction among those who do not get as much help as they want.

One increasingly popular approach is to target corporate contributions *strategically* to meet the needs of the donor as well as the recipient. **Strategic philanthropy** refers to corporate giving that is linked directly or indirectly to business goals and objectives. In this approach, both the company and society benefit from the gift:

> For example, Cisco Systems, a manufacturer of hardware for the Internet, has established a Networking Academy to train computer network administrators. From a modest start in 1997 in a high school near the company's headquarters in San Jose, California, by 2006 the program had expanded to include more than 10,000 sites in high schools and community colleges in 50 states and more than 150 countries, and had trained more than 1.6 million students. The academy initiative benefits communities throughout the world by providing job training for young people, many of whom go on to successful careers in systems administration. But it also benefits the company, by assuring a supply of information technology professionals who can operate Cisco's complex equipment.[32]

A study in the *Harvard Business Review* identified four areas in which corporate contributions were most likely to enhance a company's competitiveness, as well as the welfare of the community.[33] Strategic contributions focus on

- *Factor conditions,* such as the supply of trained workers, physical infrastructure, and natural resources. Cisco's Networking Academy is an example of philanthropy that helps the donor by providing skilled employees both for Cisco and for its corporate customers.
- *Demand conditions,* those that affect demand for a product or service. When Microsoft provides free software to libraries and universities, new generations of young people learn to use these programs and are more likely later to buy computers equipped with the company's products.
- *Context for strategy and rivalry.* Company donations sometimes can be designed to support policies that open markets and enable fair competition. For example, contributions to an organization such as Transparency International that opposes corruption may help a company gain access to previously unreachable markets.
- *Related and supporting industries.* Finally, charitable contributions that strengthen related sectors of the economy may also help companies, as shown in the following example:

> The Marriott Resort and Beach Club on the island of Kauai in Hawaii had a problem. The luxury resort wanted to offer its guests native cuisine prepared

---

[32] More information about the Networking Academy is available at *http://cisco.netacad.net.*

[33] Michael E. Porter and Mark R. Kramer, "The Competitive Advantage of Corporate Philanthropy," *Harvard Business Review,* December 2002.

with locally grown produce. But the island, which had long been dominated by sugarcane plantations, then in decline, did not have a diversified farming sector. The resort partnered with a local food bank to create a successful program to teach underemployed local residents to grow fruits and vegetables on their own land and to market their produce cooperatively. Today, the Hui meai'ai ("club of things to eat") provides employment for 56 local growers and supplies 25 businesses, including the Marriott.[34]

Of course, not all corporate contributions benefit their donors directly, nor should they. But most, if handled correctly, at least build goodwill and help cement the loyalty of employees, customers, and suppliers who value association with a good corporate citizen.

Specialists in corporate philanthropy recommend four other strategies to help companies get the most benefit from their contributions:[35]

- *Draw on the unique assets and competencies of the business.* Companies often have special skills or resources that enable them to make a contribution that others could not. For example, Google, Inc., provides free advertising on its search engine to nonprofit organizations in many countries. Donations to Direct Relief International, just one of many charities supported in this way, increased more than tenfold after it joined Google's program.[36]

- *Align priorities with employee interests.* Another successful strategy is to give employees a say in deciding who will receive contributions. An advantage of this approach is that it strengthens ties between the company and its workers, who feel that their values are being expressed through the organization's choices. For example, PacifiCare, a large health services corporation, recruits employee volunteers to serve on its foundation's regional allocation committees. "They are the true heroes of our philanthropy," said the president of the PacifiCare Foundation.[37]

- *Align priorities with core values of the firm.* McDonald's Corporation, the fast-food giant, focuses its philanthropic contributions on children's programs. One of the company's major charities is the Ronald McDonald Houses, facilities where families can stay in a homelike setting while their children receive treatment at a nearby hospital. The program operates 284 houses in 52 countries, including new programs in Latvia and Thailand. McDonald's believes that this initiative is consistent with its mission to "make a difference in the lives of children."[38]

- *Use hard-nosed business methods to assess the impact of gifts.* Increasingly, companies are using standard business tools to assess their investments in philanthropy, just as they would any other investment. For example, they might establish goals for a particular charitable gift, and then check to make sure these goals have been met. Underperforming projects would be dropped, and successful ones would receive continued funding. These efforts are sometimes part of a broader social audit, as described in Chapter 7.

[34] "A Productive Partnership: The Kauai Marriott Resort and Beach Club and the Kauai Food Bank," *In Practice* (Chestnut Hill: The Center for Corporate Citizenship at Boston College, 2002).

[35] See, for example, David Hess, Nikolai Rogovsky, and Thomas W. Dunfee, "The Next Wave in Corporate Community Involvement: Corporate Social Initiatives," *California Management Review* 44, no. 2 (Winter 2002).

[36] "Google Grants Success Profile," *www.google.com/support/grants;* and "Google Starts Up Philanthropy Campaign," *The Washington Post,* October 12, 2005.

[37] See *www.socalgrantmakers.org.*

[38] "2004 Worldwide Corporate Responsibility Report," *www.mcdonalds.com.*

In short, businesses today are taking a more strategic approach to all kinds of corporate giving. They want to make sure that gifts are not simply made randomly, but rather are targeted in such a way that they are consistent with the firm's values, core competencies, and strategic goals.

Building Collaborative Partnerships

The term *partnership,* introduced in Chapter 6, refers to a voluntary collaboration among business, government, and civil society organizations to achieve specific objectives. The need for such **collaborative partnerships** is very apparent when dealing with community problems.

One arena in which collaborative partnerships among business, government, and communities have been particularly effective is education. As mentioned earlier in this chapter, community relations managers count education as the most critical challenge they face. Many school districts and colleges in the United States face an influx of new students from the so-called "echo boom" generation, increasing class sizes and making it more difficult to give students the individual attention they need. Many schools are challenged to educate new Americans, immigrants from other parts of the world who often do not speak English as their native language. More children are living in poverty, and many come from single-parent homes. A fast-changing economy demands that the technological tools accessible to students be greatly expanded. All these challenges must be met in many states under conditions of extreme fiscal constraint, as tax revenues fall and budget crises loom. The difficulties faced by schools are of immediate concern to many companies, which rely on educational systems to provide them with well-trained employees equipped for today's high-technology workplace.

Business has been deeply involved with education reform in the United States for over two decades. A series of studies by The Conference Board identified four waves, or distinct periods, in corporate involvement in education reform from the 1980s to the present.[39] The first wave was characterized by *direct involvement* with specific schools. For example, a company might "adopt" a school, providing it with cash, equipment, and volunteer assistance, and promising job interviews for qualified graduates. The second wave focused on the *application of management principles* to school administration. Business leaders assisted schools by advising administrators and government officials who needed training in management methods, such as strategic planning and performance appraisal. The third wave emphasized advocacy for *public policy initiatives* in education, such as ones calling for school choice and adoption of national testing standards. The fourth wave, which is ongoing, focuses on *collaboration for systemic reform.* This involves collaborative partnerships among business organizations, schools, and government agencies. In such collaborations, all partners bring unique capabilities and resources to the challenge of educational reform. The result is often outcomes that are better than any of them could have achieved acting alone.[40]

A leading example of a corporation deeply involved in collaborative partnerships to improve education is IBM. Through its "Reinventing Education" initiative, IBM has partnered with schools in many states and eight countries, including

---

[39] Susan Otterbourg, *Innovative Public–Private Partnerships: Educational Initiatives* (New York: The Conference Board, 1998); and Sandra Waddock, *Business and Education Reform: The Fourth Wave* (New York: The Conference Board, 1994).

[40] For a discussion of the benefits of collaborative partnerships, see Bradley K. Googins and Steven A. Rochlin, "Creating the Partnership Society: Understanding the Rhetoric and Reality of Cross-Sectoral Partnerships," *Business and Society Review* 105, no. 1 (2000), pp. 127–44.

Brazil, Vietnam, Mexico, and Ireland, to apply technology to improve student achievement and performance. Since the program's launch in 1994, IBM has donated more than $75 million in cash and high-tech equipment. But the program goes far beyond traditional philanthropy. According to an independent evaluation by the Center for Children and Technology, Reinventing Education "engages researchers, corporate managers, and educators in a long-term partnership, committed to serious sustained collaboration to improve schools." Successful experiments are spread, through the program, to many other schools. Among the partnership's many accomplishments have been the development of a communications network connecting schools and parents, electronic portfolios to display student work, and online "learning villages" where novice teachers can work with experienced mentors. The Center for Children and Technology evaluation found that the partnership had produced "significant performance gains" for students in affiliated schools.[41]

The success of IBM's initiative illustrates the potential of collaborative partnerships that allow business to contribute its unique assets and skills to a broader effort to solve significant community problems.

Communities need jobs, specialized skills, executive talent, and other resources that business can provide. Business needs cooperative attitudes in local government, basic public services, and a feeling that it is a welcome member of the community. Under these circumstances much can be accomplished to upgrade the quality of community life. The range of business–community collaborations is extensive, giving businesses many opportunities to be socially responsible.

Like education, other community challenges are, at their core, people problems, involving hopes, attitudes, sentiments, and expectations for better human conditions. Neither government nor business can simply impose solutions or be expected to find quick and easy answers to problems so long in the making and so vast in their implications. Moreover, neither government nor business has the financial resources on their own to solve these issues. Grassroots involvement is needed, where people are willing and able to confront their own needs, imagine solutions, and work to fulfill them through cooperative efforts and intelligent planning. In that community-oriented effort, government, nonprofit organizations, and businesses can be partners, contributing aid and assistance where feasible and being socially responsive to legitimately expressed human needs.

Summary

- The *community* refers to an organization's area of local influence, as well as more broadly to other groups that are impacted by its actions. Businesses and their communities are mutually dependent. Business relies on the community for services and infrastructure, and the community relies on business for support of various civic activities.

- Addressing a community's needs in a positive way helps business by enhancing its reputation, building trust, and winning support for company actions. Like other forms of corporate social responsibility, community involvement helps cement the loyalty of employees, customers, and the public.

[41] "Reinventing Education: IBM's Award-Winning Model School Reform Program" (2008) and Center for Children and Technology, "The Reinventing Education Initiative from an Evaluation Perspective" (2004), both at *www.ibm.com/ibm/ibmgives*.

- Many corporations have established community relations departments that respond to local needs and community groups, coordinate corporate giving, and develop strategies for creating win–win approaches to solving civic problems.

- Corporate giving comprises gifts of cash, property, and employee time. Donations currently average about 1.8 percent of pretax profits. Philanthropic contributions both improve a company's reputation and sustain vital community institutions.

- Many companies have adopted a strategic approach to philanthropy, linking their giving to business goals. Corporate giving is most effective when it draws on the unique competencies of the business and is aligned with the core values of the firm and with employee interests.

- The development of collaborative partnerships has proven to be effective in addressing problems in education and other civic concerns. Partnerships offer an effective model of shared responsibility in which businesses and the public and nonprofit sectors can draw on their unique skills to address complex social problems.

Key Terms

civic engagement, *413*
collaborative partnerships, *427*
community, *412*
Community Reinvestment Act, *415*
community relations, *414*
community relations manager, *415*
corporate foundations, *421*
corporate philanthropy (corporate giving), *418*
in-kind contributions, *422*
license to operate, *414*
social capital, •••
strategic philanthropy, *425*
volunteerism, *423*

Internet Resources

www.bcccc.net	The Center for Corporate Citizenship at Boston College
http://bwnt.businessweek.com/interactive_reports/philanthropy_corporate	*BusinessWeek*'s list of corporate philanthropy's biggest givers (periodically updated)
www.corporatephilanthropy.org	Committee Encouraging Corporate Philanthropy
www.givingusa.org	Giving Institute and Giving USA Foundation
http://go.worldbank.org/VEN7OUW280	World Bank (social capital)
www.onphilanthropy.com	Resources for nonprofit and corporate professionals working in the philanthropic sector
http://philanthropy.com	Chronicle of Philanthropy
www.pointsoflight.org	Points of Light Foundation

Discussion Case: *Corporate Philanthropy and the Arts*

Nonprofit arts organizations are an integral part of the cultures of all nations. Art museums, theaters, dance companies, orchestras, nonprofit filmmakers, and arts educators enrich the quality of life of communities and deepen people's understanding of one another. The arts also help drive local economies. Cultural institutions in the United States, for example, provide 5.7 million jobs and contribute $166 billion to the economy annually, according to one study.

Historically, corporations have been significant supporters of the arts. As the recession deepened in 2008 and 2009, however, many businesses cut back their contributions. Americans for the Arts, a nonprofit organization, forecast a decrease in overall business giving in 2009. The proportion of corporate giving directed to the arts was also falling, as more went to health, education, and basic social services. "It's tough out there," said one theater manager. "The arts are . . . [the] thing that can be cut, because we need . . . our soup kitchens."

As funding from businesses fell off, many arts organizations were hit hard. The Metropolitan Museum of Art in New York, which had relied heavily on gifts from Wall Street firms, cut 74 jobs. The Detroit Institute of Arts, similarly dependent on the beleaguered auto industry, had to absorb a $6 billion budget cut. In 2009, 10,000 arts organizations in the United States—about 10 percent of the total—were at risk of closing. In the United Kingdom, the Arts Council announced that more than 200 arts organizations were in danger of losing all or some of their funding.

In light of changed circumstances, nonprofits explored what value they could offer corporate donors, and companies explored the bottom-line benefits of their philanthropy. Consider the following examples:

- Time Warner, the media company, in 2008 decided to extend its sponsorship of the City Center Fall for Dance program in New York City. The international dance festival attracts audiences of many ages and ethnicities—many of whom have never before attended a dance concert. The company's logo appears on thousands of subway posters, bus ads, brochures, and ticket envelopes for the event.

- Germany's Deutsche Bank has amassed one of the largest private art collections in the world, with more than 53,000 original works in more than 100 offices around the world. It periodically lends pieces to art museums for public exhibition. The firm, which provides services to many wealthy clients, says its aim is to "make the offices more stimulating." The bank's unusual collection attracts customers and employees interested in fine arts and, not incidentally, are often good investments.

- Panasonic donated its jumbo screen in New York's Times Square for a simulcast of the Metropolitan Opera's performance of *Madame Butterfly,* and also provided smaller Panasonic-brand screens in the Met's lobby where latecomers could watch performances. The opera's general manager welcomed the partnership, saying, "It's up to institutions like ours to create opportunities for sponsors."

- The British hearing aid maker Scrivens Groups often supports live musical performances. The company stated that its motivations included "generating a national profile for the message that hearing loss need not be a barrier to the enjoyment of music."

- In 2009, Intel announced a partnership with the nonprofit Public Broadcasting System (PBS). The company agreed to support the NewsHour, as well as a series of documentaries on innovation. An Intel spokesperson explained, "[T]here are many similarities to the way the NewsHour does its reporting and the way Intel approaches its business."

- Sweetwater Sound of Fort Wayne, Indiana, is a retailer of musical instruments and technology. The company encourages its employees, many of whom are musicians, to recommend in-kind and cash contributions to arts organizations, and many employees also volunteer directly. In its headquarters, Sweetwater built a new 250-seat auditorium that it donates for public concerts and fund-raisers.

These, and many other, businesses have concluded that their contributions to the arts are worth it, even in tough times.

Sources: "Intel Joins the NewsHour as Corporate Sponsor," press release, April 2, 2009; "Arts Groups Lose Out in Fight for Funds," *The Wall Street Journal,* March 18, 2009; "Art Business: With Financial Institutions in Turmoil, Will Banks Renowned for Spending on Art Tighten the Purse Strings?" *Apollo,* November 2008; "Art Business: What Is the Future for Corporate Sponsorship of the Arts in the Current Economic Downturn?" *Apollo,* September 2008; "Philanthropy: A Special Report: Firm Decisions: As Companies Become More Involved in Giving, Charities Are Glad to Get Aid Faster and with Less Red Tape," *The Wall Street Journal,* December 10, 2007; "As Corporate Support Shifts Its Focus, Arts Organizations Are Adjusting" *The New York Times,* February 21, 2007; "Giving Back: Firms Funding Arts Seek a Return," *The Wall Street Journal,* February 9, 2007; and Gerald Burstyn, "Hidden Agenda," *Stanford Social Innovation Review,* Spring 2005. See also the Web site of Americans for the Arts, *www.americansforthearts.org.*

Discussion Questions

1. In what ways do businesses benefit from locating in communities with vibrant arts organizations and a rich cultural life?

2. What evidence do you see in this case of the three kinds of corporate philanthropy discussed in this chapter: contributions of cash, in-kind products or services, and employee time?

3. What are the benefits to the businesses discussed here of their contributions to arts organizations? Would you consider their contributions to represent strategic philanthropy, as defined in the chapter? Why or why not?

4. If you were a manager charged with evaluating corporate contributions, what criteria would you use to decide whether or not to give to a particular arts organization?

5. If you were a manager of an arts organization, are there any circumstances under which you would turn down, or restrict in some way, a corporate contribution? What would these circumstances be?

CHAPTER NINETEEN

Managing Public Relations

How the general public perceives a business firm can have a major effect on its performance. Therefore, building a positive relationship with the public through the management of the firm's public relations is of great importance. Most companies maintain a public relations office, whose job is to formulate public relations strategy, interact with the media and with the public directly, and respond to unanticipated crises. When a business attends to this important stakeholder relationship with the public, it helps both its reputation and its bottom line.

This Chapter Focuses on These Key Learning Objectives:

- Examining the structure and activities of a public relations department, both domestically and globally.
- Designing an effective public relations strategy using new technological innovations.
- Evaluating strategies used by business organizations to influence public opinion.
- Identifying government regulatory agencies charged with protecting the public from illegal business practices.
- Assessing effective crisis management plans.
- Evaluating techniques available for employees to capably manage the organization's media image.

Subway, highway, and river traffic in the greater Boston area came to screeching halt on January 31, 2007, when 40 blinking electronic signs promoting the Cartoon Network series *Aqua Teen Hunger Force* were set up near bridges and depots. The police feared that these were acts of terrorism and stopped traffic until they could analyze and remove the equipment. Later it was explained that this was a new form of public relations—guerilla advertising. The authorities did not take this public relations stunt lightly, and they arrested the two men hired to put up these signs. Turner Broadcasting, the parent company behind this campaign, paid $1 million to reimburse federal, state, and local agencies for their expenses and pledged an additional $1 million in "goodwill funds" to be used for emergency training and public outreach. The president and general manager at the Cartoon Network, Jim Samples, resigned under pressure a month after the public relations fiasco.

Two Domino's Pizza employees thought it would be fun to videotape themselves preparing sandwiches. They put cheese up their noses and then sneezed the cheese onto the sandwiches and committed other health code violations. When they posted their video to *YouTube,* thanks to the power of the social media, the company had to deal with millions of angry and worried customers who had seen the disgusting prank. "We got blindsided by two idiots with a video camera and an awful idea," said a Domino's spokesperson. "Even people who've been with us as loyal customers for 10, 15, 20 years, people are second-guessing their relationship with Domino's and that's not fair." The employees were charged with felony counts of delivering prohibited food. Domino's quickly realized that social media has the reach and speed to turn tiny incidents into public relations nightmares.

Companies are turning to new ways to get their names out into the public. Supermarket eggs featured the names of CBS's television shows. Subway turnstiles were printed with messages from Geico, the auto insurance company. Chinese food cartons promoted Continental Airlines. US Airways sold ads on motion sickness bags. Trays used in airport security lines publicized the name Rolex. While marketers used to focus on selling their products to potential customers while they were at home, people's viewing habits have become so scattered that marketers have had to change their methods of catching the eyes of future consumers. "We never know where the consumer is going to be at any point in time, so we have to find a way to be everywhere," said Linda Kaplan Thaler, chief executive of a New York City advertisement agency. "Ubiquity is the new exclusivity." Apparently it is never too early to attract consumers. Some school buses played radio ads meant for children. Disney marketed a new movie for preschoolers by advertising on paper liners of examination tables in 2,000 pediatricians' offices.[1]

While businesses seek publicity and spend millions of dollars annually to improve their image among the public, there are minefields for public relations officers and company executives to navigate as they compete for the public's attention and dollars.

The General Public

The **general public** is broadly defined as an organizational stakeholder composed of individuals and groups found in society. As described in Chapter 1, the general public does not deal with business organizations through an economic exchange with the firm, but

[1] "Settlement in Terror Scare Is $2 Million," *The New York Times*, February 6, 2007, *www.nytimes.com;* "Cartoon Network Chief Quits Over Boston Marketing Incident," *The New York Times*, February 9, 2007, *www.nytimes.com;* "Video Prank at Domino's Taints Brand," *The New York Times*, April 16, 2009, *www.nytimes.com;* and "Anywhere the Eye Can See, It's Likely to See an Ad," *The New York Times*, January 15, 2007, *www.nytimes.com.*

does affect the firm through its opinions of the firm's activities or performance, which in turn help shape the firm's public image or reputation, as discussed in Chapter 3.

The public may utilize its own stakeholder networks—consumer advocacy groups, employee labor unions, or local community action groups—and engage with government agencies, special interest groups, or the media to demand a certain level of performance or to condemn or praise a firm.

> After a series of privacy breaches and exposure of personal information for thousands of consumers in the EU, public outcry in the United Kingdom called for legislation to better protect consumers and the public citizenry in general. According to a survey conducted by the information security firm Symantec, 96 percent of the public wanted to be notified by businesses or the government if their personal information was stolen or lost. The public and the company apparently held different views on this issue. The same poll revealed that 9 of 10 U.K. information technology managers believed that the general public should *not* be informed if a data breach occurred.[2]

Companies should be aware of public positions on important issues, especially since the public may not always share the same views as the firm.

Similarly, the firm can affect the general public's values, attitudes, and actions through various communication channels, such as television, billboards, the Internet, blogs, and other such vehicles, as will be discussed later. Just as the firm's responsible actions can enhance the quality of life for members of the public, so too can its hazardous behavior place the public at risk.

Public Relations in an Emerging Digital World

Given the importance of the general public to business and the potential for business to significantly benefit or harm the public, firms often create public relations departments, appoint public relations officers, and develop public affairs strategies to manage their relationship with the public. Bill Nielsen, former corporate vice president of public affairs at Johnson & Johnson, clearly articulated the importance of an effective public relations approach for businesses:

> In today's increasingly global world of business, there is a clear and, I believe, pressing agenda for public relations and corporate communications. . . . The agenda is all about the critical components of reputation that have to do with values and trust—trustworthiness being the ultimate condition of public approval that we seek for our companies, our clients, and our profession—on a global scale and wherever in the world we operate.[3]

An effective public relations program is fundamental to any organization's relationship with the public. A good **public relations** program sends a constant stream of information from the company to the public and opens the door to dialogue with stakeholders whose lives are affected by the company's operations. As one group of scholars has written, the essential role of the public relations program "appears to be that of a *window out of the corporation* through which management can perceive, monitor, and understand

---

[2] "Public Demand Data Breach Legislation," *Incisive Media Limited*, June 6, 2008, *www.v3.co.uk.*

[3] Bill Nielsen, "The Singular Character of Public Relations in a Global Economy," International Distinguished Lecture at the Institute for Public Relations, October 11, 2006, p. 1. Entire address is available at *www.instituteforpr.com.*

external change, and simultaneously, a *window in* through which society can influence corporate policy and practice. This boundary-spanning role primarily involves the flow of information to and from the organization."[4]

A public relations program should be proactive, not reactive. Channels of communication with the media should be established on a continuing basis, not just after a problem has arisen. Specific techniques on how to best train employees to communicate using the media are discussed later in this chapter.

Public Relations Department

The role of the **public relations department** is to manage the firm's public image and, more generally, its relationship with the public. This department may also be called *media relations,* since much of its work involves interacting with the media. It does so through direct communications with the public (for example, through its Web site) and indirect communications with them through various media outlets, such as newspapers, television, radio, and magazines. The first public relations department was created by George Westinghouse in 1889 when he hired two men to publicize his pet project, alternating current (AC) electricity. James Grunig, a professor at the University of Maryland, has described public relations as "building good relationships with strategic publics," requiring public relations managers to be "strategic communication managers rather than communication technicians."[5] Figure 19.1 shows the major activities carried out by public relations managers.

Senior leaders understand that these activities are central to the basic operations of an organization and contribute to the company's bottom line. Bill Nielsen explained,

> In fact, I am beginning to believe that public relations people ought to consider themselves as owners of organizational values—"owners" in the sense of carrying the responsibility for the articulation of values, as well as for being the strong and persistent "voice" in the organization for behavior that is consistent with its values.[6]

FIGURE 19.1
Public Relations Activities

Source: "Corporate Survey 2006," *PRWeek*, October 9, 2006, p. 21.

Public Relations Activity	Percentage of Respondents Indicating That the Activity Describes Their Work
Media relations	79.5 %
Crisis management	62.6
Employee communications	59.4
Online communications	58.0
Community relations	55.7
Reputation management	54.8
Public affairs/governmental relations	35.2
Issues advertising	31.1
Monitoring blogs	20.5
Writing blogs	12.3

[4] Boston University Public Affairs Research Group, *Public Affairs Offices and Their Functions: A Summary of Survey Results* (Boston: Boston University School of Management, 1981), p. 1.

[5] James Grunig (ed.), *Excellence in Public Relations and Communications Management* (Hillsdale, NJ: Lawrence Erlbaum Associates, 1992).

[6] Nielsen, "The Singular Character of Public Relations," p. 4.

Exhibit 19.A

Public Relations Professional Associations

The *Public Relations Society of America* (PRSA) is a professional association of public relations officers committed to "the fundamental values of individual dignity and free exercise of human rights." The PRSA believes that "the freedom of speech, assembly, and the press are essential to the practice of public relations." In serving its clients' interests, the PRSA is dedicated to "the goals of better communication, understanding, and cooperation among diverse individuals, groups, and institutions of society." To this end, the PRSA adopted a Member Code of Ethics in 2000, replacing previous standards and codes for the industry in place since 1950. The new code presented six professional core values for its members and the public relations profession: advocacy, honesty, expertise, independence, loyalty, and fairness.

Founded in 1970, the *International Association of Business Communicators* (IABC) provides a professional network of almost 16,000 business communication professionals in over 70 countries. IABC's professional network serves as a resource for its members to have a greater impact in their public relations job, assist in locating opportunities in the job market, enhance the members' public relations skills through various training programs, and enable members to identify new clients and make new friends.

The *International Public Relations Association* (IPRA), founded in 1955, proclaims as its mission "to be the world's most relevant, resourceful, and influential professional association for senior international public relations executives. IPRA provides intellectual leadership in the practice of international public relations and makes available to its members services enabling them to meet their professional responsibilities and to succeed in their careers. This allows the IPRA to increase its membership, grow financially, and create a virtuous circle of success."[7]

Most public relations officers have close links with top managers. According to a recent study by the University of Southern California's Annenberg Center, more than two-thirds of the public relations officers surveyed report directly to the chief executive officer or chief operating officer of the company. The report states that this clear reporting line to the top of the organization indicates that their CEOs believe public relations contributes to the company's market share, financial success, and sales.[8]

Assisting the public relations officer are numerous professional organizations, as described in Exhibit 19.A.

New Technology-Enhanced Channels for Public Relations

Historically, public relations officers worked mostly through contact with traditional media outlets. An organization worked to enhance its public image by seeking positive coverage in news reports and feature stories, or by paid advertisements via television, radio, magazines, newspapers, or billboards. Public relations still involves these interactions, but as new technologies have emerged, the variety of available channels of communication has grown dramatically.

Darren Herman, president of Varick Media Management in New York, spent his day conducting marketing research. But rather than looking at dozens of print advertisement layouts typically placed in newspapers or magazines, he studied graphs and Excel spreadsheets of the Internet ads he had just run for his client Vespa, the scooter company, to determine which ad had the most appeal and to

---

[7] This information is from the following professional associations' Web sites: Public Relations Society of America, *www.prsa.org;* International Association of Business Communicators, *www.iabc.com;* and International Public Relations Association, *www.ipra.org.*

[8] "Annenberg Releases Fifth Annual PR Study," *new influencer,* May 29, 2008, *www.newinfluencer.com.*

whom. His data revealed that the $0 down offer attracted 71 percent more online responses than the average for all Vespa ads, and the offer of a free T-shirt generated 29 percent fewer responses. "It's nice to be able to tell your brand manager or the chief marketing officer which audience is interacting with the unit, what time of day, what day of the week, and what the response is on certain types of offers," said Herman. Where the data technology guys were once an afterthought in the marketing presentation, now they are at the core of the online strategy. "What's more," said Herman, "they can help advertisers save money in traditional media by testing different phrases or images online to see what works before producing an expensive television commercial or magazine ad."[9]

More and more people are finding their news, marketing, or other public relations information through Internet-related vehicles, such as blogs, moblogs, vlogs, e-mails, social networking, podcasts, cell phones, personal digital assistants, and other technology-based communication sources. CEOs and other senior executives are some of the key participants in a new form of business communication—blogging. Figure 19.2 lists the top CEO bloggers and corporations, according to the rankings calculated by Technorati, Inc., and blogger Mario Sundar.

Sun Microsystems' CEO Jonathan Schwartz's blog presented video clips and text messages on a wide range of topics, including new products being rolled out by Google (Java One in 2009), but was careful to avoid forbidden issues, such as pending litigation or current government investigations (such as the antitrust investigation triggered by Google's effort to take over Oracle). Craig Newmark, CEO of Craig's List, took on controversial issues such as health care reform and food safety in his blog. He also provided links to the health care reform discussion at the American Association of Retired People (AARP)'s Web site, admitting "I'm a member. I'm old." The blog also featured photos of contaminated food to draw attention to the public issue of food safety. Mark Cuban's blog, at *blogmaverick.com,* not only focused on his ownership of the Dallas Mavericks professional basketball team, but also encouraged readers to support the Fallen Patriot Fund to aid families of U.S. military personnel who were killed or seriously injured during Operation Iraqi Freedom. Cuban's blog also had links to other CEOs' blogs, such as "Michael's Insights," directing people to the site of Michael Willner, CEO of Insight Communication.[10]

	CEO Bloggers	Corporate Blogs
1	Jonathan Schwartz, CEO, Sun Microsystems	Google
2	Craig Newmark, CEO, Craig's List	O'Reilly Radar
3	Mark Cuban, Owner, Dallas Mavericks	Yahoo! Search
4	Ross Mayfield, CEO, Socialtext	Tom Peters
5	Matt Blumberg, CEO, Return Path	Ask.com
6	Alan Meckler, CEO, Jupiter Media	Adobe Software
7	Kevin Lynch, Chief Software Architect, Adobe	GM Fast Lane
8	Robin Hopper, CEO/Founder, iUpload	SunBelt Software
9	Jason Calacanis, CEO, Weblogs	English Cut
10	John Dragoon, CMO, Novell	The Otter Group

FIGURE 19.2
Top CEO Bloggers and Corporate Blogs

Sources: Mario Sundar, "Top 10 CEO Blogs," July 9, 2006; and "Top 10 Corporate Blog Rankings," July 16, 2006, *mariosundar.wordpress.com.*

[9] "Put Ad on Web; Count Clicks; Revise," *The New York Times,* May 31, 2009, *www.nytimes.com.*
[10] See these CEOs' blogs at *blogs.sun.com/jonathan, www.cnewmark.com,* and *blogmaverick.com.*

The Internet-based communication revolution has significantly benefited smaller businesses as well.

Smaller business enterprises and emerging entrepreneurs find the Internet to be an inexpensive and powerful method to share their information. According to comScore, a provider of digital intelligence, the total number of individuals, aged 15 and older, who accessed the Internet from their home or work computers surpassed 1 billion in December 2008. Companies can talk to this new audience in "real time"—that is, instantaneously rather than waiting for the next edition of the newspaper or when their television or radio spot is aired. Small businesses can reach as many potential customers, job applicants, and new suppliers or the general public as easily and quickly as the largest business organizations by using the Internet.[11]

The Council for Research Excellence reported that adults are exposed to screens—televisions, cell phones, and even global positioning systems (GPSs)—for about 8.5 hours on any given day. Although television remains the primary vehicle for businesses to communicate with the public, online advertising supplanted the radio in 2009 as the second most common media outlet for business. Print sources ranked fourth.[12] Businesses accordingly are changing how they reach out to the public and increasingly using the Internet to promote their products, image, and various social issues.

Campbell Soup Company's Pepperidge Farms launched "connecting through cookies" in 2007 in an effort to help their primary consumer audience, women, improve their lives. Women often frequented the Pepperidge Farms Web site for product information. Campbell Soup decided to add a new social networking dimension to make the site more interactive. The Pepperidge Farms home page proclaimed, "Our friendships with our girlfriends make our lives so much richer. Visit our new section about keeping those connections strong." The $3 million campaign featured video clips of American women discussing the importance of friendships and enabled visitors to talk to one another about recipes and other issues of interest. According to the company's spokesperson, this public relations campaign was an effort to "move our communications with our customers from telling them about us to having a dialogue with them," and to help them talk to each other too. Ultimately, the program was intended to develop a more loyal customer base for Pepperidge Farm's products.[13]

One firm has abandoned all traditional public relations vehicles in favor of the Internet, as described in Exhibit 19.B.

Large organizations, too, are finding new public relations opportunities through use of the Internet.

Like many businesses, Walmart turned to the media to bolster its tarnished public image after being stung by criticism regarding its labor policies, expansion plans, and other business practices. In the past, Walmart had used more traditional media to broadcast its public relations message. But in 2006, the company turned toward a new media form to communicate with the public—blogging.

---

[11] See "Check Your Trust Barometer: How Social Networking Sites Can Enhance Your Public Image," *hrtools*, 2008, *www.hrtools.com*.

[12] "8 Hours a Day Spent on Screens, Study Finds," *The New York Times*, March 27, 2009, *www.nytimes.com*.

[13] "Making Social Connections and Selling Cookies," *The New York Times*, November 21, 2007, *www.nytimes.com*.

Holly Dunlap was a struggling New York shoe and dress designer in 2003 when she hired a well-known public relations firm at $6,500 a month to help her company, Hollywould. For that price, said Dunlap, her expectations were very high. "For us, it was a lot to pay. We did not have a lot of patience for that amount of money. We needed to see results on a daily basis." Five months later, Dunlap fired the public relations firm. She believed that she could do better and was already beginning to see results by using a newly created Web site to build her company's image. Dunlap launched *www.ilovehollywould.com.*

The Web site featured a diary written by Dunlap that was full of juicy details about her personal life, from late-night partying in downtown Manhattan to jetting through Europe. The attractive and gregarious designer drew attention to her Web site by boldfacing names of famous people she had encountered in her social journeys. "Girls read from all over the country and they see the pictures and they have a connection to the brand and will place orders," explained Dunlap. Rather than paying $6,500 a month, Dunlap spends $700 a month on Web maintenance and records an average of 20,000 visitors a week. Dunlap succeeded in placing her products in high-end stores such as Saks Fifth Avenue, Neiman Marcus, and Harrods of London, and in 2006 had estimated sales of $6 to $8 million.

Source: "How to Get Attention in a New-Media World," *The Wall Street Journal*, September 25, 2006, *online.wsj.com.*

In one instance the blogger was a non-Walmart employee, Brian Pickrell, but the message was definitely Walmart's. Pickrell posted to his Web site a note attacking state legislation that would force Walmart stores to spend more on employee health insurance. This note was identical to dozens of other notes found on other blog sites and to an e-mail distributed by Walmart's public relations firms to numerous bloggers. Mona Williams of Walmart justified this action: "As more and more Americans go to the Internet to get information from varied, credible, trusted sources, Walmart is committed to participating in that online conversation."[14]

Global Public Relations

Public relations strategies increasingly assume a global focus, since business interactions with the public through media channels frequently transcend national boundaries. Therefore, global businesses have extended their public relations strategies globally, as shown in the following example:

Dow Chemical created a global public relations management team to deal with issues surrounding chlorine, a chemical widely used in manufacturing. (Chlorine is a highly toxic gas that can irritate the respiratory system leading to severe coughing, vomiting, and in some cases lung cancer. Thus governments closely regulate business use of this chemical.) As one of the world's largest producers of chlorine, Dow had a very large stake in proposals to ban or regulate its use. Members of the global management team were drawn from the United States, Europe, and Asia-Pacific and included scientists, plant managers, and managers from Dow's manufacturing businesses. The global management team analyzed

[14] "Wal-Mart Enlists Bloggers in P.R. Campaign," *The New York Times*, March 7, 2006, *www.nytimes.com.*

scientific studies of chlorine, tracked government actions across the world, coordinated research into various aspects of the problem, and worked with company government relations staff to ensure that Dow "spoke with one voice" when talking about chlorine.[15]

When public relations strategies take on a global perspective, new challenges emerge. For example, public relations managers must be sensitive to cultural disparities, as well as similarities, in crafting press releases and interactions with the media. The impact of the organization's public relations program could vary from country to country given the culture, social mores, political system, or history. A public relations manager must be able to communicate with local media and other stakeholder groups in their native language and avoid embarrassing or misleading communication due to poor translations. All of the basic public relations tasks are more complex in an international business environment.[16]

Businesses must also ensure that sufficient funding is allocated globally for a positive and effective public affairs impact. Some U.S.-based firms allocate a percentage of their public relations budget equivalent to the percentage of revenue generated from their overseas operations to global PR operations. But they sometimes fail to understand that *more* effort, and thus additional resources, may be necessary to combat anti-American sentiment or to build a public relations presence where there has never been one.

Some businesses decentralize their global public relations programs and establish officers in each of the locations where they have operations. This helps to ensure that the local public relations strategy is in tune with local customs and emerging issues.[17] "Forward-thinking companies will become more decentralized in their . . . communications. They will increasingly put tools out there to arm influencers, peers, enthusiasts, customers, and prospects, as well as employees—and then get out of the way and let the magic happen," explained Bob Geller, senior vice president at Fusion Public Relations.[18]

Influencing Public Opinion

Business organizations or industry associations may choose to influence or change public opinion on a variety of social or political issues that might affect an organization or industry. Using the powerful outreach of the media, messages are crafted to enlighten or educate the public regarding businesses' viewpoint or how the issue might affect the public.

Public Service Announcements

Since 1942, the Ad Council has been the leading producer of **public service announcements** (PSAs), addressing critical social issues for generations of Americans and global citizens. The Ad Council has created some of the most memorable slogans, such as its inaugural campaign of "Loose Lips Sink Ships," promoting secrecy of military operations during World War II, to the more recent "Friends Don't Let Friends Drive Drunk" and "A Mind Is a Terrible Thing To Waste." More recently, PSA campaigns have ranged

---

[15] See Dow Chemical's company Web site, *www.dow.com/commitments.*

[16] For a thorough discussion of these issues see Craig S. Fleisher, "The Development of Competencies in International Public Affairs," *Journal of Public Affairs* 3, no. 3 (March 2003), pp. 76–82.

[17] For an excellent and thorough presentation of effective global public relations strategies, see Lou Hoffman, "Ten Pitfalls of International PR," *The Firm Voice,* June 11, 2008, *www.firmvoice.com.*

[18] "From 'Command and Control' to a Decentralized Marketing Tool," *Flack's Revenge blog,* February 23, 2009, *www.flacksrevenge.com.*

from disaster relief and energy efficiency to arts education and the prevention of child-hood obesity. The longest-running PSA in American history, introduced in 1944 and con-tinuing today, features Smokey the Bear and his famous warning: "Only You Can Pre-vent Forest Fires." The forest fire prevention campaign has reduced the number of acres lost annually from 22 million to less than 10 million.[19]

Modeled after the actions taken by the Ad Council, businesses have discovered that public service announcement–like advertisements are an effective means for promoting various social issues or topics that resonate with the public, as demonstrated by Starbucks.

> Starbucks has a long tradition of being cutting-edge and attracting customers that are politically and socially informed. In September 2008 Starbuck stores began offering customers a free flyer called "The Good Sheet." The Good Sheet was first printed in 2006 to bring to the public a debate on issues of philanthropy and activism through their editorials and presentation of important facts. The Good Sheet offered in Starbucks stores discusses one issue at a time, such as carbon emissions, health care, or education. According to Terry Davenport, senior vice president for marketing at Starbucks, "We thought, boy, if we could distribute some of those [The Good Sheet] in the stores, it's a quick way—without sitting down and reading a five-page article—a quick way to join the conversation." The Good Sheet is not intended to be biased toward one particular viewpoint. We are not telling people that "you should vote this way or that way . . . but simply in a way that says you should get involved, be informed," said Jonathan Greenblatt, chief executive at *Good,* the company that produces The Good Sheet.[20]

Image Advertisements

Image advertisements are used by business organizations to enhance their public image, create goodwill, or announce a major change such as a merger, acquisition, or new prod-uct line. These ads promote the image, or general perception, of a product or service, rather than promoting its functional attributes. They target the public's emotions and seek to influence the consumers' imaginations.

A good example of an image ad campaign was that used by Domino's Pizza. Their slogan "You get fresh, hot pizza delivered to your door in 30 minutes or less—or it's free" did not identify any specific type of pizza but attempted to convince the public and potential customers of the reliability of the company and its ability to provide you with fresh, hot pizza fast. Coca-Cola's classic advertisement campaign, "It's the real thing," publicized an image, not the attributes of the products it was selling.[21] In the 2000s, many companies touted their concern for the planet and the need for sustainability practices through image advertising.

> Chevron, one of the world's largest energy companies, developed a "Power of Human Energy" image ad campaign that appeared on its Web site and in a range of other media, including television, magazines, and billboards. The company recognized that energy was one of the defining challenges of the 21st century,

---

[19] See the Ad Council's Web site, *www.adcouncil.org.*

[20] "Ice-Breaker at Starbucks: The Good Sheet," *The New York Times,* September 8, 2008, *www.nytimes.com.*

[21] Examples of how business organizations try to develop their corporate social responsibility reputation through image advertising are discussed in Alan Pomering and Lester W. Johnson, "Constructing a Corporate Social Responsibility Reputation Using Corporate Image Advertising," *Australian Marketing Journal* 17, no. 2 (2009), pp. 106–14.

and it wanted to tell the story of how individuals around the world—employees, customers, and others—were seeking to respond to the challenge. For example, one ad showed a person saying, "I will leave my car at home more," and another showed a different person saying, "I will reuse things more." The company's Web site proclaimed, "As we strive to improve standards of living around the world, the demand for energy is soaring as never before. Where will the energy come from? While many answers are yet to be found, we know one thing for sure. Finding newer, smarter, cleaner ways to power the world begins with the one energy source we have in abundant supply: the power of Human Energy."

Issue Advertisements

Some businesses use their public relations' outreach in ways to influence the public's opinion of a political or legislative issue of concern to the company through **issue advertisements**. (These advertisements are also called advocacy advertisements and are discussed in Chapter 9 as a political action tactic.) Such was the case in the 1970s and 1980s, when Mobil Oil Company regularly placed full-page ads in most of the major newspapers in America to promote its political agenda. When consumers in the United States were experiencing unprecedented increases in gasoline prices in 2006 and 2007, America's oil and natural gas industry decided that it was time to explain the situation to the American public and promote its side of the issue in an effort to avoid government regulation of gasoline prices or increased taxation on the industry. The industry ran issue advertisements in 2007 in city newspapers across the country. The ads explained,

> Where does your gasoline dollar go? 56% crude oil, 26% refining, distribution, and service stations, and 18% taxes. In 2006, the industry earned 9.5 cents on each dollar of sales. According to the Federal Trade Commission, the global price of crude oil is the single most important factor in what you pay for fuel at the pump. Since 1992, America's oil and natural gas industry has invested more than $1 trillion in exploration, development, production, and distribution of oil and gas.[22]

The oil and natural gas industry also provided readers of its ads with the industry's Web site (*www.api.org*), inviting the public to research in greater depth what constituted the rising price of gasoline at the pumps.

Conversely, a group called "The People of America's Oil and Gas Industry" warned the American public in 2009 that the new energy taxes proposed by the Obama administration were "a sure way to hobble America's ailing economy" in big, bold letters in their full-page newspaper ads. These issue ads called on taxpayers to let their congressional representatives know that this was a bad idea since the action Congress was considering would impose new taxes and fees on the country's oil and natural gas industry that "could easily exceed $400 billion." The advertisements said that "these unprecedented taxes and fees would reduce investment in new energy supplies at a time when nearly two-thirds of Americans support developing our domestic oil and natural gas resources." The ads concluded, "With our economy in crisis, this is not the time to burden Americans with massive energy costs."[23] Another issue ad, featuring two memorable characters, Harry and Louise, is discussed in Exhibit 19.C.

---

[22] "The Price at the Pump," America's Oil and Natural Gas Industry ads, April 11, 2007.

[23] For more information on these image ad campaigns see the following Web sites: *thecapsolution.org* and *EnergyTomorrow.org*.

Exhibit 19.C

Harry and Louise Return

In the mid-1990s, the U.S. health insurance industry attempted to thwart President Clinton's proposed government-backed health care reform plan by introducing the American public to two middle-class citizens, Harry and Louise, through more than a dozen television commercials. At a cost of more than $14 million, Harry and Louise began to talk to the American public about health care. "It was done to get the attention of policymakers," said Charles N. Kahn III, who oversaw the advertisement campaign as the executive vice president of the Health Insurance Association of America. Harry and Louise were credited with helping kill Clinton's plan by making powerful statements in their commercials, such as "Having choices we don't like is no choice at all."

Nearly two decades later, Harry and Louise reappeared in 2009 in another issue ad campaign—this time *in support of* the U.S. government's overhaul of the medical system promoted by President Obama. The ad sponsors included the drug manufacturing industry trade association and Families USA, a nonprofit group advocating affordable medical care. "A little more cooperation, a little less politics," said Louise to her husband, Harry, in the new television spot—along with "We can get the job done this time," an obvious reference to their 1990s appearance. Not only the message has changed in 20 years; so have Harry and Louise. Harry Johnson and Louise Caire Clark (the actors, who play characters with the same names) are now nearly senior citizens, and their banter was meant to evoke concern for the uninsured in America who would be covered under the new health care reform.

Evan Tracey, CEO of Campaign Media Analysis Group, who tracks political advertising, credits Harry and Louise with setting the standard for issue advertisements. "Since that time [the mid-1990s], there hasn't been a major piece of policy, federal or state, that hasn't had an issue advocacy campaign. That's what, in essence, Harry and Louise gave birth to."

Source: "Harry and Louise Return, with a New Message," *The New York Times*, July 17, 2009, *www.nytimes.com*.

Protecting the Public through Government Regulation

Government regulation seeks to protect the public by controlling business's use of the media, although policymakers have been careful to not infringe upon the U.S. Constitution First Amendment's right to free speech, which applies to business organizations as well as private citizens. Yet, the right to free speech is not an unrestricted right and this activity does come with the obligation of acting in the best interest of the public and adhering to ethical principles. As discussed elsewhere, businesses must communicate *honestly* with various stakeholders, such as stockholders (Chapter 14), consumers (Chapter 15), and the community (Chapter 18).

Advertising used to promote the organization and its products must meet both ethical expectations and legal requirements. Thomas Jefferson, the author of the U.S. Constitution, warned, "Advertisements contain the only truth to be relied on in a newspaper." The Federal Trade Commission (FTC) is entrusted with ensuring that honesty and fairness are found in company advertising. The FTC attempts to ensure that the public is protected and guards against the following unethical business practices: the use of deception to distort the truth, the lack of fairness in information, and the use of fraud to manipulate. (The issue of deceptive advertisement is further discussed in Chapter 15.)[24]

The FTC jurisdiction applies to advertising in any medium, including online advertisements. In a 1998 FTC report to Congress, the government agency noted that over

---

[24] See FTC Commissioner Mary L. Azcuenaga's presentation before the Turkish Association of Advertising Agencies, April 8, 1997, for a thorough analysis of the FTC's role and the ethical principles it uses to guard against business's misuse of advertising at *www.ftc.gov/speeches/azcuenaga/turkey97.shtm*.

85 percent of all Web sites collected personal consumer information, yet only 14 percent of these sites provided any information to the consumer as to how this information would be used or protected. This report led to public concern over consumer privacy and later an increase in company privacy policies, as discussed in Chapters 13 and 15. The FTC has been vigilant in ensuring that consumers' rights to privacy are protected. In 2000, the Children's Online Privacy Protection Act (COPPA), discussed in Chapter 13, gave the FTC new powers to ensure privacy protection for children.

Another government agency with responsibility for regulating corporations' public relations activities is the **Federal Communications Commission (FCC)**. This agency was created in 1934 and charged with regulating interstate and international communications by radio, television, wire, satellite, and cable. The FCC regulates business advertisements, for example, by prohibiting all television stations from airing obscene programming at any time and indecent programming or profane language except after 10 p.m. The FCC also promotes open competition in the communications industry. The 1996 Telecommunications Act was passed to allow virtually any business to enter the telecommunications industry. Businesses were encouraged to become involved in providing telephone service, including local and long distance, cable programming and other video services, broadcast services, and services to schools. Thus, the FCC believed its role was not only to guard against inappropriate business activity that might harm the public, but also to foster a more competitive business environment.[25]

The government also monitors the dissemination of information to stockholders. The Securities and Exchange Commission (SEC), as discussed in Chapter 14, attempts to ensure that information distributed to all potential and current investors is timely and accurate. It operates under the belief that all investors, whether large institutions or private individuals, should have access to basic certain facts about an investment prior to buying it and as long as they hold it. Recently, greater transparency regarding company performance was mandated by the SEC for all publicly traded firms, increasing the public's knowledge of the financial risks faced by businesses. Some of the important issues focusing on how one company's CEO communicated with the public are covered in the discussion case at the end of the chapter.

Other government regulatory areas that affect the public include consumer product information, such as fuel mileage efficiency or the safety of pharmaceuticals or food, or environmental issues, such as air quality or the safety of nuclear power plants. Many of these issues, and the regulatory agencies charged with enforcing these regulations, are discussed in other chapters.

Crisis Management

A critical function of the public relations manager is *crisis management*. Every organization is likely to face a crisis at some time that forces management and its employees to act on a difficult issue quickly and without perfect information, such as in the chapter's introductory examples involving Turner Broadcasting and Domino's Pizza. A **corporate crisis** is a significant business disruption that stimulates extensive news media or social networking coverage. The resulting public scrutiny can affect the organization's normal operations and also can have a political, legal, financial, and governmental impact on its business. A crisis is any event with the potential to negatively affect the health,

---

[25] For more information on the FCC's regulatory role, see *www.fcc.gov.*

reputation, or credibility of the organization. The Institute for Crisis Management breaks down corporate crises into four groups:

- Acts of God—earthquakes, tornados, violent storms, volcanic eruptions.
- Mechanical problems—breakdowns of or faulty equipment, metal fatigue.
- Human errors—through miscommunication, improper employee behavior.
- Management decision or indecision—often involving a cover-up or lack of urgency.[26]

A corporate crisis can take many different forms. It might be a terrorist attack, poor financial results, the death of a key executive or government official, employee layoffs, a charge of sexual harassment, or the filing of class-action lawsuits brought by injured customers. Or it might be something bizarre and unique, such as the crisis that confronted Wendy's that is described in Exhibit 19.D. But crises, by definition, are often unique. To prepare for these unexpected events and sometimes tragedies, an organization must develop a crisis management plan.

Crisis management is the process organizations use to respond to short-term and immediate corporate crises. Some businesses or industries are more prone to corporate crises than others. According to the Institute for Crisis Management, medical and surgical manufacturers, pharmaceutical companies, and software manufacturers (because of the sophisticated technology found in their products and the potential for disruptive impact on consumers' lives) are at the top of a recent list of crisis-prone industries.

Often the corporate crisis quickly escalates, producing intense pressures and many suggestions about what the company should do or not do from outside experts, politicians, and observers. Sometimes, as shown in the following example, allowing the wrong or incorrect message to be sent out can have devastating negative consequences.

In 2006, an explosion in a Sago, West Virginia, coal mine trapped 13 miners. As is often the case when a mine collapses, little was known right away to tell the trapped miners' families and throngs of news reporters desperately seeking information. The International Coal Group (ICG), owner of the Sago Mine, wanted to avoid raising false hopes, while attempting to satisfy the hundreds of community residents and dozens of news crews' quest for updates. But after hours of no news, a report spread like wildfire: rescuers had found 12 miners alive. Relatives of the trapped miners, understandably, rejoiced, management at ICG breathed a sigh of relief, and the news media had its story—which was immediately broadcast globally. Then, minutes later, the real news emerged: only one miner had survived, and the others were dead. The joy and celebration turned to grief, anguish, and, of course, anger. The foremost crisis management blunder had occurred: false information was disseminated, and the worst kind, false information regarding who is alive. Weeks of investigation after the disaster revealed that ICG was simply unable to control all rumors that were circulating during the disaster. But, more importantly, ICG's management did not step up when the rumor spread to say that they had no corroborating evidence to confirm this report. Clearly, a critical element of the crisis management strategy—controlling rumors and verifying all information—had failed.[27]

[26] From the Institute for Crisis Management's Web site, *www.crisisexperts.com.*
[27] For a complete account of the crisis management effort by the International Coal Group during the Sago Mine disaster see "Sago Mine: A Hard Lesson in Crisis Communication," *American Thinker,* January 6, 2006, *www.americanthinker.com.*

Exhibit 19.D

Excuse Me, There Is a Finger in My Chili!

On March 22, 2005, Denny Lynch, senior vice president for communications at Wendy's, one of the country's largest fast-food restaurant chains, received a shocking and unexpected call. A customer, Anna Ayala, claimed she had bitten down on a severed finger while eating a cup of chili purchased at a Wendy's restaurant in San Jose, California. Lynch knew that he had to act quickly, since this incident would certainly be the top story on the evening news and in the headlines of every major newspaper the next day. A public relations nightmare had emerged, and Lynch, on behalf of Wendy's, had to prepare a response. Within days Wendy's Northern California restaurants lost 20 to 50 percent of their normal business, estimating their losses at $1 million per day. "We need closure," said Lynch. "Until then, there is lingering doubt."

In response, Wendy's immediately assembled its crisis management team in its regional headquarters in Sacramento, California. Lynch prepared a statement for the press, instructed that the company's Web site be frequently updated, and began coordinating with the San Jose police department, which was already involved in the case. According to Lynch, "It went nonstop the next two or three days. Even when the Pope passed away, it still got coverage."

In the wake of the immediate crisis, Wendy's focused on trying to discover what had really happened. Through an internal investigation, Lynch learned that a 10-year veteran and trusted employee had prepared the chili for Ayala; he assured Lynch there was nothing improper in the food preparation. Wendy's also turned to the public and offered a $100,000 reward for information about the case.

Investigators initially were unsure if the finger came from a living or dead person. The finger's DNA did not match anything in the police computer files, and a search for the fingerprint failed to turn up a match in the FBI's 50-million-print database. Further, the police still had not determined if the finger had been cooked, and if so, for how long. A thoroughly cooked finger might indicate that it came through Wendy's food supply chain, but if uncooked, it was likely that the finger was added to the chili after preparation.

While Lynch and his team worked furiously around the clock to discover the truth, Ayala, the woman who had made the accusation, was a guest on numerous morning and late night television shows. Yet, it was soon discovered that Ayala had a litigious history that included a settlement for medical expenses for her daughter, who had claimed she became sick at an El Pollo Loco restaurant in Las Vegas.

The public relations break Lynch and Wendy's needed occurred exactly one month after the initial incident, when Anna Ayala was arrested in her Las Vegas home for attempted grand larceny, accused of trying to extort $2.5 million from Wendy's. The finger in her chili was a hoax. "The true victims are Wendy's owners and operators," said San Jose chief of police Rob Davis. Forensic evidence proved that the finger was not cooked at 170 degrees for three hours—the typical preparation of Wendy's chili. It was later discovered that Ayala acquired the finger through her husband's workplace, where a fellow worker had lost part of his finger in an industrial accident.

In September 2005, Ayala and her husband, Jaime Plascencia, pleaded guilty to attempted grand larceny and conspiring to file a false claim. Ayala was sentenced to 9 years in prison and her husband, who supplied the finger, was sentenced to 12 years and 4 months in prison.

Sources: "At CSI: Wendy's, Tracking a Gruesome Discovery," *The New York Times,* April 22, 2005, *www.nytimes.com;* "Finger in Chili Is Called Hoax; Las Vegas Woman Is Charged," *The New York Times,* April 23, 2005, *www.nytimes.com;* and "Stiff Sentences for Wendy's Chili-Finger Couple," *Bay City News,* January 18, 2006, *www.SFGate.com.*

Unfortunately it is very costly to develop a strategic response once a crisis is upon an organization. Most experts recommend that organizations develop a crisis management plan ahead of time, citing the biblical wisdom: Noah built his ark *before* it began to rain. Since the first 24 hours during a crisis are the most crucial, having a plan ready for implementation when a crisis occurs is imperative.

According to experts, an effective crisis management plan must include these steps:

- *Get ready before the crisis hits* by creating an internal communication system that can be activated the moment a crisis occurs. Key employees must be identified in advance so that they are ready to address the issue. Scenario-based press releases, key discussion points, and procedures to activate the organization's Web site (to use the Internet to announce any news, product recalls, etc.) should be at the ready. Many organizations create a **dark site**, a Web site that is fully developed and uploaded with critical information, contacts for the media, and other useful details, ready to be activated at the moment it is needed. Wendy's, for example (see Exhibit 19.D), already had plans to scramble its crisis management team into action well before the crisis emerged and had key talking points ready for its conversations with the media.

- *Communicate quickly, but accurately.* Firms facing a crisis must communicate with the media and others promptly. Communications must always be honest and disclose fully what the company knows—even if it does not know the full story. Wendy's, for example, effectively communicated with the public even when it did not yet know how the finger got in the chili; the managers at Sago Mine, by contrast, at first failed to communicate and then allowed false information to circulate. The media have excellent resources and will find the truth whether the organization speaks it or not. It is often best to take the offensive and be the first to comment on a situation affecting the organization, thus placing the organization in greater control.

- *Use the Internet* to convey the public affairs message to minimize the public's fears and provide assistance. In addition to face-to-face press releases, Wendy's frequently updated its company Web site to communicate to the public and others what the company was doing about the crisis situation.

- *Do the right thing.* Often the true test of an organization is how it reacts in a time of crisis. Public relations managers should not try to minimize the seriousness of a problem or make excuses. It is possible for the organization to accept responsibility without accepting liability. It also is important that the organization be sympathetic. For example, Wendy's clearly expressed regret over its customers' fears and advised the public that it was doing everything possible to investigate.

- *Follow up* and, where appropriate, make amends to those affected. Seek to restore the organization's reputation. Wendy's relentless pursuit of the truth resulted in vindication for the company and assisted law enforcement in the prosecution of those making the false claims. With proper planning and effective implementation of a crisis management program, an organization may emerge from a crisis in a stronger condition.[28]

From multinational corporations to small businesses, organizations of any size at any location can face crisis situations, some more devastating and affecting more lives than others, and they all need a plan for what to do when handling any crisis as it unexpectedly occurs. A *crisis management guide* describing a series of critical crisis management checkpoints is shown in Exhibit 19.E.

---

[28] Adapted from Ronald J. Levine, "Weathering the Storm: Crisis Management Tips," *Metropolitan Corporate Counsel*, March 2002, pp. 3–4; and Mark Herford, "Crisis Make or Break—The First 24 Hours," *International Public Relations Association*, April 2009, *www.ipra.org*.

Exhibit 19.E

1. Create and document policies and procedures and circulate them widely.
2. Know the policies and procedures and follow them.
3. Be prepared with a continuity plan to provide for continuing operations during crisis management.
4. Work as a team with assigned responsibilities and a clear leader and practice, practice, practice in mock drills.
5. Identify and understand the organization's vulnerabilities; most importantly, correct shortcomings.
6. Let your conscience be your guide, follow good ethical practice and remember the "front-page test." (Or, better yet, consider this: What would Grandma say?)
7. Beware of dangerous and distorted minds and protect coworkers and facilities.
8. Put all phases of the event under a microscope and track and record activities.
9. Handle all records, samples, information, materials, and evidence with care.
10. Know the media and how to handle them. NEVER lie, cover up, or obfuscate.
11. Keep your eyes on the law and contact legal counsel; don't make decisions simply to avoid lawsuits.
12. Provide timely updates to coworkers and provide follow-up meetings and counseling.

Source: FosterHyland, Inc., *www.fosterhyland.com*. Used with permission, 2009.

Media Training of Employees

An important public relations step organizations can take is to provide **media training** to executives and employees who are likely to have contact with the media. Media training is necessary because communicating with the media is not the same as talking with friends or coworkers.

As an organization's representative, an employee is normally assumed to be speaking for the organization or is expected to have special knowledge of its activities. Under these circumstances, the words one speaks take on a special, official meaning. In addition, news reporters sometimes challenge an executive or spokesperson, asking penetrating or potentially embarrassing questions and expecting instant answers. Even in more deliberate news interviews, the time available for responding to questions is limited to a few seconds. Moreover, facial expressions, the tone of one's voice, and body language can convey both positive and negative impressions.

Many large business organizations routinely send a broad range of their employees to specific courses to improve their media skills—public relations experts, consumer service representatives, communications specialists, government liaison officers, and others that typically interact with external organizational stakeholders. Media communication experts generally give their clients the following advice:

- Be honest. Always tell the truth and explain why you cannot discuss a particular subject.
- Be current. The media want to speak with you because of your up-to-date knowledge. If you do not have current information, promise to find out and get back to the media.
- Be accessible. A spokesperson is expected to be on-call and promptly respond to demands made by the media, as long as the demands are reasonable.

- Be helpful. If you do not know the answer to a question, say so and offer to find out. Try to make the media's job easier; they will print or broadcast anyway, so if you are helping them there is a better chance of your message being heard.
- Be understanding. Understand the needs of the media, their pending deadline, or the importance of their acquiring background information.
- Be cool, courteous, and professional. You are representing your organization in the eyes of the media and the public. Remember, nothing is really ever "off the record."

Employees trained to interact with the media should know the basic message points that the organization wants communicated. These key points need to be reinforced with facts, such as statistics, when possible, and elaborated upon in an interview or press conference. Many times the audience is not aware of or knowledgeable about the organization's operations or product or whatever is the focus of the press conference. Therefore, it is important to be clear and avoid jargon or technical language. Finally, the spokesperson should close the interview by reiterating the organization's key message.

While the organization's spokesperson likely knows a lot of information about an issue, it is important to remember the final audience for the message. Typically the news media are looking for a **sound bite**, a short (often 30 seconds or less) clip of information that can be broadcast to the public. Sometimes the media do not print or broadcast what the spokesperson wants but rather what is controversial or sensational. The spokesperson needs to remember to keep on point and keep it short.

When the media ask a particularly tough question, the organization's spokesperson needs to shift the focus to the key message or use the question as a platform to return to the organization's agenda for the press conference. Some of the best techniques to assist a spokesperson to stay on point when challenged by a reporter with a tough question are the following:

- *Hooking.* Grab the reporter's attention by making a statement that influences the next question. For example, "We are undertaking a program to correct the situation." Typically the reporter will follow up by asking about the organization's new program.
- *Bridging.* Answer the challenging question but quickly move on to the key message. For example, "Yes, but . . . " or "What I can tell you is . . . " or "While that is true, what is important to know is . . . "
- *Flagging.* Emphasize key points and guide the reporter to them. For example, "Your listeners may not know that . . . " or "This is important news because . . . "

No matter how prepared a person is to handle the media, during a crisis situation it is often very difficult to clearly and calmly convey the organization's message. Some businesses practice with mock press conferences, as they do with their crisis management plans, so that spokespeople can experience what it is like to answer the media's tough questions under pressure, better preparing them for the real thing.

Summary

- A well-crafted public relations department can open up a dialogue between the organization and the public, providing a window out from the organization to the public and a window in for the organization from the public. The public relations function must have both a domestic and global focus and activities for a global business organization.
- An effective public relations strategy should incorporate the use of new technological innovations, such as blogs, e-mails, social networking, cell phones, PDAs, and other technology-based communication sources.

- Business organizations can influence or change public opinion through public service announcements and image advertisements.
- Numerous regulatory agencies are charged with protecting the public, including the Federal Trade Commission, Federal Communications Commission, and Securities and Exchange Commission. These agencies govern the timely and accurate flow of information from business through their advertisements or company reports to various stakeholder groups.
- An effective crisis management plan is one that is ready to be implemented before the crisis occurs, enables the organization to quickly and accurately communicate to the media, utilizes the Internet to convey critical information to the public, and always remains focused on the organization's ethical responsibilities to its stakeholders.
- A business organization needs to conduct media training for employees likely to interact with the media so that the organization's message is heard and image is maintained, especially during a crisis.

Key Terms			
corporate crisis, *444*	general public, *433*	public relations	
crisis management, *445*	image advertisements, *441*	department, *435*	
dark site, *447*	issue advertisements, *442*	public service	
Federal Communications	media training, *448*	announcements, *440*	
Commission (FCC), *444*	public relations, *434*	sound bite, *449*	

Internet Resources		
www.cerp.org	European Public Relations Confederation
www.cprs.ca	Canadian Public Relations Society
www.fcc.gov	U.S. Federal Communications Commission
www.iabc.com	International Association of Business Communications (IABC)
www.instituteforpr.org	Institute for Public Relations (IPR)
www.ipra.org	International Public Relations Association (IPRA)
www.prsa.org	Public Relations Society of America (PRSA)
www.prwatch.org	Center for Media and Democracy—PR Watch
www.sourcewatch.org	Source Watch
www.spinwatch.org	Spinwatch—Monitoring PR and Spin

Discussion Case: *Whole Foods' CEO—Free Speech or Public Relations Manipulation?*

From 1999 to 2006, John Mackey, CEO of Whole Foods Market, posted numerous messages on Yahoo! Finance stock forums, a publicly accessible Web site. Like many individuals, Mackey posted his thoughts online as a way to engage in dialogue with others interested in similar issues. What made Mackey's activity worrisome is that he posted under the name "Rahodeb" (an anagram of his wife's name, Deborah), thus disguising his identity, and discussed issues central to the financial well-being of Whole Foods.

Whole Foods Market, Inc., was the world's leading natural and organic food retailer with more than 270 stores in the United States and United Kingdom. Its core values emphasized "selling the highest-quality natural and organic products available, satisfying and delighting our customers, supporting team member happiness and excellence, caring about our communities and our environment, and creating ongoing win–win partnerships with our suppliers." The firm proudly proclaimed, "Everyone around here strives to honor this golden rule of environmental stewardship: reduce, reuse and recycle."[29] Some people began to question if Whole Foods' top management believed in and practiced these core values when they learned about the Web postings by the firm's CEO.

In his posting, Rahodeb (Mackey) cheered Whole Foods' impressive financial results and praised himself. "While I'm not a 'Mackey groupie,' I do admire what the man has accomplished—building a $1.6 million business from scratch is quite an achievement," said Rahodeb (Mackey) in 2000. He also defended Whole Foods in response to others who criticized the company online, arguing that "quarterly cash flow variance isn't statistically meaningful because the time period is too short."

Rahodeb also attacked Whole Foods' main competitor, Wild Oats Market. Rahodeb questioned, "Who would buy OATS [Wild Oats' stock symbol]? Almost surely not at current prices. What would they gain? OATS locations are too small." Rahodeb speculated that Wild Oats would slide into bankruptcy and would be sold after its stock price fell below $5 a share. A month later, Rahodeb wrote that Wild Oats' management "clearly doesn't know what it is doing . . . OATS has no value and no future."

In February 2007, Whole Foods announced plans to purchase Wild Oats Markets for $565 million, or $18.50 a share. The merger would create a powerful organization in the natural and organic food retailing industry. The Federal Trade Commission (FTC), believing that the merger would violate antitrust law since it would reduce competition and raise prices for consumers, sued Whole Foods, blocking the purchase of Wild Oats. Mackey responded, this time under his own name, saying that the government "has failed to recognize the robust competition in the supermarket industry, which has grown more intense as competitors increase their offerings of natural, organic, and fresh products." In March 2009, Whole Foods announced it had reached an agreement with the FTC and sold 31 of its stores and relinquished the rights to the Wild Oats brand to reduce its alleged monopoly of the natural foods industry.

In preparation for a 2007 FTC hearing, Whole Foods was required to provide millions of documents, including Internet postings by Mackey under the name Rahodeb. When the Securities and Exchange Commission (SEC) discovered these documents, the agency launched its own investigation into Mackey's actions. The SEC's examination focused on whether Mackey's comments contradicted what company officials had said publicly and if Whole Foods Market had selectively disclosed corporate financial information, a violation of the laws requiring full disclosure.

The next day Mackey issued an apology. "I sincerely apologize to all Whole Foods Market stakeholders for my error in judgment in anonymously participating on online financial message boards. I am very sorry and I ask our stakeholders to please forgive me." Mackey also explained that he used an alias to avoid having his comments associated with Whole Foods and to avoid others' placing too much emphasis on his remarks.

Whole Foods' board of directors formed a special committee and conducted an internal investigation of Mackey's actions but determined that the CEO had not violated any company policy. The SEC, likewise, concluded that no wrongdoing had occurred and announced that it was not pursuing any action against Mackey or Whole Foods. However, the incident may have negatively affected the firm, whose 2009 first-quarter profits fell

---

[29] See Whole Foods Market Web site at *www.wholefoodsmarket.com*.

by 17 percent. Mackey responded to the financial news optimistically, saying, "We believe our results demonstrate we can operationally adjust to lower sales volumes and believe that this flexibility, combined with our improved balance sheet, will allow us to successfully manage through these difficult economic times and emerge a stronger company over the long run." Mackey also returned to active blogging, this time using his real name, saying, "I cannot tell you how good it feels to be able to write in my blog again."

Sources: Quotations and other material used in this case are from "Whole Foods CEO Mackey Posted Comments on Stock Message Board," *The Wall Street Journal*, July 11, 2007, *online.wsj.com;* "Whole Foods Launches Probe into CEO Mackey's Web Posts," *The Wall Street Journal*, July 17, 2007, *online.wsj.com;* "Whole Foods to Sell 31 Stores in FTC Deal," *The Wall Street Journal*, March 7, 2009, *online.wsj.com;* and "Whole Foods' Net Slips," *The Wall Street Journal*, February 19, 2009, *online.wsj.com.* Also see "Rahodeb's Greatest Hits," *The Wall Street Journal*, July 16, 2007, *online.wsj.com,* for an extensive collection of e-mail postings by Mackey.

Discussion Questions

1. Do you think that Mackey used an appropriate public relations channel to share his thoughts about his own company and its competitor?

2. Do you think Mackey did anything illegal or unethical by posting messages under the name Rahodeb?

3. Were Mackey's actions described in this case consistent with the comments earlier in the chapter from Bill Nielsen, where Nielsen calls for public relations officers to uphold their organization's values?

4. Under what circumstances should company executives share their thoughts in various online forums? Is it ever appropriate for them to do so under an alias?

Cases in Business and Society

Moody's Credit Ratings and the Subprime Mortgage Meltdown

On October 22, 2008, Raymond W. McDaniel Jr. raised his right hand to be sworn as a witness before the U.S. House of Representatives Committee on Oversight and Government Reform. The topic of the day's hearing was the role of the credit rating agencies in the financial crisis on Wall Street. McDaniel, 50, was chairman and CEO of Moody's, one of the leading credit rating agencies in the world. The word "credit" came from the Latin verb *credere,* meaning to believe or to trust. Credit rating agencies, such as Moody's, had the job of evaluating bonds issued by governments, companies, and investment banks. The world's financial markets relied heavily on their assurances that various borrowers could be trusted to pay their debts on time. Now, however, Moody's and other credit rating agencies had come under strong criticism, as many questioned the accuracy of their ratings and their role in the widening financial crisis.

In late 2008, the world faced what many believed was the deepest financial crisis since the Great Depression of the 1930s. As the housing bubble burst and home prices began falling across the United States, billions of dollars worth of securities backed by their mortgages had plummeted in value, straining the balance sheets of venerable Wall Street investment banks. Lehman Brothers, Bear Stearns, and Merrill Lynch had either failed or been sold off. Prominent commercial banks and mortgage lenders, including Washington Mutual, Countrywide, and Wachovia, had collapsed and been sold to the highest bidder. Now credit had seized up, as surviving banks became afraid to lend to businesses and individuals. Consumers were reining in their spending, and jobless rates were rising. Hundreds of thousands of homes bought with easy credit and an assumption of ever-rising values were in foreclosure. In a single year, investors had lost some $7 trillion, as the value of their stocks and bonds fell precipitously.

The causes of the financial crisis were complex, and many parties bore a share of the responsibility. But some analysts pointed to a critical role played by Moody's Corporation and other credit-rating agencies. Over the previous several years, Moody's had rated thousands of bonds made up of bundles of "subprime" mortgages—home loans to people with low incomes and poor credit histories, who were buying houses they probably could not afford. Now many of these buyers were failing to make their monthly payments. Their loans were going bad at an alarming rate, and Moody's had downgraded its ratings on many mortgage-backed bonds. Some blamed Moody's for having misjudged the risk inherent in these securities. Henry Waxman, the chair of the oversight committee, was one such critic. He opened the hearing with a broad condemnation. "The story of the credit rating agencies is a story of colossal failure," he told the hearing. "The credit rating agencies occupy a special place in our financial markets. Millions of investors rely on them for independent, objective assessments. The rating agencies broke this bond of trust, and federal regulators ignored the warning signs and did nothing to protect the public." The result," he added, "is that our entire financial system is now at risk."[1]

Moody's Corporation

The company that McDaniel had come to Congress to defend was the oldest credit rating agency in the world. Moody's had been founded in 1909 by John Moody, who got his start as an errand boy at a Wall Street bank. Observing the growing popularity of corporate bonds, the young entrepreneur recognized that investors needed a source of reliable information about their issuers' creditworthiness. Moody's first manual, on the safety of railroad bonds, proved highly popular, and by 1918 Moody and his firm were rating every bond then issued in the United States. By 2008, Moody's had become the undisputed "aristocrat of the ratings business."[2] The company was composed of two business units. By far the largest was Moody's Investors Service, which provided credit ratings; it earned 93 percent of the company's revenue. The other was Moody's KMV, which sold software and analytic tools, mainly to institutional investors. In 2007, Moody's reported revenue of $2.3 billion and employed 3,600 people in offices in 29 countries around the world.[3]

Moody's core business was rating the safety of bonds—debt issued by companies, governments, and public agencies. For example, if a state government issued a bond to build new classroom buildings at a public university, Moody's would evaluate the likelihood that the government would pay back the bondholders on time. (When a bond issuer was unable to make timely payments, this was known as a default.) Then Moody's would rate the bond according to a scale from Aaa—"triple A," with a very low chance of default—to C, already in default, with some 19 steps in between. (Credit ratings were technically considered opinions on the probability of default.) Moody's ratings, along with those of its competitors, enabled buyers to evaluate the risks of various fixed-income investments.

Over the years, Moody's business model had shifted. For many decades after its founding, Moody's had charged investors for its ratings through the sales of publications and advisory services. As a Moody's vice president explained in 1957, "We obviously cannot ask payment [from the issuer] for rating a bond," he wrote. "To do so would attach a price to the process, and we could not escape the charge, which would undoubtedly come, that our ratings [were] for sale."[4] In 1975, however, the Securities and Exchange Commission (SEC) changed the rules of the game. The SEC designated three companies—Moody's, Standard & Poor's (now a unit of the McGraw-Hill Companies), and Fitch (now a unit of Fimalac SA)—as Nationally Recognized Statistical Rating Organizations, or NRSROs. In effect, the government officially sanctioned these three rating agencies and gave them a

---

[1] Congress of the United States, House of Representatives, Committee on Oversight and Government Reform, "Credit Rating Agencies and the Financial Crisis," October 22, 2008, Opening Statement of Rep. Henry A. Waxman, p. 4.

[2] Michael Lewis, "The End," *Portfolio,* December 2008.

[3] *http://ir.moodys.com;* and various annual reports at *www.moodys.com.*

[4] Edmund Vogelius, writing in the *Christian Science Monitor,* quoted in "Debt Watchdogs: Tamed or Caught Napping?" *The New York Times,* December 8, 2008.

quasi-regulatory role. At this time, Moody's and the other two NRSROs began charging bond issuers to rate their products. (In 2008, Moody's market share was about 40 percent; S&P had 40 percent; and Fitch had between 10 and 15 percent.)

The new SEC rules changed the relationship between bond issuers and rating agencies. Because ratings strongly influenced the market value of the bond, issuers had a strong incentive to shop for the best possible ratings. For their part, rating agencies also had a strong incentive to compete for market share by catering to their clients. In 2000, Moody's was spun off from its parent, Dun & Bradstreet (which had acquired Moody's in 1962), becoming once again an independent, publicly owned firm. The spin-off further increased pressure on Moody's managers to increase revenues and improve shareholder returns. A former Moody's executive later recalled that in the early 2000s "things [became] a lot less collegial and a lot more bottom-line driven" as top executives sought to make the firm more responsive to clients.[5]

The Rise of Structured Finance

As Moody's business model was changing, so were the kinds of products the company was asked to evaluate. For many years, Moody's rated mainly plain-vanilla corporate and municipal, state, and federal government bonds. Wall Street investment banks, however, were becoming more innovative. Barriers to the global flow of capital were falling. New techniques of quantitative analysis permitted the creation of increasingly sophisticated financial products, known as structured finance. This term referred to the practice of combining income-producing assets—everything from conventional corporate bonds to credit card debt, home mortgages, franchise payments, and auto loans—into pools, and selling shares in the pool to investors. Instead of buying a simple IOU from a company, say, an investor would buy a share of income and principal payments flowing from a complex financial product made up of many loans.

One structured finance product that became particularly popular in the early 2000s was the residential mortgage-backed security, or RMBS. An RMBS started with a lender—a bank such as Washington Mutual or a mortgage company such as Countrywide Financial—that made home loans to individual borrowers. The lender (or another intermediary) would then bundle several thousand of these loans and sell them to a Wall Street investment bank such as Lehman Brothers or Merrill Lynch. (This gave the lender fresh cash with which to make more loans.) The Wall Street firm would then create a special kind of bond, based on a pool of underlying mortgage loans. Buyers of this bond would receive a share of the income flowing from the homeowners' monthly payments. (The investment banks also held some of these securities on their own books, a fact that contributed to their later difficulties.)

In order to make the RMBS more attractive to investors, the investment bank usually divided them into separate "tranches" (a French word meaning "slice"), with varying degrees of risk. If any homeowners defaulted on their loans, the lowest ("subordinated") tranches would absorb the losses first, and so on, up to the highest tranches. (The lower tranches earned higher interest, commensurate with their higher risk.) This is where the rating agencies, such as Moody's, came in: They were asked to rate the creditworthiness of various tranches of the mortgage-backed securities. Reflecting their greater complexity, Moody's charged more for rating structured products—around 11 basis points, or $11 for every $10,000 in value—compared with traditional corporate bonds (4.25 basis

---

[5] Jerome S. Fons, testimony before the House Committee on Oversight, October 22, 2008, p. 4; and Eliot Blair Smith, "Bringing Down Wall Street as Ratings Let Loose Subprime Scourge," *Bloomberg.com*, September 24, 2007.

	Year Ended December 31				
	2003	2004	2005	2006	2007
Total revenue	$1,246.6	$1,438.3	$1,731.6	$2,037.1	$2,259.0
Revenue from structured finance	474.7	553.1	708.7	883.6	885.9
Structured finance as % of revenue	38.5	34.1	40.9	43.4	39.2
Operating income	663.1	786.4	939.6	1,259.5	1,131.0
Operating margins (operating income as % of total revenue)	53.2	54.7	54.3	61.8	50.1

	Year Ended December 31			
	1999	2000	2001	2002
Total revenue	$564.2	$602.3	$796.7	$1,023.3
Revenue from structured finance	172.4	199.2	273.8	384.3
Structured finance as % of revenue	30.6	33.1	34.4	37.6
Operating income	270.4	288.5	398.5	538.1
Operating margins (operating income as % of total revenue)	47.9	47.9	50.0	52.6

Note: All amounts in millions of dollars, except for percentages.

Source: Moody's Annual Reports, 2001–2008. Where relevant, the most recently corrected figures have been used.

points). For example, to rate an RMBS worth $500 million, Moody's would receive about half a million dollars in fees.[6]

Credit ratings were especially important to investors in mortgage-backed securities, because these products were so difficult to understand. As a former managing director at Moody's explained,

> First, RMBSs and their offshoots offer little transparency around the composition and characteristics of the underlying loan collateral. Potential investors are not privy to the information that would allow them to understand the quality of the loan pool. Loan-by-loan data, the highest level of detail, are generally not available to investors. Second, the complexity of the securitization process requires extremely sophisticated systems and technical competence to properly assess risk at the tranche level. Third, rating agencies had a reputation, earned over nearly one century, of being honest arbiters of risk.[7]

In other words, investors had almost no way to assess independently the safety or security of these products, so they based their judgment wholly on the agencies' ratings.

Rating structured financial products, such as RMBSs, proved to be a highly lucrative business for Moody's. Exhibit A presents selected financial results for Moody's Investors

[6] Estimates of fees for rating various products are drawn from Smith, "Bringing Down Wall Street as Ratings Let Loose Subprime Scourge."

[7] Jerome S. Fons, testimony, p. 2.

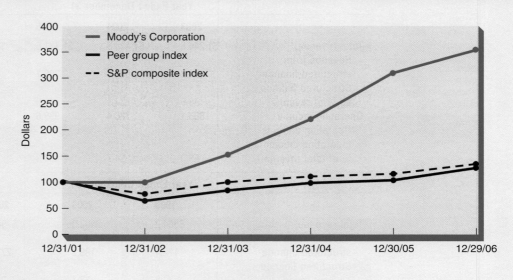

	Period Ending					
	12/31/2001	12/31/2002	12/31/2003	12/31/2004	12/30/2005	12/29/2006
Moody's Corporation	100	104.01	153.07	220.51	313.63	354.23
Peer group index	100	61.80	81.57	96.18	100.97	127.43
S&P composite index	100	77.90	100.25	111.15	116.61	135.03

Source: *Moody's Annual Report,* March 1, 2007, p. 13. The performance peer group is composed of Dow Jones & Company, Inc., The McGraw-Hill Companies, Pearson PLC, Reuters Group PLC, Thomson Corporation, and Wolters Kluwer nv. Figures assume reinvestment of all dividends.

Service for 1999 to 2007. Revenue from structured finance grew as a proportion of Moody's overall revenue throughout much of this period, peaking at 43 percent in 2006, contributing to the company's exceptional profitability. Operating margins (the percentage of revenue left after paying most expenses) during this period ranged from 48 to 62 percent, an unusually high level. In fact, for five years in a row, Moody's had the highest profit margin of any company in the S&P 500, beating even such consistently successful companies as Microsoft and Exxon.[8]

These stellar financial results rewarded Moody's shareholders with an outstanding total return in the early 2000s, relative to the company's peer group and to the broader stock market, as shown in Exhibit B. (Moody's financial results cannot be compared directly to those of S&P and Fitch, since the latter two are both part of larger companies that report consolidated results.)

[8] "Debt Watchdogs"; and Rep. Henry Waxman, statement.

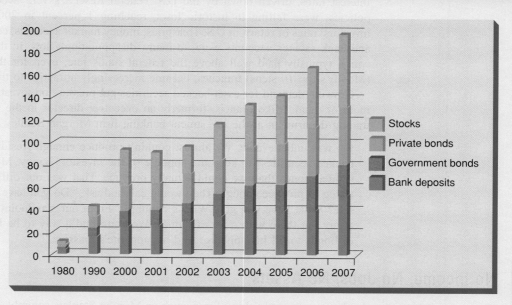

Source: McKinsey Global Institute, *Mapping Global Capital Markets,* 5th Annual Report, October 2008, p. 9. Used by permission.

Reflecting the company's success, Moody's top executives were well compensated. In 2007, for example, Moody's chairman and CEO Raymond McDaniel earned total compensation of $7.4 million, according to *Forbes.*[9]

The Giant Pool of Money

In the 2000s, the total global volume of financial assets—money available worldwide to purchase stocks and bonds, as well as more complex structured financial products created by Wall Street—grew by leaps and bounds. As shown in Exhibit C, global financial assets grew from $94 trillion in 2000 to $196 trillion in 2007. Until the advent of the credit crisis, private bonds (fixed-income securities, including mortgage and other asset-backed securities) were one of the fastest-growing asset classes, growing 10 percent a year between 2000 and 2007, when their global value stood at $51 trillion.

Several factors contributed to the growth of what National Public Radio, on the program "This American Life," vividly dubbed this "giant pool of money." Big pension plans, private hedge funds, individuals saving for retirement, and foreign governments all sought safe investments with good returns. Emerging economies, including China, India, United Arab Emirates, and Saudi Arabia, built up substantial reserves selling oil and manufactured goods to the United States and other developed nations. China grew particularly rapidly; by 2007 it had become the third-largest financial market in the world.

At the same time that the pool of money was growing, many classes of assets were becoming less attractive to investors. In the early 2000s, the stock market was languishing in the wake of the bust of the high-tech bubble and the collapse of Enron and WorldCom.

[9] "Profile: Raymond W. McDaniel," *www.forbes.com.*

Interest rates, driven down by the U.S. Federal Reserve's very accommodative interest policies, were falling to historic lows, reaching 1 percent in 2004. This meant that investors' rates of return in U.S. Treasuries, money market accounts, certificates of deposit, and bank savings accounts were, to many, disappointingly low. In this context, RMBSs, which typically paid well above the federal funds rate, even for the investment grade (Moody's top 10 steps) tranches, became increasingly attractive to the world's investors.

Growing demand for asset-backed securities put pressure on investment banks to create more of them. Mike Francis, formerly an executive director in the residential mortgage trading department at the investment banking firm Morgan Stanley, told a reporter,

> [I]t was unbelievable. We almost couldn't produce enough [residential mortgage-backed securities] to keep the appetite of the investors happy. More people wanted bonds than we could actually produce. That was our difficult task, was trying to produce enough. They would call and ask, "Do you have any more fixed rate? What have you got? What's coming?" From our standpoint it's like, there's a guy out there with a lot of money. We gotta find a way to be his sole provider of bonds to fill his appetite. And his appetite's massive.[10]

No Income, No Jobs, No Assets

As the investment banking firms, such as Morgan Stanley, scrambled to produce enough asset-backed securities to meet global demand, they put pressure on mortgage originators to produce more loans. This, in turn, encouraged lenders to weaken the standards they used to qualify borrowers. Traditionally, when a person applied for a home loan, he or she would be required to have good credit, money for a down payment, and proof of income and assets—all indicators of creditworthiness. Increasingly, in the rush to make loans, lenders began overlooking these requirements—taking on borrowers with poor credit, low-paying jobs, few assets, and no money to put down. These borrowers—and the loans made to them—were known as *subprime*.

Lenders' willingness to weaken their underwriting standards appeared consistent with public policy. The administrations of both Presidents Bill Clinton and George W. Bush had pursued policies designed to expand home ownership, particularly among minorities. In an effort to make housing more affordable, the government had helped first-time buyers with down payments and closing costs and allowed borrowers to qualify for federally insured mortgages with no money down. It also encouraged Freddie Mac and Fannie Mae, the two government-sponsored mortgage lenders, to buy RMBSs that included loans to low-income borrowers.[11]

The industry developed tongue-in-cheek acronyms for loans made to poorly qualified borrowers, such as NINAs—no income, no assets—and NINJAs—no income, no assets, and no job. Mike Francis, the former Morgan Stanley executive, described these loans:

> No income no asset loans. That's a liar's loan. We are telling you to lie to us. We're hoping you don't lie. Tell us what you make, tell us what you have in the bank, but we won't verify? We're setting you up to lie. Something about that feels very wrong. It felt wrong way back when and I wish we had never done it. Unfortunately, what happened . . . we did it because everyone else was doing it.

---

[10] National Public Radio, "The Giant Pool of Money," at *www.thislife.org/extras/radio/355_transcript.pdf.*

[11] "Don't Blame Bankers, It's Down to a Man Called Bill," *The Evening Standard (London),* October 2, 2008; and "White House Philosophy Stoked Mortgage Bonfire," *The New York Times,* December 21, 2008.

The industry also began to write more nontraditional mortgages. Instead of fixed-rate loans, under which a borrower made a stable payment every month for many years, the industry developed products with lower monthly payments to allow less qualified buyers to get into the market. These included adjustable-rate loans with low introductory "teaser" rates (which reset after three or five years at a much higher rate); interest-only loans (where the borrower was required to pay only the interest, not also a portion of the principal each month); and payment-option loans (where the borrower could choose to make a full payment, an interest-only payment, or a minimum payment that would actually cause the principal owed to increase). From 2003 to 2005, the subprime and low-documentation share of mortgage originations tripled from 11 percent to 33 percent. These loans were particularly popular in states where housing prices were going up the fastest—the so-called "sand states" of Nevada, California, Arizona, and Florida.[12]

Some banks and mortgage companies became particularly aggressive in pushing loans on poorly qualified borrowers. An investigative report for *The New York Times* examined the practices of one such lender, Washington Mutual (which later collapsed in the largest bank failure in U.S. history). WaMu, as it was known, operated a "boiler room" culture in which bank employees were under tremendous pressure to generate loan volume—and were rewarded handsomely if they did. *The New York Times* reported,

> WaMu pressed sales agents to pump out loans while disregarding borrowers' incomes and assets, according to former employees. The bank set up what insiders described as a system of dubious legality that enabled real estate agents to collect fees of more than $10,000 for bringing in borrowers, sometimes making agents more beholden to WaMu than they were to their clients.
>
> WaMu gave mortgage brokers handsome commissions for selling the riskiest loans, which carried higher fees, bolstering profits and ultimately the compensation of the bank's executives. WaMu pressured appraisers to provide inflated property values that made loans appear less risky, enabling Wall Street to bundle them more easily for sales to investors.
>
> "It was the Wild West," said [a founder of an appraisal company that worked with WaMu]. "If you were alive, they would give you a loan. Actually, I think if you were dead, they would still give you a loan."[13]

Of course, on the other side of each of these transactions was a borrower. The producers for *This American Life* interviewed one such individual—who had received a home loan for more than half a million dollars. At the time, this man was working three irregular part-time jobs and making around $45,000 a year. By the time he was interviewed, he had, not surprisingly, fallen behind in his payments, and his home was in foreclosure. The homeowner recalled,

> It's almost like you pass a guy in the street and say, [can you] lend me five hundred and forty thousand? He says, what do you do? Hey, I got a job. OK. It seems that casual . . . I wouldn't have loaned me the money. I know guys who are criminals who wouldn't loan me that and they break your knee-caps. I don't know why the bank did it . . . Five hundred and forty thousand dollars to a guy with bad credit . . . I'm not trying to absolve myself of anything . . . The bank made an imprudent loan. I made an imprudent loan. We're partners in this.[14]

[12] *FDIC Outlook,* Summer 2006, *www.fdic.gov.*

[13] Peter S. Goodman and Gretchen Morgenson, "Saying Yes, WaMu Built Empire on Shaky Loans," *The New York Times,* December 28, 2008.

[14] National Public Radio, *This American Life,* Program #355, transcript.

In many cases, the borrowers knew they were getting in over their heads—or ought to have. But in other cases, borrowers were misled by bank officers or mortgage brokers, did not understand their loan's terms, or simply believed that they would be able to sell or refinance in a year or two when, they assumed, their home would be worth more.

As the quality of mortgage loans deteriorated, some regulators tried to sound the alarm. In 2005, the Office of the Comptroller of the Currency (OCC), the arm of the Treasury Department that oversees most commercial banks, considered new regulations that would have limited risky mortgages and required clearer explanations to borrowers and warnings to buyers of RMBSs. Mortgage lenders and investment banks, however, lobbied strenuously against these rule changes, and federal regulators backed off.[15] Officials in North Carolina, Iowa, Michigan, Georgia, and other states attempted to rein in lenders, but were overruled by federal officials who argued that federal regulation preempted state regulation. The OCC brought only one enforcement action related to subprime lending between 2000 and 2006.[16]

The Collapse

In 2006, the market for residential mortgage-backed securities began to unravel. Interest rates began to rise, and housing prices began to drop. As loans began to reset, homeowners found that they were unable to make the new, higher payments—or to refinance or sell their property. Increasing numbers of homeowners realized they were "under water"—that is, they owed more than their home was worth. Lenders coined a new term—"jingle mail"—to describe what happened when borrowers simply dropped the keys in the mail and walked away from their homes. As they did so, their mortgages became worthless—and the value of securities based on them swooned.

In July 2007, Ben Bernanke, chairman of the Federal Reserve, testified in the Senate that he anticipated as much as $100 billion in losses in the market for subprime-backed securities. That month, Moody's stopped rating new RMBSs and began a series of what *Barron's* magazine called "express train downgrades, since there are no stops between Blue Chip Land and oblivion."[17] By the following summer, Moody's had downgraded more than 5,000 mortgage-backed securities, with a value in the hundreds of billions of dollars, including 90 percent of all asset-backed securities it had rated in 2006 and 2007.[18,19]

In April 2008, Roger Lowenstein, reporting for the *New York Times,* took a close look at one of many poorly performing RMBSs that had been rated by Moody's and downgraded around this time. This particular security, which he called Subprime XYZ, was comprised of 2,393 mortgages collectively worth $430 million. A West Coast mortgage lender had issued these loans in early 2006, at the height of the housing bubble. All of the borrowers were subprime—people with poor credit histories and high debt-to-income ratios. Three-quarters of the borrowers had taken adjustable-rate mortgages with low initial rates, and almost half had provided no written proof of their incomes. By early 2007, just a year after this security was created, 13 percent of the loans were delinquent. By early 2008, 27 percent of these mortgage holders were no longer paying.[20]

[15] Matt Apuzzo, "Anatomy of the Lending Crisis," *San Francisco Chronicle*, December 2, 2008.

[16] Robert Berner and Brian Grow, "They Warned Us about the Mortgage Crisis," *BusinessWeek*, October 9, 2008.

[17] Jonathan R. Laing, "Failing Grade," *Barron's*, December 24, 2007.

[18] Gretchen Morgenson, "Debt Watchdogs: Tamed or Caught Napping?" *The New York Times*, December 11, 2008.

[19] Eliot Blair Smith, "Race to Bottom at Moody's, S&P Secured Subprime's Boom, Bust," *Bloomberg.com*, September 25, 2008.

[20] Roger Lowenstein, "Triple-A Failure," *The New York Times Magazine*, April 27, 2008.

As Moody's began downgrading bonds like Subprime XYZ, many institutional investors—whose holdings of mortgage-backed securities were suddenly worth much less—became irate. Mary Elizabeth Brennan, a Moody's vice president, got an earful when she called several RMBS investors in the summer of 2007, as the problem was beginning to become obvious. According to internal documents, a portfolio manager at Vanguard, a leading money management company, told Brennan that the rating agencies had "allow[ed] issuers to get away with murder." She added, "Rating agencies aren't helping me make the right decisions." A representative of PIMCO, another money management firm, told her that Moody's "doesn't stand up to Wall Street." "Someone up there just wasn't on top of it," he added. The chief investment officer of Fortis Investments took the initiative to phone Moody's with what the manager who took the call called a "few choice words":

> If you can't figure out the loss ahead of the fact, what's the use of your ratings? You have legitimized these things [subprime mortgage-backed securities] . . . leading people into dangerous risk. If the ratings are b.s., the only use in ratings is comparing b.s. relative to more b.s.[21]

A Slippery Slope

As criticism poured in and the downgrades continued—and Moody's own stock dropped in value—the company's executives began a tough reevaluation of Moody's own practices. On September 10, 2007, McDaniel convened a town hall meeting with his managing directors (top managers). As revealed in a transcript later released to a Congressional investigation, McDaniel started out by acknowledging the criticism that "the rating agencies got it wrong." The CEO offered the following explanation of the subprime mortgage crisis:

> Looking at the subprime crisis specifically . . . We had historically low [interest] rates. We had very easy credit conditions for a number of years. We had official and market-based support for adjustable-rate mortgages. It created what I think is an overdone condition for the U.S. housing [market]. This was a condition that was supported by U.S. public policy in favor of home ownership. And as I once said, once housing prices started to fall, we got into a condition in which people can't refi[nance], can't sell, can't afford their current mortgage.[22]

Later, during the question and answer period, McDaniel reflected on the industry environment in which Moody's had rated many RMBSs:

> What happens is, as long as things are going extremely well, no one cares . . . [It] was a slippery slope . . . What happened in '04 and '05 with respect to the subordinated tranches is that our competition, Fitch and S&P, went nuts. Everything was investment grade. It didn't really matter . . . We rated . . . 20 to 25 percent of that market. We tried to alert the market. We said we're not rating it. This stuff isn't investment grade. No one cared because the machine just kept going.[23]

After the meeting, McDaniel invited attendees to submit any additional comments they wished to make electronically. One managing director commented,

> Really no discussion of why the structured [finance] group refused to change their ratings in the face of overwhelming evidence they were wrong.[24]

[21] Quotations are drawn from internal e-mails, released to Congress on October 22, 2008.

[22] Moody's Investors Service, "Managing Directors Town Hall Meeting," September 10, 2007, transcript, pp. 6–8.

[23] Ibid., pp. 62–63.

[24] "Moody's Managing Director Town Hall Feedback," September 2007, p. 1.

Another managing director asked rhetorically,

> [W]hat really went wrong with Moody's subprime ratings leading to massive downgrades and potential more downgrades to come? We heard 2 answers yesterday: 1. people lied, and 2. there was an unprecedented sequence of events in the mortgage markets. As for #1, it seems to me that we had blinders on and never questioned the information we were given . . . As for #2, it is our job to think of the worst-case scenarios and model them . . . Combined, these errors make us look either incompetent at credit analysis, or like we sold our soul to the devil for revenue, or a little bit of both.[25]

A month later, on October 21, McDaniel made a confidential presentation to his board of directors, also later disclosed to Congress. The subject of his briefing was credit policy— the overall standards governing the rating process. With respect to ratings quality, McDaniel told the board,

> The real problem is not that the market [under weights] ratings quality but rather that, in some sectors, it actually penalizes quality . . . Unchecked, competition on this basis can place the entire financial system at risk. It turns out that ratings quality has surprisingly few friends: issuers want high ratings; investors don't want rating downgrades; short-sighted bankers labor short-sightedly to game the rating agencies for a few extra basis points on execution.

Under the topic heading "rating erosion by persuasion," he commented,

> Analysts and MDs [managing directors] are continually "pitched" by bankers, issuers, investors—all with reasonable arguments—whose views can color credit judgment, sometimes improving it, other times degrading it (we "drink the kool-aid"). Coupled with strong internal emphasis on market share and margin focus, this does constitute a "risk" to ratings quality.

He also noted the inherent tension between market share and ratings quality:

> Moody's for years has struggled with this dilemma. On the one hand, we need to win the business and maintain market share, or we cease to be relevant. On the other hand, our reputation depends on maintaining ratings quality (or at least avoiding big visible mistakes). For the most part, we hand the dilemma off to the team MDs [managing directors] to solve. . . . I set both market share and rating quality objectives for my MDs, while reminding them to square the circle within the bounds of the code of conduct.

Later in the meeting, he reflected,

> The RMBS and derivatives teams are comprised of conscientious bright people working long hours. They are highly desirous of getting the rating right. But a certain complacency sets in after a prolonged period of rating success. . . . Organizations often interpret past successes as evidencing their competence and the adequacy of their procedures rather than a run of good luck.[26]

---

[25] Ibid., p. 3.

[26] "Credit Policy Issues at Moody's," Raymond McDaniel, confidential presentation to the board of directors, October 21, 2007.

What Should Be Done?

Now, on October 22, 2008, the House of Representatives Committee on Oversight and Government Reform had convened a hearing to question executives of the top credit rating agencies about their role in the nation's financial crisis. Testimony at the hearing revealed broad disagreement over the culpability of the agencies, and what if anything should be done about them.

Jerome S. Fons, managing director for credit policy at Moody's until August 2007, testified,

> My view is that a large part of the blame can be placed on the inherent conflicts of interest found in the issuer-pays business model and rating shopping by issuers of structured securities. . . . A drive to maintain or expand market share made the rating agencies willing participants in this shopping spree. It was also relatively easy for the major banks to play the agencies off one another. . . . Originators of structured securities typically chose the agency with the lowest standards, engendering a race to the bottom in terms of rating quality. . . . [T]he business model prevented analysts from putting investor interests first.

Fons recommended a "wholesale change at the governance and senior management levels of the large rating agencies." He also proposed eliminating the SEC's NRSRO designations, an increased reliance on "common sense" in the rating process, and "taming the conflicts posed by the issuer-pays model."[27]

Raymond McDaniel, who addressed the hearing on behalf of Moody's, strongly disputed the view that the business model was to blame. He pointed out the investors—as well as issuers—had an interest in influencing bond ratings. "[J]ust as an issuer has an interest in the rating to improve the marketability of its bonds, investors seeking to improve their existing bond portfolio values or to establish new portfolio positions on more favorable terms have an interest in the rating of a bond," he said. He also noted that bond issuers, such as investment banks, were themselves also often investors, weakening the distinction between the two. Companies such as Lehman Brothers issued asset-backed securities, but also held them on their books. Finally, he argued, switching to an investor-pay model would deprive individual investors of access to ratings, because only big institutional investors could afford to pay.

Rather, Moody's favored various methods of actively managing potential conflicts. The company's code of conduct, McDaniel pointed out, already required that bonds be rated by a committee, rather than by an individual, who might be swayed by personal interest. Analysts were barred from owning stock in companies whose bonds they rated, and compensation was not based on revenue associated with entities analysts rated. McDaniel concluded,

> The events of the past 15 months have demonstrated that markets can change dramatically and rapidly. Such change brings important lessons. The opportunity to improve market practices, including credit analysis and credit rating processes, must be pursued vigorously and transparently if confidence in credit markets and their healthy operation are to be restored.[28]

[27] Jerome Fons, testimony, pp. 3–6.

[28] Testimony of Raymond W. McDaniel, House Committee on Oversight and Government Reform, October 22, 2008, p. 19.

Discussion Questions

1. What did Moody's do wrong, if anything?
2. Which stakeholders were helped, and which were hurt, by Moody's actions?
3. Did Moody's have a conflict of interest? If so, what was the conflict, and who or what were the principal and the agent? What steps could be taken to eliminate or reduce this conflict?
4. What share of the responsibility did Moody's and its executives bear for the financial crisis, compared with that of home buyers, mortgage lenders, investment bankers, government regulators, policymakers, and investors?
5. What steps can be taken to prevent a recurrence of something like the subprime mortgage meltdown? In your answer, please address the role of management policies and practices, government regulation, public policy, and the structure of the credit ratings industry.

Google in China

On July 15, 2005, Google's board of directors gathered for its regular meeting at the company's headquarters in Mountain View, California. On this occasion, CEO Eric Schmidt's presentation to directors was divided into three parts—"Highlights," "Making Slow Progress/Watch List," and "Lowlights/Serious Concerns." Schmidt had much positive news to report. Google, the world's premier provider of Internet search services, was producing strong advertising sales in the United States and Europe, generating innovative new products, and expanding its service in Ireland, India, and other countries. Schmidt had one major worry, however. Under the heading "Lowlights/Serious Concerns," the first item listed was "China."[1]

The question at hand was whether or not Google should directly enter the Chinese market for search. In 2000, the company had established a Chinese-language version of its popular search engine, hosted on servers outside China. When a searcher accessed google.com from inside the country, the company's servers would automatically deliver results in Chinese translation.[2] This service left much to be desired, however; it was unreliable, and Chinese censors routinely removed search results. As Google's senior policy counsel and a member of the company's core China team, Andrew McGlaughlin described the problem in his blog:

> Google users in China today struggle with a service that, to be blunt, isn't very good. Google.com appears to be down around 10% of the time. Even when users can reach it, the Web site is slow, and sometimes produces results that when clicked on, stall out the user's browser. Our Google News service is never available; Google Images is accessible only half the time. At Google we work hard to create a great experience for our users, and the level of service we've been able to provide in China is not something we're proud of.[3]

The issue had recently become more urgent because Google had been losing market share, particularly to Baidu, a Chinese firm. At the same time, the number of Internet users in China—and with it the potential for online advertising—had been growing almost exponentially. Google seemed to be missing a huge opportunity.

[1] Google board meeting, Friday, July 15, 2005, confidential presentation slides, pp. 5–9. Google released these slides, with portions redacted pursuant to a stipulated protective order, in connection with a lawsuit filed by Microsoft Corporation alleging violation by Google, Inc., and Dr. Kai-Fu Lee, a former Microsoft executive, of Dr. Lee's noncompete agreement (Microsoft v. Lee, 05-2-23561-6, King County Superior Court, Seattle, Wash.).

[2] Google's early efforts to provide service to the Chinese are described in Clive Thompson, "Google's China Problem (and China's Google Problem)," *The New York Times Magazine,* April 23, 2006.

[3] http//googleblog.blogspot.com/2006/01/google-in-china.html.

Yet serious ethical questions remained unresolved. China operated the most far-reaching and sophisticated system of Internet censorship in the world. Any Internet firm doing business there would have to filter content that the communist regime considered offensive. Moreover, the Chinese government had demanded that other U.S. firms identify individuals who had used the Internet to criticize the authorities, and at least one dissident had been jailed as a result. Would it be possible for Google to enter China, while remaining true to its informal corporate motto, "Don't Be Evil"?

Google, Inc.[4]

Google defined itself as "a global technology leader focused on improving the ways people connect with information." In 2005, the company was the leading provider of Internet search services in the world. Its search engine offered a variety of specialized features, including the ability to search for images, videos, maps, news, products, and phone numbers. The company also provided free e-mail, instant messaging, and blogging services, and hosted all kinds of groups. One of the world's most recognized brands, the company's name had become a verb in many languages as people around the globe "googled" in search of information. In 2005, Google had more than 4,000 full-time employees and earned $1.5 billion on $6.1 billion in revenue; its market capitalization that year exceeded $80 billion.

Google was founded by Larry Page and Sergey Brin, who met in 1995 when both were enrolled in the doctoral program in computer science at Stanford. As part of a research project, Page developed a search engine algorithm he called PageRank. The problem that intrigued him was that leading search engines at the time, including Alta Vista and Yahoo!, ordered search results based on matches between words in a query and those on a Web site. This method produced results that were often poorly matched to the searcher's intent. Page's critical innovation was to rank search results based on the number and importance of backward links to a particular Web site—that is, how often it was cited by others. This enabled him to prioritize results based on likely relevance to the user. In 1997, Page and Brin offered their search service to the Stanford community under the domain name google.stanford.edu, where it attracted an enthusiastic following.

Page and Brin continued to work on the nascent search engine—which they named Google after *googol*, a mathematical term referring to the number 1 followed by 100 zeros—to improve its functionality. One idea was to "crawl" the Internet and download the entire contents of the Web in a cache where it could be readily retrieved to return superfast results to searchers. Because the two graduate students had little cash, they bought cheap PCs from a local discount chain and wrote their own software to build a makeshift supercomputer. This necessity later turned into a competitive advantage, as they were able to spread computing tasks over multiple computers, building redundancy into the system. Another idea was to add a "snippet" for each search result—several lines that highlighted the parts of a Web site relevant to the user's query. The two also developed the simple, clean design that became a hallmark of the Google site.

Page and Brin's original idea for commercializing Google was to license their technology to other Internet companies. However, the companies they approached were uninterested. At the time, Alta Vista, Yahoo!, America Online, and other portals believed their competitive advantage lay not in superior search, but rather in offering a range of attractive

---

[4] Except as noted, this history of Google is largely drawn from David A. Vise and Mark Malseed, *The Google Story* (New York: Random House, 2005).

services, such as e-mail, shopping, news, and weather. Forced to move ahead independently, the two graduate students incorporated Google in September 1998 and raised initial capital from several angel investors. In 1999, the venture capital firms Kleiner Perkins and Sequoia Capital jointly invested $25 million, and John Doerr of Kleiner Perkins and Michael Moritz of Sequoia joined Google's board. In 2001, the company hired Eric Schmidt, CEO of Novell, to be its chief executive. Google went public in an initial public offering in August 2004. Page and Brin, each of whom owned about 15 percent of the company, retained control through their ownership of Class B shares.

The Business Model

In 2005, Google's business model was based almost entirely on revenue from paid advertising. The company made money mainly in two ways:

- *AdWords.* Under this program, launched in 2000, text-based advertisements—called "sponsored links"—appeared on the right-hand side of the Google screen, separated from search results (which appeared on the left-hand side of the screen) by a vertical line. The ads were for products or services deemed relevant to words in the search query. For example, a search for "women's shoes" might produce an ad from zappos.com, an online retailer that billed itself as "the Web's most popular shoe store." When AdWords first launched, advertisers paid based on the number of times their ad was displayed. In 2002, Google began charging advertisers based on the actual number of times a user clicked on their ad. The price was set in an online electronic auction; advertisers, in effect, bid for click-throughs by Google searchers.

- *AdSense.* In 2005, Google introduced AdSense. This program placed advertisements on the Web sites of other content providers, with the Web site operator and Google sharing resulting revenue. Participants in what the company called the "Google Network" ranged from major companies such as America Online to small businesses and even individuals who operated Web sites devoted to personal interests or hobbies.

In the six months ending June 30, 2005, 99 percent of Google's revenue came from advertising; 1 percent came from licensing fees and other revenue. Of the ad revenue, 53 percent came from AdWords and 47 percent came from AdSense.[5]

In 2005, the company's foreign advertising revenue was growing faster than its domestic advertising revenue. As of June 30, 2005, international (non-U.S.) revenue was up 143 percent over the prior year; U.S. revenues were up 74 percent during this period. Even so, advertising revenue relative to usage elsewhere continued to lag the United States. By mid-2005, more than half of Google's user traffic—but only 39 percent of its revenue—came from abroad.[6]

Mission and Values

Google declared on its Web site that its mission was "to organize the world's information and make it universally accessible and useful." In their founders' letter to prospective investors, issued in advance of the initial public offering in 2004, Brin and Page further elaborated on Google's core values:

Google is not a conventional company. We do not intend to become one.

Throughout Google's evolution as a privately held company, we have managed

[5] Google Inc., Form 10-Q, quarterly report for the period ended June 30, 2005, p. 18.

[6] Ibid., pp. 12, 17, and 19.

Google differently. We have also emphasized an atmosphere of creativity and challenge, which has helped us provide unbiased, accurate, and free access to information for those who rely on us around the world. . . . Serving our end users is at the heart of what we do and remains our number one priority.[7]

Google's espoused commitment to its end users was reflected in its code of conduct. Declaring that the company had "always flourished by serving the interests of our users first and foremost," the code called for usefulness, honesty, and responsiveness in the company's dealings with customers. The code also addressed the issues of respect, avoidance of conflicts of interest, confidentiality, reporting procedures, protection of company assets, and legal compliance.

In 2001, a group of employees met to discuss the values of the company. An engineer at the gathering proposed the admonition "Don't Be Evil." This phrase stuck as an informal corporate motto. Later, when asked exactly what this meant, Schmidt remarked, perhaps a bit ruefully, "Evil is whatever Sergey says is evil."[8] In a 2004 interview with *Playboy* magazine, Google cofounders Brin and Page were questioned directly about the implications of the "Don't Be Evil" motto for the decision whether or not to enter China. The reporter asked, "What would you do if you had to choose between compromising search results and being unavailable to millions of Chinese?" Brin replied, "These are difficult questions, difficult challenges. Sometimes the 'don't be evil' policy leads to many discussions about what exactly is evil. One thing we know is that people can make better decisions with better information."[9]

China—A Major Player

China, the nation that posed a "serious concern" for Google's board of directors and a potential challenge to the company's commitment to do no evil, was one of the most economically dynamic countries in the world. With 1.3 billion people, it was also by far the most populous. In his book *China, Inc.*, Ted C. Fishman described the challenge posed by the rising Asian nation in the mid-2000s this way:

China is everywhere these days. Powered by the world's most rapidly changing large economy, it is influencing our lives as consumers, employees, and citizens. . . . No country has ever before made a better run at climbing every step of economic development all at once. No country plays the world economic game better than China. No other country shocks the global economic hierarchy like China. . . . If any country is going to supplant the United States in the world marketplace, China is it.[10]

After World War II, the Chinese Communist Party under the leadership of Mao Zedong had established an autocratic, single-party state that imposed strict controls on China's society and economy. In the 1970s, Mao's successors had initiated a series of reforms that had gradually opened the nation to world trade. The CIA described these reforms:

[7] Google Founders Letter, *www.ipogoogle.org/founders-letter.htm*.

[8] Vise and Malseed, *The Google Story*, p. 211.

[9] David Sheff, "Playboy Interview: The Google Guys," *Playboy*, September 2004.

[10] Ted C. Fishman, *China Inc.: How the Rise of the Next Superpower Challenges America and the World* (New York: Scribner, 2005).

China's economy during the last quarter century has changed from a centrally planned system that was largely closed to international trade to a more market-oriented economy that has a rapidly growing private sector and is a major player in the global economy. Reforms started in the late 1970s with the phasing out of collectivized agriculture, and expanded to include the gradual liberalization of prices, fiscal decentralization, increased autonomy for state enterprises, the foundation of a diversified banking system, the development of stock markets, the rapid growth of the non-state sector, and the opening to foreign trade and investment.[11]

As a result of these reforms, China's GDP grew tenfold over three decades. By 2005, China had become the second largest economy in the world after the United States, as measured by purchasing power.

Despite its rapid integration into the world economy, China remained a single-party dictatorship. In April and May 1989—as communism was crumbling throughout eastern and central Europe—students, intellectuals, and labor activists organized pro-democracy demonstrations across China. These culminated in a mass protest in Tiananmen Square, a large plaza in the center of Beijing. On the night of June 3 and the morning of June 4, the Chinese government responded with a massive display of military force. Tanks overran the square and the streets leading to it, and soldiers opened fire on protesters, killing as many as 3,000 and injuring thousands more. The crackdown—known as the June 4th incident or sometimes simply as Six-Four—effectively suppressed the pro-democracy movement. In 2005, the Chinese communist party faced an ongoing challenge: how to maintain its tight control of all major institutions, while allowing the free flow of money and information required in a market economy.

Internet Access[12]

The Internet first became commercially available in China in 1995. In less than a decade, as shown in Exhibit A, the number of Internet users in China soared from virtually none to 103 million, according to government estimates. This number was second only to the United States (with 154 million active users) and represented 11 percent of all Internet users worldwide.[13] Charles Zhang, chairman and CEO of Sohu.com, a leading Chinese Internet portal, argued that government estimates were too low because they were based on polls conducted over telephone land lines. "Young people do not use fixed line phones," Zhang pointed out. "They all have mobile phones."[14] Other estimates put the number of Internet users in China in 2005 as high as 134 million.[15]

Approximately 46 million computers in the country were connected to the Web, and a rapidly growing portion of these had DSL or cable access; by 2005, as shown in Exhibit A, more than half of all Web users had a high-speed connection. Sixty-nine percent of users had access at home and 38 percent at work. A quarter of all users logged on at Internet cafés. Average time online was 14 hours a week; users went online, on average, four days out of the week.

---

[11] "China," *World Fact Book 2006*, www.cia.gov.

[12] Data in this section, unless otherwise noted, are drawn from the *16th Statistical Survey Report on the Internet Development in China* (China Internet Network Information Center), July 2005, at *www.cnnic.cn*.

[13] "Worldwide Internet Users Top 1 Billion in 2005," Computer Industry Almanac Inc., press release, January 4, 2006, at *www.c-i-a.com*. U.S. data are for January 2006.

[14] "China Surpasses U.S. in Internet Use," Forbes.com, April 3, 2006, *www.forbes.com*.

[15] "Net User Tally in China Nears 134 Million," *South China Morning Post*, February 4, 2005.

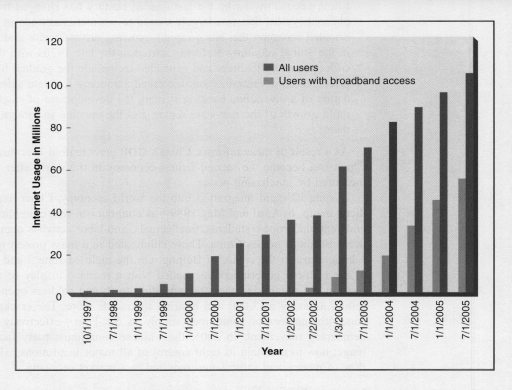

Source: China Internet Network Information Centre, *16th Statistical Survey Report on Internet Development in China,* July 2005, *www.cnnic.cn,* and earlier semiannual reports. An Internet user is a Chinese citizen who uses the Internet at least one hour per week. Users in Hong Kong, Macao, and Taiwan are not included.

Web access and usage were not evenly distributed across demographic groups or geographically. In 2005, 60 percent of Chinese Internet users were male and 40 percent female. Most were young, with the largest group (38 percent of all users) being 18–24 years old; 7 in 10 were 30 years old or younger. Internet users were a well-educated group: well over half had at least some college education. Judging from domain name registration, most Internet usage was concentrated in populous cities and coastal provinces. Twenty-one percent of domain names registered under ".cn" were in Beijing; 15 percent in Guangdong province in booming southeast China; and 10 percent in Shanghai.

Patterns of Internet Usage

What were all these people doing online? In 2005, the most common use of the Internet in China was for entertainment. Thirty-eight percent of users said this was their primary reason for going online.[16] Chinese Web surfers downloaded music, watched movies, and played online games. E-mail, instant messaging, online chat, and discussions were

[16] *16th Statistical Survey Report on the Internet Development in China.*

also very popular. Sina.com, a Chinese portal, reported that 4 million people used its forums every day. *New York Times* correspondent Clive Thompson offered the following vivid description of a typical Internet café in Beijing, which was populated mostly by teens:

> Everyone in the café looked to be settled in for a long evening of lightweight entertainment: young girls in pink and yellow Hello Kitty sweaters juggled multiple chat sessions, while upstairs a gang of young Chinese soldiers in olive-drab coats laughed as they crossed swords in the medieval fantasy game World of Warcraft. On one wall, next to a faded kung-fu movie poster, was a yellow sign that said, in Chinese characters, "Do not go to pornographic or illegal Web sites." The warning seemed almost beside the point; nobody here looked even remotely likely to be hunting for banned Tiananmen Square retrospectives.[17]

Others went online looking for news and information. Charles Zhang of Sohu.com explained, "People log onto the Internet and Sohu.com because, in China, there is no *Forbes,* Reuters, or *The Washington Post.* Print media are all state-controlled and official, and the Internet filled this void."[18] Nearly as many users reported they went online primarily to get information as said they were seeking entertainment. When asked how they obtained information online, 58 percent said they used search engines; 36 percent used known Web sites. A majority of respondents to a 2005 survey by the Chinese Academy of Social Sciences agreed that by using the Internet, people would have a better knowledge of politics and more opportunities to criticize government policies. In addition, a majority felt that government would be more aware of people's views and better able to serve citizens.

In contrast to patterns in the United States and Europe, shopping was not part of the online experience for most Chinese. Only 1 in 650 people in China had a credit card, and fewer than a quarter of Internet users had ever made an online purchase. Perhaps for this reason, search engines had not attracted many advertisers. In 2005, the annual revenue generated by search in China—for all companies combined—was just $140 million, according to Morgan Stanley's Hong Kong office.[19]

Internet Censorship

Although by 2005 many Chinese were online, their access to information and freedom of expression were restricted by a sophisticated and comprehensive system of government censorship. The authorities enforced this system on three interconnected levels: firewall devices at the border, government-mandated self-censorship by Internet service and content providers, and self-discipline exercised by individual users.

The Great Firewall of China

All information flowing in and out of China on the Internet had to traverse one of five main fiber optic pipelines that connected the infrastructure of the Chinese Internet to the outside world. The Chinese government required the operators of these pipelines to install

---

[17] Thompson, "Google's China Problem (and China's Google Problem)."

[18] "China Surpasses U.S. in Internet Use."

[19] "Google Searches for a Home in China," *BusinessWeek Online,* June 27, 2006.

sophisticated router switches—many made by the U.S. firm Cisco Systems—to block information flowing to or from specific sites as it crossed the border.[20] These devices were widely known as "the Great Firewall of China." As Jack Goldsmith and Tim Wu explained in their book, *Who Controls the Internet,*

> China has surrounded itself with the world's most sophisticated information barrier, a semi-permeable membrane that lets in what the government wants and blocks what it doesn't. In technical terms, it is a "firewall," rather similar to the security firewalls placed around corporations. Only this one is placed around a whole country.[21]

The government provided a blacklist of banned IP addresses and URLs featuring information and news about politically or culturally sensitive topics and required operators to block access to them. Users who attempted to access blocked sites would receive a non-specific error message, such as "the page cannot be displayed."

Self-Censorship by Internet Service and Content Providers

Chinese government regulations prohibited use of the Internet "to harm national security; disclose state secrets; harm the interests of the State, of society, or of a group; or to take part in criminal activities."[22]

In order to obtain a business license, all providers of Internet service within China had to provide the government with customers' account numbers, phone numbers, and IP addresses. Under the terms of a required "Public Pledge of Self-Regulation and Professional Ethics," they also had to track what sites users visited and turn over information to the government if asked. Moreover, service providers had to set up an "editor responsibility system" to monitor content and to remove and report illegal postings on any sites they hosted.[23] These regulations applied not only to Chinese firms but also to foreign firms doing business there; Yahoo!, for example, had agreed to the Public Pledge in 2002. For their part, individual subscribers had to register with the local police bureau, register any Web sites they created, and use their real names when e-mailing, blogging, or messaging.

The Chinese authorities required Internet cafés to install software to block Web sites with subversive or pornographic content and to keep records of the sites patrons visited for at least 60 days. Patrons had to present identification and register under their real names to use equipment at cafés.

Human rights activists reported that the Chinese government had launched an $800 million surveillance system known as Golden Shield to monitor civilian use of the Internet. The Security Ministry employed 35,000 Internet police whose jobs were "to monitor and censor Web sites and chat rooms in China," according to Harry Wu, publisher of the China Information Center.[24]

---

[20] In testimony before the House of Representatives, Mark Chandler, senior vice president and general counsel of Cisco Systems, responded to criticism of his company's actions in China: "Cisco does not customize, or develop specialized or unique filtering capabilities, in order to enable different regimes to block access to information. Cisco sells the same equipment in China as it sells worldwide." (House Committee on International Relations, Subcommittee on Africa, Global Human Rights, and International Operations, and the Subcommittee on Asia and the Pacific, February 15, 2006.)

[21] Jack Goldsmith and Tim Wu, *Who Controls the Internet: Illusions of a Borderless World* (New York: Oxford University Press, 2006), p. 92.

[22] OpenNet Initiative, *Internet Filtering in China in 2004–2005: A Country Study,* p. 13, at *www.opennetinitiative.net.*

[23] Ibid., p. 10.

[24] Testimony of Harry Wu, Publisher, China Information Center, before the House Committee on International Relations, Subcommittee on Africa, Global Human Rights, and International Operations, and the Subcommittee on Asia and the Pacific, February 15, 2006.

Individual Self-Discipline

Finally, the censorship regime depended on individual decisions not to engage in prohibited conduct or speech online. In some regions of the country, two cartoon police officers known as JingJing and ChaCha appeared on the screen to remind users "to be conscious of safe and healthy use of the Internet, self-regulate their online behavior, and maintain harmonious Internet order together." Fear was a powerful deterrent; individuals sought to avoid prosecution by staying away from sensitive content and not expressing views that could be construed as subversive.

Use of the Internet to Repress Dissent

The Chinese government did more than block access to content; it also used the Internet to collect information about dissidents and to prosecute them. The Electronic Frontier Foundation, an NGO that described itself as "the leading and the oldest organization working to promote freedom online," noted the ominous potential of the Internet as a tool for identifying dissidents:

> [W]ithout careful planning, Internet routers can be turned into powerful wiretapping tools; Web e-mail servers can become a honeypot of stored communications plundered by state police to identify dissidents; and blogging services and search engines can turn from aids to free speech to easily censorable memory holes.[25]

Two prominent incidents highlighted the Chinese authorities' capacity and willingness to use the Internet in this manner, as well as the inclination of U.S.-based firms to cooperate with them.

- *Shi Tao:* In April 2005, journalist Shi Tao was sentenced to 10 years in prison for disclosing "state secrets" overseas. Shi was head of the news division of *Contemporary Business News* in Hunan Province. A year earlier, Shi had been briefed on a Communist Party directive instructing the media how to respond to the upcoming 15th anniversary of the government crackdown on pro-democracy demonstrators in Tiananmen Square. That evening, Shi had used his personal Yahoo! e-mail account to send a description of this directive to a New York Web site called Democracy Forum.[26] Amnesty International subsequently reported, on the basis of a review of the court transcript, that Yahoo! had provided account-holder information that was used as evidence against Shi.[27] A Yahoo! senior executive testified in a congressional hearing in 2006 that "the facts of the Shi Tao case are distressing to our company, our employees, and our leadership." He also noted, however, that Yahoo! was "legally obligated to comply with the requirements of Chinese law enforcement. . . . Ultimately, U.S. companies in China face a choice: comply with Chinese law, or leave."[28]

---

[25] Open Letter to the House Committee on International Relations, Subcommittee on Africa, Global Human Rights, and International Operations, and the Subcommittee on Asia and the Pacific, from the Electronic Frontier Foundation, February 15, 2006, at *www.eff.org*.

[26] Human Rights in China, "Case Highlight: Shi Tao and Yahoo," at *http://hrichin.org*.

[27] "Journalist Shi Tao Imprisoned by 10 Years for Sending an Email," in Amnesty International, *Undermining Freedom of Expression in China: The Role of Yahoo!, Microsoft and Google* (London: Amnesty International, 2006), p.15.

[28] Testimony of Michael Callahan, Senior Vice President and General Counsel, Yahoo! Inc., before the House Committee on International Relations, Subcommittee on Africa, Global Human Rights, and International Operations, and the Subcommittee on Asia and the Pacific, February 15, 2006.

- *Zhao Jing:* In 1998, Zhao—then working as a hotel receptionist—began writing essays under the pseudonym Michael Anti for online discussion boards. A prolific and popular blogger, Zhao soon developed a loyal following. *The New York Times* later hired Zhao as a writer in its Beijing bureau. In 2005, in response to a request from the Chinese government, Microsoft shut down Zhao's blog on MSN Spaces—not only in China, but everywhere. A Microsoft officer later stated, "Although we do not think we could have changed the Chinese government's determination to block this particular site, we regret having to do so." He also noted that "it is a well-established principle of international jurisdiction that global Internet companies have to follow the law in the countries where they provide access to local citizens, even when those laws are different from those in their country of origin."[29]

Reporters Without Borders estimated in 2006 that 81 journalists and cyberdissidents were imprisoned in China.[30]

Human Rights Activism

Intellectuals and activists around the world worked both to gauge the extent of Internet censorship in China and to circumvent it. The OpenNet Initiative (ONI), a collaborative partnership involving researchers at the University of Toronto, Harvard Law School, and University of Cambridge, conducted a series of experiments in 2002 and 2005 to test the extent of Internet filtering in China. Using a network of trusted volunteers, ONI attempted to access various URLs and domains from multiple locations both inside and outside the Chinese firewall. The researchers also created test Web logs on several popular Chinese ISPs and sent a series of test e-mails to and from Chinese accounts. The purpose was to reveal what content was filtered and what sites were blocked.

The study concluded that filtering of content was both extensive and growing in sophistication. Tests showed that censors blocked information on a wide range of sensitive topics, including Falun Gong (a spiritual movement deemed subversive), Tibet independence, Taiwan independence, "human rights," "democracy," "anti-Communism," and the Tiananmen Square incident of June 4, 1989. In 2005, compared with earlier tests in 2002, ONI found greater specificity in Internet censorship, as the regime had apparently moved to allow greater access to neutral content on topics such as Tibet and democracy, while blocking more politically sensitive treatment of them.[31]

Activists both inside and outside China had worked hard to thwart the Chinese censors. Sometimes referred to as hackivists, these groups and individuals had developed a number of increasingly sophisticated techniques for defeating the firewall. Many used proxy servers as intermediaries between Chinese users and blocked Web sites. For example, Human Rights in China, an international NGO, in 2003 began a program of establishing regularly changing proxy sites through which Chinese citizens could access an unfiltered Internet. Technology that enabled users to anonymize their identities was also popular. In a project funded by the Open Society Institute, researchers at the University of Toronto developed software called *Psiphon* to allow users to send encrypted messages

---

[29] Testimony of Jack Krumholtz, Associate General Counsel and Managing Director, Federal Government Affairs, Microsoft Corporation, before the House Committee on International Relations, Subcommittee on Africa, Global Human Rights, and International Operations, and the Subcommittee on Asia and the Pacific, February 15, 2006.

[30] Testimony of Lucie Morillon, Reporters Without Borders, before the House Committee on International Relations, Subcommittee on Africa, Global Human Rights, and International Operations, and the Subcommittee on Asia and the Pacific, February 15, 2006.

[31] *Internet Filtering in China in 2004–2005: A Country Study.*

to a trusted computer in another country and receive encrypted information in return.[32] A company called Dynamic Internet Technologies sponsored a service called *DynaWeb* that allowed Chinese citizens to access the "Nine Commentaries on the Communist Party," first published in the United States by *The Epoch Times,* and to renounce their party membership.[33] Global Internet Freedom Technology (GIFT), available from Ultra-Reach Internet, was another such service.[34]

Radio Free Asia and Voice of America maintained Web sites in Mandarin, Cantonese, Uyghur, and Tibetan. The president of Radio Free Asia described its strategy for circulating content to individuals living under the censorship regime:

> [W]e are creating a widening network of human proxies, so informal that it has no visible shape but is very much alive. Message boards, e-mails, blogs, and instant messages pick up where the government has cut us off. Friends and family based in third countries post our articles on their own Web sites and then pass on the Web address.[35]

Chinese Google.com

At the time Google was seriously considering direct entry into the China market, the company already had about five years of experience with the Chinese censorship regime.

In 2000, Google had launched a Chinese-language version of google.com, hosted in the United States, which could be accessed from abroad by Chinese users. By 2002, this service had captured about one-quarter of the Chinese market for online search. However, service was erratic as search queries attempted to traverse the firewall. The company experienced particular difficulties with its Google News China division. Users inside China who attempted to click on stories published by blocked news sources, such as CNN and *The New York Times,* received repeated error messages.

Then, in September 2004, the Chinese authorities abruptly shut down access to the entire google.com site. After about two weeks, service was restored. When the site came back online, the blocked news sources had been omitted. The company issued the following statement:

> On balance we believe that having a service with links that work and omits a fractional number is better than having a service that is not available at all. It was a difficult trade-off for us to make, but the one we felt ultimately served the best interests of our users located in China.[36]

But as Elliot Schrage, Google's vice president for global communications and public affairs, later explained, Google's troubles in China were hardly over:

> [We] soon discovered new problems. Many queries, especially politically sensitive queries, were not making it through to Google's servers. And access became often slow and unreliable, meaning that our service in China was not something

---

[32] http://psiphon.civisec.org.

[33] http://www.dit-inc.us/dynaweb.php.

[34] www.ultrareach.com.

[35] Testimony of Libby Liu, President, Radio Free Asia, before the House Committee on International Relations, Subcommittee on Africa, Global Human Rights, and International Operations, and the Subcommittee on Asia and the Pacific, February 15, 2006.

[36] "China, Google News, and Source Inclusion," at http://googleblog.blogspot.com/2004/09/china-google-news-and-source-inclusion.html.

we felt proud of. Even though we weren't doing any self-censorship, our results were being filtered anyway, and our service was being actively degraded on top of that. Indeed, at times, some users were even being redirected to local Chinese search engines.[37]

Whatever compromises Google might have made in late 2004 to keep its service available in China, by early 2005 its market share, never dominant, was under increasing pressure. Google's toughest competition came from the rapidly growing Chinese firm Baidu, sometimes referred to as the "Chinese Google." The word *baidu,* meaning "100 times," was linked to an ancient poem about a man searching for his lover. In 2005, Baidu had around 400 employees, only 30 of whom had been with the company more than three years.[38] Baidu had made very fast inroads among Chinese users; between 2003 and 2005 its share of the market for search had ballooned from 3 percent to 46 percent. During this period, Google's share of the market for search increased slightly from 24 percent to 27 percent; Yahoo! (which had partnered with the Chinese firm Alibaba) and the Chinese portals Sina and Sohu had all seen significant erosion. Some suspected that one of Baidu's competitive advantages was its close relationship with the Chinese government. Liu Bin, an analyst with BDA China, a research firm, commented,

> Baidu works with the government more closely than other search companies. They launch[ed] a more aggressive system to censor their key words. They started to censor their search service earlier and more extensively than others. That's why the government likes Baidu.[39]

"Figuring Out How to Deal with China"

Now, at the July 2005 board meeting, the issue of what to do about China was coming to a head. After the board had taken up various other agenda items, Sukhinder Singh Cassidy, Google's vice president for Asian, Pacific, and Latin American operations, took the floor to present her analysis of the China question.[40]

The Chinese market for search, Cassidy said, was highly competitive. The company's research showed that Google was losing market share. Its main Chinese rival, Baidu, had succeeded in attracting younger, better-educated users, many of them students. In part, this was because Baidu offered a full range of services, such as entertainment. In part, it was because Baidu's search quality was perceived as superior. The Chinese used Google mainly for searching sources *outside* China and used Baidu mainly for searching sources *inside* China, evidence showed.

The most popular Internet activities in China, Cassidy reported, were online chatting; downloading music, TV shows, and movies; and playing online games. Reading the news, searching for information, and sending and receiving e-mail were also popular, although somewhat less so. Messaging, entertainment, news, and e-mail were applications that Google did not offer in China, she pointed out.

[37] Testimony of Elliot Schrage, Vice President, Global Communications and Public Affairs, Google, Inc., before the House Committee on International Relations, Subcommittee on Africa, Global Human Rights, and International Operations, and the Subcommittee on Asia and the Pacific, February 15, 2006.

[38] "Baidu's IPO and New Riches," Comtex News Network, June 21, 2005.

[39] "Google Searches for a Home in China," *BusinessWeek Online,* June 27, 2006.

[40] The following summary of Cassidy's presentation is drawn from Google Board Meeting, Friday, July 15, 2005, confidential presentation slides with portions redacted, op. cit., pp. 72–109.

Google's own research showed that the company was perceived in China as an international brand and technology leader, but "a little distant to average Chinese users." More than half of Internet users who knew about Google could not spell the name correctly, and more than half thought the company should have a Chinese name. By contrast, Baidu was perceived as being a Chinese brand with good technology, "friendly," "closer to average Chinese people's life," and as having entertainment products.

In China, Cassidy noted, "we are a premium brand, not considered a brand for mainstream users. People don't know much about us; there is a perception gap between who we are and how we are perceived in China." In addition, Google was perceived as a "foreign company [that] is not in China." On a slide titled "Key Learnings/Key Issues," Cassidy stated to the board, "[We] need to be there."

Discussion Questions

1. For Google in 2005, from a business perspective, what are the arguments for and against entering China?

2. From an ethical perspective, what are the arguments for and against entering China?

3. If Google decides to enter China, how can it do so while mitigating adverse ethical impacts? In answering this question, please formulate possible options and evaluate their strengths and weaknesses.

4. What do you think Google should do, and why?

Merck, the FDA, and the Vioxx Recall

In 2006, the pharmaceutical giant Merck faced major challenges. Vioxx, the company's once best-selling prescription painkiller, had been pulled off the market in September 2004 after Merck learned it increased the risk of heart attacks and strokes. When news of the recall broke, the company's stock price had plunged 30 percent to $33 a share, its lowest point in eight years, where it had hovered since. Standard & Poor's had downgraded the company's outlook from "stable" to "negative." In late 2004, the Justice Department had opened a criminal investigation into whether the company had "caused federal health programs to pay for the prescription drug when its use was not warranted."[1] The Securities and Exchange Commission was inquiring into whether Merck had misled investors. By late 2005, more than 6,000 lawsuits had been filed, alleging that Vioxx had caused death or disability. From many quarters, the company faced troubling questions about the development and marketing of Vioxx, new calls for regulatory reform, and concerns about its political influence on Capitol Hill. In the words of Senator Charles Grassley, chairman of a congressional committee investigating the Vioxx case, "a blockbuster drug [had become] a blockbuster disaster."[2]

Merck, Inc.

Merck, the company in the eye of this storm, was one of the world's leading pharmaceutical firms. As shown in Exhibit A, in 2005 the company ranked fourth in sales, after Pfizer, Johnson & Johnson, and GlaxoSmithKline. In assets and market value, it ranked fifth. However, Merck ranked first in profits, earning $7.33 billion on $30.78 billion in sales (24 percent).[3]

Merck had long enjoyed a reputation as one of the most ethical and socially responsible of the major drug companies. For an unprecedented seven consecutive years (1987 to 1993), *Fortune* magazine had named Merck its "most admired" company. In 1987, Merck appeared on the cover of *Time* under the headline, "The Miracle Company." It had consistently appeared on lists of best companies to work for and in the portfolios of social investment funds. The company's philanthropy was legendary.

By Anne T. Lawrence. Copyright © 2006 by the author. All rights reserved. An earlier version of this case was presented at the Western Casewriters Association Annual Meeting, Long Beach, California, March 30, 2006. This case was prepared from publicly available materials.

[1] "Justice Dept. and SEC Investigating Merck Drug," *The New York Times*, November 9, 2004.

[2] "Opening Statement of U.S. Senator Chuck Grassley of Iowa," U.S. Senate Committee on Finance, Hearing, "FDA, Merck, and Vioxx: Putting Patient Safety First?" November 18, 2004, *http://finance.senate.gov.*

[3] A history of Merck may be found in Fran Hawthorne, *The Merck Druggernaut: The Inside Story of a Pharmaceutical Giant* (Hoboken, NJ: John Wiley & Sons, 2003).

Company	Sales ($bil)	Profits ($bil)	Assets ($bil)	Market Value ($bil)
Pfizer	40.36	6.20	120.06	285.27
Johnson & Johnson	40.01	6.74	46.66	160.96
Merck	**30.78**	**7.33**	**42.59**	**108.76**
Novartis	26.77	5.40	46.92	116.43
Roche Group	25.18	2.48	45.77	95.38
GlaxoSmithKline	34.16	6.34	29.19	124.79
Aventis	21.66	2.29	31.06	62.98
Bristol-Myers Squibb	19.89	2.90	26.53	56.05
AstraZeneca	20.46	3.29	23.57	83.03
Abbott Labs	18.99	2.44	26.15	69.27

Source: Forbes 2000, *www.forbes.com*. Listed in order of overall ranking in the Forbes 2000.

In the 1940s, Merck had given its patent for streptomycin, a powerful antibiotic, to a university foundation. Merck was especially admired for its donation of Mectizan. Merck's scientists had originally developed this drug for veterinary use, but later discovered that it was an effective cure for river blindness, a debilitating parasitic disease afflicting some of the world's poorest people. When the company realized that the victims of river blindness could not afford the drug, it decided to give it away for free, in perpetuity.[4]

In 1950, George W. Merck, the company's long-time CEO, stated in a speech, "We try never to forget that medicine is for the people. It is not for the profits. The profits follow, and if we have remembered that, they never fail to appear. The better we have remembered that, the larger they have been."[5] This statement was often repeated in subsequent years as a touchstone of the company's core values.

Merck was renowned for its research labs, which had a decades-long record of achievement, turning out one innovation after another, including drugs for tuberculosis, cholesterol, hypertension, and AIDS. In the early 2000s, Merck spent around $3 billion annually on research. Some felt that the company's culture had been shaped by its research agenda. Commented the author of a history of Merck, the company was "intense, driven, loyal, scientifically brilliant, collegial, and arrogant."[6] In 2006, although Merck had several medicines in the pipeline—including vaccines for rotavirus and cervical cancer, and drugs for insomnia, lymphoma, and the effects of stroke—some analysts worried that the pace of research had slowed significantly.

Estimating the company's financial liability from the Vioxx lawsuits was difficult. Some 84 million people had taken the drug worldwide over a five-year period from 1999 to 2004. In testimony before Congress, Dr. David Graham, a staff scientist at the Food and Drug Administration, estimated that as many as 139,000 people in the United States had had heart attacks or strokes as a result of taking Vioxx, and about 55,000 of these

---

[4] Merck received the 1991 Business Enterprise Trust Award for this action. See Stephanie Weiss and Kirk O. Hanson, "Merck and Co., Inc.: Addressing Third World Needs" (Business Enterprise Trust, 1991).

[5] Hawthorne, *The Merck Druggernaut,* pp. 17–18.

[6] Ibid., p. 38.

had died.[7] Merrill Lynch estimated the company's liability for compensatory damages alone in the range of $4 to $18 billion.[8] However, heart attacks and strokes were common, and they had multiple causes, including genetic predisposition, smoking, obesity, and a sedentary lifestyle. Determining the specific contribution of Vioxx to a particular cardiovascular event would be very difficult. The company vigorously maintained that it had done nothing wrong and vowed to defend every single case in court. By early 2006, only three cases had gone to trial, and the results had been a virtual draw—one decision for the plaintiff, one for Merck, and one hung jury.

Government Regulation of Prescription Drugs

In the United States, prescription medicines—like Vioxx—were regulated by the Food and Drug Administration (FDA).[9] Before a new drug could be sold to the public, its manufacturer had to carry out clinical trials to demonstrate both safety and effectiveness. Advisory panels of outside medical experts reviewed the results of these trials and recommended to the FDA's Office of Drug Safety whether or not to approve a new drug.[10] After a drug was on the market, the agency's Office of New Drugs continued to monitor it for safety, in a process known as "postmarket surveillance." These two offices both reported to the same boss, the FDA's director of the Center for Drug Evaluation and Research.

Once the FDA had approved a drug, physicians could prescribe it for any purpose, but the manufacturer could market it only for uses for which it had been approved. Therefore, companies had an incentive to continue to study approved drugs to provide data that they were safe and effective for the treatment of other conditions.

In the 1980s, the drug industry and some patient advocates had criticized the FDA for being too slow to approve new medicines. Patients were concerned that they were not getting new medicines fast enough, and drug companies were concerned that they were losing sales revenue. Each month an average drug spent under review represented $41.7 million in lost revenue, according to one study.[11]

In 1992, Congress passed the Prescription Drug User Fee Act (PDUFA). This law, which was supported by the industry, required pharmaceutical companies to pay "user fees" to the FDA to review proposed new medicines. Between 1993 and 2001, the FDA received around $825 million in such fees from drug makers seeking approval. (During this period, it also received $1.3 billion appropriated by Congress.) This infusion of new revenue enabled the agency to hire 1,000 new employees and to shorten the approval time for new drugs from 27 months in 1993 to 14 months in 2001.[12]

Despite the benefits of PDUFA, some felt that industry-paid fees were a bad idea. In an editorial published in December 2004, the *Journal of the American Medical Association (JAMA)* concluded, "It is unreasonable to expect that the same agency that was responsible for approval of drug licensing and labeling would also be committed to

---

[7] "FDA Failing in Drug Safety, Official Asserts," *The New York Times,* November 19, 2004. The full transcript of the hearing of the U.S. Senate Committee on Finance, "FDA, Merck, and Vioxx: Putting Patient Safety First?" is available at *http://finance.senate.gov.*

[8] "Despite Warnings, Drug Giant Took Long Path to Vioxx Recall," *The New York Times,* November 14, 2004.

[9] A history of the FDA and of its relationship to business may be found in Philip J. Hilts, *Protecting America's Health: The FDA, Business, and One Hundred Years of Regulation* (New York: Alfred A. Knopf, 2003).

[10] Marcia Angell, *The Trust About the Drug Companies* (New York: Random House, 2004), ch. 2.

[11] Merrill Lynch data reported in "A World of Hurt," *Fortune,* January 10, 2005, p. 18.

[12] U.S. General Accounting Office, *Food and Drug Administration: Effect of User Fees on Drug Approval Times, Withdrawals, and Other Agency Activities,* September 2002.

actively seek evidence to prove itself wrong (i.e., that the decision to approve the product was subsequently shown to be incorrect)." *JAMA* went on to recommend establishment of a separate agency to monitor drug safety.[13] Dr. David Kessler, a former FDA Commissioner, rejected this idea, responding that "strengthening postmarketing surveillance is certainly in order, but you don't want competing agencies."[14]

Some evidence suggested that the morale of FDA staff charged with evaluating the safety of new medicines had been hurt by relentless pressure to bring drugs to market quickly. In 2002, a survey of agency scientists found that only 13 percent were "completely confident" that the FDA's "final decisions adequately assess the safety of a drug." Thirty-one percent were "somewhat confident" and 5 percent lacked "any confidence." Two-thirds of those surveyed lacked confidence that the agency "adequately monitors the safety of prescription jobs once they are on the market." And nearly one in five said they had "been pressured to approve or recommend approval" for a drug "despite reservations about [its] safety, efficacy or quality."[15]

After the FDA shortened the approval time, the percentage of drugs recalled following approval increased from 1.56% for 1993–1996 to 5.35% for 1997–2001.[16] Vioxx was the ninth drug taken off the market in seven years.

Influence at the Top

The pharmaceutical industry's success in accelerating the approval of new drugs reflected its strong presence in Washington. The major drug companies, their trade association PhRMA (Pharmaceutical Research and Manufacturers of America), and their executives consistently donated large sums of money to both political parties and, through their political action committees, to various candidates. The industry's political contributions are shown in Exhibit B.

Following the Congressional ban on soft money contributions in 2003, the industry shifted much of its contributions to so-called stealth PACs, nonprofit organizations that were permitted by law to take unlimited donations without revealing their source. These organizations could, in turn, make "substantial" political expenditures, providing political activity was not their primary purpose.[17]

In addition, the industry maintained a large corps of lobbyists active in the nation's capital. In 2003, for example, drug companies and their trade association spent $108 million on lobbying and hired 824 individual lobbyists, according to a report by Public Citizen.[18] Merck spent $40.7 million on lobbying between 1998 and 2004.[19] One of the industry's most effective techniques was to hire former elected officials or members of their staffs. For example, Billy Tauzin, formerly a Republican member of Congress from Louisiana and head of the powerful Committee on Energy and Commerce, which oversaw

---

[13] "Postmarketing Surveillance—Lack of Vigilance, Lack of Trust," *Journal of the American Medical Association* 92, no. 21 (December 1, 2004), p. 2649.

[14] "FDA Lax in Drug Safety, Journal Warns," November 23, 2004, *www.sfgate.com*.

[15] 2002 Survey of 846 FDA scientists conducted by the Office of the Inspector General of the Department of Health and Human Services, *www.peer.org/FDAscientistsurvey*.

[16] "Postmarketing Surveillance."

[17] "Big PhRMA's Stealth PACs: How the Drug Industry Uses 501(c) Nonprofit Groups to Influence Elections," *Congress Watch*, September 2004.

[18] "Drug Industry and HMOs Deployed an Army of Nearly 1,000 Lobbyists to Push Medicare Bill, Report Finds," June 23, 2004, *www.citizen.org*.

[19] Data available at *www.publicintegrity.org*.

Election Cycle	Total Contributions	Contributions from Individuals	Contributions from PACs	Soft Money Contributions	Percentage to Republicans
2006	$5,187,393	$1,753,159	$3,434,234	N/A	70%
2004	$18,181,045	$8,445,485	$9,735,560	N/A	66%
2002	$29,441,951	$3,332,040	$6,957,382	$19,152,529	74%
2000	$26,688,292	$5,660,457	$5,649,913	$15,377,922	69%
1998	$13,169,694	$2,673,845	$4,107,068	$6,388,781	64%
1996	$13,754,796	$3,413,516	$3,584,217	$6,757,063	66%
1994	$7,706,303	$1,935,150	$3,477,146	$2,294,007	56%
1992	$7,924,262	$2,389,370	$3,205,014	$2,329,878	56%
1990	$3,237,592	$771,621	$2,465,971	N/A	54%
Total	$125,291,328	$30,374,643	$42,616,505	$52,300,180	67%

Source: Center for Responsive Politics, *www.opensecrets.org.*

the drug industry, became president of PhRMA at a reported annual salary of $2 million in 2004.[20]

Over the years, the industry's representatives in Washington had established a highly successful record of promoting its political agenda on a range of issues. In addition to faster drug approvals, these had more recently included a Medicare prescription drug benefit, patent protections, and restrictions on drug imports from Canada.

The Blockbuster Model

In the 1990s, 80 percent of growth for the big pharmaceutical firms came from so-called "blockbuster" drugs.[21] Blockbusters have been defined by *Fortune* magazine as "medicines that serve vast swaths of the population and garner billions of dollars in annual revenue."[22] The ideal blockbuster, from the companies' view, was a medicine that could control chronic but usually nonfatal conditions that afflicted large numbers of people with health insurance. These might include, for example, daily maintenance drugs for high blood pressure or cholesterol, allergies, arthritis pain, or heartburn. Drugs that could actually cure a condition, and thus would not need to be taken for long periods, or were intended to treat diseases, like malaria or tuberculosis, that affected mainly the world's poor, were often less profitable.

Historically, drug companies focused most of their marketing efforts on prescribing physicians. The industry hired tens of thousands of sales representatives—often, attractive young men and women—to make the rounds of doctors' offices to talk about new products and give out free samples.[23] Drug companies also offered doctors gifts—from free meals to tickets to sporting events—to cultivate their goodwill. They also routinely

[20] "Rep. Billy Tauzin Demonstrates That Washington's Revolving Door Is Spinning Out of Control," *Public Citizen,* December 15, 2004, press release.

[21] "The Waning of the Blockbuster," *BusinessWeek,* October 18, 2004.

[22] "A World of Hurt," p. 20.

[23] In 2005, 90,000 sales representatives were employed by the pharmaceutical industry, about one for every eight doctors. *The New York Times* revealed in an investigative article ("Give Me an Rx! Cheerleaders Pep Up Drug Sales," November 28, 2005) that many companies made a point of hiring former college cheerleaders for this role.

sponsored continuing education events for physicians, often featuring reports on their own medicines, and supported doctors financially with opportunities to consult and to conduct clinical trials.[24] In 2003 Merck spent $422 million to market Vioxx to doctors and hospitals.[25]

During the early 2000s, when Vioxx and Pfizer's Celebrex were competing head-to-head, sales representatives for the two firms were hard at work promoting their brand to doctors. Commented one rheumatologist of the competition between Merck and Pfizer at the time, "We were all aware that there was a great deal of marketing. Like a Coke–Pepsi war."[26] An internal Merck training manual for sales representatives, reported in *The Wall Street Journal,* was titled "Dodge Ball Vioxx." It explained how to "dodge" doctors' questions, such as "I am concerned about the cardiovascular effects of Vioxx." Merck later said that this document had been taken out of context and that sales representatives "were not trained to avoid physicians' questions."[27]

Direct-to-Consumer Advertising

Although marketing to doctors and hospitals continued to be important, in the late 1990s the focus shifted somewhat. In 1997, the FDA for the first time allowed drug companies to advertise directly to consumers. The industry immediately seized this opportunity, placing numerous ads for drugs—from Viagra to Nexium—on television and in magazines and newspapers. In 2004, the industry spent over $4 billion on such direct-to-consumer, or DTC, advertising. For example, in one ad for Vioxx, Olympic figure skating champion Dorothy Hamill glided gracefully across an outdoor ice rink to the tune of "It's a Beautiful Morning" by the sixties pop group The Rascals, telling viewers that she would "not let arthritis stop me." In all, Merck spent more than $500 million advertising Vioxx.[28]

The industry's media blitz for Vioxx and other drugs was highly effective. According to research by the Harvard School of Public Heath, each dollar spent on DTC advertising yielded $4.25 in sales.

The drug companies defended DTC ads, saying they informed consumers of newly available therapies and encouraged people to seek medical treatment. In the age of the Internet, commented David Jones, an advertising executive whose firm included several major drug companies, "consumers are becoming much more empowered to make their own health care decisions."[29]

However, others criticized DTC advertising, saying that it put pressure on doctors to prescribe drugs that might not be best for the patient. "When a patient comes in and wants something, there is a desire to serve them," said David Wofsy, president of the American College of Rheumatology. "There is a desire on the part of physicians, as there is on anyone else who provides service, to keep the customer happy."[30] Even some industry executives expressed reservations. Said Hank McKinnell, CEO of Pfizer, "I'm beginning to think that direct-to-consumer ads are part of the problem. By having them on

---

[24] The influence of the drug industry on the medical professional is documented in Katharine Greider, *The Big Fix: How the Pharmaceutical Industry Rips Off American Consumers* (New York: Public Affairs, 2003).

[25] ""Drug Pullout," *Modern Healthcare,* October 18, 2004.

[26] "Marketing of Vioxx: How Merck Played Game of Catch-Up," *The New York Times,* February 11, 2005.

[27] "E-Mails Suggest Merck Knew Vioxx's Dangers at Early Stage," *The Wall Street Journal,* November 1, 2004.

[28] IMS Health estimate reported in "Will Merck Survive Vioxx?" *Fortune,* November 1, 2004.

[29] "With or Without Vioxx, Drug Ads Proliferate," *The New York Times,* December 6, 2004.

[30] "A 'Smart' Drug Fails the Safety Test," *Washington Post,* October 3, 2004.

Exhibit C

Vioxx Sales in the United States, 1999–2004

	U.S. Prescriptions Dispensed	U.S. Sales	U.S. Sales of Vioxx as % of Total Merck Sales
1999	4,845,000	$372,697,000	2.2%
2000	20,630,000	$1,526,382,000	7.6%
2001	25,406,000	$2,084,736,000	9.8%
2002	22,044,000	$1,837,680,000	8.6%
2003	19,959,000	$1,813,391,000	8.1%
2004*	13,994,000	$1,342,236,000	5.9%

*Withdrawn from the market in September 2004.

Sources: Columns 1 and 2: IMS Health (*www.imshealth.com*); column 3: Merck *Annual Reports* (*www.merck.com*).

television without a very strong message that the doctor needs to determine safety, we've left this impression that all drugs are safe. In fact, no drug is safe."[31]

The Rise of Vioxx

Vioxx, the drug at the center of Merck's legal woes, was known as "a selective COX-2 inhibitor." Scientists had long understood that an enzyme called cyclo-oxygenase, or COX for short, was associated with pain and inflammation. In the early 1990s, researchers learned that there were really two kinds of COX enzyme. COX-1, it was found, performed several beneficial functions, including protecting the stomach lining. COX-2, on the other hand, contributed to pain and inflammation. Existing anti-inflammatory drugs suppressed both forms of the enzyme, which is why drugs like ibuprofen (Advil) relieved pain, but also caused stomach irritation in some users.

A number of drug companies, including Merck, were intrigued by the possibility of developing a medicine that would block just the COX-2, leaving the stomach-protective COX-1 intact. Such a drug would offer distinctive benefits to some patients, such as arthritis sufferers who were at risk for ulcers (bleeding sores in the intestinal tract).[32] As many as 16,500 people died each year in the United States from this condition.[33]

In May 1999, after several years of research and testing by Merck scientists, the FDA approved Vioxx for the treatment of osteoarthritis, acute pain in adults, and menstrual symptoms. The drug was later approved for rheumatoid arthritis. Although Merck, like other drug companies, never revealed what it spent to develop specific new medicines, estimates of the cost to develop a major new drug ran as high as $800 million.[34]

Vioxx quickly became exactly what Merck had hoped: a blockbuster. At its peak in 2001, Vioxx generated $2.1 billion in sales in the United States alone, contributing almost 10 percent of Merck's total sales revenue worldwide, as shown in Exhibit C. The retail

[31] "A World of Hurt," p. 18.

[32] "Medicine Fueled by Marketing Intensified Troubles for Pain Pills," *The New York Times,* December 19, 2004.

[33] "New Scrutiny of Drugs in Vioxx's Family," *The New York Times,* October 4, 2004.

[34] This estimate was hotly debated. See, for example, "How Much Does the Pharmaceutical Industry Really Spend on R&D?" ch. 3 in Angell, *The Trust About the Drug Companies;* and Merrill Goozner, *The $800 Million Pill: The Truth Behind the Cost of New Drugs* (Berkeley: University of California Press, 2004).

price of Vioxx was around $3.00 per pill, compared with pennies per pill for older anti-inflammatory drugs like aspirin and Advil. Of course, Vioxx was often covered, at least partially, under a user's health insurance, while over-the-counter drugs were not.

Safety Warnings

Even before the drug was approved, some evidence cast doubt on the safety of Vioxx. These clues were later confirmed in other studies.

Merck Research: Internal company e-mails suggested that Merck scientists might have been worried about the cardiovascular risks of Vioxx as early as its development phase. In a 1997 e-mail, reported in *The Wall Street Journal,* Dr. Alise Reicin, a Merck scientist, stated that "the possibility of CV (cardiovascular) events is of great concern." She added, apparently sarcastically, "I just can't wait to be the one to present those results to senior management!" A lawyer representing Merck said this e-mail had been taken out of context.[35]

VIGOR: A study code-named VIGOR, completed in 2000 after the drug was already on the market, compared rheumatoid arthritis patients taking Vioxx with another group taking naproxen (Aleve). Merck financed the research, which was designed to study gastrointestinal side effects. The study found, as the company had expected, that Vioxx was easier on the stomach than naproxen. But it also found that the Vioxx group had nearly five times as many heart attacks (7.3 per thousand person-years) as the naproxen group (1.7 per thousand person-years).[36] Publicly, Merck hypothesized that these findings were due to the heart-protective effect of naproxen, rather than to any defect inherent in Vioxx. Privately, however, the company seemed worried. In an internal e-mail dated March 9, 2000, under the subject line "Vigor," the company's research director, Dr. Edward Scolnick, said that cardiovascular events were "clearly there" and called them "a shame." But, he added, "there is always a hazard."[37] At that time, the company considered reformulating Vioxx by adding an agent to prevent blood clots (and reduce CV risk), but then dropped the project.

The FDA was sufficiently concerned by the VIGOR results that it required Merck to add additional warning language to its label. These changes appeared in April 2002, after lengthy negotiations between the agency and the company over their wording.[38]

Kaiser/Permanente: In August 2004, Dr. David Graham, a scientist at the FDA, reported the results of a study of the records of 1.4 million patients enrolled in the Kaiser health maintenance organization in California. He found that patients on high doses of Vioxx had three times the rate of heart attacks as patients on Celebrex, a competing COX-2 inhibitor made by Pfizer. Merck discounted this finding, saying that studies of patient records were less reliable than double-blind clinical studies.[39] Dr. Graham later charged that his superiors at the FDA had "ostracized" him and subjected him to "veiled

---

[35] "E-Mails Suggest Merck Knew Vioxx's Dangers at Early Stage."

[36] "Comparison of Upper Gastrointestinal Toxicity of Rofecoxib and Naproxen in Patients with Rheumatoid Arthritis," *New England Journal of Medicine,* 2000, p. 323.

[37] "E-Mails Suggest Merck Knew Vioxx's Dangers at Early Stage."

[38] At one of the early Vioxx trials, the plaintiff introduced a Merck internal memo that calculated that the company would make $229 million more in profits if it delayed changes to warning language on the label by four months (*The New York Times,* August 20, 2005). The FDA did not have the authority to dictate label language; any changes had to be negotiated with the manufacturer.

[39] "Study of Painkiller Suggests Heart Risk," *The New York Times,* August 26, 2004.

threats" if he did not qualify his criticism of Vioxx. The FDA called these charges "baloney."[40]

APPROVe: In order to examine the possibility that Vioxx posed a cardiovascular risk, Merck decided to monitor patients enrolled in a clinical trial called APPROVe to see if those taking Vioxx had more heart attacks and strokes than those who were taking a placebo (sugar pill). This study had been designed to determine if Vioxx reduced the risk of recurrent colon polyps (a precursor to colon cancer); Merck hoped it would lead to FDA approval of the drug for this condition. The APPROVe study was planned before the VIGOR results were known.

Merck Recalls the Drug

On the evening of Thursday, September 23, 2004, Dr. Peter S. Kim, president of Merck Research Labs, received a phone call from scientists monitoring the colon polyp study. Researchers had found, the scientists told him, that after 18 months of continuous use individuals taking Vioxx were more than twice as likely to have a heart attack or stroke than those taking a placebo. The scientists recommended that the study be halted because of "unacceptable" risk.[41]

Dr. Kim later described to a reporter for *The New York Times* the urgent decision-making process that unfolded over the next hours and days as the company responded to this news.

> On Friday, I looked at the data with my team. The first thing you do is review the data. We did that. Second is you double-check the data, go through them and make sure that everything is O.K. [At that point] I knew that barring some big mistake in the analysis, we had an issue here. Around noon, I called [CEO] Ray Gilmartin and told him what was up. He said, "Figure out what was the best thing for patient safety." We then spent Friday and the rest of the weekend going over the data and analyzing them in different ways and calling up medical experts to set up meetings where we would discuss the data and their interpretations and what to do.[42]

According to later interviews with some of the doctors consulted that weekend by Merck, the group was of mixed opinion. Some experts argued that Vioxx should stay on the market, with a strong warning label so that doctors and patients could judge the risk for themselves. But others thought the drug should be withdrawn because no one knew why the drug was apparently causing heart attacks. One expert commented that "Merck prides itself on its ethical approach. I couldn't see Merck saying we're going to market a drug with a safety problem."[43]

On Monday, Dr. Kim recommended to Gilmartin that Vioxx be withdrawn from the market. The CEO agreed. The following day, Gilmartin notified the board, and the company contacted the FDA. On Thursday, September 30, Merck issued a press release, which stated in part,

[40] "FDA Official Alleges Pressure to Suppress Vioxx Findings," *Washington Post*, October 8, 2004.

[41] "Painful Withdrawal for Makers of Vioxx," *Washington Post*, October 18, 2004. Detailed data reported the following day in *The New York Times* showed that 30 of the 1,287 patients taking Vioxx had suffered a heart attack, compared with 11 of 1,299 taking a placebo; 15 on Vioxx had had a stroke or transient ischemic attack (minor stroke), compared with 7 taking a placebo.

[42] "A Widely Used Arthritis Drug Is Withdrawn," *The New York Times*, October 1, 2004.

[43] "Painful Withdrawal for Makers of Vioxx."

Merck & Co., Inc. announced today a voluntary withdrawal of VIOXX®. This decision is based on new data from a three-year clinical study. In this study, there was an increased risk for cardiovascular (CV) events, such as heart attack and stroke, in patients taking VIOXX 25 mg compared to those taking placebo (sugar pill). While the incidence of CV events was low, there was an increased risk beginning after 18 months of treatment. The cause of the clinical study result is uncertain, but our commitment to our patients is clear. . . . Merck is notifying physicians and pharmacists and has informed the Food and Drug Administration of this decision. We are taking this action because we believe it best serves the interests of patients. That is why we undertook this clinical trial to better understand the safety profile of VIOXX. And it's why we instituted this voluntary withdrawal upon learning about these data. Be assured that Merck will continue to do everything we can to maintain the safety of our medicines.

Discussion Questions

1. Do you believe that Merck acted in a socially responsible and ethical manner with regard to Vioxx? Why or why not? In your answer, please address the company's drug development and testing, marketing and advertising, relationships with government regulators and policymakers, and handling of the recall.

2. What should or could Merck have done differently, if anything?

3. What is the best way for society to protect consumers of prescription medicines? Specifically, what are the appropriate roles for pharmaceutical companies, government regulators and policymakers, patients and their physicians, and the court system in assuring the safety and effectiveness of prescription medicines?

4. How should the present system be changed, if at all, to better protect patients?

Ventria Bioscience and the Controversy over Plant-Made Medicines

"Ventria is dedicated to leading the development of plant-made pharmaceuticals that promise affordable human health products for the global community."

Scott Deeter, president and CEO, Ventria Bioscience

It was a warm, sunny day in mid-July 2004—perfect conditions for growing rice in California's lushly irrigated Sacramento Valley. But *their* rice was not in the ground, thought Scott Deeter with mounting frustration. Deeter was the president and CEO of Ventria Bioscience, a Sacramento, California–based biotechnology firm. The 20-person start-up had developed an innovative process to produce pharmaceutical proteins in the seeds of genetically modified rice. Ventria believed that its first product—a medicine designed to lessen the severity of childhood diarrhea—held great promise for public health, particularly in the developing world. The company had tested its bioengineered rice in small test plots near its headquarters. That spring, it had sought to plant at least 120 acres to begin commercial-scale production. But in its effort to obtain the necessary permits, Ventria had been stymied at nearly every turn. Facing vigorous opposition from environmentalists, food safety activists, consumer advocates, and rice farmers, the California Secretary of Agriculture had denied the company's request to plant rice on a commercial scale. Now Deeter had to figure out the best way forward for the fledgling, venture capital–backed firm.

Ventria Bioscience

Ventria Bioscience (originally called Applied Phytologics) was founded in 1993 by Dr. Raymond Rodriguez, a molecular biologist on the faculty of the University of California–Davis. In the early 1980s, Rodriguez and his graduate students had embarked on an ambitious research program aimed at improving the productivity of rice, a crop he recognized as being of great importance to human nutrition worldwide. With the support of a state government grant to encourage the commercialization of basic scientific

By Anne T. Lawrence. Copyright © 2008 by the author. All rights reserved. An earlier version of this case was presented at the 2008 annual meeting of the North American Case Research Association. The author is grateful to Dr. Raymond Rodriguez for his assistance in the preparation of this case. The author also gratefully acknowledges research funding provided by the Don and Sally Lucas Foundation.

research, Rodriguez began to develop techniques to "express" medically useful proteins in rice plants, from which they could be extracted and purified. He explained,

> We were working on expression technology—taking a gene that encodes for a medical protein and using recombinant DNA technology to produce that protein in the plant. The key technology for Ventria was the ability to express a protein abundantly in a harvestable organ or tissue. That was the breakthrough. Roots or tubers like a potato, fruits like a tomato, ears of corn, or grains of rice—those are harvestable. Expressing the protein of interest in stems and leaves is a waste of effort and resources. If you can focus your overexpression technology on a harvestable organ, you are way ahead in terms of efficiency. Very few research labs or ag biotech companies could do this at that time.

In 1993, Rodriguez incorporated Applied Phytologics to commercialize his techniques for producing medical proteins in rice. In his search for funding, he approached Dr. William Rutter, the founder and board chairman of the Emeryville biotechnology firm Chiron, with whom he had earlier worked as a postdoctoral fellow at the University of California–San Francisco. Rutter was immediately attracted to the potential of the new venture. Rodriguez recalled,

> [Rutter and I] both like disruptive technologies. Neither of us was interested in incremental improvements in yield and cost efficiencies. We *were* excited, however, by the prospects of order-of-magnitude improvements—thousand-fold increases in yield with similar fold decreases in costs. For a technology-based industry, that's really critical. We wanted to revolutionize the biopharmaceutical industry by putting production on a metric ton scale instead of a gram or kilogram scale.

With the help of an early "angel" investment from Rutter, Rodriguez opened a lab in Sacramento in 1994 and recruited a small staff of scientists and technicians, including some of his former graduate students. Within a few years, the new company launched research on around 15 different medical and industrial proteins, filed dozens of patent applications, and continued to improve its core technology, which eventually became known as the "ExpressTec System." In the venture's early years, Rodriguez chaired the board, as well as overseeing the company's R&D activities.

As the venture continued its research and development, Dr. Rodriguez gradually built a board of directors of biotech leaders and seasoned entrepreneurs. Early board members included Dr. William J. Rutter and Dr. Pablo Valenzuela, cofounders of Chiron Corporation and early pioneers in biotechnology; William H. Rutter, an attorney and venture capitalist; Ron Vogel, president of Great Western Malting; and bioentrepreneur Dr. Roberto Crea. In 2000, Thomas N. Urban, the former chairman and CEO of Pioneer Hi-Bred International, Inc., a leading agricultural seed company, was recruited to chair the board. Melvin Booth, the former CEO of MedImmune, later became a director. So did William W. Crouse, a general partner of HealthCare Ventures, and David Dwyer, a general partner in Vista Ventures; both venture capital funds specialized in biotechnology. Members of the board and their organizations collectively provided more than 85 percent of the company's financing.

Overseeing the company's day-to-day operations was a management team consisting of Frank E. Hagie, Jr., president and CEO; Dr. Delia R. Bethell, a biologist and Ventria's vice president of clinical development; and Dr. Ning Huang, a molecular biologist and vice president of research and development. (Dr. Huang had received his Ph.D. from Dr. Rodriguez in 1990.) In 2000, Dr. Rodriguez resigned from the board to devote more time to his university research and teaching. As chairman emeritus, Dr. Rodriguez continued to support the company but did not participate directly in its day-to-day operations or governance.

Plant-Made Medicines

Designing plants to produce pharmaceuticals—the work that Rodriguez and his colleagues were pursuing—represented the second wave of agricultural biotechnology. The first wave concentrated on adding traits, such as insect resistance and herbicide tolerance, to edible crops—such as corn, canola, and soybeans—and to fiber crops such as cotton. For example, "RoundUp-Ready" soybeans, developed by Monsanto, were genetically engineered to be impervious to the herbicide RoundUp, allowing farmers to spray the field with weedkiller without hurting the soybean crop. "YieldGuard" corn plants were genetically engineered to resist the corn borer, a common insect pest. The second wave, of which Ventria was part, involved the use of genetic engineering to "phytomanufacture" protein pharmaceuticals and other commercially valuable compounds in plants.

Plant-made medicines, particularly those made in rice, held many real and potential benefits. First, it was too expensive to chemically synthesize anything but the smallest proteins. Most therapeutic proteins, therefore, were produced in mammalian or microbial cell cultures. This was costly and sometimes dangerous, as animal tissues could transmit viruses or prions (such as the infectious agents that caused "mad cow" disease). Second, plant-grown medicines could also be produced much less expensively than they could be using conventional, mammalian cell-culture technology. Third, rice and other agricultural crops could be stored at room temperature from months to years, allowing processing facilities to operate year-round and respond quickly to customer demand. Fourth, the well-established existing infrastructure for harvesting, storing, and milling rice could support the production of rice-based medical proteins. A final advantage of using rice was that medical proteins produced in food crops could be delivered orally without extensive purification. The hypoallergenic and hyperdigestible rice starch served as an ideal natural medium for the recombinant protein.[1]

On the other hand, the technology also carried potential risks. Most plant-made medicines were grown in crops also used for food, posing the danger that pharmacologically active plants might become mistakenly commingled with and contaminate the human or animal food supply. Pharmaceutical plants might crossbreed with wild plants or food crops, creating unwanted hybrids, or pose a threat to insects. Also, since the modified genes being transferred into plants often originated as human or animal genes, the potential ethical issues were profound. The public's reactions to plant-made pharmaceuticals were likely to be extreme, given the high benefits, potential risks, and deep moral quandaries posed by these new technologies.

One earlier incident, in particular, had highlighted the potential risk. In 2001, ProdiGene, a Texas biotech company, had planted a test plot of corn that had been genetically engineered to produce a pig vaccine. The following year, the same field was planted with conventional soybeans, which became contaminated by volunteer corn that had sprouted from the previous season's seeds. By the time this was discovered, the soybeans had been harvested and stored in a silo containing 500,000 bushels. The genetically modified corn tainted the entire lot of soybeans, which had to be destroyed. ProdiGene was fined $250,000 and had to pay for the cleanup. Although the contaminated soybeans never reached the food supply, some saw the incident as a warning of the possible risks of commingling.[2]

---

[1] Scott Deeter, "Prepared Remarks," House of Representatives, Small Business Committee, Hearing on Different Applications for Genetically Modified Crops, June 29, 2005.

[2] "Pharming Reaps Regulatory Changes," *http://pewagbiotech.org/buzz.*

In 2004, seven companies and research organizations in the United States held permits for field tests of genetically engineered pharmaceutical plants.[3] Most, like Ventria, were small, private firms that relied mainly on venture capital as they worked toward the goal of an initial public offering or acquisition by a larger firm. Many were thinly capitalized. In 2004, according to the Biotechnology Industry Organization (BIO), an industry trade association, 60 percent of all biotechnology firms had less than a two-year supply of cash on hand and 30 percent had less than a one-year supply. Reflecting a high concentration of professionals, wages in the biotechnology industry were relatively high, averaging $65,775 in 2004; top companies invested $130,000 per employee in research and development. With high wages and research costs, many of these firms had high burn rates. A successful product launch, according to BIO, could take 10 to 15 years and cost as much as $1 billion in private investment.[4]

Lactiva and Lysomin

In April 2002, Ventria's board appointed Deeter to succeed Hagie as president and CEO. Born in Kansas, Deeter had completed his undergraduate work in economics at the University of Kansas and had then gone on to earn an MBA at the University of Chicago and a Masters of Science at the London School of Economics. He had begun his career in the technology and life sciences group of the Wall Street investment bank Salomon Brothers. He then took a position with the agribusiness firm Cargill, where he worked on a joint venture with Hoffman LaRoche to make human health products from soybeans. From Cargill, Deeter moved to Koch Industries as vice president for agriculture, where he was involved in negotiations to buy Purina Mills in 1998. In 1999, Deeter left Koch to launch CyberCrops, a venture capital–backed Web site that hosted an online grain exchange service and provided news, weather, and other information to farmers. Deeter sold the business in April 2001, after the dot-com firm was unable to attract additional capital.[5]

Deeter's first task as the new CEO of Ventria was to help Rodriguez and the board winnow down the professor's long list of projects to one or two that had the greatest likelihood of successful commercialization. Deeter and his team analyzed some two dozen possible medically active proteins. They asked three key questions of each one. Did it meet a demonstrated need? Was another company already working on it? Could it be delivered orally or topically, as opposed to injected? Rodriguez later recalled,

> What we were looking for was a protein that was extremely valuable to human health and in extremely short supply, with no competition, that could be administered orally in a partially purified form.

---

[3] "Regulation of Plant-Based Pharmaceuticals," Congressional Research Service Report for Congress, March 8, 2005, p 1. Other sources give a higher figure for the number of organizations involved in biopharming. See, for example, "Biopharming: The Emerging World Market of Plant-Based Therapeutics," *Theta Reports,* November 2002; "The Transgenic Plant Market—Profits from New Products and Novel Drugs," Drug and Market Development Corp., August 2002; and "World Agricultural Biotechnology: Transgenic Crops," Freedonia Industry Study, March 2002, cited in the *Federal Register* 68, no. 151 (April 6, 2003), p. 46435.

[4] "Biotechnology Industry Facts" and "Importation of Prescription Drugs," Biotechnology Industry Organization, *http://www.bio.org.* These figures provided by BIO are for the biotechnology industry as a whole, of which plant-made pharmaceuticals represent only a small fraction.

[5] Biographical information on Deeter appears at *http://www.ventria.com* and in press materials released in connection with the Kansas Day of Innovation, September 7, 2006, *http://www.kansasbio.org/news/pdf/8.7_panel.pdf.*

The proteins Deeter and his team selected were *lactoferrin* and *lysozyme,* two compounds naturally found in human breast milk. Medical researchers had long recognized that breast-fed babies suffered less from diarrhea than did bottle-fed babies. They had hypothesized that lactoferrin and lysozyme—both considered "natural antibiotics"—conferred some protection against bacterial gastrointestinal illness. Rodriguez had developed a process for producing these compounds abundantly in the grains of genetically modified rice plants. Since the 1960s, the standard treatment for severe diarrhea had been oral rehydration solution (ORS), a mixture of salts and sugars that had been credited with saving the lives of millions. Ventria's scientists believed that adding lactoferrin and lysozyme to ORS would improve the effectiveness of this commonly used therapy for gastrointestinal illness. The company branded its lactoferrin and lysozyme products *Lactiva* and *Lysomin,* respectively.

The potential market for such a product was huge, the company reasoned. The World Health Organization estimated that the world's children suffered 4 billion episodes of diarrhea each year. Nearly 2 million of these children died annually from complications of the disease, chiefly dehydration and malnutrition. Just 65 acres of pharmaceutical rice could generate 1,400 pounds of lactoferrin, enough to treat 650,000 children with dehydration, the company estimated.[6] It also believed that these compounds might be of value in the treatment of diarrhea suffered by tourists and military personnel and in the treatment of inflammatory bowel disease.[7] The company believed early adopters might include infant formula companies, drug companies that produced oral rehydration solution, and public health organizations like the Red Cross.

Regulation of Farmed Pharmaceuticals

In order to move forward with its plans to commercialize Lactiva and Lysomin, Ventria needed both federal and state regulatory approval. In 2004, the regulatory rules covering plant-made pharmaceuticals were complex and evolving. At the federal level, three agencies held partial jurisdiction over plant-made medicines.

FDA: The Food and Drug Administration (FDA) was responsible for the safety and effectiveness of food and medicines. Normally, a medicine produced in a genetically modified plant was subject to the same mandatory premarket approval procedures as any other medicine. However, Ventria had sought classification of Lactiva and Lysomin as "generally recognized as safe" (GRAS) food additives, which required a lower threshold for approval. A panel of scientific experts commissioned by the company had concluded that Lactiva and Lysomin met the GRAS standard, and the company had submitted these results to the FDA. In 2004, however, the FDA had not yet cleared Ventria's products for commercial sale. The FDA also maintained a "zero-tolerance" standard for pharmaceutical crop products in any food intended for animals or humans; any commingling of pharmaceutical crops and food crops was strictly forbidden. The FDA considered fields in which pharmaceutical crops were grown to be manufacturing facilities, and the agency had a right to inspect them. If necessary, it could condemn contaminated food and enjoin the manufacturer.

---

[6] "Tending the Fields: State and Federal Roles in the Oversight of Genetically Modified Crops," Pew Initiative on Food and Biotechnology, *http://pewagbiotech.com*, p. 97.

[7] Scott Deeter, "Prepared Remarks," House of Representatives, Small Business Committee, Hearing on Different Applications for Genetically Modified Crops, June 29, 2005.

EPA: The Environmental Protection Agency (EPA) was responsible for the environmental safety of food crops genetically engineered to contain pesticides or other substances potentially harmful to the environment. The agency's rules required pesticides—including those engineered into a plant—to have "no unreasonable adverse impact on the environment." Pesticide-containing plants required experimental use permits for most field tests. Because Ventria's rice did not contain pesticides, these rules did not apply to it.

USDA: For its part, the U.S. Department of Agriculture's Animal and Plant Health Inspection Service (known as APHIS) had oversight of genetically modified crops being tested in fields. Plants that were genetically modified to produce pharmaceuticals always required an APHIS permit, which generally specified acceptable field testing, storage, transportation, chain of custody, and auditing requirements. APHIS forwarded its permits to the relevant state agency, which could add its own requirements. The service also conducted its own field inspections; it inspected all pharmaceutical field trials at least annually.[8] Since 1997, Ventria had applied for and received dozens of permits from APHIS to field-test its pharmaceutical crops.

In 1986, the federal government adopted a Coordinated Framework for the Regulation of Biotechnology, which proposed to use existing agencies and laws to regulate the products of biotechnology. Michael Rodemeyer, former executive director of the Pew Initiative on Food and Biotechnology, explained the complexities of this regulatory approach for both regulators and those they regulated:

> On one level . . . the Coordinated Framework is very easy to describe. The FDA is responsible for food safety, the EPA is responsible for microbes and pesticides, and APHIS is responsible for all plants. In practice, however, it is much more complex than that. Why? In part, because some products fall into multiple categories. For example, a corn plant that has been engineered to produce its own pesticide is a plant, a pesticide, and a food, so it falls under the purview of all three agencies. In addition, each of the three agencies uses different laws to govern the products of biotechnology, and most of these laws were passed well before the advent of biotechnology.[9]

The consequence of this system, for biotechnology firms, was a complex regulatory landscape with multiple, overlapping requirements.

California Rice Industry

In California, genetically engineered rice required the approval not only of federal and state regulators, but also indirectly of the rice industry itself.

California was home to a major rice industry. The state was the leading producer of short- and medium-grain rice in the United States and second only to Arkansas in total volume of rice produced. (Other major rice-producing states were Missouri, Texas, Louisiana, and Mississippi.) In 2003, California produced 1.75 million tons of rice on 507,000 acres. Almost all of the state's rice fields lay in a swath of land abutting the Sacramento River, a broad valley that relied on the river and its tributaries for irrigation. The crop generated annual sales of more than $500 million.

---

[8] "Regulation of Plant-Based Pharmaceuticals," CRS Report for Congress, p. 4.

[9] "Opportunities and Challenges: States and the Federal Coordinated Framework Governing Agricultural Biotechnology," Pew Initiative on Food and Biotechnology, May 2006, pp. 9–10.

Forty percent of California rice was exported, mainly to Japan, Taiwan, Korea, and Turkey. The rest was consumed domestically in food, pet food, and beer. Although the United States produced only 2 percent of the world's rice, it accounted for 14 percent of the international rice trade; the nation was second only to Thailand and Vietnam in rice exports.[10] However, the U.S. share of the world rice trade was declining; it had dropped from 28 percent in 1975 to 12 percent in 2003.[11]

Rice producers in California, as in much of the developed world, used highly sophisticated technology. Farmers used laser-guided grading equipment to position perimeter levees and level their fields precisely to enable an even covering of five inches of water during the growing season. From the fourth week in April to the second week in May, weather permitting, skilled pilots used low-flying, small aircraft guided by global positioning systems to deposit pregerminated seeds onto the flooded fields. Within a few days, the plants would emerge above the surface of the water, and within a few weeks the fields would be densely covered with bright green, grasslike stalks. The grains of rice—the plant's seeds—developed in late summer, when the rice was about three feet tall. When the rice matured in September and early October, farmers drained the fields and harvested the crop with combines, which separated the grain from the stalks. After the harvest, the rice was transported to a drying facility and from there to a mill. At the mill, the rice was processed to remove the inedible hull and then either sold as brown rice or further polished into white rice. Many mills used laser sorters to remove broken or immature grains.[12]

The two stages of rice production, farming and milling, defined the two major segments of the industry. California was home to more than 2,000 rice farmers, many of whom continued to operate as family-owned businesses. They were organized through their trade association, the Rice Producers of California. Rice mills, which required significant capital investment, tended to be owned by larger organizations. Leading millers in California included agribusiness giants ADM, Far West Rice, Pacific International, and Sun West. The Farmers Rice Cooperative, owned by a cooperative of 800 growers, also operated several mills.

To protect the interests of its rice industry, the California state government had established a body known as the California Rice Commission (CRC), declaring, "The production and milling of rice in this state is . . . affected with a public interest."[13] The commission's work was supported by an assessment on farmers and millers, based on their volume of production. The CRC was authorized by law to "promote the sale of rice, educate and instruct the wholesale and retail trade with respect to the proper handling and selling [of] rice, and conduct scientific research."[14]

In 2000, California had passed the Rice Certification Act (known as AB 2622), empowering the CRC to appoint an advisory board, which would have the right to review any varieties of rice "having characteristics of commercial impact," except for rice planted for research purposes on 50 or fewer acres. The enabling legislation stated,

> There is a growing need to maintain the identity of various types of rice to satisfy
> increasing consumer demand for specialty rices. This demand requires providing
> the industry with the ability to establish the terms and conditions for the production

---

[10] California Rice Commission Statistical Report, May 1, 2005.

[11] "Tending the Fields," p. 92.

[12] Information from the California Farm Bureau Federation, the U.S. Rice Foodservice, and personal observation.

[13] California Food and Agricultural Code, Section 71005.

[14] California Legislative Counsel's Digest, *http://www.leginfo.ca/gov.*

and handling of rice in order to minimize the potential for the commingling of various types of rice, and in order to prevent commingling where reconditioning is infeasible or impossible.[15]

By statute, the advisory board was composed of four producers (farmers), four handlers (millers), and four public representatives.[16] The job of the advisory board was to recommend to the Secretary of Agriculture "proposed regulations [on] planting, producing, harvesting, transporting, drying, storing, or otherwise handling rice . . . including, but not limited to, seed application requirements, field buffer zones, handling requirements, and identity preservation requirements." Once the secretary had received a recommendation from the advisory board, he was required within 30 days to issue the proposed regulation, decline and give the advisory board a written explanation, or request additional information.[17] Although the advisory board could not legally prohibit the production of any particular rice, including genetically modified rice, as a practical matter its recommendations to the secretary carried considerable weight. As the CRC itself pointed out, "No other commodity in the U.S. has a similar mechanism to protect its industry."[18]

The CRC Advisory Board Considers Ventria's Protocol

In 2003, as Ventria ramped up to commercial-scale production, Deeter and his team made plans to expand their acreage of rice planted. Their goal was to plant 120 acres during the 2004 growing season, an amount that, for the first time, exceeded the 50-acre rule and therefore fell under the CRC advisory board's authority. Accordingly, the company began discussions with members of the advisory board to develop an acceptable production protocol. During these talks, Ventria stipulated that its rice had a "commercial impact" and agreed to a number of provisions to address the rice industry's concerns. For example, the company agreed to establish buffer zones around its plots, to transport its rice in covered trucks, and to use dedicated processing equipment.

On Monday, March 29, 2004, the advisory board of the CRC held its regular meeting at the Best Western Bonanza Inn in Yuba City, in the heart of the Sacramento Valley rice belt. Heading the agenda was a discussion of Ventria's draft protocol. Discussion was animated. Members who had been involved in the discussions with Ventria recommended that the board approve the draft protocol. Several farmers, however, expressed concern that the presence of genetically modified rice in California posed a serious commercial threat, particularly to the state's export markets. Their concern seemed to be validated by the Japanese Rice Retailers Association, which wrote the advisory board:

> From the viewpoint of rice wholesalers and retailers in Japan, it is certain that the commercialization of GM [genetically modified] rice in the U.S. will evoke a distrust of U.S. rice as a whole among Japanese consumers, since we think that it is practically impossible to guarantee no GM rice contamination in non-GM U.S. rice. As you know, most Japanese consumers react quite negatively to GM

---

[15] Ibid.

[16] The public representatives were drawn, one each, from the California Crop Improvement Association, the California Warehouse Association, the California Cooperative Rice Research Foundation, and the University of California.

[17] Legislative Counsel's Digest.

[18] "California Rice Certification Act," California Rice Commission: *Serving the California Rice Industry* [newsletter], 6, no. 3 (March/April 2004).

crops. If the GM rice is actually commercialized in the U.S., we shall strongly request the Japanese government to take necessary measures not to import any California rice to Japan.[19]

Representatives from Californians for GE-Free Agriculture[20] and the Center for Food Safety both submitted written comments expressing opposition to the protocol.

After further debate and the passage of several amendments to strengthen the protocol—including a provision that Ventria plant its rice in southern California, far from the Sacramento Valley—the advisory board voted 6 to 5 to approve Ventria's protocols. Voting in favor were all four public members, one farmer, and one miller. Most of the farmers and millers voted "nay."[21] Whether for or against, all seemed to agree that the industry was moving into uncharted water. "There's a learning curve here for producers," said Ronald Lee, a farmer. "Some have some knowledge. Some have very little. We're entering new territory here."[22]

At the request of the company, the CRC recommended "emergency status" for Ventria's protocol review. This designation would give the California Secretary of Agriculture 10 days to approve or reject it, without a period of public comment, so the company could move forward in time for the spring 2004 planting season. Over the next 10 days, the Secretary of Agriculture was lobbied from both sides. The Biotechnology Industry Association expressed its support for the emergency status:

> [We] are writing to express strong support for your authorization of a protocol approved by the California Rice Commission. . . . Plant-made pharmaceuticals offer an exciting approach to scalable, economically attractive biopharmaceutical manufacturing, producing broad access to exciting new health products to address many of the most prevalent human diseases.[23]

Several environmental and consumer groups asked the secretary to deny the request for an emergency exemption. A number of rice farmers also spoke out in the press. "Consumers in Japan and many of California's other major rice export markets have already shown strong resistance to GM crops," said Greg Massa, a grower of organic rice. "Approval of this [Ventria] rice could shatter our years of hard work in building these markets and spell trouble for all California rice farmers."[24] Joe Carrancho, a grower and former president of the Rice Producers of California, commented, "If the Japanese have the perception—underline perception—that our rice has [genetically modified organisms] in it, then we're done. You can put a bullet in our head." He and environmentalists "may be apart on some issues, but on this one we're together," he said.[25]

On April 9, the Secretary of Agriculture rejected the recommendation for emergency status for the protocol review, saying, "It is clear that the public wants an opportunity to comment prior to any authorization to plant."[26] He called for more information about federal permits and asked the CRC to consult with affected groups.

---

[19] Quoted in Greg Massa, "Pharmaceutical Rice Is a No-Grow," *Sacramento Bee,* May 14, 2004.

[20] In this context, GE refers to "genetically engineered."

[21] Minutes of the March 29, 2004, AB 2622 Advisory Board, provided to the author by the president of the California Rice Commission.

[22] "State's Rice Farmers Fear Biotech Incursion," *San Francisco Chronicle,* April 8, 2004.

[23] Biotechnology Industry Association, letter to the Honorable A. G. Kawamura, April 5, 2004.

[24] "Plan Calls for Altered Rice Crops in State," *San Diego Union-Tribune,* March 27, 2004.

[25] "State's Rice Farmers Fear Biotech Incursion."

[26] "Modified Rice Won't Be Planted," *San Francisco Chronicle,* April 10, 2004; "Protein Rice Suffers Setback," *Sacramento Bee,* April 10, 2004.

Ventria's Opponents Mobilize

Even after the secretary's decision, the controversy continued to mount. In July, four advocacy organizations—Friends of the Earth, the Center for Food Safety, Consumers Union, and Environment California—produced a detailed report detailing their concerns about pharmaceutical rice in California. The groups submitted their report to the California Department of Food and Agriculture, the California EPA, and the California Department of Health Services, as well as to the public. In the document, the groups called for "a moratorium on the cultivation of Ventria's pharmaceutical rice and other pharm crops."[27]

The activist alliance made four arguments for a moratorium on pharmaceutical rice. First, it argued that contamination of food rice by genetically modified pharmaceutical rice grown outdoors was "inevitable," because of multiple potential pathways:

> Contamination of human foods with plant-made pharmaceuticals can occur through dispersal of seed or pollen. Wildlife, especially waterfowl, can transport seeds for long distances, as can extreme weather events such as floods or tornadoes. Harvesting equipment can carry seed residues to conventional fields, seeds can be spilled from trucks, or unharvested seeds can sprout as volunteers amid the following year's crop. Cross-pollination occurs at considerable distances in high winds or by insect, even with self-pollinating crops such as rice.[28]

The report argued that Ventria's protocols did not offer sufficient protection against contamination:

> The lack of detailed plans to prevent birds from spreading the pharm rice is particularly disturbing. California's Central Valley is one of the most important wintering areas for waterfowl in North America. Viable seed are known to pass through the gut of many waterfowl species, making waterfowl effective dispersal agents for many wetland plant species, including rice. . . .
>
> Ventria's protocol also does not deal with the possibility of seed dispersal through flooding. . . . Historical records show that floods of various magnitude occur not infrequently in the Sacramento Valley. . . .
>
> Ventria's . . . one-year fallow period following cultivation of its pharm rice means a greater likelihood of pharm rice volunteers contaminating a commercial rice crop grown subsequently in the same field. . . .
>
> The 100-foot isolation distance from food-grade rice . . . may not be adequate to prevent cross-pollination.[29]

What would happen if Ventria's rice did contaminate the food supply? Once commingling had occurred, the report continued, the potential for adverse impacts to human health was great. Possible consequences included infections, allergies, and autoimmune disorders:

> While human lactoferrin has antimicrobial properties, it paradoxically poses the potential hazard of exacerbating infections by certain pathogens capable of using it as a source of needed iron. Such pathogens include bacteria that cause

---

[27] "Pharmaceutical Rice in California: Potential Risks to Consumers, the Environment, and the California Rice Industry," Friends of the Earth, Center for Food Safety, Consumers Union, and Environment California, July 2004, p. 1.

[28] Ibid., p. 6.

[29] Ibid., p. 7.

gonorrhea and meningitis, as well as [those] implicated in causing ulcers and certain forms of stomach cancer. . . . Ventria's rice-expressed lysozyme and lactoferrin have two characteristics of proteins that cause food allergies: resistance to digestion and to breakdown by heat. . . . Pharmaceutical proteins generated by inserting human genes into plants . . . are usually different from their natural human counterparts. These differences may cause the body to perceive them as foreign, resulting in immune system responses.[30]

Finally, Ventria's rice could have serious environmental consequences if it cross-bred with existing weed species, creating noxious "super weeds," the report argued:

Ventria's rice-produced pharmaceuticals have antibacterial and antifungal properties. If these traits are passed to related weed species such as wild and annual red rice, they could lend these weeds a fitness boost, promoting their spread.[31]

Moving Forward

In discussions with representatives of the CRC advisory board over the past year and a half, Deeter and his team had offered numerous concessions to address the concerns of rice farmers and others. The company had agreed to grow rice many miles away from any rice grown for food. It had promised to use dedicated equipment for field production, storage, and transportation and to use only processing equipment that was restricted to bioengineered rice or had been thoroughly sanitized before reuse. The company had agreed to keep detailed logs and to allow third-party inspections. None of this, however, had been enough to satisfy the company's critics. In biotechnology, things always seemed to take longer, cost more, and face hurdles that could not have been anticipated when the company was started. Now another planting season had come and gone, and Ventria's investors appeared no closer to successful commercialization than they had been a year earlier.

Discussion Questions

1. What is the problem facing Scott Deeter and Ventria?
2. What groups have a stake in Ventria's actions? Identify the relevant stakeholders and for each, state its interests and sources of power.
3. What options might emerge from a dialogue between Ventria and its relevant stakeholders?
4. If Ventria chooses to employ a political action strategy, how might it go about influencing relevant regulators?
5. If Ventria chooses not to engage in dialogue or political action (or dialogue and political action are unsuccessful), what other options does the company have?
6. What do you think Ventria should do now, and why?

[30] Ibid., p. 3.
[31] Ibid., p. 3.

Hewlett-Packard's Secret Surveillance of Directors and Journalists

On September 28, 2006, members of Congress, their staff, reporters, prospective witnesses, and the curious public packed the wood-paneled hearing room of the U.S. House Committee on Energy and Commerce. The subject of the day's hearing, called by the Subcommittee on Oversight and Investigations, was "Hewlett-Packard's Pretexting Scandal."[1] At issue were methods the technology firm had used to investigate the unauthorized disclosure of nonpublic information to the press by members of its board of directors. Hewlett-Packard (HP) apparently had hired investigators who had used a technique known as pretexting, calling the phone company and posing as someone else in order to obtain that person's records. *Newsweek* had summed up the situation in a cover story published 10 days earlier: "Lying, spying, name-calling, finger-pointing—all of it is a tragicomedy that Shakespeare might've penned if he had gotten an MBA."[2]

Hewlett-Packard and its board chairman, Patricia Dunn, had initially defended the company's investigation of directors and journalists, saying aggressive efforts to ferret out the source of leaks were fully justified. But in the past few weeks, the situation had begun to spin out of control, as the Securities and Exchange Commission and the California Attorney General had opened probes into the company's actions.[3] Now nearly two dozen of HP's top executives, directors, lawyers, and investigators—including the company's CEO Mark Hurd—had been called before Congress to account for their firm's possibly out-of-bounds behavior and to explain what they intended to do about it. Shortly before the September hearing, Dunn had agreed to resign from the board, and HP's general counsel, Ann Baskins—who had supervised the investigation—had left the firm. Now Dunn faced the daunting challenge of defending her actions, and Hurd, as CEO and newly appointed board chairman, had to chart a way forward for the company.

This is an abridged version of a longer case, Anne T. Lawrence, Randall D. Harris, and Sally Baack, "Unauthorized Disclosure: Hewlett-Packard's Secret Surveillance of Directors and Journalists," *Case Research Journal* 28, no. 1 (Winter 2008). All materials in this case, unless otherwise noted, are drawn from internal company documents submitted by Hewlett-Packard in connection with the hearing, "Hewlett-Packard's Pretexting Scandal," held on September 28, 2006, before the Subcommittee on Oversight and Investigations of the Committee on Energy and Commerce, House of Representatives, Serial No. 109-146, or from the transcript of this hearing. Full references are available upon request. Copyright © 2008 by the *Case Research Journal* and Anne T. Lawrence, Randall D. Harris, and Sally Baack. All rights reserved.

[1] "Probing the Pretexters: Congress Grills Hewlett-Packard Executives over 'Sleaze' Investigative Tactics," *The Wall Street Journal,* September 29, 2006.

[2] David A. Kaplan, "HP Scandal: The Boss Who Spied on Her Board," *Newsweek,* September 18, 2006.

[3] "H-P Faces Probe over Its Inquiry into Board Leaks," *The Wall Street Journal,* September 7, 2006.

Corporate Governance at Hewlett-Packard

Hewlett-Packard described itself as a "technology solutions provider to consumers, businesses, and institutions globally."[4] Founded in 1939 in a garage near the Stanford University campus by David Packard and Bill Hewlett to make test and measurement instruments, the company had grown to become a leader in the information technology industry. HP had four main business units, focusing on information technology infrastructure, imaging and printing, business services, and personal computers and devices. Headquartered in Palo Alto, California, the company in 2005 earned $3.5 billion on revenues of $86.7 billion.[5] It employed around 150,000 people and had a presence in more than 170 countries.

In 2006, an 11-person board of directors had overall responsibility for HP's strategy and policies. Patricia Dunn, who had joined the board in 1998, served as chairman from February 2005 until her resignation in September 2006. Dunn, who held a degree in journalism, had begun her career as a secretarial assistant. She had risen rapidly to become, at age 42, CEO of Barclays Global Investors, a firm that managed more than $1 trillion in assets, mainly for institutions. At Barclays, Dunn was known for her customer focus and adherence to strict ethical standards in the stewardship of others' money. In 2002, Dunn stepped down as Barclays' CEO after being diagnosed with cancer. Another prominent member of HP's board was Thomas Perkins, a partner in the powerful Silicon Valley venture capital firm Kleiner Perkins Caufield & Byers. Perkins had a long association with HP; he had headed the company's research labs and later its computer division. George (Jay) Keyworth II, the board's longest-serving member, was a nuclear physicist and chair of the Progress & Freedom Foundation. (Exhibit A presents members of the board from 1999 to 2006 and indicates which board members were insiders.)

HP's board had a recent history of turmoil and turnover. In 2002, Carly Fiorina, CEO since 1999, had initiated a merger with computer maker Compaq. Although most of the board supported the move, Walter Hewlett, a son of company founder Bill Hewlett and a long-time director, opposed it, saying the merger would destroy the egalitarian culture that was a core element of his father's legacy. Hewlett and his allies led a bruising proxy fight in which they worked to mobilize institutional investors to vote against the acquisition. Despite opposition from both the Hewlett and Packard families, stockholders ultimately approved the merger in a close vote, and Hewlett subsequently left the board.[6]

Shortly after the merger, Perkins rejoined the HP board (on which he had earlier served briefly), moving over from Compaq's board. One of Perkins's first actions as a director was to help organize a new technology committee "to make recommendations to the board as to scope, direction, quality, investment levels, and execution of HP's technology strategies."[7] Initial members of the committee included Keyworth; Lawrence Babbio, the president of Verizon; and Richard Hackborn, HP's former executive vice president of computer products. According to James B. Stewart, writing in *The New Yorker,* the technology committee soon came to function as a virtual "board-within-the-board,"

---

[4] *www.hp.com/hpinfo.*

[5] Hewlett-Packard Form 10-K for the fiscal year ending October 31, 2005, p. 71.

[6] The story of the merger proxy vote is told in Peter Burrows, *Back-Fire: Carly Fiorina's High-Stakes Battle for the Soul of Hewlett-Packard* (Hoboken, NJ: John Wiley & Sons, 2003); and George Anders, *Perfect Enough: Carly Fiorina and the Reinvention of Hewlett-Packard* (New York: Penguin, 2004).

[7] "Hewlett-Packard Company Board of Directors Technology Committee Charter," *www.hp.com/hpinfo/investor/technology.pdf.*

Exhibit A

Hewlett-Packard Board of Directors, 1999–2006

	1999	2000	2001	2002	2003	2004	2005	2006
Richard A. Hackborn	A	A	A	A	A	A	A	A
George A. Keyworth	A	A	A	A	A	A	A	A
Robert P. Wayman(*)	A	A	A	A	A		A	A
Sam Ginn	A	A	A	A				
Walter B. Hewlett(**)	A	A	A	A				
Susan Packard Orr(**)	A	A						
Thomas E. Everett	A							
John B. Fery	A							
Jean-Paul G. Gimon	A							
David M. Lawrence	A							
David W. Packard(**)	A							
Lewis E. Platt(*)	A							
Paul F. Miller								
Phillip M. Condit	A	A	A	A	A			
Patricia C. Dunn	A	A	A	A	A	A	A	A
Robert E. Knowling		A	A	A	A	A	A	
Carleton S. Fiorina(*)		A	A	A	A	A		
Lawrence T. Babbio					A	A	A	A
Lucille S. Salhany					A	A	A	A
Sanford M. Litvack					A	A		
Thomas J. Perkins					A		A	A
Robert L. Ryan						A	A	A
Sari M. Baldauf								A
John H. Hammergren								A
Mark V. Hurd(*)								A
Total Directors	14	10	9	9	11	9	9	11

Note: A = Active board membership at the time of annual meeting. Board membership changed between meetings during this time period. Lewis E. Platt completed his term as chairman in 1999. Carly Fiorina served as chairman from 1999 to 2005. Patricia Dunn served as chairman from February 2005 to September 2006. Mark Hurd became chairman in September 2006.

(*) Inside director (i.e., HP employee at the time of board service). Richard Hackborn and Thomas Perkins were former HP employees at the time of board service.

(**) Member of one of the founding families (Hewletts and Packards).

Source: HP proxy statements.

taking up key strategic issues, including market entry and exit, mergers and acquisitions, and competitor and partner relationships.[8]

A Leak of Confidential Board Deliberations

The original unauthorized disclosure—leak of confidential board deliberations—that initiated the chain of events leading to the September 28 hearings had occurred 20 months earlier, before Dunn had become chairman. On January 21, 2005, Fiorina received an urgent e-mail from HP's press office, saying that the *The Wall Street Journal* was planning to run a story about an off-site strategic planning meeting of the board that had

[8] James B. Stewart, "The Kona Files," *The New Yorker,* February 19 and 26, 2007, p. 155.

taken place several days earlier. The reporter had apparently talked with several directors about the board's discussions. Fiorina later recalled in her memoir,

> It is hard to convey how violated I felt. Until a board makes a decision, its deliberations are confidential. . . . Trust is a business imperative. No board or management team can operate effectively without it. . . . I sent an e-mail message to the board. I informed them of the leak. I said this was completely unacceptable behavior by a board member. I convened a conference call for Saturday morning. I was as cold as ice during the call. I said the board could not operate in this way and I would not. . . . Jay [Keyworth], Dick [Hackborn], and Tom [Perkins] all acknowledged that the reporter had contacted them. They all denied they had spoken with her.[9]

On Monday morning, *The Wall Street Journal* ran an article on page A1 by Pui-Wing Tam. The article reported,

> Directors of Hewlett-Packard Co., unhappy with the uneven performance of the giant printer and computer maker, are considering a reorganization that would distribute some key day-to-day responsibilities of Chairman and Chief Executive Carly Fiorina among other executives, said people familiar with the situation. At its annual planning meeting between Jan. 12 and Jan. 15, H-P's board discussed giving three senior executives more authority and autonomy over key operating units, according to people familiar with the matter. . . . The board's concerns, according to these people, include the mediocre performance of the PC business, which ekes out thin profits, and the perception that H-P holds weak market positions against IBM and Dell.[10]

The board agreed to ask the company's outside counsel to conduct an investigation of possible leaks. Over the next several days, the attorney interviewed all members of the board. He reported his results to the board in a conference call on January 27. Fiorina recalled,

> [The attorney] informed us that two, possibly three, board members had leaked confidential board conversations. His report named only one member, because only Tom Perkins was honest enough to admit that he'd spoken to the press, although he was adamant that he had been a "second source." Although I appreciated Tom's candor, I was deeply disturbed when no one else spoke up. As the call progressed, all but one board member [Keyworth] asked questions or made comments.[11] . . . Everyone on that call knew that both Tom and Jay were the sources. They were allies. They were the ones pushing for the reorganization described in the article. I was clear and unequivocal that this was unacceptable behavior. They didn't like that.[12]

The next meeting of the board was held on February 7 at the Chicago Airport, an off-site location chosen to avoid further press speculation. After some brief preliminaries, Dunn asked Fiorina if she had anything to say. Fiorina spoke to the group about her views on strategy and other matters. Dunn then asked her to leave the room. When Fiorina was called back three hours later, Dunn and Robert Knowling informed her she had been fired. At their meeting, the board had also decided to name Dunn non-executive chairman and Robert Wayman, HP's chief financial officer, as interim chief executive while they conducted a search for a new CEO.

---

[9] Carly Fiorina, *Tough Choices: A Memoir* (New York: Penguin, 2006), pp. 290–92.

[10] "Hewlett-Packard Considers a Reorganization; Management Move Stems from Performance Concerns; Helping Fiorina 'Succeed,'" *The Wall Street Journal*, January 24, 2005.

[11] *Tough Choices*, p. 293.

[12] Quoted in Stewart, "The Kona Files," p. 155.

"Something Had to Be Done"

Dunn believed that one of her first priorities as chair was to address the board leaks. She recalled,

> Not surprisingly, given [the] breakdown of boardroom sanctity and continued disclosures of board-level information making their way into print over the ensuing week, many directors expressed to me their strong opinion that something had to be done to determine their source and bring them to an end. In fact, the majority of directors told me during my first few weeks as chairman that, next to leading the board's CEO search, coming to grips with HP's famously leaky board should be my top priority.[13]

Dunn believed that a vigorous leak investigation was imperative. She commented,

> The most fundamental duties of a director—the duties of deliberation and candor—rely entirely upon the absolute trust that each director must have in one another's confidentiality. This is true for trivial as well as important matters, because even trivial information that finds its way from the boardroom to the press corrodes trust among directors. . . . The most sensitive aspects of a company's business come before its board: strategy; executive succession; acquisitions; business plans; product development; and key supplier relations. That is exactly the type of information a company's competitors and those who trade in its stock would love to have before that information becomes public. Boards have an unquestionable obligation to take appropriate steps to prevent this happening.[14]

Dunn sought the advice of Wayman, who referred her to HP's chief of global security. He, in turn, referred her to Ron DeLia, whose firm, Security Outsourcing Solutions (SOS), based in Massachusetts, had done contract investigative work for HP for several years. Dunn later referred to DeLia's firm as a "captive subsidiary."[15] In April, Dunn and DeLia exchanged several phone calls and e-mails, putting in motion an investigation to identify the source of the leaks.[16] Dunn proposed to refer to the investigation by the code name Project Kona, after the location of her vacation home in Hawaii. By this time, the focus of the investigation had expanded to include several other journalists who had published articles in *BusinessWeek* and *The New York Times*. These articles had included information that had possibly been leaked following a board meeting in March, at which the board had discussed the selection of Mark Hurd as Fiorina's successor.

DeLia subcontracted part of the investigative work for Project Kona to the Action Research Group (ARG) of Melbourne, Florida. DeLia had known and worked with ARG for more than two decades and had often used the firm to obtain phone and fax records for persons of interest. ARG, in turn, sometimes subcontracted work to other individuals. In addition to analyzing phone records, DeLia reviewed articles written by the journalists

---

[13] Patricia C. Dunn, "My Role in the Hewlett-Packard Leak Investigation," written testimony provided to the Subcommittee on Investigations of the House Energy and Commerce Committee, p. 2.

[14] Ibid., pp. 3–4.

[15] "Interviews of Ron DeLia—DRAFT," August 21, 2006, by attorneys conducting an investigation of the investigation, Hearing Documents, p. 630; Dunn, "My Role," p. 9. DeLia's background is further described in "HP Investigator Has Contentious Past; Forays into Other Ventures Have Sparked Disputes over Business, Finance," *The Wall Street Journal*, September 14, 2006, p. A18.

[16] DeLia to Dunn, e-mail, April 19. 2005, Hearing Documents, p. 237.

and researched patterns of "potential affiliation" among the journalists and HP directors. On June 14, Security Outsourcing Solutions delivered its preliminary findings to Dunn. The report described the firm's methods, and indicated it had not found the source of the leaks. Although the investigation had not succeeded, Dunn was hopeful that the investigation itself had had a dampening effect, as by this time no leaks from the boardroom had occurred for some time.

A New "Major Leak"

From January 19 to 21, 2006, the board met again for its annual off-site strategic planning meeting. Soon after, Dunn received an e-mail from the head of HP's public relations department, saying there had been a "major leak." The article in question had appeared on CNET, an online technology publication. In an article published on January 23, reporters Dawn Kawamoto and Tom Krazit had written,

> Hewlett-Packard executives are mulling plans to improve over the next 18 months the technology the company uses to manage its direct sales, while it continues with commercial printing efforts and acquisitions of software companies. . . .
>
> HP CEO Mark Hurd, the company's board of directors and senior executives gathered at the computer giant's annual management retreat to discuss long-term strategies. . . .
>
> According to the source, HP is considering making more acquisitions in the infrastructure software arena. Those acquisitions would include security software companies, storage software makers, and software companies that serve the blade server market.[17]

Dunn circulated the CNET article to the board. To Perkins, she sent this e-mail:

> Tom, this will disturb you as much as it disturbs me. For our discussion. Break out the lie detectors. Regards, Pattie.[18]

Perkins responded,

> This is incredible! I can't believe that this has happened again. But, in reading it, I don't think it damages the company too much—it's just that the news should come from us when we want it to, and not when it is leaked. I doubt if this came from a board member. Frankly, I don't think a board member would have remembered this much detail . . . I think Mark [Hurd] must put the fear of God (i.e. Mark Hurd) . . . to stop this.[19]

This time, Dunn consulted Ann Baskins, HP's general counsel. Baskins recommended that the investigation be turned over to Kevin Hunsaker, a senior attorney in HP's legal department who had responsibility for overseeing investigations into violations of standards of business conduct, including employee wrongdoing.[20]

"All Investigative Alternatives"

On Monday, January 23—the day the article appeared—Hunsaker assembled a team to carry out the second leak investigation, which became known as Kona II.

---

[17] "HP Outlines Long-Term Strategy," CNET, January 23, 2006.

[18] Stewart, "The Kona Files," p. 152.

[19] Ibid., p. 154. Perkins apparently provided these e-mails to Stewart, who does not give their exact dates.

[20] Susan Beck, "Where Will the Troubles End for Sonsini and HP?" *Law.com*, December 6, 2006, at *www.law.com*.

The Kona II team went to work immediately. They assigned undercover operatives to Keyworth (whom they suspected from the beginning), following him to Boulder, Colorado, from January 30 to February 1, where he was giving a lecture at the University of Colorado. Surveillance teams later separately followed Keyworth's wife and Dawn Kawamoto, the CNET journalist. These activities turned up nothing of relevance; the operatives observed Mrs. Keyworth playing bingo at a local community center, and Kawamoto picking up her child after school.

Fred Adler, a member of HP's IT security team, examined the company's internal telephone and Internet records for evidence of contact with Kawamoto and her associates at CNET. This effort turned up nothing other than some routine contacts between CNET and HP's public relations department.

The following day, Thursday, February 2, the team provided an initial briefing to Dunn in HP's Palo Alto offices. The presentation slides reported that the team was considering "all investigative alternatives." It also noted, "While time is of the essence, the investigation must be comprehensive, accurate, and in compliance with all laws and accepted investigative principles."[21]

"Subject: Phone Records"

As the team in California proceeded with their work, DeLia—working from Massachusetts—once again mobilized the Action Research Group. He instructed the Florida investigators to obtain the home phone, office phone, cell phone, and fax records of Kawamoto, as well as those of seven current and former board members (including Keyworth and Perkins), two HP employees, eight other journalists, and in some cases those of their family members. ARG quickly began producing results, sending DeLia detailed logs of phone records, showing numbers called and the time and duration of the calls.

> **HUNSAKER TO GENTILUCCI,** January 30, 2006 [e-mail]. Subject: Phone Records: Hi Tony, How does Ron [DeLia] get cell and home phone records? Is it all above board? [Anthony Gentilucci was manager of global security investigations for HP and a member of the Kona II team.]
>
> **GENTILUCCI:** The methodology used is social engineering. He has investigators call operators under some ruse, to obtain the cell phone records over the phone. It's verbally communicated to the investigator, who has to write it down. In essence the operator shouldn't give it out, and that person is liable in some sense. Ron can describe the operation obviously better, as well as the fact that this technique since he, and others, have been using it, has not been challenged. I think it's on the edge, but above board. We use pretext interviews on a number of investigations to extract information and/or make covert purchases of stolen property, in a sense, all undercover operations.
>
> **HUNSAKER:** I shouldn't have asked . . . [ellipses in original]

DeLia later told attorneys hired by HP to investigate the Kona II activities that he subscribed to proprietary databases, available only to licensed investigators and law enforcement officials, which provided Social Security numbers along with other information about individuals. The interview summary stated, "DeLia supplied ARG with Social Security numbers for all subjects of pretexting. DeLia thought that ARG used the last four digits of the numbers as required." Perkins later asked AT&T, his phone service

---

[21] "Project Kona II," presentation slides, Hearing Documents, p. 315.

provider, whether or not his phone records had been pretexted during this period. AT&T responded,

> [T]he third-party pretexter who got details about Perkins's local home telephone usage was able to provide the last four digits of Perkins's Social Security number and that was sufficient identification for AT&T. The impersonator convinced an AT&T customer service representative to send the details electronically to an e-mail account at yahoo.com that on its face had nothing to do with Perkins.[22]

By February 10, DeLia's operatives had obtained information for more than 240 telephone, cell phone, and fax numbers.

"A Key Piece of the Puzzle"

On Monday evening, February 6, DeLia provided the team with an apparently critical piece of evidence: telephone logs supplied by his investigator that showed several calls from Kawamoto to Keyworth's home shortly before her article came out. Even though it was after hours, some members of the team were apparently checking their e-mails and seemed immediately to recognize the information's importance.

> **GENTILUCCI TO HUNSAKER, DeLIA, NYE, and ADLER,** 9:33 p.m. [e-mail]: . . . appears to be a "key" piece of the puzzle, "worth" a lot of weight in this case. Sorry, I couldn't help myself. Lets keep on moving forward with the plan. Good work team. [Vince Nye and Fred Adler were HP employees and members of the Kona II team.]

> **HUNSAKER TO DeLIA, GENTILUCCI, NYE, AND ADLER,** 9:36 p.m. [e-mail]: Do we have the outbound calls from Keyworth's home from that date, so we can confirm that he and/or his wife . . . were at home? . . . Do you know what time of day the call went from Kawamoto to the Keyworth residence? . . . I'm starting to get excited . . .

The next morning, a junior member of the investigation team, Vince Nye, contacted two of his superiors.

> **NYE TO GENTILUCCI, cc TO HUNSAKER,** February 7, 2006, 9:32 a.m. [e-mail]: Tony: I have serious reservations about what we are doing. As I understand Ron's methodology in obtaining the phone record information it leaves me with the opinion that it is very unethical at the least and probably illegal. If it is not totally illegal, then it is leaving HP in a position that could damage our reputation or worse. I am requesting that we cease this phone number gathering method immediately and discount any of its information. I think we need to re-focus our strategy and proceed on the high ground course.

He also wrote Fred Adler, a fellow investigator.

> **NYE TO ADLER,** February 7, 2006, 1:30 p.m. [e-mail]: Fred: This information is too detailed to obtain via voice over the phone by a pretense operative . . .

He wrote again a few minutes later.

> **NYE TO ADLER,** February 7, 2006, 1:46 p.m. [e-mail]: Its clear from the earlier call, that this is "Don't ask Don't tell" with regard to Ron's role . . . Kevin

---

[22] David A. Kaplan, "Intrigue in High Places," *Newsweek*, September 18, 2006, paraphrasing a letter from AT&T to Perkins and provided by Perkins to the SEC and to *Newsweek*.

thinks . . . He doesn't want to go make sure she knows . . . This is the guy who is suppose to keep us above the board!!!!!!!

ADLER TO NYE, February 7, 2006, 2:42 p.m. [e-mail]: Agreed, I am VERY concerned about the legality of this information.[23]

"In Compliance with the Law"

Sometime that day the investigation team met to review their progress. Adler later testified before Congress:

[A]t that meeting . . . both myself and Mr. Nye . . . started questioning Mr. Gentilucci and Mr. DeLia and Mr. Hunsaker about the pretext calling and how the information was being obtained and whether it was in compliance with the law.

Hunsaker apparently followed up on his team members' concerns about the legality of the methods used by DeLia's contractors, because he received the following e-mail from DeLia:

DeLIA TO HUNSAKER, February 7, 2006, 2:12 p.m: Kevin: I sent an email to my source in FL and asked them if there were any state laws prohibiting pretexting telephone companies for call records. Following is their response. We are comfortable there are no Federal laws prohibiting the practice. Note: The Federal Trade Commission has jurisdiction. The firm has been in business for over 20 years and is properly licensed in FL and other states. I have been utilizing their services for approximately 8 to 10 years. Ron. "As of right now there are no laws against pretexting. We are on top of everything going on regarding this issue and if any law were to pass we will be the first to let you know." [underlining in original]

An attorney conducting an internal probe for HP later reported on an interview with Hunsaker about his research on the legality of pretexting:

. . . after Nye and Adler expressed concern about the legality of pretexting . . . [Hunsaker] asked DeLia . . . to confirm the method's legality with the Florida investigators. . . . Asked about the scope of his [own] research, Hunsaker said he did about an hour's worth of online research on the legality of pretexting . . .

Ann Baskins, HP's general counsel, later recalled that during a meeting with Hunsaker in or around early March she had specifically asked him to consult a legal expert to confirm the legality of pretexting. Hunsaker delegated this task to Gentilucci, who contacted an attorney he knew in Boston. This attorney advised the team that pretexting of financial institutions was prohibited by statute, but that no law specifically banned the pretexting of phone records.

"The Overwhelming Weight of Evidence"

On March 10, 2006, Hunsaker issued an 18-page draft report of the investigation, addressed to Dunn, Hurd, and Baskins. The executive summary concluded that the investigation had likely found the source of the leaks:

[T]he overwhelming weight of evidence reviewed by the Investigation Team indicates that the source of the leak is HP Board member George Keyworth II.

---

[23] From the context, the "she" in Nye's e-mail appears to be Ann Baskins.

Specifically, the content of each of the articles citing a "source" written by Kawamoto in the past 4 years, the numerous connections made the Investigation Team tying Keyworth to the leaks, and the telephonic contact between Kawamoto and Keyworth in January and February of 2006, all clearly identify and establish Keyworth as the only feasible source of the leaks.

The report concluded by posing, but not answering, the question "whether Keyworth should be interviewed in conjunction with the investigation" and, if so, by whom and to what purpose.

The following week, HP's directors and many top executives gathered in Los Angeles for the annual shareholders' meeting. On the evening of March 18, Hurd, Dunn, and Baskins were in the lounge of the Park Hyatt Hotel when they noticed Keyworth, the board member they suspected, sitting at the bar. Hurd told his companions, "I'll take care of this."[24] Dunn later recalled,

> Mr. Hurd . . . has related many times to me and to others that he tried in every way he could to get Mr. Keyworth to come forward and admit his culpability. Ms. Baskins and I were sitting near them during this meeting, which occurred over cocktails in the hotel lobby, and I could see that Mr. Hurd was intensely engaged with Mr. Keyworth. Mr. Hurd subsequently described to me . . . that, although he gave Mr. Keyworth several chances to come forward, Mr. Keyworth declined to acknowledge his culpability.[25]

"But One Board Seat from Which to Resign"

On May 18, the board gathered in Palo Alto for its regular meeting. Ten directors were present. Immediately prior to the meeting, Robert Ryan, chairman of the audit committee, met with Keyworth privately to inform him about the findings of the investigation. Dunn recalled this exchange:

> Mr. Ryan reported [to Hurd, Dunn, Baskins, and HP's outside counsel] after his interview with Mr. Keyworth that Mr. Keyworth's immediate response to hearing the investigation's results was to admit he was the leaker, followed by the question, "Why didn't you just ask me?" All of us were flummoxed by this response, as it was clear to all of us that for the prior 15 months Mr. Keyworth could have come forward at any time to acknowledge his culpability.[26]

According to the minutes of the May 18 meeting, the first item on the agenda was the findings of the leak investigation. Dunn reported that the investigation had been conclusive and then turned to Ryan, who summarized the report for the board and stated that Keyworth had been identified as the leaker and had, that morning, acknowledged being the source for the CNET article. After some further discussion, Keyworth addressed the group. The minutes of the meeting summarized his statement:

> [Keyworth] described the circumstances under which he became acquainted with Dawn Kawamoto, explaining that he initially established contact with Kawamoto at the request of former CEO Carly Fiorina, who asked Keyworth to speak with certain members of the media in support of the Compaq merger. He added that

---

[24] Stewart, "The Kona Files," p. 162.

[25] Dunn, "My Role," p. 21.

[26] Ibid., p. 23.

Kawamoto emerged as an influential reporter who reported favorably on HP. He said that his intent in describing the January board meeting to Kawamoto was to help the company and in particular to convey that HP and its CEO were addressing key growth opportunities and other important strategies rather than narrowly focused on cost-cutting efforts. Dr. Keyworth assured the board that he had not been a source for other stories by different reporters, including articles written by Pui-Wing Tam of *The Wall Street Journal*. He indicated that he would not make unauthorized disclosures to the media in the future.

Keyworth then left the room. After a discussion that lasted about 90 minutes, the board voted by secret ballot, 6 to 3, to ask for Keyworth's resignation. Dunn later recalled this discussion and its aftermath:

> Mr. Perkins became very agitated when it became clear that a majority of the board did not think Mr. Keyworth had handled his response to the board appropriately and thus were strongly leaning toward asking for his resignation. A secret ballot, suggested by another director, was taken, in which a strong majority of the board voted to ask Mr. Keyworth to resign, which later in the meeting he refused to do. At that point Mr. Perkins erupted in great anger. Mr. Perkins's anger was directed entirely at me, and centered on the "betrayal" he alleged at my not having abided by an agreement that he said we had to cover up the name of the leaker. I had little opportunity to respond to this outburst except to say, "Tom, we had no such agreement." . . . At no point during Mr. Perkins's outburst did he make any statements whatsoever about the leak investigation—including its justification and methods. Mr. Perkins told the board he resigned and he left the room, at which point a director put a motion on the table to accept his resignation, which was then seconded and carried unanimously.[27]

Several days later, Perkins wrote a confidential memo to the members of the board of the News Corporation, on which he served, to explain his actions, in which he stated,

> I was very angry at the time, but now that over a week has passed, I think that I did the right thing, and to paraphrase the Revolutionary War hero, Nathan Hale ("I regret that I have but one life to give to my country"), I regret that I have but one HP board seat from which to resign.

On May 22, HP filed a Form 8-K with the SEC reporting Perkins's resignation, as required by law, giving no reason for his action.

"Untoward and Illegal Practices"

On July 28, Perkins wrote Baskins, with a copy to Hurd and HP's outside counsel, saying he could not accept the minutes of the May 18 board meeting as written. One of his main points was that the minutes did not convey his concerns about the legality of the leak investigation.

> An essential point, which I explicitly made, questioned the legality of the surveillance of director's communications by the chairman's outside experts. I specifically questioned this at the time of the meeting and question it still. As written the minutes state that I concurred in the nature of the investigation—this

---

[27] Ibid., pp. 24–25.

is not true. I was under the impression that the investigation involved examining calendars, travel schedules, and such. I had no idea that personal communications were involved, and had I known that this was the case I would have brought the matter (of the intrusive nature of the investigation) to the board, for full examination, well in advance of the May 18th meeting.

On August 16, after an exchange of correspondence with AT&T, his telephone service provider, Perkins wrote again, this time asking that HP provide a copy of his letter to the SEC. "I have direct proof of these untoward and illegal practices," he stated. "My personal phone records were 'hacked.'"

Baskins wrote back, indicating that the board had decided it would not amend the minutes or the filings with the SEC noting Perkin's resignation, because they were accurate. Perkins's attorney responded, threatening to "take appropriate action."[28] Shortly thereafter, the SEC, the FBI, and the California Attorney General began investigations.

In early September, the story broke wide open in the media. On September 18, *Newsweek* ran a cover story, "Intrigue in High Places: To Catch a Leaker, Hewlett-Packard's Chairwoman Spied on the Home-Phone Records of Its Board of Directors." The author, who was writing a book about Perkins's yacht, had interviewed Perkins extensively for the piece. Articles in *BusinessWeek, The Wall Street Journal,* and other leading publications also appeared around this time, and congressional staffers contacted the company about a possible House of Representatives inquiry.

"The Final Story"

Now, facing members of Congress, the press, and the public, just four of the potential witnesses called to the hearing—Dunn, Adler, Hurd, and HP's outside counsel—agreed to testify. The others—Baskins, Gentilucci, Hunsaker, DeLia, and various investigators from Florida, Colorado, Texas, and Georgia—all pleaded their Fifth Amendment rights against self-incrimination.

Dunn vigorously defended her actions and stated, "I do not take personal responsibility for what happened." She continued,

> I am neither a lawyer nor an investigator, and in this matter, I relied on the expertise of people in whom I had full confidence based upon their positions with the company and my years of experience working with them. I deeply regret that so many people, including me, were badly let down by this reliance. . . .

In her written testimony, she offered this reflection:

> When the final story is written on what happened at HP, I believe that its roots will be understood as emanating from a clash between the old and the new cultures of the boardroom, driven importantly by Sarbanes-Oxley and related regulatory changes. The clash is perhaps particularly poignant in Silicon Valley, where the culture of innovation, freedom of maneuver, and creativity are seen as essential to value creation.[29]

---

[28] Stewart, "The Kona Files," p. 165.
[29] Dunn, "My Role," p. 29.

The final witness of the day was Mark Hurd, HP's CEO. He testified,

> HP is a company that has consistently earned recognition for our adherence to standards of ethics, privacy, and corporate responsibility, and yet these practices that we have taken such pride in have recently been violated by people inside the company and by people outside the company with whom we contracted. This committee rightfully wonders what happened.
>
> What began as a proper and serious inquiry into leaks to the press of sensitive company information became a rogue investigation that violated our own principles and values. There is no excuse for this aberration. It happened; it will never happen again. . . .
>
> The question remains: how did such abuse of privacy occur in a company renowned for its commitment to privacy? It is an age-old story. The ends came to justify the means. The investigation team became so focused on finding the source of the leaks that they lost sight of the values that this company has always represented.

Discussion Questions

1. What was the problem or problems facing HP's board of directors?
2. What stakeholders were affected by the actions of HP's board and chairman, and how were they affected?
3. Were the actions taken by HP's chairman, legal department, and investigators to find the source of the leaks ethically justifiable, or not? What method or methods of ethical reasoning support your view?
4. How would you evaluate the actions of HP's board of directors relative to accepted standards of good corporate governance? In your response, you may wish to consider the board's structure, function, and process.
5. Put yourself in the role of Mark Hurd, as of the date of the congressional hearing of September 28, 2006. What actions would you take now, with respect to ethics, governance, and legal compliance?

The Solidarity Fund and Gildan Activewear, Inc.

In late 2003, officers of the Solidarity Fund, a large pension fund operated by the Québec Federation of Labor (QFL), met to discuss what to do about their investments in Gildan Activewear, a Montreal-based textile and garment company.

Over the previous year, public controversy had swirled around the company's labor practices in its manufacturing plants in Central America. In January 2002, a television documentary aired by the Canadian Broadcasting Corporation (CBC) charged that Gildan's workers in Honduras earned less than a living wage, worked long shifts, had excessively high production quotas, and breathed air filled with fabric dust. Just a few months later, a labor rights group issued a report claiming Gildan had fired Honduran workers who had tried to organize a union. These charges presented the Fund, which owned 14 percent of Gildan, with a difficult dilemma. The textile company had been an excellent investment; its stock had risen in value from just over $2 (Canadian) per share when the fund first invested in 1995 to nearly $12. However, if the allegations were true, the company's practices would run counter to the basic values of the Fund. Should the pension fund try to influence Gildan's conduct? Should it sell its shares in protest? Or should it do neither?

The Solidarity Fund

The Québec Federation of Labor (QFL), an alliance of unions in the Canadian Province of Québec representing more than half a million workers, founded the Solidarity Fund in 1983. At the time, Québec was mired in a deep recession. High interest rates had put many small and medium-sized businesses into bankruptcy, and nearly a quarter of the province's young people and more than 14 percent of its workforce were unemployed. In an effort to rethink the role of unions in promoting economic development, the QFL launched a new fund designed to invest its members' retirement savings in local companies. With the unionization rate in Québec above 40 percent (compared with around 30 percent in Canada as a whole and around 13 percent in the United States), the federation believed it could have a significant impact.

The Solidarity Fund had two central goals. Its first goal was to democratize access to professionally managed retirement accounts. A network of volunteer local representatives signed up shareholders who directed savings to the Fund. Unionized workers made up close to 60 percent of the Fund's shareholders (the rest were unaffiliated individuals). Participants typically used the Fund as a supplement to an employer-provided pension.

This case was written by Pierre Batellier and Emmanuel Raufflet, HEC Montreal, and abridged and edited by permission of the authors by Anne T. Lawrence. Copyright 2009 © by the authors. All rights reserved.

Under law, savings invested in the Fund were locked in until retirement, except in special circumstances such as job loss or periods of retraining. The Fund's second mission was to support job growth in Québec, either through long-term investment in small and medium-sized local companies or by investing in outside companies whose activities benefited the province.

Although the Fund sought to give its shareholders a fair return, it also used nonfinancial criteria in selecting investments. Its managers looked to invest in companies with good working conditions, positive relations with local communities, and a commitment to environmental responsibility. It also looked for companies that were open to partnering with institutional shareholders, such as the Fund. The Fund did not, however, have an absolute requirement that a company in which it invested be unionized.

As part of its due diligence, when it first invested in a company—and later when it increased its investment or divested—the Fund prepared a social audit. Between 1983 and 2002, the Fund team prepared nearly 2,000 social audits. Fund specialists would visit a company to gather data, observe working conditions, and meet with company managers and employee representatives. The social audits, which were not made public, sometimes identified issues of concern and made recommendations for improvement, which were often addressed in collaboration with the company's management. Once invested, the Fund played an active role in the company as a shareholder, sometimes by placing a member on the board of directors.

Many of the Fund's 400 employees, particularly its development officers and subscription staff, came from a union background and were loyal to the interests of organized labor. The Fund's financial officers, by contrast, were generally trained in the field of finance and saw their main goal as meeting the Fund's financial goals. Major investment decisions often reflected a creative tension between the unionists and the financiers. The final decision, however, rested with the Fund's 17-person board, 11 of whom were union representatives. The president, general secretary, and other executives of the QFL often came from high positions in QFL-affiliated unions, such as those representing metalworkers, Canadian public service employees, and construction workers.[1]

Some two decades after its launch, the Solidarity Fund had 500,000 shareholders and net assets of more than $4.6 billion, making it a crucial financial player in Québec's economy. (This dollar amount, and all others cited later in this case, are given in Canadian dollars, unless otherwise noted.) It had invested in the start-up, development, and growth of 1,800 Québec companies, some of them leading success stories, such as the transport company Transforce, the pharmaceutical company Biochem Pharma, the travel agency Transat, and the insurance firm SSQ. One of its biggest success stories was Gildan Activewear, Inc.

Gildan Activewear, Inc.

Glenn and Greg Chamandy, two brothers from a family of textile entrepreneurs, and their associate Edwin B. Tisch founded Gildan Textiles, Inc., in Montreal in 1984. (The company later changed its name to Gildan Activewear, or—in French—*Les Vêtements de Sport Gildan.*) The company's goal was "to be the world leader in quality knitwear for the North American and international markets, with the lowest operating costs."[2] The company's core business was producing low-cost T-shirts and fleece garments that could

[1] Solidarity Fund QFL Board of Directors, *www.fondsftq.com/internetfonds.nsf/vWebTAN/AprCon.*
[2] *www.gildan.com.*

be customized by institutional clients such as schools, universities, and companies with their own logos and designs. Its strategy was to compete on the basis of low prices, good quality, and fast delivery times through vertical integration of its supply chain. In contrast to many textile manufacturers, which relied on subcontractors, Gildan generally owned and operated its own factories. When it did turn to subcontractors, it required that the subcontractor be a dedicated operation, supplying to it alone.

In its early years, Gildan maintained all its operations in Québec, which had been home to a thriving textile industry throughout much of the 20th century. The manufacture of T-shirts required multiple steps: the fabric had to be knitted, washed, and dyed, and then cut and sewn into garments. Gildan operated three factories in Montreal, one each for knitting, dyeing, and sewing, as well as a corporate headquarters; collectively, these operations at their peak employed more than 1,000 workers. But in the early 1990s, in an effort to compete with its main rivals, Fruit of the Loom and Hanes, Gildan began moving some assembly operations, particularly sewing, to subcontractors in Mexico. In addition, the company decided it wanted its own manufacturing capability abroad, and it devised a plan to buy or build several state-of-the art factories in Honduras, a small country in Central America. This was a risky move in the short term, and several banks Gildan approached for financing turned the company down.

In 1995, Gildan contacted the Solidarity Fund for help in financing its expansion. In reviewing this request, the Fund recognized that Gildan's expansion abroad would likely cost some production jobs in Québec, but thought it would also protect and possibly expand Canadian jobs in design, marketing, finance, and other headquarters functions. Some manufacturing would also remain, it concluded. In early 1996, the Fund invested $3 million directly in Gildan stock and lent the company another $3 million.

Gildan's operations, both in North America and Latin America, proved to be extremely efficient, and in the years from 1996 to 2001, Gildan's annual growth ranged from 20 to 30 percent. Very quickly, Gildan took market share from its two leading competitors, Fruit of the Loom and Hanes. Feeling threatened, those companies launched major advertising campaigns to counter their new Canadian rival, but to no avail. Gildan's stack of contracts grew, and in 1998, its sales reached nearly $200 million with a market share of more than 10 percent.

The same year, Gildan was listed for the first time on the Toronto and New York stock exchanges. Hoping to raise an additional $60 million in capital through its initial public offering, Gildan was disappointed to obtain only $30 million. Once again, Gildan turned to the Fund, which provided a loan in 1998 worth $15 million (on top of $12 million in 1997). In 1998 and 1999, Gildan purchased two factories in Rio Nance and El Progreso, Honduras, which were equipped with new equipment and modern technology. Gildan began to transfer jobs from Montreal to Honduras and had soon doubled its production and sales volume.

Gildan pursued a vertical integration strategy, organizing different stages of production to exploit the relative competitive advantages of various locales. The sewing was done in Mexico and Honduras, where labor was cheap; the cutting, in the United States to reduce customs duties; and the dyeing and knitting, in Québec where water and electricity were abundant. The company's acquisition in 2001 of a spinning mill in Long Sault, Ontario, which guaranteed a steady supply of cotton yarn, was the final step in its vertical integration strategy.

By the end of 2001, Gildan was producing 14 million dozen T-shirts annually. The company had 8,000 employees in North and Central America. With sales of more than $500 million, it for the first time surpassed its leading competitor, Fruit of the Loom, which filed for Chapter 11 bankruptcy protection the same year. During the 2002 financial year,

Gildan posted record profits of $42 million, despite closing its factory on Clark Street in Montreal. The same year, salaries of its three top executives collectively rose from $1.5 million to $13.3 million—an increase of more than 800 percent. Gildan's president, Greg Chamandy, earned $5.8 million (mainly in stock options), going from 110th to 6th on the list of best-paid business executives in Québec.[3]

Gildan was proving to be an excellent business partner for the Fund; it repaid principal and interest on the Fund's loans in good time, and its stock continued to appreciate. The Fund felt it had contributed to the growth of a Québec company that was undergoing strong expansion and had a solid financial base characterized by limited debt and significant cash flow.

Honduras

Gildan believed that much of its success hinged on its decision to move a large share of its production to Honduras. In the early 2000s, Honduras, a small nation in Central America with a population of 6 million, remained one of the poorest countries in the Western Hemisphere, with a GDP per capita of less than $1,000 (U.S.) per year. Two-thirds of Hondurans lived below the poverty level, and 44 percent lived on less than $2 (U.S.) a day. In 2000, Honduras ranked 119th (out of 179) in the world on the Human Development Index (HDI).[4]

In the early 1990s, the government of Honduras began to set up export processing zones (EPZs), designated areas in which foreign companies were exempt from import duties, taxes on equipment, property and capital, and national and municipal taxes on revenues for the first 10 years of operation. Companies could return home with no limits on repatriating profits or capital. In 1998, the government extended those advantages across its entire territory. Some 30 industrial parks were built, most of them private, mainly near Puerto Cortes, the leading Caribbean seaport, and in San Pedro Sula, one of the country's major ground transportation hubs. The industrial parks and the EPZs were considered offshore operations, and duties were charged on products made there for sale in Honduras.

The clothing and textile industry was quick to respond to these incentives and, by 2002, accounted for 90 percent of the companies operating in the EPZs. The garment industry created 100,000 jobs in Honduras between 1992 and 2002. Eighty percent of them were held by women, most between 18 and 25 years of age. During this period, Honduras became the third largest exporter of textiles and apparel to the United States.[5] In a country where unemployment reached 28 percent in 2001, the *maquiladoras* (foreign-owned factories) and the more than 125,000 jobs they provided had become a vital part of the Honduran economy.

In 2002, the basic minimum hourly wage was 63 cents (97 cents, all costs included), or $5.58 (U.S.) per day. Under Honduran law, the maximum allowable workday was 13 hours, and the maximum allowable workweek was 44 hours for daytime work. Overtime and night shift work were compensated at a rate that was 25 percent above the regular wage. Employees also received social security contributions, as required by Honduran law, and an extra 13th month's pay (called an *Aguinaldo)*, traditional in many Latin American countries.[6]

---

[3] SEDAR, Circulaire de la direction, Gildan, February 9, 2003.

[4] Panorama de l'espace Caraïbes 2004, INSEE, *www.insee.fr/fr/insee_regions/guadeloupe/publi/pano_economie.htm.*

[5] The investment climate in Honduras is described at *http://strategis.ic.gc.ca/epic/internet/inimr-ri.nsf/fr/gr123052f.html.*

[6] Central American Business Consultants: *http://www.ca-bc.com/zip_internacional.*

Although unions were permitted in Honduras, they were generally weak. In 1954, a general strike had laid the basis for the Honduran union movement and led to a new labor code that guaranteed workers' right to form unions. But in the early 2000s, only about 20 poorly trained inspectors enforced the labor code. The high turnover of both firms and workers in the *maquiladoras* tended to limit union success. Mounting violence associated with youth gangs (*maras*) established a climate of fear and mistrust that also discouraged union organizing. Within the *maquiladoras,* only about 1 in 10 workers were union members (compared with about 25 percent in Honduras as a whole). Many workers had turned to other institutions for protection, including local development agencies, labor support groups, and churches.[7]

By 2002, Gildan had more than 5,000 employees in Honduran factories that it owned directly. Some of those jobs had been transferred from factories in Montreal, including one on Clark Street that shut down permanently in 2002. At the time of that closing, Gildan's management talked publicly about "problems in finding labor to work in [our Canadian] sew[ing] factories. In the South meanwhile, there is a pool of desperate labor."[8] The Canadian workers were more productive, but the difference in salary was enormous: an employee in Montreal earned more in one hour than a Honduran did in one day.

The Solidarity Fund's Social Audits of Gildan

In 1999, Solidarity Fund's management, concerned about the transfer of jobs from Québec to Honduras, asked Daniel Bourcier, one of the Fund's development officers, to undertake a new social audit of the company.

After visiting the Montreal factory on Clark Street as a basis for comparison, Bourcier left for a week's visit to Honduras, accompanied by Gildan's executive vice president, Edwin B. Tisch. Gildan put a car and driver at Bourcier's disposal and gave him full access to its staff, facilities, and books. During that week, the Fund officer visited three Gildan facilities and three subcontractors in the San Pedro Sula area and another in Tegucigalpa and also met with Gildan's local managers.

During his visit, Bourcier was pleasantly surprised by Gildan's newly constructed factories. Located in closed compounds with armed guards at the gate, the modern buildings were equipped with good lighting and up-to-date sewing machines. However, Bourcier identified three issues of concern. The first was dilapidated facilities and substandard working conditions in plants that supplied Gildan. The audit recommended that Gildan cease all dealings with these contractors. The second issue was the high level of cotton dust in the plants—well above standards acceptable under Canadian occupational safety laws.

The third issue involved the production system in the Gildan factories, under which workers were paid based on the productivity of their team of 12 people. The more each team produced, the higher the pay of each member. Each team was responsible for its own discipline. A quick worker would be given a green flag, and one who was slower, an orange flag. If a worker was much slower than her colleagues, the work team could give her a red flag and send her back to the sewing school, causing her a significant loss of income. The social audit found it unacceptable that Gildan had transferred responsibility for discipline from management to the work team.

---

[7] UN Committee on Economic, Social, and Cultural Rights, July 2001.

[8] Katia Gagnon, "Gildan, les rois du t-shirt (Gildan: the T-Shirt Kings)," *La Presse,* March 24, 2001.

After the audit had been completed, the Fund presented its concerns to management. Gildan's responded that its production system was completely legal, and sending people for retraining was rare. Gildan also insisted that its system gave workers salaries much higher than the minimum wage. Moreover, the company said, the workers could always form a union if they were dissatisfied. The Solidarity Fund decided after this conversation to maintain its investments in Gildan, at least for the time being, but it remained concerned.

Public Controversy

In 2002, the Canadian Broadcasting Corporation (CBC) television program *Disclosure* ran an exposé entitled "Sewing Discontent." The show's producers had investigated allegedly deplorable working conditions in Gildan's El Progreso factory in Honduras. The report mentioned extremely high production quotas, wages that did not cover even basic needs, wages based on productivity, supervised breaks, 11-hour days, poor air quality in the shops, illegal firings, and forced pregnancy tests. In one scene, the program showed young women working at a furious pace in noisy and dusty conditions.

Mackie Vadacchino, Gildan's vice president for corporate affairs, denied these allegations, saying,

> We do have excellent working conditions. . . . Many people want to work for Gildan because of our wages, because of our benefits, because of our facilities. . . . One of the visions of [the founders] has always been to prove to the world that this industry can be profitable, and not just profitable but very profitable, and maintain excellent working conditions for their employees. . . . We've become an industry leader in a relatively short period of time. However, there are others that aren't so happy about us having gained that market share. . . . I think that [the employees] lied to you. . . . I think that they were coerced by someone, coached by someone, to say things to you to make us look bad.[9]

After the CBC exposé, the Maquila Solidarity Network (MSN), a North American labor rights organization, and Equipo de Monitorio Independiente de Honduras (EMIH), an independent nonprofit monitoring agency in Honduras, undertook a review of Gildan's practices in Honduras. Several months later, MSN gave Gildan its preliminary report and asked for comments. Their findings included

> . . . wages that do not meet basic needs, excessively high production targets, the impact of the 4 × 4 work schedule (4 consecutive 11-hour workdays), and the effects of the intensive pace of production on women workers' health and family life, failure to provide day care and nursing facilities as required by law, lack of freedom of association, and workers' belief that new employees are tested for pregnancy and those found to be pregnant would be fired.[10]

That same month, MSN also received reports from Honduras that 38 workers at the company's El Progreso factory had been fired shortly after applying to the Ministry of Labor to register a union. At MSN's request, EMIH interviewed the workers and drafted a report on the circumstances surrounding the firings. When MSN representatives met with Gildan to discuss the findings, the company denied that union activity had been the

---

[9] "The Gildan Story," *Disclosure*, CBC, *www.cbc.ca/disclosure/archives/0222_gildan/story.html.*

[10] MSN Gildan Campaign Updates Gildan, *http://en.maquilasolidarity.org/gildan.*

cause of any dismissals at the El Progreso plant. It also refused to reinstate the fired workers or to contact the Ministry of Labor to determine if the workers had applied to register their union prior to the firings. MSN called on the company to cooperate with an independent investigation into the firings and other workplace issues documented in the MSN/EMIH report.

Gildan's Social Responsibility Initiatives

Gildan itself—as well as some others in government and the community—held a contrary view that the firm was an exemplary employer.

In 2003, Gildan accepted the Award for Excellence in Corporate Social and Ethical Responsibility. Sponsored by the Nexen Corporation, this award was given to companies that had directly helped developing countries or countries in transition to progress socially and economically. In announcing the award, Susan Whelan, Canada's Minister for International Cooperation, praised the company as

> a prime example of how a company can combine business success with corporate social responsibility. Gildan's employees and business partners benefit from a code of ethics and behavior that values diversity, dignity, fairness, and equal opportunity for all.[11]

Whelan referred to Gildan's own code of ethics, which it attached to contracts given to its business partners and subcontractors. Those partners and sources had to comply with the code or risk the cancellation of their contract. The company had introduced an audit procedure to check for compliance. Gildan management described the process of auditing: "The various factories undergo several inspections a month. We make sure they employ no one under 18 years of age, and that the environment is acceptable and safe and comfortable."[12]

In its 2003 annual report, Gildan emphasized that it offered its employees in Honduras

> well-paying jobs with attractive benefits. . . . Gildan's Honduran employees work in modern air-conditioned and clean facilities and their wages are generally twice the national minimum wage for the apparel sector. The company provides many benefits, such as access to free medical assistance, subsidized transportation to and from work, subsidized meals, and filtered water. The company also empowers workers by providing them the opportunity to upgrade their skill sets and education levels. School classes are offered so employees can earn their diplomas, and extensive on-the-job training is also provided to employees. In addition, Gildan sponsors family days, where employees are encouraged to invite relatives to visit the facility and share lunch with them at the company's expense, in order to foster employees' pride about their jobs and for their relatives to better understand the type of work they do.[13]

Above all, Gildan insisted, it provided jobs in a country with rampant unemployment, especially among women. At the same time, Gildan highlighted its environmental achievements. According to the 2003 annual report, these included

---

[11] Gildan *2003 Annual Report*, p. 23, *http://gildan.com/corporate/downloads/annual_report_2003_en.pdf*.

[12] Campaign Updates.

[13] Gildan *2003 Annual Report*.

the operation of biological wastewater treatment systems in Honduras, the production of environmentally friendly products, and the use of safe, clean, and energy-efficient manufacturing procedures and inputs. . . . All chemicals, dyes, and materials that are used in Gildan production facilities are selected and monitored to ensure that they have been approved for use by the appropriate regulatory authorities, and that they present no adverse effects to health or the environment. In addition, production processes are controlled to ensure reduced energy and water consumption and to minimize effluent discharge.[14]

The Controversy Continues

Even as Gildan touted its own social and environmental responsibility, it continued to attract criticism from NGOs and activists. At the 2003 annual shareholders' meeting, MSN, Oxfam Canada, and Amnesty International publicly accused Gildan of illegally firing employees for union organizing at Gildan's El Progreso factory. They also cited Gildan's failure to give a reason for the firings, threats by supervisors regarding union activities, and failure to respond to three summons from government workplace inspectors. The Solidarity Fund, along with bulk purchasers of Gildan products, including the state of Maine and several universities, joined the NGOs in requesting an independent, third-party investigation of the firings for union organizing, and recommended to Gildan that it speed up its application for membership in the SA8000 (a set of standards developed by Social Accountability International). (Gildan had earlier indicated it planned to do so.)

Under pressure to allow an independent investigation of the allegations at El Progreso, Gildan's management asked the Fund whether, as a long-time partner and investor, it would be willing to conduct the investigation. Although this was not the Fund's preferred approach, it nevertheless agreed to do so. At the end of March 2003, Fund officers Bourcier and Audette left for their week's mission in Honduras. The first few days were devoted to gathering information at meetings with representatives from the union, the main labor federation, EMIH, and the Jesuits (a Catholic religious order), as well as with labor law experts. They collected documentation, including photocopies of the request for unionization filed by the workers with their signatures. The final day was devoted to factory visits and an examination of internal documents, made available by Gildan management. Recalled Bourcier,

> In the documents we obtained, we had the list of fired workers and the list of signatories to the request for union accreditation. The names were the same.
> So we opened the files, and found copies of the severance checks made out to the workers. I could see they all had the same letter of resignation, almost to the letter.

After checking that the productivity of the workers who had been let go was at least as high as the average, the Fund's auditors were convinced that the workers had been fired for trying to form a union.

Pressure on the company grew even stronger in July 2003, when EMIH and MSN released their report, *A Canadian Success Story? Gildan Activewear: T-Shirts, Free Trade and Worker Rights,* which detailed their evidence of bad-faith practices and abuses of worker rights. The report reiterated the request that Gildan apply corrective measures, including rehiring the fired workers.

[14] Ibid, pp. 24–25.

Gildan categorically denied the charges made by both the Fund and MSN/EMIH, explaining that the firings were the result of a downturn in the industry. In addition, Gildan reiterated that it maintained high social standards and directly challenged the investigative methods used by MSN and EMIH, and threatened to sue the two groups. Gildan argued that local unions were unreliable, and it denounced the labor code as antiquated.

The Solidarity Fund and Gildan

In November 2003, three Solidarity Fund officers, Bourcier, Audette, and Laporte, sat down to talk. The intense media focus on the allegations against Gildan had created a serious dilemma for the Fund, which was heavily invested in a company that appeared not to respect the values that lay at the very core of its operations. The officers needed to make a recommendation to the board and top management of the Fund within the next few days on what to do about their investments in Gildan Activewear.

One option was for the Fund to continue doing what it had been doing—to keep fully invested in the company and to continue its regular social audits. Another option was to divest completely—to sell its stock holdings in the company and to call in its loans. Selling would give the Fund a more than 1,000 percent return on its investment over seven years; but that return could potentially be even higher if it stayed invested. A final option was to keep its shares and to step up its efforts to influence the company's behavior. The officers were aware that the Fund enjoyed significant leverage: it was a major shareholder, had a representative on the board, and had worked closely with the company for many years. But it had already been working for many months to influence the firm's practices. In the Fund's officers' view, they had received, at best, mixed messages from the company—and mixed results in their efforts to shape its behavior.

Discussion Questions

1. What is the purpose of the Solidarity Fund? Do you think it represents an example of social investment? Why or why not?

2. Do you believe the evidence in the case shows Gildan Activewear to be a socially responsible company, or not?

3. What evidence do you find in the case of the benefits and of the costs of globalization?

4. In what ways did the Solidarity Fund attempt to use its position as an institutional investor to try to influence Gildan Activewear?

5. What are the arguments for and against a decision by the Solidarity Fund to divest from (sell its investments in) Gildan Activewear?

6. What do you think the Solidarity Fund managers should do now, and why?

Kimpton Hotels' EarthCare Program

Michael Pace faced a dilemma. He was Kimpton Hotels' West Coast Director of Operations and Environmental Programs, General Manager of its Villa Florence Hotel in San Francisco, and the main catalyst for implementing its EarthCare program nationally. He was determined to help the boutique hotel chain "walk the talk" regarding its commitment to environmental responsibility, but he also had agreed not to introduce any new products or processes that would be more expensive than those they replaced. They were already successful in introducing nontoxic cleaning products, promotional materials printed on recycled paper, towel and linen reuse programs, and complimentary organic coffee and had made substantial progress in recycling bottles, cans, paper, and cardboard. Now that the initial phase of the program was being implemented nationwide, he and the company's team of eco-champions were facing some difficult challenges with the roll-out of the second, more ambitious, phase.

For example, the team had to decide whether to recommend the purchase of linens made of organic cotton, which vendors insisted would cost at least 50 percent more than standard linens. It would cost an average of $100,000 to $150,000 to switch out all the sheets, pillowcases, and towels in each hotel. If they couldn't negotiate the price down, was there some way they could introduce organic cotton in a limited but meaningful way? All linens were commingled in the laundry, so they couldn't be introduced one floor at a time. Maybe they could start with pillowcases—though the sheets wouldn't be organic, guests would be resting their heads on organic cotton. Would it even be worth spending so much on linens? The team would face similar issues when deciding whether to recommend environmentally friendly carpeting or furniture.

There were also issues with their recycling initiatives. The program had been field-tested at Kimpton hotels in San Francisco, a singular city in one of the most environmentally aware states in the United States. Now the eco-champions team had to figure out how to make it work in cities like Chicago, which didn't even have a municipal recycling program in place. In Denver, recycling actually cost more than waste disposal to a landfill, due to the low cost of land in eastern Colorado. Pace knew that the environmental initiatives most likely to succeed would be those that could be seamlessly implemented by the General Managers and employees of the 39 unique Kimpton hotels around the country. The last thing he wanted to do was to make their jobs more difficult by imposing cookie-cutter standards. At the same time, he knew that recycling just 50 percent of Kimpton Hotels' waste stream would save over $250,000 per year in waste disposal costs.

Kimpton had recently embarked on a national campaign to build brand awareness by associating its name with each unique property. Pace knew that the success of Kimpton's strategy would rest heavily on its ability to maintain the care, integrity, and uniqueness that customers had come to associate with its chain of boutique hotels. Other hotel companies had begun investing heavily in the niche that Kimpton had pioneered. To differentiate itself, the company had to continue to find innovative ways to offer services that addressed the needs and values of its customers, and EarthCare was a crucial part of its plans. But could Pace find a way to make it happen within Kimpton's budget, and without adversely affecting the customer experience? Would Kimpton be able to keep the promises made by its new corporate brand?

The Greening of the U.S. Hotel Industry

The U.S. hotel industry—with its 4.5 million rooms, common areas and lobbies, conventions, restaurants, laundry facilities, and back offices—had a significant environmental impact. According to the American Hotel and Lodging Association, the average hotel toilet was flushed 7 times per day per guest, an average shower was 7.5 minutes long, and 40 percent of bathroom lights were left on at night. A typical hotel used 218 gallons of water per day per occupied room. Energy use was pervasive, including lighting in guestrooms and common areas, heating and air conditioning, and washing and drying towels and linens. The hotel industry spent $3.7 billion per year on electricity.[1]

Hotels had other environmental impacts, as well. Guestrooms generated surprisingly large amounts of waste, ranging from one-half pound to 28 pounds per day, and averaging 2 pounds per day per guest. Nonrefillable bottles of amenities, such as shampoo and lotion, generated large amounts of plastic waste, and products used to clean bathrooms and furniture contained harmful chemicals. Paints contained high levels of volatile organic compounds. Back office and front desk activities generated large amounts of waste paper. And furniture, office equipment, kitchen, and laundry appliances were rarely selected for their environmental advantages.

Opportunities for reducing a hotel's environmental footprint were plentiful, and many could yield bottom-line savings. Reduced laundering of linens, at customer discretion, had already been adopted enthusiastically across the spectrum of budget to luxury hotels; 38 percent of hotels had linen reuse programs. Low-flow showerheads could deliver the same quality shower experience using half the water of a conventional showerhead. Faucet aerators could cut water requirements by 50 percent. A 13-watt compact fluorescent bulb gave the same light as a 60-watt incandescent, lasted about 10 times longer, and used about 70 percent less energy. Waste costs also could be significantly reduced. For many hotels, 50–80 percent of their solid waste stream was compostable, and a significant part of the remaining waste was composed of recyclables, such as paper, aluminum, and glass.

In addition to bottom-line savings, environmental programs held the potential to generate new business. Governmental bodies and NGOs, corporations, and convention/meeting planners were showing increased interest in selecting hotels using environmental criteria. California, which had an annual travel budget of $70 million, had launched a Green Lodging Program and encouraged state employees to select hotels it certified. The criteria for certification include recycling, composting, energy- and water-efficient fixtures and lighting, and nontoxic or less toxic alternatives for cleaning supplies. State governments in Pennsylvania, Florida, Vermont, and Virginia also had developed green lodging programs.

---

[1] California Green Lodging Program, *www.Ciwmb.ca.gov/epp/*.

CERES, a well-respected environmental nonprofit, had developed the Green Hotel Initiative, designed to demonstrate and increase demand for environmentally responsible hotel services. Some major corporations had endorsed the initiative, including Ford Motor Company, General Motors, Nike, American Airlines, and Coca-Cola. CERC, the Coalition for Environmentally Responsible Conventions, and the Green Meetings Industry Council were encouraging meeting planners to "green" their events by, among other things, choosing environmentally friendly hotels for lodging and meeting sites.

Despite all this potential, environmental progress in the U.S. hotel industry had been very limited. With a few exceptions, most hotels were doing very little beyond easy-to-implement cost-saving initiatives. These hotels had reduced their environmental footprint as a consequence of their cost-cutting efforts, but they were not necessarily committed to a comprehensive environmental program. During a 1998 effort by Cornell University's School of Hotel Administration to identify hotels employing environmental best practices, researchers were "surprised by the dearth of nominations."[2] In contrast to their U.S. counterparts, hotels in Canada and Europe seemed to be embracing the hotel greening process.

Kimpton Hotels

Kimpton Hotels was founded in 1981 by the late Bill Kimpton, who once said, "No matter how much money people have to spend on big, fancy hotels, they're still intimidated and unsettled when they arrive. So the psychology of how you build hotels and restaurants is very important. You put a fireplace in the lobby and create a warm, friendly restaurant, and the guest will feel at home."

Credited with inventing the boutique hotel segment, Kimpton Hotels had built a portfolio of unique properties in the upscale segment of the industry.[3] By 2005, Kimpton had grown to include 39 hotels throughout North America and Canada, each one designed to create a unique and exceptional guest experience. Every hotel lobby had a cozy fireplace and plush sitting area, where complimentary coffee was served every morning, and wine every evening. Guestrooms were stylishly decorated and comfortably furnished, offering amenities such as specialty suites that included Tall Rooms and Yoga Rooms. Every room offered high-speed wireless Internet access and desks with ample lighting. Rather than rewarding customer loyalty with a point program, Kimpton offered customization and personalization. "We record the preferences of our loyal guests, "said Mike Depatie, Kimpton's CEO of real estate. "Someone may want a jogging magazine and a Diet Coke when they arrive. We can get that done."

Business travel (group and individual) accounted for approximately 65 percent of Kimpton's revenues, and leisure travel (tour group and individual) the other 35 percent. The selection of hotels for business meetings and conferences was through meeting and conference organizers. Around 35 percent of all rooms were booked through Kimpton's call center, 25 percent through travel agents, and 25 percent through their Web site, and the remainder "came in off the street." The Internet portion of their business continued to grow, but they didn't cater to buyers looking for the "steal of the century." Rather, they were increasingly being discovered by the 25 percent of customers that market researchers called *unchained seekers,* many of whom used the Internet to search for unique accommodations that matched their particular needs or values.

---

[2] Cathy A. Enz and Judy A. Siguaw, "Best Hotel Environmental Practices," *Cornell Hotel and Restaurant Administration Quarterly,* October 1999.

[3] Gene Sloan, "Let the Pillowfights Begin," *USA Today,* August 27, 2004.

Historically, Kimpton had prospered by purchasing and renovating buildings at a discount in strategic nationwide locations that were appropriate for their niche segment. The hotel industry in general had been slow to enter the boutique niche, and Kimpton enjoyed a substantial edge in experience in developing value-added services for guests. "All hotels are starting to look alike and act alike, and we are the counterpoint, the contrarians," explained Tom LaTour, Kimpton president and CEO. "We don't look like the brands, we don't act like the brands, and as the baby boomers move through the age wave, they will seek differentiated, experience-oriented products."

Kimpton's top executives took pride in their ability to recognize and develop both undervalued properties and undervalued people. Kimpton's hotel general managers were often refugees from large branded companies who did not thrive under hierarchical, standardized corporate structures. At Kimpton, they were afforded a great deal of autonomy, subject only to the constraints of customer service standards and capital and operating budgets.

This sense of autonomy and personal responsibility was conveyed down through the ranks to all 5,000 Kimpton employees. Kimpton's flexible corporate structure avoided hierarchy, preferring a circular structure where executives and employees were in constant communication.[4] Steve Pinetti, senior vice president for sales and marketing, liked to tell the story of a new parking attendant who had to figure out how to deal with a guest who felt that he had not been adequately informed of extra charges for parking his car at the hotel. The attendant decided on the spot to reduce the charges, and asked the front desk to make the necessary adjustments. He had heard his general manager tell everyone that they should feel empowered to take responsibility for making guests happy, but he fully expected to be grilled by his GM, at the very least, about his actions. A sense of dread took hold as he was called to the front of the room at a staff meeting the very next day, but it dissipated quickly when his general manager handed him a special award for his initiative.

Commitment to Social and Environmental Responsibility

An important part of Kimpton's history was its longstanding commitment to social and environmental responsibility. Staff at each hotel had always been encouraged to engage with local community nonprofits that benefit the arts, education, the underprivileged, and other charitable causes. Kimpton maintained these local programs even in periods of falling occupancy rates and industry downturns. These local efforts evolved into the companywide Kimpton Cares program in 2004, as part of the company's corporate branding effort. At the national level, Kimpton supported the National AIDS Fund (in support of its Red Ribbon Campaign) and Dress for Success (which assisted economically disadvantaged women struggling to enter the workforce) by allotting a share of a guest's room fee to the charity. At the global level, Kimpton embarked in a partnership with Trust for Public Land (TPL), a nonprofit dedicated to the preservation of land for public use. In 2005, Kimpton committed to raising $15,000 from its total room revenues to introduce the TPL Parks for People program, and created eco-related fund-raising events in each of its cities to further support the campaign.

Kimpton also introduced EarthCare, a comprehensive program of environmental initiatives intended for rollout to all the chain's hotels. "As business leaders, we believe we have a responsibility to positively impact the communities we live in, to be conscious

---

[4] Liz French, Americanexecutive.com, December 2004.

about our environment, and to make a difference where we can," said Niki Leondakis, Kimpton's Chief Operating Officer. Kimpton's top executives considered the Kimpton Cares program, and its EarthCare component, essential parts of the company's branding effort. Steve Pinetti noted, "What drove it was our belief that our brand needs to stand for something. What do we want to stand for in the community? We want to draw a line in the sand. We also want our impact to be felt as far and wide as it can. Hopefully, through our good deeds, we'll be able to influence other companies."

Anecdotal evidence suggested that Kimpton's early efforts had already had financial payoffs. Kimpton was receiving significant coverage of its EarthCare program in local newspapers and travel publications. "We've booked almost half a million dollars in meetings from a couple of corporations in Chicago because of our ecological reputation," said Pinetti. "Their reps basically told us, 'Your values align with our values, and we want to spend money on hotels that think the way we do.'" Kimpton believed that companies that identified with being socially responsible would look for partners like Kimpton that shared those values and that certifications like the California Green Lodging Program would attract both individuals and corporate clientele.

However, Pinetti noted, "The cost-effectiveness wasn't clear when we started. I thought we might get some business out of this, but that's not why we did it. We think it's the right thing to do, and it generates a lot of enthusiasm among our employees."

Kimpton's Real Estate CEO Mike Depatie believed that incorporating care for communities and the environment into the company's brand had been a boon to hiring. "We attract and keep employees because they feel that from a values standpoint, we have a corporate culture and value system that's consistent with theirs," he commented. "They feel passionate about working here." While the hotel industry was plagued with high turnover, Kimpton's turnover rates were lower than the national averages.

Rolling Out the EarthCare Program

Pinetti and Pace realized that they were too busy to handle all the planning and operational details of the national rollout, so they turned to Jeff Slye, of Business Evolution Consulting, for help. Slye was a process management consultant who wanted to help small and medium-sized business owners figure out how to "ecofy" their companies. He had heard that Kimpton was trying to figure out how to make its operations greener and integrate this effort into its branding effort. When they first met in October 2004, Pinetti and Pace handed Slye a 10-page document detailing their objectives and a plan for rolling out the initiative in phases. Kimpton's program was to have the following eco-mission statement:

> Lead the hospitality industry in supporting a sustainable world by continuing to deliver a premium guest experience through nonintrusive, high-quality, eco-friendly products and services.
>
> Our mission is built upon a companywide commitment toward water conservation; reduction of energy usage; elimination of harmful toxins and pollutants; recycling of all reusable waste; building and furnishing hotels with sustainable materials; and purchasing goods and services that directly support these principles.

Slye worked with Pinetti and Pace to fill various gaps in their plan and develop an ecostandards program, a concise report outlining a strategy for greening the products and operational processes that Kimpton used. In December 2004, Pinetti asked Slye to present the report to Kimpton's COO, Niki Leondakis. Leondakis greeted the proposal enthusiastically, but noted that it needed an additional component: a strategy for communicating the program both internally (to management and staff) and externally (to guests, investors, and the press). As important as the external audiences were, Slye knew that the internal communications strategy would be particularly crucial, given the autonomy afforded each Kimpton hotel, each with its own set of local initiatives. Getting everyone on board would require a strategy that respected that aspect of Kimpton's culture.

Slye, Pace, and Pinetti decided to create an ad hoc network of eco-champions throughout the company. The national lead (Pace) and co-lead (Pinetti) would head up the communications effort and be accountable for its success. Each of five geographic regions (Pacific Northwest, San Francisco Bay Area, Central U.S., Washington D.C., and Northeast/Southeast), covering six or seven hotel properties, would also have a lead and co-lead who would help communicate the program to employees, and be the local point persons in the chain of command. One of their key roles would be to solicit employee suggestions regarding ways to make products and processes greener.

In addition, a team of national eco-product specialists would be key components of the network. These specialists would be responsible for soliciting staff input, and identifying and evaluating greener products as potential substitutes for existing ones. Products would be tested for effectiveness and evaluated on the basis of their environmental benefits, effect on guest perceptions, potential marketing value, and cost. Pinetti and Pace determined that specialists would be needed initially for six product categories: beverages, cleaning agents, office supplies, engineering, information technology, and room supplies. Meanwhile, Pace and Pinetti asked all general managers to report on their existing environmental initiatives, to get baseline feedback on what individual hotels were doing already. They turned the results into a matrix they could use to identify gaps and monitor progress for each hotel.

By February 2005, the network of eco-champions was in place, and everyone had agreed on the basic ground rules for the transition. No new product or service could cost more than the product or service it replaced, nor could it adversely affect customer perceptions or satisfaction. All leads, co-leads, and product specialists began meeting via conference call every Friday morning to discuss the greening initiative and share accounts of employee suggestions, progress achieved, and barriers encountered.

To help communicate the program's goals and achievements, and to help motivate employees seeking recognition, the team began to post regular updates and success stories in Kimpton's internal weekly newsletter, *The Word,* which was distributed throughout the organization and read by all GMs. They also ran an EarthCare contest to further galvanize interest, which generated over 70 entries for categories such as Best Eco-Practice Suggestion, Most EarthCare Best Practices Adopted, and Best Art and Humor Depicting EarthCare. The team also communicated the environmental benefits of their activities to the staff. For example, printing on 35 percent postconsumer recycled paper would save 24,000 pounds of wood, and recycling 100 glass bottles per month would save the energy equivalent of powering one hundred 100-watt lightbulbs for 60 days.

The team of eco-champions also quickly learned that the national rollout effort would have its share of potential operational risks and challenges, which would need to be addressed:

- *Potential resistance by general managers (GMs) to a centralized initiative.* A green management program mandated by corporate headquarters might threaten Kimpton's culture of uniqueness and autonomy. GMs might chafe at what they saw as corporate intrusion upon their autonomy and would want the flexibility to adapt the program to local requirements.

- *Potential resistance by hotel staff to new products and procedures.* Kimpton's relatively low turnover meant that some employees had been working there for many years and had become accustomed to familiar ways of doing things. Informal queries by management, for example, revealed that many cleaning staff equated strong chemical odors with cleanliness. Also, many of the service staff did not speak English fluently, and might have difficulty understanding management's reasons for switching to new procedures or greener cleaning products.

- *A slower payback period or a lower rate of return for green investments, relative to others.* The gains in operating costs achieved by installing longer-life and more energy-efficient fluorescent lighting could take years to pay off, while higher acquisition costs could inflate short-term expenses. The same logic applied to water conservation investments. Would corporate executives and investors be patient? What if consumer tastes or Kimpton's branding strategies changed before investments had paid off?

- *Benefits intangible to customers.* Unless informed, guests would not be aware that their rooms had been painted with low-VOC paints. Likewise, organic cottons would likely not feel or look superior to traditional materials.

- *For some products, required investments might exceed existing budgets or fail to meet the cost parity criterion.* For example, the eco-specialists learned that one of Kimpton's vendors did have a Green Seal certified nontoxic line, but the products were selling at a 10–15 percent premium over standard products. They discovered that virtually every product they were interested in was more expensive than those currently used. At the extreme, eco-friendly paper products were priced 50 percent above standard products. Would additional budget be provided? Would savings in other areas be allowed to pay for it?

- *Marketing the program could prove challenging.* How should the EarthCare program be promoted, given customer concerns regarding the impact of some environmental initiatives on the quality of their guest experience? Guests might be concerned, for example, whether low-flow shower heads or fluorescent lighting would meet their expectations. According to the American Automobile Association's Diamond Rating Guidelines, some water-saving showerheads and energy-saving lightbulbs could lower a hotel's diamond rating.[5]

- *Regional variations in customer values.* Environmental awareness and concern varied considerably by geographic region, from very high on the West Coast and in the Northeast, to considerably lower in the South and Midwest.

- *Regional differences in recycling infrastructure and regulatory environment.* California had a mandated recycling program requiring 70 percent recycling of solid waste by 2007, so San Francisco's disposal service provided free recycling containers. Other localities might not be so generous.

Even in the face of these challenges, Kimpton executives believed that the EarthCare program was the smart, as well as the "right," thing to do. According to Tom LaTour, chairman and CEO,

> It's good business. It's not just because we're altruistic, it's good for business. Otherwise the investors would say, what are you guys doing? A lot of people think it's going to cost more. It's actually advantageous to be eco-friendly than not.

---

[5] *AAA Lodging Requirements & Diamond Rating Guidelines* (Heathrow, FL: AAA Publishing, June 2001).

Niki Leondakis, COO, saw the program's impact on marketing and employee retention:

> Many people say we're heading toward a tipping point: If you're not environmentally conscious, your company will be blackballed from people's choices. Also, employees today want to come to work every day not just for the paycheck but to feel good about what they're doing. . . . It's very important to them to be aligned with the values of the people they work for, so from the employee retention standpoint, this helps us retain and attract them so we can select from the best and the brightest.[6]

Discussion Questions

1. What are the benefits of Kimpton's environmental sustainability initiatives? What are its costs?
2. How would you justify the EarthCare program to Kimpton's board of directors and stockholders? That is, what is the business case for this program?
3. What challenges face the EarthCare program, and how might Kimpton overcome them?
4. What further steps should Kimpton take to institutionalize its environmental commitments?
5. How would you measure the success of the EarthCare program, and how should it be reported to stakeholders?

---

[6] Carlo Wolff, "Environmental Evangelism: Kimpton Walks the Eco-Walk," *Lodging Hospitality*, March 1, 2005.

Mattel and Toy Safety

On September 12, 2007, members of Congress, their staff, reporters, prospective witnesses, and curious members of the public gathered in a U.S. Senate hearing room to consider the issue of toy safety. In the weeks leading up to the hearing, Mattel, Inc., one of the world's leading toy makers, had ordered a series of recalls of children's playthings that had been found to be coated with lead paint. Lead—a heavy metal sometimes added to paint to intensify color, speed drying, and increase durability—was a potent neurotoxin and potentially dangerous to children who might ingest bits of paint. The toy recalls had alarmed parents and consumer activists, as well as the toy industry, retailers who marketed their products, and product safety regulators. Now, as the holiday shopping season approached, everyone wanted to make sure that toys—80 percent of which were made in China—were safe. "It's scary," said Whitney Settle, a mother from Petroleum, West Virginia. "I have a 2-year-old boy who chews on everything. I doubt I am going to buy [Mattel toys] anymore—or it's going to make me look twice."[1]

Mattel, Inc.

Headquartered in El Segundo, California, Mattel, Inc., was the global leader in the design, manufacture, and marketing of toys and family products. Mattel toy lines included such best-selling brands as Barbie (the most popular fashion doll ever introduced), Hot Wheels, Matchbox, American Girl, Radica, and Tyco, as well as Fisher-Price brands, including Little People, Power Wheels, and a wide range of entertainment-inspired toys. Mattel had long enjoyed a reputation as a responsible company. *Forbes* magazine had recognized Mattel as one of the 100 most trustworthy U.S. companies, and CRO magazine had ranked the company as one of the 100 Best Corporate Citizens. Mattel employed more than 30,000 people in 43 countries and territories and sold products in more than 150 nations. In 2006, the company earned $592 million on sales of $5.6 billion.

In 2007, Mattel manufactured about 65 percent of its toys in China. When the company first began shifting production to Asia in the 1980s, it used outside contractors. Mattel soon became concerned, however, that outsourcing put the company's intellectual property at risk, as outsiders could learn to make imitation Barbie dolls and other trademarked

By Anne T. Lawrence and James Weber. Copyright © 2008 by the authors. All rights reserved. An earlier version of this case was presented at the 2008 annual meeting of the Western Casewriters Association. The authors developed this case for class discussion rather than to illustrate effective or ineffective handling of the situation. Materials in this case are drawn from testimony at the hearing on toy safety held by the Senate Appropriations Committee, Subcommittee on Financial Services and General Government, on September 12, 2007, and from articles appearing in *The Wall Street Journal, New York Times, Boston Globe, BusinessWeek, The Guardian, Forbes, Reuters, International Business Times,* and the trade press.

[1] "Amid Recalls, Toy Makers Tout Quality," *Boston Globe,* August 19, 2007.

products. Believing it could handle manufacturing more securely by operating its own factories, in the 1990s Mattel built or acquired production facilities in China, Hong Kong, Indonesia, Malaysia, the Philippines, and Singapore. In 2007, nearly 50 percent of the company's toy revenue came from core products made in these company-run plants, which included five factories in China. Mattel also contracted production to between 30 and 50 Chinese firms, many of which had relationships with other subcontractors. In 2007, production throughout the toy industry was shifting toward China, in part because the weakening Chinese currency made goods manufactured there increasingly cost-competitive.

In 1997, Mattel had developed a detailed code of conduct, called its Global Manufacturing Principles. Covering both Mattel's factories and those of its contractors and suppliers, the principles addressed a wide range of labor issues. These included wages (at least minimum wage or local industry standard, whichever was higher), child labor (workers had to be at least 16 years old or the local minimum, whichever was higher), and health and safety (compliant with the standards of the American Conference of Government Industrial Hygienists). In a move that was at the time unprecedented, the company hired S. Prakash Sethi, a professor at Baruch College in New York, to carry out independent audits to assure compliance with these standards. Mattel gave Professor Sethi a generous budget, access to all facilities and records of the company and its contractors, and permission to make the results of his inspections public. Since 1999, the International Center for Corporate Accountability (ICCA), the nonprofit organization headed by Professor Sethi, had conducted audits of facilities operated by Mattel and its contractors at least once every three years and more often if it found problems. Over the years, Mattel had terminated several dozen suppliers for noncompliance and made numerous changes in its own plants.[2]

Although its Global Manufacturing Principles focused exclusively on working conditions, Mattel also took steps to ensure product quality and safety. In China, Mattel tested products both at its own facilities and in special test labs. The company had specific standards with respect to lead in paint. Robert A. Eckert, Mattel's CEO, described the company's safety protocols for paint:

> For years, Mattel has required vendors to purchase paint from a list of certified suppliers or test the paint that they used to ensure compliance with the established standards; audited the certified paint suppliers to ensure compliance with lead level standards; periodically audited vendors to ensure that they are complying with paint requirements; conducted lead level safety tests on samples drawn from the initial production run of every product; and had protocols for further recertification testing for lead on finished products.[3]

The Toy Recalls

On August 1, 2007, Mattel issued a voluntary recall of 1.5 million Chinese-made, Fisher-Price products, including the popular Big Bird, Elmo, Diego, and Dora the Explorer characters, after the company learned that they contained too much lead. The company had begun a special investigation in July after a European retailer found lead paint on a

---

[2] The ICCA audits are available online at *www.mattel.com/about_us/Corp_Responsibility.*

[3] Testimony of Robert A. Eckert, submitted to the Senate Committee on Appropriations, Subcommittee on Financial Services and General Government, September 12, 2007.

Mattel product. Two weeks later, Mattel recalled another 436,000 toys—the Sarge toy from the Cars die-cast vehicle line—again because of high levels of lead. The second recall also included 18.2 million toys, such as Barbie, Batman, Polly Pocket, and Doggie Daycare play sets, that contained small but powerful magnets that could fall out of the toys and be swallowed by young children. Once ingested, these magnets could attract each other and cause a potentially fatal intestinal perforation or blockage. Mattel's ongoing investigation continued to turn up problems, and in early September the company issued a third recall of 11 different products—eight pet and furniture play sets sold under the Barbie brand and three Fisher-Price toys.

As it issued one recall after another, Mattel sought to reassure its customers. The company told the public that it was aggressively working with the Consumer Product Safety Commission in the United States and other regulatory agencies worldwide that governed consumer product safety. It provided a comprehensive list of all recalled products on its Web site and a toll-free number to respond to consumer questions regarding the safety of its products. The company also placed full-page ads in *The Wall Street Journal, The New York Times,* and *USA Today.* It also issued many press releases, including one that said, "Mattel has rigorous procedures, and we will continue to be vigilant and unforgiving in enforcing quality and safety. We don't want to have recalls, but we don't hesitate to take quick and effective action to correct issues as soon as we've identified them to ensure the safety of our products and the safety of children."

Mattel instructed customers who had purchased the recalled products to take them away from their children, and it provided them with a prepaid mailing label to return affected toys for a refund or safe replacement product. Although Mattel did not reveal how many toys were actually returned, past recalls of inexpensive toys had yielded return rates below 5 percent, according to product safety experts. The company indicated that it would safely dispose of the returned products and recycle some materials into other products, such as park benches.

What Had Gone Wrong?

In its investigation, Mattel learned that some of its external vendors and their subcontractors were cutting corners to save money and time. Lead paint was at least 30 percent cheaper than unleaded paint, and some thought that it produced a richer color and was easier to apply. Mattel discovered, for example, that the main supplier of the Cars product, the focus of the second recall, was a Chinese contractor called Early Light Industrial. This firm had subcontracted the painting of the toy to another company, Hong Li Da. Although the subcontractor was supposed to use paint provided by Early Light Industrial (which had had been inspected and approved for use in toys exported to the United States), instead it substituted lead paint. "Early Light, the vendor, is every [bit as] much the victim as Mattel is," Eckert later commented. "The subcontractor chose to violate the rules."[4] In another instance, Lee Der Industrial, a contractor, had used paint supplied by another firm and had apparently failed to test it for lead. In total, Mattel's investigation uncovered seven contractors that had been involved in making the lead paint–coated products.

In its investigation of the problem with the small magnets, Mattel found that the problem lay in the toys' design, not their production. While the company routinely put its products through rigorous stress tests, it did not anticipate that if two or more high-powered magnets were ingested at once they could close off the intestines if they became

[4] "What Went Wrong at Mattel," *BusinessWeek*, August 15, 2007.

attached inside a young child. Once it discovered this possibility, Mattel changed the design of the toy; in the newer versions the magnets were locked into the products so that a child could not break them free and accidentally ingest them. (The Consumers Union reported that one toddler had died and 12 children had been injured as a result of swallowing magnets, but did not say if Mattel toys, in particular, had caused these injuries.)

Regulation in the United States and China

In the United States, the Consumer Product Safety Commission (CPSC) had responsibility for protecting the public from unreasonable risks of serious injury and death from more than 15,000 types of consumer products, including children's toys. The commission's mandate included developing uniform safety standards for various products and, if necessary, issuing a voluntary recall of unsafe products. Some observers believed that the CPSC was underfunded and understaffed, relative to the breadth of its mission. In 2007, the commission had an annual budget of $62 million and employed around 400 people (down from a high of around 900), including about 15 investigators charged with visiting ports of entry to inspect imports and 100 charged with monitoring products on store shelves. According to the Consumers Union, an advocacy organization, Chinese products in 2007 accounted for two-thirds of the products the CPSC regulated and 60 percent of all product recalls, compared with 36 percent in 2000.

When Mattel announced its first recalls in August, the CPSC's acting commissioner, Nancy A. Nord, attempted to reassure the public. She told the press that she was negotiating with representatives from the toy industry to conduct broader testing of imported toys and urged consumers not to overreact to news of the recalls. "In today's environment, it is easy to take recalls out of proportion. By no means is it the largest recall this agency has done, and it represents only a tiny fraction of the hundreds of millions of toys that are sold in the United States every year."[5]

In China, government standards required that paint intended for household or consumer product use contain no more than 90 parts of lead per million. (By comparison, U.S. regulations allowed up to 600 parts per million, although they banned the use of lead paint in toys entirely.) However, enforcement of the lead standard in China was lax, according to some observers. "There is a national standard on the lead level in toys," said Chen Tao, sales manager for a toy factory in Shantou, in southern China, "but no one really enforces it. Factories can pick whatever paint they want."[6] Whether lead-based paint was used or not was generally left up to the customer. "It depends on the client's requirements," explained a manager at another Shantou manufacturer. "If the prices they offer make it impossible to use lead-free paint, we'll tell them that we might have to use leaded paint. If they agree, we'll use leaded paint. It totally depends on what the clients want."[7]

In the wake of the toy recalls, Chinese officials and regulators took several steps. In mid-August, the Beijing government established a cabinet-level committee, headed by Vice Premier Wu Yi, to improve the quality and safety of Chinese products. It suspended the export licenses of two companies, Hanshen Wood Factory (which had made some

---

[5] "Mattel Recalls 19 Million Toys Sent from China," *The New York Times,* August 15, 2007.

[6] "Why Lead in Toy Paint? It's Cheaper," *The New York Times,* September 11, 2007.

[7] Ibid.

lead-painted Thomas & Friends toys recalled by another company) and Lee Der Industrial. Zhang Shuhong, one of the owners of Lee Der Industrial, reportedly killed himself by hanging in a factory warehouse shortly afterward.[8] In September, the government introduced a new food and toy recall system and announced a "special war" to crack down on poor-quality products and unlicensed manufacturers. Beijing's largest state-run television network began broadcasting a special called "Believe in Made in China," featuring interviews with government regulators, reports on China's biggest companies, and segments on foreign buyers of Chinese goods. The government also agreed to prohibit the use of lead paint on toys exported to the United States, to increase inspections of its exports, and to hold regular talks with American safety regulators.

The Senate Hearings

In September 2007, as the hearings commenced, many of the key players in the toy safety crisis gathered to offer their perspectives to members of the Senate. Those testifying included representatives of the Consumer Product Safety Commission, the consumer advocacy organization Consumers Union, the American National Standards Institute, the Toy Industry Association, the retailer Toys "R" Us, and Mattel.

Consumer Product Safety Commission

Acting Commissioner Nancy A. Nord offered the following comments at the hearing:

> I would like to report to you in more detail today on the initiatives that the CPSC has undertaken in recent years to address the growth in imports and to relate to you what actions we are planning for the future. . . .
>
> The issue of Chinese imports cannot be adequately addressed by any one remedy but rather requires a multi-pronged approach to the problem. The CPSC's plan of action includes dialogue and initiatives with the Chinese government; working with the private sector including Chinese manufacturers directly; increased surveillance and enforcement activities at the borders and within the marketplace; and modernization of our governing statutes.
>
> [We are working with Chinese regulators on] specific cooperative actions . . . to improve the safety of consumer products: training; technical assistance; a mechanism to provide for "urgent consultation" when necessary; information exchanges; and the creation of Working Groups to address issues in four priority areas [including toys].
>
> The second prong of our plan to address Chinese imports is to work with the private sector including Chinese manufacturers. One of the commission's first initiatives in responding to the growth in imports was to establish the Office of International Programs and Intergovernmental Affairs to support a comprehensive effort to ensure that imported consumer products complied with recognized American safety standards. . . .
>
> A major emphasis of this program is working with foreign manufacturers to establish product safety systems as an integral part of their manufacturing process. We have found that many overseas manufacturers, particularly those from the developing world, are either ignorant of existing voluntary and mandatory standards or simply choose not to design and manufacture their products to those standards.

---

[8] "Scandal and Suicide in China: A Dark Side of Toys," *The New York Times,* August 23, 2007.

The CPSC has also conducted industry-specific safety seminars and retail and vendor training seminars in China. . . .

The third prong of our plan of action for Chinese imports is increased surveillance and enforcement activities. . . . CPSC obviously attempts to keep dangerous products from entering into the country in the first instance. However, in the event a defective product does enter the stream of commerce, CPSC has been taking stronger measures to effectively remove such products from the marketplace. . . .

CPSC staff is also working with various domestic and international associations and standards groups to assure that a strong message is being delivered to Chinese manufacturers and exporters. . . .

The fourth prong of our plan of action for Chinese imports is the modernization of our governing statutes to better allow us to address the large influx of imports. . . . For example, . . . [we propose to make] it unlawful to sell a recalled product in commerce.

Consumers Union

Sally Greenberg, senior product safety counsel for the Consumers Union, a private consumer advocacy organization and the publisher of *Consumer Reports* magazine, testified,

Unfortunately, the system in place to protect consumers—especially children—from unsafe products has broken down. The recent avalanche of toy recalls, involving Chinese-made toys made with excessive lead levels in the paint, has exposed millions of children to a highly toxic substance and created a crisis of confidence among consumers who feel that they can trust neither the toy industry nor our government to keep their children safe. . . .

Never in its history has the CPSC been so challenged as an agency. . . . [W]e believe the agency's leadership has failed to use the regulatory authority it has to fine companies that violate its rules, has refused to request more funding and resources even while admitting it cannot carry out core functions, and has opposed efforts by consumer groups to provide the commission with the funding and tools it needs to keep consumers safe. In addition, further exacerbating the CPSC's weakened state, the current administration has instead imposed additional cuts on the already woefully underfunded and understaffed agency. . . .

[W]e recommend that Congress set a goal of funding the CPSC at least to reach 700-plus employees, [which] the agency had when its doors opened in 1974. Consumers Union commends the toy industry, including retail giants such as Toys "R" Us, for embracing the idea of third-party testing and inspecting, and for welcoming the federal regulatory involvement in making testing and inspection mandatory.

Greenberg also took the opportunity to press for a proposal backed by her organization to protect consumers from unsafe Chinese-made products.

On July 18 of this year, Consumers Union . . . [proposed] eight steps that should be taken to help safeguard the health and safety of American consumers from the onslaught of unsafe Chinese-produced consumer products and foods. That list included the following steps:

1. Provide increased resources to government safety agencies to prevent unsafe products from crossing our borders.

2. Hold suppliers, importers, distributors, as well as manufacturers accountable for bringing unsafe products to the market by requiring preshipment inspections and testing to ensure product safety.

3. Develop U.S. government–administered, third-party safety certification programs for all products.

4. Develop a product traceability program for country-of-origin labeling for both food and consumer products as well as for all components and ingredients.

5. Require that importers post a bond to ensure they have sufficient resources to recall their products should they prove dangerous or defective.

6. Give all agencies with enforcement authority the power to levy meaningful civil penalties for manufacturers, importers, distributors, and retailers who fail to comply with regulations, and criminal penalties for those who knowingly and repeatedly jeopardize public safety.

7. Authorize mandatory recall authority for all government agencies.

8. Require all government agencies to publicly disclose information pertaining to safety investigations and reports of adverse events.

She later added a comment on recall effectiveness:

> Recall notices rarely reach the very people who most need it—parents and care-givers. There is no law requiring manufacturers to try to find purchasers of the product or to notify parents or day care centers if a product proves dangerous and must be recalled. Further, there is no requirement that manufacturers adver-tise a product recall in the same way they advertised the product in the first place—toys with lead paint and magnets, high chairs, cribs, strollers, infant swings, and carriers often continue to be used for months or years after they have been recalled. In an effort to improve recall effectiveness, consumer groups peti-tioned the CPSC, asking that the commission require simple registration cards on products intended for use by children. While not a panacea, registration cards are one way to facilitate recalls.

American National Standards Institute

The president and CEO of the American National Standards Institute (ANSI), S. Joe Bhatia, also spoke before the Senate Committee. ANSI is a private nonprofit organiza-tion that coordinates the development of voluntary standards to protect consumer safety in a wide range of industries; it collaborates internationally with the International Orga-nization for Standardization (ISO). Bhatia testified,

> Standards are important for everyone because they influence the design, safety, manufacturing, and marketing of many products worldwide. Standards are not only developed in response to injuries, hazard, or other identified safety risks, but more often in a proactive manner to prevent injuries from known hazards. . . .
>
> This hearing is necessary not because there is an issue with standards. It is necessary because some suppliers—particularly those who are exporting products to U.S. soil—are not complying with the rigorous standards and regulations that have been established to keep our citizens safe.
>
> Products manufactured in accordance with U.S. toy safety standards provide greater protection to our children. Testing and inspection systems must be strengthened so that compliance with these standards can be verified before unsafe products get into this country. . . .

The system must be efficient, consistent, and sustainable. It must focus on improving how products are evaluated and assessing who is conducting the evaluations. . . .

ANSI wants to help reassure consumers that the products they find on the shelves of their local retailer have been tested and found to be safe—regardless of country of origin. In order for the Institute to accomplish the objective:

- Standards and conformity assessment resources that are already in place must be used more efficiently;
- Government and industry need to work at a single purpose to identify gaps in the current systems of testing and inspection of products imported to the United States;
- New human and financial resources must be brought to bear to strengthen existing systems and fill any identified gaps.

Toy Industry Association

Carter Keithley, president and CEO of the Toy Industry Association—an industry association representing companies that provides 85 percent of the toys sold in the United States—also testified. He said,

> At the outset, I would like to note the U.S. has among the strictest, most comprehensive toy safety systems in the world. U.S. toys have, for years, been ranked among the safest of all consumer products in the home. In fact, many nations around the world emulate the U.S. system and understand our toy safety standards to be the premier standards. This is not to say there is no room for improvement. It is our mission to continuously search for new ways to further strengthen our safety systems and standards. . . .
>
> As we entered the summer months and up until as late as last week, toy recalls were in the headlines daily. These recent recalls clearly demonstrated our safety system needed to be strengthened. Although, as I stated, we have some of the best standards in the world, we were left wanting in assuring the application of the standards. This lack of assuring application of standards left our companies, the industry, and most importantly our children exposed. . . .
>
> As companies continue to test current product to clear violative product from their supply chains, TIA has, with the approval of our member companies, set out to provide a long-term program to address the "assurance gap." To that end, I would like to share the framework for our new mandatory testing program for toys sold in the United States.

> The new mandatory program will
> 1. Require all toys manufactured for the U.S. market to be tested to U.S. standards;
> 2. Standardize procedures that will be used industrywide to verify that products comply with U.S. safety standards;
> 3. Establish criteria to certify that testing laboratories are qualified to perform testing to U.S. standards using industrywide protocols;
> 4. Require the development of testing protocols and certification criteria through the cooperation of all stakeholders and apply them consistently;
> 5. Necessitate that TIA work with Congress, CPSC, and ANSI to implement the legislation, rules, and protocols to ensure industrywide adherence.

> It is the toy industry's strong belief that with this new mandatory testing program our industry will be even better equipped to protect the integrity of our products and the safety of American children.

Toys "R" Us

Jerry Storch, chairman and CEO of Toys "R" Us, a toy and baby products retailer operating in 35 countries, with 842 stores in the United States, testified,

> As the recalls this year unfolded, it became clear to us that change was needed. Like many of you, we were frustrated by some of the large recalls earlier this year, especially by what appeared to be an unacceptably long time frame between discovery of a problem and the actual consumer recall. . . .
>
> It is our belief that a combination of strong safety practices when toys are manufactured and reinforcing federal legislation can help provide the answer. We also believe a strong, well-financed Consumer Product Safety Commission (CPSC) is needed, rather than a patchwork quilt of potentially contradictory state legislation.
>
> [W]e believe the recall process itself could be improved in two ways: First, we support legislation shortening the time frames during the period between identification of a problem and the eventual recall of that product. We are troubled by the possibility that we could be continuing to sell toys that someone knows may have a problem, while we remain unaware until we receive word that a recall is coming—usually just a day or two at most before the recall.
>
> Second, we believe that production code stamping of products and packaging would significantly help in tracing potential safety issues. It would make it easier for retailers and parents to identify recalled product, and avoid the guessing game when a mom or dad is trying to remember whether they bought the product before or after the recall date.
>
> To our knowledge, based on the recalls this year, the problem was not that testing wasn't happening, or that testing wasn't being done properly, but rather that testing was not done frequently enough. Prior to recent events, toy makers would test the initial batch of a product, then periodically retest batches to make sure the factory was still complying. What appears to have happened in the recent cases is that someone replaced the compliant paint with noncompliant paint at an unknown point between tests. Therefore, while we have long required testing from our vendors, we are moving to require that our vendors submit to us certification of testing for each batch coming to Toys "R" Us, and we have been told many vendors are already moving to this practice. To reinforce this direction, we strongly support strengthening third-party testing requirements. Specifically, we advocate for legislation requiring accredited certification of testing facilities. It is a sensible way for all of us—including retailers and consumers—to know that the manufacturers have or use quality testing facilities.

Mattel

Mattel also took its message to Capitol Hill. Robert A. Eckert, Mattel's CEO, told the committee,

> Like many of you, I am a parent. I, like you, care deeply about the safety of children. And I, like you, am deeply disturbed and disappointed by recent events. As to lead paint on our products, our systems were circumvented, and our standards were violated. We were let down, and so we let you down. On behalf of Mattel and its nearly 30,000 employees, I apologize sincerely. I can't

change the past, but I can change the way we do things. And I already have. We are doing everything we can to prevent this from happening again.

Eckert continued later in his remarks,

Obviously, we know that parents are looking to us to see what we're doing to improve our system to make people live up to their obligations and meet our standards. We have acted quickly and aggressively by implementing a strengthened 3-point safety check system to enforce compliance with all regulations and standards applicable to lead paint. . . .

I would like to conclude by reiterating my personal apology on behalf of Mattel and to emphasize our commitment to parents. The steps we have taken will strengthen the safety of our products. Parents expect that a toy carrying the Mattel brand is safe. Ensuring safety is crucial to the long-standing trust this company has built with parents for more than 60 years. There is simply nothing more important to Mattel than the safety of children.

Discussion Questions

1. Do you believe that Mattel acted in a socially responsible and ethical manner with regard to the safety of its toys? Why or why not? What should or could Mattel have done differently, if anything?

2. Who or what do you believe was responsible for the fact that children were exposed to potentially dangerous toys? Why do you think so?

3. What is the best way to ensure the safety of children's toys? In responding, please consider how the following groups would answer this question: government regulators (in the United States and China); consumer advocates; the toy industry; children's product retailers; and standard-setting organizations. What might explain the differences in their points of view?

4. What do you think is the best way for society to protect children from harmful toys? Specifically, what are the appropriate roles for various stakeholders in this process?

The Collapse of Enron

On December 2, 2001, Enron Corporation filed for bankruptcy. The company's sudden collapse—the largest business failure in U.S. history to date—came as a shock to many. Just months earlier, *Fortune* magazine had named Enron the most innovative company in America for the sixth consecutive year. The Houston, Texas–based firm, ranked seventh on the *Fortune* 500, was widely considered to be the premier energy trading company in the world. At its peak in 2000, Enron employed 19,000 people and booked annual revenues in excess of $100 billion. At a meeting of executives in January 2001, chairman and CEO Kenneth Lay had said the company's mission was no longer just to be the world's greatest energy company; rather, its mission was to become simply "the world's greatest company."[1]

The pain caused by Enron's abrupt failure was widely felt. The company immediately laid off 4,000 employees, with more to follow. Thousands of Enron employees and retirees saw the value of their 401(k) retirement plans, many heavily invested in the company's stock, become worthless almost overnight. "We, the rank and file, got burned," said one retiree, who lost close to $1.3 million in savings. "I thought people had to treat us honestly and deal fairly with us. In my neck of the woods, what happened is not right."[2] Shareholders and mutual fund investors lost $70 billion in market value. Two banks—J. P. Morgan Chase and Citigroup—faced major write-downs on bad loans. Not only did Enron creditors, shareholders, and bondholders lose out, confidence also fell across the market, as investors questioned the integrity of the financial statements of other companies in which they held stock.

In the aftermath, many struggled to unravel the messy story behind Enron's collapse. Congressional committees initiated investigations, prosecutors brought criminal charges against Enron executives and their accountants for obstruction of justice and securities fraud, and institutional investors sued to recoup their losses. Some blamed Arthur Andersen, Enron's accounting firm, for certifying financial statements that arguably had wrongfully

By Anne T. Lawrence. Copyright © 2003 by the author. All rights reserved. Sources for this case include articles appearing in *The Wall Street Journal, The New York Times, BusinessWeek, Fortune, Houston Chronicle, Newsweek, Time,* and *U.S. News & World Report.* Primary documents consulted include various Enron annual reports; "Report of the Investigation by the Special Investigative Committee of the Board of Directors of Enron Corp.," February 1, 2002 (the Powers Committee Report); William S. Lerach and Milberg Weiss Bershad Hynes & Lerach LLP, "In Re: Enron Corporation Securities Litigation" (consolidated complaint for violation of the securities laws), 2002; and transcripts of hearings before the U.S. House of Representatives Committee on Financial Services and Committee on Energy and Commerce and the U.S. Senate Committee on Governmental Affairs and Committee on Commerce, Science, and Transportation. Secondary sources consulted include Peter C. Fusaro and Ross M. Miller, *What Went Wrong at Enron* (Hoboken, NJ: John Wiley & Sons, 2002); Robert Bryce, *Pipe Dreams: Greed, Ego, and the Death of Enron* (New York: PublicAffairs/Perseus Books, 2002); Malcolm S. Salter, Lynne C. Levesque, and Maria Ciampa, "Innovation Corrupted: The Rise and Fall of Enron," Working Paper Series, No. 02-102, 2002; and Mark Jickling, "The Enron Collapse: An Overview of Financial Issues," Congressional Research Service, February 4, 2002.

[1] "Enron's Last Year: Web of Details Did Enron In as Warnings Went Unheeded," *The New York Times,* February 10, 2002. Revenue data are from Enron's *2000 Annual Report.*

[2] "Enron's Collapse: Audacious Climb to Success Ended in Dizzying Plunge," *The New York Times,* January 13, 2002.

concealed the company's precarious financial situation; some blamed the board of directors for insufficient oversight. Others pointed to a go-go culture in which self-dealing by corrupt executives was condoned, or even admired, while others faulted government regulators, industry analysts, and the media for failing to uncover the company's weaknesses. It would likely take years for the courts to sort through the wreckage.

Enron Corporation

Enron Corporation was formed in 1985 through a merger of Houston Natural Gas and InterNorth of Omaha, Nebraska. The union created a midsized firm whose main asset was a large network of natural gas pipelines. The company's core business was distributing natural gas to utilities.

The central figure from the outset of Enron's history was Kenneth L. Lay. The son of a Baptist minister from rural Missouri, Lay trained as an economist at the University of Missouri and the University of Houston and briefly taught college-level economics. After a stint with Exxon, Lay accepted a post in the Nixon administration, serving in the Federal Energy Commission and, later, in the Interior Department as deputy undersecretary for energy. Following the Watergate scandal, Lay returned to the private sector in 1974, taking the first in a series of executive positions at various energy companies. Lay became CEO of Houston Natural Gas in 1984, and he assumed the top job at Enron in 1986, shortly after the merger. One observer described Lay as a man of "considerable charm, homespun roots, and economic expertise" who tended to play an "outside" role, leaving the day-to-day management of his company in the hands of others.[3]

A strong proponent of free markets, Lay felt that the deregulation of the 1980s presented an opportunity for the fledgling company. Historically, the U.S. energy industry had been highly regulated. Utilities were granted monopolies for specific regions, and regulators controlled the prices of electricity and natural gas. Pipeline operators could transport only their own natural gas, not that of other producers. In the 1980s, however, a series of legislative actions at both federal and state levels removed many of these restrictions. For the first time, energy producers were free to compete, buy and sell at market prices, and use each other's distribution networks. The promise of deregulation, touted by lawmakers at the time, was that competition would lead to greater efficiencies, lower prices, and better service for consumers.

Deregulation caused problems for both producers and users of energy, however, because prices for the first time became highly volatile. In the past, energy users (an industrial company or regional utility, for example) could buy extra natural gas or electricity from producers on the spot market on an as-needed basis. Once prices were free to fluctuate, however, this approach became riskier for both parties. The customer did not want to be forced to buy when prices were high, and the producer did not want to be forced to sell when prices were low.

Enron moved to provide an ingenious solution: The company would leverage its large network of pipelines to set up a "gas bank" that would act as the intermediary in this transaction, reducing market risk. Enron would sign contracts with producers to buy their gas on a certain date at a certain price and other contracts with users to sell them gas on a certain date at a certain price. Presuming that both parties were willing to pay a slight premium to insure against risk, Enron could make money on the spread. Enron had clear advantages as a market maker in natural gas: It owned pipelines that could be

---

[3] Peter C. Fusaro and Ross M. Miller, *What Went Wrong at Enron* (Hoboken, NJ: John Wiley & Sons, 2002), p. 9.

used to transport the product from producer to user, and it had strong institutional knowledge of how markets in the industry operated.

The idea man behind this innovation was Jeffrey Skilling. A graduate of the Harvard Business School and a partner in the consulting firm McKinsey & Company, Skilling had been brought in by Lay in the late 1980s to advise Enron on the company's response to deregulation. The gas bank, in itself, was a clever idea, but Skilling went further. He developed a series of other products, called energy derivatives, for Enron's trading partners. These products included *options,* which allowed companies to buy gas in the future at a fixed price, and *swaps,* which allowed them to trade fixed prices for floating prices and vice versa. In 1990, Skilling left McKinsey to become CEO of Enron Gas Services, as the gas bank came to be known. In 1996, he was promoted to the position of president and chief operating officer of Enron and, in February 2001, to CEO.[4]

We Make Markets

Enron's core gas services division was highly profitable, but by the mid-1990s its growth had begun to level out, as competitors entered the market and both buyers and sellers became more sophisticated and thus able to drive harder bargains. The challenge, as Skilling saw it, was to maintain Enron's growth by extending the business model that had worked so well in natural gas into a range of other commodities. As he later explained this strategy to an interviewer, "If you have the same general [market] characteristics, all you have to do is change the units. Enron has a huge investment in capabilities that can be deployed instantly into new markets at no cost."[5]

In particular, Skilling sought to trade commodities in industries with characteristics similar to those of natural gas—ones that were undergoing deregulation, had fragmented markets, maintained dedicated distribution channels, and in which both buyers and sellers wanted flexibility.[6]

- *Electricity.* One of the most obvious markets for Enron to enter was electric power. Deregulation of electric utilities in many states—most notably, California—presented an opportunity for Enron to use its trading capabilities to buy and sell contracts for electricity. Enron already owned some gas-fired power plants, and it moved to build and buy facilities designed to supply electricity during periods of peak demand. Enron also moved to expand this business internationally, especially in nations undergoing energy deregulation or privatization.

- *Water.* In 1998, Enron acquired Wessex Water in the United Kingdom and changed its name to Azurix, with the ambitious goal of operating water and wastewater businesses globally.

- *Broadband.* The company formed Enron Broadband Services in January 2000. Portland General Electric, which Enron acquired in 1997, provided the core fiber optic network for this service. The idea was to supply customers with access to bandwidth at future dates at guaranteed prices. Enron believed these contracts would appeal to

---

[4] Enron's early history is described in two cases, "Enron: Entrepreneurial Energy," Harvard Business School case 700-079, and "Enron's Transformation: From Gas Pipelines to New Economy Powerhouse," Harvard Business School case 9-301-064.

[5] Darden School of Business videotape, May 25, 2001, cited in Joseph Bower and David Garvin, "Enron's Business and Strategy," unpublished paper, Harvard Business School, April 10, 2002.

[6] Malcolm S. Salter, Lynne C. Levesque, and Maria Ciampa, "Innovation Corrupted: The Rise and Fall of Enron," Harvard Business School Working Paper Series, No. 02-102, 2002..

customers who did not want to rely on the public Internet or build their own telecommunications networks.

• *Pulp, paper, and lumber*. Enron launched *clickpaper.com*, an online market for the purchase of contracts for the delivery of wood products, and bought a newsprint company to ensure a ready source of supply.

Skilling told an interviewer from *Frontline* in March 2001, "We are looking to create open, competitive, fair markets. And in open, competitive, fair markets, prices are lower and customers get better service. . . . We are the good guys. We are on the side of the angels."[7]

By 2001, Enron was buying and selling metals, pulp and paper, specialty chemicals, bandwidth, coal, aluminum, plastics, and emissions credits, among other commodities. At the height of its power, 1,500 traders housed in Enron's office tower in Houston were trading 1,800 different products. As *The New York Times* later noted in an editorial, Enron was widely viewed as "a paragon of American ingenuity, a stodgy gas pipeline company that had reinvented itself as a high-tech clearinghouse in an ever-expanding roster of markets."[8] Reflecting the general enthusiasm, Skilling replaced his automobile vanity license plate, which had read WLEC (World's Largest Energy Company) with WMM (We Make Markets).[9]

Insisting on Results

In his 1999 letter to shareholders, Lay described the company's attitude toward its employees this way: "Individuals are empowered to do what they think is best. . . . We do, however, keep a keen eye on how prudent they are. . . . We insist on results."[10]

Enron used a recruitment process designed to hire individuals who were smart, hardworking, and intensely loyal. The company preferred to hire recent graduates. After an initial screening interview, candidates were brought to the Houston office for a "Super Saturday," during which they were individually interviewed for 50 minutes by eight interviewers, with only 10-minute breaks between interviews.

Even candidates who survived this strenuous hiring process, however, could not count on job security. Within the company, management used a "rank and yank" system in which new recruits were ranked every six months, and the 15 or 20 percent receiving the lowest scores were routinely terminated. Enron's highly competitive and results-oriented culture "created an environment," in the words of one observer, "where most employees were afraid to express their opinions or to question unethical and potentially illegal business practices."[11]

On the other hand, employees were encouraged to take initiative and were handsomely rewarded when their efforts paid off. Louise Kitchen, chief of the European gas trading unit, for example, organized a team to develop an online trading system. When it was adopted as the basis for a companywide division, Kitchen was promoted to president of Enron Online.

[7] "Enron's Many Strands: The Company Unravels; Enron Buffed Image Even as It Rotted from Within," *The New York Times,* February 10, 2002.

[8] "The Rise and Fall of Enron" [Editorial], *The New York Times,* November 2, 2001.

[9] Fusaro and Miller, *What Went Wrong,* p. 70.

[10] *1999 Enron Annual Report.*

[11] Fusaro and Miller, *What Went Wrong,* p. 52. Enron's "rank and yank" system is described in Malcolm Gladwell, "The Talent Myth," *The New Yorker,* September 16, 2002.

	Base Salary	Bonus	Other	Stock Options	Total	Stock Options as % of Total
Lay	1.3	7	.4	123.4	132.1	93
Skilling	.9	5.6	—	62.5	69.0	91

Note: All figures are in millions of dollars, rounded to the nearest $100,000. "Stock options" represents stock options exercised and sold in 2000, not granted in 2000. These figures do not include the value of perquisites, such as personal use of company aircraft.

Sources: Enron, SEC Schedule 14A (proxy statement), March 27, 2001, p. 18; and Dan Ackman, "Executive Compensation: Did Enron Execs Dump Shares?" *Forbes.com,* March 22, 2002.

Executive compensation was also results-based. According to Enron's 2001 proxy statement,

> The basic philosophy behind executive compensation at Enron is to reward executive performance that creates long-term shareholder value. This pay-for-performance tenet is embedded in each aspect of an executive's total compensation package. Additionally, the philosophy is designed to promote teamwork by tying a significant portion of compensation to business unit and Enron performance.[12]

Executive compensation was primarily composed of salary, bonus, and stock options, as shown in Exhibit A. In addition, the company routinely lent money to top executives, forgiving the loans if the terms of their contracts were fulfilled. Enron also awarded some executives equity stakes in various business units, which could be converted into stock or cash under certain conditions. For example, Skilling held a 5 percent stake in the retail energy unit, which he converted into $100 million worth of stock in 1998.[13]

During Enron's final years, many top executives sold significant blocks of company stock. Between October 1998 and November 2001, according to a lawsuit later filed by shareholders, Lay sold $184 million worth of Enron stock; Skilling, $71 million; and Andrew Fastow, Enron's CFO, $34 million. All three men sold large blocks in late 2000 or early 2001.[14]

Politics as Usual

Political action was an important part of Enron's overall strategy. The company's primary policy goal was to promote deregulation and reduce government oversight in the range of markets in which it traded. It maintained an office in Washington, DC, staffed by over 100 lobbyists and also used outside lobbyists for specialized assignments. The company spent $2.1 million on lobbying in 2000 alone.[15] Enron was also a major campaign contributor. From 1994 on, Enron was the largest contributor to congressional campaigns in the energy industry, giving over $5 million to House and Senate candidates, mostly to Republicans (see Exhibit B). In 2000, it gave $2.4 million in political contributions.

[12] Enron, SEC Schedule 14A (proxy statement), March 27, 2001, p. 15.

[13] "Enron Compensation Raised Questions," *Dow Jones Newswires,* March 26, 2002.

[14] Insider trading data computed by Milberg Weiss Bershad Hynes & Lerach LLP; available at *www.enronfraud.com.*

[15] "The Fall of the Giant: Enron's Campaign Contributions and Lobbying," Center for Responsive Politics, *www.opensecrets.org.*

Election Cycle	Total Contributions	Soft Money Contributions	Contributions from PACs	Contributions from Individuals	% to Democrats	% to Republicans
1990	$163,250	N/A	$130,250	$33,000	42%	58%
1992	$281,009	$75,109	$130,550	$75,350	42	58
1994	$520,996	$136,292	$189,565	$195,139	42	58
1996	$1,141,016	$687,445	$171,671	$281,900	18	81
1998	$1,049,942	$691,950	$212,643	$145,349	21	79
2000	$2,441,398	$1,671,555	$280,043	$489,800	28	72
2002	$353,959	$304,909	$32,000	$17,050	6	94
Total	$5,951,570	$3,567,260	$1,146,722	$1,237,588	26	74

Note: Soft money contributions were not publicly disclosed until the 1991–92 election cycle. Soft money contributions were banned in 2002.

Source: Center for Responsive Politics, based on Federal Election Commission data; available at www.opensecrets.org/news/enron/enron_totals.asp.

Enron CEO Kenneth Lay also had close personal ties with the Bush family. In 1992, Lay had chaired the host committee for the Republican National Convention in Houston at which George H. Bush was nominated to run for a second term as president. Enron donated $700,000 to George W. Bush's various campaigns between 1993 and 2001. Lay and his wife personally donated $100,000 to the younger Bush's presidential inauguration.

Over the years, Enron's efforts to influence policymaking enjoyed significant success, as illustrated by the following examples:

- *Commodities futures regulation.* The job of the Commodities Futures Trading Commission (CFTC), a federal agency, is to regulate futures contracts traded in an exchange. From 1988 to 1993, the CFTC was chaired by Wendy Gramm, an economist and wife of then-Congressman Phil Gramm (Republican, Texas). In 1992, Enron petitioned the CFTC to exempt energy derivatives and swaps—such as those in which it was beginning to make a market—from government oversight. In January 1993, just days before President Clinton took office, Wendy Gramm approved the exemption. The following month, after she had left office, Gramm was invited to join Enron's board of directors. According to Enron's filings with the SEC, Gramm received somewhere between $.9 and $1.8 million in salary, fees, and stock option sales and dividends for her service on the board between 1993 and 2001.[16]

- *Securities and Exchange Commission (SEC).* In 1997, the SEC granted Enron an exemption for its foreign subsidiaries from the provisions of the Investment Company Act of 1940, a law designed to prevent abuses by utilities. The law barred companies it covered from shifting debt off their books, and barred executives of these companies from investing in affiliated partnerships. After it had failed to win the exemption it wanted from Congress in 1996, Enron hired the former director of the investment management division at the SEC as a lobbyist to take the company's case directly to his former colleagues. He was successful. The year 1997 was the last in which the SEC conducted a thorough examination of Enron's annual reports.[17]

[16] Blind Faith: *How Deregulation and Enron's Influence over Government Looted Billions from Americans* (Washington, DC: Public Citizen, December 2001).

[17] "Exemption Won in 1997 Set Stage for Enron Woes," *The New York Times,* January 23, 2002.

- *Commodity Futures Modernization Act.* This law, passed by Congress in late 2000, included a special exemption for Enron that allowed the company to operate an unregulated energy trading subsidiary. Senator Phil Gramm, chair of the powerful banking committee, was instrumental in getting this provision included in the bill despite the opposition of the president's working group on financial markets. Over the years, Enron had been the largest single corporate contributor to Gramm's campaigns, with $260,000 in gifts since 1993.[18]

Reviewing the history of Enron's efforts to limit government oversight, one reporter concluded, "If the regulators in Washington were asleep, it was because the company had made their beds and turned off the lights."[19]

Off the Balance Sheet

As Enron forged ahead in the late 1990s as a market maker in a wide range of commodities, it began to assume increasing amounts of debt. Even though Skilling had touted the value of an "asset light" strategy, entry into markets for such varied commodities as water, steel, and broadband required that Enron buy significant hard assets. Enron's aggressive new business ventures required, by some estimates, on the order of $10 billion in up-front capital investments. Heavy indebtedness, however, posed a problem, because creditworthiness was critical to the company's ability to make markets in a wide range of commodities. Other parties would be unwilling to enter into contracts promising future delivery if Enron were not viewed as financially rock-solid, and the company had to maintain an investment-grade credit rating to continue to borrow money on favorable terms to fund its new ventures. A complicating factor was that several of the company's major new initiatives fell far short of expectations, and some—broadband in particular—were outright failures.

Beginning in 1997, Enron entered into a series of increasingly complex financial transactions with several special purpose entities, or SPEs, evidently with the intention of shifting liabilities (debt) off its books. After the bankruptcy, these transactions were investigated by a special committee of the Enron board, which released its findings in a document now known as the Powers Committee Report.

Under standard accounting rules, a company could legally exclude an SPE from its consolidated financial statements if two conditions were met: (1) an independent party had to exercise control of the SPE, and (2) this party had to own at least 3 percent of the SPE's assets. The independent party's investment had to be "at risk"—that is, not guaranteed by someone else.[20] The obvious problem was that if Enron intended to burden the SPEs with debt, no truly independent party would want to invest in them.

A key figure in many of these transactions was Andrew S. Fastow. Described as a "financial whiz kid," Fastow had joined Enron Finance in 1990. He developed a close relationship with Skilling and rose quickly, becoming chief financial officer (CFO) of Enron in 1998, at age 37. Speaking of Fastow's selection, Skilling told a reporter for *CFO* magazine, "We needed someone to rethink the entire financing structure at Enron from soup to nuts. We didn't want someone stuck in the past. . . . Andy has the intelligence and youthful exuberance to think in new ways."[21]

[18] *Blind Faith.*

[19] "Enron's Collapse: Audacious Climb to Success Ended in Dizzying Plunge."

[20] A. Christine David, "When to Consolidate a Special Purpose Entity," *California CPA*, June 2002.

[21] "Andrew S. Fastow: Enron Corp.," *CFO Magazine*, October 1, 1999.

The SPEs Enron set up in the five years leading up to its bankruptcy included the following:

- *Chewco.* In 1997, Enron created Chewco, an SPE named after the Star Wars character Chewbacca. Fastow invited a subordinate, Michael Kopper, to become the required "independent" investor in Chewco. Kopper and a friend invested $125,000 of their own funds and, with Enron providing collateral, got an $11 million loan from Barclays Bank. Between 1997 and 2000, Kopper received $2 million in management fees for his work on Chewco. In March 2001, Enron repurchased Chewco from its "investors"; Kopper and his friend received more than $10 million. The Powers Committee concluded, "Our review failed to identify how these payments were determined or what, if anything, Kopper did to justify the payments."[22]
- *The LJM Partnerships.* In 1999, Enron created two partnerships known as LJM1 and LJM2 (the initials of Fastow's wife and children). Unlike Chewco, where he had delegated this role to a subordinate, Fastow himself served as general partner and invested $1 million of his own money. Enron proceeded to transfer various assets and liabilities to the LJMs, in a way that benefited its bottom line. For example, in the second half of 1999, the LJM transactions generated "earnings" of $229 million for Enron (the company reported total pretax earnings of $570 million for that period).
- *Raptor Partnerships.* In 1999 and 2000, Enron established four new even more ambitious SPEs, collectively known as the Raptor Partnerships, with such fanciful names as talon, timberwolf, bobcat, and porcupine. In a series of extremely complex financial maneuvers in the final five quarters before declaring bankruptcy, Enron conducted various transactions with and among the Raptors and between the Raptors and the LJMs that generated $1.1 billion in "earnings" for the firm. Among other actions, Enron lent large blocks of its own stock to the Raptor partnerships in exchange for promissory notes, which were then posted to Enron's balance sheet as notes receivable.

Fastow made out handsomely on these deals. According to the Powers Committee Report, he eventually received almost $50 million for his role in the LJM partnerships and their transactions with the Raptors, in addition to his regular Enron compensation. In its review of Enron's SPE transactions, the Powers Committee Report concluded,

> These partnerships . . . were used by Enron management to enter into transactions that it could not, or would not, do with unrelated commercial entities. Many of the most significant transactions apparently were designed to accomplish favorable financial statement results, not to achieve bona fide economic objectives or to transfer risk. . . . They allowed Enron to conceal from the market very large losses resulting from Enron's merchant investments.[23]

Manipulating Revenue

Moving liabilities off the books was one way to make the company's financial condition look better than it was. Another way was to manipulate revenue. In the period preceding its collapse, Enron used a number of accounting practices apparently aimed at inflating revenues or reducing their volatility:

- *Mark-to-market accounting.* Mark-to-market (MTM) is an accounting procedure that allows companies to book as *current earnings* their expected *future revenue* from certain

---

[22] Powers Committee Report, p. 8.

[23] Ibid., p. 4.

assets. The Financial Accounting Standards Board (FASB), the organization that establishes generally accepted accounting principles, approved MTM in the early 1990s. Aggressively using this procedure, Enron counted projected profits from many deals in the year they were made. For example, in 2000 Enron entered into a partnership with Blockbuster to deliver movies on demand to viewers' homes over Enron's broadband network. The venture fell apart within a few months, after pilot projects in four U.S. cities failed. Nonetheless, Enron booked $110 million in profits in late 2000 and early 2001, based on the anticipated value of the partnership over 20 years.[24] In 2000, mark-to-market gains accounted for over half of Enron's reported pretax earnings.[25]

- *Sham swaps.* In the wake of its collapse, Enron was investigated by the SEC for possible sham swaps. For example, on the last day of the third quarter 2001, as the company's stock price was falling, Enron entered into an agreement with the telecommunications firm Qwest to exchange assets. Qwest and Enron agreed to buy fiber optic capacity from each other, and the two companies exchanged checks for around $112 million to complete the swap. According to *The New York Times,* "The deal enabled Enron to book a sale and avoid recording a loss on . . . assets, whose value in the open market had dropped far below the price on Enron's books."

- *Prudency accounts.* Enron traders routinely split profits from their deals into two categories—one that was added directly to the company's current financial statements, and the other that was added to a reserve fund. These so-called prudency accounts, according to Frank Partnoy, an expert in finance who testified before the U.S. Senate Committee on Governmental Affairs, functioned as "slush fund[s] that could be used to smooth out profits and losses over time." The use of prudency accounts made Enron's revenue stream appear less volatile than it actually was. As Partnoy noted, "Such fraudulent practices would have thwarted the very purpose of Enron's financial statements: to give investors an accurate picture of a firm's risks."[26]

The Best Interests of the Company

The two groups most responsible for overseeing the legal and ethical integrity of the company's financial reporting were Enron's board of directors and its auditors, Arthur Andersen's Houston office. In January 2001, Enron's board was made up of 17 members. Of the 15 outside members, many had long personal and business associations with Lay and were considered loyal supporters of his policies. Although the board included only two insiders (Lay and Skilling), other members of top management frequently attended, sitting around the edge of the boardroom.[27] The full board typically met five times a year. Members of Enron's board were unusually well compensated. In 2001, for example, each director received $381,000 in total compensation. (By comparison, the average director compensation for the top 200 companies that year was $152,000; and for companies in the petroleum and pipeline industries, it was $160,000.)[28]

---

[24] "Show Business: A Blockbuster Deal Shows How Enron Overplayed Its Hand—Company Booked Big Profit from Pilot Video Project That Soon Fizzled Out," *The Wall Street Journal,* January 17, 2002; and Robert Bryce, *Pipe Dreams: Greed, Ego, and the Death of Enron* (New York: PublicAffairs/Perseus Books, 2002), pp. 281–83.

[25] "Question Mark to Market: Energy Accounting Scrutinized," *CFO.com,* December 4, 2001.

[26] Testimony of Professor Frank Partnoy, Senate Committee on Governmental Affairs, January 24, 2002, *www.senate.gov/~gov_affairs/012402partnoy.htm.*

[27] Jay W. Lorsch, "The Board at Enron," unpublished paper, Harvard Business School, April 10, 2002, p. 1.

[28] Pearl Meyer and Partners, 2001 *Director Compensation: Boards in the Spotlight: Study of the Top 200 Corporations,* 2002. Data are rounded to the nearest thousand dollars.

The quality of the company's financial reporting was the responsibility of the audit and compliance committee. Chaired by Robert Jaedicke, emeritus professor of accounting and former dean of the Stanford Business School, the committee also included Wendy Gramm and four others.[29] The audit committee typically met for an hour or two before the regular board meetings, often for discussions with the company's professional auditors.

The board's first substantive involvement with the SPEs run by Fastow and his associates came in 1999.[30] Fastow's dual roles as both CFO and general partner of the LJM partnerships potentially violated Enron's code of ethics, which prohibited an officer from owning or participating in "any other entity which does business with . . . the company." An exception could be made if the participation was disclosed to the chairman and CEO and was judged not to "adversely affect the best interests of the company." Accordingly, in June and again in October, the board reviewed and approved the LJM partnerships and voted to suspend its code of ethics in this instance to permit Fastow to run the partnerships.

However, the board seemed sufficiently concerned that it put additional controls in place: it required both an annual board review and that the chief accounting officer and chief risk officer review all transactions with the partnerships. In October 2000, the board added additional restrictions, including provisions that Skilling personally sign off on all related approval sheets. In May 2001, an Enron attorney discovered that Skilling had not signed these documents, as the board had required, so he sent a message to the CEO that he needed to sign the papers at his convenience. Skilling never replied.[31] As for the mandated board review, the Powers Committee later concluded that although the audit committee had periodically reviewed the SPEs, "these reviews appear to have been too brief, too limited in scope, and too superficial to serve their intended function."[32]

In its oversight function, the board and its audit committee relied heavily on the professional advice of Enron's auditor, Arthur Andersen, which repeatedly told the board it was "comfortable" with the partnership transactions. Founded in 1913 and Enron's auditor since 1985, Andersen was one of the Big Five accounting firms. Since the early 1990s, Andersen's Houston office had acted both as the company's external and internal auditors, in an arrangement called an "integrated audit," in which Enron subcontracted much of its "inside" work to the firm.[33] Andersen also did considerable consulting and nonauditing work for its client. All told, Enron was a very important client of the Houston office. In 2000, for example, Andersen received $25 million for audit and $27 million for nonaudit services from Enron. Between 1997 and 2001, Andersen received around $7 million for its accounting work on the Chewco, LJM, and Raptors transactions.

Relations between Enron and Arthur Andersen were unusually close. Many Andersen accountants had office space at Enron and easily mingled with their coworkers. "People just thought they were Enron employees," said one former Enron accountant.[34] Moreover, mobility between Andersen and its client was high; indeed, at the time of the bankruptcy,

---

[29] Other members of the audit committee were John Mendelsohn, president of the M.D. Anderson Cancer Clinic; Paolo V. Ferraz Pereira, former president of the State Bank of Rio de Janeiro; John Wakeham, former British Secretary of State for Energy; and Ronnie Chan, chairman of a large property development group in Hong Kong.

[30] Earlier, the board had provided a cursory review of Chewco, but had apparently been unaware of Kopper's role.

[31] "Enron's Many Strands."

[32] Powers Committee Report, p. 24.

[33] "Court Documents Show Andersen's Ties with Enron Were Growing in Early '90s," *The Wall Street Journal*, February 26, 2002.

[34] "Were Enron, Andersen Too Close to Allow Auditor to Do Its Job?" *The Wall Street Journal*, January 21, 2002.

the company's chief accounting officer, Richard Causey, had formerly been in charge of Andersen's Enron audit.

Andersen's own structure gave considerable autonomy to local offices like the one in Houston. Like other big accounting firms, Andersen had a professional standards group (PSG) at its corporate headquarters whose job was to review difficult issues that arose in the field. Unlike others, however, Andersen's PSG did not have the authority to overrule its field auditors in case of disagreement. An investigation by *BusinessWeek* showed that on four different occasions, the Enron audit team went ahead despite PSG objections to various aspects of its accounting for the Enron partnerships. Finally, Enron requested that its chief critic be removed from the PSG. Andersen headquarters complied.[35]

Later, responding to criticism of its actions as Enron auditors, Andersen simply stated that it "ignored a fundamental problem: that poor business decisions on the part of Enron executives and its board ultimately brought the company down."[36]

A Wave of Accounting Scandals

On March 5, 2001, *Fortune* magazine published a cover story, written by reporter Bethany McLean, under the title "Is Enron Overpriced?" In the article, McLean challenged the conventional wisdom that Enron stock—which had returned 89 percent to investors the previous year and was selling at 55 times earnings—was an attractive buy. Calling Enron's financial statements "nearly impenetrable," she interviewed a number of stock analysts who, although bullish on Enron stock, were unable to explain exactly how the company made money. One called the company's financial statements "a big black box."[37]

What *Fortune* did not know at the time was that the fragile structure of partnerships Enron had constructed rested on the high price of the company's stock. Much of the partnerships' assets consisted of Enron stock or loans guaranteed by Enron stock. If the share price declined too far, this would trigger a need for more financing from the company. Before Enron's announcement of first-quarter 2001 results, and then again prior to the second-quarter results, Andersen worked furiously to restructure the partnerships to prevent the necessity of consolidating them with Enron's books. The Powers Committee later commented that these efforts were "perceived by many within Enron as a triumph of accounting ingenuity by a group of innovative accountants. We believe that perception was mistaken. . . . [The] Raptors were little more than a highly complex accounting construct that was destined to collapse."[38]

In late July, Enron's stock slid below $47 a share—the first "trigger" price for the partnerships. On August 14, Skilling abruptly resigned as president and CEO, citing undisclosed personal reasons. Lay, who had been serving as chairman, resumed the role of CEO. In a memo to Enron employees that day, Lay assured them,

> I have never felt better about the prospects for the company. All of you know that our stock price has suffered substantially over the last few months. One of my top priorities will be to restore a significant amount of the stock value we have lost as soon as possible. Our performance has never been stronger; our business model has never been more robust; our growth has never been more certain; and most importantly, we have never had a better nor deeper pool of

---

[35] "Out of Control at Andersen," *BusinessWeek*, April 8, 2002.

[36] "Enron's Doomed 'Triumph of Accounting,'" *The New York Times*, February 4, 2002.

[37] "Is Enron Overpriced?" *Fortune*, March 5, 2001.

[38] Powers Committee Report, pp. 131–32.

talent throughout the company. We have the finest organization in business today. Together, we will make Enron the world's leading company.[39]

The following day, Sherron S. Watkins, an accountant and Enron vice president who worked under Fastow, wrote a memo to Lay to express her concerns about the company's accounting practices. She stated frankly,

> I am incredibly nervous that we will implode in a wave of accounting scandals. My 8 years of Enron work history will be worth nothing on my résumé; the business world will consider the past successes as nothing but an elaborate accounting hoax. Skilling is resigning now for "personal reasons" but I think he wasn't having fun, looked down the road, and knew this stuff was unfixable and would rather abandon ship now than resign in shame in 2 years.

She added,

> I have heard one manager . . . say, "I know it would be devastating to all of us, but I wish we would get caught. We're such a crooked company."

After a detailed review of the "questionable" accounting practices of the SPEs, Watkins recommended that Lay bring in independent legal and accounting experts to review the propriety of the partnerships and to prepare a "clean-up plan."[40]

Lay followed Watkins's advice—to a point. He brought in attorneys from Vinson & Elkins, the Houston law firm that had long been Enron's outside counsel and that had helped prepare the legal documents for the partnerships. In his instructions, Lay indicated that he saw no need to look too closely into the accounting. The lawyers interviewed Fastow, Enron's auditors, and several others, and then reported back to Lay on September 21 that although the accounting was "creative" and "aggressive," it was not "inappropriate from a technical standpoint."

Yet, despite these assurances, the partnerships were unraveling as Enron's stock price dropped (see Exhibit C) and could no longer be supported by even the most aggressive accounting. On October 16, under pressure from its auditors, Enron announced a charge against earnings of $544 million and a reduction in shareholders' equity of $1.2 billion related to transactions with the LJM partnerships. On October 22, the SEC initiated a probe of the SPEs; Fastow was fired the following day. Then, on November 8, Enron further shocked investors by restating *all* of its financial statements back to 1997 because "three unconsolidated entities [i.e., the partnerships] should have been consolidated in the financial statements pursuant to generally accepted accounting principles." These restatements had the effect of reducing income for 1997 to 2000 by $480 million, reducing shareholders' equity by $2.1 billion, and increasing debt by $2.6 billion.[41]

Company executives frantically went searching for a white knight to purchase the company. Dynegy, another Houston-based energy trader and longtime rival, initially agreed to buy Enron for $8.9 billion on November 9. After Dynegy's CEO and board had taken a careful look at Enron's books, however, they changed their minds and withdrew the offer. The rating agencies immediately downgraded Enron to junk status, and the stock dropped below $1 a share and was delisted from the New York Stock Exchange.

---

[39] The full text of Lay's memo appears in Fusaro and Miller, *What Went Wrong*, p. 201.

[40] The full text of Watkins's memo appears in Fusaro and Miller, *What Went Wrong*, pp. 185–91.

[41] Based on data reported in the Powers Committee Report, p. 6.

Exhibit C

Enron Stock Price and Trading Volume, 1998–2002

Source: *bigcharts.com.*

As the company imploded, Enron tried to call in its political chits in one last Hail Mary move. Lay and other top executives placed urgent calls to Commerce Secretary Donald Evans, Treasury Secretary Paul O'Neill, and other administration officials, reportedly asking them to lean on banks to extend credit to the company. They declined to do so. Later asked why he had not helped Enron, Evans said it would have been an "egregious abuse" to have intervened. O'Neill simply stated, "Companies come and go. . . . Part of the genius of capitalism is, people get to make good decisions or bad decisions, and they get to pay the consequence or enjoy the fruits of their decisions."[42]

Discussion Questions

1. Who were the key stakeholders involved in, or affected by, the collapse of Enron? How and to what degree were they hurt or helped by the actions of Enron management?

2. Considering all aspects of the case, what factor or factors do you believe most contributed to the collapse of Enron? In your answer, please consider both external and internal factors.

3. What steps should be taken now by corporate managers, stakeholders, and policy makers to prevent a similar event from occurring in the future?

[42] "Enron Lessons: Big Political Giving Wins Firms a Hearing, Doesn't Assure Aid," *The Wall Street Journal,* January 15, 2002.

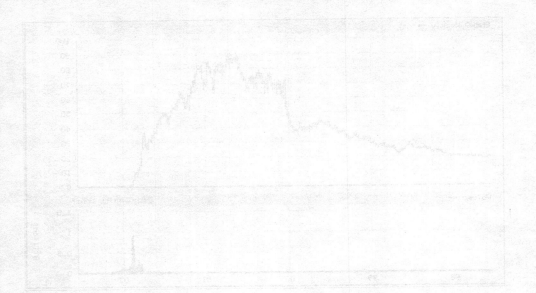

This glossary defines technical or special terms used in this book. Students may use it as a quick and handy reference for terms that may be unfamiliar without having to refer to the specific chapter(s) where they are used. It also can be a very helpful aid in studying for examinations and for writing term papers where precise meanings are needed.

A

acid rain   Rain that is more acidic than normal; occurs when emissions of sulfur dioxide and nitrogen oxides from utilities, manufacturers, and vehicles combine with water vapor in the air.

ad hoc coalitions   The bringing together of diverse groups to organize for or against legislation or regulation.

advocacy advertising   A political tool used by companies to promote their viewpoint through the media.

affirmative action   A positive and sustained effort by an organization to identify, hire, train if necessary, and promote minorities, women, and members of other groups who are underrepresented in the organization's workforce.

air pollution   When more pollutants, such as sulfur dioxide or particulates, are emitted into the atmosphere than can be safely absorbed and diluted by natural processes.

alternative dispute resolution   A method for resolving legal conflicts outside the traditional court system, in which a professional mediator (a third-party neutral) works with the two sides to negotiate a settlement agreeable to both parties.

annual stockholders' meeting   A yearly meeting called by a corporation's board of directors for purposes of reporting to the company's stockholders on the current status and future prospects of the firm.

anti-Americanism   Opposition to the United States of America, or to its people, principles, or policies.

antitrust laws   Laws that promote competition or that oppose trusts, monopolies, or other business combinations that restrain trade.

B

balanced scorecard   An approach focusing on a set of key financial and nonfinancial indicators to account for an organization's short-term and long-term accomplishments.

biodiversity   The number and variety of species and the range of their genetic makeup.

biotechnology   A technological application that uses biological systems or living organisms to make or modify products or processes for specific use.

bioterrorism   The use of deadly bioengineered diseases and poisons by terrorists.

blogs   Web-based journals or logs maintained by an individual containing commentaries, descriptions, graphics and other material.

blowing the whistle   (See whistleblowing.)

board of directors   An elected group of individuals who have a legal duty to establish corporate objectives, develop broad policies, and select top-level personnel for a company.

bottom line   Business profits or losses, usually reported in figures on the last or bottom line of a company's income statement.

bottom of the pyramid   The world's poor; also refers to creative business actions to develop products and services that meet the needs of the world's poor.

boundary-spanning departments   Departments, or offices, within an organization that reach across the dividing line that separates a company from groups and people in society.

bribery   A questionable or unjust payment often to a government official to ensure or facilitate a business transaction.

bundling   The collection of political contributions made by an organization's stakeholders to increase the organization's ability to influence a political agent.

business   An organization that is engaged in making a product or providing a service for a profit.

business and society   The study of the relationship between business and its social environment.

business ethics   The application of general ethical ideas to business behavior.

C

campaign finance reform   Efforts to change the rules governing the financing of political campaigns, often by limiting contributions made or received.

cap-and-trade   Allows businesses to buy and sell permits that entitle the bearer to emit a certain amount of pollution. The government issues these permits and caps the total amount of pollution that may be produced.

carbon neutrality   When an organization or individual produces net zero emissions of greenhouse gases.

carbon offsets (carbon credits)   Investments in projects that remove carbon dioxide or its equivalent from the atmosphere.

carrying capacity   The maximum population that the Earth's ecosystem can support at a certain level of technological development.

cellular telephones (or cell phones)   A mobile devices using radio technology that enables users to place calls from anywhere.

central state control (system)   A socioeconomic system in which economic power is concentrated in the hands of government officials and political authorities. The central government owns the property that is used to produce goods and services, and most private markets are illegal.

CERCLA   (Comprehensive Environmental Response, Compensation, and Liability Act). The major U.S. law governing the cleanup of existing hazardous-waste sites, popularly known as Superfund.

charity principle   The idea that the wealthier members of society or profitable businesses should contribute to those less fortunate or to organizations that provide community services.

chief information officer   Manager who has been entrusted with the responsibility to manage the organization's technology with its many privacy and security issues.

child care   The care or supervision of another's child, such as at a day-care center; offered as a benefit by some employers to working parents.

citizenship profile   Choosing a configuration of citizenship activities that fits the setting in which the company is working.

civic engagement   The active involvement of businesses and individuals in changing and improving communities.

civil society   Nonprofit, educational, religious, community, family, and interest-group organizations; social organizations that do not have a commercial or governmental purpose. See also nongovernmental organization.

collaborative partnerships   Alliances among business, government, and civil society organizations that draw on the unique capabilities of each to address complex social problems.

command and control regulation   A regulatory approach where the government "commands" companies to meet specific standards (such as amounts of particular pollutants) and "controls" the methods (such as technology) used to achieve these standards. This approach is often contrasted with market-based regulatory approaches where the government establishes general goals and allows companies to use the most cost-effective methods possible to achieve them.

commons   Traditionally, an area of land on which all citizens could graze their animals without limitation. The term now refers to any shared resource, such as land, air, or water, that a group of people use collectively.

community   A company's area of local business influence. Traditionally, the term applied to the city, town, or rural area in which a business's operations, offices, or assets were located. With the rise of large, complex business organizations, the meaning of the term has expanded to include multiple localities.

community relations   The organized involvement of business with the communities in which it conducts operations.

community relations manager (or community involvement manager)   Manager delegated to interact with local citizens, develop community programs, manage donations of goods and services, work with local governments, and encourage employee volunteerism.

Community Reinvestment Act   A federal law requiring banks to reinvest a portion of their depositors' money back into the local community, through low-income lending programs, and to provide annual reports to the public.

competition   A struggle to survive and excel. In business, different firms compete with one another for customers' dollars, employees' talents and other assets.

competitive intelligence   The systematic and continuous process of gathering, analyzing and managing external information on the organization's competitors.

Comprehensive Environmental Response, Compensation, and Liability Act (CERCLA)   (See CERCLA and Superfund.)

computer hackers   Individuals often with advanced technology training who, for thrill or profit, breach a business' information security system.

conflicts of interest   Occur when an individual's self-interest conflicts with acting in the best interest of another, when the individual has an obligation to do so.

constructive engagement   When transnational corporations operate according to strong moral principles and become a force for positive change in other nations where they operate.

consumer affairs officer   Manages the complex network of consumer relations.

consumer movement   A social movement that seeks to augment the rights and powers of consumers. (Also known as consumerism.)

consumer privacy   A consumer's right to be protected from the unwanted collection and use of information about that individual for use in marketing.

consumer protection laws   Laws that provide consumers with better information, protect consumers from possible hazards, encourage competitive pricing, protect privacy, or permit consumer lawsuits.

consumer rights   The legitimate claims of consumers to safe products and services, adequate information, free choice, a fair hearing, competitive prices, and privacy.

consumerism   (See consumer movement.)

corporate citizenship   This term broadly refers to putting corporate social responsibility into practice through stakeholder partnerships, serving society, and integrating financial *and* social performance.

corporate crisis   A significant business disruption that stimulates extensive news media or social networking coverage.

corporate culture   A blend of ideas, customs, traditional practices, company values, and shared meanings that help define normal behavior for everyone who works in a company.

corporate foundations   Organizations chartered as nonprofits, and funded by companies, for the purpose of donating money to community organizations, programs, and causes.

corporate giving   (See corporate philanthropy.)

corporate governance   The system of allocating power in a corporation that determines how and by whom the company is to be directed.

corporate philanthropy   Gifts and contributions made by businesses, usually from pretax profits, to benefit various types of nonprofit and community organizations.

corporate political strategy   Those activities taken by an organization to acquire, develop, and use power to achieve a political advantage.

corporate power   The strength or capability of corporations to influence government, the economy, and society, based on their organizational resources.

corporate social responsibility   The idea that businesses should be held accountable for any of its actions that affect people, their communities, and their environment.

corporate volunteerism   A program wherein a company engages its employees in community service as a way to improve the company's image as well as serve the communities in which the business operates.

corporation   Legally, an artificial legal "person," created under the laws of a particular state or nation. Socially and organizationally, it is a complex system of people, technology, and resources generally devoted to carrying out a central economic mission as it interacts with a surrounding social and political environment.

cost-benefit analysis   A systematic method of calculating the costs and benefits of a project or activity that is intended to produce benefits.

crisis management   The process organizations use to respond to short-term or intermediate-term, unexpected, and high consequences shocks, such as accidents, disasters, catastrophes, and injuries.

cyberchondriacs   People who leap to the most dreadful conclusions while researching medical matters online.

cyberspace   A virtual location where information is stored, ideas are described, and communication takes place in and through an electronic network of linked systems.

D

dark site   A Web site developed and uploaded with critical information but remains dormant or "dark" until activated by the firm when needed in response to a crisis.

debt relief   The idea that the world's richest nations should forgive poor nations' obligation to pay back loans.

deceptive advertising   An advertisement that makes false or misleading claims about the company's own product or its competitor's product, withholds relevant information, or creates unreasonable expectations; generally illegal under U.S. law.

democracy   A form of government in which power is vested in the people and exercised by them directly or by their elected representatives.

department of corporate citizenship   A department created in a business to centralize under common leadership wide-ranging corporate citizenship functions.

deregulation   The removal or scaling down of regulatory authority and regulatory activities of government.

design for disassembly   Designing products so that they can be disassembled and their component parts recycled or reused at the end of their useful life.

digital divide   The gap between those that have technology and those that do not.

digital medical records   The electronic storing of a patient's medical records so that they are accessible by other medical providers.

Digital Millennium Copyright Act   The U. S. law that made it a crime to circumvent antipiracy measures built into most commercial software agreements between the manufacturers and their users.

directors   (See board of directors.)

discrimination (in jobs or employment)   Unequal treatment of employees based on non–job-related factors such as race, sex, age, national origin, religion, color, and physical or mental handicap.

diversity   Variation in the characteristics that distinguish people from one another, such as age, ethnicity, nationality, gender, mental or physical abilities, race, sexual orientation, family status, and first language.

diversity council   A group of managers and employees responsible for developing and implementing specific action plans to meet an organization's diversity goals. (See also diversity.)

divestment   Withdrawing and shifting to other uses the funds that a person or group has invested in the securities (stocks, bonds, notes, etc.) of a company. Investors sometimes have divested the securities of companies doing business in countries accused of human rights abuses.

dividend   A return-on-investment payment made to the owners of shares of corporate stock at the discretion of the company's board of directors.

drug testing (of employees)   The testing of employees, by the employer, for the presence of illegal drugs, sometimes by means of a urine sample, saliva, or hair follicle analyzed by a clinical laboratory.

E

e-business   Electronic business exchanges between businesses and between businesses and their customers.

eco-efficiency   Occurs when businesses or societies are simultaneously economically efficient and environmentally responsible.

ecological footprint   One method of measuring the earth's carrying capacity, and how far human society has exceeded it.

ecologically sustainable organization (ESO)   A business that operates in a way that is consistent with the principle of sustainable development. (See also sustainable development.)

ecology   The study of how living things—plants and animals—interact with one another in the Earth's unified natural system or ecosystem.

economic leverage   A political tool where a business uses its economic power to threaten to relocate its operations unless a desired political action is taken.

economic regulation   The oldest form of regulation in the U.S., aimed at modifying the normal operations of the free market and the forces of supply and demand.

ecosystem   Plants and animals in their natural environment, living together as an interdependent system.

egoist   (See ethical egoist.)

elder care   The care or supervision of elderly persons; offered as a benefit by some employers to working children of elderly parents.

electronic monitoring (of employees)   The use by employers of electronic technologies to gather, store, and monitor information about employees' activities.

emissions charges or fees   Fees charged to business by the government, based on the amount of pollution emitted.

employee assistance programs (EAPs)   Company-sponsored programs to assist employees with alcohol abuse, drug abuse, mental health and other problems.

employee ethics training   Programs developed by businesses to further reinforce their ethical expectations for their employees.

employment-at-will   The principle that workers are hired and retained solely at the discretion of the employer.

enlightened self-interest   The view that holds it is in business's self-interest in the long run to provide true value to its stakeholders and behave responsible as a global corporate citizen.

environmental analysis   A method managers use to gather information about external issues and trends.

environmental audit   A company audit, or review, of its progress toward meeting environmental goals, such as reducing carbon emissions.

environmental intelligence   The acquisition of information gained from analyzing the multiple environments affecting organizations.

environmental justice   The efforts to prevent inequitable exposure to risk, such as from hazardous waste.

environmental partnerships   A voluntary, collaborative partnership between or among businesses, government regulators, and environmental organizations to achieve specific environmental goals.

Environmental Protection Agency (EPA) The U.S. federal government agency responsible for most environmental regulation and enforcement.

environmental scanning Examining an organization's environment to discover trends and forces that could have an impact on the organization.

environmental standards Standard amounts of particular pollutants allowable by law or regulation.

equal employment opportunity The principal that all persons otherwise qualified should be treated equally with respect to job opportunities, workplace conditions, pay, fringe benefits, and retirement provisions.

Equal Employment Opportunity Commission (EEOC) The U.S. federal government agency charged with enforcing equal employment opportunity laws and executive orders.

ergonomics Adapting work tasks, working conditions, and equipment to minimize worker injury or stress.

ethical climate An unspoken understanding among employees of what is and is not acceptable behavior.

ethical egoist A person who puts his or her own selfish interests above all other considerations, while denying the ethical needs and beliefs of others.

ethical principles Guides to moral behavior, such as honesty, keeping promises, helping others, and respecting others' rights.

ethical relativism A belief that ethical right and wrong are defined by various periods of time in history, a society's traditions, the specific circumstances of the moment, or personal opinion.

ethics A conception of right and wrong conduct, serving as a guide to moral behavior.

ethics audit An assessment used by an organization to target the effectiveness of their ethical safeguards or to document evidence of increased ethical employee behavior.

ethics and compliance officer A manager designated by an organization to investigate breaches of ethical conduct, promulgate ethics statements, and generally promote ethical conduct at work.

ethics policies or codes A written set of rules used to guide managers and employees when they encounter an ethical dilemma.

ethics reporting mechanisms A program that enables employees, customers or suppliers to report an ethical concern directly to someone in authority in an organization.

European Union (EU) The political and economic coalition of countries located in the greater European region.

executive compensation The compensation (total pay) of corporate executives, including salary, bonus, stock options, and various benefits.

extended product responsibility The idea that companies have a continuing responsibility for the environmental impacts of their products and services, even after they are sold.

F

fair labor standards Rules that establish minimum acceptable standards for the conditions under which a company's employees (or the employees of its suppliers or subcontractors) will work. For example, such standards might include a ban on all child labor, establishment of maximum work hours per week, or a commitment to pay wages above a certain minimum level.

family-friendly corporation A company that fully supports both men and women in their efforts to balance work and family responsibilities.

family leave A leave of absence from work, either paid or unpaid, for the purpose of caring for a family member.

Federal Communications Commission The U.S. federal government agency created in 1934 to regulate interstate and international communications; specifically regulates business advertisement.

fiscal policy The patterns of spending and taxation adopted by a government to stimulate or support the economy.

527 organizations Groups organized under section 527 of the Internal Revenue Service tax code for the purpose of donating money to candidates for public office and influencing elections.

flextime A plan that allows employees limited control over scheduling their own hours of work, usually at the beginning and end of the workday.

foreign direct investment When a company, individual or fund invests money in another country.

fraud Deceit or trickery due to the pursuit of economic gain or competitive advantage.

free enterprise system A socioeconomic system based on private ownership, profit-seeking business firms, and the principle of free markets.

free market A model of an economic system based on voluntary and free exchange among buyers and sellers. Competition regulates prices in all free market exchanges.

G

general public   Broadly defined as individuals or groups in society.

general systems theory   A theory that holds that all organisms are open to, and interact with, their external environments.

genetic engineering   The altering of the natural make-up of a living organism, which allows scientists to insert virtually any gene into a plant and create a new crop, or an entire new species.

genetically modified foods   Food crops grown from genetically engineered seeds or food processed from such crops.

glass ceiling   An invisible barrier to the advancement of women, minorities, and other groups in the workplace.

glass walls   An invisible barrier to the lateral mobility of women, minorities, and other groups in the workplace, such as from human resources to operations, which could lead to top management positions.

global codes of conduct   Codes of conduct that seek to define acceptable and unacceptable behavior for today's transnational corporations.

global corporate citizenship   Refers to putting an organization's commitment to social and environmental responsibility into practice worldwide.

global warming   The gradual warming of the earth's climate, believed by most scientists to be caused by an increase in carbon dioxide and other trace gases in the earth's atmosphere resulting from human activity, mainly the burning of fossil fuels.

globalization   The movement of goods, services, and capital across national borders.

greening of management   The process by which managers become more proactive with respect to environmental issues.

green marketing   A concept that describes the creation, promotion, and sale of environmentally safe products and services by business.

greenhouse effect   The warming effect that occurs when carbon dioxide, methane, nitrous oxides, and other gases act like the glass panels of a greenhouse, preventing heat from the earth's surface from escaping into space.

greenwashing   When an organization misleads consumers regarding the environmental benefits of a product or service.

H

harmonization   The coordination of laws and enforcement efforts among nations.

hazardous waste   Waste materials from industrial, agricultural, and other activities capable of causing death or serious health problems for those persons exposed for prolonged periods. (See also toxic substance.)

honesty testing   Written psychological tests given to prospective employees that seek to predict their honesty on the job.

human genome   Strands of DNA developing a unique pattern for every human.

human rights   An ethical approach emphasizing a person or group's entitlement to something or to be treated in a certain way, such as the right to life, safety, or to be informed.

I

ideology   A set of basic beliefs that define an ideal way of living for an individual, an organization, or a society.

image advertisements   Used by businesses to enhance their public image, create goodwill, or announce a major change, such as a merger, acquisition or new product line.

incumbents   Individuals who are seeking re-election to their political office.

industrial ecology   Designing factories and distribution systems as if they were self-contained ecosystems, such as using waste from one process as raw material for another.

information phase   The fifth phase of technology; emphasizes the use and transfer of knowledge and information rather than manual skill.

in-kind contributions   Corporate charitable contributions of products or services, rather than cash.

innovation   Creating a new process or device that adds value.

insider trading   Occurs when a person gains access to confidential information about a company's financial condition and then uses that information, before it becomes public knowledge, to buy or sell the company's stock; generally illegal.

institutional investor   A financial institution, insurance company, pension fund, endowment fund, or similar organization that invests its accumulated funds in securities offered for sale on stock exchanges.

institutionalized activity (ethics, social responsiveness, public affairs, etc.) An activity, operation, or procedure that is such an integral part of an organization that it is performed routinely by managers and employees.

intangible assets Nonphysical resources of the organization that enable it to achieve its goals and objectives, including intellectual property and corporate reputation.

intellectual property Ideas, concepts, and other symbolic creations of the human mind that are recognized and protected under a nation's copyright, patent, and trademark laws.

interactive social system The closely intertwined relationships between business and society.

international financial and trade institutions Institutions, such as the World Bank, International Monetary Fund, and World Trade Organization, that establish the rules by which international commerce is conducted.

International Monetary Fund An international financial institution that lends foreign exchange to member nations so they can participate in global trade.

internet A global network of interconnected computers, enabling users to share information.

iron law of responsibility The belief that those who do not use their power in ways that society considers responsible will tend to lose their power in the long run.

issue advertisements A technique used by businesses to influence the public's opinion of a political or legislative issue of concern to the company.

issue management The active management of public issues once they come to the attention of a business organization.

issue management process A five-step process where managers identify the issue, analyze the issue, generate options, take action and evaluate results.

J

justice An ethical approach that emphasizes whether the distribution of benefits and burdens are fair among people, according to some agreed-upon rule.

K

Kyoto Protocol An international treaty negotiated in 1997 in Kyoto, Japan, that committed its signatories to reduce emissions of greenhouse gases, such as carbon dioxide.

L

labor force participation rate The proportion of a particular group, such as women, in the paid workforce.

labor standards Conditions affecting a company's employees or the employees of its suppliers or subcontractors.

labor union An organization that represents workers on the job and that bargains collectively with the employer over wages, working conditions, and other terms of employment.

laws Society's attempt to formalize into written rules the public's ideas about what constitutes right and wrong conduct in various spheres of life.

legal challenges A political tool that questions the legal legitimacy of a regulation.

legal obligations A belief that a firm must abide by the laws and regulations governing the society.

license to operate The right to do business informally conferred by society on a business firm; must be earned through socially responsible behavior.

life-cycle analysis Collecting information on the lifelong environmental impact of a product in order to minimize its adverse impacts at all stages, including design, manufacture, use, and disposal.

living wage The moral obligation for a company to pay its employees enough to achieve a decent family standard of living.

lobbying The act of trying to directly shape or influence a government official's understanding and position on a public policy issue.

M

marine ecosystems This term refers broadly to oceans and the salt marshes, lagoons, and tidal zones that border them, and well as the diverse communities of life that they support.

market-based mechanism A form of regulation, used in environmental policy, that uses market mechanisms to control corporate behavior.

market failure Inability of the marketplace to properly adjust prices for the true costs of a firm's behavior.

market stakeholder A stakeholder that engages in economic transactions with a company. (Also called a primary stakeholder.)

M-commerce   Commerce conducted by using mobile or cell telephones.

media training   The education of executives and employees, who are likely to have contact with the media, in how to effectively communicate with the press.

military dictatorship   A repressive regime ruled by a dictator who exercises total power through control of the armed forces.

monetary policy   Government actions to control the supply and demand of money in the economy.

monopoly   Occurs when one company dominates the market for a particular product or service.

Montreal Protocol   An international treaty limiting the manufacture and use of chlorofluorocarbons and other ozone-depleting chemicals. (See also ozone.)

moral development stages   A series of progressive steps by which a person learns new ways of reasoning about ethical and moral issues. (See stages of moral development.)

morality   A condition in which the most fundamental human values are preserved and allowed to shape human thought and action.

N

nanotechnology   The application of engineering to create materials on a molecular or atomic scale.

natural monopolies   Where a concentration of the market is acquired by a few firms due to the nature of the industry rather than because of company practices.

negative externalities (or spill-over effects)   When the manufacture or distribution of a product gives rise to unplanned or unintended costs (economic, physical or psychological) borne by consumers, competitors, neighboring communities or other business stakeholders.

nongovernmental organizations (NGOs)   Organizations that do not have a governmental or commercial purpose, such as religious, community, family, and interest-group organizations. Also called civil society or civil sector organizations.

nonmarket stakeholder   A stakeholder that does not engage in direct economic exchange with a company, but is affected by or can affect its actions. (Also called a secondary stakeholder.)

nonrenewable resources   Natural resources, such as oil, coal, or natural gas, that once used are gone forever. (See also renewable resources.)

O

Occupational Safety and Health Administration (OSHA)   The U.S. federal government agency that enforces worker safety and health standards.

occupational segregation   The inequitable concentration of a group, such a minorities or women, in particular job categories.

ownership theory of the firm   A theory that holds that the purpose of the firm is to maximize the long-term return for its shareholders. (Also called the property or finance theory of the firm.)

ozone   A gas composed of three bonded oxygen atoms. Ozone in the lower atmosphere is a dangerous component of urban smog; ozone in the upper atmosphere provides a shield against ultraviolet light from the sun. (See also Montreal Protocol.)

P

parental leave   A leave of absence from work, either paid or unpaid, for the purpose of caring for a newborn or adopted child.

pay gap   The difference in the average level of wages, salaries, and income received by two groups, such as men and women (called the gender pay gap) or whites and persons of color (called the racial pay gap).

performance-expectations gap   The perceived distance between what a firm wants to do or is doing and what the stakeholder expects.

pharming   A hacking technique that redirects a user's computer from a legitimate Web site to another site.

philanthropy   (See corporate philanthropy.)

phishing   The practice of duping computer users into revealing their passwords or other private data under false pretenses.

political action committee (PAC)   An independently incorporated organization that can solicit contributions and then channels those funds to candidates seeking political office.

pollution prevention   (See source reduction.)

pornography   Adult-oriented, sexual material of an offensive nature.

privacy   (See right of privacy.)

privacy policy   Business policies that explain what use of the company's technology is permissible and how the business will monitor employee activities.

privacy rights   Protecting an individual's personal life from unwarranted intrusion by the employer.

private property   A group of rights giving control over physical and intangible assets to private owners. Private ownership is the basic institution of capitalism.

privately held corporation   A corporation that is privately owned by an individual or a group of individuals; its stock is not available for purchase by the general investing public.

product liability   The legal responsibility of a firm for injuries caused by something it made or sold.

product recall   Occurs when a business firm, either voluntarily or under an agreement with a government agency, removes a defective or sometimes dangerous product from consumer use and from all distribution channels.

profits   The revenues of a person or company minus the costs incurred in producing the revenue.

proxy   A legal instrument giving another person the right to vote the shares of stock of an absentee stockholder.

proxy statement   A statement sent by a board of directors to a corporation's stockholders announcing the company's annual meeting, containing information about the business to be considered at the meeting, and enclosing a proxy form for stockholders not attending the meeting to vote.

public   (See general public.)

public affairs management   The active management of an organization's interactions with government at all levels to promote the firm's interests in the political process.

public issue   An issue that is of mutual concern to an organization and its stakeholders.

public policy   A plan of action undertaken by government officials to achieve some broad purpose affecting a substantial segment of the public.

public-private partnerships   Community-based organizations that have a combination of businesses and government agencies collaborating to address important social problems such as crime, homelessness, drugs, economic development, and other community issues.

public relations   A program that sends a constant stream of information from the company to the public and opens the door to dialogue with stakeholders whose lives are affected by company operations.

public relations department   Manages the firm's public image and, more generally, its relations with the public.

public service announcements (PSAs)   Advertisements that address critical social issues.

publicly held corporation   A corporation whose stock is available for purchase by the general investing public (as contrasted with a privately held firm).

Q

quality management   Measures taken by an organization to assure quality, such as defining the customer's needs, monitoring whether or not a product or service consistently meets these needs, analyzing the quality of finished products to assure they are free of defects, and continually improving processes to eliminate quality problems.

questionable payments   Something of value given to a person or firm that raises significant ethical questions of right or wrong in the host nation or other nations.

R

racial harassment   Harassment in the workplace based on race, such as ethnic slurs, derogatory comments, or other verbal or physical harassment that creates an intimidating, hostile, or offensive working environment or that interferes with an individual's work performance. (See also sexual harassment.)

rain forest   Woodlands that receive at least 100 inches of rain a year. They are among the planet's richest areas in terms of biodiversity.

regulation   The action of government to establish rules by which industry or other groups must behave in conducting their normal activities.

renewable resources   Natural resources, such as fresh water or timber, that can be naturally replenished. (See also nonrenewable resources.)

reputation   The desirable or undesirable qualities associated with an organization or its actors that may influence the organization's relationships with its stakeholders.

reregulation   The increase or expansion of government regulation on activities where regulatory activities had previously been reduced.

reverse discrimination   The unintentional discrimination against an individual or group in an effort to help another individual or group.

revolving door   The circulation of individuals between business and government positions.

right (human)   A concept used in ethical reasoning that means that a person or group is entitled to something or is entitled to be treated in a certain way.

right of privacy   A person's entitlement to protection from invasion of his or her private life by government, business, or other persons.

S

Sarbanes-Oxley Act   U.S. law passed in 2002 that greatly expanded the powers of the SEC to regulate information disclosure in the financial markets and the accountability of an organization's senior leadership regarding the accuracy of this disclosure. (See also Securities and Exchange Commission.)

Securities and Exchange Commission (SEC)   The U.S. federal government agency whose mission is to protect stockholders' rights by making sure that stock markets are run fairly and that investment information is fully disclosed.

semantic phase   A phase of technology that began around 2000; characterized by the development of processes and systems that enable organizations and people to navigate through the expanding amount of information on the Internet.

sexual harassment   Unwanted and uninvited sexual attention experienced by a person, and/or a workplace that is hostile or threatening in a sexual way. (See racial harassment.)

shareholder   (See stockholder.)

shareholder resolution   A proposal made by a stockholder or group of stockholders and included in a corporation's notice of its annual meeting that advocates some course of action to be taken by the company.

shareholder lawsuit   A lawsuit initiated by one or more stockholders to recover damages suffered due to alleged actions of the company's management.

social assistance policies   Government programs aimed at improving areas such as health care and education.

social auditing   A systematic study and evaluation of an organization's social and ethical performance. (See also social performance audit.)

social capital   The norms and networks that enable collective action; goodwill engendered by social relationships.

social contract   An implied understanding between an organization and its stakeholders as to how they will act toward one another.

social equity   Determined by assessing the company's social benefits and costs, as revealed by a social performance audit.

social investment   The use of stock ownership as a strategy for promoting social objectives. (Also called socially responsible investing.)

social networking   A system using technology to enable people to connect, explore interests, and share activities around the world.

social performance audit   A systematic evaluation of an organization's social, ethical, and environmental performance.

social regulation   Regulations intended to accomplish certain social improvements such as equal employment opportunity, on-the-job safety and health, and the protection of the natural environment.

social responsibility   (See corporate social responsibility.)

social responsibility shareholder resolution   A resolution on an issue of corporate social responsibility placed before stockholders for a vote at a company's annual meeting, usually by social activist groups.

society   Refers to human beings and to the social structures they collectively create; specifically refers to segments of humankind, such as members of a particular community, nation, or interest group.

soft money   Funds donated to a political party to support party-building activities such as televised commercials that do not specify a candidate, get-out-the-vote drives, and opinion polling; corporate soft money contributions were outlawed in the United States by the Bipartisan Campaign Reform Act of 2002.

software piracy   The illegal copying of copyrighted software.

sound bite   Information, often 30 seconds or less, used by the media in its broadcast to the public.

source reduction   A business strategy to prevent or reduce pollution at the source, rather than to dispose of or treat pollution after it has been produced. (Also known as pollution prevention.)

spam   Unsolicited e-mails (or junk e-mails) sent in bulk to valid e-mail accounts. (See unsolicited commercial e-mails.)

spirituality (personal)   A personal belief in a supreme being, religious organization, or the power of nature or some other external, life-guiding force.

stages of moral development   A sequential pattern of how people grow and develop in their moral thinking, beginning with a concern for the self and growing to a concern for others and broad-based principles.

stakeholder   A person or group that affects, or is affected by, a corporation's decisions, policies, and operations. (See also market stakeholder and nonmarket stakeholder.)

stakeholder analysis   An analytic process used by managers that identifies the relevant stakeholders in a particular situation and seeks to understand their interests, power, and likely coalitions.

stakeholder coalitions   Alliances among company's stakeholders to pursue a common interest.

stakeholder dialogue   Conversations between representatives of a company and its stakeholders about issues of common concern.

stakeholder engagement   An ongoing process of relationship building between a business and its stakeholders.

stakeholder interests   The nature of each stakeholder group, its concerns, and what it wants from its relationship with the firm.

stakeholder map   A graphical representation of the relationship of stakeholder salience to a particular issue.

stakeholder networks   A connected assembly of concerned individuals or organizations defined by their shared focus on a particular issue, problem or opportunity.

stakeholder power   The ability of one or more stakeholders to achieve a desired outcome in their interactions with a company. The four types are voting power, economic power, political power, and legal power.

stakeholder salience   A stakeholder's ability to stand out from the background, to be seen as important, or to draw attention to itself or its issue. Stakeholders are more salient when they possess power, legitimacy and urgency.

stakeholder theory of the firm   A theory that hold that the purpose of the firm is to create value for society.

stem-cell research   Research on nonspecialized cells that have the capacity to self-renew and to differentiate into more mature, specialized cells.

stewardship principle   The idea that business managers, as public stewards or trustees, have an obligation to see that everyone—particularly those in need or at risk—benefits from the company's actions.

stockholder   A person, group, or organization owning one or more shares of stock in a corporation; the legal owners of the business. (Also known as shareholder.)

stock option   A form of compensation. Options represent the right (but not obligation) to buy a company's stock at a set price for a certain period of time. The option becomes valuable to its holder when, and if, the stock price rises above this amount.

stock screening   Selecting stocks based on social or environmental criteria.

strategic philanthropy   A form of corporate giving that is linked directly or indirectly to business goals or objectives.

streaming   A customized, on-demand radio or video service that allows the user to download the material to a computer and save it on a hard drive.

strict liability   A legal doctrine that holds that a manufacturer is responsible (liable) for injuries resulting from the use of its products, whether or not the manufacturer was negligent or breached a warranty.

Superfund   A U.S. law, passed in 1980, designated to clean up hazardous or toxic waste sites. The law established a fund, supported mainly by taxes on petrochemical companies, to pay for the cleanup. (Also known as the Comprehensive Environmental Response, Compensation, and Liability Act [CERCLA].)

sustainability officer   Manager given the authority to direct the organization's environmental policies and programs.

sustainability report   A single report integrating a business's social, economic, and environmental results.

sustainable development   Development that meets the needs of the present without compromising the ability of future generations to meet their own needs.

sweatshop   Factories where employees—sometimes including children—are forced to work long hours at low wages, often under unsafe working conditions.

T

technology   A broad term referring to the practical applications of science and knowledge to commercial and organizational activities.

technology cooperation   Long-term partnerships between companies to transfer environmental technologies to attain sustainable development.

The Business Roundtable   Founded in 1972, an organization of chief executive officers from leading corporations involved in various public issues and legislation.

tissue engineering   The growth of tissue in a laboratory dish for experimental research.

toxic substance   Any substance used in production or in consumer products that is poisonous or capable of causing serious health problems for those persons exposed. (See also hazardous waste.)

tradable permits   A market-based approach to pollution control in which the government grants companies "rights" to a specific amount of pollution (permits), which may be bought or sold (traded) with other companies.

trade association   A coalition of companies in the same or related industries seeking to coordinate their economic or political power to further their agenda.

transnational corporation   Corporations that operate and control assets across national boundaries.

transparency   Clear public reporting of an organization's performance to various stakeholders.

triple bottom line   The measurement of an organization on the basis of its economic results, environmental impact, and contribution to social well-being.

U

United Nations Global Compact   Voluntary agreement of business, labor, and nongovernmental organizations to work for sustainable development goals.

unsolicited commercial e-mails (or junk e-mail)   Unrequested e-mail messages sent in bulk to valid e-mail accounts. (See spam.)

U.S. Corporate Sentencing Guidelines   Standards to help judges determine the appropriate penalty for criminal violations of federal laws and provide a strong incentive for businesses to promote ethics at work.

U.S. Foreign Corrupt Practices Act   Federal law that prohibits businesses from paying bribes to foreign government officials, political parties, or political candidates.

utilitarian reasoning   An ethical approach that emphasizes the consequences of an action and seeks the overall amount of good that can be produced by an action or a decision.

utility (social)   A concept used in ethical reasoning that refers to the net positive gain or benefit to society of some action or decision.

V

values   Fundamental and enduring beliefs about the most desirable conditions and purposes of human life.

virtue ethics   Focuses on character traits to define a good person, theorizing that values will direct a person toward good behavior.

vlogs   Video Web logs produced by a digital camera that captures moving images and then transferred to the Internet.

volunteerism   The uncompensated efforts of people to assist others in a community.

W

Wall Street   A customary way of referring to the financial community of banks, investment institutions, and stock exchanges centered in the Wall Street area of New York City.

water pollution   When more wastes are discharged into waterways, such as lakes and rivers, than can be naturally diluted and carried away.

whistleblowing   An employee's disclosure of alleged organizational misconduct to the media or appropriate government agency, often after futile attempts to convince organizational authorities to take action against the alleged abuse.

white collar crime   Illegal activities committed by corporate managers or business professionals, such as fraud, insider trading, embezzlement or computer crime.

workforce diversity   Diversity among employees, a challenge and opportunity for business. (See also diversity).

World Bank   An international financial institution that provides economic development loans to member nations.

World Business Council for Sustainable Development (WBCSD)   A group of companies from several nations whose goal is to encourage high standards of environmental management and to promote cooperation among businesses, governments, and other organizations concerned with sustainable development.

World Trade Organization   An organization of member nations that establishes the ground rules for trade among nations.

Z

zombie   A hijacked computer that can be remote controlled by the attacker to respond to the attacker's commands.

BIBLIOGRAPHY

Part One: Chapters 1–3

Ackerman, Robert. *The Social Challenge to Business.* Cambridge, MA: Harvard University Press, 1975.

Albrecht, Karl. *Corporate Radar: Tracking the Forces That Are Shaping Your Business.* New York: American Management Association, 2000.

Bakan, Joel. *The Corporation: The Pathological Pursuit of Profit and Power.* New York: Free Press, 2004.

Barth, Regine and Franziska Wolff, eds. *Corporate Social Responsibility in Europe—Rhetoric and Realities.* Cheltenham, UK: Edward Elgar Publishing, 2009.

Bendell, Jem. *The Corporate Responsibility Movement: Five Years of Global Corporate Responsibility Analysis from Lifeworth, 2001–2005.* Sheffield, UK: Greenleaf Publishing, 2009.

Boutilier, Robert, *Stakeholder Politics: Social Capital, Sustainable Development, and the Corporation.* Sheffield, UK: Greenleaf Publishing, 2009.

Bowen, Howard R. *Responsibilities of the Businessman.* New York: Harper, 1953.

Chamberlain, Neil W. *The Limits of Corporate Social Responsibility.* New York: Basic Books, 1973.

Clarkson, Max B.E., ed. *The Corporation and Its Stakeholders: Classic and Contemporary Readings.* Toronto: University of Toronto Press, 1998.

European Academy of Business in Society. *Developing the Global Leader of Tomorrow.* United Kingdom: Ashridge Publishing, December 2008.

Frederick, William C. *Values, Nature, and Culture in the American Corporation.* New York: Oxford University Press, 1995.

———. *Corporation Be Good!* Indianapolis, IN: Dog Ear Publishing, 2006.

Freeman, R. Edward. *Strategic Management: A Stakeholder Approach.* Marshfield, MA: Pitman, 1984.

Freeman, R. Edward, Jeffrey S. Harrison, and Andrew C. Wicks, *Managing for Stakeholders: Survival, Reputation, and Success.* New Haven: Yale University Press, 2007.

Grayson, David and Adrian Hodges. *Corporate Social Opportunity: 7 Steps to Make Corporate Social Responsibility Work for Your Business.* Sheffield, UK: Greenleaf Publishing, 2004.

Isaacs, William. *Dialogue: The Art of Thinking Together.* New York: Doubleday, 1999.

Kolb, Robert W., ed. *Encyclopedia of Business Ethics and Society.* Thousand Oaks, CA: SAGE Publications, 2008.

McElhaney, Kellie. *Just Good Business: The Strategic Guide to Aligning Corporate Responsibility and Brand.* San Francisco: Berrett-Koehler, 2008.

McGonagle, John J.; and Carolyn M. Vella. *Bottom Line Competitive Intelligence.* New York: Praeger, 2002.

Post, James E., Lee E. Preston, and Sybille Sachs, *Redefining the Corporation: Stakeholder Management and Organizational Wealth.* Palo Alto, CA: Stanford University Press, 2002.

Phillips, Robert. *Stakeholder Theory and Organizational Ethics.* San Francisco: Berrett-Koehler Publishers, Inc., 2003.

Reich, Robert B. *Supercapitalism: The Transformation of Business, Democracy, and Everyday Life.* New York: Alfred A. Knopf, 2007.

Svendsen, Ann. *The Stakeholder Strategy: Profiting from Collaborative Business Relationships.* San Francisco: Berrett-Koehler Publishers, 1998.

Vogel, David. *The Market for Virtue: The Potential and Limits of Corporate Social Responsibility.* Washington, DC: Brookings Institution Press, 2005.

Waddock, Sandra, et al., eds. *Unfolding Stakeholder Thinking.* Sheffield, UK: Greenleaf Publishers, 2002.

Waddock, Sandra and Charles Bodwell. *Total Responsibility Management: The Manual.* Sheffield, UK: Greenleaf Publishers, 2007.

Wall, Caleb. *Buried Treasure: Discovering and Implementing the Value of Corporate Social Responsibility.* Sheffield, UK: Greenleaf Publishing, 2008.

Yankelovich, Daniel. *The Magic of Dialogue: Transforming Conflict Into Cooperation.* New York: Simon & Schuster, 1999.

Zakhem, Abe J., Daniel E. Palmer, and Mary Lyn Stoll, *Stakeholder Theory: Essential Readings in Ethical Leadership and Management.* Amherst, NY: Prometheus Books, 2008.

Part Two: Chapters 4–5

Callahan, David. *The Cheating Culture.* Orlando: Harcourt, 2004.

Cavanaugh, Gerald F. *American Business Values: With International Perspectives,* 6th edition. Upper Saddle River, NJ: Prentice-Hall, 2009.

Ciulla, Joanne B., ed. *Ethics, the Heart of Leadership,* 2nd ed. Westport, CT: Praeger, 2004.

Colby, Anne, and Lawrence Kohlberg. *The Measurement of Moral Judgment: Volume I, Theoretical Foundations and Research Validations.* Cambridge, MA: Harvard University Press, 1987.

Cortright, S.A. and Michael J. Naughton, eds. *Rethinking the Purpose of Business: Interdisciplinary Essays from the Catholic Social Tradition*. Notre Dame, IN: University of Notre Dame Press, 2002.

Donaldson, Thomas, and Thomas W. Dunfee. *Ties that Bind: A Social Contracts Approach to Business Ethics*. Cambridge, MA: Harvard Business School Publishing, 1999.

Giacalone, Robert A. and Carole L. Jurkiewicz, eds. *Handbook of Workplace Spirituality and Organizational Performance*. Armonk, NY: M.E. Sharpe, 2003.

Goodpaster, Kenneth E. *Conscience and Corporate Culture*. Malden, MA: Blackwell, 2007.

Jackall, Robert. *Moral Mazes: The World of Corporate Managers*. New York: Oxford University Press, 1988.

Leipziger, Deborah, ed. *SA8000: The First Decade*. Sheffield, UK: Greenleaf Publishers, 2009.

McLean, Bethany, and Peter Elkind. *The Smartest Guys in the Room: The Amazing Rise and Scandalous Fall of Enron*. New York: Penguin Books, 2003.

O'Brien, Thomas and Scott Paeth, eds. *Religious Perspectives on Business Ethics: An Anthology*. Lanham, MD: Rowman & Littlefield Publishers, 2007.

Pauchant, Thierry C. *Ethics and Spirituality at Work*. New York: Praeger, 2002.

Price, Terry L. *Leadership Ethics, An Introduction*. New York: Cambridge Press, 2008.

Rawls, John. *A Theory of Justice*. Cambridge, MA: Harvard University Press, 1971.

Rosenthal, Sandra B., and A. Rogene Buchholz. *Rethinking Business Ethics: A Pragmatic Approach*. New York: Oxford University Press, 1999.

Solomon, Robert C. *A Better Way to Think About Business*. New York: Oxford University Press, 1999.

Stone, Christopher D. *Where the Law Ends: The Social Control of Corporate Behavior*. Prospect Heights, IL: Waveland Press, 1975.

Vagelos, Roy and Louis Galambos. *The Moral Corporation, Merck Experiences*. New York: Cambridge University Press, 2006.

Werhane, Patricia H., and R. Edward Freeman. *The Blackwell Encyclopedic Dictionary of Business Ethics*. Malden, MA: Blackwell, 1997.

Part Three: Chapters 6–7

Andriof, Joerg, and Malcolm McIntosh. *Perspectives on Corporate Citizenship*. Sheffield, UK: Greenleaf Publishing, 2001.

Bhagwati, Jagdish. *In Defense of Globalization*. New York: Oxford University Press, 2007.

Burke, Edmund M. *Managing a Company in an Activist World: The Leadership Challenge of Corporate Citizenship*. Westport, CT: Praeger, 2005.

Coicaud, Jean-Marc et al., eds. *The Globalization of Human Rights*. New York: United Nations University Press, 2003.

Crane, Andrew, Dirk Matten and Jeremy Moon. *Corporations and Citizenship*. Cambridge, UK: Cambridge University Press, 2008.

Elkington, John. *Cannibals With Forks: The Triple Bottom Line of 21st Century Business*. London: Thompson, 1997.

Epstein, Mark J. *Making Sustainability Work: Best Practices in Managing and Measuring Corporate Social, Environmental, and Economic Impacts*. San Francisco: Berrett-Koehler, 2008.

Fombrun, Charles. *Reputation*. Boston, MA: Harvard Business School Press, 1996.

Friedman, Thomas L. *The Lexus and the Olive Tree*. New York: Anchor Books, 2000.

———. *The World Is Flat: A Brief History of the Twenty-First Century*. New York: Farrar, Straus and Giroux, 2005.

Googins, Bradley K., Philip H. Mirvis and Steven A. Rochlin. *Beyond Good Company: Next Generation Corporate Citizenship*. New York: Palgrave Macmillan, 2007.

Kaplan, Robert and David Norton. *The Balanced Scorecard*. Boston, MA: Harvard Business School Press, 1996.

Kiggunda, Moses N. *Managing Globalization in Developing Countries and Transition Economies*. New York: Praeger, 2002.

Korten, David C. *When Corporations Rule the World*, 2nd ed. San Francisco: Berrett-Koehler, 2001.

Margolis, Joshua Daniel; and James Patrick Walsh. *People and Profits? The Search for a Link Between a Company's Social and Financial Performance*. Mahwah, NJ: Erlbaum, 2001.

McIntosh, Alastair, *Soil and Soul: People Versus Corporate Power*. London: Aurum Press, 2004.

Orlitzky, Marc and Diane Swanson. *Toward Integrative Corporate Citizenship: Research Advances in Corporate Social Performance*. New York: Palgrave Macmillan, 2008.

Porter, Michael. *The Competitive Advantage of Nations*. New York: Basic Books, 1991.

Prahalad, C.K. *The Fortune at the Bottom of the Pyramid: Eradicating Poverty through Profits*. Philadelphia, PA: Wharton School Publishing, 2006.

Savitz, Andrew W. and Karl Weber. *The Triple Bottom Line: How Today's Best-Run Companies Are Achieving Economic, Social, and Environmental Success—And How You Can Too*. San Francisco: Jossey-Bass, 2006.

Sethi, S. Prakash. *Setting Global Standards: Guidelines for Creating Global Codes of Conduct in Multinational Corporations.* New York: John Wiley & Sons, 2003.

Soros, George. *On Globalization.* New York: Perseus Books, 2002.

Stiglitz, Joseph E. *Making Globalization Work.* New York: W.W. Norton, 2007.

Waddock, Sandra. *Leading Corporate Citizens: Vision, Values, and Value Added,* 2nd ed. New York: McGraw-Hill, 2006.

Williams, Bob. *The Sustainability Advantage: Seven Business Case Benefits of a Triple Bottom Line.* Gabriola Island, British Columbia: New Society Publishers, 2002.

Williams, Oliver F., ed., *Peace Through Commerce: Responsible Corporate Citizenship and the Ideals of the United Nations Global Compact.* South Bend, IN: University of Notre Dame Press, 2008.

Wood, Donna J., Jeanne M. Logsdon, Patsy G. Lewellyn and Kim Davenport. *Global Business Citizenship.* Armonk, NY: M.E. Sharpe, 2006.

Yaziji, Michael and Jonathan Doh. *NGOs and Corporations: Conflict and Collaboration.* New York: Cambridge University Press, 2009.

Part Four: Chapters 8–9

Epstein, Edwin M. *The Corporation in American Politics.* Englewood Cliffs, NJ: Prentice-Hall, 1969.

Foundation for Public Affairs, *The State of Corporate Public Affairs 2008–2009.* Washington, DC: Foundation for Public Affairs, 2008.

Harris, Phil and Craig S. Fleisher, eds. *Handbook of Public Affairs.* Thousand Oaks, CA: Sage Publications, 2005.

Judis, John B. *Paradox of American Democracy: Elites, Special Interests, and the Betrayal of the Public Trust,* New York: Random House, 2001.

Lodge, George C. *The New American Ideology.* New York: Alfred A. Knopf, 1978.

———. *Comparative Business-Government Relations.* Englewood Cliffs, NJ: Prentice-Hall, 1990.

Lodge, George C. and Ezra F. Vogel, eds. *Ideology and National Competitiveness.* Boston: Harvard Business School Press, 1998.

Mitnick, Barry M., ed. *Corporate Political Agency: The Construction of Competition in Public Affairs.* Thousand Oaks, CA: Sage Publications, 1993.

Preston, Lee E. and James E. Post, *Private Management and Public Policy.* Englewood Cliffs, NJ: Prentice Hall, 1975.

Sachs, Jeffrey D. *The End of Poverty: Economic Possibilities for Our Time.* New York: Penguin Press, 2005.

Schier, Steven E. *By Invitation Only: The Rise of Exclusive Politics in the United States,* New York: Random House, 2001.

Vogel, David. *Kindred Strangers: The Uneasy Relationship between Politics and Business in America.* Princeton, NJ: Princeton University Press, 1996.

Woodstock Theological Center. *The Ethics of Lobbying: Organized Interests, Political Power, and the Common Good.* Washington, DC: Georgetown University Press, 2002.

Part Five: Chapters 10–11

Anderson, Ray C. *Mid-Course Correction: Toward a Sustainable Enterprise.* Atlanta, GA: Peregrinzilla Press, 1998.

Arnold, Matthew B. and Robert M. Day. *The Next Bottom Line: Making Sustainable Development Tangible.* Washington, DC: World Resources Institute, 1998.

Daly, Herman E. *Beyond Growth: The Economics of Sustainable Development.* Boston: Beacon Press, 1996.

Dunphy, Dexter, Suzanne Benn, and Andrew Griffiths. *Organisational Change for Corporate Sustainability.* New York: Routledge, 2003.

Esty, Daniel C. and Andrew S. Winston. *Green to Gold: How Smart Companies Use Environmental Strategy to Innovate, Create Value, and Build Competitive Advantage.* New Haven, CT: Yale University Press, 2006.

Foreman, Jr., Christopher H. *The Promise and Perils of Environmental Justice.* Washington, DC, Brookings Institution, 2000.

Frankel, Carl. *In Earth's Company: Business, Environment, and the Challenge of Sustainability.* Gabriola Island, British Columbia: New Society Publishers, 1998.

Friedman, Frank B. *Practical Guide to Environmental Management,* 9th ed. Washington DC: Environmental Law Institute, 2003.

Friedman, Thomas L. *Hot, Flat, and Crowded: Why We Need a Green Revolution—and How It Can Renew America.* New York: Farrar, Strauss, and Giroux, 2008.

Hammond, Allen. *Which World? Scenarios for the 21st Century.* Washington DC: Island Press, 1998.

Hart, Stuart L. *Capitalism at the Crossroads: The Unlimited Business Opportunities in Solving the World's Most Difficult Problems.* Philadelphia, PA: Wharton School Publishing, 2005.

Hawken, Paul, Amory Lovins, and L. Hunter Lovins. *Natural Capitalism: Creating the Next Industrial Revolution.* Boston: Little Brown, 1999.

Hertsgaard, Mark. *Earth Odyssey: Around the World in Search of Our Environmental Future.* New York: Broadway Books, 1998.

Hoffman, Andrew J. *Competitive Environmental Strategy: A Guide to the Changing Business Landscape.* Washington DC: Island Press, 2000.

Holliday, Charles O., Jr., et al. *Walking the Talk: The Business Case for Sustainable Development.* Sheffield, UK: Greenleaf Publishing, 2002.

Long, Frederick J., and Matthew B. Arnold. *The Power of Environmental Partnerships.* Fort Worth, TX: Dryden Press, 1995.

Marcus, Alfred A. et al. *Reinventing Environmental Regulation: Lessons from Project XL.* Washington, DC: Resources for the Future, 2002.

Nattrass, Brian and Mary Altomare. *The Natural Step for Business: Wealth, Ecology and the Evolutionary Corporation.* Gabriola Island, British Columbia: New Society Publishers, 1999.

Sharma, Sanjay, and J. Alberto Aragon-Correa, eds. *Corporate Environmental Strategy and Competitive Advantage.* Northampton, MA: Edgar Elgar Academic Publishing, 2005.

Schendler, Auden. *Getting Green Done: Hard Truths from the Front Lines and Sustainability Revolution.* New York: Foundation for Public Affairs, 2009.

Speth, James Gustaveth, *The Bridge at the Edge of the World.* New Haven, CT, Yale University Press, 2008.

Stead, Jean Garner and W. Edward Stead. *Management for a Small Planet,* 3rd edition. Armonk, NY: M.E. Sharpe, 2009.

Winston, Andrew S. *Green Recovery.* Boston: Harvard Business Press, 2009.

Worldwatch Institute. *State of the World 2009: Into a Warming World,* New York: W.W. Norton, 2009.

Part Six: Chapters 12–13

Bynum, Terrell Ward and Simon Rogerson. *Computer Ethics and Professional Responsibility.* Malden, MA: Blackwell, 2003.

DeGeorge, Richard T. *The Ethics of Information Technology and Business.* Malden, MA: Blackwell, 2002.

Heinberg, Richard. *Cloning the Buddha: The Moral Impact of Biotechnology.* San Juan Capistrano, CA: Quest Books, 1999.

Larquin, Paul. *High Tech Harvest.* Cambridge, MA: Westview Press, 2008.

Mannion, Michael. *Frankenstein Foods: Genetically Modified Foods and Your Health.* London: Welcome Rain, 2001.

Marshall, Stewart, Wallace Taylor and Xinghuo Yu, eds. *Closing the Digital Divide: Transforming Regional Economies and Communities with Information Technology.* New York: Praeger, 2003.

McClure, Stuart, Joel Scambray and George Kurtz. *Hacking Exposed: Network Security Secrets and Solutions.* New York: McGraw-Hill, 2009.

Micek, Deborah and Warren Whitlock. *Twitter Revolution.* Las Vegas, NV: Xeno Press, 2008.

Miller, Henry I. and Gregory Conko. *The Frankenfood Myth.* Westport, CT: Praeger, 2004.

Safko, Lon and David K. Brake. *The Social Media Bible: Tactics, Tools and Strategies for Business Success.* New York: John Wiley & Sons, 2009.

Shaw, Michael J., ed. *E-Commerce and the Digital Economy.* Armonk, NY: M.E. Sharpe, 2006.

Sherlock, Richard; and John D. Morrey, eds. *Ethical Issues in Biotechnology.* Lanham, MD: Rowman Littlefield, 2002.

Straub, Detmar, Seymour Goodman and Richard Baskerville, eds. *Information Security: Policy, Processes, and Practices.* Armonk, NY: M.E. Sharpe, 2008.

Weasel, Lisa H. *Food Fray: Inside the Controversy over Genetically Modified Food.* New York: American Management Association, 2009.

Yeh, Raymond T. with Stephanie H. Yeh. *The Art of Business in the Footsteps of Giants.* Olathe, CO: Zero Time Publishing, 2004.

Zook, Matthew. *The Geography of the Internet Industry.* Malden, MA: Blackwell, 2005.

Part Seven: Chapters 14–19

Andvliet, Luc, and Mary B. Anderson, *Getting It Right: Making Corporate-Community Relations Work.* Sheffield, UK: Greenleaf, 2009.

Bebchuk, Lucian A., and Jesse M. Fried. *Pay without Performance: The Unfulfilled Promise of Executive Compensation.* Cambridge, MA: Harvard University Press, 2004.

Carter, Colin B. and Jay W. Lorsch. *Back to the Drawing Board: Designing Corporate Boards for a Complex World.* Boston: Harvard Business School Press, 2004.

Cohan, William D., *House of Cards: A Tale of Hubris and Wretched Excess on Wall Street.* New York: Doubleday, 2009.

Crystal, Graef S., Ira T. Kay, and Frederic W. Cook. *CEO Pay: A Comprehensive Look,* New York: American Compensation Association, 1997.

Davidson, Kirk D. *Selling Sin: The Marketing of Socially Unacceptable Products.* New York: Praeger, 2003.

Dine, Philip M. *State of the Unions: How Labor Can Strengthen the Middle Class, Improve Our Economy, and Regain Political Influence.* New York: McGraw-Hill, 2008.

Domini, Amy L. *Socially Responsible Investing: Making a Difference and Making Money.* Chicago: Dearborn Trade, 2001.

Edley, Christopher, Jr. *Not All Black and White: Affirmative Action and American Values.* San Francisco: Noonday Books, 1998.

Featherstone, Liza. *Selling Women Short: The Landmark Battle for Workers' Rights at Wal-Mart.* New York: Basic Books, 2004.

Greenhouse, Steven. *The Big Squeeze: Tough Times for the American Worker.* New York: Anchor Books, 2009.

Hilts, Philip J. *Protecting America's Health: The FDA, Business, and One Hundred Years of Regulation.* New York: Alfred A. Knopf, 2003.

Eichenwald, Kurt. *Conspiracy of Fools: A True Story.* New York: Broadway Books, 2005.

Grunig, Larissa A., James E. Grunig, and David M. Dozier. *Excellent Public Relations and Effective Organizations.* Mahwah, NJ: Erlbaum, 2002.

Jennings, Marianne. *The Board of Directors: 25 Keys to Corporate Governance.* New York: Lebhar-Friedman Books, 2000.

Kelly, Marjorie. *The Divine Right of Capital: Dethroning the Corporate Aristocracy.* San Francisco: Berrett-Koehler Publishers, Inc., 2003.

Leana, Carrie and Denise Rousseau. *Relational Capital.* New York: Oxford University Press, 2000.

Mitroff, Ian I. *Crisis Leadership: Planning for the Unthinkable.* New York: John Wiley and Sons, 2004.

Monks, Robert A. G. and Nell Minow. *Corporate Governance*, 3rd ed. Malden, MA: Blackwell Publishers, 2004.

Nestle, Marion. *Food Politics: How the Food Industry Influences Nutrition and Health.* Berkeley: University of California Press, 2002.

Rose, Stephen J., and Heidi I. Hartmann. *Still a Man's Labor Market: The Long-Term Earnings Gap.* Washington DC: Institute for Women's Policy Research, 2004.

Rosen, Jeffrey. *The Unwanted Gaze: The Destruction of Privacy in America.* New York: Random House, 2000.

Sagawa, Shirley, Eli Segal, and Rosabeth Moss Kanter. *Common Interest, Common Good: Creating Value Through Business and Social Sector Partnerships.* Cambridge, MA: Harvard Business School, 1999.

Schepers, Donald. *Socially Responsible Investing.* Florence, KY: Routledge, 2007.

Schlosser, Eric. *Fast Food Nation: The Dark Side of the All-American Meal.* New York: Perennial, 2002.

Smallen-Grob, Diane. *Making It in Corporate America.* New York: Praeger, 2003.

Smith, Denis and Dominic Elliott, eds. *Key Readings in Crisis Management.* Florence, KY: Routledge, 2006.

Sorkin, Andrew Ross. *Too Big to Fail: The Inside Story of How Wall Street and Washington Fought to Save the Financial System—and Themselves.* New York: Viking, 2009.

Sriramesh, Krishnamurthy and Dejan Vercic, eds. *The Global Public Relations Handbook: Theory, Research and Practice.* Mahwah, NJ: Erlbaum, 2003.

Van Den Berghe, L. and Liesbeth De Ridder. *International Standardisation of Good Corporate Governance: Best Practices for the Board of Directors.* Dordrecht, The Netherlands: Kluwer Academic Publishers, 1999.

Whitman, Marina, V.N. *New World, New Rules: The Changing Role of the American Corporation.* Boston: Harvard Business School Press, 1999.

Additional **McGraw-Hill** International Editions
are available in the following subjects:

Accounting	Geology and Mineralogy
Agriculture	Industrial Arts and Vocational Education
Biological Sciences	Mathematics
Business and Industrial Management	Mechanical Engineering
Chemistry and Chemical Engineering	Medicine
Civil Engineering	Meteorology
Economics	Physics
Education	Political Science
Electrical Engineering	Psychology
Electronics and Computer Science	Sociology
Finance	

Some ancillaries, including electronic and print components, may not be available to customers outside the United States.

The **McGraw·Hill** Companies

ISBN: 978-007-128936-8
MHID: 007-128936-4

9 780071 289368